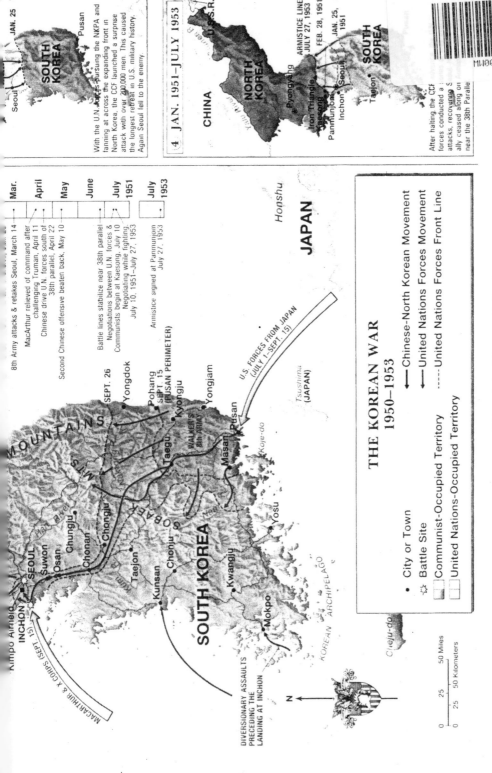

JAN. 25

SOUTH
KOREA

Seoul

Pusan

With the U.N. forces pursuing the NKPA and
fanning at across the expanding front in
North Korea, the CCF launched a surprise
attack with over 200,000 men. This caused
the longest retreat in U.S. military history.
Again Seoul fell to the enemy.

4 JAN. 1951–JULY 1953

CHINA

U.S.S.R.

NORTH
KOREA

Pyongyang

Kaesong

Iron Triangle

Panmunjom

Inchon

Seoul

Taejon

SOUTH
KOREA

ARMISTICE LINE
JULY 27, 1953

FEB. 28, 1951

JAN. 25,
1951

After halting the CCF
forces conducted a
attacks, recovering S
ally ceased along on
near the 38th Paralle

Mar.

April

May

June

July
1951

July
1953

8th Army attacks & retakes Seoul, March 14

MacArthur relieved of command after
challenging Truman, April 11
Chinese drive U.N. forces south of
38th parallel, April 22

Second Chinese offensive beaten back, May 10

Battle lines stabilize near 38th parallel
Negotiations between U.N forces &
Communists begin at Kaesong, July 10
Negotiating while fighting,
July 10, 1951–July 27, 1953

Armistice signed at Panmunjom
July 27, 1953

Honshu

JAPAN

U.S. FORCES FROM JAPAN
(JULY 1–SEPT. 15)

Tsushima
(JAPAN)

SEPT. 26

Yongdok

Pohang
SEPT. 15
(PUSAN PERIMETER)

Yongjam

Taegu

Kyongju

WALKER'S
8th ARMY

Masan

Pusan

Koje-do

THE KOREAN WAR
1950–1953

• City or Town
☆ Battle Site
☐ Communist-Occupied Territory
☐ United Nations-Occupied Territory

→ Chinese-North Korean Movement
→ United Nations Forces Movement
----- United Nations Forces Front Line

MOUNTAINS

S.

MTS.

SOBAEK

Seoul

Suwon

Osan

Chonan

Chungju

Chongju

Taejon

Chonju

Kwangju

Kunsan

Chonju

Mokpo

Yosu

SOUTH KOREA

Kimpo Airfield

INCHON

MACARTHUR & X CORPS (SEPT. 15)

DIVERSIONARY ASSAULTS
PRECEDING THE
LANDING AT INCHON

KOREAN ARCHIPELAGO

Cheju-do

N

0   25   50 Miles
0   25   50 Kilometers

Map Courtesy of West Point Museum Collection

RED DRAGON
THE SECOND ROUND

FACES OF WAR II

190 VETERANS OF THE KOREAN WAR RECALL
The years 1952 through 1954
OF THAT FORGOTTEN WAR

THEIR EXPERIENCES AND THOUGHTS
and
WARTIME PHOTOGRAPHS OF THAT ERA
BY

Arthur W. Wilson..Editor & Author
Captain, Infantry AUS
Heavy Mortar Company
31st Infantry Regiment
7th Infantry Division
Korea 1950-1951

&

Norman L. Strickbine..Photographer
Sergeant and Battalion Photographer
13th Combat Engineer Battalion
7th Infantry Division
Korea 1950-1951

COVER PAINTING BY NORMA STRICKBINE

THIS BOOK IS DEDICATED TO THE GALLANT MEN OF ALL SERVICES
ARMY..MARINE CORPS..NAVY..AIR FORCE..MERCHANT MARINE
WHO IN SACRIFICE OF THEIR LIVES MADE IT POSSIBLE FOR
WE SURVIVORS TO RETURN ALIVE TO THIS GREAT NATION.

Published in 2003 by Artwork Publications LLC
Post Office Box 25105
Portland, Oregon 97298
Fax 1-503-297-5163
Web page <www.artworkpub.com>

E-Mail:
Wilson<artwilsn@easystreet.com>
Strickbine <norms@tek-web.com>

Printed by Josten's Printing and Publishing, Inc.
Post Office Box 991
Visalia, California 93279

We gratefully acknowledge the contributions to this book
by fellow Korean War veterans named in these vignettes
and for permission to recount a memorable war experience from
their period of service in the Korean War 25 June 1950-27 July 1953.

ISBN 0-9653120-3-8

LIBRARY OF CONGRESS Cataloging- in- Publication Data

Korean War 1950-1953 Campaigns North Korea Chosin (Changjin)
Reservoir 1950 & DMZ 1951-1953   1954-1968
South Korea All Campaigns, 1950-1953 Regimental Histories,
United States Army & United States Marine Corps.

RED DRAGON, The Second Round, FACES OF WAR II [VOLUME 2]
KOREAN VIGNETTES, THE YO-YO WAR, FACES OF WAR I [VOLUME 1]
Editor: Wilson, Arthur W. Captain Infantry AUS 31st Infantry Regiment 7th Infantry Division
Photographer: Strickbine, Norman L. Sergeant 13th Engineers(C) Battalion 7th Infantry Div

TABLE OF CONTENTS

PAGE	FACES OF WAR	UNIT
6	Jae-won Lee	Fox Co 32d Inf Regt 7th Inf Div & 5th Regimental Combat Team
11	Bae-sun Lee	10th Fighter Wing ROK AF Republic of Korea
13	Keun-sup Yoon	Maintenance Officer ROK AF Republic of Korea
15	Gerald D. Gingery	H Co 5th Cavalry Regiment 1st Cavalry Division
17	Harry Wiedmaier	USS Mansfield DD278 United Sates Navy
19	Donald D. Down	3d Platoon Co F 2d Bn 7th Cavalry Regiment 1st Cavalry Division
21	Benjamin S. Luci	C & D Batteries 3d AAA Automatic Weapons Battalion Self Propelled
23	Richard P. Roderick	Headquarters 5th Air Force United States Air Force
25	John Covach	Co A 31st Infantry Regiment 7th Infantry Division
27	Louis W. Bontempo	G Co 32d Infantry Regiment 7th Infantry Division
29	John P. McBride	Easy Co 7th Cavalry Regiment 1st Cavalry Division
31	Charles C. Rakestraw	A Co 32d Infantry Regiment 7th Infantry Division
33	Bae-suk Lee	3d Military Police Company 3d Infantry Division
35	John Covach	Co A 31st Infantry Regiment 7th Infantry Division
38	Larry M. Casilac	Fox Co 9th Infantry Regiment 2d Infantry Division
41	Jean F. McCrady	B Co 31st Infantry Regiment 7th Infantry Division
43	Glenn V. Ellison	Fox Co 27th Infantry Regiment 25th Infantry Division
45	James P. Ramsey	Able Co 32d Infantry Regiment 7th Infantry Division
47	Kenneth G. Crump	36th FBS 8th Fighter Bomber Wing 5th Air Force USAF
50	Clarence A. White	B Co 32d Infantry Regiment 7th Infantry Division
53	William L. Ward	1st Plat Love Co 1st Bn 32d Infantry Regiment 7th Infantry Division
55	Charles W. Edmond	Co B 15th Infantry Regiment 3d Infantry Division
58	Tay S. Kim M.D.	Love Co 8th Cavalry Regiment 1st Cavalry Division & 24th Inf Div
61	Richard Eyre Coote	16th New Zealand Field Artillery Regiment New Zealand
64	Paul A. Freeburger	Intell & Reconn Platoon 14th Infantry Regiment 25th Infantry Division
68	Hung-bae Park	Lt Col Ret Med Corps ROK Air Force Republic of Korea
71	Leonard LaRue (Brother Marinus OSB)	MSTS "Meredith Victory"
73	James R. Grove	Baker Co 13th Engineers(C), 7th Infantry Division
75	Bae-suk Lee	2d Battalion 15th Infantry Regiment 3d Infantry Division
77	David Ralph Hughes	King Co 7th Cavalry Regiment 1st Cavalry Division
79	Maurice Siskel Jr.	Heavy Mortar Co 31st Infantry Regiment 7th Infantry Division
81	John T. Carrig	1st Platoon A Co 1st Bn 17th Infantry Regiment 7th Infantry Division
83	Paul E. Bouchard	Co A 7th Cavalry Regiment 1st Cavalry Division & 6147 TAC Air Sqdn
85	Kerstin Jonasson	Swedish Red Cross Field Hospital Based in Pusan, South Korea
87	John D. Matthews	Co's E & G 2d Battalion 7th Cavalry Regiment 1st Cavalry Division
89	Marvin L. Pearson	17th Heavy Tank Co 17th Infantry Regiment 7th Infantry Division
91	Donald A. Chase	B Co 19th Infantry Regiment 24th Infantry Division
93	Richard E. Coate	Easy Company 15th Infantry Regiment 3d Infantry Division
95	LaFayette F. Keaton	Love Co 1st Battalion 187th Airborne Regimental Combat Team
97	James F. Byrne	George Co 3d Battalion 1st Marine Regiment 1st Marine Division
99	Joseph J. Bennett	D Btry 15th AAA Automatic Weapons Battalion (Self Propelled)
101	Boris R. Spiroff	G Co 7th Cavalry Regiment 1st Cavalry Division
103	James H. Appleton	Item Co 3d Battalion 5th Marine Regiment 1st Marine Division
105	Angelo Rosa	Service Battery 955th Field Artillery Battalion Eighth Army
107	Kenneth F. Barwise	12 Platoon Dog Co Princess Patricia's Canadian Light Infantry Regt.
109	Richard E. Coate	E Company 15th Infantry Regiment 3d Infantry Division
111	John Covach	Co A 31st Infantry Regiment 7th Infantry Division
112	Arthur F. Dorie	M Company 3d Battalion 23d Infantry Regiment 3d Infantry Division
119	Pat N. Westfall	Heavy Mortar & Fox Cos 31st Infantry Regiment 7th Infantry Division
121	Donald A. Chase	B Co 19th Infantry Regiment 24th Infantry Division
123	Levi O. Haire	HQ & Service Co 13th Engineer (C) Battalion 7th Infantry Division

TABLE OF CONTENTS

PAGE	FACES OF WAR	UNIT
125	James H. Appleton	Item Co 3d Battalion 5th Marine Regiment 1st Marine Division
127	Lulan E. Gregg	8076 MASH (Mobile Army Surgical Hospital)
129	Charles L. Grove	USS Ajax (AR6) United States Navy
131	Melvin James Boland	Baker Co 1st Bn 1stMarines 1st Mar Div
133	Donald A. Chase	B Co 19th Inf Regt 24th Inf Div
135	James H. Appleton	Item Co 5th Marine Regt 1st MarDiv
137	James H. Appleton	Item Co 5th Marine Regt 1st MarDiv
139	David F. Link	HQ Co 2d Bn 17th Infantry Regiment 7th Infantry Division
141	James A. Jones	Item Co 3d Bn 7th Marines 1st Marine Division
143	James H. Appleton	Item Co 5th Marine Regiment 1st Marine Division
145	John Covach	Co A 31st Infantry Regiment 7th Infantry Division
147	Jacques K. Doyle	179th Infantry Regiment 45th Infantry Division US National Guard
150	Ronald C. Feldkamp	Heavy Mortar Co 31st Infantry Regiment 7th Infantry Division
153	Peter T. Aguilar	Heavy Mortar Co 31st Infantry Regiment 7th Infantry Division
155	James H. Appleton	Item Co 3d Battalion 5th Marine Regiment 1st Marine Division
157	Chesley Q. Yahtin	Ambulance Co 7th Medical Battalion 7th Infantry Division
159	James H. Appleton	Item Co 3d Battalion 5th Marine Regiment 1st Marine Division
161	Donald M. Cohen	Charlie Co 1st Battalion 38th Infantry Regiment 2d Infantry Division
164	Fred E. Proft	1st Field Artillery Observation Battalion X Corps
167	Ashok Banerjee	60th Indian Field Ambulance Company Republic of India
169	Joaquin B. Benitez	Item Co 3d Battalion 7th Marine Regiment 1st Marine Division
171	Blaine B. Wallin	Fox Co 31st Infantry Regiment 7th Infantry Division
173	William V. Palizzolo	Baker Co 1st Battalion 7th Marine Regiment 1st Marine Division
176	Billie G. Kanell	Company I 35th Infantry Regiment 25th Infantry Division
179	James H. Appleton	Item Co 3d Battalion 5th Marine Regiment 1st Marine Division
181	James H. Appleton	Item Co 3d Battalion 5th Marine Regiment 1st Marine Division
183	Anthony Tavilla	Fox Co 2d Bn 23d Infantry Regiment 2d Infantry Division
185	Dale W. Kember	1092 Engineers(Combat) Battalion 8th Army
187	Daniel Northup	A Co 31st Infantry Regiment 7th Infantry Division
189	Henry D. Buelow	16th Reconn, 1st Cavalry Division & 45th Reconn, 45th Inf Div & USN
191	Joseph C. Violette	Tank Co 31st Infantry Regiment 7th Infantry Division
193	James H. Appleton	Item Co 5th Marine Regiment 1st Marine Division
195	Joseph W. Russo	1st Plat A Co 15 th AAA & 2d Ranger Co & 32d Inf Regt 7th Inf Div
197	Melvin W. Bromby	Motor Torpedo Boat Squadron 1 & MTB Sqdn 2 United States Navy
199	Dennis D. Strickbine	C Co 1st Motor Transport Battalion 1st Marine Division
201	Richard E. Fordyce	Charlie Company 31st Infantry Regiment 7th Infantry Division
203	Roger G. Baker	3d Platoon A Co 1st Tank Battalion 1st Marine Division
205	Roger G. Baker	3d Platoon A Co 1st Tank Battalion 1st Marine Division
207	Lynn W. Dorsey	343d Squadron 98th Bombardment Wing United States Air Forve
209	Emery A. Vallier	Easy Co 7th Cavalry Regiment 1st Cavalry Division
211	James J. Hon	Headquarters & Service Co 1092 Engineers (C) Bn I Corps
213	Esper K. Chandler	2d Platoon Able Co 27th Infantry Regiment 25th Infantry Division
215	James D. Kennicutt	Mike Co 279th Infantry Regiment 45th Infantry Division
217	Gerald E. Lawrence	Item Co 3d Battalion 31st Infantry Regiment 7th Infantry Division
219	Lawrence Hochfeld	504th Transportation Truck Company US Army
221	Paul Z. Hinson	3d Platoon Fox Co 279th Infantry Regiment 45th Infantry Division
223	Roger J. Lueckenhoff	A Co 160th Infantry Regiment 40th Infantry Division
225	John W. Hill	Fox Co 279th Infantry Regiment 45th Infantry Division
227	Jacques K. Doyle	179th Infantry Regiment 45th Infantry Division US National Guard
230	Glenn E. White	Love Co 279th Infantry Regiment 45th Infantry Division
233	Han Chae-Soo	Korean War Correspondent for Seoul Newspaper

TABLE OF CONTENTS

PAGE	FACES OF WAR	UNIT
235	Theodore S. Perry	George Co 223d Infantry Regiment 40th Infantry Division
237	James H. Appleton	Item Company 3d Battalion 5th Marine Regiment 1st Marine Div
240	James J. Hill	Co H 2d Bn 196th Regimental Combat Team Alaska
243	John Covach	A Company 31st Infantry Regiment 7th Infantry Division
245	Max R. Reynolds	Headquarters Co 2d Engineer Battalion(C) 2d Infantry Division
247	Thomas Riley Bunner	Item Co 3d Battalion 223d Infantry Regiment 40th Infantry Division
249	Robert L. Riggs	M Co 160th Infantry Regiment 40th Infantry Division
251	John O. Rem	Battery B 780th Field Artillery Battalion Eighth Army
253	James H. Appleton	Item Co 3d Battalion 5th Marine Regiment 1st Marine Division
255	Edwin E. Marshall	How Co 160th Infantry Regimental Combat Team 40th Infantry Div
257	Christopher E. Sarno	1st Tank Battalion 1st Marine Division Fleet Marine Force USN
260	Hwang Ha-Lyong	Guerilla Intel: KLO G-2, KMC G-2, HID, SOU 105, AISS 6006-SAU 53
263	James H. Appleton	Item Co 3d Battalion 5th Marine Regiment 1st Marine Division
265	Denzil Batson	2d Platoon F Co 2d Bn 15th Infantry Regiment 3d Infantry Division
267	Edward H. Utley	Weapons Co 1st Battalion 1st Marine Regiment 1st Marine Division
269	Carl L. Hempen	2d Chemical Mortar Bn 8th Army
271	Arnoldo A. Muniz	Service & Tank Companies 224th Infantry Regt 40th Infantry Division
273	John A. Lynn	King Co 3d Bn 31st Infantry Regiment 7th Infantry Division
275	Carl L. Hempen	2d Chemical Mortar Bn 8th Army
277	John A. Lynn	King Co 3d Battalion 31st Infantry Regt 7th Infantry Division
280	Chun-sun Ma	Heavy Mortar Co 31st Infantry Regiment 7th Infantry Division
281	Sung-sup An	Tank Co 31st Infantry Regiment 7th Infantry Division
283	Donald F. Gardner	George Co 2d Bn 223d Infantry Regiment 40th Infantry Division
285	David B. Bleak	Medical Co 223d Infantry Regiment 40th Infantry Division USNG
287	George F. Bray	Baker Co 1st Battalion 180th Inf Regt 45th Inf Division USNG
289	Walter Kosowan	54th Transport Coy 2d Royal Canadian Regiment CANADA
291	Jacques K. Doyle	179th Infantry Regiment 45th Infantry Division US National Guard
293	Boyed H. Burnley	Attached Love Co 279th Infantry Regiment 45th Infantry Division
295	Robert A. Gannon	VMA 132 United States Navy
297	Marion C. Wheeler, Jr.	C Co 728th Military Police Battalion Eighth Army
299	Jay E. Hibberts	1st Squad 3d Platoon Fox Co 279th Regimental Combat Team
301	Arthur F. Dorie	Mike Co 3d Battalion 23d Infantry Regiment 3d Infantry Division
303	Lloyd R. Moses	Commanding Officer HQ 31st Infantry Regiment 7th Infantry Div
305	George W. Langdale	2d Platoon Able Co 27th Infantry Regiment 25th Infantry Division
307	Stanley Stoyanof	3dTMRS Transportation Corps 8th Army
309	William J. Dillon	Mike Co 15th Inf Regiment 3d Inf Div & 5th Cav Regt 1st Cav Div
311	Ernest L. Buschjost	2d Chemical Mortar Bn Attached Charlie Co 461st Infantry Battalion
313	Benito Martinez	Co A 27th Infantry Regiment 25th Infantry Division
315	LeVern E. Sundet	Able Co 27th "Wolfhounds" Infantry Regiment 25th Infantry Division
317	John J. Stevenson	Item Co 223d Infantry Regiment 40th Infantry Division USNG
319	Paul G. Myatt	Able Co 27th "Wolfhounds" Infantry Regiment 25th Infantry Division
321	Richard E. Fordyce	Charlie Co 31st Infantry Regiment 7th Infantry Division
323	Clarence D. Beaver	Headquarters Company 31st Infantry Regt 7th Infantry Division
325	Robert B. Campbell	Weapons Co 1st Battalion lst Marine Regiment 1st Marine Division
327	Roy E. Zittle	C Co 1st Battalion 224th Infantry Regiment 40th Infantry Division
329	Paul A. Freeburger	Intelligence & Reconnaissance Platoon 14th Infantry 25th Inf Division
331	James W. Davis	Easy Co 2d Battalion 5th Marine Regiment 1st Marine Division
333	James W. Newland	Don't remember
335	Peter J. Worthington	12 Platoon Dog Co 3d Bn Princess Patricia's Light Inf. CANADA
337	Thomas M. Nielsen	4th Fighter Interceptor Wing 5th Air Force United States Air Force

TABLE OF CONTENTS

PAGE	FACES OF WAR	UNIT
339	Donald A. Chase	Item Company 3d Battalion 15th Infantry Regiment 3d Infantry Division
341	Harley Bogart	539th Quartermaster Laundry Company QM Corps 8th Army
343	Lee Bae-Sun	10th Fighter Wing Air Force Republic of Korea
345	Ivan H. Holshausen	2 Squadron South African Air Force Republic of South Africa
347	Robert E. Levulis	B & HQ Cos 1st Battalion 279th Infantry Regiment 45th Infantry Division
349	Keith E. Roberts	2d Field Artillery Battalion 4.2 inch Rockets US Army
351	Gilbert H. Clausen	Headquarters Company 187th Airborne Regimental Combat Team (Airborne)
353	Leroy I. Strope	Baker Company 15th Infantry Regiment 3d Infantry Division
355	LeVern E. Sundet	Able Co 27 "Wolfhounds" Infantry Regt 25th Infantry Division
357	Herbert L. Scheer	61st Searchlight Company 8th Army
359	Ronald J. Demers	1st Field Artillery Observation Battalion
361	Robert D. Hunt	HU-1 United States Navy
363	Richard A. Rhinehart	185th Engineer(C) Battalion Eighth Army
365	William G. Hawkins	2d Platoon Able Co 1st Battalion 5th Marine Regiment 1st Marine Division
367	Jeremiah G. Crise	16th Fighter Interceptor Sqdn 51st FIG 51st Fighter Interceptor Wing USAF
369	James W. Newland	Don't remember
371	William J. Dillon	Mike Co 15th Infantry Regiment 3d Infantry Div & 5th Cav Regt 1stCavDiv
373	Herbert L. Scheer	61st Searchlight Company Eighth Army
375	Jerome Konsker	Love Co 32d Infantry Regt HQ 7th Div & 7th Signal Co 7th Infantry Division
377	Leonard O. Loethen	45th MASH (Mobile Army Surgical Hospital) 8th Army
379	David P. Whisnant	1st Squad 1st Platoon Baker Co 1st Bn 31st Infantry Regiment 7th Inf Division
381	Christian E. Markey, Jr.	4th Battalion 11th Marine Regiment 1st Marine Division
383	William J. Nelson	Easy Co 223 Inf Regt & HQ Co 224 Infantry Regiment 40th Infantry Division
385	Rollin B. Noble	5th Military Police POW Command #5 Eighth Army
387	Arthur George Elkington	Headquarters Co 3d Battalion 65th Infantry Regiment 3d Infantry Division
389	Hubert S. Coose	Battery A 75th Field Artillery Battalion
392	James A. Brettell	Able Co 13th Combat Engineer Bn 7th Infantry Division
395	Robert C. Wickman	Item Co 3d Battalion 7th Marine Regiment 1st Marine Division
397	David S. Mueller	George Co 2d Battalion 224th Infantry Regiment 40th Infantry Division
399	James L. Pitzer	How (Weapons) Co 3d Battalion 7th Marine Regiment 1st Marine Division
401	Dan D. Schoonover	Company A 13th Engineer Combat Battalion 7th Inf Division
403	James H. Vitali	75th FA Bn-(155mm howitzer) 8th Army
405	Austin H. Glass	Item Co 3d Battalion 1st Marine Regiment 1st Marine Division
407	Donald A. Chase	Item Company 3d Battalion 15th Infantry Regiment 3d Infantry Division
409	William H. Funchess	C Company 1st Battalion 19th Infantry Regiment 24th Infantry Division
411	Nyle T. Jones	Btry D 15th Automatic Anti Aircraft Bn SP Atchd 31st Inf Regt 7th Inf Div
413	Paul F. Carroll	428th Engineer Water Supply Co 378th Eng Utility Detachment 8th Army
415	Jarvis M. Barrett	868th Field Artillery (Atomic) Battalion (Germany)
417	Richard L. Johnston	Co 2 KCZLLSG US Signal Corps US Army
419	Charles W. Bowar	B Company 24th Infantry Regiment 25th Infantry Division
421	Charles N. Phillips	Kearsarge CVA 33 1953-'55 (Taiwan Combat Zone) USNavy
423	Walter Cox Benton	3d Military Police Company 3d Infantry Division
425	Eugene P. Moser	Headquarters & Headquarters Company 1st Bn 38th Inf Bde (Brigade)
428	Choi Kee-Tae	12th Infantry Division ROK Army Republic of Korea
431	Jean Kirnak nee Bowen	8076 MASH (Mobile Army Surgical Hospital)
434	Maurice Siskel, Jr.	Heavy Mortar Co 31st Infantry Regiment 7th Infantry Division
438	Thomas F. Marker Sr.	Heavy Mortar Co 31st infantry Regiment 7th Infantry Division
439	TFM,Sr & General Alexander M. Haig, Jr.	Then 1st Lt, Aide to Major Gen Ned Almond X Corps US Army, Cmdg.

ACKNOWLEDGMENTS

The pictorial history of the Korean War is enhanced by the reality of the many battlefield photos provided by those veterans who allowed publication of their own wartime photographs. It is our hope their gift of these scenes to posterity will serve as a sobering reminder of the brutality and ugliness of war and the bonding lifetime comradeship resulting from shared military experiences.

We are highly indebted to Master Sergeant Roger J. Leuckenhoff of Able Company 160th Infantry Regiment, 40th Division. Sergeant Leukenhoff contacted former regiment and division comrades of the Korean War with the request that he be permitted to furnish their names to us for contact and possible inclusion of their memories of the Korean War in the book *Red Dragon*. Without his assistance we could not have obtained appropriate representation of the service of men in the 40th Infantry Division of the California National Guard during its service in Japan and Korea.

We also wish to express our gratitude to readers of *The Graybeard*,
National magazine of the Korean War Veterans Association,
who responded to our notice of intent to publish Red Dragon.

We are also indebted to editors of several regimental news letters
Who printed our "Message to Garcia."

We also express our sincere appreciation to those poets of the Korean War
who granted permission to include their verse in this book.

Any book that purports to record the experiences of veterans of any war
must include the poetry and doggerel verse composed in times of rest,
and sung around camp fires in a rear area encampments

AT ARLINGTON

BENEATH THE SOD AT ARLINGTON
OUR COUNTRY'S HEROES REST
THE GRASSY PLAINS OF GETTYSBURG
EMBRACE A NATION'S BEST.

BUT FAR BEYOND OUR SACRED SHORES
ARE MANY UNMARKED GRAVES
IN BITTER SAND ON FOREIGN LAND
OR UNDER TOSSING WAVES.

THERE ALSO SLEEP OUR GALLANT ONES
WHOSE LONELY RESTING PLACE
HATH NO BLOOM OR RIBBONED WREATH
OR FRIENDS TO GATHER ROUND

THERE IS NO STONE TO MARK THE SPOT
WHERE FIGHTING FIERCE THEY FELL,
LOOKED THEIR LAST AS EYES GREW DIM
ON BATTLE SCENES FROM HELL.

NO BUGLE SINGS THEIR EPITAPH
NO HEAD IS BOWED IN PRAYER
NO PROUD SALUTE OF RIFLE FIRE
BREAKS THE SILENT AIR.

AND YET, THEY ARE WITH US STILL
AS SURELY AS WE STAND
UPON THIS BLESSED AND HOLY SOIL
THAT IS THEIR NATIVE LAND.

THEIR COURAGE IS OUR HERITAGE
THEIR SACRIFICE IS OUR SHIELD
SYMBOLIC OF THOSE NOBLE HEARTS
THAT KNEW NOT HOW TO YIELD.
OUR DEAD WERE LAID TO REST
WHILE THE BUGLER SOUNDED TAPS
IN HONOR OF THE NATION'S BEST.

VALOR

THERE IS A DECORATION
WHICH STANDS ABOVE THE REST
TO CITE OUTSTANDING BRAVERY
AMONG OUR NATION'S BEST/

THIRTEEN STARS ARE CLUSTERED
ON A BAND OF SOFTENED BLUE
AND THE MEDAL IT EMBRACES
IS HELD BY VERY FEW.

THIS HONORED STAR OF VALOR
SPEAKS OF COURAGE WITHOUT PEER
AND OF SELFLESS DEDICATION
WHEN HELL AND DEATH DREW NEAR

ITS METTLE HAS BEEN TESTED
ON THE FIERY FIELD OF WAR
ON JUNGLE TRAILS, IN MOUNTAIN VALES
AND TO THE OCEAN FLOOR

ITS SPIRIT HAS SHONE BRIGHTLY
WHERE HAWKS AND EAGLES FLY
AND WHERE MEN WHO RODE THE THUNDER
HAVE GONE TO FIGHT AND DIE.

IN MANY TIMES, IN MANY CLIMES
ENGAGED IN MORTAL STRIFE
THE ACT THAT GAINED THE MEDAL
BROUGHT TO END A GALLANT LIFE

AND TO THOSE FEW WHO CARRY ON
THERE IS NO TRIBUTE WE CAN PAY
NO ACCOLADE TO GIVE
THEY DO NOT SEEK FOR WORLDLY GAIN
FOR HONORS, PRAISE, OR LAND
BUT JUST TO KNOW THEY SERVED SO WELL
THEIR COUNTRY AND THEIR GOD.

AT ARLINGTON

VALOR

BENEATH THE SOD AT ARLINGTON
OUR COUNTRY'S HEROES REST
THE GRASSY PLAINS OF GETTYSBURG
EMBRACE A NATION'S BEST.

BUT FAR BEYOND OUR SACRED SHORES
ARE MANY UNMARKED GRAVES
IN BITTER SAND ON FOREIGN LAND
OR UNDER TOSSING WAVES.

THERE ALSO SLEEP OUR GALLANT ONES
WHOSE LONELY RESTING PLACE
HATH NO BLOOM OR RIBBONED WREATH
OR FRIENDS TO GATHER ROUND

THERE IS NO STONE TO MARK THE SPOT
WHERE FIGHTING FIERCE THEY FELL,
LOOKED THEIR LAST AS EYES GREW DIM
ON BATTLE SCENES FROM HELL.

NO BUGLE SINGS THEIR EPITAPH
NO HEAD IS BOWED IN PRAYER
NO PROUD SALUTE OF RIFLE FIRE
BREAKS THE SILENT AIR.

AND YET, THEY ARE WITH US STILL
AS SURELY AS WE STAND
UPON THIS BLESSED AND HOLY SOIL
THAT IS THEIR NATIVE LAND.

THEIR COURAGE IS OUR HERITAGE
THEIR SACRIFICE IS OUR SHIELD
SYMBOLIC OF THOSE NOBLE HEARTS
THAT KNEW NOT HOW TO YIELD.

OUR DEAD WERE LAID TO REST
WHILE THE BUGLER SOUNDED TAPS
IN HONOR OF THE NATION'S BEST

THERE IS A DECORATION
WHICH STANDS ABOVE THE REST
TO CITE OUTSTANDING BRAVERY
AMONG OUR NATION'S BEST/

THIRTEEN STARS ARE CLUSTERED
ON A BAND OF SOFTENED BLUE
AND THE MEDAL IT EMBRACES
IS HELD BY VERY FEW.

THIS HONORED STAR OF VALOR
SPEAKS OF COURAGE WITHOUT PEER
AND OF SELFLESS DEDICATION
WHEN HELL AND DEATH DREW NEAR

ITS METTLE HAS BEEN TESTED
ON THE FIERY FIELD OF WAR
ON JUNGLE TRAILS, IN MOUNTAIN VALES
AND TO THE OCEAN FLOOR

ITS SPIRIT HAS SHONE BRIGHTLY
WHERE HAWKS AND EAGLES FLY
AND WHERE MEN WHO RODE THE THUNDER
HAVE GONE TO FIGHT AND DIE.

IN MANY TIMES, IN MANY CLIMES
ENGAGED IN MORTAL STRIFE
THE ACT THAT GAINED THE MEDAL
BROUGHT TO END A GALLANT LIFE

AND TO THOSE FEW WHO CARRY ON
THERE IS NO TRIBUTE WE CAN PAY
NO ACCOLADE TO GIVE

THEY DO NOT SEEK FOR WORLDLY GAIN
FOR HONORS, PRAISE, OR LAND
BUT JUST TO KNOW THEY SERVED SO WELL
THEIR COUNTRY AND THEIR GOD

THE POEMS *AT ARLINGTON* AND *VALOR* ARE QUOTED BY PERMISSION OF THE AUTHOR
ROBERT A. GANNON, FROM HIS BOOK OF VERSE.....*THE LAUGHTER AND THE TEAR*S ©1997

OLD SOLDIERS NEVER DIE, THEY JUST FADE AWAY

Gen. Douglas A. MacArthur in the twilight of his life gave this speech to US Military Academy cadets at West Point in January 1962 two years before his death 5 April 1964. Born 26 January 1880, he graduated in 1903 from West Point in 1903 with a scholastic record yet to be equaled. He spanned the transition from American Frontier to Space Age. His life was filled with the grandeur and sorrow of a soldier who sees his country from both sides of the coin of birth and death. One of the truly great Americans.

"No human being could fail to be deeply moved by such a tribute, coming from a profession I have served so long and a people I have loved so well. It fills me with an emotion I cannot express. This award is not intended primarily for a personality, but symbolizes a great moral code, the code of conduct and chivalry of those who guard this beloved land of culture and ancient descent. "Duty," "honor," "country" those three hallowed words reverently dictate what you want to be, what you can be, what you will be. They are your rallying point to build courage when courage seems to fail, to regain faith when there seems to be little cause for faith, to create hope when hope becomes forlorn. Unhappily, I possess neither that eloquence of diction, that poetry of imagination, nor that brilliance of metaphor to tell you all that they mean. The unbelievers will say they are but words, but a slogan, but a flamboyant phrase. Every pedant, every demagogue, every cynic, every hypocrite, every troublemaker, and, I am sorry to say, some others of an entirely different character will try to downgrade them, even to the extent of mockery and ridicule.

"But these are some of the things they build. They build your basic character. They mold you for your future roles as the custodians of the nation's defense. They make you strong enough to know when you are weak, and brave enough to face yourself when you are afraid. They teach you to be proud and unbending in honest failure, but humble and gentle in success; not to substitute words for action; not to seek the path of comfort, but to face the stress and spur of difficulty and challenge; to learn to stand up in the storm, but to have compassion on those who fall; to master yourself before you seek to master others; to have a heart that is clean, a goal that is high; to learn to laugh, yet never forget how to weep; to reach into the future, yet never neglect the past; to be serious, yet never take yourself too seriously; to be modest so that you will remember the simplicity of true greatness; the open mind of true wisdom, the meekness of true strength. They give you a temperate will, a quality of imagination, a vigor of the emotions, a freshness of the deep springs of life, a temperamental predominance of courage over timidity, an appeti enture over love of ease. They create in your heart the sense of wonder, the unfailing hope of what next, and the joy and inspiration of life. They teach you in this way to be an officer and a gentleman.

"And what sort of soldiers are those you are to lead? Are they reliable? Are they brave? Are they capable of victory? Their story is known to all of you. It is the story of the American man at arms. My estimate of him was formed on the battlefields many, many years ago, and has never changed. I regarded him then, as I regard him now, as one of the world's noblest figures; not only as one of the finest military characters, but also as one of the most stainless.

"His name and fame are the birthright of every American citizen. In his youth and strength, his love and loyalty, he gave all that mortality can give. He needs no eulogy from me, or from any other man. He has written his own history and written it in red on his enemy's breast. In 20 campaigns, on a hundred battlefields, around a thousand campfires, I have witnessed that enduring fortitude, that patriotic self-abnegation, that invincible determination which have carved his statue in the hearts of his people. From one end of the world to the other, he has drained deep the chalice of courage. I do not know the dignity of their birth, but I do know the glory of their death. They died unquestioning, uncomplaining, with faith in their hearts, and on their lips the hope that we would go on to victory. Always for them: duty, honor, country. Always their blood, sweat, and tears, as they saw the way and the light.

"As I listened to those songs in memory's eye I see those staggering columns of the First World War, bending under soggy packs on many a weary march, from dripping dusk to drizzling dawn, slogging ankle deep through mire of shell-pocked roads; to form grimly for the attack, blue-lipped, covered with sludge and mud, chilled by the wind and rain, driving home to their objective, and for many, to the judgment seat of God. And 20 years after, on the other side of the globe, against the filth of dirty foxholes, the stench of ghostly trenches, the slime of dripping dugouts, those boiling suns of the relentless heat, those torrential rains of devastating storms, the loneliness and utter desolation of jungle trails, the bitterness of long separation of those they loved and cherished, the deadly pestilence of tropic disease, the horror of stricken areas of war. Their resolute and determined defense, their swift and sure attack, their indomitable purpose, their complete and decisive victory, always victory, always through the bloody haze of their last reverberating shot, the vision of gaunt, ghostly men, reverently following the guidance of your password, duty, honor, country.

You now face a new world, a world of change. The thrust into outer space of the satellite spheres and missiles marks a beginning of another epoch in the long story of mankind. In the five or more billions of years the scientists tell us it has taken to form the earth in the three or more billion years of development of the human race, there has never been a more abrupt or staggering evolution. We deal now, not with things of this world alone, but with the illimitable distances and yet unfathomed mysteries of the universe. We are reaching out for a new and boundless frontier. We speak in strange terms of harnessing the cosmic energy, of making winds and tides work for us; of the primary target in war, no longer limited to the armed forces of an enemy, but instead to include his civil population; of ultimate conflict between a united human race and the sinister forces of some other planetary galaxy; such dreams and fantasies as to make life the most exciting of all times.

Everything else in your professional career is but corollary to this vital dedication. All other public purpose, all other public projects, all other public needs, great or small, will find others for their accomplishments; but you are the ones who are trained to fight. And through all this welter of change and development your mission remains fixed, determined, inviolable. It is to win our wars. Yours is the profession of arms, the will to win, the sure knowledge in war there is no substitute for victory, if you lose, the Nation will be destroyed, the very obsession of your public service must be duty, honor, country.

"Others will debate the controversial issues, national and international, which divide men's minds. But serene, calm, aloof, you stand as the Nation's war guardians, as its lifeguards from the raging tides of international conflict, as its gladiators in the arena of battle. For a century and a half you have defended, guarded and protected its hallowed traditions of liberty and freedom, of right and justice. Let civilian voices argue the merits or demerits of our processes of government. Whether our strength is being sapped by deficit financing indulged in too long, by federal paternalism grown too mighty, by power groups grown too arrogant, by politics grown too corrupt, by crime grown too rampant, by morals grown too low, by taxes grown too high, by extremists grown too violent; whether our personal liberties are as firm and complete as they should be. These great national problems are not for your professional participation or military solution.

"Your guidepost stands out like a tenfold beacon in the night: duty, honor, country. You are the leaven which binds together the entire fabric of our national system of defense. From your ranks come the great captains who hold the Nation's destiny in their hands the moment the war tocsin sounds. The long gray line has never failed us. Were you to do so, a million ghosts in olive drab, in brown khaki, in blue and gray, would rise from their white crosses, thundering those magic words: duty, honor, country. This does not mean that you are warmongers. On the contrary, the soldier above all other people prays for peace it is he who must suffer and bear the deepest wounds and scars of war. But always in our ears ring the ominous words of Plato, wisest of all philosophers: "Only the dead have seen the end of war."

The shadows are lengthening for me. The twilight is here. My days of old have vanished tone and tints. They have gone glimmering through the dreams of things that were. Their memory is one of wondrous beauty, watered by tears and coaxed and caressed by the smiles of yesterday. I listen with thirsty ear, for the witching melody of faint bugles blowing reveille, of far drums beating the long roll. In my dreams I hear again the crash of guns, the rattle of musketry, the strange, mournful mutter of the battlefield. But in the evening of my memory I come back to West Point. Always there echoes and re-echoes: duty, honor, country. Today marks my final roll call with you. But I want you to know that when I cross the river, my last conscious thoughts will be of the corps, and the corps, and the corps.

HOMECOMING

NO BUGLES BLEW WHEN HE CAME HOME NO TRUMPET SANG HIS PRAISE NO ROLLING DRUMS OF VICTORY RECALLING HIS NOBLEST DAYS.	NO LAUREL LEAF WAS ON HIS BROW NO SCEPTER IN HIS HAND NO WILDLY WAVING BANNERS ABOVE HIS NATIVE LAND.
NO PROUDLY SMILING BROTHERS NO SISTER'S HAPPY FACE NO COMRADE'S CHEERFUL GREETING NO LOVER'S WARM EMBRACE.	JUST A SILENT GUARD OF HONOR WHERE HIS SHATTERED BODY LIES JUST A FLAG ON HIS CASKET AND A MOTHER'S MISTY EYES.

THE HILLS OF KOREA

The American soldier fought three tough enemies in the Korean War. Two, Chinese and North Korean, were human. Terrain and climate were, in an impersonal and very impartial way, almost as deadly as the shot and shell of the human foe. The thirty to fifty degree below zero winter temperatures exacted a heavy toll in frostbite casualties in the winter. But in every season, from freezing cold to broiling sun, the Korean hills were always there. Based on the age-old military maxim, "Control the high ground," ferocious battles were fought to dominate the high terrain in every sector. Good observation meant artillery fire could be directed accurately. Further, control of the high ground meant the enemy must climb in the attack while under fire. Mountain climbing is hard tiring, work. Soldiers are exhausted by the climb before they can close with the enemy. The attacker of the "high ground" will pay a 4 to 1 price in dead and wounded. Both sides vied in this deadly contest. 'Hills' do not sound high to Americans who measure their hills in feet. Hill 1179 measured in meters, towers to a height of 3,595 feet. Nor, at first, do they sound high to a soldier until, as a member of a fatigue party, he climbs several times daily in the role of human pack mule, replenishing ammunition, water, food, medical supplies, all the miscellaneous equipment needed daily by thousands of soldiers existing in fox holes and bunkers. As noted elsewhere in his book, it has been said with some degree of truth, "If the 'hills' of Korea were hammered flat, it would be the largest country on earth."

HILLS OF BATTLE IN THE KOREAN WAR 1950-1953 EAST TO WEST

Hill Name	Height in Meters	Grid Coordinates	Geographic Location	REMARKS
Anchor Hill Area	Hill	414472	East coast	Enemy held
	Hill 339		Just south of Anchor Hill	
	Hill 269		South of Anchor Hill	
	Hill 346		South of Anchor Hill	
	Hill 350		South of Anchor Hill	
	Hill 854		NE of Punchbowl	
	Hill 812		North of Punchbowl	
	Hill 755		North of Punchbowl	
	Hill 673		North of Punchbowl	
	Hill 749		North of Punchbowl	
Punchbowl Area		240370		Assembly area for invasion of Seoul
	Hill 841			Just north of Punchbowl
	Hill 673			North of Punchbowl
	Hill 749			North of Punchbowl
	Hill 1179		West edge of Punchbowl,	Taeusan
Bloody Ridge	Hill 983		South of Heartbreak Ridge	
	Hill 940		Near Punchbowl	
	Hill 773		Near Punchbowl	
Heartbreak Ridge	Hill 894,931,851	142403	West of Punchbowl	
Noname Ridge	Hill......		Near Heartbreak Ridge	
	Hill 1220		West of Heartbreak Ridge	
	Hill 689			
Christmas Hill	Hill.....	055428	East of Kumwha	
Wire Ridge	Hill.....	'970461'		
Capitol Hill	Hill......	'905493'	East of Kumwha	
Finger Ridge	Hill......	878498	East of Kumwha	
	Hill 394		East of Kumwha	
Sniper ridge	Hill 598	677426	ENE of Kumwha, South of Kumsong	
OP 51	Hill......		5th RCT site, overrun by Chinese	
OP 52	Hill......		5th RCT site, overrun by Chinese 13 Jul '53	
Jane Russell	Hill......	664424	NE of Triangle Hill	
Sandy Ridge	Hill......	668413		
Triangle Hill	Hill 598	660418	3 miles N of Kumwha	
Lightning Hill	Hill......		NE, between Kumwha and Kumsong	
Papa San Mtn	Hill 1162	649459	6 miles N of Kumwha	

Hills of Korea compiled by Art Elkington PO Bx 8346 Kalispell, MT 59904. He would appreciate correction and additional input data.

HILLS OF BATTLE IN THE KOREAN WAR 1950-1953 EAST TO WEST

Hill Name	Height in Meters	Grid Coordinates	Geographic Location	REMARKS
Sugar Loaf	Hill 105	630476	NW of Papa San	
Boomerang	Area	613424	East flank of Iron Triangle near Papa San	
Pikes Peak	Hill 454	642428	2 ½ miles NNW of Kumwha City	
Iron Triangle		525515	North, near City of Pynoggang	
Iron Triangle		430350	West, near City of Chorwon	
Iron Triangle		656388	East, Near City of Kumwha	
OP Harry	Hill 528	508421	Center of Iron Triangle	
Star Hill	Hill 478	507426	NNW of OP Harry	
Hill 412		518420	NNE of OP Harry	
OP Howe	Hill 361	508405	1 mile S of OP Harry	
	Hill 717	536453	NNE of OP Harry	
	Hill 682	552457	4 miles NE of OP Harry	
North Star	Hill 478	501434		
	Hill 528	543431	NE of OP Harry	
	Hill 589	534346	5 miles SSE of OP Harry	
Jackson Heights	Hill......	476435	West flank of Iron Triangle	
OP Tom	Hill 270	471426		
OP Dick	Hill......	488422		
Iron Horse Mt	Hill 391	477433	North of Jackson Heights	
Reserve Area	Hill 456	534326		
Chorwon Hill	Hill 362	419348		
	Hill 284	406397	West of Chorwon city	
Hadicoll view point	Hill......	384338	Chorwon Valley panorama	
Whitehorse Mt	Hill 396	381398	5 miles NW Chorwon City	
Arrowhead	Hill 281	352385	5 miles WNW ofChorwon City	
Twin Peaks	Hill......	354350	Just East of Hill 292	
Twin Peaks	Hill	357349		
	Hill 477	334316		
	Hill 487	347338		
Alligator Hill	Hill 324	326361		
Alligator Jaws	Hill......	315370	1 mile NW of Hill 324	
The T-Bone	Hill 290	285376	2 miles west of Alligator Jaws	
Arsenal	Hill......	295355	Just south of T-Bone	
OP Erie	Hill 191	297349	South end of Arsenal	
	Hill 200	295358	Between T-Bone and Arsenal	
Yoke	Hill......	315355	Just south of Alligator Jaws	
Uncle	Hill......	310350	Just south of Yoke	
Snook, OP 9	Hill......	286346	½ mile SW Hill 191 -OP Erie	
Spud	Hill......	295362	West of Alligator Jaws at the T-Bone	
Pork Chop OP 10	Hill 255	261353	OP 10 located on Pork Chop South of T-Bone	
Old Baldy OP 11	Hill 266	255321	South of Pork Chop Hill	
	Hill 206		4 miles N of Ancien	
Queen	Hill.......	216274	SW of Old Baldy	
	Hill 179		SW of Queen on Imjin River	
Bak Area		214260	South, next to Hill 279	
Hannah	Hill......	211267	South of Bak on the Imjin River	
Big Nori	Hill......	215235	South of Bak on the Imjin River	
Little Nori	Hill......	216235	South of Bak on the Imjin River	
Betty	Hill......	210223	South of Bak on the Imjin River	
Tessie	Hill......	203266	South of Bak on the Imjin	

Hills of Korea compiled by Art Elkington PO Bx 8346 Kalispell, MT59904. Additional input data&corrections desired.

HILLS OF BATTLE IN THE KOREAN WAR 1950-1953,   EAST TO WEST

OP Kelly	Hill......	197223	West of Imjin River and Little Nori
Dagmar	Hill 355		West of Yonchon
	Hill 238		2500 yards west of Dagmar
Little Gibralter	Hill......		SW of OP Kelly
The Hook	Hill......	103104	East of Kaesong
Detroit Hill......			East of Kaesong
Boulder City Complex	Hill 119		
OP Berlin	Hill 111	003081	
OP East Berlin	Hill......	088082	East of Kaesong
Nevada City	Hill......		East of Kaesong
Vegas	Hill......		East of Kaesong
Reno	Hill......	068079	East of Kaesong
Elko	Hill......	067075	
Carson	Hill......	064075	East of Kaesong
Ungok	Hill 101		
	Hill 58		1/4 mile NE of Bunker Hill
Bunker Hill	Hill 122	015042	
	Hill 916		200 yards in front of Bunker Hill
	Hill 800		South of ridge on Bunker Hill
	Hill 754		South of ridge on Bunker Hill
Hedy	Hill......	014036	
	Hill 67		
	Hill 90		
	Hill 812		
	Hill 754		
	Hill 755		
	Hill 520		
	Hill 1151		
	Hill 543		
	Hill 1147		Near Chipon
	Hill 393		Near Waegwon
	Hill 283		
	Hill 454		Near Hill 200
OP Victor	Hill......		

The above numbered hills were ON or Near the MLR as it was constituted in spring-summer of 1953. The compiler of this list, Arthur Elkington, would appreciate any input in the way of correction of the above listing. Any additional information concerning the hills listed below as to "name" of the hill as was used on patrol maps or artillery concentrations would be welcomed also. The information requested in his research is limited to the period 1 January to 27 July 1953. He is seeking the *name of the Hill or the OP*, *the Hill Height*, the *Map Grid Coordinates* and the *General Location*. Your supplementary comments would be most helpful to his project.

HILLS BY NUMBER. ALL NUMBERS ARE IN METERS

981, 466, 500, 284, 456, 600, 283, 453, 454, 303, 1147, 543, 1151, 520, 755, 689, 394, 528, 346, 67, 90, 812, 754 , 238, 206, 396
Also Hills in other sectors of the MLR: 600, 456, 453, 238, 206, 346, 284, 396, 812, and 406

HIS ADDRESS
Arthur G. Elkington
PO Box 8346
Kalispell, MT 59904

ABBREVIATIONS & ACRONYMS

AAA	Antiaircraft Artillery
AFPS	Armed Forces Press Service
ANGLICO	Air-Naval Gunfire Liaison Company
AP	Armor-piercing
Arty	Artillery
Asst	Assistant
BAR	Browning Automatic Rifle
BGen	Brigadier General
Bn	Battalion
BOQ	Batchelors Officer's Quarters
Btry	Battery
(C)	Combat
C/S	Chief of Staff
Capt	Captain
Cav	Cavalry
CCF	Chinese Communist Forces
CG	Commanding General
Chicom(s)	Chinese Communist Forces
CINCFE	Commander in Chief, Far East
Cmdr	Commander
Co, Coy	Company
CO	Commanding Officer
Col	Colonel
Comp C	Composition C- A plastic military explosive.
CP	Command Post
DA	Department of the Army
Div	Division
DOA	Department of the Army. Also, Dead on Arrival.
DOW	Died of Wounds
DUKW	Amphibious Truck
EM	Enlisted Man *or* men
Eng	Engineer
ETO	European Theatre of Operations
EUSAK	Eighth US Army in Korea
1st Sergeant	First Sergeant, Ranking Co NCO, "Top Kick", "First Soldier'
F-51	Air Force Mustang fighter-bomber
F4U	Marine Corsair fighter-bomber
FA	Field Artillery
FAC	Forward Air Controller
FDC	Fire Direction Center
FEAF	Far East Air Forces
FEC	Far East Command
54RR 57mm	54mm Recoilless Rifle. A squad weapon in Korea
FECOM	Far East Command-- Gen MacArthur's command in Asia
FMF	Fleet Marine Force
FO	Forward Observer (artillery or mortar)
Fuse VT	Variable Time Set Fuse.
Fuse Quick	Shell with fuse set to explode on instant of impact.
G-1	Army, Corps or Div Personnel Section
G-2	Army, Corps or Div Intelligence
G-3	Plans & Operations, Army, Corps or Div

ABBREVIATIONS & ACRONYMS

G-4	Supply& Logistics Army, Corps or Div
GCR	Ground Control Radar
Gen	General
GHQ	General Headquarters
GO	General Orders
Gy Sgt, "Gunny"	Gunnery Sergeant USMC
H&S, HQ & Svc	Headquarters and Service
HE	High explosive
HEAT	High explosive anti tank
HMG	Heavy Machine Gun, water cooled, cal .30
HM	Heavy Mortar, rifled mortar, 4.2" diameter, firing a 25 lb shell.
HQ	Head quarters
Inf	Infantry
KATUSA	Korean Army Troops with United States Army
KIA	Killed in action
KMAG	Korean Military Advisory Group
L-17, L-19	Single wing prop planes, observation & "jack of all work."
LCI	Landing Craft, Infantry
LCP	Landing Craft Personnel
LCVP	Landing Craft, Vehicle and Personnel
LMG	Light Machine Gun, cal. 30, air cooled,highly maneuverable.
LP	Listening Post
LSD	Landing Ship Dock
LSMR	Landing Ship, Medium, Rocket
LST	Landing Ship Tank
LSV	Landing Ship, Vehicle
Lt	Lieutenant
Lt Col	Lieutenant Colonel
LVT	Landing vehicle, tracked
M-1	Garand rifle, std .30 cal weapon of US Infantry in WWII & Korea
M-16	Armored half track vehicle mounting Quad .50 cal MG's
M-19	Armored track vehicle mounting Dual 40mm quick firing cannon
M-2 boat tail	30. cal rifle ammunition muzzle velocity of approx 2000 ft/sec
MAG	Marine Air Group *or* Military Advisory Group
Maj	Major
MarDiv	Marine division
MATS	Military Air Transport Service
MC	Medical Corps
METO	Machine gun
Mgen	Major General
MIA	Missing in Action
MLR	Main line of resistance
MP	Military Police
Msgt	Master Sergeant
MSR	Main Suppl;y Route
NCO	Non Commissioned Officer-Corporals & Sergeants.
NK	North Korean
NOKO, NoKo	North Korean Soldier
NKPA	North Korean Peoples Army
O	Officer

ABBREVIATIONS & ACRONYMS

OJT On Job Training, ironic military term- the learning curve in battle.

OP	Observation Post, also Out Post
OPL, OPLR	Outpost Line of Resistance
Pfc, PFC	Private first class
PLA	Peoples Liberation Army (China)
Plat, Plt	Platoon
POL	Petroleum, Oil & Lubricants
POW, PW	Prisoner of war
Primacord	A military high explosive in cord form. Used in demolition.
PROV	Provisional
Proximity Fuse	Shell designed to explode on close passage to trees, rocks, etc.
Pvt	Private
Quad 50	Four .50 caliber MGs fired as an integral unit
RCT	Regimental Combat Team.
Recon	Reconnaissance {British, Recce} {US Marines, often, Reconn}
RJ	Road Junction
ROK	Republic of Korea
ROKS, ROKs	South Korean soldiers
RTO	Radio-Telephone Operator
S/Sgt	Staff Sergeant
S-1	Adjutant (personnel) Regt or Bn
S-2	Intelligence, Regt or Bn
S-3	Plans & Operations, Regt or Bn
S-4	Supply, Regt or Bn
SCR	Set, complete radio
SFC	Sergeant first class
75RR	75mm Recoilless Rifle. A Bn weapon, often asgd to a rifle Co.
Sgt	Sergeant
SITREP	Situation report
SMaj	Sergeant major
SP	Self propelled
T/O	Table of Organization
TOT	Time on Target, simultaneous massed fire on a target
T/O&E	Table of Organization and Equipment
Tetryl	A military high explosive used in demolitions
TF	Task Force
TSgt	Technical Sergeant
TSMG	Thompson Sub Machine Gun
Twin 40' s	Dual 40mm quick firing cannon
UDT	Underwater Demolition Team
UN	United Nations
USA	United States Army
USAF	United States Air Force
USMC	United States Marine Corps
USN	United States Navy
VMF	Marine Fighter Squadron
VT	Variable Time Fuse
WIA	Wounded in Action
WP	White Phosphorus
XO	Executive officer, officer second in command of a military unit.
YAK-9	WW II Russian low level attack plane used by North Korea.

MEDALS & AWARDS

ACM	Army Commendation Medal
ACM	American Campaign Medal WWII
ACSM	American Campaign Service Medal
ADM	American Defense Medal WWII
ADSM	American Defense Service Medal
AFOUA	Air Force Award
AFRM	Armed Forces Reserve Medal
AFUC	Air Force Unit Citation
AM	Air Medal
APCM	Asiatic Pacific Campaign Medal, WWII
ARCOM	Army Commendation Medal w/ pendent
BS	Bronze Star
BSM	Bronze Star Medal
CIB	Combat Infantry Badge
CM	Commendation Medal
CMB	Combat Medical Badge
CMH	Congressional Medal of Honor
DFC	Distinguished Flying Cross
DSCN	Distinguished Service Cross, Navy. "Navy Cross."
DSC	Distinguished Service Cross
DSM	Distinguished Service Medal
EAME	Europe, Africa, Middle East Campaign Medal WWII
GC	*British*-Good Conduct Badge
GCM	Good Conduct Medal
KCSM	Korean Campaign Service Medal
KPUC	Korean Presidential Unit Citation
KWSM	Korean War Service Medal
KPM	Korean Peace Medal
LM	Legion of Merit.
LSM	*British*-Long Service medal
MCGCM	Marine Corps Good Conduct Medal
MOH	Medal of Honor (Congressional)
NCA	Navy Commendation Award
NDSM	National Defense Service Medal
NGSM	*British*-Naval General Service Medal
NPUC	Navy Presidential Unit Citation
OM,J	Occupation Medal Japan after WWII
OM,G	Occupation Medal Germany after WWII
PH	Purple Heart
PUC	Presidential Unit Citation
PWM	Prisoner of War Medal
ROK PUC	Republic of Korea Presidential Unit Citation
SS	Silver Star
SSM	Silver Star Medal
UNSM	United Nations Service Medal
USNGCM	US Navy Good Conduct Medal
VM	Victory Medal WWII
VSCM	Viet Nam Campaign

ABOUT THIS BOOK

The legacy of this book is an inheritance from *Korean Vignettes, Faces of War*©, a book well received by Korean War veterans. In the memories of those whose vignettes were portrayed, the book gave a realistic view of the Korean War panorama. *Red Dragon, The Second Round, Faces of War II* , had a different origin and a much more difficult birth. Both the Editor and Photographer, two amateurs, had grappled with the complexities of invading the turf of an established publishing industry. By the time we had successfully shot our way through the many roadblocks encountered, we vowed, "Never Again!" We held to that oath for four years, giving the same answer to those urging emphasis on the history of the latter half of the Korean War in a second book. We faced the same query every year at reunions of the 31st Infantry Regiment. We had the same answer for those who noted we had not mentioned the contribution of the 40th and 45th National Guard Divisions. This was an unintended slight, reflecting a lack of knowledge by the editors whose Korean War experience was limited to the period June 1950 through year end 1951.

Guilt gnawing at our collective conscience finally resulted in a decision to correct the unintended slight to the two National Guard Divisions. Preliminary research revealed a historical lack of detail. The detailed history "bible" of the Korean War, *The Forgotten War* by Clay Blair, devotes 941 pages to the period 25 June 1950 through 10 July 1951. The remaining 35 pages cover 11 July 1951 to war's end, 27 July 1953. However, those 35 pages are devoted solely to 'Peace Talks" and difficulties of POW exchange. Truly his "Forgotten War" title applies literally only to the latter half of the Korean War. We did not have the means to explore the extensive material available at Carlisle Barracks, or other repositories of military information. We resorted to use of the same device we had pioneered in Korean Vignettes, memories of those who were there in the making of military history, the veterans who fought it.

Conversation with members of the 31st Infantry at annual reunions soon revealed a wealth of anecdotal memories detailing activities in the latter part of the war. We finally decided to go ahead with the project. Initially, we projected two books. One, devoted to mid 1951 through mid 1952, the second, from mid 1952 to war's end. As we waded into our second year of work, we decided to limit our effort to one book in a wrap up of our effort to save for posterity the persona of the Korean War soldier. This decision was twofold. First, we had bitten off more that we could realistically chew, considering the mortality table statistics applying to the Editors' ages.

The second reason was mundane. We had blithely decided to place all work, including photos, on CDs for safety in case of a hard drive crash. A check was made with the printer to ascertain if CDs were acceptable for book printing. Little did the Editors know! We failed to check out the intricacies involved in transfer of data from CD to a printer's computer. Too late, we found special software programs were needed. By the time we were aware of this, two years had elapsed. The work was well on the way. Discretion was weighed against valor. Discretion tipped the balance, sights were lowered to aim at one book. To obtain the most wordage placed on a single page of text, Ariel Narrow 11 was adopted as the type and font. With all text completed the printer returned to the editor a sample print page. Catastrophe! Were *Red Dragon* to be printed in the same size book as *Korean Vignettes*, it would have been necessary to include a magnifying glass with each book. The larger book you hold in your hands is the unforeseen result of using Ariel Narrow 11 as a type font. Amateur publishers with limited guidance, the Editors learned the hard, hard way.

Previous experience was of great help in obtaining suitable individuals to cooperate in jointly working up war memories into the Bio form- vignette format used in Korean Vignettes. Vincent A. Krepps, Editor of The Graybeard, the Korean War Veterans Association bimonthly magazine, most kindly and graciously published our request for contributors. Several Regimental Associations published similar requests. We lucked out in a contact with M/Sgt Roger J. Leuckenhoff. He had served in A Co, 160th Infantry, 40th Division California US National Guard. Roger must have been acquainted with half the members of the 40th Division! He was instrumental not only enabling us to contact members of the 40th Division, but of other units as well. What a recruiting sergeant he would have made, had he chosen to stay in service. From draftee to M/Sgt in 22 months tells his story. We can never thank him adequately.

Gathering information and talking to the individuals who constitute these two books has been the most instructive experience of my life. The sheer hardihood and down right guts exhibited by the fighting men, and those women serving in the ANC in Korea, occupy, in my opinion, a unique position in the military annals of the United States. From the elite of the US Marine Corps right down to those last young men drafted with serial numbers US 5x,xxx,xxx in mid 1953, they gave full measure of courage, devotion and honor to their country. In my reading of US military history, comparing the trials, tribulations, length of campaigns without relief, cold, hunger and numerical superiority of the enemy, I find parallels only in the ranks of Robert's Rangers, the Continentals at Valley Forge, and the shoeless, hungry, ragged, yet faithful men of the Confederacy who followed "Marse" Lee all the way to the bitter end at Appomattox.

Red Dragon, like Korean Vignettes, will have a two tier price system. To veterans, immediate members of veteran's families, and those in active military service, the military price will be $9.00 lower than the $36.95 cover price, plus $5 standard S & H charge.

Your comments are welcomed in correction of any errors noted.

Faces of War II

The Red Chinese Dragon with it's hordes now enter,
with plans for the destruction of the U. N. defenders.

But these brave men of valor, have decided to stand.
To protect South Korea from the Communist hand.

The battles are endless, bloody, and savage,
But the Dragon is stopped, no more to ravage.

South Korea is saved from total desolation,
and is now among the world's Free Nations.

[Freedom Is Not Free]
Anonymous

MEMORIAL TO THE DEAD   -   KOREAN WAR MUSEUM   -   SEOUL, KOREA

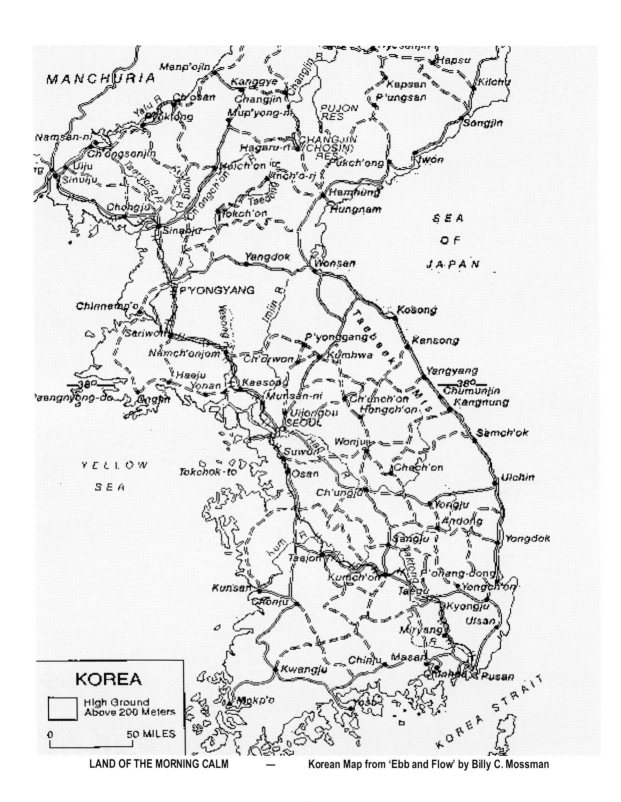

KOREA

High Ground
Above 200 Meters

0   50 MILES

LAND OF THE MORNING CALM   —   Korean Map from 'Ebb and Flow' by Billy C. Mossman

American forces land at Inchon to take the Japanese surrender, 8 Sept. 1945. Upper left photo shows Wolmi Island beneath the wing of photo plane from the USS Intrepid with causeway leading into Inchon city. In lower photo the Infantry goes ashore in long lines of LCI's, with causeway in upper left. Above the Stars and stripes are run up, while below the Japanese flag is lowered at ceremony in Seoul, Korea. Sept. 9, 1945.

Photos National Archives.

The USS Boxer visits Korea April, 1950, and welcome signs go up in Seoul, Korea. Photo National Archives.

Photos courtesy of Tom Marler.

G.I.s on occupation duty 'make like cowboys.' These were combat engineers and the horses were not issued.

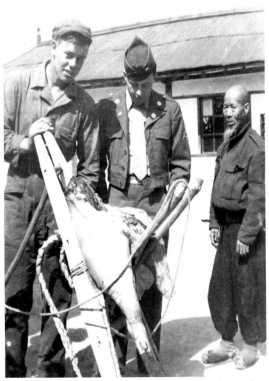

A hog that is being taken to market is inspected, possibly to be confiscated for a bar-b-que.

4

U.S. and Russian soldiers on the 38th Parallel at close of WW-2 [1945]

G.I. at 38th Parallel check point checks citizens before border is closed.

All photos courtesy Jae Won Lee.

ROK Army enters Yeosu after Communist rebellion. [1948-1949]

Captured North Korean guerilla leaders from the Chiri Mountains.

RED DRAGON
The SECOND ROUND
FACES OF WAR II

Jae-won		Lee	Civilian
First Name	MI	Last Name	Serial Number
None		13 May 1926	Interpreter, US Army
Nickname	MOS	Birthday	Grade / Rank
Fox Co 32d Inf, 7thDiv & 5th RCT		1946-1950	Kaesong, No. Korea
Unit (s)		Duty Tour (s)	Home Town

Medals & Awards

PRELIM TO WAR

In 1945 Korea was divided at the 38th parallel between the Soviet Union and the United States. At the Potsdam Conference, it was agreed the Soviets would declare war on Japan. The partition extending into the offshore waters was conceived as a method of preventing accidental clashes between American and Russian air and sea forces. A straight line on a map, it made a highly impractical and indefensible border between two divergent and hostile political philosophies. For example, the line ignored such barriers as the mountains of eastern Korea, the sea inlets of the west coast or other natural topography features such as rivers. It cut through small towns such as Ong-Jin, Chong-Dan and Pack-Jone. These towns became OPs 4,7, 9 & 10 respectively on the daily patrols I made as interpreter with Fox Co of the 32d Inf beginning in late September after the US and Russia linked up at Kaesong on 15 Sept 1945. Our patrols to the Ong-jin Peninsula had to go through the Russian zone. Initially we were grudgingly allowed to pass through the city of Ha-jiu to reach Ong-Jin, south of the 38th. The company patrol team was based at Yonan on the 38th about 80 miles from Seoul. Korea, north of the 38th had a population of 9 million, the south a population of 19 million.

The north was occupied by 120,000 Russian soldiers under General Chistakov, the south by 50,000 men in the US 24th Corps, commanded by Lt General John Hodge. The parallel was patrolled by the 1st Bn of the 32d Inf based at Uijongbu and by the 2d Bn operating out of Moon-san. The line was meant to be a temporary expedient. The Soviets took a firm grasp of northern Korea, disarming and interning Japanese soldiers and colonial government officials, transporting many as prisoners to the Soviet Union. The Russians soon brought in a contingent of 300 Korean troops under Kim-Il Sung, and, as an additional security measure, numerous Korean politicians trained in the Communist philosophy. Within months the Russians had frozen the 38th into a permanent border blocking transport of goods and services as well as disrupting the economic and administrative unity of the country. Patrols began blocking passage by people across the 'border.'

Moscow announced a plan for international trusteeship over Korea in December 1945. South Korean communist support was convenient for the Soviets, but the majority of South Koreans rejected the idea. The United States took the matter to the United Nations. The UN passed a resolution calling for elections throughout Korea in the spring of 1947. The Soviets refused to allow UN observers north of the 38th parallel. Seventy year old Syngman Rhee (1875-1965) returned to Korea after a 33 year exile. His credentials as a Korean patriot gave him 90% support in elections. On 15 August he was seated as President with the proclamation of the Republic of South Korea. Ambassador John Muccio replaced Gen Hodge as chief of US mission to South Korea. The Soviets responded by proclaiming the Democratic Peoples Republic of Korea with Kim Il-Sung as Premier. Kim's regime was recognized by all nations of the Russian dominated Communist Bloc.

In the years 1945 through 1948, South Korea's economic crisis was worsened by inflation which multiplied tenfold the cost of rice, basic food of South Korea. A thriving black market was rampant, fueled by the tons of military equipment brought by US troops into Korea. In one year, over 1000 jeeps were stolen. Americans found it easier to buy spare parts on the black market than order through regular channels. Many economic problems were exacerbated by the American occupying power. For example, with good intentions, but bad results, military government offices sold lumber supplied by Japanese firms. Cigarettes, collected from nonsmoking American soldiers were sold. The money so raised, was used to bolster the payroll fund for unpaid Korean government employees. General Hodge, a bluff and capable infantry commander tried hard to carry out his orders when he arrived in Seoul. He ordered Japanese officials, including police, to retain their arms and maintain order. Some Japanese army units were also employed to keep the peace.

The situation was ripe for exploitation by the Communists. Communist party members soon moved to take advantage by arousing agents already placed in the city to spread anti-American propaganda. An armed force of 4000 guerillas led by Lt Kim Ji-Hae, a defector from the 14th Regiment, ROK Army, with recruits from Cheju-do Island, gathered at Jiri Mountain. They were joined by another group commanded by a former Korean officer of the Japanese army, Kim Dal-sam. Both groups congregated at Jiri Mountain.

In the southwest, the Communist political organ was the South Korean workers party, a twin to the so called workers party created on Cheju-do Island. The two groups maintained close contact until they coalesced at Jiri Mountain. Their common goal was the unification of all Korea under Communist domination. Many noncommunist Koreans, angered at the continued presence of an occupying foreign army on their soil, added to the political turmoil. In the American zone a remarkable number of Koreans reacted to the prospect of liberty by anointing themselves to lead the new nation. By 1947 more than 200 political parties had been formed, some of them representing no more that one man and his family. Lyun-woon Hiung headed the only party to formulate a complete government structure. He drew little support as most South Koreans believed his Korea Peoples Republic Party to be pro-Communist.

In the American military government, General Hodge tried to delegate as much responsibility to civilian government as possible. His task was immensely complicated by the simple fact that he did not have a pool of trained government employees to draw upon. The Japanese in 40 years of colonial rule were chiefly to blame for Korea's stunted development. All but the most trivial of government positions were off limits to Koreans. For example, 75% of all teaching positions in Korean colleges and in university level administrative jobs were reserved for Japanese nationals. It was therefore nigh impossible to find people with the requisite background required to handle the many administrative jobs which enable a government to function smoothly and equably.

All during this period I accompanied, in my role of interpreter, the daily patrols operated from Moon-san by the 2d Bn 32d Infantry. Our patrols on an almost daily basis met with increasingly hostile situations on the border between the two Koreas. Several times, these confrontations erupted in gunfire. When not on patrol, I occupied my time studying for university entrance exams.

On 1 January 1949 the Soviet Union announced withdrawal of the last of their troops from Korea. General MacArthur, Far East Commander, ordered a new unit, the 5th RCT, to be formed from men of the 7th Division. The new unit was the sole American combat unit left in Korea, all that remained of General Hodge's once mighty 50,000 man US 24th Corps. The 5th RCT was activated at Sam Kackjee, Yongsan in South Korea. The remainder of the stripped 7th Division was transferred to Japan. Outposts along the 38th parallel and patrols covering the line of demarcation kept the 5th RCT in touch with the Korean people when gunfights erupted between South Korean Constabulary and North Korean Army units. On 29 January, the North Koreans raided and burned the police station at Paekchon. I was with the patrol that found the 7 dead South Korean police officers killed in his action.

KMAG, Korean Military Advisory Group, announced it was seeking volunteers to train with the ROK Army. There was no great rush of volunteers. The unit had a strength of 182 officers and 293 enlisted men under Ambassador John Muccio. One of my friends, Capt Kane served as advisor to the ROK 17th Regiment at Ong-jin Peninsula. In May 1949 a force of two reinforced North Korean battalions attacked the 11th ROK Regiment, commanded by Lt Col Che Keyong-nock at Kaesong, 40 miles north of Seoul. After a furious engagement a suicide team of 10 men from the 11th Regiment succeeded in repulsing the newly designated NKPA (North Korean Peoples Army). The 10 men in the suicide squad were all killed, but were successful in accomplishing their mission. With the looming departure of the 5th RCT for Hawaii, I went to work for KMAG as an interpreter, assistant to 1st Lt Bill Conger in training of rifle platoons for the 3d Brigade of the ROK Army. The ROK regiment then in training at Taegu was commanded by Col Che Duck-shin.

At the end of June, 1949 the US 5th RCT departed from Inchon leaving a 475 man KMAG force to operate under the supervision of Ambassador Muccio. Left behind were $110 million dollars of military equipment for the use of the South Korean Constabulary. That equipment included rifles, machine guns, mortars, bazookas and trucks, but no artillery or combat aircraft. This materiel was deemed sufficient to equip 50,000 men of the 65,000 man South Korean army, which in the minds of those Americans making the decisions, would be adequate to deal with North Korean guerillas who were the only military problem with which South Korea would have to cope.

North Korea, in comparison, boasted heavy artillery, T-34 tanks, 110 fighter and bomber aircraft, and an army of 200,000 men. Its ground forces included an estimated 40,000 Koreans who had fought as members of Mao Tse Tung's Chinese Eighth Route Army. These men had been transferred from the Chinese Army to the NKPA by his order. The South Korean Army, gradually building up to 100,000 men, lacked the combat experience of the hardened veterans returned by China as soldiers to fill the ranks of the NKPA.

25 June 1950, at onset of the first rains of the season, the NKPA hurled itself across the 38th parallel. In the first few hours there was little contact between the two armies. Invading NKPA tanks rolled forward at will. Russian built fighter-bombers strafed Seoul the first day. ROK units stationed between Seoul and the 38th were no match for the invaders. They were quickly overrun. In two days the NKPA reached the outskirts of Seoul. Ambassador Mucio had already ordered evacuation of women and children. He scrapped a long standing air evacuation plan out of concern the NKPA fighter planes might shoot down the evacuating aircraft. On 26 June, 682 people were loaded aboard a Norwegian fertilizer ship in Inchon harbor. The ship had accommodations for only 12 passengers. After a miserable 3 day sea voyage to Fukuoka in Japan, 50 of the evacuees were removed from the ship on stretchers. Their ordeal marked the beginning of an initially frustrating 3 months of trial- by-arms for American military forces soon to be engaged on Korean soil under orders from President Truman. Not until the Inchon landing on 14/15 September 1950 would American forces regain the initiative.

Exhausted ROK troops during the long retreats of early July 1950.   -------   Truman Library Collection.

Below. A ROK Officer gets his troops ready to assault a hill.
August 13, 1950.   U.S. Army photograph..

Right. A wounded ROK soldier is being comforted by his
buddy at a 'make-shift' aid station.   Truman Library.

South Korean civilians flee from advancing North Korean troops. These were from the Pohang area.   July -1950.
Thousands that did not flee were brutally murdered by the North Korean Communist troops.   <u>Archives Photos.</u>

ROK troops move a small anti-tank gun to the front to try to stop the North Korean T-34's. Brave but hopeless !

Left. Troops from the 24th and 25th Infantry Divisions disembark at the port of Pusan. **Above.** Japanese LSTs land part of the 1st Cavalry Division at Pohang **Below.** The 'Faces of War' are quick to appear, as wounded troopers from the 1st Cavalry Division get treatment at a crude aid station. Yongdong, 21 July 1950. **U.S. Army Photos.**

RED DRAGON
The SECOND ROUND
FACES OF WAR II

Bae-Sun		Lee		O-50839 ROK AF	
First Name	MI	Last Name		Serial Number	
None	Fighter Pilot	28 Jun 1931		Col, then Lt	Nicknamenmn
	MOS	Birthday		Grade / Rank	
10th Fighter Wing AF ROK		1952 & 1953		Hamhung, No. Korea	
Unit (s)		Duty Tour (s)		Home Town	
Air Medal Republic of Korea		93 Combat Missions			
Medals & Awards					

DEFECTOR

In 1948 I was a 17 year old North Korean student living in Hamhung, South Hamgyung Province under the harsh and despotic rule of the Communists. The past two years had convinced our family that all freedom and liberty were in process of being taken from us. In my particular case, I had applied at Kim IL Sung University as a physics and math major. Although I had passed my entry exams with an outstanding score, admittance was refused because my father was a "bourgeois" businessman. In late 1948 North Korea was in the final stages of tightening border controls. Escape, though difficult, was still possible. After long planning, my 60 year old uncle and I left for the South before dawn on November 1, 1948. On my back I carried 40 dried fish for my older brother who was studying medicine at Yonsei University in Seoul. My mother packed for me a large package of 'yut', a sweet taffy beloved by all Koreans. In disguise, I grew a mustache, a beard and dressed as a manual laborer. If caught, my punishment would be severe, ranging from death to hard penal labor in a slave camp. My trip to the South was guided by a professional border crosser. We were a party of 5, the guide, my uncle, two teen age girls, and I. We were lucky, our guide was honest. Once paid, he did his best to get us all across the border.

We took the train from Hamhung to Wonsan, then transferred to the Chulwon train, the closest rail station to the 38th parallel. Hearing that inspection at Chulwon was rigorous, we got off at Pyunggang, and walked to Chulwon. From there we took a street car to Kimwha, last station before the border. Our route thereafter was on rough mountain trails into an area later termed by American troops 'The Iron Triangle.' This trail was used by farmers taking their cattle to South Korea where they received a three times better price than in the North. There was no trail map, we followed cow dung on the trail. By nightfall we were to reach our halfway point at a small hut near the center of the mountain range. Our last lap the second day would take us to the South Korean village of Pochon- ni.

My first day was almost a disaster. I had been told to eat a hearty breakfast, but had not felt hungry. At the end of the second hour my uncle collapsed. He could not go on. He said he would return to Hamhung, but urged me to continue. With reluctance, I did. Two hours later it began to snow, the trail became slippery and dangerous. I was exhausted. My legs refused to move. The guide yelled at me to get up. I could not. He and the girls went on. Despondent, hungry, I sat in the snow. I soon thought of the "yut" in my pack. I cracked it into pieces with a stone. Chewing on it, I could feel the energy flowing into my body. I got up, still chewing, and soon caught up with the others. With the heavy snowfall, the dung trail disappeared. The guide became panicky. He told us to shout for help. What irony! To hope that North Korean patrols rescue us! We yelled, fortunately, no reply. I realized for the first time that the will to live overrides all other emotions. Calming, the guide remembered he had matches. We built a small fire and huddled around it the rest of the night, dried our clothing, boiled and ate some of the fish I had brought. I awakened at sunrise. The snow had stopped.

Our guide realized we had strayed from the path. We retraced our footsteps frozen in the snow and located the main path. It had been recently used, there was fresh cow dung. To us, it was like sighting date palms in the desert! We reached mid point about 3 PM. Tired out, we stayed three days. The hut was in the north, but so rugged was the terrain we did not sight anyone except a farmer and his cows. We hiked another day, reaching Pochon-ni late at night. Bidding farewell to the guide and the two girls, I walked on a country road toward Seoul. Reaching a police station, I voluntarily reported that I was a defector from the North. The police checked my belongings consisting of a hand made South Korean flag and some dried fish. The 'yut' was long gone. The police were satisfied I was a bona fide defector, not a spy. They gave me a certificate to that effect. I walked out of that police station as the newest citizen of the Republic of South Korea.

A kind truck driver gave me a ride to Seoul. Arriving at a street car station, I could feel the difference between the people here and in Hamhung. There were more smiles, people did not look worried, nor were they afraid to talk to each other. I had stayed with an aunt in 1945, so knew the city of Seoul well. I caught a street car to the address I had carried in my pocket. As I got off the street car, there was my oldest brother waiting to get on! What odds would a gambler give that two North Korean brothers would meet in such a circumstance? As soon as I saw him I began to cry like a baby, but it was with happiness! All the misery of the trip fell from my shoulders as the experience flashed like a kaleidoscope through my mind. I left my home town on Nov. 1, 1948 and arrived in Seoul on November 7. It was a test of nerve and will. It laid a foundation for the tough soldier I was to become.

11

Two G.I.s from the 1st Cavalry Division compare the almost worthless 2.36 with the new 3.5 Bazooka. The 3.5 proved to be an effective T-34 'stopper'.

A G.I. views some of the thousands of civilians murdered by North Korean Communist. Over 7,000 civilians, ROKs and G.I.s, were tied up and shot at Taejon alone.   <u>U.S Army Photo.</u>

RED DRAGON
The SECOND ROUND
FACES OF WAR II

Keun Sup		Yoon	O- 50088 ROK AF
First Name	MI	Last Name	Serial Number
None	Unknown	24 Dec 1925	Col, then 1st Lt/Cpt
Nickname	MOS	Birthday	Grade / Rank
ROK Air Force Maintenance Officer		1947-1967	Yuchon, North Korea
Unit (s)		Duty Tour (s)	Home Town
Japanese Air Force 1942-1945--Flight Engineer--Republic of Korea 1947-1967			
Medals & Awards			
Chung Mu Military Merit Medal			

THE MIRACLE OF DESPERATION

In September 1945, I returned to my home in North Korea following release from the Japanese Air Corps, in which as a draftee, I had unwillingly served as a flight engineer. As a Christian, I daily celebrated my release from the strictures of Japanese control. I was home, a free man! It took very little time to recognize that I was not free, but under the whip of a godless communist dictatorship regime incorporating the worst features of Japanese colonialism. One Sunday morning, as the reverberating peal of the church bell echoed in my ears, I felt the Lord call me to work in His Church. I began teaching in a public school and organized a Sunday school. Because of these activities I was accused of being a reactionary counter revolutionist by the Red Communist authorities. To avoid imminent arrest, I fled my home town, crossed the 38th parallel to take sanctuary in South Korea. I later learned my mother and sister were murdered, brutally buried alive, because they were Christians. I have often wondered if it was not also in revenge of my flight.

I joined the South Korean Army Air Corps as a maintenance officer. At the start of the Korean War, we were but a cadre, nominal in strength and in process of establishing the ROK Air Corps as an independent military service. The Air Corps consisted of several unarmed AT-6 trainers and small L type aircraft. The L type planes were hand-me-down surplus which had seen service as artillery "spotter" planes by the American military, also in observation, rescue and courier missions. Very ironic, the ROK Army as yet had no artillery! Our few aircraft had been donated by citizens of various organizations. There were a few trained pilots and support personnel like myself who came from Japanese military backgrounds. Several hundred airmen were in training. Our Air Force Academy had just enrolled its first class of air cadets. During the first few days of the war, the situation was completely chaotic. Confusion, anxiety and demoralization resulted from the surprise attack by Russian trained North Koreans on a raw, in-training South Korean military force. South Korea was taken by surprise. We paid dearly in blood and suffering for that over the next three years.

South Korean Army soldiers fought bravely to defend our country against the overwhelming might of a Russian trained and equipped invader. The outcome was inevitable, it pitted a lightly armed constabulary against a heavily armed, highly trained regular military force supported by air, heavy artillery, tanks and armored units. The South Korean Air Force with its few training planes and pilots could not provide meaningful support to the desperately fighting front line soldiers. The best we could do was drop grenades and a few home made bombs. Just flying over the front boosted morale of army soldiers who saw the markings of the South Korean flag.

By end of the second day, enemy forces had reached Seoul. We flew twice that morning and in the afternoon were ordered to 'bomb' the Imjin bridge north of Seoul to delay the enemy advance. We installed ten 30 kilo hand made bombs under the wings of an AT-6 trainer. As maintenance officer I knew all aspects and mechanics of the flight aircraft. I flew rear seat for 2d Lt Du Man Kim, the pilot who volunteered although he had no training in this aircraft. He was a Japanese trained pilot who later flew 200 missions as an F-51 pilot, then went on to become a 4 star Air Force general. Our mission was a desperate gamble. Personal safety meant nothing. We had to do something to help fellow soldiers who were battling hard in an attempt to stem the onrush of the North Korean invaders.

As flight engineer I sat in the rear seat to start the engine, to help in take off, and bring in the landing gear. Lt Kim concentrated on flying. Overloaded, we barely got off the ground. Once in the air we flew without further problem along the Han River until we reached the Imjin . As we banked in preparation to dive on target, the aircraft lurched and began to drop uncontrollably in a swinging motion, nose down. Lt Kim and I were helpless, we could do nothing. As we approached the ground, I cried out to the Lord, "Oh Lord, help us, Oh Lord." In my ears a voice sounded, "Drop the bombs!" Not sure what would happen, I told Lt Kim, "Drop the bombs."

The bombs dropped, load on the airplane was reduced, we wobbled away to be pushed upward by a tremendous blast from the bomb explosions. I turned my head to see the demolished bridge. Mission accomplished. Lt Kim regained control of the airplane. Heading back through heavy enemy fire we returned safely to base. I have thought on this incident many times. We were in God's hands. I believe Our Lord protected and guided us in those desperate, dangerous moments. Beyond human comprehension, it was a miracle.

Top. Korean refugees flee the Communist in the Taegu area. -- Middle. North Korean troops killed by napalm in a battle in the Taegu area, August 1950. -- All above photos courtesy Ben Luci.

Bottom. G.I.s check out a destroyed T-34 tank near Waegwan. July 1950. -- Photo National Archives.

RED DRAGON
The SECOND ROUND
FACES OF WAR II

Gerald	D.	Gingery	RA 16298972
First Name	MI	Last Name	Serial Number
Ginger	1745/3060	3 Sept 1931	Cpl
Nickname	MOS	Birthday	Grade / Rank
H/5th Cav/1st Cav Div	18 Jul '50-2 Nov '50	Clare, MI
Unit (s)	Duty Tour (s)	Home Town
Combat Infantry Badge Purple Heart Good Conduct Medal Occpn Medal-J Nat'l Def Svc Medal
Medals & Awards
Korean Campaign Service Medal, 2stars ROK SKM ROK Presidential UnitCitation UN Medal

COOK CUM INFANTRYMAN

I took my basic 8 week training at Ft Knox, Ky. On completion of infantry training, I was assigned to Cooks & Bakers School, graduating as the Honor Student in a class of 48. Volunteering for overseas duty, I shipped to Japan on the troop transport USS General Hodge. There I was assigned to H Company, 5th Cavalry Regiment as a cook. In June 1950 I was on furlough at a Japanese resort on Mt Fuji. Returning to Camp McGill on 25 June, I was surprised to find the camp on a war footing. North Korea had invaded South Korea. The next several days were hectic. We lost 25 men by transfer to the 24th Infantry Division, already processing for war duty in Korea. We were put through a stepped up training program on infantry weapons with emphasis on the bayonet. White clothing was dyed olive drab. A Landing Craft Vehicle Personnel [LCVP] took us to Korea. Passing through the straits between Honshu and Kyusha, we saw rusted hulks of ships sunk in WW II. It was obvious war resulted in some very final acts. We landed unopposed at Pohang-dong, north of Pusan 18 July 1950. The invaders had not as yet reached that far south. We advanced north to meet them. Our progress was hindered by hordes of pitiful refugees.

It was a sad sight, mothers, tiny babies, children carrying tots almost as big as they were, some without parents. A few were wounded, all were hungry. As we halted to eat, children would gather. Few of us could withstand their pleading looks. We gave away most of our C-Rations, resulting in a hungry couple of days until rations caught up with us. North Koreans began sending their soldiers through our lines in peasant garb, carrying arms and radios in their bundles. They formed guerila groups and began ambushing rear echelon units. We initiated use of metal detectors on refugee groups and soon stopped that tactic. Finally all refugees had passed through our lines. We were then free to engage anything in front of us as enemy. In this war of movement, cooks were not needed. Assigned to duty as a runner, I delivered messages between Bn HQ, line companies and platoons. I had my first wound of the war from a grenade encounter with a North Korean night patrol. It was slight, of little consequence. I returned to duty within hours. In the stifling heat of July, I suffered sunstroke while digging a trench. Returning from a Pusan hospital to duty, I saw a South Korean recruiting party in action. A two man Drum and Bugle Corps, as it were, one soldier banging a drum, the other blowing a bugle. Soldiers with the party, spotting a likely looking candidate, would dart into the crowd and grab him. Quite an effective Selective Service System!

The next two months we were engaged in incessant battle with North Koreans trying to force us into the sea. We suffered many casualties. I was one of the lucky survivors of our unit when we made the break out from the Naktong perimeter 18 Sept. We drove northward, linking up on 25 Sept with the 7th Division which had landed at Inchon. Our drive north continued. By now, the only items of equipment I still carried were my rifle, bayonet, steel helmet, canteen and items on my web belt. Supplies began to catch up. We received new clothing, had a few hot meals and a chance for bath, courtesy of the QM dept. We quickly went from a scruffy outfit to a well equipped, high morale unit of soldiers. We halted at Kaesong, near Seoul, just south of the 38th parallel. On 10 Oct we were ordered to pursue retreating North Koreans. Our advance was met by stiff resistance, roads were heavily mined. I was now a member of an 81mm mortar squad in H Company. As soon as we hit resistance we would dismount from our trucks and set up our four 81's to fire support of the rifle companies. I always admired the infantry as they jumped off their trucks, and with fixed bayonets went charging up hill, routing the enemy. By the end of October we had taken the capitol, Pyongyang. On the 28th we again headed north, this time for Yongsan-dong a few miles from Manchuria. That night the 8th Cavalry, a sister regiment, came under heavy attack. We were sent to support them. The Chinese and North Korean enemy were in massive force as they launched their joint attack on us.

It was the afternoon of 2 Nov 1950 when my luck ran out. The battle was at its height, the noise was deafening. All our artillery, 60mm mortars to 155 howitzers and everything in between, was firing as quickly as gunners could feed their weapons. The Air Force and Navy fighters were in full support with rockets, MGs strafing, bombs and napalm. The Chinese, in spite of the terrible carnage inflicted, kept coming. I was passing 81mm mortar shells to my gun crew when I was hit. A .31 bullet hit to the left of my nose, knocking out many teeth, exiting my neck, barely missing the jugular vein and spine. Immediate medical attention, numerous pints of blood and medics who wiped blood out of my mouth kept me from suffocating. Evacuation hospital surgeons saved my life. I spent the next nine months in hospitals from Osaka, Japan to Atterbury, Indiana. I returned to duty. I was alive and had beat the odds, thanks to the Medics and my Maker.

__Above__ A U.S. Navy destroyer plows through heavy seas off the Korean coast.   On standby to fire missions in support of U.N. forces ashore.

__Left__ All hands were required to replenish ammo supply that was constantly being expended on North Korean targets ashore.

Below.   North Korean fishermen are picked up for interrogation.   __All photos from National Archives__

RED DRAGON
The SECOND ROUND
FACES OF WAR II

			784-87-15
Harry	O.	Wiedmaier	O-503350 (Korea)
First Name	MI	Last Name	Serial Number
None	1100 (Line Officer)	11 July 1927	Capt USNR Ret, *then* Ensign
Nickname	MOS	Birthday	Grade / Rank
USS Mansfield (DD-728		Jul-Nov 1950 & Aug '51-Jan '52	Portland, OR
Unit (s)		Duty Tour(s) in Korea	Home Town
Submarine Dolphins	Navy Unit Citation	Asiatic Pacific Theater	WWII Victory Medal

Medals & Awards

KCSM 3 stars   NDSM   UN Medal   Numerous awards accumulated in 38 years of service

DUNKED USAF PILOT SAVED BY DD-728

On graduation from Oregon State University , 5 June 1950, I was commissioned an Ensign in the US Navy. Having jointly embraced the idea of a naval career, Sara Mae Addis and I married 12 June. We were enjoying a blissful honeymoon when the North Korean Communists invaded South Korea 25 June. On that date the Mansfield, the DeHaven and the light cruiser Juneau assisted in the removal of diplomatic personnel and KMAG dependents from Seoul before the city was overrun by the North Korean Communist invaders. An odd coincidence in my life, it was on that same date in 1945 I was first sworn into the US Navy. The honeymoon ended abruptly on my receipt of orders to report to Moffit Field in California. I flew out of Travis AFB bound for Tokyo on the Fourth of July.

 My orders were to report to USS Mansfield DD-728. Squadron 9 consisted of 8 destroyers with the USS Mansfield as flagship flying the Commodore's pennant. Arriving in Tokyo I took a train to Sasebo, arriving 11 July just in time to see the Mansfield come in to replenish ammunition, fuel and supplies. Reporting aboard, I was immediately 'drafted' for "All Hands Evolution,"a naval term meaning all hands, including officers of lesser rank than Lt Commander, were included in the work party. Ammo loading was underway, five inch shells weighing 54 lbs and propellant canisters weighing 37 lbs were carefully passed, chain gang fashion, man- to-man from dock to separate ammunition stowage lockers below deck. The next morning we were underway, wending passage through mine fields to return to the bomb line at Yongdok-po north of Pohang. This was the northeast corner of the Pusan Perimeter.

My assigned duties aboard ship were Asst. Combat Information Center and Communications Officer. Other duties were Registered Publication Information Officer. Cryptoanalysis, SECRET materials, their proper storage and security, Daily Signals, codes and charts were also my responsibility. I made a quick trip to Fukukoa to get 1895 Japanese Army maps of Korea for the Yondok-po and Pohang areas. These were the most up to date maps available. We "hand drew" these maps onto our charts to provide shore bombardment forward observers with map grid coordinates for transmission of fire data to CIC. Our next problem was'Glove 26 Oboe,' our FO, who needed a reliable radio system. That problem was solved by using Army SCR 300 radios. With the FO on one SCR, the receiving SCR 300 was set up next to our plotting table, in navy terms, DRT for Dead Reckoning Trace.

This device has the capability of using a moving light point (our position) under the map overlaid on our naval chart. This accurately showed the Mansfield's movements as to latitude and longitude. One day "Glove 26 Oboe" called for a fire mission giving us coordinates and "Fire for Effect." Our ships XO took the hand mike before we could 'WILCO' the message. He told the FO, "That is YOUR position you are asking us to fire on!" The FO came right back with noticeable urgency and raised voice to say, "Fire, Godamit, Fire!" The XO gave us an immediate "GO." We fired 30 rounds. We were vastly relieved when Glove 26 Oboe came back on the circuit saying, "Damn good shooting. We're OK." We kept up shore bombardment for the next two weeks interrupted only by several trips to Sasebo to replenish ammunition.

We maintained 24 hour radio guard on 142.5 megacycles and 500 kilocycles, SOS distress circuits. We received a "May Day, May Day" from a USAF P- 51 pilot. Our topside lookouts confirmed the P-51 was having engine problems. We received a message from topside that the plane's propeller had sheared off. It was making lazy loops as it fell seaward as could be plainly seen from the bridge. The pilot, a Lt Tubbs, turned his plane back towards the Mansfield. He was forced to bail out before reaching us. The ship was put to flank speed. Lt Tubbs, tangled in his chute in ice cold 38 degree water, was fighting to stay afloat. The Mansfield boasted two husky Bosun's Mates, friendly competitors in ship's duties. As the Mansfield, slowing from flank speed, approached the pilot, both Bosuns dove from the bow and swam toward the struggling pilot. From the deck it appeared dubious whether they could reach him in time. By now we had a cargo net over the side. Our lifeboat had been lowered but was not yet underway when the swimmers towed the pilot to the net. With much tugging and grunting the pilot was pulled aboard. As the flagship, we had the only doctor in the squadron. Dr Lee and the ships medics soon had him warmed up. He was taken to Pusan where AF Medics placed him in an Air Force hospital.

My "Sitting Ducks" destroyer division of 9 Squadron, USS Mansfield, USS Swenson, USS DeHaven and USS Collet supported the Inchon invasion. On 13 Sept 1950, Day minus 2, we steamed within point blank range of NK shore batteries to draw their fires to disclose their positions. Next day we found and exploded mines in the harbor approaches. The recovery of South Korea had begun.

Stretcher bearers carry wounded Marine to a forward aid station. August 1950.

A 105 mm howitzer from the 64th F.A. Bn., of the 25th Division fires on North Korean positions near Uirson, 27 August 1950 Photos from National Archives.

N.K. prisoner taken near No Name ridge and the Naktong River, Sept. 1950. G.I. watches and billfolds in his possession indicates he may have murdered GI P.O.W.s.

Russian T-34 tanks destroyed in the battle for the Pusan perimeter, July - August 1950.

RED DRAGON
The SECOND ROUND
FACES OF WAR II

Donald	D.	Down	RA 15 279 288
First Name	MI	Last Name	Serial Number
Don	2745	12 Sept 1931	SFC, then Pvt
Nickname	MOS	Birthday	Grade / Rank
Fox3 2d Bn 7th Cav Regt 1stCav Div		22 Jul '50-15 Apr '51	Lorain, OH
Unit (s)		Duty Tour (s)	Home Town
Combat Infantry Badge Bronze Star with 2OLC & 2V devices Purple Heart, 2OLC GC Medal			
Medals & Award			
KCSM,4stars AOM, Japan &Germany NDSM UNSM ROK Pres Unit Citation & War Svc Medal			

BAND OF HEROS

I enlisted in the Regular Army on 3 November 1948, shortly after I turned 17. After 8 weeks basic training at Ft Knox, Ky, I was sent to Ft Lawton, WA for overseas duty in FECOM. Arriving in Japan 1st week of April '49, I was assigned to 1st Plt, F Co, 7th Cavalry Regiment, 1st Cav Div. At the outbreak of the Korean War we were in training status with only two battalions in each regiment, four rifle companies in each battalion. Instead of 17,000 men in the division, we mustered but few more than 11,000. To worsen the situation, over 700 NCOs had been transferred to beef up the 24th and 25th Divisions, both divisions preceded us to Korea. Our 1st Cav Div was despatched to Korea beginning 18 July with the 8th Cav landing at Pusan, followed by the 5th and lastly by my regiment evening of 22 July 1950, one month after the North Korean invasion began. We immediately moved forward to engage the attacking North Korean Army. Seven days later, on 29 July, we were positioned on the right flank of our battalion, near a double set of RR tracks.

The North Koreans were firing the 85 mm tank guns of a number of Russian T-34 tanks from positions about 1500 yards to our front. Their gun fire had punished us severely all that day. About 2330 hours that night my squad leader, Cpl Alfred Clair, received one of the new 3.5 inch rocket launchers and four rockets. It proved to be a godsend, replacing the obsolete 2.36 inch WW II bazooka. Those WW II version rockets just bounced off the thick armor of the T-34 tanks. At about 0100, Cpl Al Clair accompanied by asst sqd ldr Cpl Ralph Bernotas, collared Elzonda Berryman, the best rifle shot in the company and myself, a BAR man. He wanted us to come with them on a tank hunting raid to give him and Bernotas covering fire. He said his plan had been OK'd by Plt M/Sgt Lucas. All four of us were to be volunteers. We went armed for bear. I had my BAR, Al Clair also carried a BAR, extra BAR ammo and a rocket round, Ralph carried the 3.5 bazooka, three rockets on a pack board plus his rifle, while sniper Elzondo carried extra rifle ammo bandoliers. We each carried two or three grenades. Both Al and I carried 20 full clip BAR magazines in our waist belts and ammo bags.

On our way to the target area we walked in a hollow between some separated RR tracks. Nearing the targeted tanks, possibly 250 yards away, we came to a bridge culvert. There we reviewed the details of Al's plan. Al and Ralph would get as close as possible to the North Korean tanks while Elzondo and myself would hang back at the culvert to give covering fire. If they could not get back to us, Elzondo and I were to return to company lines without trying to help them. They went forward, we learned later, to within about 50 yards of the closest two enemy tanks. At about 0345 hours we heard a loud explosion and 15 minutes later, another. In support of our bazooka team we placed fire on the scurrying enemy figures moving in the light of the burning tank. Tank motors started up, we heard the noise of tanks rumbling away, the chatter of a BAR and the bark, bark of an M-1 rifle. It began to break daylight. A heavy mist hovered close to the ground. Al and Ralph had not returned and we could make out no sight of them. In accord with Al's orders, we began the return to our platoon positions. We had forgotten the password so went slowly as we got close to our lines. Thankfully, we heard American voices giving mortar fire orders. We shouted our names. Luckily, we were recognized and told to come on in.

About 1000 hours we heard a whistle being blown in front of our lines. It was Cpls Clair and Bernotas, running madly toward our positions shouting and waving arms in hope of recognition. They came in safely. That afternoon we heard what else had happened. Their first rocket missed the tank target. After the second rocket hit one of the T-34s which was firing on our company, they opened fire on enemy infantry, forcing them to take cover. They quickly moved to a new position and fired their third rocket at an enemy tank, hitting it in the right track assembly. It moved a short distance, then exploded and burned. They started a return to our lines but when they reached the culvert where they expected to find me and Berryman, they found an enemy MG crew set up in the culvert. They knocked it out with grenades. Hearing tank engines start up, and with one rocket left, they decided on one more try. Their last round, fired from about 100 yards at a brush camoflouged tank, missed the target. They opened up with BAR and M-1 fire causing the tank to button up, then ran like hell to get away. Running and concealing themselves, they worked their way back to the company position.

An 11 year persistent effort by Al Clair and the help of Sen Chuck Hagel of Nebraska resulted in Berryman, Bernotas and myself being awarded Bronze Stars with V device. On 28 May 2002, Sen Hagel advised us that Al Clair had been awarded the Bronze Star with V.

Above Left. M-16's of the 3rd AAA-AW Bn. are moved by rail to the Pusan perimeter and go into action August 21, 1950.

Above. An M-19 is dug into position.   Photos by Ben Luci.

Left. A train load of barb wire is also moved up to the perimeter.

Below. Before integration the all black 24th Regiment is moved into the lines July 18, 1950 .   U.S. Army Photo.

RED DRAGON
The SECOND ROUND
FACES OF WAR II

Benjamin	S.	Luci	RA 13 317 283
First Name	MI	Last Name	Serial Number
Ben	1602 Tk Gunner/Driver	11 Feb 1933	Sgt
Nickname	MOS	Birthday	Grade / Rank
C & D Batteries 3dAAA-AW-Bn (SP)	20 Aug 1950-15 Aug 1951		Altoona, PA
Unit (s)	Duty Tour (s)		Home Town

Combat Infantry Badge   Good Conduct Medal   Korean Campaign Service Medal, 4stars

Medals & Awards

National Defense Service Medal   United Nations Medal   ROK Korean War Service Medal

M-19 TWIN FORTY RAPID FIRE

I enlisted in the US Army 16 August 1949 using a date altered birth certificate, changing my birth year to 1932. My deception had been caught by both the Marines and the Navy, but my third attempt with the Army was successful. Practice made me a better forger. Upon completion of basic training at Ft Dix, NJ, I was assigned to 3d Division, 3dBn AAA(AW) SP at Ft Benning, GA. Each squad in the 4 squad platoon consisted of an M-19 Tank and a M-16 Half Track. The M-19 full track tank mounted a turret with twin 40mm fast firing AA cannon. The M-16 {Quad .50} was armed with 4x.50 cal MGs, swivel mounted to fire as a unit. Both weapons fired full circle. Their only limitation was their guns could not be depressed below the gun carriages in event of close-in infantry attack. The M-19 was originally developed as a mobile Anti-Aircraft weapon during WW II. The M-16 had been modified from its original intended use as a tank destroyer, substituting four .50 cal MGs for a 75 mm cannon. The M-19 weighed 19 tons. It was powered with reliable twin Cadillac engines giving it adequate power on its full tracks to maneuver the lower hills and rice paddies of Korea's valleys with ease. Used as direct fire weapons against infantry, both weapons had lethal firepower and proved invaluable in offense and defense.

In July of 1950, C Co was detached from 3d Division and sent to Korea. We landed at Pusan 20 August 1950 to be attached to the 65th Inf Regt of the 2nd Division. Our first night of action, 21 August, near Taegu was frightening and full of confusion. We were green and not yet acquainted with personnel in the regiment were supporting. The infantry unit we were supporting was dug in. They had placed trip flares forward of our positions. Mixed in with the flares were white phosphorus grenades also rigged with trip wires. About 0100 hours one of the parachute flares was tripped forward of our position. Everyone on our tank immediately took his combat position. We could hear oriental voices and the rattle of ammunition boxes. Firing broke out in a crescendo, screaming and yelling, North Koreans came charging up the hill. Small arms fire zinged around us, rattling off our tank armor, while mortar rounds added their detonations to the fury of their assault. We opened fire with our twin 40's, as did on our M-16 Quad 50 on our right flank.

At one point in the midst of the fight, tracers seemed to be visible from all directions as if we were surrounded. Their attack was apparently coordinated with other enemy attacks on our left flank. These attacks on our left flank seemed to be more intense, specifically so in the case of mortar fire. The enemy pulled back for a short time. As they did so, enemy mortar fire came in heavier, abating as the North Koreans mounted a second, then a third attack, all of which were repulsed. By 0500 hours it was all over, the enemy retreated, leaving, by my count, 75 dead bodies to our front. My memory of that first night and the fear and horror I felt then remains with me to this day.

In the week following the Inchon invasion in mid September, we moved swiftly up the peninsula, chasing fleeing enemy groups. Crossing the Han River was a difficult challenge. The combat engineers put a pontoon bridge into place, only to have it knocked out by mortar fire. The third attempt was the charm. We assisted in their effort by roaring along the embankment at speeds of up to 45 mph, drawing mortar fire which took some heat off the engineers. As we moved farther north we heard that General MacArthur had said the war was over and that we would be home by Christmas. By mid November the 3d Division was in North Korea in support of the 1st Marine Division and 7th Infantry Division attacking northward near and north of the Chosin reservoir.

When the Chinese entered the war, attacking in force on 27 November with an Army of a half million men, we knew General MacArthur was going to have to celebrate Christmas all by himself in Tokyo, we would not be joining him in his festivities. For almost a month the 3d Division maintained a cordon around the city of Hamhung and the port of Hungnam. Battles and skirmishes were fought every day to prevent the Chinese from taking possession of Hungnam which would have prevented withdrawal of the1st Division Marines and the 7th Division from North Korea. Our particular platoon was one of the last to leave the port of Hungnam Christmas Eve, 24 December 1950.

Landing at Pusan, we regrouped, and in January began a drive north to retake South Korea from the Chinese. In the months following we moved all over the Korean Peninsula furnishing supporting fire to other units, often operating detached from our parent 3d Bn AAA (AW) SP. One newsman, chronicling the Korean War, observing the effect of our fire on the Chinese during the 1951 UN Offensive, described our guns as "Scythes of Death." In August I rotated, attending Cadre School at Ft Edward, then assigned as an instructor at Camp Stewart, GA. I was discharged 25 Sept 1952, ready for civil life, no longer enamored of a military life of blood and death.

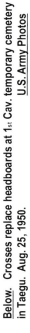

Above. The 5th Cav. displays some of it's captured N. K. weapons. Near Waegwan, South Korea, July 1950.

Below. Crosses replace headboards at 1st Cav. temporary cemetery in Taegu. Aug. 25, 1950. <u>U.S. Army Photos</u>

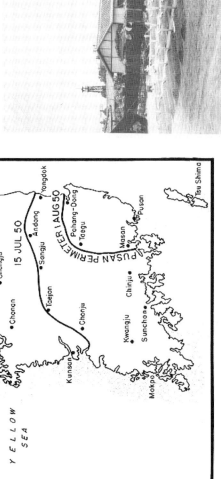

North Korean invasion of South Korea showing progress, before finally being stopped at the Pusan perimeter.   Map from the Internet.

RED DRAGON
The SECOND ROUND
FACES OF WAR II

Richard	P.	Roderick	14 258 280 USAF
First Name	MI	Last Name	Serial Number
Rod	671-97170	16 Sept 1929	E-6
Nickname	MOS	Birthday	Grade / Rank
HQ 5th Air Force		Jul '50-Dec '51	St. Petersburg, FL
Unit (s)		Duty Tour (s)	Home Town
Air Force Commendation Ribbon with Medal Pendant			United Nations Medal
Medals & Awards			
Korean Campaign Service Medal with 6 bronze stars			National Defense Service Medal

THE FURNACE MURDERS

At the onset of the war in Korea, I was assigned to Itazuke Air Force Base in Japan. I had served there since Oct 1949. South Korea was invaded by the armed forces of Communist North Korea on 25 June 1950. Within 15 days of the invasion, 5th Air Force HQ was established in Taegu under command of Major General Earl Partridge. I was assigned to the security Detachment. In Sept, General Douglas MacArthur's planned invasion at Inchon in South Korea was launched to cut supplies and communications to the North Korean forces still in attack on the Naktong perimeter. The perimeter had held for better than two months while the Army, Marines and Air Force assembled sufficient strength to strike back. American troops, hastily assembled from occupation forces in Japan, had been tossed into the Korean cauldron with orders to hold the North Korean Army at any cost until help could arrive.

On September 14 American Marines began landing at Inchon. Four days later, Army troops in the Naktong perimeter broke through the encircling North Korean forces that had invested the Naktong redoubt. The North Koreans fled in pell -mell retreat to escape being caught in the vise of American troops attacking both their front and rear. On September 28, troops of the 7th Infantry Division driving south linked up at Osan-ni with troopers of the 1st Cavalry Division driving northward. Marines of the 1st Marine Division were in the last stages of their attack to free Seoul, some 30 miles north of Osan-ni. Many North Koreans were isolated from their parent units in the retreat, setting the stage for a year of guerilla warfare before they were cleaned out of rear areas. These actions enabled the 5th Air Force to move from Taegu forward to Seoul and establish air bases there in close support of the advancing American infantry. The move took the better part of a week since it was necessary to maintain air operations during the transfer from Taegu to Seoul.

With the liberation of Seoul complete and the city swept of enemy stragglers, 8th Army and 5th Air Force HQ were established in the city. Several airbases were also set up in nearby areas. 5th Air Force HQ was assigned for operational activities, offices and billets into buildings that had formerly been occupied by the University of Korea Medical School. I and several other members of the Security Detachment were ordered to search the grounds for 'booby traps' and for anything else that could pose a threat to HQ personnel or interrupt operational flight procedures. We searched throughly, 'mapping' areas that were 'clean' as we proceeded.

On the second day we made a discovery which gave me the greatest shock of my life. For the first time in this war I had a horrifying glimpse into the mind set of the North Korean enemy. Searching the basement area of the Medical School, I opened the furnace door. I was stunned to see a number of bodies stacked like cordwood in the fire box. Too jolted at the time, I did not make an accurate count. Later it was determined there were ten bodies, both men and women, sex discernable by clothing. They had all been shot in the back of the head. Furnace doors opened in smaller buildings of the complex, led to discovery of another eighteen bodies. The shock here was even worse. All these people too had been shot in the back of the head, not only men and women, but children as well. It was truly a scene out of the depths of hell. Air Force Police located civilian survivors who identified the bodies as municipal employees of the city of Seoul. Best we could determine, when these employees were rounded up they were accompanied by their children. Was it just easier to murder the children on the basis that the dead can tell no tales? Or was it just sheer barbaric cruelty?

Our search turned up a hand crank portable phonograph with about a dozen 78 rpm records. One of the records was Mel Torme singing "Tampico." We enjoyed his singing on an almost daily basis until Seoul was evacuated in January 1951. The phonograph was abandoned as a spoil of war to the Chinese and North Korean armies when Seoul was taken for the second time. I left my name and address in the phonograph. I have never received a thank you or any comment from the Chinese on Mel Torme's singing.

To quote Kipling, AND THE MEASURE OF OUR TORMENT
IS THE MEASURE OF OUR YOUTH
GOD HELP US FOR WE KNEW
THE WORST TOO SOON

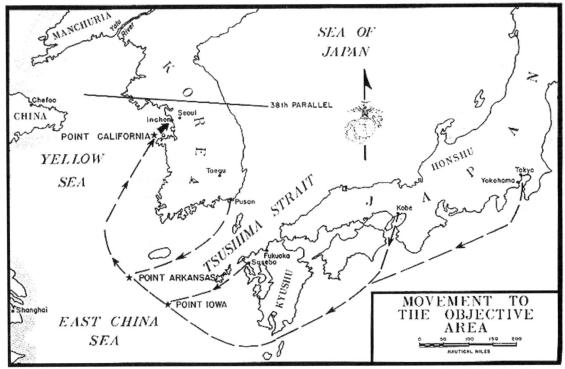

Above. Invasion route to Inchon, Sept. 15 1950.   Map from National Archives.

Troops from the 7th Infantry Division go down the nets at the Inchon invasion.   Photo by Lloyd Mielenz.

A loaded LST heads for the beach at evening high tide. Sept. 15, 1950.   U.S. Navy Photo.

RED DRAGON
The SECOND ROUND
FACES OF WAR II

John	NMI	Covach	O-61893
First Name	MI	Last Name	Serial Number
None	1542	17 March 1929	Col USA Ret, Then Lt
Nickname	MOS	Birthday	Grade / Rank
Co A 31st Inf Regt 7th Inf Div		17 Sept 1950-Feb 1952	St Clair, PA
Unit (s)		Duty Tour (s)	Home Town
Combat Infantry Badge		Bronze Star, V for Valor 2 OLC	Purple Heart Medal with OLC
Medals & Awar			

Numerous other Medals & Awards for the Korean War and the later Vietnam War.

BAPTISM OF FIRE

The same scene of combat viewed by different soldiers seems always to exhibit the "Roshamon effect." Only in broad outline do they agree. Whether this is an idiosyncracy of human memory, or merely the result of observations from different perspectives, is best left to the psychologists. What soldiers know is that participants generally describe a combat action in sharply different detail. This combat action at Hill 113 is viewed through the eyes of two men, one of 1st platoon, the other of 2d platoon A Company, 31st Inf Regt. It was in this action at Hill 113 near Osan-ni on 28 Sept 1950 that men of the Polar Bear Regt earned the Combat Infantry Badge.

When we landed at Inchon my platoon was composed roughly half and half of GIs and Koreans. We marched on dirt roads south to Suwon, eating dust for two days. The September weather was hot, drinking water was at a premium. We were a green outfit. At night we dug in on the heights above the road. Every night, our green troops blasted away at an imaginary enemy. We shot up our own Tank Company one night. Thank God they were buttoned up. I was forever running from one position to another to see what the hell my men were shooting at. This madness ended with our first casualty. Squad leader Gale Ferguson was shot by men in B Company who mistook us for the enemy! I had been ordered by my CO, Capt Hirtle to take my platoon, assume command of a tank platoon and make a reconn to the south. No one had notified B company. A lot of bullets flew at us until my gutsy plat Sgt, Roy Clanton, stood up in the hail of gunfire, waved his white kerchief and yelled, "We surrender." Miraculously he was not hit. Next evening as we neared the Suwon airfield we were strafed by US aircraft. We plowed on and secured the airfield with no opposition except our own Air Force. We had not yet located the enemy. Unknown to us, the remnants of a NK Armored Division lay but a few hundred yards south of us.

We had dug in at the southern edge of the airfield. That night all hell broke loose as a NK tank unit tried to break through our positions. At daylight, I counted 7 Russian T-34 tanks knocked out along the road. Our artillery had so many flares above us that night was turned into day. The hard hit enemy fell back on Osan-ni and holed up on Hill 113 through which ran twin railroad tunnels. We received orders to bypass the twin tunnels hill mass in a flanking move and mount an attack on Hill 113 from the south. We left Suwon under cover of darkness. My designated area of attack was across hundreds of yards of open rice paddies with the enemy atop the hill looking down our throats. Sure enough, we soon came under fire. Luckily, they were firing AT rounds which hit the hard ground and whizzed off without exploding. I recalled an old PMS&T instructor who counseled the best method of stopping close in enemy artillery fire is to close on his position. In a Civil War scenario, we made a skirmish line, charging directly at the guns. The tactic worked. No casualties. The NK guns could not, at that close range from above, lower gun elevation enough to fire effectively at us.

M/Sgt Charles Lonsford, plat Sgt 2d platoon A Co, in the "Roshamon effect," remembers the action differently. He recalls 2d platoon led the attack into Suwon along a road from the northwest, my 1st platoon following. He also recollects the 1st platoon had the additional mission of protecting his right flank. We both agree that our A Co objective was Hill 113 and that our initial attack was made on a low scrub covered ridge that ran almost perpendicular to our front. This assault was no contest, the NKs had moved to higher ground. That afternoon F-80s worked over Hill 113 with napalm, bombs and cannon fire. We moved around the hill to the side that faced Suwon, from where we mounted a final attack the next morning at first light. Another bloodless victory. All we found were dead bodies all over the area amid the wrack of war. The survivors had fled. We linked up that day with the 1st Cavalry Division driving northward after their breakout from the Naktong perimeter. They had pushed the NK Armored Division remnants into our attack zone.

M/Sgt Lonsford was soon awarded a field commission as 2d Lt. A year later, on rotation home, he was a Captain. He was forever doing things that earned him medals, respect and plaudits of his fellow soldiers as the most decorated soldier in the 31st Reg't. He was later described to me by Lt General McCaffrey, then our Regimental Commander, as the bravest man he ever knew. At one time or another he commanded each of the three 1st Bn rifle companies. He seemed to relish tough assignments, attracted to them as if by gravity. He ended his 13 months of Korean duty on the regimental staff. At the time Col McCaffrey assigned him to that duty, the good Colonel was overheard to remark that he was not about to see him killed so close to his rotation date. Charlie Lonsford was a legend in his own time.

Above. Troops of the 31st Regt.,7th Division aboard an LST head for shore at Inchon. Sept. 1950. <u>Archives Photo</u>.

Lt. Baldomero Lopez leads Marines over the sea wall at Red Beach. He was killed shortly after this photo was taken while assaulting a bunker. Sept. 15, 1950. <u>U.S.M.C. Photo</u>.

Troops from the 31st Regt. pass through Suwon on their way to link up with the 1st Cavalry Division at Osan. Sept. 1950. Photo by Lloyd Mielenz.

Louis	W.	Bontempo	RA 12 297 705
First Name	MI	Last Name	Serial Number
Lou	1745	9 June 1929	Cpl
Nickname	MOS	Birthday	Grade / Rank
G Co 32d Inf 7th InfDiv		Sept 1950-Sept 1951	New York, NY
Unit (s)		Duty Tour (s)	Home Town
Silver Star Medal Combat Infantry Badge Korean Campaign Service Medal, 5***** ROK PUC			
Medals & Awards			
Army Presidential Unit Citation Navy Presidential Unit Citation NDSM UN Medal KWSM			

INVASION PLUS THREE

The Inchon Landing, really an invasion of a North Korean conquered South Korea, has gone down in history as one of the most brilliant campaigns in the annals of warfare. For those of us in the 32d Inf Regt however, it was "hurry up and wait." Arriving on 16 Sept, our ship lay at anchor awaiting orders which never came, to take part in the amphibious assault. A vast flotilla of US Navy ships lay around us, gun batteries belching fire. Smoke billowed from the besieged city. Other troop transports also lay at anchor, awaiting word to unload their cargo of infantrymen. One shipboard rumor was the Marines had already taken Inchon. Time passed slowly, we cleaned weapons, adjusted heavy ammo cans to pack boards and in general "shot the breeze of idle troops." Lurking though, in the back of everyone's mind, was the reality we would soon face the North Korean enemy. On the morning of 18 Sept our call to action came.

Laden with gear, we went down cargo nets draped over shipside into amphibs for the half mile trip to a muddy beach. The ramp gate clattered down. We were ashore, feet barely wet. All 4 platoons assembled, moving out behind our company commander, Capt Anthony Reynolds. What we saw was devastation, houses riddled with bullets, blasted by shell fire, flattened by bombs. Our route took us eastward, away from the invasion and Inchon. Each winding road turn showed more ugliness of war, the bloated body of a dead man lying on his back, a battered truck, discarded equipment and broken weapons. Indeed, war had been here before we arrived. On we went at a blistering pace set by Capt Reynolds. I began to feel the effects of the heavy load of 2 MG ammo cans strapped on my pack. We were now in an area of rolling hills and barren countryside. There were no rest breaks. In the third hour we began climbing a winding track over hilly ground. Then it began. One of our Korean soldiers ahead of me staggered, stumbled and fell flat. He crawled to the side of the narrow road and lay there, panting for breath. Ten minutes later another Korean fell to his knees, exhausted. Not surprising, they were smaller men, not as well fed as Americans. Most of us managed to summon just enough energy to continue.

After 5 hours of a brutal forced march, we in the ranks were cursing Capt Reynolds, the Army, the war and our own stupidity in enlisting. Mercy finally intervened. The column halted. Plt Sgt Ferguson bellowed for us to fall out. I knew if I heard the call 'Saddle Up, Move out' I would not be able to get on my feet. The short respite revived us a bit. Sgt Ferguson pointed at some small knolls facing the road, "Dig in up there facing the road. We stay here for the night." He paced off distance between foxholes. Wearily, we began to dig in. "Light your cigarettes deep in your hole, cup 'em in your hand. The gooks can see the glow for miles." I was first up for guard. At midnight I roused my buddy Comieux. The clang of mess kits awakened me about 4 AM. "Sure is cold for September. Cooks are set up down the road ready to serve breakfast. Get your ass into gear, buddy," Comieux said as he dug his mess kit out of his pack. Morning of 19 Sept we quickly ate a pancake breakfast and hurried back to our foxhole to build a warm up fire. The fire had no sooner begun to blaze when the call came to form up. I thought to myself, hope today will not be like yesterday! As if in answer to my thoughts, Capt Reynold with his HQ guide, Tom Collier, and company runner, Hal Dietz passed by us and moved up the road followed by 1st and 2d platoons in column of twos. Third platoon fell in behind, 4th platoon at the rear. Unlike yesterday, there was a lot of starting and stopping. We hiked up and down rolling waves of hills, often losing sight of the head of the column in the rocky countryside. By late afternoon we were in a vast wasteland of high grass, at the end of which were a number of straw thatched Korean farmhouses.

We entered the high grass in diamond formation, not knowing what was in store for us. We were in an old dried up rice paddy, when a loud boom and black smoke 100 yards away, followed by a thud ahead of us, and another behind, told me we had been bracketed by enemy mortar gunners. More rounds crashed around us. For 15 minutes we huddled in fear. Then came a short burst from a burp gun, followed within 30 seconds by the staccato rat-a-tat of American LMG fire, accompanied by the bang-bang-bang of M-1 rifles. The fire exchange lasted less than 5 minutes. Word came to move up. As we reached the cluster of small farmhouses, Capt Reynold sent 3d and 4th plts to scout behind the knolls ahead. While we waited, Plt Sgt Marion Snow told sqd ldr Billy Rinker what had happened. "Cap'n told me to send a sqd up and flush the gooks out of those houses. Alvarez volunteered to take the lead. He made a mad dash toward the straw thatched houses. As he came within a few yards of the houses he was hit, dropping to the ground head first. A nice young Mexican kid, just 22 years old, became our first fatality of the war. One single shot from an enemy rifle was all it took.

A G. I. from the 5th Regt. checks over the battlefield on Hill 268 near Waegwan. Sept. 1950.

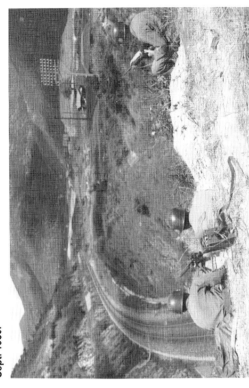

M.P. s from the 519th M.P. company cover a railroad with a .30 cal. M.G. Pusan Perimeter Sept., 1950.

Photos U.S. Army Archives

A machine gun from the 7th Cav. Regt. covers the Naktong River. Aug. 26, 1950.

An American soldier keeps a close eye on some recently captured Communist guerillas July, 1950.

RED DRAGON
The SECOND ROUND
FACES OF WAR II

John	P.	McBride	O-58501
First Name	MI	Last Name	Serial Number
None	1542	23 March 1925	1st Lt
Nickname	MOS	Birthday	Grade / Rank
Co.E/ 7th Cav/ 1st Cav Div		Aug 1950- Oct 1950	Coeur d'Alene, ID
Unit (s)		Duty Tour (s)	Home Town

Bronze Star, V device,3 Oak Leaf Clusters   Purple Heart Medal   Combat Infantry Badge

Medals & Awards

Korean Campaign Service Medal, 2 stars   United Nations Medal   ROK Presidential Unit Citation

FIRST SERGEANT

As we wend our way along life's journey, one is sometimes privileged to meet a man who stands out like an illuminating seashore beacon in his affect on the lives of those with whom he is in contact. Homer K. Leacock, First Sergeant, Easy Company of the 7th Cavalry Regiment was such a man. I had been assigned to the First Cavalry Division after my hurried plane trip from the United States where I had been stationed. The outbreak of the Korean War had caught the United States by surprise, both within the military services as well as in our diplomatic assessment of the world political situation. The First Cavalry Division was one of three American divisions which had been hurriedly mustered from scattered occupation duty posts in Japan. These units, at two thirds wartime strength, had been sent to Korea piecemeal and thrown into action to halt the onrushing attack of the North Korean Army which had invaded South Korea in a Sunday morning surprise attack on 25 June 1950. By the time I arrived in Korea in August, American troops, reinforced by a American Marine Brigade from the United States, had been able to halt the invasion. Almost all of South Korea was in the grip of the North Koreans except for the area east of the Naktong River and the northeast countryside around the deep sea port of Pusan.

On that August day, following my assignment to Easy Company, I was waiting at 2d Bn HQ for a ride to the company CP. A jeep drove up. The driver was a rugged, large framed man, red headed, with a chiseled face. His bright blue eyes made his stern soldierly appearance less threatening. I was grateful for the warm welcome with which he greeted me. His greeting and kindly manner did much to assuage the ripples in my stomach. This was not my first war. I had served in the ranks of an infantry company during the World War II Ardennes Battle of the Bulge, in December and early January of 1945. I was very aware of the duties of an infantry platoon leader as well as the high casualty rates associated with the leadership of a platoon of infantrymen. The warm welcome indicated that I would be serving in an outfit that valued the soldierly virtue of comradeship. My past military experience had shown me that the 1st Sgt usually sets the overall tone of an infantry company. It was a good beginning for a war that lasted longer than many people expected.

The Naktong Perimeter defending the port of Pusan was vital to the survival of South Korea. Through Pusan flowed the supplies and reinforcements from the United States which were to keep South Korea in the ranks of the world's free nations. I would occasionally see Sgt Leacock as unit positions would change in the course of battle. Different terrain features would change the daily defensive tactics of my platoon. On the day of 17 September my platoon was in reserve. We had for the past several nights been engaged in a series of night patrols. In a daylight attack on Hill 184, the attacking platoon was forced back. The company commander, his executive officer, a platoon leader and a number of soldiers were wounded, including Sgt Leacock. As the company began a hasty reorganization, Sgt Leacock refused evacuation until all his administrative company duties had been transferred to another NCO. That was the last time I saw him in Korea. He was evacuated and the attack on the company objective was successfully completed.

It was ten years before I saw him again. I had joined the Jesuit Order and was studying in Toronto. On a trip to the States, I had an overnight stop in Washington. The newspaper noted that the First Cavalry Division was meeting in a downtown hotel. It was here that life's journey would again link the first sergeant and the future priest. We kept in contact with cards and letters throughout the years. He eventually retired and I was ordained. In a trip to California, I visited with him and his wife in Salinas. Our friendship continued to flourish and prosper through the years. It was a special blessing to both of us. In the mid '80s I was a Chaplain at the Federal Penitentiary in Lompock, CA. He and his wife visited me there for breakfast and dinner in my quarters. It was our last meeting. He died of lung cancer several years later. He was a special friend, a soldier's soldier, so to speak. We became tightly bonded in a way characteristic of old military comrades who survive bullets of an enemy. He loved his country and served it bravely, head held high.

"THIS STORY THE GOOD MAN SHALL TEACH HIS SON AND THE FEAST OF CRISPIAN SHALL NE'ER GO BY FOR HE THAT OUTLIVES THIS DAY AND COMES SAFE HOME WILL STAND A TIP-TOE WHEN THIS DAY IS NAMED. FROM THIS DAY TO THE ENDING OF THE WORLD WE IN IT SHALL BE REMEMBERED. THEY SHALL BE FAMED FOR THERE THE SUN SHALL GREET THEM AND DRAW THEIR HONOURS REEKING UP TO HEAVEN. FOR HE TODAY THAT SHEDS HIS BLOOD WITH ME SHALL BE MY BROTHER. WE FEW, WE HAPPY FEW, WE BAND OF BROTHERS.   HENRY V ACT IV

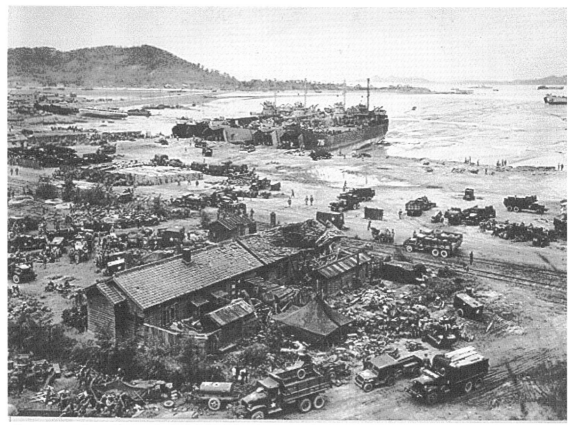

Troops pour ashore at Inchon, Sept. 15, 1950. Able to land only twice a day due to the 30 foot tides, these LSTs make the
most of it and unload huge piles of material.   <u>Photo from National Archives</u>.

Also a sad Face of War is this child,
abandoned in the rubble of Inchon.

Marines are busy at the deadly game of clearing the enemy from the
capitol city of Seoul, Sept. 1950.   Marine Corps Photo.

RED DRAGON
The SECOND ROUND
FACES OF WAR II

Charles	C.	Rakestraw	RA 24 889 451
First Name	MI	Last Name	Serial Number
Chuck	3745	24 Nov 1928	SFC, then Pfc
Nickname	MOS	Birthday	Grade / Rank
A Co 32d Inf 7th Div		16 Sept 1950-3 Dec 1950	Blue Springs, MI
Unit (s)		Duty Tour (s)	Home Town

Combat Infantry Badge Purple Heart Medal Korean Campaign Service Medal,3stars ROK PUC

Medals & Awards

Presidential Unit Citation(Navy) Natl Def Svc Medal UN Medal ROK Korean War Service Medal

THE COMPANY COMMANDER WHO WASN'T

I transferred into the 7th Div in mid August 1950 and assigned to A Co of the 32d Inf Regt. After training site on Mt Fuji we landed in mid September at Inchon. Ashore, we fought up the Inchon-Seoul highway, crossing the Han River on 24 Sept. Ordered to clear some low hills on the eastern outskirts of Seoul, we stumbled upon an old Japanese horse stable. Stored in it was a cache of new Model 1903 Jap rifles and hundreds of Samurai swords. Many men took one as a souvenir, only to later toss them away at the 'Frozen Chosin,' as a useless encumbrance. In a residential area we dug in to await orders. One of our ROKs was talking to the house owner while eating a plate of food brought out to him. The ROK loaded his rifle, handed it to the Korean who went inside. I yelled at him, chewing him out for letting go of his M-1. I never finished. There was a shot, the Korean civilian came out and handed over the rifle. Laughing, the ROK said "He wife no damn good, she communist." I thought, "My God, what kind of people are we dealing with?"

Next we were told to secure a large hill studded with big oak trees overlooking the city, supposedly heavily defended. Our attack was made with walking assault fire. Not a shot was fired at us, the enemy had vanished. My favorite way to take a hill--no opposition! None of us were sorry, if defended, our cost could have been very high. On the forward slope of the hill below the crest machine guns were spaced about 50 feet apart. Each gun had 6 boxes of ammo neatly stacked adjacent to it, all booby trapped. My boots were worn out, laces digging into my foot causing infection. When we reassembled on the road, I asked the 1st Sgt for permission to see the medic. Our brand new Company Commander thought I wanted to duck out, go on sick call. "No sir, all I want is to have the medic dress my feet with gauze and sulfa." He wouldn't hear of it. Made me the company runner. Never did understand how he decided being a runner would be easier on my feet! Anyway, I had lost. I collared the medic on the QT. He took one look and fixed me up.

We next moved downhill to a dirt road leading to a broad avenue which separated residences from the business district. Intersections were blocked by sandbag barricades leaving an opening for one vehicle. Building walls held Communist posters of Josef Stalin. The company commander never questioned any of the civilians about enemy activities, nor did any volunteer. We marched to the barricaded end of the street. Beyond the barricade was a park area with an intersecting dirt road. To the right was a small hill, on the left a bigger hill. We halted while the CO radioed Bn for new orders. The platoon I was with halted. It was a quiet scene; the platoon Sgt was showing pictures of his daughter's wedding, a M/Sgt from Stars & Stripes was interviewing several soldiers. He wore no helmet. The CO ripped into him, told him to put on his helmet. In compliance, he was halfway back to his jeep when a machine gun opened up, wiping out our rifle squad posted across the street. One of the four light tanks with us fired on the MG, knocking it out. Men scrambled for cover. The plat Sgt ran to the barricade and began firing beyond it. He paid no attention to his platoon, it was like he was fighting a one man war. The CO, hearing the firing, ran up screaming orders at everyone, but to no one in particular. Then the CO, with no knowledge of the situation, ordered Sgt Buckly's squad with my best friend, Thomas Laxton on point, to flank the barricade. The plat Sgt yelled, "Stop!" His last word was still in his mouth when he and Tom both took bullets in the head.

The CO told me to fire my rifle grenades at a MG position up hill. I had a perfect position on the hillside, but the CO ordered me down to the street to adjust my sights. Lead was flying everywhere, but orders are orders. I fired one round and returned to the hillside to fire my last two grenades. My last grenade got the MG. I returned to the street The CO asked me who was in charge. I pointed to the dead plat Sgt. "Where's the asst plat Sgt?" "Hiding behind the building, sir," "Go tell him I want him!" I found the Sgt leaning against a wall, smoking a cigarette. "Tell that stupid asshole I'll be there in a minute!" I trotted back with his literal answer, then took up a firing position. A pregnant looking woman came down the street. Someone shot her. The bullet ricocheted off her belly, stripping away some of her garments. She was loaded as heavily as a pack mule with ammo belts. Our tanks came up forcing the North Koreans to retreat. The platoon guide showed up. The CO put him in charge. We fought through to a train station. We had 59 casualties, 14 KIA in the action. The CO was wounded, as was Lt Fox. We never saw the CO again. The platoon guide made M/Sgt. On 2 Oct we started the move back to Pusan and on to 'Frozen Chosin.' The Army was the same old Army, nothing had changed.

Above. More than 300 innocent civilians that were sealed in a cave by North Korean Army to suffocate. Hamhung. October 1950. Right. A family mourns their father murdered by North Korean invaders at Chongju, Sept. 27, 1950. Lower Left. A GI from the 27th Regiment, who was wounded by mortar fire, gets a little rest on a hospital train bound for Pusan. July 27, 1950. Lower Right. This GI from the 21st Regiment was wounded while crossing the Naktong River. Sept. 19, 1950. All Photos from U.S. Army Archives. ---- More of the horrible FACES

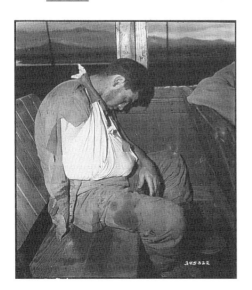

RED DRAGON
The SECOND ROUND
FACES OF WAR II

Bae Suk		Lee	52903 ROK AF
First Name	MI	Last Name	Serial Number
None	Civilian Interpreter	Nov 20, 1929	Civilian
Nickname	MOS	Birthday	Grade / Rank
3d MP Co		Sept 1950-June 1951	Hamhung, No. Korea
Unit (s)		Duty Tour (s)	Home Town

Medals & Awards

TRAGEDY

I was born in Hamhung, Hamkyong Province, North Korea when all Korea was under Japanese occupation. The end of WW Two in August 1945 saw our country divided at the 38th parallel. North Korea under Russian sponsored Dictator Kim Il Sung, dedicated its energies into a military buildup which, by conquest of South Korea, would create a single Korean totalitarian government uniting both countries. One year of tyrannical rule convinced me that I must leave my native homeland. I adopted South Korea as my country when I fled communist enslavement August 1946 , crossing the 38th parallel into freedom. My younger brother fled also in 1948. We both stayed at the home of our aunt in Seoul. I finished my last year of high school then entered Medical Scool at Yensi University. My brother soon enlisted in the Korean Air Force. During the initial 3 month occupation of Seoul after the 25 June 1950 attack, I hid to evade imprisonment by North Korean invaders. My aunt and her husband who was a music teacher and their five children, including twins less than a year old, were imprisoned. They were like my own parents. They were murdered by Communists, leaving five orphan children, when the Communists under attack by American forces landing at Inchon, retreated from Seoul.

When Korean and US Marines entered the outskirts of Seoul, I came out of hiding and joined the Korean Marines. I did not accompany them as they prepared for the Wonsan invasion on the east coast. In late October, I saw a poster seeking Korean interpreters for work with the US 10th Corps. I was one of three selected as interpreters. In early December after the Chinese intervention, we three interpreters were flown by C-54 to Yonpo Airbase at Hungnam. Marines guarded huge stacks of supplies piled at edges of the runway. To the north we could see Navy Corsairs in dive bomb attacks over the mountainous land at the Chosin Reservoir. We were taken to a warehouse site just evacuated by HQ X Corps in preparation for the move back to South Korea. After a few days we were transferred to Hamhung where HQs 3d Inf Div was located. I was assigned to the 3d MP Company. I could not have had better luck! Hamhung was my home town, all my family and relatives still lived here. At first I did not tell my fellow MPs that Hamhung was my birthplace, their thinking was all North Koreans were Communists. I was put on guard duty at one of the two bridges linking the city to the two main roads, west and south to the sea. In my role as soldier and interpreter pulling both day and night guard duty, I soon became friends with other MPs. As with all soldiers, they were interested in talking about their home towns. Learning I had fled North Korea to escape communism and my family yet lived here, they were helpful in arranging for me to see them in off duty time.

The 3d day of my assignment as bridge guard, we received an order prohibiting all civilian traffic across the two bridges. They were being rigged for demolition as a deterrent to the advancing Communist forces. All transport, even Korean Army trucks, were checked. If civilians were aboard, they were forced to unload. I was helpless to aid my fellow Koreans, old and young, in their cries and pleas to be allowed to continue their flight from Communist rule. Strict enforcement of the order resulted in permanent separation for many families were in different parts of the city. I was assigned duty to announce this order in Korean as we toured the city on a jeep mounted loud speaker. It came as a total surprise to the city's inhabitants. Finishing my loud hailer tour of the city, I grasped the opportunity to visit my family home. I found my family packed and ready to move south. They were waiting for my youngest sister, who at the time of the bridge closure, was on a visit beyond the bridge. My father refused to leave without my sister. She was unable to return. The family faced a dilemma, either stay under communist rule as the Chinese surged south, or abandon my sister. This happened in many different, yet similar situations, to hundreds of thousands of families in the first year of the Korean War. Again my good luck held. I was assigned to the guard post at the bridge my sister needed to cross to join the family.

When I explained the desperate situation to my MP friends, they were happy to help. Wasting no time, our MP jeep was driven to the house of the relative my sister was visiting. She was returned to the bosom of the family. When I went back the next day, our home was deserted. I was not aware where they were. I later learned tthey joined the exodus of the 119,000 North Korean refugees from Hungnam taken aboard the fleet of merchant ships evacuating Hungnam of troops and supplies. Several months later I located them in a refugee camp on Koje Island off the coast of South Korea, alive and happy to be together. I worked with the UN Civil Assistance Command Korea (UNCACK) for three years in support of my family before returning to medical school to finish my education.

Upper Left. A South Korean LST runs aground near Changsadong while creating a diversion for the Inchon invasion. Upper Right. A well aimed bomb by the US Air Force scores a bridge and a T-34 with one shot.
Lower Left. Inchon harbor at low tide. Sept. 1950.
Lower Right. Lt. Covach with interpreter, Soo-Koon Ai, in the Suwon area. September 1950. Photo by John Covach. All other photos from the National Archives.

RED DRAGON
The SECOND ROUND
FACES OF WAR II

John	NMI	Covach	O-61893
First Name	MI	Last Name	Serial Number
None	1542	17 March 1929	Col USA Ret, Then Lt
Nickname	MOS	Birthday	Grade / Rank
Co A 31st Inf Regt 7th Inf Div		17 Sept 1950-Feb 1952	St Clair, PA
Unit (s)		Duty Tour (s)	Home Town
Combat Infantry Badge		Bronze Star,V for Valor 2 OLC	Purple Heart Medal with OLC
Medals & Awards			

Numerous other Medals & Awards for the Korean War and for the Vietnamese War

COMRADES

The very nature of warfare has from time immemorial engendered a close knit comradeship among fighting men, linking them with iron bonds. This is the story of two men, born in the year 1929, but on opposite sides of the globe. John Covach, born to immigrant parents in a small coal mining town in Pennsylvania, and Soo-Koon Ai, son of distinguished family in Suwon, South Korea. Their lives meshed as a result of the June 1950 invasion of South Korea by the Russian supported communists of North Korea. John Covach, on graduation from Pennsylvania Military College, had accepted a Regular Army commission. His first assignment posted him to Korea. There, in the 31st Inf Regt, he commanded A Co's 1st plat of 45 men, 25 GIs and 20 KATUSA, none of whom spoke English.

Soo-Koon Ai fled Seoul ahead of the invading North Koreans, walking to his ancestral home in Suwon about 25 miles south of Seoul. He decided to stay with his parents, but also resolved to fight the North Koreans as a partisan. He cajoled a group of local young men into meeting on a nearby mountainside to explain the necessity of resistance. The meeting had just begun when it was surrounded by North Korean soldiers. He was betrayed by two men in the group who were acting as informers. Denial and resistance were useless. Guarded by two soldiers, he was marched off, headed for the local gaol in Suwon. He knew on arrival he would be tortured, interrogated and finished off with a bullet in the head. With nothing to lose, he took a desperate gamble. In the star studded darkness, he could make out a sheer dropoff on the trail. He jumped. Within 20 feet his feet hit a steep slope. As he plunged downhill he stripped off the disguise of the white peasant farmer shirt which made him a clear target. None of the guard's shots hit him. He did not go home, knowing it would only jeopardize his parents. He and a friend dug a cleverly camoflouged hole near a ball diamond south of Seoul, stocking it with water and provisions given by relatives of both men. They stayed in their self imposed prison for seven weeks, emerging in the aftermath of the Inchon landing when they heard English speaking voices near their rubbish covered hideout.

The morning after the Inchon landing, Covach's platoon headed south to take part in the attack on Suwon and its critical airfield. At a halt while the plat was being supplied with C rations, Lt Covach was approached by a Korean speaking flawless English. It was Soo-Koon Ai, proposing that he join the platoon as an irregular. To Lt Covach, desperately needing an interpreter, he was God's gift. East and West had met to fight a common enemy. Soo was at Covach's side when the plat took its first casualty, Sgt Gale Ferguson. Together, in evening twilight near Suwon they took cover from strafing by friendly aircraft. Both were atop a Sherman tank in the attack of an enemy position near Osan-ni when the tank broke through a log bridge. Both were thrown clear, badly bruised. Together they crossed rice paddies in the face of enemy machine gun and cannon fire. Together they viewed the excavated shallow grave of American soldiers, hands bound behind their back, taken prisoner in war's first days, murdered by North Korean captors. Together, on 28 Sept they stormed and overran the North Korean stronghold. In the forge of close combat, they became brothers, welded by the fires of war. They parted 31 Oct, Soo to US Army General HQ, John to take ship for Iwon and the battle of the Chosin Reservoir.

Years passed, they maintained a desultory correspondence. In the stress of duty in Germany when the Berlin wall was being built, the two comrades lost contact. In 1967 John served in Vietnam as a Lt Col on Gen Abrams staff. At the same time Koon-Soo was a frequent Saigon visitor, working as a contractor in supply of the two Korean divisions fighting there in support of their American allies. They never met. In retirement, John decided to try and contact his lost wartime friend. It was an exercise in frustration. He received information and misinformation. "Your friend has died." Then in March 1998, John made the acquaintance of Woo Sung-Han, an *LA Korean Times* reporter who used the Internet to locate soldiers who had served with Col Young Oak Kim. Col Kim had been John's Bn CO while in Korea, commander, friend and mentor. Woo published an article about Col Kim, adding that Col John Covach was trying to locate an old Korean war comrade, Soo-Koon Ai. The second caller was Soo's nephew. Soo-Koon called the next day. The two friends planned to meet in September at a veterans reunion in Seoul. Fate intervened. John was diagnosed with stomach cancer. Soo, in Manila on business, learned of this. Soo-Koon Ai and his wife immediately flew to John's bedside in Fairfax, VA. They stayed with John and his wife Waldtraut for several days prior to the operation. The operation went well. John and Soo plan their next reunion in Korea. They will tramp the ground where so many men in their youth, East and West, fought and died those many years ago.

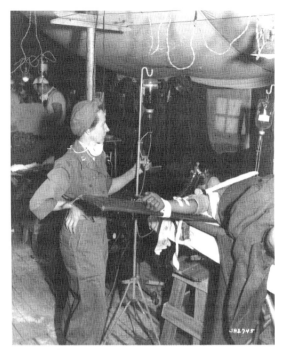

Above. A nurse at a field hospital gives blood to a wounded G.I. while other GIs are flown to Japan for further treatment. Right. A machine gun crew from the 1st Cav. at work near Taejon,

Sept. 22, 1950. Lower left.. A 4.2 mortar in action near Chochiwon. Lower Right. A battery of 90MM guns fire in support of the 5th RCT. near Taegu. All photos are from the U.S. Army Archives.

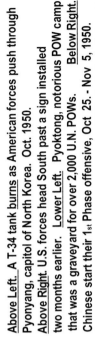

Above Left. A T-34 tank burns as American forces push through Pyonyang, capitol of North Korea. Oct. 1950.

Above Right. U.S. forces head South past a sign installed two months earlier. Lower Left. Pyoktong, notorious POW camp that was a graveyard for over 2,000 U.N. POWs. Below Right. Chinese start their 1st Phase offensive, Oct 25. - Nov 5, 1950. CCF photo from Internet.

RED DRAGON
The SECOND ROUND
FACES OF WAR II

Larry	M	Casilac	RA 19329116
First Name	MI	Last Name	Serial Number
None	745	12 Oct 1931	Private
Nickname	MOS	Birthday	Grade / Rank
Fox/9/2Div		Oct '50-Jul '53	San Francisco, CA
Unit (s)		Duty Tour (s)	Home Town
Silver Star	Bronze Star	Purple Heart Combat Infantry Badge	Good Conduct Medal
Medals & Awards			
Occupation Medal, Japan		National Defense Service Medal	United Nations Medal

THE LONG MARCH

I was almost 19 years old when I was assigned as a bazooka man to Fox Company, 9th Infantry, then at Sunchon, North Korea. The 9th arrived at Sunchon late afternoon 1 November 1950. We had pushed up from Pyongyang, Capitol of North Korea, meeting with little resistance from the NKPA. The division halted in Pyongyang for resupply before driving further into North Korea. Sunchon, a small village 40 miles NNE of Pyongyang, was the nexus of a north-south, east-west road and rail network. It was a critical supply point. Holding it crippled the efforts of the NPKA to regroup. On 2 November, air observation reported heavy mechanized forces in the Sunchon 9th Inf sector area. I was the bazooka man in a 14 man patrol reconnoitering the area to locate the tank group. My bazooka was WWII, a 2.36" shoulder held weapon needing two men to operate it. My assistant would load the rocket into the rear end of the bazooka, wrap two firing wires to two posts, then tap my helmet to signal, 'ready to fire.' His next maneuver was to move aside lest he killed or burned by the back blast. We were good. The task required teamwork. We had spent many hours in practice.

We saw T-34 Russian tanks coming down the road. The riflemen took high ground above the road. My loader and I picked a spot where the road made an S curve. It put me in position to fire into the tread mechanism of the oncoming tanks. My first rocket stopped the leading tank cold. The tank crew came boiling out of the turret,to be picked off by the riflemen of our patrol on the hill. The scenario was repeated with the second tank as it attempted to push the first tank off the road. The third tank left the road, rumbled across the paddy field heading for us. I fired our third rocket head on as the turret cannon and coaxial machine gun began swiveling in an aiming pattern straight at us. The third rocket bounced like a tennis ball off the heavy six inch frontal armor of the T-34. Before the turret quit swiveling, my loader and I took to our heels. We had not yet been equipped with the new 3.5" bazooka which was a T-34 killer. The newer weapon would have allowed us to continue the fight. It was a miserly post WWII military budget saver which cost the lives of good men that day, others would follow in days yet to come. We took unnecessary casualties because of antiquated WW II weapons. We were up against an enemy supplied with the latest Russian military hardware, machine guns, mortars, rapid fire machine pistols and assualt rifles. We did not acquire matching weaponry until mid 1951, I was later to learn.

Machine gun fire stitched a pattern in my loader's back, missing me. I stopped to pick up the bazooka rockets, ran to a new spot to fire the rest of the rockets. I now had to lay the bazooka down, insert a rocket, tie wires to posts, then hoist it to my shoulder without disturbing connections. As I fired the last rocket, Chinese infantry advanced at a run toward me. I pulled my Colt .45 and started firing. While I was changing the clip to reload, a Chinese soldier charged at me with fixed bayonet. I grabbed his rifle behind the bayonet. While he was tugging on his rifle, I stabbed him in the side with my carbine bayonet after jerking it loose from my pistol belt. Picking up his rifle, runnning and awkwardly shooting backward, I rejoined what was left of our 14 man patrol. Air strikes were called in on the Chinese tank column. The fighter planes strafed, dropped napalm, and for a time, dispersed the tank column.

My CO said he was going to recommend the Silver Star. I told him I did not deserve it. I had left my loader to die. Because I had not knocked out that third tank, six other men in our patrol died as well. I carry that guilt to this day. On 18 Nov 1950, our 9th Inf HQ group relocated a mile NE of Kunu-ri. The village of Kunu-ri was 50 miles almost due north of Pyongyang. It was another important choke point of road traffic in North Korea, straddling the primary rail and road networks into Manchuria. We were now in daily contact with the Chinese. At dusk, 18 November, my squad engaged in a running fire fight with Chinese troops. I was hit. It was dark. Separated from my squad, I gritted my teeth and waited for help. Hearing footsteps, I called, "I'm hit, I need a medic." The footsteps were Chinese. They went through my pockets, taking everything. Two of them grabbed me, one by my wounded leg. I passed out. When I came to, I was being bandaged by an American artillery officer. There were 20 of us in a school house. We were joined by 40 other American prisoners, half of them walking wounded. I was helped by other POWs in the 3 mile march to a collection center. The barn was so tiny only half of the wounded could get inside. My bleeding leg wound was tended by a black medic who still had his aid kit. He poured peroxide into the wound. It was a cold 20 degrees below. Those outside could not build a fire. Boiled soybeans was the evening meal. All 60 of us ate with our hands. More POWs arrived. The Chinese frisked us once more, taking what little warm clothing we still had to cover our shivering bodies. They stripped us as clean as plucked chickens.

One man slept in wet clothing. He was rigid the next morning, frozen stiff. He was not the last to die of freezing cold on that terrible trip. Many others died as our clothing was inadequate for sub-zero temperatures.

The guards brought a sack of boiled field corn. Wounded were fed first, what was left was divided. We were told we would move 2 miles to a larger collection center. Stretchers were rigged out of rice bags to carry wounded. In the absence of a doctor, the black medic was doing his best until the Chinese confiscated his medic bag, also each man's first aid kit. Someone gave me a tree branch so I could hobble along. We arrived at the IP for the long march to a POW camp later christened "The Bean Camp." Here we were told the wounded must be left behind. Some POWs favored carrying the wounded, others were afraid all would be killed if the wounded slowed the march pace set by the Chinese. A Chinese officer named Liu Zeh of the 17th Regt said he would lead us to a wonderful prison camp, concrete barracks, heated, with electric lights and many books to read. There were 320 of us including 17 officers. Officers were forced to march in front of the column and, not allowed to mingle with us. We moved at night. The Chinese awakened villagers to line village streets. North Koreans would spit on us and throw rocks. We got water once every 24 hours.

At dawn we would stop to sleep. We were fed cracked corn, splintered, not ground. This half boiled pig mash had sharp edges which tore at our guts. A little soy bean paste was added to the corn so it could be made into a ball. We got one ball in the morning, another at dusk, nothing else. Men began coming down with diarrhea from eating dirty snow or drinking ditch water. We were not allowed to stop and relieve ourselves on the nightly 10 hour march. A man hoarded what strength he had, ran to the front of the column, relieved himself, pulled up his pants and retook his place in the column. If he was late rejoining the column or still squatting, the rear guard gave him a butt stroke with his rifle. Several men went off their rocker and began screaming. A guard would bash him. If the man did not get up, the column was forced to march over his body. He would be left behind. A bit later we would hear a shot.

Crossing on a high bridge over a frozen river, one man fell to his death. He was left there. The guards would herd us to the road side when a column of Chinese troops came by. Orders were given that the wounded were not be carried. We marched in total silence except for the moans of wounded men. If a man stumbled or coughed the guard gave him a bash to the head. It was an obvious tactic to rid themselves of the weaker men who were slowing the column. Every day the column was shorter as men too weak to get to their feet were left, never to be heard from again. One day while asleep in a village, a flight of our F-80's made a dozen strafing runs.

The building we were in began to burn. A bunch of our men were shot. The guy next to me took a bullet in the eye, it came out his cheek, making a crease in my jacket. One officer was killed, another hit in the leg. We were let out of the burning building. The village was afire, explosions everywhere. A camouflaged Russian truck was parked by the side of each building. The village was a Chinese ammo dump! Nearing the camp, we were allowed to carry our wounded. Stretchers were rigged, but most men refused to carry them. They would walk away, each in his own private hell, fearful of using his dwindling strength to help, lest tomorrow, he not able to keep up, left to freeze in the dark. It fell to the officers to be stretcher bearers. The way they handled the job showed me why they had been chosen as leaders of men. Another long 4 days of marching brought us to the "Bean Camp." The trek was over. Of the 320 men that started that long march, 120 survived. Shades of Bataan! Americans never hear of the hellish Korean War atrocities.

Another ordeal now began. A year of prison camp filled with daily propaganda lectures and a starvation diet existence. During that period I witnessed many comrades die of disease, neglect and inhumane treatment. I was luckier. The Chinese included me in a POW exchange. I was skin and bones, weak and frail due to starvation and barbaric prison camp conditions. Three weeks of good hospital care and adequate food allowed me to be flown home. A lifetime since of stress, bad dreams, feelings of guilt, and constant insecurity based on nothing I can put a finger on haunts me to this day. Weekly psychiatric treatments for PTSD provided by the VA have recently begun to be of help. I was discharged for 'Convenience of the Government', 2 December 1952, four years and a day since I enlisted for a four year hitch. My DD 214 discharge noted 'most significant duty assignment as HQ Battery 38th Field Artillery'!

I had never been even close to that outfit. Were my records lost in that disastrous retreat from Kunu-ri? The separation center, working with what they had, did their best. Fortunately, my name was located on a Division Special Order listing names awarded the Silver Star. Otherwise, I might never have gotten my records straight. My company commander had been a man of his word. I do not remember his name but he must have survived to carry out his promise. I am glad that he was not one of those nameless dead left on the battlefields of Kunu-ri. My DD 214 also listed me as having been awarded the Combat Infantry Badge.

This was another proof I was an infantryman. The personnel of the separation center were certainly not combat veterans. They would not have made that mistake! Neither a 'redleg', army slang for an artilleryman, nor any member of any other branch of the Army is ever awarded the CIB. The CIB is reserved for the dogface infantryman in recognition of his status as the point of our nation's spear.

None of this concerned me for quite a few years. I spent that time in a psychiatric ward in the state of California. With what I suppose were good intentions, I was given electroshock treatments. It took quite a few years following release from 'therapy" before I was able to unscramble my thinking from the wreckage of electroshock treatment and return to a world which had passed me by. With the help of a loving wife and assistance from a reconstructed Veterans Administration that now exists to serve veterans rather than bureaucratic employees, I hope to live out my remaining years and gain the peace of mind that has eluded me for half a century.

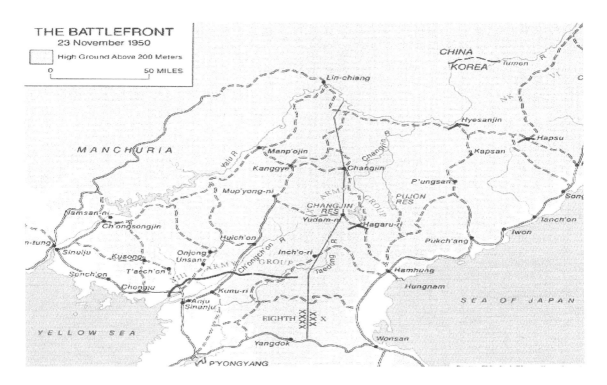

THE BATTLEFRONT
23 November 1950

High Ground Above 200 Meters

0   50 MILES

Above. Map of North Korea shortly before the Chinese intervention. It shows the separation between 8th Army and X Corps, and shows places that are remembered in nightmares to this day.   Map from Ebb and Flow.
Below. U.N. prisoners are herded north by Chinese troops. Many will not survive these brutal forced marches. Still more will perish in the ' hell hole' POW gulags along the Yalu River.   Chinese Photo from the Internet.

RED DRAGON
The SECOND ROUND
FACES OF WAR II

Jean	F.	McCrady	RA 13 291 483
First Name	MI	Last Name	Serial Number
Mac	1745	19 Jan 1931	M/Sgt, then Pfc
Nickname	MOS	Birthday	Grade / Rank
B Co 31st Inf 7th InfDiv		17 Sept '50- July 1951	Keller, VA
Unit (s)		Duty Tour (s)	Home Town

BS,V CIB,star Air Assault Badge Air Medal, 2 Cdn Medal,3 clstrs POW Medal GCM,6knots
Ocpn Medal,J&G NDSM,clstr KCSM,5stars VNSM,3stars Viet Nam Cross of Gallantry,palm UN
Medal VNCM,60 device Army PUC(3) Navy PUC(2) ROK PUC(2) & KWSM VN PUC VNGC PUC

Medals & Awards

NEVER SAY DIE

I was born in the small town of Keller on the Accomack peninsula in the Old Dominion state of Virginia. The Accomack juts southward out of the state of Maryland like a severed finger, sliced off at the 38th parallel by an arbitrary colonial survey. The western side of the peninsula fronts Chesapeake Bay, the eastern side on the Atlantic. It bears a striking similarity to the Korean Peninsula in that it is isolated from the rest of Virginia as is Korea from mainland Asia. Both peninsulas have a map boundary at the 38th parallel.

When the Korean War broke out, I was in the 172d Station Hospital. My hospital release assigned me to a security unit with light duty for a 6 month recuperation period. I went AWOL and made my way to Sasebo where my 17th Inf outfit was already aboard ship. My 1st Sgt, his company muster roster full as a result of the recent assignment of KATUSA soldiers, arranged for my transfer to B Company of the 31st Infantry. En route to the Inchon landing, I was assigned as a sniper as my WD 20 record showed "Expert." When the orders aboard ship came out, I found I had been promoted to Cpl. My feet after my sojourn in the hospital were soft and tender. The march south to Suwon raised a lot of blisters, turning my feet into raw meat. The platoon medic dusted my feet with sulfa powder and wrapped them in bandages, dusted with talc, which got me by until the blisters turned into good infantry calluses.

On 20 November 1950 after landing at Iwon on the east coast of North Korea, I was promoted and given the 3 stripes of a buck sergeant. We conducted 12 days of motorized patrols after the landing. We were then ordered to join the rest of the 31st Regiment at the Fusen Reservoir. There we received further orders to move to the east side of the Chosin Reservoir and relieve the 5th Marine Regiment. We arrived at Koto-ri 28 November. On the morning of 29 November, B Company 31st Inf and the 41st Independent Commando, British Royal Marines, were combined and reconstituted into a Task Force. The Task Force was ordered to attack up the MSR to relieve Hagaru-ri. We fought all day long, breaking through 5 of the 9 Chinese roadblocks between Koto-ri and Hagaru-ri. When my squad leader was killed, I took over. At the 5th roadblock when the Chinese attack severed the column, I used the truck mounted .50 cal MG with deadly effect, turning back the first wave of the enemy attack, allowing time for formation of a hasty defense. The gun jammed. I was not able to clear the stoppage. In the second wave attack, I was hit with mortar shrapnel. I resorted to my sniper rifle to pick off the enemy until I was wounded by mortar shrapnel, destroying my rifle and rendering me unconscious.

When I came to, a USMC major ordered me to place some men in the rear to defend from an attack in that direction. I did so, and was collecting ammunition from the wounded to supply the only remaining automatic weapon we still had in operation when I was surprised by 2 Chinese who took me prisoner. They led me to a house away from the immediate area, taking my shoe pacs from my feet. They left after a couple of hours. About 2 hours later I checked outside the house. No guards. My shoe pacs were outside the house! I put them on and took off, weaponless and fearful of being shot by either side as I made my way back to rejoin my unit. I could tell the fight was still going on by the sound of gunfire. Back with my own people, I found a rifle and was again collecting ammo from the wounded when I was hit with a grenade fragment, paralyzing my right leg. Fortunately, the paralysis gradually wore off.

I had so much blood on my clothing that men thought I was badly wounded. Some of it was mine, but much of the blood came from wounded men while I was collecting their ammo. We had been cut down to less than platoon strength when the Chinese gave us an ultimatum, "Surrender or die!" Our pusillanimous company commander decided to surrender. I had no wish to be a Chinese prisoner, so I said to the men who had been fighting with me at the tail of the column, "We're better dead than a prisoner of these Chinese. Let's head south and try to fight our way out of this." My men all agreed. We fought our way over the hills back to Koto-ri, arriving there about 1400 hours on the 30th of November. The Marines of Chesty Puller's outfit assigned me to a machine gun section. I stayed with the Marines as a part of their fighting force in Koto-ri until the 10th of December when we headed south down the MSR back to Hamhung. I walked all the way, gimping along on my wounded right leg which was well along in the process of healing.

My three wounds in the fight to relieve Hagaru never got into my service record. I was lucky in Viet Nam, not wounded in that war!

<u>Above.</u> A 1st Cav. convoy makes it's way through a small village on the way to the Pusan Perimeter, Aug 3,1950.   <u>Above.</u> Crossing the 38th parallel this tank-infantry team pursues the NK forces, 14 miles north of Kaesong, Oct. 1950. <u>Lower Left.</u> British troops are in hot pursuit of the enemy north of Sariwon, N.K., Oct. 1950. <u>Lower Right.</u> Marine tanks fire on Hill 296 near Sinchon, Oct. 2, 1950.   Photos from National Archives.

RED DRAGON
The SECOND ROUND
FACES OF WAR II

Glenn	V.	Ellison	RA 17253897
First Name	MI	Last Name	Serial Number
None	1745	29 Jan 1931	M/Sgt, then Cpl
Nickname	MOS	Birthday	Grade / Rank
F/27/25		July 1950-June 1951	Austin, MN
Unit (s)		Duty Tour (s)	Home Town

Bronze Star w/V for Valor   Combat Infantry Badge   Good Conduct Medal   Occpn. Medal, Japan

Medals & Awards

Korean Campaign Service Medal w/5stars   NDSM   UN Medal   PUC ,2OLC   ROK PUC ,3OL

FIRST TO FIGHT

When the Korean War began on 25 June 1950, I was stationed at Camp Crawford near the city of Sapporo on the island of Hokkaido, northernmost island of the Japanese Archipelago. The entire 31st Infantry Regt, one of three regiments of the 7th Infantry Division, was posted at Camp Crawford. I was a soldier in Item Co, 3d Bn. As was the case with all occupation units in Japan, we were at two thirds combat strength. The 25th Infantry Division, also under strength, was immediately shipped incrementally to Korea in an attempt to stop the invading North Korean Army from conquest of all South Korea. As one of those 'drafted' from other units to beef up the units already in Korea, on 10 July 1950, I joined Fox Co/27th Infantry in Korea. My regiment, the "Wolfhounds," fought the North Koreans tooth and nail on the Naktong Perimeter until we broke the backs of the North Koreans in mid September. The next two months were spent in continuous attack to finish off the invaders. By Thanksgiving Day, that year on 23 November, we were far into North Korea. Our feeling was that the North Koreans were defeated, just a little mopping up to be done, an easy ride!

Tank-infantry team Task Force Dolvin, had moved to the northeast to continue the offensive. Halted for the night at Ipsok, N.K. their movement uncovered our divarty positions. MGen Kean ordered our 2d Bn into reserve to cover the artillery and put out any fires that TF Dolvin couldn't handle. The night of 26 Nov passed quietly. Unkown to us, TF Dolvin was under heavy fire. The battle noises heard were attributed to NoKos making a final stand. We were in for a rude shock. About 1 AM 27 Nov, we came under attack in our reserve position. Easy Co had accompanied TF Dolvin which left Fox and George to carry the Bn load. Col Murch ordered a platoon from Fox to protect TF Dolvin HQ. That night, a company of Chinese cut through Fox positions and took possession of Hill 216. 2d Bn in its 'reserve' position was surrounded. It was not considered comical when a Chinese soldier stumbled in with a surrender leaflet in his hand. He was out of luck--he could take potluck with the rest of us! To complete the bad news we learned the Ranger Company had been wiped out. Easy CO, Capt Desiderio, had been killed. He was posthumously awarded the MOH. Our cool headed company commander, Capt Gough, wasn't sure what was going on. One thing for sure, we were now fighting the Chinese.

At daylight the decision was made to withdraw TF Dolvin. Fox 1st and 3d platoons would attack and take Hill 216 to clear the Chinese roadblock. Our second platoon sent to protect the TF HQ was lost. They never showed up. The remnants of Task Force Dolvin would join us. Together, we would attempt to fight our way out. The artillerymen in their gun pits to our rear were trying to fight off the Chinese swarming around them. We took Hill 216 with light loss. The Chinese opened up on us with their mortars. Casualties were heavy even though we took cover in Chinese dug foxholes. At the crest of the hill, Lonzo Mosier found an abandoned Chinese .50 cal MG which he turned on the Chinese with devastating effect. As Capt Gough said, "Beautiful, just beautiful!" A tank was sent around the base of the hill to fire into a draw where the Chinese had fled for cover. A Chinese soldier with a bangalore torpedo made a run for the tank. Mosier nailed him with his captured .50 cal MG. The courageous Chinese soldier and his torpedo went skyhigh together in one big bang. Task Force Dolvin, with help of our fire from the hill above was able to pass below Hill 216, although still under fire from the Chinese. We put our wounded on their vehicles. The situation for survival did not look promising for any of us.

Our Air Force received high marks that day. They strafed and bombed with great precision at very close quarters without injury to us, driving the Chinese eastward and away from us. We made our break and went down the road at a trot along with the vehicles and tanks. New orders were given to establish a defense position south of Ipsok. We were to hold our ground to allow our 35th Regiment to cross over the only bridge behind us and over the Kuryong River. This would enable them to withdraw with the rest of our division. By this time battle casualties had thinned our ranks considerably. While attempting to set up in position, the Chinese, right on our heels, took us under fire. The battle raged on throughout the night. We were about to be overrun under the overwhelming attack of Chinese manpower when the 35th cleared the bridge. The order to pull out and resume withdrawal was sure welcome. When the ordeal was over, we had marched 60 miles through mountains, gone four days without sleep, with only what food we happened to have on us. Water was at a premium. We drank from sources we knew would cause medical problems later. We had no choice. Our losses were catastrophic. We left behind many dead that we could not recover. North Korea, a cold, hard land, was their final resting place. May God grant them peace forever as they rest in eternity far from the country of their birth.

Right. A South Korean minesweeper is destroyed while sweeping Wonsan Harbor. Right Center. The 7th Division makes its second invasion at Iwon Oct. 29, 1950. Below. Capt. Ed Stamford, USMC, Forward Air Controller for Task Force Faith. Bottom. The CCF 79th or 80th Division attacks the 1st Bn. 32nd Regt. East of Chosin. Dec. 1950 CCF photo from the Internet. All others from the National Archives.

RED DRAGON
The SECOND ROUND
FACES OF WAR II

James	P.	Ramsey	RA 17 249 527
First Name	MI	Last Name	Serial Number
Jim	1745	4 Oct 1930	Cpl
Nickname	MOS	Birthday	Grade / Rank
A/32/7		Sept '50-Dec '50	Springfield, MO
Unit (s)		Duty Tour (s)	Home Town
Combat Infantry Badge	Purple Heart	Good Conduct Medal	UN Medal ROK PUC
Medals & Awards			
O-M Japan Korean Campaign ServiceMedal,3stars NDSM Expert: Rifle, Pistol, Machine Gun			

THE AGONY OF FROSTBITE

I enlisted in the Army with two friends, Roy James and Bill Newberry, 1 Sept 1948. After 8 week Basic Training program at Ft Knox I was given 7 day delay en route for a visit home. The Seattle POE where we boarded the troop transport General MM Patrick for occupation duty in Japan was my next stop on my free world tour given to Army volunteers, courtesy of the American people. In Japan, I was assigned to the 12th Cavalry Regt, soon deactivated, then transferred to Camp Haugen at Hatchinoke, home of the 32d Infantry Regiment. Our daily training schedule, looking back, was too easy. The occupation program did not train us for the rigors of war. Within a month after the Korean War began, my company was stripped of its older NCOs and its few WW II veterans. These men were sent to beef up the 3 American divisions holding the Naktong Perimeter. The loss of these men made a bad situation worse.

All companies were at 2/3 strength. We were poorly equipped with worn, outdated equipment left over from WW II.. We did not yet know we would be fighting a North Korean Army equipped with the latest Russian military gear. Camp McNair at the base of Mt Fuji was the training area where we received 100 South Korean civilians. We paired with these men in a "buddy" system, charged with turning them into soldiers. Most of these men would become good soldiers once the communication problem of languages was licked. We called our Korea bound transport "Aching Victory" for its side-to-side rolling motion. Landing at Inchon, 15 Sept 1950, we met with stiff resistance from the NK Army. We attacked east of Seoul to support the flank of the 1st MarDiv then attacking Seoul.

Seoul taken, the regiment headed south by truck and rail for Pusan. A training schedule more suitable for the realities of war was begun for daily training. At night we slept aboard ship. Early November we left Pusan for the Iwon landing in North Korea. Not a shot was fired in opposition. Next day we loaded into trucks and headed south for Hamhung on our way north to the Chosin Reservoir. A poor road system and high mountains in between dictated a southern detour. Thanksgiving was celebrated at a place we called "Happy Valley." The sun was shining brightly, a nice day. We received mail and had a turkey dinner with all the trimmings. It was the last sunny day and decent meal in Korea. The weather turned colder as we climbed to 4300 feet at the east side of the Chosin Reservoir where our 1st Bn relieved the 5th Marines. Spread thin, we felt no concern as we had already taken the measure of the NK Army. That changed drastically night of 27 Nov when the Chinese struck in a two division attack. I and my asst gunner, Sammie Hubbell, killed the next night, were out on a hillside finger, our LMG set in cross fire. As the attack mounted in fury, we moved back into the company where I took a TSMG bullet in the hip. The aid station bandaged me, the full extent of my medical attention.

Many wounded, all were in bad condition, made worse by frostbite. The temperature ranged as low 35 degrees below zero, with the wind chill factor doubling that. The morning of 1 Dec I was placed in a truck loaded with wounded. So many of us, we were stacked 5 and 6 deep. Other trucks in the convoy were as bad. The morning of 2 Dec, the truck I was in was hit, driver killed. The truck rolled over on its side into a ditch. The truck behind was hit, blocking the road. That ended the convoy. If we, the wounded, wanted to live our only recourse was to fight our way out. Some were so seriously wounded that they were helpless. I could crawl. None of the weapons I picked up would fire. Oil in the mechanism had frozen solid. The wounded were again being wounded or killed by Chinese fire. I crawled out on the ice of the Reservoir. No gloves, the pain was excruciating. Then numbness set in. A wounded Lt led us as we crawled toward the Marine base at Hagaru. I looked back. Our trucks were burning. The Chinese had thrown gasoline on the shattered convoy, wounded and all. We reached Hagaru that morning. My hands and feet were numb, absolutely no feeling in them.

The Marines took me into one of their warming tents. Later that day we were evacuated by plane. As the plane took off it was hit by enemy fire. The plane turned on its side and crashed. No one was killed. The pilots had some facial cuts. We had crashed in the edge of a mine field. Marines led us through the mine field and placed us on another plane. Landing at Hungnam we were taken to USMC tents, boots were pulled off, we were covered with blankets. It was the first time I had been warm in days, but oh, how the warmth did make my hands and feet hurt! Under morphine, I slept, not to awaken until I was being taken off a litter aboard the hospital ship. My wound was dressed, but my hands and feet were horribly swollen. The skin was board stiff. The pain was terrible. I was taken to Tokyo General Hospital and forwarded by circuitous routings to several hospitals, ending up at Percy Jones Hospital in Battle Creek, MI. I was there for 7 months being treated for frostbite. I recovered from my wound, but the after effects of frostbite are with me to this day. Cold weather reminds me forcibly as pain recurs and incessant itching worsens. My big toes are numb with little feeling.

Above.   This M-16 Quad .50, part of the airfield security, is a welcome sight to this Air Force Mechanic.
Center. British troops of the 1st Bn. Middlesex Regt prepare to cross the Chongchon River near Sinanju. 24 Oct. 1950. Below. This Air Force P-51 Mustang takes off from a flooded air field to furnish close air support for the Infantry. The P-51 was a real work horse. Top and Bottom Photos from Natl. Archives, Center Photo from the Internet.

RED DRAGON
The SECOND ROUND
FACES OF WAR II

Kenneth	G.	Crump	AF 19326024
First Name	MI	Last Name	Serial Number
Ken	Photographer	25 January 1931	Sgt.
Nickname	MOS	Birthday	Grade / Rank
36FBS 8thFBW 5th AF		Aug '50-Jan '52	Red Bluff, CA
Unit (s)		Duty Tour (s)	Home Town
Good Conduct Medal		Korean Campaign Service Medal w/4 stars	NDSM
Medals & Awards			
Presidential Unit Citation		Occupation Medal, Japan UN Svc Medal	ROKPUC

BED CHECK CHARLIE

Outbreak of war in Korea found me covering maneuvers of the 101st Airborne at Fort Campbell, KY. Thirty days later, I was covering a real war in which real bullets, aimed to kill, were being used. My assignment as photographer-gun camera specialist with the 8th Fighter Bomber Group, 5th AF, was from Aug '50 through Jan '52. Our pilots initial flew WWII Mustangs but later were equipped with F-80 Shooting Star jets. We flew from Itazuke and Tsuiki airbases in Japan and later from Korean airfields at Taegu, Pohang, Suwon, Kimpo and Pyongyang. Our landing fields changed with the ebb and flow of battle. Our airfields with exception of Pyongyang were usually safe from attack. American fighter pilots controlled Korean airspace. An exception was "Bed Check Charlie."

"Bed Check Charlie" was the name applied to Russian PO-2 biplanes used effectively against German armies in WWII. In Korea they were used as night raiders to harass US controlled airfields. "Bed Check Charlie" was a name coined in 1942 by US Marines on Guadalcanal, pinned on a light Jap bomber that kept a nightly bombing schedule at 2200 hours. The name stuck, being applied to any light bomber engaged in a harassing, nuisance type of attack. Each PO-2 was equipped with two bombs, about 250 pounds each. Occasionally, 'Charlie' got lucky and destroyed an American plane on a parking ramp. Slow, flying at low altitude, they cut engine power and glided in, gunning their motors for a quick get-a-way after dumping their bombs. They did not always get away.

The first time I witnessed "Bed Check Charlie" was at the airstrip in the North Korean capitol of Pyongyang. My outfit, the 35th FB Sqdn of 8th FB Group had been flying P-51 Mustangs from the captured airstrip since mid Nov in support of the 8th Army offensive that began day after Thanksgiving day, 23 Nov. The airfield was located adjacent to a massive European style Russian built barracks. The barracks and nearby government buildings had obviously been hurriedly evacuated shortly before our arrival. Communist Party Cards were stacked beside a printing press in one room. In one of the buildings we found glass plate negatives of Russian soldiers. We printed these out in a makeshift dark room. They still exist to this day, another proof of Russian involvement in the Korean War.

The Pyongyang airfield was little more than a dirt strip. It had been heavily bombed before we took possession. This caused severe problems in getting aircraft quickly airborne. By mid-November the strip was in good operational condition. North Korean intelligence was aware of this. Local Communists had passed on information we were mounting air strikes as quickly as planes could take off. In any event, "Bed check Charlie"again sprang into action 26 Nov when the Chinese launched an all out attack on 8th Army.

That night a PO-2 dropped two bombs near barracks where our pilots and airman had bedded down to escape the weather which over night turned bitterly cold, presaging a winter that was to be the coldest since 1905 when theJapanese began keeping records. One airman was killed, two wounded, several planes were damaged. "Bedcheck" continued his nightly sneak raids. The PO-2 was a comparatively silent aircraft. These attacks were intended to demoralize, damage aircraft and harass personnel. He did inflict damage, but never hurt our morale. His 'luck' ran out the night of 3 December when an Army Bofors twin 40mm AA gun from an Army AAA SP Bn filled the air with explosive shells, knocking him out of the sky. Later, at Kimpo and Suwon airfields, "Charlie's' raids became more frequent, often with damaging results to aircraft lined up for early morning missions.

The Chinese surprise offensive caused our forces to retreat in an effort to consolidate positions. On Dec 3d, the 2d US Division and the Commonwealth Brigade with its huge Centurion tanks passed our airstrip, followed by elements of the US 24th and 25th Divisions. The next day was ominously silent. About 1600 hours a dust cloud was visible to the north. Was it the point of the Chinese Armies? It turned out to be the Turkish Brigade. They camped by our airstrip and warmed up at our fires. One of our pilots, Capt Howard Tanner, drove a jeep loaded with C-Rations which he passed them out to the hungry Turks. They smiled their gratitude. They were gone in the morning. Later that day C-54 cargo planes airlifted us back to Seoul airport. We had spent 47 days in our foray into North Korea. "Bed check Charlie's" cousins were soon back at his old stand. We had not lost him in North Korea!

Above. Enemy dead in the great killing grounds of North Korea, Oct. 1950. Above Right. An F-80 Shooting star goes hunting with a full load of napalm. Below. The Valley Forge and it's F4Us are hampered by vicious winter weather. Below Right. Fleeing refugees in Jan 1951 block withdrawal route of ROK 1st Corps, near Kangnun. All photos from National Archives Archives.

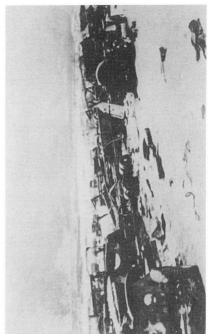

Above. After 4 days and 5 nights of battle, CCF troops move through destroyed American positions at the inlet. **Below.** The remains of Task Force Faith near Hill 1221, where 30 truck loads of badly wounded GIs were murdered by the CCF 79th and 80th Divisions. CCF photos from the Internet.

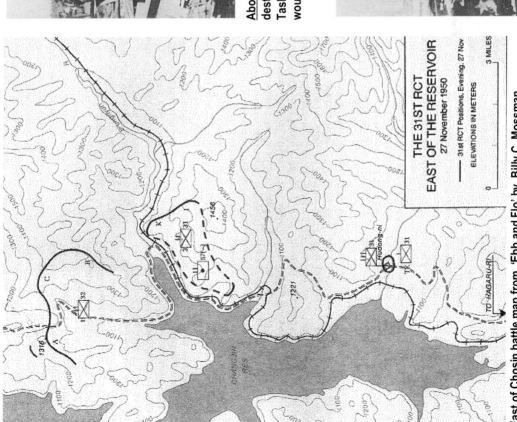

THE 31ST RCT
EAST OF THE RESERVOIR
27 November 1950

—— 31st RCT Positions, Evening, 27 Nov

ELEVATIONS IN METERS

0   3 MILES

East of Chosin battle map from 'Ebb and Flo' by Billy C. Mossman

RED DRAGON
The SECOND ROUND
FACES OF WAR II

Clarence	A.	White	RA 14 281 063
First Name	MI	Last Name	Serial Number
None	4745	28 Feb 1932	CSM, then S/Sgt
Nickname	MOS	Birthday	Grade / Rank
B/32/7		17 Sept '50-13 Sept '51	Elizabeth City, NC
Unit (s)		Duty Tour (s)	Home Town

Silver Star(2) Bronze Star (3) Commendation Medal w/V Purple Heart(3) CIB w/star ROKPUC
Medals & Awards

Legion of Merit(2) Good Conduct(8) KCSM,6stars Presidential Unit Citation (3) NSDM UN Medal

SAGA OF AN AMERICAN SOLDIER

We were the first Army unit ashore at Inchon on 17 Sept 1950, following the Marine landings on 15 Sept which secured the beachhead. The Regt was ordered to attack east of Seoul to relieve NKPA pressure on the Marines' right flank. In my job of company supply sgt, I spent my time in the front line making sure men in our rifle companies had ammo, food and equipment needed to do their job. I was blessed with a good supply clerk who brought our supply truck close to the firing line. In that two week period of combat I came to know most of the officers in the Bn. After Seoul fell, we trucked to Pusan and trained for 3 weeks, then took ship for the Iwon landing on the east coast of North Korea. Our new mission was to push north in our regimental sector destroying the fleeing, demoralized NKPA in the east coast area of North Korea. This operation had barely begun when X Corps ordered us to turn around and head for the eastern shore of the Chosin Reservoir to take over an area held by the 5th Marine Regiment. We bivouaced there 26 Nov 1950

We were now part of a composite unit designated Task Force MacLean commanded by Col MacLean, CO 31st CO 31st Inf Regt. The task force consisted of Hq Co(-) 31/7, HM(-)/31/7and two Inf Bns, 1st of the 32d and 3d of the 31st, of the 7th Division. Attached was a platoon of HM32/7 which, with 8 mortars of HM/31(-), gave the task force the 12 tubes of a heavy mortar company. I could not help but wonder if two under strength Army Bns were up to the task of replacing a Marine regiment twice our manpower. We soon learned! That first day we moved 4 miles north of the Reservoir. That was as far as we ever got into North Korea, 68 miles from the Yalu River. That night, 27 Nov at 2300 hours, the Chinese struck. We were badly surprised. Men in their sleeping bags were bayoneted.

It was cold, 30 degrees below zero, a windy night of blowing snow. In spite of heavy losses we barely managed to maintain our perimeter. By morning we were in full retreat, on our way back south to link up with 3dBn/31. During this running fight LTC Faith called me over and said, "White, you are no longer a supply sgt. You are now a plat sgt. Take over B Co HQ plat, cover the withdrawal of B Company." LTC Faith was unreal, he was anyplace and everywhere. We did our best to cover B company while they maneuvered to give flank protection to movement of our vehicles. In evading MG fire, I fell over a 20 foot cliff onto the road, breaking the stock of my carbine, injuring my arm and butt. When I tried to get to my feet the machine gunner would open fire on me. I belly wiggled off the road onto a finger leading down to the Reservoir. As I slid across the ice, I could see our vehicles pull into the Reservoir inlet where our 105 howitzers were set up. I also saw a figure run out onto the ice. Using arm movements, he gestured, "Come On". I saw him shot and fall to the ice. I did not then know it was our Task Force CO, Col MacLean. The Chinese came out on the ice and picked up the body, dead or alive, I could not tell. As I neared the 'Inlet' I was so covered with ice and snow as to be unrecognizable. I was now a target of my own men! I yelled as I got closer, hoping for recognition. I was lucky, made the perimeter without getting shot. First person I saw was Col Faith, "White, I thought you were dead. Wondered what happened to you. Welcome back. You don't have a CO. See your 1st Sgt. Get to work, we've a job to do!" I laughed in bravado, "It will take more than a few Chinese to finish me."

Bill Van Marter and I shared the a foxhole in front of HQ plat B Co CP. Bill was a company cook who had dropped his pots, grabbed his M-1 and turned infantryman when we fought east of Seoul. We were in a draw which drew the Chinese like a magnet into our perimeter as they launched mass attacks, wave after wave. I don't know how else, except for the help of the Lord, not one Chinese breached the perimeter at our location. After the first day we piled dead Chinese in back of our foxhole so we would not waste ammo on the dead. We also placed a couple of the expired Sons of Han in front for protection. The ground was rocky, frozen solid. Frozen bodies gave us almost as good protection as if we had been able to dig in. We did these chores when we had overhead air cover provided by Marine Corps fighter planes. It was the only time we could get out of our foxhole without a Chinese sniper trying to kill us. The Chinese hit their holes when the Marine pilots were overhead. During the breakout from the Inlet, B Co was flank guard on the left of the column, A/32 was on the right and in the lead. The 3/31 was rear guard in the column. A Marine fighter pilot mistakenly napalmed column point. It demoralized the head of the column, almost stopping progress. The Chinese, approaching as close as 50 yards to the convoy, used this confusion against us. They opened fire on the trucks loaded with wounded. As Ralph Boughman and I passed a Koreaan hut, three Chinese stepped out behind us and took us prisoner. One wanted to kill us, two did not. They took our trigger finger mittens and cigarettes and were in the process of taking our boots when a sortie of Marine Air passed overhead.. The Chinese dove for cover. We took advantage and lit out. A machine gun from the hill above fired on us, hitting Ralph in the back. He yelled at me, "I'm hit!." I turned. As I did a slug hit me in the helmet. The bullet was deflected, coming out the back, creasing my head just deep enough to make it bleed. The wound soon froze in the sub-zero temperature. The bleeding stopped. I fell on top of Ralph. His last words were, "Clarence, don't leave me." I told him, "Ralph, I'll be here as long as you need me." We lay there for about 5 minutes until he died. I was then a little guy, he was twice my heft. I left him, couldn't carry his heavy weight. It has been a sorrow to me for 50 years. I finally got back to the convoy. Capt Erwin Bigger, CO our 1st Bn Weapons Company was organizing an attack on Hill 1221. He had suffered several wounds. He walked with aid of two aiming stakes he used as canes. We rallied under his direction, assaulted the hill, killing or running off the Chinese who held it. except for a MG on the military crest at the east end of the hill.

The fire from this weapon was devastating to the convoy as vehicle after vehicle was singled out as they were pulled across the first blown bridge by Quad .50 MG tracked gun carriers. I had broken my carbine in the attack, but picked up an M-1. With its greater range I was able to pick off many Chinese as they ran from the west end of Hill 1221 to the protection of the MG at the eastern end. We held them off until darkness set in at about 1630 hours. Another disaster hit us. In the fading light a last Marine air sortie of the day strafed us, thinking us Chinese. We lost a number of men we could ill afford. Our numbers were dwindling. Capt Biggers, I later learned, led a number of wounded men down the south side of Hill 1221 onto the ice of the Chosin Reservoir. They crawled across the ice toward the USMC position at Hagaru-ri. Many men were saved by US Marines who went out on the ice to pick them up.

In the confusion arising from strafing by our own air cover, the Chicoms hit us hard. Bill Van Marter and I dove into a deep Chinese slit trench. We pulled a dead Chinese on top of us, playing dead. Their sing-song voices were all around us. Hours later, the voices faded away. Rolling the dead Chink off us, we quietly moved down the south side of the hill onto the ice, following foot tracks in the snow. We had no gloves, we ate snow for water Exhausted, hungry and miserable, we scarcely cared whether we lived or died. We only wanted to get warm. We kept walking, it helped to warm us up a bit. Soon the moon came out. It had quit snowing. Looking back, we could see other soldiers following us. Several times, Chinese soldiers, one an officer, came out on the ice and made motions for us to surrender. We were in no mood to surrender after all we had been through. Rightly or wrongly, we shot them and kept on trudging toward the Reservoir's south shore. We finally reached Marine lines about 2 AM on 2 Dec. Both of us were wounded. I did not know if mine was serious. Bill been hit in the left shoulder. We had long since used our First Aid packets on other soldiers.

The Marines took us into one of their company field kitchens. It felt warm inside that tent! The Marine cooks gave us the best meal of our lives, hot corned beef hash and hot coffee. We thought we were in heaven, even though we were surrounded by the Chinese. They fitted us with warm Marine Corps clothing into which we changed, while gnawing on Tootsie Rolls which they gave us. We saved some for the march out which we were told would get under way as soon as all Marines farther north had closed on Hagaru. We did not get our wounds attended. An aid man told us that there were a lot more serious cases ahead of us. We were assigned to a Marine unit and were, of course, glad to be with a fighting group and not left to shift for ourselves. We heard a 'Provisional Army Battalion' composed of men from both the 32d and 31st Infantry Regiments was being organized by Major Bob Jones, the S-1 of our 1st Bn/32d. We knew him for an outstanding officer who had served as a paratrooper in WW II. We felt that under his leadership we had as good a chance at survival as we would have by staying with the Marines. So we thanked the Marines and joined up with Major Jones.

The Provisional Bn, including Bill and I, was assigned to the left flank providing cover for movement southward to Hamhung. The Marines had the right flank. It was our job to clear out Chinese positions blocking on our side of the road. This meant that we had to take, clear and hold the high ground on the left above the MSR allowing passage of vehicles and troops heading south. It was a cold, arduous, nasty business. From a personal viewpoint, we were better off with Major Jones' Provisional Bn than with the Marines who had a tougher job. I have no idea when we left Hagaru or when we got to Koto-ri. How many days we were on left flank guard on the movement southward to Hamhung is another memory loss in a very confused period of time for me. I just remember the cold.

I remember watching as bridging sections were dropped to replace the blown bridge over a canyon spanning a deep gorge. The big pipes that carried water down the mountain to the electric power plant were in this gorge. That was south of Koto-ri, I think. The installation of that bridge was itself a miracle. I remember watching a bulldozer dig a mass grave for truckloads of dead American and South Korean soldiers. I don't remember where that was either. We finally reached the port city on 10 December. God had to be watching over us, else we would not have survived. We walked every step of the way down those mountains. On the morning of 11 December, just three of us from Baker Co 32dInf assembled for roll call, our unwounded 1st /Sgt, Bill Van Marter and myself. The "First Soldier" took us to the aid station where dried blood was washed off and our wounds dressed. Several months later we received Purple Heart Medals. I would like to revisit that area, but doubt North Korea will permit a return visit from an old enemy.

In my Army career, I was a 30 year soldier. I enlisted at 16, retiring as a Command Sergeant Major in 1978. In Viet Nam, I picked up 2 more Silver Stars, 2 Purple Hearts and 23 Air Medals for helicopter flight duty plus sundry other decorations. Looking back on a lifetime of military service, I am glad I chose a career of worth to my country, a career which jibed with my own personal values.

Above.   Chinese prisoners taken during the battle at the Chosin Reservoir.   The weather did not play favorites.   Below.   American dead at Hellfire Valley. Chinese had stripped boots and clothes from the bodies.   Both photos from the National Archives.

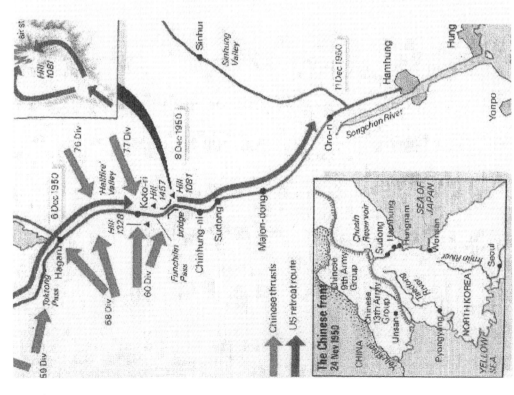

Map insert show positions before the Chinese intervention.
The larger map shows the American escape route from Chosin.
Arrows mark the major Chinese attacks.

52

RED DRAGON
The SECOND ROUND
FACES OF WAR II

William	L.	Ward	RA 15378956
First Name	MI	Last Name	Serial Number
Bill	1745	2 Apr 1932	Cpl
Nickname	MOS	Birthday	Grade / Rank
L1/32/7		17 Sep '50-20 Feb '51	Wallins Creek, KY
Unit (s)		Duty Tour (s)	Home Town

Combat Infantry Badge   Korean Campaign Service Medal with 3 Bronze stars

Medals & Award

National Defense Service Medal   United Nations Service Medal   Republic of Korea Peace Medal

A CHINESE ATROCITY

It must have been either the night of 15 or 16 December 1950 that it happened. It was my worst experience of the Korean War. Not because it happened to me, but to SFC Raymond Penland, a duty sgt in HQ Platoon, Love Company 32d Infantry. He met his death as a subject of torture by his Chinese captors during the siege of Hungnam. War in itself is a nightmare of horror, but to torture another human being goes beyond horror. I have no words in my vocabulary to express the degradation of the human spirit which allow such actions. Sgt Penland, already a career soldier in WW II, had dedicated his life to the US Army in service of his country.

I met Sgt Penland shortly after being assigned to Love Company. As soldiers do, we traded experiences. He had been in the US 5th Division in WW II and had fought in France at St Lo. I had an uncle who had also been in the Red Diamond Division and had been wounded at St. Lo. I asked him if he had by odd chance known a James Howard? He thought for a moment and said, "Yeah, I think so. Did he step on a mine, and was he from someplace in Kentucky that had a creek as part of its name?" "Wallins Creek?" "Yeah, so he was your uncle? I knew him for the better part of two years. If you fit his boots, you will turn out to be one fine soldier!" Penland was from Tennessee, and was now in his mid thirties. He had been a Regular Army soldier for 17 years.

Love Company had been assigned to the defense of the Hungnam Perimeter, holding the port secure for withdrawal of the 1st Marine and 7th Infantry Divisions from the Chosin Reservoir area. We were occupying a hill to the rear of the Hungnam beachhead. We did not see much of the Chinese during the day, but could tell they were close by. The whole area smelled like a garlic farm. My Sqd Ldr, Sgt Melvin Bell, had me keep up a steady fire with my BAR into no-mans land to discourage the Chinks from coming closer. Lt Jack Thomas, Sgt Penland and Cpl Quirino Bianco made a late morning Jeep run into the ammo dump at Hungnam. En route, they were ambushed. Lt Thomas, although wounded, dove into a ditch and crawled away. Cpl Bianco played dead and got away with it, minus his boots. He was wounded in the neck. After the Chinese left the ambush scene, taking Sgt Penland with them. Bianco made his way back to friendly lines to report what had happened. The Korean night settled in with an early darkness about 4 PM. From our position, for several hours at widely spaced intervals we heard single shots, then screams of agony.

While we did not then know what was going on, we recognized Sgt Penland's voice as coming from someone undergoing some form of torture. He sounded as if he were being slowly murdered. His screams sent us into a frenzy. We were powerless to do anything. Sgt Moore, our Platoon Sgt, pep talked us regarding surrender, "You can hear what happens to a prisoner of the Chinese! If you are out of ammo, use your bayonet, throw rocks at them, spit on them, use your fists, do anything and everything except surrender. Better to die than be taken prisoner!" We were all overwhelmed by anger and emotion. We cheered and rallied with him, "Come on and finish us! Were here, what are you waiting for? Come and get us!" We were one wild bunch of frustrated, angry soldiers.

Early in the morning at false dawn we saw masses of men heading up the draw toward us. We thought the Chinese were starting a human-sea attack to give us the coup-de-grace. We held our fire until they were closer. Fortunately so, since at 200 yards it turned out they were members of the 65th Puerto Rican Reg't, 3d Div. coming to reinforce the perimeter. We were sure happy to see them!

That morning, during daylight, a patrol retrieved Penland's body. It looked as if he had been in an amateur's butcher shop. His feet had been mutilated, almost shot off at the ankles, his hands at the wrist, his legs at the knees. Our Company Commander, Captain Harry McCaffrey, had the company file by Sgt Penland's body in small groups so that we could all see what kind of enemy we faced. It was an atrocious, dreadful scene I have never forgotten.. I had never imagined such barbarity could be visited by one human being on another. It still haunts me in my dreams after all these years.

I hated the Chinks for a whole lot of moons, but as I have reached my twilight years, I don't hate anymore. I don't recall who said it, "War produces no winners." What I do know is that war does produce lifelong memories that are better forgotten.

Above. Marines put Hagaru to the torch before withdrawing to Koto-ri. **Below.** American dead are unloaded for a mass burial at Koto-ri. **Below Left.** Survivors of the battle of Chosin load on board landing craft at Hungnam. <u>Photos, National Archives.</u>

X CORPS
EVACUATION PLAN

--- --- Trace of X Corps Perimeter, 11 Dec
———— Evacuation Phase Lines

0   10 MILES

SEA OF JAPAN

Above. Hungnam evacuation plan showing shrinking perimeter defenses.

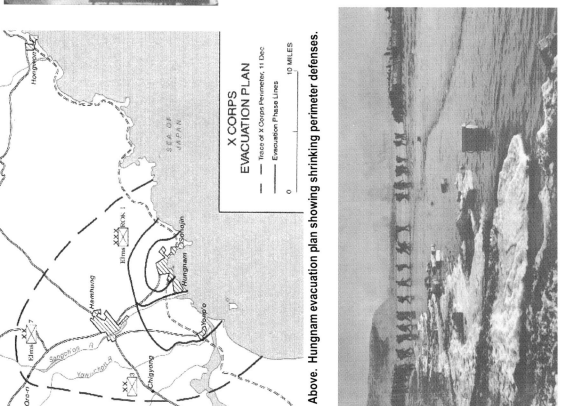

RED DRAGON
The SECOND ROUND
FACES OF WAR II

			O-193 60 24 (Vietnam)
Charles	W	Edmond	RA 15 233 556(Korea)
First Name	MI	Last Name	Serial Number
Ed	1745-Rifleman	23 Oct 1927	Corporal
Nickname	MOS	Birthday	Grade / Rank
Co "B" 15th Inf Regt 3d InfDiv		7 Dec 1950-24 June 1951	Ashland, KY
Unit (s)		Duty Tour (s)	Home Town

DFC(for Valor) Bronze Star Purple Heart Air Medal w/ 7 clusters Army Commendation Medal

Medals & Awards

Combat Infantry Badge   KCSM,3stars NDSM   Vietnam Service Medal   UN Medal   ROK KWS

HUNGNAM PERIMETER

7 December 1950. I could see the cold, bleak coastline of the North Korean peninsula from our anchorage in Hungnam harbor. The transport ship I was on was loaded with replacements for various combat units fighting in North Korea. Before disembarking we had been told to wear as much clothing as we could pile on. With blizzard like winters where 35 degrees below zero is common, it was sound advice. Once off the ship we crowded like cattle into Army trucks referred to as 'Deuce and a Half.' These ubiquitous 4 wheel drive trucks were the army work horses. An hour later we stumbled half frozen from the trucks stopped in front of a church. A grizzled old sergeant told us, "Sleep here tonight. Tomorrow you'll be assigned to your units." Inside the unheated church described in a letter home as "cold as a well diggers ass," I opened a can of frozen beans and franks, chipping out single bites using a bayonet point, as ice picks were not yet an item of army issue. At dawn we were roused by the same bull voiced sergeant who had probably performed the same reveille service for Grant's men at Appomattox. A night on an ice cold floor had so crippled me it took 5 minutes of "side straddle hop" to limber up. Another truck ride in 20 below weather took us to a process center where we stood in line, stamping feet and running in place, while waiting to be processed for next of kin info, insurance and other gory reminders of our new combat status.

In trucks again, we were now on the way to our company units. I went to "B" Co. En route we were given a break to answer calls of nature. Trucks were parked by the roadside, laden with what looked to be sleeping bags. A closer look shocked me. The objects were bodies frozen in the rigor of death. Many were still fully clothed. Although I loathed the idea of robbing the dead, it was a time to be practical. We could use the winter clothing they no longer needed. I grabbed a fleece lined parka, a winter sleeping bag and a pair of trigger finger mittens. Scurrying back to the truck, I mumbled a prayer for the souls of the departed ones who in death again helped their living comrades. Late that day we reached the company CP. At the HQ tent was a sign, "Audie Murphey's Company." A big yardstick! A Warrant Officer examined my records. Noticing my 120 AGCT score, he said, "We need a clerk in the CP. Stay here, we can use you to better advantage than as a rifleman on the line." "Thank you, sir, No, sir." Little did I know what lay ahead. My reply might have been different! I was off to my platoon. At that time each rifle plt had 4 squads of 9 men each, 2 men with BAR's, 7 with M-1 rifles. Plt Head Quarters usually consisted of a Lieutenant, a platoon sgt, platoon guide, an RTO(radio-telephone operator), 2 wire men, a medic and a messenger.

An officer shortage placed SFC Spragglin in charge of the platoon. He was a big man, 30 or so, affable, but a strict disciplinarian. After a month in the platoon, I concluded an officer could have done no better. He placed me in the 3d squad. Four GIs in the platoon hung together from a time of training at Ft Benning. They were veterans, having seen combat at the Wonsan landing. Initially they kept a distance. That changed over the next couple of weeks. There were 4 ROKs also in the squad. I remember one ROK in particular, Kim Dong Ho. He was better educated than the other 3 who were simple farm boys. After an all day march we set up a defense line behind a dike-like rice paddy berm. Hungrily we ate the last of our rations, not knowing that it would be 3 days before we ate again. To the front, we had clear fields of fire for our automatic weapons. The night was eerily quiet. About 9 PM we could see thousands of Chinese outlined in the light of flares we had been sending up since dark. Good foresight by Bn and Regt had set up artillery concentrations to be fired on demand.

In the light of flares, Chinese soldiers would drop in slow motion to the ground. Was this ruse supposed to make them less visible? It didn't work! We opened fire, watching bodies convulse, jerk and drop. Artillery tore great gaps in their formations as they rushed us. We were supported also by mortars and tank cannon fire. MGs were set about every 30 feet, riflemen only a few feet apart. These combined fires were devastating. The Chinese assault continued all night long. Bodies were stacked in heaps and windrows. Still they came, getting at times as close as 20 feet. They threw grenades, none of which exploded, whether due to cold or faulty fuses we did not know. At daybreak they quit. We exploded the dud grenades with rifle fire lest they be picked up and thrown again. Our planes bombed and strafed every possible target as they covered our daylight retreat, Chinese close on our heels. That night we set up another defense line. It was a repeat of the night before, as was the next night. On the third day we arrived at the outskirts of Hungnam where we obtained rations. Here, the Chinese made probing attacks only, not in force. On December 21st, covered by naval gunfire we withdrew from the port. On the 24th we evacuated Hungnam, celebrating Christmas aboard ship. It was over.

Left. F4Us aboard the carrier Valley Forge also suffer from foul weather. Below Left. Some of the huge supply dump at Hungnam is being loaded on to LSTs for removal to South Korea. Below. A Chaplain prays over American dead at Koto-ri.

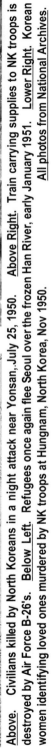

Above. Civilians killed by North Koreans in a night attack near Yonsan, July 25, 1950. Above Right. Train carrying supplies to NK troops is destroyed by Air Force B-26's. Below Left. Refugees once again flee Seoul over the frozen Han River, early January 1951. Lower Right. Korean women identifying loved ones murdered by NK troops at Hungnam, North Korea, Nov 1950. All photos from National Archives.

RED DRAGON
The SECOND ROUND
FACES OF WAR II

Tay	S.	Kim M.D.	None
First Name	MI	Last Name	Serial Number
None	Interpreter	28 Nov 1929	Civilian volunteer
Nickname	MOS	Birthday	Grade / Rank
L/8/1st Cav Div & 24th Inf Div		1950-1951	Seoul, Korea
Unit (s)	Duty Tour (s)	Home Town	
Dr Kim is now a citizen of the U. S.		He practices medicine in Los Angeles.	
Medals & Awards			
He served 3 years in US Army Medical Corps with rank of Lt Col.			

HEGIRA

I was a sophomore in Pre-Med when North Korea invaded, 25 June 1950. I hid in our cellar to escape North Korean press gangs who were shanghaiing young men into the NK Army. A few days later my mother was told our home was to be requisitioned by the NK Army as a communications center. That night we fled to Osan to lodge with relatives. In mid September, the US Army landed at Inchon. American troops came through Osan-ni. As the only English speaker in Osan I was assigned to make placards "Welcome US Soldiers." A Lt in a reconn jeep of the 1st Cavalry stopped , took me to his company commander. He had 100 KATUSA who did not speak English, nor did the Americans speak Korean. I was asked to accompany him as interpreter. I gladly accepted as the Americans were here to fight the North Korean invaders and keep us free from communism. It was my country and I wanted to help.

On the road we passed a group of about 100 forlorn young girls who had been 'used' by the NK Army, but abandoned in the NK retreat. I saw a few familiar faces, girls from Ewha Women's College. We passed 3 burned out tanks with charred bodies lying around. Other war wreckage littered the roadsides. Going through Seoul, next to a NK police station, were hundreds of dead bodies, civilians shot as "undesirables" by the retreating NK Army. As the American column moved north we saw many young and middle aged men coming down from the mountains where they had hidden from the NK Army. Near Uijong-bu we were shelled by NK tanks. We halted, then pulled back. The tanks were destroyed by American artillery. It was the last fire we received until the Chinese intervention in December. Pushing north, we stopped for 7 days in Pyong Yang, capitol of North Korea where we received supplies.

Leaving Pyong Yang we advanced to Sinan-Ju, passing through Unsan where Korea's largest gold mine was located. It had been developed by American mining engineers. Near Sinan-Ju we made a fortified base by building bunkers around a large rice field. On 5 December Chinese troops from the north advanced and cut off road traffic. A truck of wounded soldiers came into camp. It stopped to gas up. We were told to write letters home as this was the last truck that might still have time to get through. I wrote to my family. I later learned they received it. The truck with its wounded must have made it safely back. My letter did. We stayed 3 more days. The first day many infantry GIs joined in defense of the base. It was relatively quiet during the day, but night was filled with noise of machine gun fire, Chinese signal flutes and bugles. On the 3d day the Company CO introduced me to the Regimental CO. He told me that no help would be forthcoming, "Pass the word." As dark set in, we made an orderly departure following front line soldiers who set a rapid pace southward. It was a rainy dark night. A group of us, 7 GIs, a South Korean soldier and myself became separated from the main group. About 2 AM we decided to rest under a tree to keep off some of the rain and sleep for a few hours.

It was about 10 AM, clear daylight, when we awakened. All nearby farm houses were empty. The Korean soldier broached the idea that we should dump the GIs, and change to civilian clothes. "It is our only chance. We will never make it home with these blue eyed soldiers." While I realized he was probably right, I also realized that these GIs too were here, possibly unwillingly, several thousand miles from home to fight communism in our defense. To cold heartedly desert them in enemy territory was more than my conscience would allow. Without a further word to him, I ran to rejoin the GIs still rapidly marching south. We kept on, but after dark ran into a continuous flow of Chinese soldiers. Their trucks were moving without lights. We climbed a hillside taking refuge in a deserted farm house. We were cold, shivering, and very hungry, yet dared not fire up the sub floor "ondol" heating device, lest it draw attention. About 2 hours later, the house was surrounded, we heard gunshots and were told in English, "Come out! Hands up!"

Taken to a school where a Chinese HQ had been set up, we were interrogated. I told them I was an interpreter. I received "special treatment," in solitary confinement, an armed guard outside. Next day, in gangs of 20, we marched at night ,resting during the day in empty farmhouses. We were made to tidy up each farmhouse before leaving. No attempt was made to keep us in the same group each day. Reflecting on the single man, single guard result of being an interpreter, I decided to change my role. On arrival at a prison camp near the Yalu River, I lied. I was now a "forced laborer," made to carry ammunition. It worked. I was placed with other civilians, next to American prisoners in a POW cage area converted from the entire south side of a village.

In the initial days of the Chinese invasion, the Communists were probably not well coordinated with the NK Army. The Chinese cast a wide net, gathering in every man. Civilians, regional government workers, soldiers all went into the bag. Soldiers were immediately sent to Manchuria to be regrouped into regiments. Prisoners were put to work making huts to live in. We cut logs in the mountains to build two story huts. Each floor was built for 20 prisoners. It took 3 days to build with 40 of us working on our hut. 20 was a tighfit. Luckily, I was put with 15 others in the upper floor of the hut we had built. Not quite as crowded. We were fed a thin corn soup which smelled of pork, but had no pork in it. I guess we got the broth while the Chinese guards got the meat. In a daily lecture the virtues of communism were extolled; the South Korean "puppet" government and "the US Imperialists who wanted to enslave the world," were vilified. We were petrified with fear when several Americans died of a fever. I knew it was probably Typhus because we were all infested with lice. If we stayed here long enough we would all probably die of it.

About 20 December several high ranking North Korean soldiers visited the camp. Interrogations began anew the next day. There were 8 of us: a civilian truck driver of the 18th ROK Regiment, 3 South Korean civilians, 2 Katusa and myself. We agreed none of us were paid, we were all forced labor and all would definitely refuse to join the NK Army. When questioned, I said I was picked up off the street and made to carry ammunition to North Korean soldiers in the hills. I was asked if I was paid. I said, "No." If I had answered yes, I would have been treated as an army employee. He asked me to join the NK Army. He said they had already taken Seoul and that the Chinese Liberation Army was advancing toward Pusan. They would soon push the US Imperialists into the sea. I replied that since Seoul was retaken, I wanted to return to Seoul. I was worried about my family. After I had seen them and knew they were alright, I would then join the NK Army. I was wearing almost new Army boots. He was wearing canvas sneakers. I offered to exchange my boots for his sneakers. The ploy worked. He gave me a paper with a NK Central Intelligence Seal saying that "I was taken by force to North Korea by Sung Man Rhee's puppet government. He is to receive all help necessary in returning to his home." This printed official form looked very impressive. One KATUSA came out looking very pale. He had been forced to join the NK Army.

Three of us left that evening and started our walk to freedom. Using my pass, and with NK Army troops now in South Korea, it was easy to get food and a place to stay at night. We walked for 15 days, sometimes at night. I learned that each village was controlled by 5 hard core NK communists. Farmers told me that the new regime had announced it would take 30% of the harvests, the farmer could keep 70%. Communist calculations based the harvest on inflated yields. It worked out the Communists took 70%, the farmers were left with 30%. As we neared Kae Sung we were strafed by American fighter planes. I was lying prone near the corner of a house. Bullet holes stitched the house wall just a foot above my head. If a cat has nine lives, I must have had nineteen. Thinking about it in later years, I firmly believe that I am still alive as a heavenly reward for not abandoning those 7 GIs. The 3 of us finally reached Kae Sung just north of the Imjin River. It was a 15 day walk, some of it at night, from the POW camp to the Imjin. We approached a destroyed railroad bridge, still passable on foot although only one side hung drunkenly onto the support girders. We were stopped by a NK soldier armed with a Russian machine gun (Burp Gun) hung on his shoulder. He stopped us. My dream of freedom shrunk as if it were about to fade away as a dream does after awakening. However, with a serious look on my face, I handed him my pass and told him we were on a serious government mission to the people of the south. The big lie worked. He let us proceed.

Our luck continued. As we crossed the bridge we ran into several GIs, probably 24th Division. They were retrieving the body of a soldier who had stepped on a mine. We raised our hands and shouted, "Don't shoot!" We were taken to a Hawaiian Nisei Captain who interrogated us in an all night session. He said he believed our story and released us. He also said we were lucky. Regulations required that anyone crossing the front lines was to be sent south to a POW camp. Since UN forces were in retreat he had no way to process us. I later learned that deadly riots between North and South Korean factions in the Koje-do Island POW camps had cost many lives. Lucky again! We were sent to the Seoul RR station. We wept tears of joy, we were free! It was the day before Christmas.

We journeyed south to Pusan as soon as we were freed. We walked, rode in empty RR cars, and cadged truck rides. When the Chinese reached Seoul, 4 Jan 1951, I was in Pusan, had found my family, slept for 3 days and nights without knowing I was wetting my own bed! After a 3 month rest, I saw a newspaper notice that the US 8th Army would hire 30 interpreters. Of more than 300 taking the exam, I was one of the fortunate 30. After a brief training session I was sent to the US 7th Division as an assistant to the Hawaiian Nisei officers, who were division prisoner interrogators. After 6 months of this duty, I returned to school to again study medicine.

As I write these memories 50 years have passed. I reflect on the causes of our civil war. When we were divided at the 38th parallel we were not a nation, but a colony, and to the victors of WW II, pawns in a chess game soon known as The Cold War. The birth of our problems go back to brutal occupation by Japan. Japan in her evil aspiration to dominate all of Asia made us a colony. As a nation we could have stood on our own in national unity. The Korean War was a lost war for every combatant country. No one won. Today however, facts are facts. We live in a world as it is, not as we might wish. As long as the United States maintains a strong posture in Korea we of the south will stay free. If she does not, China will lower the Bamboo Curtain. We will again be a subjugated vassal colony. The hope of all South Koreans is negotiation will result in unification and a democratic government of equals. Recent events and discussions offer some slight hope of unification. It may take another fifty years before the Communists allow this.

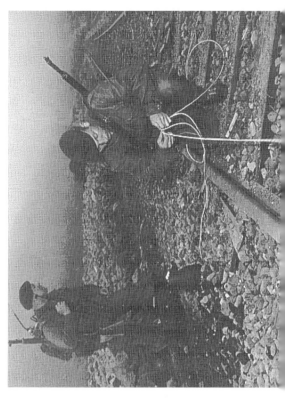

Right. Australian Sea Fury planes fly over the HMAS Sydney. Below Right. British Commandos [41st Royal Marines] destroy railroad tracks, 8 miles South of Songjin, April 10, 1951. Below Left. Refugees fleeing the Chinese, crawl over the destroyed Taedong River bridge at Pyonyang, Dec. 1950. Photos from the Internet.

RED DRAGON
The SECOND ROUND
FACES OF WAR II

Richard	Eyre	Coote	206010
First Name	MI	Last Name	Serial Number
Dick		15 April 1929	Captain
Nickname	MOS	Birthday	Grade / Rank
16th New Zealand Field Arty Regt		Dec 1950-May 1952	Nelson, New Zealand
Unit (s)		Duty Tour (s)	Home Town

Medals & Awards

A CHRISTIAN TAKES HIS FAITH TO WAR

The lasting experience of Korean war service was the realization I could not get away from God and His protection. For centuries my ancestors have been involved in wars. My father, a decorated veteran of WW I, died when I was 8. My two brothers, much older than I, served in New Zealand's WW II Armed Forces. Growing up in the troubled days of WW II, I contributed to the war effort as a solitary teen-age deer hunter in the mountains, obtaining skins needed for flying jackets before the age of synthetics. It was at this time, in close communion with my God in the solitude of the New Zealand mountains, I began the walk of a Christian path which has guided my life. In true family tradition, I was the first Kiwi to volunteer from my home town. It was a chance to share comradeship with my two brothers, to gain respect as a fellow soldier. I had nearly finished my apprenticeship as an Engineer. I was surrounded by friends. A wonderful girl, now my wife of 48 years, had consented to share her life with me. I had joined a church which, through prayer, enabled me to obtain quick healing after a bad motor bike crash. I was living in a wonderful and comfortable world!

My comfortable world underwent rapid change as I entered into military life. The euphoria of change quickly evaporated as military training in all its rigors dominated every waking hour. A working day was 14 to 16 hours. Being selected for officer training meant education in all aspects of soldiering and gunnery and learning all the responsibilities of commissioned rank. Training was intense. We double timed to visit the toilet. Prior to army service, I habitually spent some time each day reading my Bible and meditating in prayer. This not only became impossible, but made me a butt of ridicule and persecution by some. The persecution soon halted. Being a Christian does not translate as physically helpless. Persecution stopped, ridicule went underground, surfacing *sotto voce* on occasion when I would read from the small Bible my wife had given me. I continued to read, pray and meditate. No longer was I in a circle of friends. In fact, I was the only member of my faith among the 1100 men soon to depart for war in a strange country thousands of miles from all that I held dear. It was obvious my immediate future was one of uncertainty and continuous challenge!

We embarked in Wellington on the SS Ormonde for a 3 week trip to Korea. Boarding, I lugged my gear into my 4 berth cabin. To my surprise, an addressed parcel lay on my bunk. It was from the headquarters of my church in Boston, MA, USA . In it was a small pocket Bible, a text book and a letter with the name of a chaplain serving with US forces, Capt Jack Allen, APO 424 Korea. To no avail, I tried to find out who had placed the package on my bunk. Security was tight on the ship, yet none of the shipboard officers could give me an explanation. I was delighted to get this parcel, but the name of a chaplain and APO 424 was not much of an address to find him. The sea trip was great. I was able to get some undisturbed time which allowed me to discover the wonders of the 139th Psalm in which King David describes his awareness that God had created him and would be his guide and protector. I realized this Psalm must have been of tremendous strength and comfort to soldiers for over 3000 years. It comforted me as I studied its message.

We arrived in Pusan mid winter 1950. It was snowing, a bleak cold day. We moved to an encampment at Song-do, some ten miles from the wharves. En route, I noticed a painted sign, '424' on a small corrugated iron hut. It dawned on me that 424 had something to do with the address of the American Army Chaplain. Next day while in charge of a detail collecting equipment from the ship, I stopped the convoy at the hut. I saw a man sitting at a packing case desk. I asked, "What does 424 stand for?" "American Post Office 424." I said, "I have a name of a man I want to contact at APO 424." He laughed, "There are thousands of names at this address!" I responded, "Yet, by any chance do you know a Capt Jack Allen?" He rose, held out his hand ,and said, "I'm Jack Allen. It's good to meet you. Where are you from?" By sheer chance I had located the man I wanted to find on my first day in Korea!

That Sunday, Jack held the first service ever for our church in Korea. This experience confirmed for me the promises made in Psalm 139 for me and all mankind. It protected me throughout my army service as on the day on our guns fired 10,387 shells, and in months when we fired more than 72,000 rounds. In commemoration of the 50th Anniversary and on behalf of the ANZAC forces at the Korean National War Memorial at Kapyong, I read the service from the Bible my wife had given me 50 years earlier. It had been a constant Korean companion. Now reading from it, she was with me to share this moving ceremony in tribute to our fallen comrades.

Left. A radio operator with the 24th Regt. enjoys a Stars & Stripes with his rations. The headlines state that the 'super' bazooka is on the way. **Right.** A battery of 155s carry on their deadly trade.

Below Left. Traveling to Korea at his own expense, the great Al Jolson performs for the troops. This performance at Pusan on Sept. 17, 1950 would be one of his last as he died a short time later. **Below Right.** The GI favorite, Bob Hope, is surrounded by Marines. Delayed in their invasion of Wonsan, the Marines were delighted to find the Bob Hope Show awaited on the beach.

All Archive Photos.

Above. A familiar sight. Dead North Koreans litter a frozen battlefield. Photo by Ben Luci. Above Right. A tank is rafted across the Han River by Combat Engineers. Below Left. Marines on their way to the Pusan Perimeter share their ration chocolate with Korean kids. Below Right. A G.I. searches the far shore of the Naktong River for North Korean invaders. Photos from the National Archives.

63

CHINESE INTERVENTION

By the end of October 1950, six Chinese armies had crossed the Yalu River. These six Chinese armies constituted an approximate strength of 180,000 men, concentrated in front of the advancing United Nations forces. These stealthy Chinese troop buildup movements were conducted at night, in great secrecy. They had not been detected by UN forward troops, or by air reconnaissance units. Unsupported reports by prisoners of a massive Chinese build-up were not believed. At a time when thousands of organized Chinese troops were pouring across the Yalu, the Far East Command SitRep(Situation Report) showed them still poised for action in Manchuria. As the Chinese build-up developed, the US Forces continued their advance northward. In November they had reached the main North Korean enemy position between Pyongyang and the Yalu River. The Chinese launched a heavy, concerted attack along the axis of advance which turned the UN advance into a retreat. The US forces set up new defensive positions along the Imjin River north of Seoul. The New Year opened with another crushing offensive by the Chinese which forced a further general withdrawal. Seoul again fell to the Communists. A new line was established some 64 kilometers south of the former capital.

In mid-February a new UN offensive was begun. Weather was bitterly cold. Enemy resistance, as the retreat continued, increased as each valley and ridge line running east and west was taken. These mountain ridges, cutting across the axis of advance, provided the enemy with a natural line of defense. Initially, resistance by a dug in and camouflaged enemy was heavy. The UN attack slowed in a series of stubbornly fought battles. Suddenly, the enemy withdrew. It became apparent the Chinese were withdrawing across the entire front. Seoul was liberated in March by 1st ROK and 24th US Infantry Divisions advancing toward the 38th Parallel. Meanwhile, the question of crossing the 38th Parallel was being debated at both military and political levels.

Two options were considered by the United Nations, the first being to press for complete military victory which would require additional forces and extension of the conflict beyond the borders of Korea. Stabilization of the military situation combined with negotiations to end the conflict was the alternative. General MacArthur pressed for all-out effort to achieve victory, even at the risk of war with Communist China. He expressed his dissatisfaction with President Truman and the UN. Both favored negotiation. General MacArthur was relieved of his command. He was replaced by LTG Matthew B. Ridgeway. After Ridgeway assumed command, there was no change in tactics of the situation. A vigorous advance to regain all of the captured South Korean territory continued. By April of 1951 most of the UN front was north of the 38th Parallel.

Evidence began accumulating the enemy was placing his forces on the high ground north of the Imjin River. The withdrawal allowed the Chinese to replace tired troops and reorganize equipment. On the night of 22 April 1951, North Korean and Chinese forces struck the western and west-central sectors of the UN positions. The 1st and 9th Corps were ordered to withdraw. The 6th ROK Division in the 9th Corps area received the brunt of the attack. The 6th ROK division was overwhelmed and forced to retreat. It was in grave danger of being cut off and destroyed. Fortunately, the British Commonwealth Brigade, in Corps reserve, was able to provide an escape route for withdrawal of the South Koreans. During this action, a Canadian battalion was surrounded requiring resupply with parachute drops of ammunition and food. Canadian casualties were heavy, but their valiant effort saved the day.

By 1 May the enemy offensive had waned. The 1st and 9th Corps of the Eighth Army held an irregular line approximately 30 kilometers south of the 38th Parallel forming an arc north of the city of Seoul. The Canadian and Australian Regiments received the United States Presidential Unit Citation for their action in this campaign. Plans were drawn up immediately at UN Headquarters to return to the 'Kansas' Line, the name for a range of hills just north of the 38th Parallel. Simultaneously, defensive positions were strengthened against a possible new Chinese offensive. However, to the north, the Chinese shifted their forces eastward in preparation for offensive action against the Eighth Army sector. Battle tactics were determined by the relative strengths and nature of the opposing forces. With air superiority and material strength, the aim of the United Nations was not to close with the enemy and destroy him, but to force him back beyond the mountain barriers along the 38th Parallel.

Chinese tactics were dominated by their chief asset, manpower. When an offensive failed, they withdrew, awaiting reinforcements and supplies being brought forward for another attempt. During this period, the UN operations consisted of regimental groups moving forward singly or in conjunction with flanking units. On 24 May 1951, the 25th Infantry Division moved to an area northeast of the city of Uijongbu and commenced an advance through a series of phase lines to the 'Kansas' Line with combined tank-infantry battle group forces to move rapidly to seize and hold an objective until the main force arrived to establish strong defensive positions. Following the valley of the Pochon River, advancing in the face of light resistance, the division reached positions on the 'Kansas' Line on 27 May and the following day, began an advance north of the 38th Parallel.

The advance was halted near a burnt-out village at the foot of a formidable mountain barrier named Kakhul-bong (Hill 467). Kakhul-bong was vital to the Chinese supply line and their system of communication across the Chorwon Plain. Control of this salient was vital to the UN Forces since it lay close to the supply route from Seoul through Uijongbu to the Chorwon area. During the month of June, units were assigned the task of establishing and holding a patrol base in the tip of the salient.

Patrol bases of the defended areas were of battalion size, set up in no-man's land at distances ahead of forward defense positions. From these forward bases, troops maintained vigilance over a wide area, yet probe deeply into the heights beyond. By mid-June Eighth Army had broadened its salient on the east coast and advanced up the center of the Korean Peninsula. This line remained substantially here until the end of the war. In July during the summer of 1951, the Communists requested a cease fire. Negotiations were begun to end the conflict. However, almost at the outset, the truce talks quickly ran into trouble. Suspicion prevailed the Communists never intended the talks to produce an early peace, rather, they were using this period to gain military advantage. The talks, like the war itself, would drag on for the next two years. The UN Command stepped up its offensive on the 1st Corps front in September and October to achieve area defense in depth to provide better protection for the Seoul-Chorwon supply route. The 'Wyoming' line was extended from Sang-gorangpo to Chung-go to eliminate the salient created by the curve in the Imjin River. In the middle of September, all four divisions of the 1st Corps established a new front line, known as Jamestown, American divisions on the right, 1st ROK Division on the left.

Phase lines Wyoming and Kansas were to the rear of the Main Line of Resistance (MLR). The enemy took the offensive and mounted attacks with increasing intensity in the month of November. On 27 November, cease-fire negotiations were renewed. No further offensive actions were taken. Artillery action was limited to defensive fire and counter-battery bombardment. This partial cease-fire soon proved one-sided and temporary. The enemy continued to shell friendly positions and mount combat patrols. From the winter of 1951 to 1952 until the end of hostilities in 1953, a period of static warfare ensued. UN Forces held and improved their positions, reinforced defenses and maintained patrols in no-mans land. It became a war of patrol and counter-patrol, of booby traps and mines. The fighting in Korea slowly ground on, to end only with the signing of the Korean Armistice Agreement at Panmunjom, 27 July 1953.

Battlefield success requires good leadership and high morale. Many circumstances occur in war where these virtues are not enough. Timing of events, not to mention plain old fashioned good luck, also have a great deal to do with military success or failure.

Paul Freeburger   I & R Platoon   14th Inf Regt   25th Inf Div

Marines hold ceremony at Hamhung after their breakout from the Chosin Reservoir. December 13, 1950.

Above. GIs bring in North Korean stragglers on the push north of the 38th parallel. Above Right. More North Korean dead. Photo by Ben Luci. Below. This Mustang from the Australian Air Force was a little short of its air field after being hit by NK ground fire. Below Right. A chow line serves members of the 1st Cavalry Division during the early days of the Pusan perimeter battle, Aug 1950 U. S. Army Signal Corps Photos.

Above. The *Meredith Victory* ready to load refugees at the port of Hungnam.   Note AA gun position in foreground.
Below. 14,000 refugees later staunch become citizens of South Korea.   Photos courtesy Bob Lunney..

RED DRAGON
The SECOND ROUND
FACES OF WAR II

Hung-bae		Park	O-53891
First Name	M I	Last Name	Serial Number
None		10 Feb 1932	Lt Col MC AF ROK
Nickname	MOS	Birthday	Grade / Rank
Lt Col Ret AF ROK		14 Nov 1950-Sept 1952	Sonchon, North Korea
Unit(s)		Duty Tour(s)	Home Town

Student Volunteer Corps   LT Col Ret MC AF ROK   Professor Emeritus of Preventive Medicine, Hanyang College of Medicine Seoul, Korea Honorary President, Aerospace Medical Assn, Korea

VOLUNTEER SOLDIER - FIGHTING EDUCATOR

The North Korean Peoples Army inflicted a crushing blow in a surprise invasion of South Korea, June 25, 1950. This was countered by the successful Inchon landing in September by US Marines and 7th Division Army troops. Seoul was liberated on September 28, 1950, less than 3 months after the invasion. The cost in American and Korean lives had been heavy as fighting forces were brought up to strength and committed piecemeal into battle. Advancing American and Korean troops in mid November reached the Yalu River on the Chinese border. South Korea recognized the need to set up a military government which would assist the liberated people of North Korea in recovery of their identity, organizing them for self government and, through education, gain voluntary cooperation.

An Information and Education Corps was organized in battalion strength and named the 773rd I & E Bn to aid in the accomplishment of this task. Battalion personnel were made up of a 15 percent cadre from the Regular Army of the Republic of South Korea the remaining 85 percent were student volunteers. Many young students who had fled North Korea were in school in Seoul at the time of the invasion. Many of them successfully escaped the draft gangs of the North Korean Peoples Army. The liberation of Seoul freed these students to volunteer for service in the ROK Army and assignment to the I & E Bn. I was assigned to the Fifth Company. Then, the Chinese intervened in the war on 27 November 1950, committing over a half million troops in the first few days of their attack. By the time the Bn was organized, the tide of battle had turned. The joy of victory and unification evaporated leaving an atmosphere of uncertainty due to defeat and withdrawal from North Korea. We all wondered what would now be done with our battalion.

Our unit left Seoul the morning of December 5 as a military band played in honor of our departure for North Korea. The train reached Sin Mak, about 40 kilometers north of the 38th parallel where passage was halted by a heavy snowstorm. The train was then ordered to return to Seoul as North Korea was being evacuated by UN forces. A frozen rice ball was handed out as our days ration. I ate my frozen rice ball, watching my native homeland of North Korea recede farther into the distance of the engulfing snowstorm. Our hearts were heavy with sorrow. We were as gloomy as the weather. We were tired, disappointed, uncertain of the future, for ourselves and our unit in which we were so proud to serve. In Seoul we set up a temporary camp at the Duk Soo palace. We were told it was but a matter of a few days before Seoul would be in the hands of Chinese troops. Remembering the nightmare of horror and suffering caused by the North Korean capture of Seoul in June, the citizens of Seoul, including government organizations and military police, began a hurried evacuation of the city. A volunteer "do-or-die" squad was organized which would remain until the last possible moment to patrol the city and maintain order in the midst of chaos and the vacuum left by the retreating government.

On December 23, the 773d E & I Battalion evacuated Seoul. The"do-or-die" squad recruited from the 5th Company remained to patrol the city and assist in the evacuation of the civilian population. We met as a squad for the last time on New Years day 1951 to share information and intelligence before we split up to escape the advancing Chinese. On January 3 the Chinese reached the outskirts of Seoul. The roar of artillery fire was now much closer. It was time to leave but there was one last duty to perform. We regrouped.

Following orders, we visited all the major newspaper plants, dismantling and breaking the rotary presses with sledgehammers. We burnt mountains of blank newsprint. It was regrettable but we had learned that leaving these facilities intact gave the enemy the ability to use the presses as communist propaganda tools to disseminate their outrageous propaganda and deceptive lies. The newsprint went up in flames, lighting up the sky. The main streets were congested with military vehicles and fleeing civilians. The next day we went to the Han River to check information that Red Chinese patrols had entered the city.

Tens of thousands of civilian refugees were gathered at the bridge approaches waiting to cross the river. The populace that had not yet left were warned by radio and by leaflets broadcast through out the city the two previous two days that they should remain in their homes. It was of extreme military importance that civilians be screened to eliminate enemy guerillas from infiltrating UN positions.

Demolition of the bridge had been set for 2 PM. In spite of these warnings a huge crowd had gathered waiting for an opportunity to cross the river and gain refuge from the Chinese and North Korean communist troops. A temporary floating bridge had been built which could have accommodated thousands of those wishing to cross the river. The crowd was unmanageable as they pushed and shoved in competition for space. Few were able to cross. It was a scene of complete chaos, the ultimate in disorder. We all felt sympathy for the refugees and understood their suffering. The desire to escape a merciless dictatorship and their aspiration for freedom, even at the cost of their lives, goaded them on. However, fear had turned the huge crowd into an unmanageable mob.

That afternoon, machine gun fire wounded a number of civilians. The next day we saw a young women carrying a child. She had suffered a gunshot wound. She was wandering around as if she had lost her mind, as perhaps she had. All we could do was cover her wound with a compress bandage, hiding the exposed bone. We directed her back to the city in the hope that she would find medical help. There were so many scenes of suffering and grief that it is impossible to remember them all. It was one of the most agonizing experiences of my life. I was helpless to be of any real assistance to these people. The cruelty of war is indescribable.

There were many incidents during the Korean War where enemy guerillas disguised themselves as civilian refugees. They used this deceit to attack UN troops from ambush. American and Korean troops, adopting harsh measures to screen out these infiltrators, regrettably caused some civilian casualties. The Communists were ruthless in using civilians as screening shields, sacrificing these innocents without hesitation. It was part and parcel of the cruel communist dogma to do whatever it took to gain advantage and accomplish their goal of dominating all the Korean people. It was just another of the barbarities of war as practiced by North Korea. After completion of our duty in Seoul in January 1951 we moved south to Taegu in concert with UN troops. UN troops under American Army command were reorganizing new defensive lines to stop the advance of the Chinese armies. Conditions of the war had changed. As a result, a new multifaceted strategy was developed to offset the boundless manpower of the Chinese armies. Unlimited manpower and a complete disregard for human life enabled Chinese generals to employ "Human Sea" attacks in their offensives. Recognizing that it was now going to be a longer war, I &E Corps was reorganized. Our mission was changed from a civilian to a military objective. Two of us were assigned to each infantry battalion in the fighting divisions of the Army of South Korea.

Our mission was now to teach soldier illiterates to read and write in our Korean language which had been forbidden under the Japanese occupation. At this time, approximately 10 percent of our soldiers were illiterate. We functioned also as instructors to explain the causes and background of the Korean Civil War. Many of our soldiers were from the countryside, small farmers of isolated villages far from any political atmosphere which could have acquainted them with the present political situation. This was another heritage of the Japanese occupation which had encouraged political ignorance, emphasizing obedience to authority. Almost two generations had grown up in this political isolation. Part of our mission was to inform our soldiers about domestic and foreign affairs. There were many other problems and difficulties among soldiers. One of the worst personal problems some soldiers faced were psychological conflicts induced by persistent and intriguing communist propaganda criticizing the USA and its "cat's paw, the South Korean government." The Communist theme, "We will liberate the Korean people from exploitation by American Imperialism."

We were armed with captured rifles. In our new role we rotated weekly among the infantry companies in the battalion to which were assigned. In order to be effective in our mission we stayed with each company for that week, sharing the rigors of combat, living and fighting with the soldiers we were teaching. When there was a lull in the fighting we carried out moral education in the foxholes. When we were in a rear area, or in reserve, we set up classes in reading and writing for those soldiers who needed that instruction. We were given every cooperation by the battalion officers. In some few cases, I received letters from my soldier students using the knowledge of the Korean language which they had been taught. Those instances were gratifying to me, it made the effort worthwhile.

I continued as an active volunteer member of the I & E program for almost more two years. During this period I had several different assignments. Among these was duty with the 26th Inf Regt of the Capital Division, the 29th Inf Regt of the 9th Division and a punitive expedition organized to eradicate communist partisan guerillas in the Chi Ri San mountains. My job in this latter operation was to persuade the partisans who had been infiltrated into this area of the hopelessness of their cause. My role in this mission was only partially successful. The success of the overall objective was attained by implementing the classic military solution, "Kill the enemy." Even though I was not a regular Korean Army soldier, I fought together with my soldier comrades for two years. I still feel a great satisfaction and pride that by my duty performance , I contributed to defense of my homeland and the freedom which we enjoy today.

In October 1952 I returned to civil life. The war had turned into daily arguments for negotiating terms to an end of the war. The work in the military which I had been doing was no longer needed. It was time for me to return to my goal of obtaining a medical education. I became a physician, serving in the Medical Corps of the Air Force, ROK. My specialty was Preventive Medicine. After retirement from the Korean Air Force I joined the faculty of Hanyang University of Medicine, teaching there in my specialty for many years. Today as Professor Emeritus I am retired from Hanyang University and from my role as Medical Advisor to Asiana Airlines.

Left. Every type boat imaginable filled Hungnam Harbor to evacuate nearly 100,000 North Korean civilians who chose freedom. **Below Left.** Carrying everything they owned, these refugees load into LSTs in search of a better life in South Korea. **Below.** Capt. J. Robert Lunney USNR [Ret] served as a Staff Officer on the *Meredith Victory* during its rescue mission. All photos courtesy of Bob Lunney.

RED DRAGON
The SECOND ROUND
FACES OF WAR II

Leonard (1955-2001 Brother Marinus OSB)	P.	LaRue	US Maritime Service
First Name	MI	Last Name	Serial Number
None(OSB-Brother Marinus)	14 January 1914		Ship's Captain
Nickname MOS	Birthday		Grade / Rank
MSTS *Meredith Victory*	1950-1952		Philadelphia, PA
Unit (s)	Duty Tour(s) in Korea		Home Town

Presidential Unit Citation to Officers & Crew of *Meredith Victory* by President Syngman Rhee,

Medals & Award

Military Merit, *ULCHI* with Gold Star   Meritorius Service Medal   Catholic War Veteran's Medal

THE CHRISTMAS ARK

The Meredith Victory was a World War II freighter operated by Moore-McCormack SS Lines, chartered by MSTS (Military Sea Transportation Service). Captain LaRue took command of *Meredith Victory* in early July 1950. On her first voyage she carried 250 US Army trucks from Oakland, CA to Japan. She then participated in the Inchon landings, carrying men and equipment of the 32d Infantry Regt. During the Korean War she operated under military orders usually as part of a US Navy Task Force. She was 455 feet in length, 10,000 tons burden, crewed by 12 officers and 35 seamen. On 14 December 1950 she was in Hungnam, North Korea preparing to off-load her 10,000 ton cargo of aircraft jet fuel. Orders to evacuate Hungnam sent her south to unload at Pusan. On 19 December 1050, with 250 tons of jet fuel still in one hold, emergency orders were received to return immediately to Hungnam to assist in evacuation of personnel. The evening of 20 December she was back in Hungnam, now under siege by Chinese troops. A thinly held perimeter girded Hungnam and the city of Hamhung. It was vigorously manned, primarily by soldiers of the 3d US Division. Staunch defense by these troops protected both Hungnam harbor and Hamhung, southern terminus of the MSR, over which marines of the First Marine Division and soldiers of the 7th Infantry Division were making a fighting withdrawal from the Chosin Reservoir.

Two Army Colonels boarded *Meredith Victory,* one of the 193 ships in the evacuation fleet. Captain LaRue was asked to evacuate Korean refugees after the 105,000 man UN force had cleared the harbor. To quote Capt JR Lunney USN, then one of Capt LaRue's ship officers," Capt LaRue did not ask questions. He immediately agreed. He was a man of action, of great Christian devotion." In his memories of that tragic scene related to Bill Gilbert, author of *Ship of Miracles,* Capt LaRue trained his binoculars on the mass of refugees, at least 100,000 people of all ages, women, babies to stooped old men and all ages between. "I saw a pitiable scene, Korean refugees thronged the docks. Beside them, their children clustered like frightened chicks. With them was everything they could wheel, drag or carry; household furnishings, a man with a violin, a woman with a sewing machine, a young girl with triplets."

Refugees began loading afternoon of 22 December in the midst of an incessant bombardment of protective American naval gunfire targeted on the encroaching Chinese enemy. The refugees were placed on pallets and lowered like cargo into all 5 holds including the one holding the 250 tons of jet fuel. Several stretcher cases, 17 other wounded people, hundreds of babies, some separated from their families were taken aboard. By late next morning 14,000 souls had been crammed between decks and into the 5 cargo holds. To utilize all ship's space for people, refugees were not allowed to bring their possessions aboard ship, only food and water they might have on hand. The weather was sub-zero, blankets were not available. Crewmen gave their coats to women and children. Sanitary facilities did not exist. Nature's call took place in space occupied by bodies. Cramped quarters and poor ventilation made breathing difficult. Brother Marinus later commented, "There is no secular explanation why Korean people, stoic as they are, were able to stand still, silent and virtually motionless, for the 3 days they were confined below decks. This was truly a Christmas miracle."

Meredith Victory departed Hungnam harbor with its human cargo afternoon of 23 December. By some miracle she threaded her way through mine fields without the aid of a mine sweeper escort. Brother Marinus, when asked in later years how it was possible, said quietly, "It was a turning point in my life. I often think of that voyage, how so small a ship could hold so many human souls and surmount endless peril without harm to a soul. The clear message to me at that Christmastide while in cold bleak waters off the shores of Korea, 'Truly God's own hand was at the helm of my ship.'" His ship arrived in Pusan Christmas eve, to be told Pusan was trying to cope with the mass of refugees already there. He was directed to take his cargo 50 miles south to Koje-do island. *Meredith Victory* arrived Christmas Day, too late to off-load her cargo of suffering humanity. The next day, 2 LSTs were lashed shipside. Refugees clambered into them , then ferried ashore. Safe at last, there were no deaths on that voyage, however 5 babies were born!

Never before in recorded history has any nation at war ever made the effort to save so many civilians in the midst of their own battle for survival. 98,000 North Koreans escaped the Communist tyranny to become free citizens of the Republic of Korea. In 1959 Leonard LaRue, Brother Marinus OSB, took his final vows at St Paul's Abbey, Newton, NJ. He joined his maker 14 October 2001.

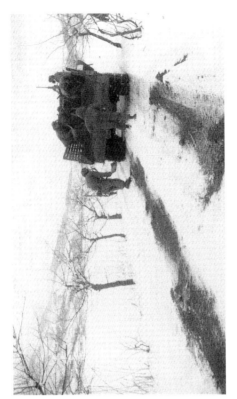

Above Left. The effects of napalm make a gruesome 'face of war'. Above. A crew from the 13th Engineers, 7th Div. spread sand on an icy stretch of the MSR. Below Left. Combat engineers try to repair a blown out road near the Manchurian border. Below Right. A jeep destroyed by a mine becomes an item of interest to these GIs. Upper Right photo from Natl. Archives. All others courtesy Roy Wilson.

RED DRAGON
The SECOND ROUND
FACES OF WAR II

James	R.	Grove	RA 13338616
First Name	MI	Last Name	Serial Number
Jim	Pioneer Engineer	22 Nov 1933	Private
Nickname	MOS	Birthday	Grade / Rank
Baker Co 13th Engrs(C), 7th Division		Sept 1950- Aug 1951	Ridgeley, WV
Unit (s)		Duty Tour (s)	Home Town

Korean Campaign Service Medal, 5 stars   Occpn Medal-Japan   National Defense Service Medal

Medals & Awards

Presidential Unit Citation   Meritorious Unit Citation   UN Medal   Korean War Service Med

BAD KOREAN MEMORIES

An experience that should bond people together for all time instead leaves bitter memories. Some friends I'll always remember, fingers of one hand is enough to count them. In Seoul, I recall rice bag road blocks across the streets 8 and 10 feet high, in double rows 3 or 4 feet apart with a space in the middle for people to get through. In the morning, nothing on the ground. Passed by in the afternoon, bodies stacked high near the opening. The ROKs thought they were NK's, and shot them. In the same time frame, my squad stopped to destroy a NK machine gun. The ROKs were talking to a kid dressed in white when bang, suddenly the bastards gut shot him. He lay there for a few minutes crying . The same SOB shot him again, not to kill him, just to make him hurt some more.

Still in Seoul, I remember a woman lying dead in the road, in itself bad enough. What really got to me was her two little kids trying to get her to move off the road to safety. Now a gripe. In all the TV shows about Korea, Marines land at Inchon, Marines take Seoul, Marines at Chosin- - -just in case no one remembers- - the Army's 32d Inf, 7th Division fought at Seoul. If the Army had not fought east of Chosin, preventing closure of the Chinese trap at Hagaru-ri, they could have used a small rowboat to evacuate all the live Marines from North Korea. Give credit where credit is due, the Marines are a great fighting outfit, but they didn't fight the war alone.

I have a jumble of memories. 15 Sept 1950, first night ashore at Inchon, we set perimeter in a little hollow just off the main valley to Seoul. Says our Plt Sgt, "There are 40,000 North Koreans up that valley." "What?" "We're gonna stop them if they want our little hollow!" I recall our platoon leader's jeep driver found a NK machine gun and two fresh dead NKs. He shoots them up with his grease gun, goes to the Lt and says, "See what I've done." Lt puts him for a Silver Star. Lt had to know they were already dead, everyone else knew it. Spring of 1951, same Lt writes up another Lt's action. He makes some changes, gets himself a Silver Star. Then, up around Samsu, my squad was working on something when this Inf Sgt comes to us, " My people are in big trouble. "Give us a hand." Sqd ldr tells him, "We can't help, we're engineers." I'd have crawled under a rock if they weren't all frozen fast to the earth.

One bitter cold night in Nov '50, our Platoon Sgt. lost his mess kit. He says one of us stole it. He falls us out in platoon formation and tells us we're going to stand there until his mess kit shows up. He goes inside the tent to keep warm, once in a while he'd come out to check on us. One of the guys from St Louis says, "If you guys will all shoot up in the air I'll kill this son-of-a-bitch." Why we didn't, I'll never know. End of Dec '50, just back from North Korea, outside of Taegu in training before going back north, our Plt Sgt was watching a platoon training problem. He tried to scratch his leg with the heel of his other foot. Trouble was, the trigger of his carbine got in the way. Could have sold tickets to that one if I had known. We thought the new Plt Sgt was a big improvement.

A more pleasant memory. In spring '51 on our way somewhere on a muddy, slippery road we passed a truck which bumped our trailer of lumber and caused it to slide partly off the road. Thinking it was going to drag the truck off the road, I bailed out. A truck behind it passed just then, I grabbed the bow which holds up the canopy and swung aboard. Damned if I didn't land in a truck filled with beer. I yelled to my squad, they came running. I tossed them several cases of beer then jumped with a case for myself. Warm beer with nothing to drink since last August! Drinking beer on a slippery road, standing on a bench to urinate, now that's living dangerously!

Odd memories crop up. While attached to Task Force Kingston near the Yalu River in November '50 I saw a twin 40 gunner fire on a North Korean who ran into a house way up on a mountainside. His first couple of rounds drifted over the house about 30 feet too high. The next two went directly into the doorway. The roof went up, the walls went out, and the North Korean, I guess, went straight to hell. I remember an infantry sergeant knocking over a bunch of North Koreans. His LT was keeping score for him. Last I heard the count was in the twenties. I recollect a big rock that the North Koreans had rolled into the road. We couldn't move it so we placed a block of C-3 to blow a bypass around it. Ground was frozen so hard, the C-3 barely made an impression on the surface. Everyone remembers the cold in Korea. There was the rain and mud of the spring and the heat and dryness of the summer. No end to it.

A lot of guys said when they left Korea, they never looked back. I looked back. I wanted to be damn sure the boat didn't turn around!

Above. F4U Corsairs take off from the USS Boxer. A beautiful sight to 'hard pressed' GIs on the beachhead. Above Right. This sailor also gets to enjoy the winter sports in a snowstorm off Hungnam. Below Left. The last troops of the 3rd Division race away from the port in LCVPs. Below Right. The USS Begor stands by as the port of Hungnam is destroyed, December 24, 1950. All photos from the National Archives.

RED DRAGON
The SECOND ROUND
FACES OF WAR II

Bae-Suk	Lee	52903 ROK AF
First Name MI	Last Name	Serial Number
Civilian Interpreter	Nov 20, 1929	Student, later Colonel
Nickname MOS	Birthday	Grade / Rank
2d Bn 15th Inf 3d Div	Jan-June 1951	Hamhung, No. Korea
Unit (s)	Duty Tour (s)	Home Town

Retired as Col, 17 years service as Flight Medical Officer, Air Force Republic of Korea
Medals & Awards

Dr. Lee is now a *US citizen. He practiced medicine in Marietta, Ohio until his retirement.

TRIUMPH

When the 3d MP Company was evacuated from Hungnam, last beachhead in North Korea, I was assigned to the 2d Bn 15th Inf Regt of the 3d Division. One of my most painful memories of the last day before evacuation was touring an outlying village to encourage all civilians to leave the area to avoid massive naval and air bombdment and the explosive demolition of all supplies in the area. There were only a few elderly, weak and apathetic people left. They were not concerned with survival and refused to leave their homes. The 2d Bn/15th Inf was the last defensive force to leave Hungnam. We were not attacked until the last day, December 24th. The Chinese were easily held off by the tremendous barrages from Navy ships and Corsair fighters. We embarked Christmas eve on an LST which transferred us to a troop ship in the harbor. The formation of many ships moving on the ocean surface, smoothly and silently, was like a scene from a Hollywood movie. The ships rails were lined with impromptu latrines to accommodate the number of troops aboard. There was no privacy for anyone. Announcements were made over the loudspeakers calling troops by units to mealtimes. We were all stamped on the wrist with indelible ink to prevent "chowhounds" from returning a second time. The stamp was changed for each meal. Within two weeks after our arrival in Pusan, the 3d Division was snaking along in convoy to the north to a new line of defensive positions. We dug our new defensive positions into the frozen ground about the middle of January 1951.

The Chinese halted their advance and cautiously probed our positions. We probed theirs in a similar manner. It was like two boxers feeling each other out. All possibilities were considered, including further retreat. I accompanied one of these platoon sized, day long patrols to examine routes of both attack and retreat. For the first time I met a group of Korean Army soldiers called HID. They were not KATUSA. They had been originally assigned to G-2, X Corps during the North Korean campaign. Their mission was to gather intelligence information behind enemy lines. This was done by stealth and infiltration. They were usually disguised as local residents and provided with 'papers' in proof of their local origin. Some were caught and shot as spies. This group left Hamhung with the 3d Division and stayed with them even after 3d Division was transferred from X Corps to 8th Army command. There was much confusion and gaps in command and communication at this time, in my case also. We were all waiting for instructions from home units and from higher command. HID continued their daily intelligence patrols. I accompanied them on some of these patrols.

In late January, American forces launched massive counterattacks to break the stalemate. Fighting was fierce. Initial advancement was slow. The Chinese were deeply dug in with orders to fight to the death. I saw hundreds of dead Chinese on one hill, and was told that there were over 900 dead and no prisoners. In this phase of action, my job was to carry ammunition boxes to the hilltop and help bring wounded soldiers to the base of the hill for further medical attention. I did not function as an interpreter at this time as I did not speak Chinese. For the next 6 months I was attached to the X Corps HID unit of the ROK Army on the central eastern front. As the battle line seesawed back and forth in the spring of 1951, the HID unit to which I was now attached moved along the front lines to gather enemy intelligence information. In the summer of 1951 I was relieved from active duty on the front and returned to civil life. There was no hassle, no bureaucratic regulations. I was a civilian volunteer, not a soldier. My next task was to look for my family and my aunt's children, last seen in Seoul. My family was in a refugee camp on Kojo Island. My aunt's children were found in Pusan.

June 1971 at age 42, I emigrated to the US. My wife was the driving force behind this decision. I started over as a doctor. At Mount Sinai Hospital in NYC, I met Dr Stanley G. Seckler who became my friend, guide and mentor. He and his family were a great source of strength as we learned the mores of our new culture. After 4 years of postgraduate training in anesthesiology, we moved to Marietta, Ohio, a beautiful old town across the Ohio River from Williamstown, WVA. It has been a rewarding and gratifying profession working with a wonderful staff in service to our patients. This has become my home, my town, my hospital and my country. We are privileged, blessed and honored to be citizens of the United States. We owe it to our fellow Americans, and specifically to American veterans who as soldiers kept the world free from communist domination. To those who died in the doing, there is no way I can bring comfort to their families, but I can say, "May our All Mighty God forever bless American veterans and the United States of America.

Above. A wounded G.I. gets tagged and evacuated. The bitter cold was also a killer.   Above Right.   A frigate from Thailand runs aground in North Korea.
Below. An Air Force flight nurse passes out candy to Korean orphans. Hundreds of these orphans were air lifted out of Seoul to save them from the approaching
Chinese Armies, 2:50 PM December 1950.   Below Right.   The port of Inchon is destroyed before the Chinese arrive.   All photos from the Archives and Internet.

RED DRAGON
The SECOND ROUND
FACES OF WAR II

David	Ralph	Hughes	O-17958
First Name	MI	Last Name	Serial Number
Dave	1542	1927	Col, then Lt&Cpt
Nickname	MOS	Birthday	Grade / Rank
K/7/1st Cav Div		Nov '50-Dec '51	Denver, CO
Unit (s)		Duty Tour (s)	Home Town
Distinguished Service Cross	Silver Star/2OLC	Bronze Star with V	Purple Heart
Medals & Awards			
CIB, star	Air Medals (14)	Legion of Merit	Joint Service Commendation Medal

"SHANKS BOOTEES"

It was in the dark days of the December retreat I first saw them. They were hanging from the muzzle of an old, battered Springfield rifle-a pair of tiny blue baby bootees. Their pale silk ribbons ended in a neat bow behind the front sight. Each little boot hung down separately, one slightly above the other, swinging silently in the cold wind. They reminded me of tiny bells, even though one had a smudge of dirt on its soft surface. The part of the ribbon that touched the barrel had lost color from scorching heat but they seemed to me to be the freshest, cleanest objects in all of drab, war torn Korea. At first the bootees had fixed my attention, but after the wonder had worn off of seeing those symbols of home in such an incongruous place, I let my eyes drift, unobserved to their owner.

He was a Lt, young, I could see, and tired, not so much from the exertion of the trudging march, but with the long days and nights in combat. He was talking to men from his platoon, all of them watching together the core of a little blaze in their midst. I could tell he was answering some of their disturbing questions about the war. There was a tone of hopelessness in the men's voices, but the Lt sounded cheerful. There was a glint in his eye, and a squint that melted into an easy smile as he spoke. As my companions moved on, I glanced back briefly to the bootees, still fresh, still swinging. Often over the next few weeks I saw the Lt, bootees swinging, as we moved southward before the Chinese armies. Around ever present warming fires I heard the simple story of the officer's bootees.

The Lt was named Shank, and he, 22 years old, led a rifle platoon. He had come over from Okinawa while the Army was clamped in the iron vise of the Pusan perimeter, short on manpower. Shank had his baptism of fire on the hills outside Taegu. His youth and fire helped keep his decimated platoon intact as the North Koreans frantically tried to crack the American lines. Then came the breakthrough, and Shank's company rode on the record breaking tank and truck dash northward. He picked up the Springfield and kept it because of its renowned accuracy and immunity to cold weather. On a violent day south of Pyongyang, Shank won a Silver Star for gallantry as he led his flesh-and-blood infantrymen against T-34 tanks, destroying three of them. The Chinese intervention into the war and the beginning of the American retreat had brought him up to where I met him, south of Kuna-ri, bootees swinging.

The bootees? That was simple. He was an expectant father. The little boots sent by his young wife reflected his whole optimistic attitude while the battle was at its darkest. I learned when the baby came it would be announced by a new piece of ribbon on the bootees, blue for a boy and pink for a girl. I forgot him as we prepared to defend Seoul from above the frozen Han River. We were hit hard by the Chinese. They streamed from the hills, charging our barbed wire. They charged again and again, their bodies piled up before our smoking guns. Days were but frantic preparation for nights. Companies dwindled, my platoon was halved as cold, sickness, wounds and death by enemy fire took their toll. I neared the end of my mental reserves. Rumors of the battle's casualties placed Shank's name s among them. I wondered where Shanks, his Springfield, and swinging little bootees were now?

Then the endless retreat from Seoul began. I and my too few men were too dulled to show emotion at the announcement. Most were too miserable to want to retreat again for twenty five miles, Chinese or no. But we did, in temperatures of 30 degrees below zero as our silent column stumbled along the hard, icy, narrow Korean road. It was the most depressing night I had ever endured - pushed by the pursuing enemy, punished by the bitter cold and the chaotic memory of the interminable bloody nights before. As a leader I was close to that mental chasm that leads to absolute despair. Only numbness of body and mind prevented me from thinking myself into mute depression. We plodded across the cracking ice of the Han River at four thirty in the morning, marching southward at ever slowing pace. Finally, the last five mile stretch was ahead. We rested briefly. As men dropped to the roadside, they fell asleep immediately. I wondered if I could get them going again. Worse, I didn't think I could go again myself - so tired, so numb and raw was my body. Then in the depths of despair, thinking of my current uselessness in a second page war, I looked up as a figure in a passing column brushed against my inert feet clad in their clumsy shoe pacs. There walked Lt Shank up that frozen Korean road, whistling softly, while every waking eye lifted to see the muzzle of his battered Springfield rifle. Swinging gaily in the first rays of the morning sun were Shank's bootees, and fluttering below them was the brightest, bluest piece of ribbon I have ever seen.

Above. An icy mountain pass near Punggi is cleared. Note tank in ditch. Left. A MG crew of the 2nd Division near the Chongchon River before the Chinese intervention. Did any survive ?
Left Bottom. A Chinese POW taken by these G.I.s from the 13th Engr., 7th Division.
Right Bottom These two GIs have discovered the A-frame is handy for hauling their gear. POW photo by Roy Wilson. All others from National Archives.

RED DRAGON
The SECOND ROUND
FACES OF WAR II

Maurice	NMI	Siskel Jr.	ER 15 246 312
First Name	MI	Last Name	Serial Number
Maury	4740 Radio Opr	30 May 1928	Cpl
Nickname	MOS	Birthday	Grade / Rank
HM/31/7		24 Dec '50-4 Jul '51	Bedford, IN
Unit (s)		Duty Tour (s)	Home Town
Parachutist's Badge	WW II Victory Medal	Combat Infantry Badge	Good Conduct Medal

Medals & Awards

Korean Campaign Service Medal, 3 stars   National Defense Service Medal   UN Medal   KWSM

THE 'GLORY' OF WAR

Too young for WW II, I enlisted in the Army after my 18th birthday in September 1946. Volunteering for Paratroop duty, I earned my Parachutist Badge as a Radio Operator in the 456th Airborne FA Bn. I completed 2 years active service, then transferred to the Enlisted Reserve. After a summer job as a foundry laborer I had begun my junior year at Indiana University. On my third day of class I received notice I was being called to active duty . I went to Ft Lewis, WA for refresher training. Three weeks later I was at the Seattle POE. The Chinese intervention led to replacements being shipped daily as transport became available. A stormy ocean trip to Pusan, Korea, then a tedious and extremely cold trip by GI 2½ ton truck which ended at the 31st Infantry Replacement Depot in Taegu, South Korea about 3 AM Christmas Eve. A 1st Lt approached the group of men milling about, all wondering where they would sleep. He called out for men trained as radio operators and FDC specialists. My 82d Airborne training as a parachutist radio operator and fire direction control specialist made me a prize catch. Heavy Mortar Company, 31st Infantry Regiment was my new home. I never did get any sleep that night. He interviewed the several of us in his hunter's bag to assign us to our duties. The 'glory' of war had begun!

The 31st Infantry was the worst hit Army unit at the Chosin Reservoir. The Lt who grabbed me turned out to be Arthur Wilson, the only surviving officer of HM Co in the Chosin Reservoir battles. He was now company commander, desperately trying to integrate 125 replacements and his remaining 45 men into a battle ready unit. The 31st Reg't was slated to jump off 25 January as one unit in a counter offensive to throw back the onrushing Chinese. First, as his RT operator where I stuck to him like a glued Siamese twin, and later as chief RadOp, I came to know him on an intimate basis. He was a first class soldier, veteran of the jungle battles in Burma against the Japanese. As with many American citizen soldiers of WW II who rose from the ranks, he had developed into a quasi-professional soldier, having learned well the hard trade of war. He knew his men. He demanded perfection. He was not easy to work for. Training went on in a rush, replacements, vehicles, radios, weapons all was at fever pitch. Hours were long, sleep short, snow and cold was the daily routine. Sleep was snatched on icy straw in unheated tents. The 'glory 'of war was now chillingly apparent!

The fighting tides of war changed in late January. Our move northward involved bypassing enemy strong points. There was not a well defined "front." Heavy Mortar company set up its own perimeter security on every halt and bivouac to prevent infiltrators. It had no infantry protection other than its own efforts. It was now a war of continuous movement. My radio truck was a 3/4 ton weapons carrier hung inside with blankets to prevent the escape of candle light at night. We operated 24 hours around the clock. A Coleman pocket stove gave us warmth, allowing us to operate the radio keys. When the unventilated stench became too strong, the back flap was opened until our fingers were numb with cold. Back to the stench. We, like everyone else, slept on the ground in sleeping bags. We all learned to sleep fully clothed and often with boots on so we could come out of the sack prepared for instant action. Sleep was grabbed as circumstance permitted, sometimes hours, sometimes minutes, but never enough! The 'glory' of war again.

My first experience of enemy fire came as a surprise. As RT OP, I was sitting in the back of the jeep. We were searching for new mortar positions to displace forward later that day. A 105 shell hit about 30 yards ahead. Lt Wilson was experienced. The driver and I were not. He yelled, "Stop the jeep, everybody bail out!" I flattened myself in a small puddle in the ditch which wet my trousers at the crotch. I took a lot of ribbing. It injured my dignity because it wasn't true! In the spring drive north, we spent 30 days as bait in front of our MLR. Thirty days of digging new perimeter positions ensued, nothing but C Rations and deadly boredom. The Chinese hit the regiment on our right flank. Boredom was over. We fired a storm with our mortars. On a later move I vividly remember a brief halt, stepping out of the jeep onto something squishy. The road was littered with Chinese dead squashed to pulp by the passage of tanks. The area earned the name of Massacre Valley from the 5000 dead Chinese in the paddy fields below. The true 'glory 'of war!

Memories. Radio truck positioned by terrain in front of mortars. Concussion hurt our ears and kept blowing out our candle with each round fired. On bivouac in a narrow river bottom, we were under several hours of incoming artillery. An overhead trajectory sent the enemy shells into the opposite bank. Noisy but not dangerous, every one except guards, slept in spite of the din. Again, on reconn we ended up in the middle of a fire fight, thus resuming our primary Infantry MOS. The 'glory' of war has little appeal to soldiers.

Above. This GI and his KATUSA buddy are bored and nigh frozen. Shows blocking position near Tanyang, Jan. 1951.   Photo by Norm Strickbine.

Below.   Captain Roberts is shown on the left shortly before his death at Tanyang. On the right is Lt. Jack Carrig.   Photo courtesy of John T. Carrig.

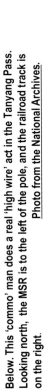

Below. This 'commo' man does a real 'high wire' act in the Tanyang Pass. Looking north, the MSR is to the left of the pole, and the railroad track is on the right.   Photo from the National Archives.

RED DRAGON
The SECOND ROUND
FACES OF WAR II

John	T.	Carrig	O-1684974
First Name	MI	Last Name	Serial Number
"Jack"	1542	17 May 1930	1st Lt
Nickname	MOS	Birthday	Grade / Rank
A1/1/17/	Nov'48-Dec'49 & Sep'50-Jun'51		Rye, NY
Unit (s)	Duty Tour (s)		Home Town

Silver Star   Combat Infantry Badge w/star   Korean Campaign Service Medal w/ 5stars

Medals & Awards

National Defense Service Medal   AFRM   UN Medal   Korean Presidential Unit Citation

THE ICY CLUTCH OF TANYANG PASS

Following our withdrawal from Hysanjin in North Korea in early December 1950, and subsequent to the 17 day battle of the Chosin Reservoir, the 17th Infantry Regt in mid December boarded the USNS Breckinridge at Hungnam for the 4 day 'vacation' voyage back to Pusan. It was old home week. We had embarked from Pusan for Iwon in initiation of our foray into North Korea. In Pusan, we spent Christmas aboard a Taegu bound troop train. Replacements had brought us up close to combat strength. In late January we began an advance north along the axis Taegu-Tanyang-Chechon to make contact with Communist forces which had forced us south. Traffic on the MSR was hampered by North Korean guerilla activity in swoops down from the mountain in swift spoiling attacks.

Leaving our "rest" area we began a trek northward. We rode in open trucks, a condition made mandatory so we might spot the enemy should he try to ambush us. In January, riding in open trucks in Korea's icy mountains was not a pleasure jaunt. To prevent frostbite, a soldier must constantly stamp his feet on the steel truck bed to enhance leg and foot circulation. It was as tiring as a forced march. Journeying through frozen Tanyang Pass, 5 miles south of the 37th parallel, we anticipated the day's trip to end at Tanyang. We anticipated, at least hoped for bivouac in a warm building, if not a warm welcome, from Bn HQ where we could 're-activate' our chilled bodies and abandon the 'comfort' of our open trucks. It was not to be. Our company commander, Capt Edmund C. Roberts, Jr. was handed new orders before he could dismount from his jeep. He transmitted this new order to us in his usual quiet fashion.

What our good captain thought about this morale breaking order will remain forever hidden. He was only 10 hours away from his own death back up at icy Tanyang Pass. A good company commander, he put a good face on the assignment just now given him. He did not say so, but gave the impression that "A" Company should feel honored to have been chosen for this difficult and dangerous task. We did not dismount from our icy 6x6 GI trucks. We made a U-turn, resuming the foot stamping routine on the twisting 10 mile journey back to the pass. At the crest of Tanyang Pass we dismounted to establish a control point on the MSR, that pitiful dirt and gravel road which passed as a main highway in prewar Japanese controlled Korea. Our mission was to "patrol vigorously" along the ridges on both sides of the MSR. At the top of the pass, a swale stretched westward of the road. There the twisting, undulating road became fairly straight. It was here we established our checkpoint and command post. It was 2030 hours when we arrived, having spent most of the preceding 36 hours walking and riding to reach this desolate place. A great effort was made to dig in, site weapons and prepare fields of fire. To establish a proper defensive position on this frozen ground was nigh impossible in frigid darkness. I was acting as Company XO. Command of my 1st platoon was in the capable hands of platoon Sgt, SFC Rene Pigeault. About midnight, an armored unit was permitted to pass our checkpoint. Shortly, two Korean Army jeeps headed down to Tanyang village. Later that night we heard distant explosions. We reported these to Bn, but were not told to investigate.

Up at 0500, the company came to life and dug into the 'sumptuous' "C" ration breakfast provided by a solicitous government for its soldiers. Capt Roberts decided to go down road toward Tanyang to investigate the explosions heard that night. He placed me in command. I was told to send the rifle platoons out on "vigorous patrolling" as ordered by Bn. Capt Roberts told me he would not go all the way to Tanyang and would return shortly. Accompanied by WOJG Marvin Petersen, he left with an EM driver and a Katusa soldier. He was followed later by two GIs in a jeep. Then, somewhat later, by a 2½ ton mess truck carrying a Sgt and two Katusa.

None returned alive. All were killed by North Korean guerillas that cold morning of 3 January. The explosions heard were guerillas attacking one of the tanks which had broken down. The ROK soldiers in the two Korean jeeps were killed. All 4 jeeps were pushed over a cliff. The tank was too heavy to push. It was later recovered by a GI tank retriever. In addition to the 8 men KIA in Capt Robert's group, we had three men WIA. The night's toll including the tankers, counted 14 GIs and 3 Katusa plus the ROK soldiers in the 2 jeeps. That night, North Korean guerrillas with an assist from the 'Icy Clutch of Tanyang Pass,' inflicted serious damage on our small patrol force in central South Korea. This experience taught us how to better deal with a determined North Korean enemy.

Above. A B-26 gets two North Korean trains in one napalm attack south of Wonsan, April 1951. Above Right. Pinpoint accuracy is displayed by another B-26 on attack of an enemy hilltop position near Taejon, Aug 1950. Below Left. Two railroad bridges are destroyed by Air Force bombers, north of Taejon, Aug 1950. Below Right. Capt. Bouchard is on the left in the photo of a flight line in Korea after the war. Other photos from National Archives & Internet.

Paul	E.	Bouchard	O 1308782 AUS
First Name	MI	Last Name	Serial Number
"Tiny"	1542	2 July 1918	Capt, then 1st Lt
Nickname	MOS	Birthday	Grade / Rank
Co A 7Cav & 6147 TAC Air Sqdn (Mosquito)		18 Jul 1950-12May 1951	Bradford, PA
Unit (s)		Duty Tour (s) Home Town	

CIB w/star	DFC, OLC	Bronze Star	Air Medal,7 OLC	ACM	ADSM	APCM, 2 stars
Medals & Award						
WWII VM	Occupation Medal-J	KCSM, 4 stars	NDSM	Army PUC	UNS	KWSM

INFANTRY SOLDIER GOES TDY TO 5th AIR FORCE

I am of French (Canadian) extraction although my parents were American citizens. In my youth I was captivated by airplanes, a fascination fueled by my admiration for a WW I veteran who was a test pilot for the Piper Aircraft Company. It was a fascination which was to stay with me all my life. He took me for an occasional ride, allowing me to taxi the Cub alone, but I was never allowed the controls while in the air. In high school I lived with my aunt who managed an apartment house. In an effort to contribute to my keep, I joined the Pennsylvania National Guard and was assigned to K Co 128th Inf, 28th Div. This high school decision spurred by need to help pay my way, led to a life long association with the US Army, both as soldier and officer, and as a civilian worker on retirement after 25 years of service. I had attained the grade of Corporal when the 28th Division Guard was nationalized 17 February 1941. I was selected for OCS in mid 1942 and graduated 21 January 1943 from The Infantry School, Ft Benning, GA as a 2d Lieutenant.

My first assignment, 17 Sept '43- 28 Oct '44, was as liaison officer to a Chinese Infantry Bn of Northern Combat Command which, after having trained in India, was now fighting the Japanese in Burma. I was transferred 29 Oct '44 to the newly activated 475th Inf Regt, as 5307Composite Unit ("Merrill's Marauders"), as now been designated. I functioned as platoon leader in A Company of the 475th until my return to the ZI , 23 March 1945. In 1946 as the Army downsized, I reverted to my enlisted rank of SFC and was assigned to recruiting duty in New York City. Recalled to active duty as an officer in mid '48, I served as Easy Co Cmdr, 507th Airborne Infantry Regiment until late March '49, then transferred to FEC in Japan. After a short stint training soldiers in certain rudiments of military discipline I was assigned as a platoon leader in the 7th Cavalry Regiment, 1st Cavalry Division. Shortly after outbreak of war, the division was despatched to Korea. Delayed by a typhoon, my regiment, the 7th Cav, was the last ashore. We debarked at Pohang on 23- 24 July 1950. My Able Company platoon was immediately committed to battle. By the time of the breakout from the Naktong Perimeter on 18 September, two months of combat had hardened our surviving young soldiers into veterans. On 23 Sept '50 I was assigned temporary duty (TDY) with the 6147th Tactical Control Squadron, 5th Air Force as a Forward Air Controller.

The 6147th Tactical Control Squadron (TAC) was an impromptu unit organized by the 5th Air Force to meet a need spawned by the nature of the enemy and the countryside. Mountainous terrain of ridges, gullies and narrow valleys, a peasant enemy adept in use of readily available natural camouflage materials made spotting an aerial target very difficult for a pilot flying at the high speeds of combat aircraft. TAC 6147 was given responsibility for gathering information about location of enemy ground forces, size, equipment, armament, and means of their transportation. The unit was a hodgepodge of the different military services, all ages and ranks. There were civilians in the unit, 'drafted' because of their skills. Pilots were all US Air Force. We assembled and erected a wooden floored 8 man squad tent city near an airfield from which we would operate. We had no TO&E to guide us, we were a 'bastard' unit which made for great difficulty in obtaining equipment and supplies. Improvisation became the order of the day. I swapped a Russian antiaircraft gun turret for a jeep equipped with a generator. That gave us a single bulb for each tent, better than the hazard of candles. Fabricated sheet metal stoves burning oil drained from our aircraft gave us a bit of warmth in the frigid Korean winter. We coped.

Observation flights were flown in T-6 Trainers equipped with belly tanks and four 2.36 smoke rockets used for marking targets as a guide for Fighter and Bomber pilots. We generally flew two sorties each day, occasionally, three. Flights were of 4 to 6 hours duration. We usually flew at altitudes of 500 feet making for 'nervous nellies' of newly arrived pilots used to flying at much a higher altitude in mountainous Korean terrain. The low altitude flown was not of bravado, but of necessity for good vision by myself and other Forward Air Controllers in spotting enemy targets. Many times we returned from a mission with riddled wings, holes in the fuselage, and in my own case, twice with an engine afire, barely making it in a controlled crash landing behind our own lines, but with the loss of an aircraft. We spotted for a Navy battleship, and relayed target observations for naval cruiser and destroyer gunfire on the east coast north and south of Wonsan. We learned targets could be anything; Korean huts, hard buildings, camouflaged installations in rice paddies and hayfields, RR tunnels, anything that looked different. Winter darkness once caught our squadron near Wonsan. We landed, playing follow the leader, each guiding on the engine exhaust of the plane ahead. The leading plane landed in the light of flares. All survived. It was more than luck. Our pilots skills had been honed to proficiency by months of low level flight.

 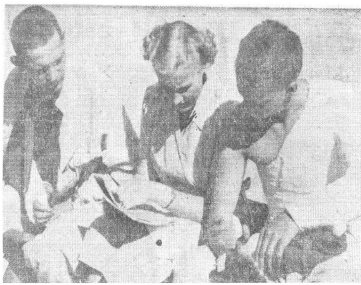

Above. Still looking ' fit for duty ' Nurse Jonasson sends a snappy salute to Korean Veterans from her home in Sweden.
Above Right.   A faded yellow clipping from a Swedish newspaper shows Nurse Jonasson reading the latest issue of
Stars and Stripes to two wounded G.I.s at the hospital in Pusan. 1950.   Above photos courtesy of Kerstin Jonasson.
Below.   A helicopter is shown landing aboard the hospital ship USS Consolation off the coast of Korea in late 1951.
Below   The helicopter and these floating hospitals saved the lives of countless wounded soldiers.   National Archives.

RED DRAGON
The SECOND ROUND
FACES OF WAR II

Kerstin	NMI	Jonasson	None
First Name	MI	Last Name	Serial Number
None	Nurse	24 Sept 1923	Major
Nickname	MOS	Birthday	Grade / Rank
Swedish Red Cross Field Hospital		23 Sept 50-12 Feb 51	Stockholm, Sweden
Unit (s)		Duty Tour (s)	Home Town
Korean War Medal		United Nations Medal	Peace Medal
Medals & Awards			

SWEDISH NIGHTINGALE

July 20 1950. The Swedish Red Cross announced on the radio that volunteers were being accepted to fill ranks of the Swedish Field Hospital for service in Korea. I was 27 years old and trained as a surgical nurse. The call for humanitarian aid was not Sweden's first response to a similar summons. Sweden had furnished a field hospital to care for Ethiopian casualties caused by the Italian invasion of Ethiopia in 1936. Similar help had been extended to Finland during WW II. Thinking I had the necessary skills and qualifications, I volunteered. Days passed quickly as we equipped, packed suitable clothing, obtained visas, had instruction on making out wills, received vaccinations and many things needed to prepare for going to a country at war. And, who knew what risks?

On 26 August the first 48 member group of what was to be a full staff of 178 medical professionals flew via SAS to the USA. We were quartered at Fort Dix, NJ for 8 days to obtain more medical equipment, additional shots and instruction on the operations of a field hospital in wartime. Then to Camp Stoneman, a POE in California, where we received more military indoctrination and information about Korea. We were also given instruction in American military organization. It was all information later found to be very useful. On 8 Sept we embarked on the "General Anderson," a troop transport carrying as fellow passengers 2000 US paratroopers destined for the ranks of the 187th Airborne RCT. During the 12 day voyage we become acquainted with other members of our now fully staffed nursing group. We numbered 34 women: 2 head nurses, 16 ward nurses, 2 medical therapeutists, one lab assistant, an assistant kitchen chef, and a laundry manager. The other 11 women were Red Cross 'Help Sisters'. Our ages ranged from 22 to 41.

In Pusan we were shown to a school. We refurbished it as a hospital. The ground floor layout consisted of an administrative office, an X-Ray room, a pre-op room, 3 operating rooms, a sterilization facility for instruments and equipment and a post-op room. For 3 days we scoured, scrubbed and sterilized what was already a clean building when assigned to us. The 2d floor had room for 150 beds. The hospital was operationally sized for 250 patients. Large rectangular pyramidal tents holding 36 cots were set up on the school grounds to accommodate less seriously wounded soldiers. A special tent was set aside for tetanus patients. We had many of these. Tetanus was endemic in the Korean countryside. It caused many deaths. Another tent was reserved for the dead. Other tents housed a kitchen, a laundry, a medical laboratory, and a small PX. A small tent used for church services was well patronized. Our sleeping quarters were crowded, bunks were stacked 3 high. Only on the top bunk could one sit. We slept three women to a cell, like nuns, either working or sleeping. Our travel bags were used as writing desks. Each cell had a chair which we used in turn. The dining room adjacent to the kitchen served also as living area when off duty (which was not often!) and as a showroom for the occasional movie. We had all the amenities of a small, well organized, but very crowded village befitting a civilized people at war.

As the war surged back and forth, we were at times almost overwhelmed by as many as 650 wounded soldiers. Looking back, I do not see how we managed. Yet I also remember on many occasions, as we scissored off the clothing of a wounded American, finding notes which said in different ways, but the same message, "If I am so badly hit that I cannot talk, take me to the Swedish Hospital." It was a poignant reminder that we had a good reputation as a fine military hospital. It stemmed, I think, from the long work days spent in the care of wounded men. To be known and appreciated by the fighting men in Korea was our reward. It was enough.

In a war anything can happen and often does. It was necessary to adapt procedures to the immediate urgency. Orders are given, then perhaps countermanded as a situation changed within minutes. The surgeons worked long hours and were often so exhausted they were near collapse. Many times we did not have enough doctors or nurses. We were a hospital to which the wounded of all 17 fighting nations were brought. I vividly remember once 13 different languages were being spoken in the hospital wards. Fortunately, good medical care is the same in all languages. As one American soldier put it, "Rest, good food and TLC from a pretty nurse will heal any GI, no matter how badly he is wounded!" Exaggerated as it was, it caused a roar of laughter in the ward. Soldiers of all nations, we found, responded better to TLC treatment and a cajoling approach than to orders. It was a lesson learned early in our stay in Korea. It made our services more palatable to the wounded men in our care. I will never forget them. Heroes all.

Above. Armor from the 25th Infantry Division crosses the Han River in the opening phase of Operation Ripper, March 1951. Right. With her brother on her back, this war weary Korean girl trudges past a stalled M-26 tank. Near Haengju, Korea June 1951. Below. These 1st Cavalry Division troopers collect Chinese POWs during Operation Killer. Feb 20 - March 6, 1951. [One was too slow getting his hands up.]

All photos from the National Archives.

RED DRAGON
The SECOND ROUND
FACES OF WAR II

John	D.	Matthews	O1 331 306
First Name	MI	Last Name	Serial Number
None	1542	31 Oct 1923	Maj,Ret then 1st Lt
Nickname	MOS	Birthday	Grade / Rank
Co's E and G 2d Bn 7th Cav 1st Cav Div		July 1950--Aug 1951	Winona, MI
Unit (s)		Duty Tour (s)	Home Town
Combat Infantry Badge	Silver Star	Bronze Star w/ V device	Commendation Medal
Medals & Awards			
Korean Campaign Service Medal, w/6 stars	NDSM	UN Medal	ROK PUC ROK KWSM

ATTACK ON HILL 554

We were in continuation of the drive north to retake South Korea from the clutches of the Chinese who had intervened in the Korean war in late November the prior year. The drive northward began 25 Jan 1951. It was given the code name, "Operation Ripper." This morning at 0730 hours 10 March 1951, our 2d Bn of the 7th Cav Regt, 1st Cav Div, was poised to attack the enemy defending Hill 554. E and G Companies were tasked with the assault. F Company, in the classic American infantry attack formation of "2 up, 1 back," was in reserve pending developments. Both of our attacking companies were on the receiving end of heavy mortar, small arms and automatic weapons fire from the Chinese Bn defending the hill. Nearing the hill crest we were met by a shower of concussion hand grenades just before we closed with the enemy in hand-to-hand combat. Patrols from the 7th Regiment's "4th" Bn, the attached Greek Bn, supported the attack by directing tank fire onto the western flank of the hill mass. Accurate tank fire resulted in destruction of several small enemy groups. The hill mass was secured by 1400 hours. Patrols quickly moved out to clear the slopes of Hill 554.

Our company commander, 1st Lt Moses, assembled his platoon leaders in a dry river bed to give a brief and concise attack order. Third Platoon, commanded by Lt Robert "Snuffy" Gray, was to attack and secure the small hill at the SW side of Hill 554, then give fire support to my 1st platoon. "Snuffy" was a 'mustang' officer who had received a battlefield commission while serving as 1st Sgt of G Company. He was well liked and highly respected by all men and officers in the company. The mission of my 1st platoon was to attack and take Hill 554. We were to delay our assault until our CO advised 3d platoon had taken the secondary objective, a small hill flanking Hill 554. The company moved up in an open squad column, 100 yards between platoons across flat lightly wooded terrain toward Hill 554 about one mile to our front. Our forward movement was covered by a vigorous preparatory artillery and mortar fire.

Third platoon moved rapidly, securing its objective meeting little resistance. Shortly, I received my attack order via radio to move to my right flank and assault Hill 554 from the south. We continued in open squad column formation a short distance up the hill, then formed a marching fire skirmish line. As we reached a point about 30 yards from the entrenched hill crest a shower of concussion grenades were thrown down at us. They looked like a flight of down swooping blackbirds. Fortunately, the command to throw was given before we came in range. They all landed short. We had no casualties. We increased our pace on the upward climb, all the while maintaining a heavy fire on the hill crest. The fire from the crest diminished after the shower of grenades had been lobbed at us.

At the crest, two Chinamen raised up out of the entrenchment. One had a burp gun. His gun on automatic, he fired a burst at Sgt Flynn, leader of my 1st squad, hitting him in his cartridge belt, spinning him around. Sgt Flynn from a distance of 2 feet, shot him dead with a round from his M-1. Sgt Humphrey shot the second before he had a chance to fire his weapon. I spotted the cap of a 3d Chinese soldier. As he raised up into firing position, I gave him a point blank burst in his upper chest with my automatic carbine. He fell back, dead. Motioning my men to squat, I unhooked a frag grenade from the lapel of my field jacket, pulled the pin, let go the handle, held it for 2-3 seconds, then lobbed it into the trench. After the grenade exploded we stood up to see one Chinaman zipping down the back slope of the hill with the speed of a running gazelle. He jumped behind a rock and escaped down the hillside. We found no other live enemy at the crest, although there were several dead. Withdrawing, they had taken their wounded with them. We could see them in retreat, moving down the two draws on the reverse side of the hill mass. Obviously, since we met with but slight resistance at the crest, they had been ordered to retreat after lobbing their grenades at us, leaving a suicide squad to delay.

The Chinese raised several white flags in surrender from the western hill mass which had been under the accurate gun fire of tanks of the Greek Bn supporting our combined attack. I reported Hill 554 secure at 1400 hours and also gave our CO, Lt Moses, the map grid coordinates of the two draws, down which the Chinese Bn was withdrawing. He gave orders placing the two draws under a sustained mortar barrage. Second platoon relieved us and were given orders to send out a patrol to clean out any Chinese who might be lurking on the western slope. We spent the night at the base of the hill. Next morning we conducted a patrol to establish contact.

Top.   A most insidious 'face of war' was the use of
the wooden box mine. This GI 3/4 ton truck hit one and
3 GIs were killed.   Above. A mine has just blown a
track off this tank.   Above Right. This tanker from the
This tanker from the 17th Regt. Hv. Tk. Co. takes a break
to finish his novel. Below Right.Sgt. Boucher and Marv
Pearson improve their minds with some outdated comic
books. Taken in the 7th Division sector, spring 1951.

Photos Marv. Pearson.

RED DRAGON
The SECOND ROUND
FACES OF WAR II

Marvin	L.	Pearson	RA 17 277 869
First Name	MI	Last Name	Serial Number
Marv	1795	7 June 1929	Sgt
Nickname	MOS	Birthday	Grade / Rank
17th Heavy Tank Co 7th Div		Sept 1950-Aug 1951	Breckenridge, MN
Unit (s)		Duty Tour (s)	Home Town

Good ConductMedal   Korean Campaign Svc Medal,5 stars   National Defense Medal   ROK PUC

Medals & Awards

Korean War Veteran Medal   Korean Disabled Veteran Medal   ROK PUC   UN Medal   ROK K

THE LIGHTER SIDE OF WAR

In April of 1950 I enlisted in the Army at Fargo, ND. I was immediately shipped to FECOM after completing basic training at Ft Ord, CA. In Japan I volunteered for tanks and was assigned to Heavy Tank Co, 17th Infantry. I was trained as a gun loader, but en route to Inchon for the September landing I was told by my platoon leader that I was now gunner. I had fired the 76mm cannon only 3 times in Japan, but in the next few weeks with live fire and more ammo, I became pretty good. I remained a tank gunner throughout my Korean service and stateside assignments until discharged in April of 1953. I lost my first tank in the hasty withdrawal from the Yalu River after the Chinese entered the war. Some 10 miles south of Kapsan in North Korea, our tank was disabled. After removing the machine guns, I placed thermite grenades in the gun breech and on the motor, poured 20 gallons of gasoline in the ammo wells and a grenade down the gun tube. I borrowed the tank of my buddy Papaleo and used his gun to fire a round of APC into it to set it afire. After that it was just a matter of hitching rides on any vehicle that had room for me on that miserably cold trip back to Hamhung.

In common with all Korean veterans, I remember bone chilling cold, the agonizing bitter cold of the Korean winters, and the heat, dust, sweat and insects of the broiling summers. I also remember the old Army game of 'hurry up and wait' and those shared moments of terror, fear, apprehension and anxiety most other veterans know only too well. Instead of dwelling on these memories of military service in the Korean War, I prefer to recount some of the lighter moments that other veterans can relate to in their own experience.

En route to the Yalu, we bivouacked near a Korean village. While on guard 0400-0600, I liberated a clucking chicken that came pecking around my feet. Off guard duty, and not being the wasteful type, I took the chicken to a Korean mama-san and asked her to cook it for me. Man, that chicken sure smelled good! Just enough for me, I didn't offer to share it. The rest of the crew could liberate their own damn chickens. I went into the farmhouse, fished in the pot with a long spoon, pulling out what I thought was a piece of chicken. Not chicken, but chicken guts. Mama-san had plucked the feathers, but everything else, feet, head and innards went into the pot! I gave the chicken to the family, Mama, Papa and three kids, then suffered the indignity of raucous laughter from my tank crew.

Later, at Hyesanjin on the Yalu River border between China and Korea, someone shot and wounded a hog. It came running toward a group of us. A Korean papa-san, presumably the hog's owner, wanted us to kill it. Sgt Boucher pulled out his Army .45 and at a distance of three feet, shot it between the eyes. The hog ran off. Sgt Boucher was flabbergasted. "How could I have missed?" Everybody stood staring for a moment, then we all broke into laughter and began kidding him. Standing next to him I saw what had happened. I reached to pick the .45 slug off the ground. The ammo was old, no good, World War I, there was just enough oomph in the primer to get it out of the gun barrel. That shook us all up. We shot off all our .45 ammo and carefully inspected the new issue to be sure it was manufactured during WW II! One of the rifle company guys later shot the pig for a squad pork chop supper.

January 1951 we again moved north, stopping one night at a Korean farm house. It had the typical layout of all Korean farmhouses. The cows, pigs, chickens live in one end of the house at ground level. The family lived on a raised level about three feet above. The fire to heat the interior in the harsh Korean winter is built at the livestock end. The flues branch under the floor but come together near the chimney at the other end. The floor, a mixture of hardened blood and clay, is polished by use to the smoothness of marble. It can be 50 below outside, but a well stoked fire can set up a sweat inside in no time at all. The Koreans build small fires using twigs, straw and small limbs. Our tank driver, a guy named Hegle from Spokane, WA spotted one of those big black iron kettles the Koreans use. Warming some bath water in it, he was bent over the kettle, his bare butt presented to the livestock at the end of the hut. We in the tank crew and the Korean family were all interested spectators. Suddenly, Hagle let out a blood curdling yell and leaped straight up onto the family floor level. Bossie, the family cow, had reached out and placed her cold wet nose on his ass. First time I had ever heard Koreans laugh. I can still see those Korean kids getting a big kick out of it. I've lost track of Hegle, but I'll bet he remembers!

That same night somebody stoked the fire with plenty of wood. I awakened, my back burning, my boots afire. I yelled everybody awake. One guy's sleeping bag caught fire. We had one hellish time convincing the supply sergeant to requisition us some new gear.

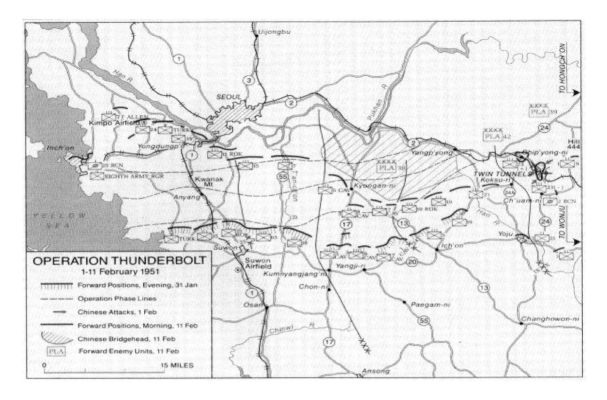

Above. Situation map during Operation Thunderbolt. Below Left. Troops of the 19th Regiment of the 24th Division take cover and wait for a Chinese assault near the Han River, 10 Feb 1951. .Below Right. A Chinese unit leader gives his instructions prior to making an attack.. Note 4 'Potato Masher' concussion grenades in the grenade carrier worn by the Chinese soldier with his back to camera . Chinese photo from the Internet Others from National Archives.

RED DRAGON
The SECOND ROUND
FACES OF WAR II

Donald	A.	Chase	RA 31 467 752
First Name	MI	Last Name	Serial Number
Don	1745	11 January 1926	Cpl
Nickname	MOS	Birthday	Grade / Rank
B Co 19th Inf Regt 24th Div		B Co 19th Inf Regt 24th Div	Natick, MA
Unit (s)		Duty Tour (s)	Home Town

Combat Inf Badge, star Bronze star, VOLC   Purple Heart, 2 OLC   GCM 2 Knots EAME, 2 stars

Medals & Awards

WW II VM   ACSM   NDSM   KCSM 5 stars   UN Medal   ROK PUC   Korean War Service Medal

INDOCTRINATION TO WAR

I had served in WW II as a rifleman in the 89th Division from January 1945 through the battles of the Rhineland and Central Europe, and in the occupation of Austria with the 83d Division. Later I served in Nome, Alaska in '46 and '47. However, I was still an unknown quantity to men of Baker Company when I reported for duty late Jan 1951. The company had just weeks before returned to offensive action after Chinese intervention in late November. The retreat from North Korea had pushed UN forces from North Korea deep into South Korea before being halted. Although a veteran of infantry warfare, I had yet to be blooded in the milieu of Korean combat.

Being a replacement is a unique experience. He is the new guy, a completely unknown individual, and for some time will stay an outsider, not admitted into the tightly bonded circle of "old men" in the squad and platoon, neither accepted or rejected. He will, if assigned to a rifle squad, most likely be appointed BAR man and saddled with its 21 lb weight plus its 20 round clip of ammo and the heavy ammo harness holding another six clips of 20 rounds each. Every infantryman loves that potent weapon but hates to carry it! Needless to say I wasn't too thrilled with my BAR assignment, but goiod sense kept my mouth shut. What often helps the new kid on the block is that there is usually one man who will say hello, explain what is going on, and aid in acceptance into the squad.

What was unique about this squad was the number of older men. They had fought in WW II, joined the reserves, never dreaming they would be called again to duty. I quickly became friendly with one man, a disgruntled "Truman Trooper," an ETO veteran, married with three children, also less than thrilled with his assignment. We had similar experiences which gave us a common bond. He explained this war was nothing like the war in Europe. The Koreans all looked alike, there was no way to tell friend from foe, the enemy seemed to be everywhere. He was killed a few weeks later while I was recouperating from wounds at the Swedish Hospital in Pusan.

I joined while the company was in reserve so had a few days to orient myself. I had my initiation into Korean combat in early February. We were issued extra ammo, grenades and C-rations, and under cover of darkness our tanks moved up. We of the infantry after a general briefing, moved up to our jump-off positions. The artillery laid down a tremendous barrage on the ridge line which was our objective. It was very cold with a scruff of snow on the icy ground. We began our assault while our artillery was still firing. We had crossed over frozen rice paddies, then a long, wearying climb up a steep slope. The tanks to our rear were firing directly into the midst of the enemy.The Chinese managed to throw a lot of lead as well as toss and roll grenades down at us. The artillery fire lifted when we were about a hundred yards or so from the top of the ridge. Fire was resumed beyond the ridge to work over the enemy fleeing from our attack. My squad reached the ridge crest to find the North Koreans had fled, taking their dead and wounded with them. Splotches of blood were scattered everywhere, damaged weapons and some discarded equipment, but no enemy dead.

During this action, I was one scared soldier. Fear was something that was with me in every action in which I participated. It never left me or abated in intensity. I kept praying that I would not suffer a wound leaving me paralyzed or blind. Those possibilities were my greatest fears. Other types of wounds I felt I could handle. In bull sessions, it seemed every soldier had his own private hell of anxieties and apprehensions gnawing at him, particularly in those harrowing hours waiting for the order to jump-off in attack. The heart beats faster, the mouth is dry, the mind conjures up a thousand horrible possibilities. The fear of death haunts every infantry soldier, yet discipline and respect for his comrades causes him to stick his head again and again into the jaws of the lions of war.

This was was but one battle of many in days to come in which I participated during my time in the 24th Infantry Division. I suppose because it was my first, the details remain sharply etched in my mind. That memory is a kaleidoscope of many sensations. The cold overcast, gloomy day, the eardrum shattering blasts from tank guns, men falling without a sound, other men gasping for breath in the arduous climb, the crash of exploding shells, the shaking ground under foot when an artilley barrage hit all at once, blasts of grenades, sping! and buzz of small arms fire in the ears, the overrun and deserted enemy position with blood stained ground and shrubbery, all capped by the relief that I was still alive, yet somberly aware it would repeat endlessly on the tomorrows yet to come.

Left. A patrol from the 19th Regt. of the 24th Division patrols 10 miles north of Seoul looking for Chinese. Below Left. An M-16 Quad 50 from the 3rd Division is also looking for a fight. Below. With the title of "Soldier's Watch" this photo by the AP of Pfc. Coate had a wide circulation, and was more recently used to publicize the Korean War Memorial.
"On Guard" photo by Dick Coate   All others from National Archives.

RED DRAGON
The SECOND ROUND
FACES OF WAR II

Richard	E.	Coate	US 52 001 171
First Name	MI	Last Name	Serial Number
Dick	4745	6 February 1929	PFC
Nickname	MOS	Birthday	Grade / Rank
E Company 15th Inf Regt 3d Div		6 Feb 1951-17 Jan 1952	Trenton, OH
Unit (s)		Duty Tour (s)	Home Town

Combat Infantry Badge   Good Conduct Medal   Korean Campaign Service Medal,3 stars

Medals & Awards

National Defense Service Medal   New York State War Medal   UN Medal   ROK PUC   KWSM

SOLDIER'S WATCH

Shortly after dawn on 4 March 1951 following a cold grueling night I had spent in a shell crater, my squad joined the rest of the platoon squatting or standing around a fire. They were warming themselves in front of an abandoned Korean farmhouse used as an assembly point for 2d Bn 15th Inf personnel returning from all night vigils on LPs (Listening Posts) and OPs (Observation Posts) on the banks of the Han River opposite Seoul. In the group was a photojournalist photographing war scenes. Of the four photos he took, I was surprised to be singled out as the subject of a photograph of a silhouetted, lonely rifleman on guard at his post. Not unlike a film director selecting a background extra player for a scene in a movie, my identity did not matter to him. Perhaps my appearance as the prototype of a bone- tired, exhausted American soldier caught his eye, one who would make an appropriate subject for the shot he was trying to obtain. Perhaps he was looking for a strong profile, a happy birth gift from my parents. Whatever, he chose me as the subject of a photograph destined to attain an unique place in the annals of the Korean War and the ensuing Cold War.

Working quickly with an eye on the changing light, few words passed between us as he placed me just inside the wide doorway of the dark, gutted interior of the thatched roofed farmhouse. A theater major in college, I had taken stage lighting design courses so I was familiar with what he was trying to do. I understood the impact a silhouette shot against early morning light would have in making an effective picture. Courses taken in Stage Direction and Art contributed to my knowledge of composition and the necessity of defining the relationship of an individual to his environment. The composition he was arranging, the silhouette of a lonely rifleman juxtaposed against a backdrop of frozen rice paddies, a distant village and a forbidding range of mountains stained blood red by the rising sun would create an interesting photographic shot of the Korean War. By now, I was intensely interested and most cooperative. When the photographer backed off to kneel, focus and adjust his lens, I struck what I thought would be a suitable dramatic pose. I extended my M-1 rifle, placing the butt on the door sill in a relaxed stance of 'Parade Rest." The photographers demeanor reflected deep concentration. Although he treated me like an object, I was not offended. There was a slight adjustment for the second shot in which I directed my gaze more toward the hills. That was the shot later published and captioned 'Soldier's Watch' in American newspapers back home. Nodding approval when the session was over, he immediately left the darkened interior of the farmhouse.

As a budding professional actor prior to my induction into the army, I had risen to the 'military' occasion. With his departure my feeling of complete exhaustion returned. Weeks of round- the- clock alert, constant patrolling, and stress of the prior night's vigil had taken their toll. About to take a quick "ten", I realized the photographer had not taken my name. I caught him in the nick of time. As I caught up with him, he was conferring with his colleague, a newspaper reporter, about moving on. "Don't you want my name and home address?" As I put it in a letter to my wife, Betty, "The plight of a rifleman, sweating the odds on a daily basis was like 'waiting for the ax to fall, 'akin to a prisoner awaiting execution. In case I didn't make it back, I sure as hell wanted my wife and my folks to know that the lonely, bone tired rifleman in that photo was me!" The photographer extracted a pencil and notepad from his pocket and noted my information as if it were a business transaction. Because of his brusque attitude and lack of apology for the oversight, I was not too fatigued to be offended. It may have shown in my manner. Stating that one of the silhouettes would probably be published, he replaced his pencil and pad in the pocket of his field jacket to walk out of my life. Relieved he had noted my name and address, I returned to the interior of the farmhouse, and dropped down on a pile of straw to catch some sleep, out like a light!

I had reason to be proud of my own creative contribution to the success of the photograph the Associated Press captioned as 'Soldier's Watch' when it was released nationwide in the Easter season of 1951. That chance encounter with the photojournalist was a milestone in my life. The photograph, along with Betty's interview appeared in the Middletown (Ohio) Journal on Easter Sunday. She was later given a glossy and a copy of the AP release. These proved to be of inestimable value when I needed a background for the story "The Unidentified Soldier" in the USO poster presented to General Richard Stilwell, Chairman of the Presidential Advisory Board and head of the fund drive for the Korean War Memorial in our nation's capital. His letter of commendation launched my successful pro bono press campaign soliciting funds for the memorial to "Help Write The Korean War Veteran Back Into History."

<u>Right</u>. Paratroopers of the 187th Abn. Regiment load up into C-119 'Flying Boxcars' of the 314th Troop Carrier Group.

<u>Below</u>. Making their second combat jump of the war, the 187th is shown parachuting into the drop zone near Munsan-ni, Korea, March 24,1951.

<u>Bottom</u>. Troopers assemble, to take up blocking positions to trap retreating Chinese forces.

<u>Upper and lower Photos courtesy of Lafayette Keaton</u>.   Center photo from National Archives

94

RED DRAGON
The SECOND ROUND
FACES OF WAR II

LaFayette	F.	Keaton	RA 16403515
First Name	MI	Last Name	Serial Number
"Laf"	11B5P	29 Oct 1927	SFC
Nickname	MOS	Birthday	Grade / Rank
L/187 Airborne RCT		1951-1952	Sandusky, OH
Unit (s)		Duty Tour (s)	Home Town
Silver Star Bronze Star Ranger Tab Combat Infantry Badge			Master Parachutist
Medals & Awards			
Pathfinder & Distinguished Pistol Shot Badges			Combat Parachutist Badge/2stars

AIRBORNE INDIAN WARRIOR

I am an American Indian born in Sandusky, Ohio where my father, an Apache veteran of WW II was stationed at Camp Perry. He had participated in all 5 of the WW II combat jumps of the 509th Parachute Infantry. He and my mother, a Cherokee Indian, had married after release of the Apache nation from Florida exile. Enlisting in early 1950 I was assigned to the 187th Airborne RCT. On 28 Feb 1951 we assembled at K-2 Airstrip near Taegu. By order of General Ridgway I was detached to work with the 2d and 4th Ranger Companies training for their first combat jump. They made 5 practice jumps, then on the 8th and 9th we participated in mass jumps of 4000 troopers. One man was killed in pre-op training. Operation Tomahawk was launched 23 March '51. Mission of the 187th RCT was to seize the Munsan-ni area and establish a block to trap the NKPA I Corps which was to be driven north by 8th Army. We would be supported by the 6th Tank Bn, 90 mm gun Patton tanks, on loan from the 24th Division. The Ranger companies would assault and take Munsan-ni. We were combat ready. If my Dad had been in the jump, he would have yelled, "Geronimo!" as he went out the door.

We took off from Taegu at 0730 on a clear sunny day. Our jump into the drop zone took place at 0900 from 135 aircraft provided by C-119 'Flying Boxcars of the 314th Troop Carrier Group and from C-46 Commando planes of the AF Reserve 437th Troop Carrier Wing. Our LMGs were jump tied to the parachutist. Each man carried two cases of ammo on pack boards which were slung over combat packs held on our knees. My estimate of weight of equipment carried by each man, including main and reserve chutes, was 300 lbs. We flew out to sea for rendezvous, then north in column. Crossing in from the coast we could see Chinese troops entrenched in depth in defensive positions in the hills overlooking Munsan-ni. The Air Force called the Munsan area "Happy Valley" because there were so many Chinese targets. We made a low altitude combat jump at 500 feet. Rifle and MG fire zinged around our ears as we floated down the last 100 feet or so. We were heavily engaged as we landed. Going into immediate attack we took the critical terrain, establishing the block position to cut off retreating enemy forces. Unfortunately, the 6th Tank Bn column was delayed by land mines and NKPA artillery fire, losing six tanks, several jeeps and a scout car in the 12 hours it took them to reach our drop zone.

Enemy dead littered the drop zone. I wondered if they were killing each other. They were in our line of fire as well as their own. They were lousy shots. We picked them off with little harm to ourselves. Their mortar fire was more accurate, peppering the area as we pushed toward our assembly point. Under our attack the enemy retreated eastward. Initially, he put up a suicidal resistance with fanatical counter attacks, blowing horns and firing flares, supported by surprisingly accurate artillery fire. His fanaticism was no match for the relentless attack of disciplined American paratroopers. The Chinese fought fiercely during daylight, but as darkness set in he tried to withdraw to higher ground. Daylight air observation enabled us to launch successful attacks on their night positions. These positions consisted of ten main units supposedly located to be of mutual support. It was a futile tactic, our night training made it easy to dispose of them. Our attacking forces seized Hill 507. With this dominant terrain feature in hand, the defense of the 234th CCF Regiment in collapsed like a house of cards on 27 March. A sweep of the area netted 8000 dispirited former Nationalist Chinese soldiers who had been conscripted by the Communists. Other Chinese and North Korean forces retreated eastward toward Uijong-bu.

Link up with American units pushing up from the south was effected by the 3d Division as they cleared the last vital approach along the Uijong-bu/Chipyon-ni axis on 28 March. On 29 March the 3d Div took over our positions. General Bowen, Commander of the 187th Airborne Regimental Combat Team moved us back to Taegu. We accomplished our mission in spite of a navigational error which put all 3 Bns of 3447 jumping paratroopers, including Rangers, into the South Drop zone. This left the North drop zone, the linkup point for the 6th Tank Bn Task Force, to be held by the 27 paratroopers of the 1st Bn HQ staff which included the Bn CO! Fortunately, the area was held by the NKPA, who for some reason, stayed in their defensive positions. The HQ group hung on by the skin of their teeth until General Bowen sent B/187 to pull the fat out of the fire. It is an axiom of combat that any operation, no matter how well planned, no matter how good the troops, if something can go wrong, it probably will go wrong, and usually does! Americans shine as soldiers because individuality is the norm. Individuality produces great gripers but also competent fighting men.

The Chinese XIII Army Group is shown here in the attack in the Hoensong area. February 12, 1951. This attack almost destroyed the ROK 8th Division. Blowing a bugle must have been painful in that sub zero weather.
CCF photo from the Internet.

This Chinese 'sniper' was credited with 214 'hits' in 32 days. Although this is certainly a possible 'score,' it seems unlikely considering the ancient rifle with no scope.
CCF photo from the Internet.

U.S. Marines on the counter attack dig these Chinese soldiers out of their holes. These were taken on the Central Front near Hoensong. March 2, 1951. Photo from the National Archives.

RED DRAGON
The SECOND ROUND
FACES OF WAR II

James	F.	Byrne	1103683 USMC
First Name	MI	Last Name	Serial Number
Jim	0300	13 May 1932	Pfc
Nickname	MOS	Birthday	Grade / Rank
G/3/1 1st Mar Div		Nov 1950-April 1951	Mill Valley, CA
Unit (s)		Duty Tour (s)	Home Town

Purple Heart Medal   Korean Campaign Service Medal w/ 3 stars   National Defense Service Medal
Medals & Awards
Navy Presidential Unit Citation   UN Medal   ROK Presidential Unit Citation   Korean Service Medal

SNIPER

On the night of 2 March 1951, Clayton Sepulveda and I had just rejoined our outfit, G-3-1, after almost three months of wound recovery spent in hospital. Sepulveda had been burned in a fire. I had been wounded (WIA) in ambushed convoy. We rejoined the company just as they were preparing to jump off in the attack. The objective was Hill 321, not a big hill as Korean hills go, but a tough one to attack due to the way the terrain was put together. The previous day the company had taken several KIAs and quite a number of WIAs, consequently the air was thick with tension. The order was given to move out. Much of the foreboding faded away as each marine struggled with his full load of combat gear to begin the climb of what seemed like an endless array of ridges and mountains.

Three months in hospital in Japan recovering from my wound had left me sadly out of shape. To make my first day of return to duty seem even worse, I had asked for shoe-pacs for my return to Korea. That was one big, big mistake. Each foot weighed 10 lbs, it seemed, after the first few minutes. Finally we reached the edge of a valley that ran east to west and was perhaps a half mile in width. We stopped to reassemble for a coordinated attack on Hill 321. Before we could get reorganized, a few mortar rounds came in on us. The rounds were close, but luckily we suffered no casualties. It was very clear we were not going to catch the enemy by surprise.

Eventually, word was passed to move out and take our objective. In the assault I ran as fast as I could because we were taking some small arms fire. In the open valley there was no cover protection. We were like sitting ducks if we did not zig and zag as we ran forward to make it more difficult for an enemy rifleman to keep us in his sights. By this time, my legs felt like they were made of lead, and I swear the shoe pacs seemed to weigh 50 lbs each. Somehow I reached the top of the hill. When I did, I dropped to the ground in complete exhaustion, utterly spent. I rolled over on my back and gasped for air. My heart was pounding as if it would burst. Within seconds a sniper zeroed in on me. I could hear the hiss of the bullet as dirt kicked up within an inch of my face. In spite of my collapse in fatigue, I rolled to my right and prayed I was out of his line of vision. My prayer was answered, he did not fire at me again.

A few minutes later, my squad leader yelled at me and Sepulveda to come with him to the forward slope of the hill. We were to form a fire team, locate the sniper and eliminate him. The sniper had been raising hell with the headquarters group which was trying to locate a site to establish a company command post(CP). Orders had been given to the 1st platoon to find him and silence his sniper activity. My squad leader had been tapped for the chore, and Sepulveda and I were the two marines anointed to accompany him.

My squad leader searched the area to his front with his binoculars while Sepulveda and I made use of our eyes in the same task. I scanned the area slowly, looking for movement or the glint of sunlight off a rifle barrel, anything that might indicate the sniper's location. Sepulveda was doing the same thing as we both had been trained to do. The sergeant was on my left and Sepulveda was on my right. There was no sequence to the following events, they occurred simultaneously. The crack of a rifle, a hollow thud which sounded to me like a huge paddle hitting a firm mattress. From the corner of my eye, I saw Sepulveda fly backwards. The sergeant and I quickly dragged him back to the reverse slope. It was too late. He was KIA the very second the bullet slammed into his chest.

The ironic thing is that apparently the sniper was trying to take out my squad leader, the man who held the binoculars to his eyes. The round went through the sleeve of his jacket, passed in front of my face and struck Clayton square in the chest. The other strange twist to this episode is that we were searching in the wrong direction! We were scanning the ridge line in front, while he was off to the side, on our left flank. We knew this a bit later as the sergeant and I pieced together the facts and correlated them. The sniper absolutely had to be on our left in order for his bullet to have the effect it did on all three of us. It was too late for Clayton Sepulveda.

The sniper kept us pinned down for the rest of the day. Just as it was getting dark the sniper struck for the last time. Pfc Hems, our machine gunner, was on the skyline digging in a position for his light Browning machine gun. In the last glimmer of light, the sniper hit Hems in the leg and knocked him halfway down the hill. We never did find that sniper, he just vanished in the night. He cost us.

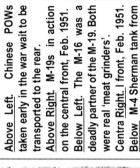

Above Left. Chinese POWs taken early in the war wait to be transported to the rear.
Above Right. M-19s in action on the central front, Feb. 1951.
Below Left. The M-16 was a deadly partner of the M-19. Both were real 'meat grinders'.
Centra Right. I front, Feb. 1951.
Below M-4 Sherman tank from the 31st Tk. Co. slides into a ditch near Hagaru-ri, Nov. 1950.

RED DRAGON
The SECOND ROUND
FACES OF WAR II

Joseph	J.	Bennett	RA 14337291
First Name	MI	Last Name	Serial Number
Jack	1502	18 Jul 1930	Sgt
Nickname	MOS	Birthday	Grade / Rank
D Btry 15th AAA AW Bn SP		Sept'50- Jul '51	Valdosta, GA
Unit (s)		Duty Tour (s)	Home Town
Bronze Star Medal	Purple Heart Medal	Good Conduct Medal	KWSM UN Medal

Medals & Awards

Korean Campaign Service Medal w/4 stars   Nat'l Defense Svc Medal   K50Medal

PLAYING FOOTSIE WITH A LAND MINE

Our outfit, 15th AA(Anti Aircraft) AW(Automatic Weapons) Bn(Battalion) SP(Self Propelled) had a name in army terminology that was as long as it was descriptive. These Bns used these old WWII armored vehicles as antiaircraft weaponry gun platforms. In Korea, they doubled in utility as weapons of infantry ground support. The 'Twin 40s' were Bofors dual 40mm quick firing antiaircraft cannon mounted on an M-19 full tracked vehicle towing an ammunition trailer. The M-16 was a half tracked vehicle originally designed as a tank destroyer, equipped with an anti tank gun. It was converted into a mobile gun platform mounting 'Quad 50s', four .50 caliber machine guns which a gunner fired on a single axis as if it were one weapon. It also pulled an ammunition trailer. These units, broken down into platoons comprising both M-16s and M-19s, were often used in infantry direct fire support. They thus served a dual role.

Their fire was deadly accurate. A high rapid rate of fire for both weapons, the ease in which guns could be traversed and aimed, line-of-sight with pin point accuracy, flexibility in quickly shifting fire from one target to another, and sheer volume of fire made them literally, a scythe of death to the enemy. They had 3 limitations. It was possible for the enemy to get beneath their line of fire, the guns could not be laid below horizontal. Rate of fire was so great that in rapid displacement, they often ran out of ammo. In the mountainous terrain of Korea their usefulness was limited to fire from positions attainable by a tracked vehicle. The sight of the M-16s and M-19s, either in attack or defense, was a real morale booster to the dogface infantryman. He knew what they could do for him.

April 6 1951 was another dismal day in a succession of dismal days of cold weather in a wet and dismal and spring. We were escorting a six gun battery of artillery to an advanced forward position so they could give better close support to the advancing infantry. This was a routine mission for us. The lesson had been well learned that artillery in convoy needed an escort. For the past month we had also been firing in support of the 31st Infantry in its forward advance. No one, certainly not the infantry had a chance for rest in that time. Infantry on our flank was in assault of a hill ahead and to our right flank. They were receiving MG fire from the enemy on higher ridge above them. The Twin 40s from one of our M-19s spotted it, knocking it out in the wink of an eye. I was glad someone on the track ahead had spotted that enemy gunfire. I'm sure that timely intervention saved several infantryman from wounds or death.

Then it happened. My right front wheel hit a land mine! Cpl Edgar Estep was adjusting the radio antenna on the right side of our half track. The explosion blew me out of the M-16. I really don't remember what happened after that. It rattled my brains enough to keep me in the hospital for a couple of weeks. Concussion was the diagnosis. For years I thought that Ed Estep had been killed. In a telephone conversation with Hode Hensley 45 years later I learned to my joy and surprise Ed had survived. Kim, my KATUSA buddy who rode shotgun with me that day, was a good friend and a very special person to me. He had been evacuated, but whether dead or live, I never learned. I hope he survived as did Ed Estep, and today still lives and enjoys life in South Korea.

On 25 May we were again on the move in the Spring Offensive. The enemy on the ridge line acted as if fleeing our fire power. We learned shortly they had been working to get behind us. We kept moving. Resistance was light. Less than 1000 yards further forward, the dam broke! The enemy seemed to appeared out of nowhere. We had a field day until they got under our field of fire. While moving, the field of fire is limited in an M-16 or M-19. The guns cannot be depressed enough to cover level terrain within fifty feet in front of the tracked gun carriers. A grenade tossed into my ammo trailer started a fire. Before the ammo explode, I jumped out and unhooked the trailer. Sometime during this excursion I received two 2 gunshot wounds in my right shoulder.

I was again evacuated to a field hospital. One slug was removed, the other had passed on through, just above the collar bone. No bones were broken. After another 'convalescent' period in the hospital, I returned to my outfit, little the worse for wear. However, I sure did not turn down the chance to return to the USA when I was notified shortly after return to duty that I was eligible to be sent home under the new rotation policy. At home I enjoyed a 30 day furlough which I spent with my family. I have read that a brain concussion as happened to me can affect a persons memory. Perhaps that is why I am blank on some things. Guess I'm not alone.

Above. A Captain from the 5th Cav. Regt. with a head wound awaits evacuation to an aid station.
Above Right. 1st Cav. troopers in a firefight in the Pyongyang train yards, Oct. 50.
Right. Hill 575 gets a large dose of WP in preparation for an attack on Hill 575, February 14, 1951.
Below. G Co. 7th Cav. Regt assaults Hill 575.
  Photos courtesy Boris Spiroff and the Archives.

RED DRAGON
The SECOND ROUND
FACES OF WAR II

Boris	R.	Spiroff	RA 6 894 579
First Name	MI	Last Name	Serial Number
RA 6 894 579	4745	14 Feb 1920	1st Sgt(E-8) then SFC
Nickname	MOS	Birthday	Grade / Rank
G Co 7th Cav 1stCavDiv		19 Sept 1950- 23 Sept 1951	Baltimore. MD
Unit (s)		Duty Tour (s)	Home Town

Bronze Star Medal w/Oak Leaf(2)   Combat Infantry Badge w/star   Army Commendation Medal

Medals & Awards

Natl Defense Svc Medal   UN Medal   ROK Victory Medal   ROK Pendant Medal   ROK KWSM

CAREER SOLDIER

A native of the 'Old Line State,' born in Baltimore, I enlisted 15 Feb 1937 at age 17 in the Regular Army, for assignment to the 14th Inf Regt serving in the Panama Canal Zone. In March 1943 I returned to the States as S/Sgt(E-6) in a regimental cadre destined to serve as one of the 3 Bns in 5307 Composite Unit (P). This outfit, also known as Merrill's Mauders, fought in WW II to open the Burma Road into China. I was plucked out of this group as I spoke the Serbian language, and sent to the Balkan Group OSS, 2671st Spec Recon Bn in Yugoslavia Jan '44 through Oct '44, part of that time with Marshal Tito's 19th Brigade. I was then transferred to the 13th Airborne Division in France in Jan 1945, but was recalled by the OSS, serving with them until VE Day 8 May 1945. I returned to the US in July 1945 for a furlough, then was assigned to a OSS unit in Burma. VJ Day, 15 Aug '45, canceled that assignment.

By January 1950 I had attained the rank of SFC(E-7) and was on duty with the 3d Armored Cavalry Regiment stationed at Ft George Mead, MD. I had met my fiancee, Cassie Schnitzlein, before going overseas in Oct '43. We decided, now in a world at peace, it was a good time to wed. It was happy five months until, on 25 June, North Korea invaded South Korea. 27 July I received orders for Camp Stoneman, CA, POE for FECOM. There I vegetated for five weeks until 8 Sept when a group of us were flown to Japan via Anchorage, AK. A small coastal vessel took us to Pusan on 19 Sept where I was assigned to Company G, 7th Cav Regt, 1st CavDiv, then on line and in action near Taegu on the Pusan Perimeter. I arrived just in time to participate in the 'Breakout' from the Perimeter on 23 Sept and begin the drive northward to link up with the American 1st Marine and Army 7th Inf Divisions of the Inchon landing invasion force.

During the month of October our Bn participated in mop up of the area around Seoul, then moved north to Kaesong to join the rest of the 7th Cav Regt. En route we met a North Korean unit which hit us with mortar and MG fire. led 2 squads of my platoon in a flanking action, wiping them out. The action awarded me a 2d Bronze Star. In mid month, the weather turned cold. Heading north to attack Pyongyang, capital of North Korea, men became casualties due to frozen hands and feet. Hungry, cold, almost frozen and without ammunition, about 100 NK soldiers surrendered. I was left with six men to guard them until DivRear moved up to take them to a POW cage. It was a hungry 2 days until MPs arrived to take them off our hands. We spent the next several days in hitching rides on the MSR to catch up with G Co. Shortly after rejoining G Co we went into action near Anju in a hot and hectic fire fight which saw us for a time surrounded and shot at from all points of the compass. The weather turned increasingly colder with harsh biting winds, weather as much a threat as the North Koreans. The medics had their hands full with wounds and frostbite. On 31 Oct we reached Unsan north of the Chongchon River. Early morning 1Nov we were under attack by uniformed Chinese troops, better disciplined than North Koreans. Badly outnumbered, we were forced to withdraw. The Chinese advanced in great swarms. Only our artillery and mortar fire kept us from being overrun. We suffered heavy casualties. G company was scattered. After regrouping, 2 of my men were missing. I reported them MIA. Our platoon medic was wounded, bad news, no idea when we might expect his replacement.

We back-tracked for three weeks. Thanksgiving Day, 23 Nov, we dug in awaiting further Chinese assault. None came that day, but what did arrive was a traditional Thanksgiving dinner of turkey with all the trimmings. It is an Army custom traditionally honored in peace and war that cause men to wonder how it is possible in circumstances like these. Our great concern is not to be flanked, then surrounded and annihilated. We must maintain contact with units on our right and left so that there can be no break through. The cold is horrible, 30 degrees and more below zero. We are in endless retreat, outnumbered many times over. The only good news on 27 Nov, Specialist J. Howard, a medic, joined us. Medics are a military necessity. A good medic is like an angel. Morale picks up.

The war continued, ups and downs for the next year through death of General "Bulldog" Walker, assumption of command by General Ridgeway, the successful drive north to retake all of South Korea and initiation of peace talks. I came home in Oct '51 to be assigned as instructor to the Maryland National Guard. Another year in the life of a career soldier. That year no bullets were aimed my way. I retired in Oct 1962 with 25 years of Army service under my belt, no longer the callow youth who had enlisted in Baltimore in 1937.

101

Above.   Sailors aboard the USS Philippine Sea battle a fire on an F4U Corsair. March 1951.   Archive photo.

Below.   This North Korean POW is getting a ride to the POW cage. He was taken near the Naktong River in August of 1950. Photo from the National Archives

Below. These tired Marines are taking a break on the way to Seoul, Korea. They have just cleared the hut of a determined North Korean sniper. Sept. 1950.   Photo from the Archives.

RED DRAGON
The SECOND ROUND
FACES OF WAR II

James	H.	Appleton	1156912 USMC
First Name	MI	Last Name	Serial Number
"Appy"	0311	26 August 1931	Corporal
Nickname	MOS	Birthday	Grade / Rank
I Co 3d Bn 5th Marines 1st MarDiv		April '51-April '52	Nashville, TN
Unit (s)		Duty Tour (s)	Home Town

Silver Star   Commendation Ribbon w Combat V   Navy PUC 1 star   USMC Good Conduct Medal

Medals & Awards

USN Occpn Medal w/Eur Clasp   NDSM   KCMS 3 stars   KSM   UN Medal   ROK PUC   KWSM

INTRODUCTION TO COMBAT

We off loaded from the attack transport USS Menard at Pusan, Korea about 0100 hours 9 April 1951. We were loaded immediately onto waiting 2 ½ ton trucks that hauled us to the Repo-Depo where we bedded down for what we thought would be a night's sleep. In the first of many surprises that day, we were awakened at 0400 for a breakfast of dehydrated eggs, hot coffee and powdered milk. Then it was back to the trucks for a quick journey to the K-1 airfield outside the city where we played the old military game of "hurry up and wait." As we passed through the city, Korean MPs standing on their concrete pedestals were waving their white gloved hands, directing traffic in the city streets. As each truck passed an MP, the driver would cut his ignition switch for a few seconds, then switch it on again just as he passed the MP. The backfire sounded like a cannon, shaking the small statured men with the blast. The Korean MPs in impotent rage were reduced to shaking their fists and yelling epithets in Korean. Their cursing made a blistering mouthful!

Daylight came, finally at 1000 hours a couple of C-54 transports landed, flown by Marine Corps master sergeants. The plane doors opened and a solid stream of tired 19, 20 and 21 year old veterans piled off the plane. We loaded aboard. The pilots did not bother to face into the wind, taking off as soon as we were aboard. We flew for 45 minutes to Hoengsong where we loaded into trucks for the trip up to the front. Off loading the plane, we were issued a bandoleer of ammo and a Mark II frag grenade. In contrast to the unmanned ring mounted .50 caliber MGs at K-1, these trucks had loaded MGs with a gunner at full alert in the ring mount. We knew we were now headed into "Harms Way." Matters could get very serious, very quickly. The trucks first went to Div HQ where we were sorted out, on to 5th Regt HQ where we sorted once again. At 3d Bn HQ I was assigned to Item Co and turned over to the company runner who guided us to the company CP. En route we were issued another bandoleer of ammo, a grenade and a second canteen.

The runner introduced me to the CO, Co Cmdr Capt McPherson, and my plat ldr, who assigned me to the 1st squad. The sqd ldr, Sgt Roberts, told me I was to be an Asst BAR man and to report to that big guy over there. The big guy turned out to be Dick Yezny from Fresno, CA. Dick Yezny became my friend and mentor in those important first few days of learning my craft as an infantryman in the US Marine Corps. He filled me in. We were engaged in Operation Ripper-Killer, similar to Sherman's "March through Georgia," burning everything that would assist the enemy in his ability to wage war. Yezny took the first watch at nightfall, awakening me from a fitful sleep at 0100. I was disoriented, scared and just knew that at any minute the entire NKPA would cross the Pukhan River and drag my sorry little Tennessee ass back to Pyongyang about 125 miles north of us. Dawn began breaking through trees to the east about 0630, I had survived my first night on the lines, managed not to shoot anybody, get myself shot, or piss anybody off.

The second day was going fine until about 1100 when the platoon was told to roll their gear and be ready to move in 30 minutes. We had been assigned as a security for a 105 artillery outfit which had deployed forward to extend its range. I thought I was in good shape, but at this pace in early spring heat I had trouble keeping up. Yezny turned back and said, "'App.'" just put one foot in front of the other, keep your eyes on my ass and we'll get there together." We crossed the Pukhan five times so wet shoes and socks were the order of the day. As we came to the artillery position, we could see another unit digging in. SNAFU, Dog Company had also sent out a unit to provide security. So it was hightail it back to Item Company. By the time we got close it was getting dark. Rather than redeploy the entire company in the dark, Item Company Skipper had us set up on a little knoll in front and dig in for the night. About 2300 our two light MGs opened up. I came out of my sleeping bag like toothpaste squirted from a tube. The firing stopped suddenly. Yezny said a pair of headlights had come barreling down the road. Turned out to be a truckload of Korean Service Corps workers that had been sent to help dig in the artillery position. Someone had neglected to inform us they would be coming back that night.

I was now a veteran combat infantryman. Out where "the rubber meets the road." Out where real bullets are shot at people, where people can get killed. I had passed my final exam in 'Introduction to Combat 101' with flying colors. I would spend many more nights in coming months, peering into darkness where a determined and elusive enemy waited to kill me and my friends. I now felt I was ready for the task ahead and for the more complex courses like "Night Patrolling" and "Ambushes" that would be required.

Above. Chinese Armies move up to the front in preparation for their 5th phase campaign, April 22, 1951. All soldiers are in camouflage. It appears that most of their vehicles are captured American 21/2 ton trucks. CCF photos from the Internet.

Below Left Again, refugees flee from the advancing Chinese Armies, April 1951. Photo by Angelo Rosa.

Below Right The 955th F.A. Bn. from Brooklyn, N.Y. move their 155 mm howitzers up to try to check the Chinese 5tg phase offensive. April 1951. Photo by Angelo Rosa

104

RED DRAGON
The SECOND ROUND
FACES OF WAR II

Angelo	NMI	Rosa	NG 21 925 232
First Name	MI	Last Name	Serial Number
Angie	4014, Auto Mechanic	9 Aug 1931	Cpl
Nickname	MOS	Birthday	Grade / Rank
Service Battery 955th FA Bn	1 Feb 1951-10 Jan 1952		Brooklyn, NY
Unit (s)	Duty Tour (s)		Home Town
Good Conduct Medal	Korean Campaign Service Medal, 2 stars		United Nations Medal

Medals & Awards

Nat'l Defense Service Medal   Korean Presidential Unit Citation   ROK Korean War Service Med

955th FA, aka 'RED LEG DEVILS'

For kicks, in 1948 I joined the 955th Field Artillery Service Battery. We drilled once each week, and each summer had a 2 week summer camp at Camp Drum in upstate New York. Lots of fun with friends and a pay check each month. On my birthday, 9 August 1950, Uncle Sugar called in his IOU. I knew fun and games were at an end when I read in the evening news the 955th had been federalized for service in the Korean "Police Action." We trained at Ft Lewis, WA for 4½ months, fleshing out our half filled ranks with cowboys from Colorado and Wyoming, Mexican-Americans from Los Angeles, southerners from the Carolinas and Georgia, and apple pickers from Washington. Many of these men in the standby reserve had recently been discharged after 2 years of service. They had been recalled before they had time to savor the flavor of civilian life. We sailed for Korea on a US Navy ship manned by naval reservists just as seasick on the voyage as were we soldiers. The only functional people were the Merchant Mariners!

We landed at Pusan 1 Feb 1951. My first night ashore I was posted as a perimeter guard and admonished to stay alert as there were 40,000 North Korean guerillas hiding in the hills around our bivouac area. That night I saw at least half of them hiding in trees and shrubs in front of me, just waiting for a chance to slit my throat. The next day we went to work guarding POWs who were unloading the ships carrying our 155mm howitzers and assorted gear. I had my first sight of the tragedy of war, seeing young Korean boys, 8 to 12 years old, shoeless, naked except for an old sack wrapped around them. The temperature was then below zero, made worse by a brisk wind. One of the battery sergeants inspecting the guard spotted two young Koreans who appeared to be school kids approaching the ammo dump. The two were searched. The school books were phony, hollowed out, filled with dynamite. The ROK MPs were alerted. The last we saw of the 'students,' they were being given a professional lesson in violence as they were led away.

We moved to an area near the Naktong River for testing by 8th Army Artillery HQ. We passed with flying colors, thanks to our battery sergeants, many of them WW II veterans. There were 3 firing batteries plus Service Battery in the Bn. C Battery whose senior NCO was Sgt Twyford a WW II ETO veteran, held the Bn firing record, 3 rounds in 11 seconds. In Korea we were assigned at different times to IX Corps and I Corps. We eventually 'settled down' in the Chorwon area of the Iron Triangle. A 'bastard outfit,' not assigned to a division, we supported 3d, 24th, 25th and 1st Cav Divisions, an RCT, and a number of foreign troop units serving under the UN flag.

15 April we boarded LSTs at Pusan, landing at Inchon. Moving north to Seoul we encountered a multitude of children, boys and girls, as we passed through the ruins of the flattened city. They crawled out of holes in the ground, from under the rubble of buildings, gaunt, many of them naked, covered with soot and dirt, haunted looks on their faces and a terrible fear in their eyes. It was the saddest thing I have ever seen and hope to never witness again. We bivouacked north of the city in a dry river bed. The next morning shells were falling in the valley, a mile or so away. A straggling line of Korean civilians were on the road, men with A-frames on their backs loaded with family possessions, women with heavy loads balanced on their heads. Accompanying them was a sea of children, babes in arms, tots carrying babies, clutching hands holding on to parents and grandparents. An ocean of suffering humanity.

Some of us were very green, but we were learning. It was the Fifth Chinese Offensive. First to flee were the civilians, behind them, our soldiers in rear guard retreat. The soldiers looked beat, they had been on line for 40 days without relief. We were eventually told to saddle up and join the move southward. The MPs were doing a fantastic job directing traffic. At a road fork we were directed left. We later learned the 555th FA Bn reached the same fork. By that time the road had been cut. Moving back north several weeks later in the attack to retake Seoul, we saw wreckage of that battle, burned out tanks and 155 howitzers, nothing but a mass of junk metal.

That fall, I came down with malaria and was sent to a MASH Hospital. Released, I hitched a ride on a 3/4 ton weapons carrier heading toward my outfit. Never made it. Hit a mine in the road, tossed me some 25 feet into the adjacent mine field. When I came to I had a bleeding head wound. I was 'ambulanced' back to the same MASH I had just left. Christmas day 1951 I was loaded aboard a Liberty ship in Pusan. Fifteen seasick days later I was in the USA, no longer the green kid of a year ago. While recuperating, awaiting discharge, I was detailed to pick up garbage and litter in the WAAC quarters at Camp Kilmer. I had the gratitude of a grateful nation.

Above. Australian troops defend Hill 159. Above Right. The 73rd Hv. Tk. Bn. Loaded for bear. Below. Engineers from the 14th ECB take cover behind their dozer. Near the Han River, March 1951. Lower Right. Canadian troops dig in and prepare for Chinese attack, April 1951. All photos from National Archives.

RED DRAGON
The SECOND ROUND
FACES OF WAR II

Kenneth	F.	Barwise	800036
First Name	MI	Last Name	Serial Number
"Ken"	Rifleman	30 July 1929	Private
Nickname	MOS	Birthday	Grade / Rank
12 Plt Dog Co, PPCLI Regt		7 Nov '50-20 Nov '51	Vancouver,BC CANADA
Unit (s)		Duty Tour (s)	Home Town
Canadian Military Medal			
Medals & Awards			

TWO CANADIAN SOLDIERS AT KAPYONG

It is 24 April 1951. Capt Mills' Twelve Platoon of "Dirty" Dog Company, Princess Patricia's Canadian Light Infantry, Commonwealth Brigade is in battle position near Kapyong, South Korea. Pvts Ken Barwise and L. P. Jobagy have their 60mm mortars set up beneath a rocky overhang on Hill 677 near Co HQ. That night, the CCF attacked in the opening salvo of their massive Fifth Offensive. The attack is so sudden that the 60mm mortars are never employed. Said Barwise, "They were on top of us right away. I would have had to shoot straight up into the air to hit them." Twelve Platoon's positions are overrun, a LMG position manned by a Vickers gun team of Pvts Maurice Carr and Bruce MacDonald keeps a deadly fire on the enemy until both die in a hail of Chinese bullets. Barwise and L/Cpl I. W. Wanniana, finding themselves together in the chaos of battle, assist in a staunch night long defense of company HQ. At dawn, the two make their way to "C" Company to guide Lt Whitaker's Eight Platoon back to "D" positions in counterattack. In the forward move, Barwise sights the bodies of his two friends in the midst of a litter of dead Chinese. Reaching the gun pit, Barwise stunned by the blast of a Chinese concussion grenade. Regaining consciousness he fires the remaining half belt of ammo at the Chinese. Ammo gone, he shoulders the Vickers and with Wanniana firing cover for both, they make a successful run to Co HQ.

Pvt Barwise and L/Cpl Wanniana were a unique fighting team. Barwise at 21, is 6' 4", a big man with a huge barrel chest. His mates liken him to "Man Mountain" Dean, the famed wrestler. L/Cpl Wanniana, a 5' 6" Cree Indian of the Alberta, Fort McMurray tribe, is a seasoned 3 year combat veteran of WW II. Although dissimilar in size, both have the same stout fighting heart and desire to be a soldierly example for their mates. In military parlance, 'born leaders'. These qualities stand them in good stead as they fight to help retake their platoon sector. Kapyong is the crucial pivot of the central sector, vital to the Main Line of Resistance. It must be held.

The day before the Chinese attack, Barwise has led Korean 'Chioggi' porters carrying ammo strapped to their A- frame back packs up hill to the company position from a point a mile west of Hill 677. This day, knowing the route well, CSM Ed Morris assigns him the duty of leading Korean porters transporting KIAs to the rear for burial. It is a grim scene that greets American troops climbing the hill to relieve the Princess Pats. Seeing the dead bodies on the canvas stretchers, an American Sgt has a slight quaver in his voice as he comments, "Rough up there, ain't it?" Barwise nods silently as he looks back at the bodies carried on stretchers. "Come on, get a move on, you guys," the Sgt shouts to his men, "We've got work to do!" the quaver gone from his voice. As the Americans go up hill and he down hill, Barwise hears the shots of battle still going on. Looking at the bodies of his friends Maurice Carr and Bruce Mac Donald, then back at the hill crest of Hill 677, he wonders if in future years anyone will remember that the Princess Pats fought here. He is bone weary, but makes many more similar trips that day as the Princess Pats prepare to turn their positions over to the relieving Americans. Three days after the battle, Barwise goes on sick call for a painful, festering ear. Major Anderson, Bde surgeon, carefully inserts tweezers into his ear to pull out a long sliver of steel. He comments, "When did this occur?" "At Kapyong," The Major nods, "Takes about 3 days for a wound to fester like this," he says as he prepares a syringe of streptomycin and penicillin.

Barwise is honored for his bravery with the Military Medal, presented at a ceremony by Brigadier John Rockingham, Commander of the 25th Canadian Infantry Brigade. During the ceremony, Barwise, in the honesty of youth, wonders in his mind why L/Cpl Wanniana who had been his comrade all through the fight is not also honored. "He did everything I did. I was a Pvt, he a L/Cpl. If only one of us is to have a medal, it should be him, since he was the leader in charge." He does not like to think so, but perhaps Wanniana was not considered for a medal because he is an Indian. Reflecting, Barwise knows that prejudice of that stripe exists in the thinking of some Canadians. In fairness, possibly it was because he was widely known and well liked in the Regiment, whereas Wanniana was quiet, unassuming and not widely known in spite of his combat record. It could also be, he thinks, the image of big Ken Barwise, securing the Vickers and humping it home under fire has painted a heroic picture in the minds of those recommending medal awards. Still, 50 years later, Ken Barwise believes Wanniana too should have been honored for his bravery at Kapyong.

Wannianna dies unknown, unhonored. Barwise makes Canada's Army and the Pats his career. He lives today in honored retirement.

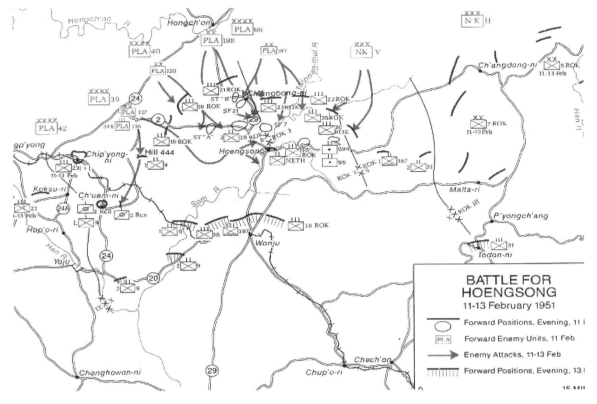

One of the costliest and least understood battles of the Korean War.   <u>Map from Ebb and Flow.</u>

GIs of the 10th Engineers, 3rd Division check out a damaged and abandoned American tank for possible 'booby traps'. Always a very 'touchy' job.   <u>Photo from the National Archives</u>.

A 3rd Division Engineer plants an anti-personnel mine field. Deadly business !   <u>Archive Photo</u>.

RED DRAGON
The SECOND ROUND
FACES OF WAR II

Richard	E.	Coate	US 52 001 171
First Name	MI	Last Name	Serial Number
Dick	4745	6 February 1929	PFC
Nickname	MOS	Birthday	Grade / Rank
E Company 15th Inf Regt 3d Div		6 Feb 1951-17 Jan 1952	Trenton, OH
Unit (s)		Duty Tour (s)	Home Town
Combat Infantry Badge	Good Conduct Medal	Korean Campaign Service Medal, 3 stars	
Medals & Awards			
National Defense Service Medal	New York State War Medal	UN Medal ROK PUC KWSM	

RETREAT

22 April 1951, our 15th Inf Regt was in I Corps reserve in the northern suburbs of Seoul. At 10 PM, at the juncture of the Imjin and Han Rivers, the Chinese attacked our sister regiments, the 7th and 65th Inf Regts and the attached units, British Gloucesters, Turks, Belgians and Filipinos. The Chinese Spring offensive was designed to drive UN Forces out of Korea. Seoul in our sector was their immediate objective. The Main Line of Resistance across Korea bent under pressure of their "'human sea" attacks. The 15th on the morning of the 24th was trucked north to a back-up position on the western MSR (Main Supply Route), bypassing UN forces retreating south. Twilight on the 25th, the 2d Bn 15th, the Filipino Bn, and the 65th Regt converged to form a defensive perimeter on a complex of 3 ridges framing a valley adjacent to the MSR. Easy Company was deployed on a low hill in a southern blocking position.

The rest of the 2d Bn was on the ridge to our left. A narrow road bisecting our ridge connected the valley to our rear where Bn HQ and 2d Bn Hvy Wpns were situated. The bulk of the 65th deployed in the valley. The Filipino Bn situated in the north valley blocking position was overwhelmed by swarming Chinese. The Filipino Bn disintegrated under a tidal wave onslaught. A fierce battle ensued, the 65th putting up a stiff resistance to the Chinese. Shortly before dawn, retreating units of the 65th passed through Easy/15 on the road below to regroup in our rear. Now under siege, we waited for the full impact of the Chinese assault.

When it became apparent the Chinese were busy realigning their forces, orders were issued to move out at first light. Our FO waited in his jeep at the base of the hill where he was joined by our commo chief, SFC Leonard Cusson. Noting the folded panels, he started back up hill when he saw the American Mosquito 'spotter' plane overhead. Sensing an impending tragedy, Cusson retraced his steps, grabbed the panels, unfolding them as he ran. The Mosquito pilot mistaking us for the enemy had alerted 3 F-80 Air Force jets. The first napalm hit near the base of the forward slope. Severe strafing followed. Were it not for the heroic action of Sgt Cusson, Easy Co. might have been even more seriously crippled. While the rest of the company ran pell-mell for cover, Sgt Cusson continued racing up the hill. Momentarily stopped by a second napalm drop on the hill crest, Sgt Cusson persevered. He placed his last 2 panels within 20 feet of the flames. There he witnessed the 3d napalm drop on an adjoining ridge occupied by Easy 65. A jet pilot, spotting the panels, rocked his wings in recognition. The jets flew off, leaving 7 dead and 12 wounded in Easy Co 15 Infantry from strafing or napalm burns. However tragic the error, the Chinese knew the same horror would be their lot if they hit us in daylight attack.

In retreat, 2d Bn/15 was designated buffer between the advancing Chinese and the rest of our regiment. We headed south for 'Line Golden,' a defensive perimeter north of Uibongju. With the Chinese on our heels, the SitRep stated 'unit in orderly retreat.' Whatever it was, it was a long line of wet, miserable American soldiers humping heavy packs in cold driving rain, mile after wretched mile. In a symphony of misery, one company leapfrogging another, we trudged back to Uibongju. The night of the 26th having reached our objective, Easy Company climbed the treacherously slippery finger of a hill, carefully planting one foot in front of the other. One misstep and a man would career down the steep slope. Feet sopping wet, we set up a defensive perimeter, listening to the dispiriting sound of Chinese bugles. Fully expectant of a Chinese assault, an unrelenting rain pelting our ponchos, we were misery personified.

By dawn of the 27th, barring a few snatch naps, we had been 72 hours without sleep. The rain subsiding shortly before daybreak, the CO permitted one platoon at a time to go down hill the into a courtyard fronting a Buddhist temple. Bleary eyed and bearded, we warmed ourselves while heating C-rations. Our mood was somber as we surveyed the peaceful scene of a huge golden Buddha within the temple, cherry trees in full bloom in the court yard, all in contrast to the horror of war. The stark contradiction was not lost on us. We were vastly outnumbered and were much relieved when we received the order to move out. As "Tail-end Charlie" in the retreat, last unit in the buffer force, nothing was between us and the Chinese. We marched on. Well inside 'Line Golden' we climbed aboard trucks. It is not without irony that during this horrific period, our only casualties were inflicted by our own Air Force. Heading south, bypassing other units defending Seoul, the roar of artillery blasted our eardrums. This convoy of weary dogface soldiers was headed for a rest. The line had held, we had played a significant role in the defense of Seoul. We had earned the right to be proud.

This trooper from the 5th Cavalry Regiment keeps a wary eye out for Chinese in early 1951. The recoilless rifle can handle any small chores that comes his way. Photo from National Archives.

On the move is a squad from the 31st Regiment Heavy Mortar Company of the 7th Infantry Division. Badly decimated at the Chosin Reservoir this unit made the Chinese pay heavily for the remainder of the war.

Set up for firing is a 4.2 mortar of the 31st Regt Heavy Mortar Co. It had a healthy appetite for ammo considering the pile of ammo cases in the background. Bottom photos by Pat Westfall.

John	NMI	Covach	O-61893
First Name	MI	Last Name	Serial Number
None	1542	17 March 1929	Col USA Ret, Then Lt
Nickname	MOS	Birthday	Grade / Rank
Co A 31st Inf Regt 7th Inf Div		17 Sept 1950-Feb 1952	St Clair, PA
Unit (s)		Duty Tour (s)	Home Town
Combat Infantry Badge	Bronze Star w/ V for Valor 2 OLC		Purple Heart Medal with OLC
Medals & Awards			

Numerous other Medals & Awards for the Korean War and for the Vietnam War

BOOTS

Sgt Jones and I became acquainted as we strolled the streets of Sapporo on "Courtesy Patrol." We were a two man team intended to tone down the exuberance of young GIs exposed to the fleshpot temptations of an oriental city. A green young 2d Lt, I was newly commissioned just before being posted to Japan. On arrival a month earlier I had been assigned to Easy Company 31st Infantry. The regiment, awaiting an imminent shipment to Korea, was in barracks at Camp Crawford, near Sapporo on Hokkaido, northernmost Island of the Japanese Archipelago. I drew duty the night of 1 Aug '50, missing the regimental birthday party. However, I knew in traditional ritual, the celebration would culminate in a toast to the President of the United States proposed by the youngest regimental officer, 2d Lt Tom Walker, a graduate of the Citadel. The toast, drunk from silver cups filled with punch, was ladled from a huge silver bowl ornately decorated with Chinese dragons. Made of melted Chinese silver dollars, it was a memento of the time the 31st deployed in Shanghai to protect American lives during the Sino-Japanese War. Every officer posted to the Regiment purchased a cup made of melted silver dollars. On departure, the cup with his name inscribed remained with the Regiment in honor of his service.

Activated in the Philippines in 1916, the 31st Infantry guarded the Trans-Siberian railroad in 1918-19 in the early years of the Russian Civil War. It participated in relief efforts to assist Japan after the devastating 1923 earthquake. Returning to the Philippines from Shanghai, it took part in the 1942 defense of Bataan. Before the surrender at Bataan, the Shanghai cups and bowl and the Regimental Colors were buried to prevent despoliation by the victorious Japanese. Retrieved after the US victory in WW II, they were again the centerpiece of regimental tradition. This unique regimental history of overseas service inspired veterans of WW I who fought in France to christen the regiment with the sobriquet "La Legion Etrangere des Etats-Unis,"- Foreign Legion of the United States.

Much of our casual conversation the early part of the evening was concerned with regimental history. We became as friendly with each other as the officer-NCO code then would allow. That night patrol really introduced me to the 'exotic' orient. Eating places, dives, bars, outdoor markets, teeming sidewalks were a kaleidoscope of activity. Melon hawkers yelled at us, girls approached us with all kinds of invitations, old mama-sans babbled words I did not understand, at the same time laughing, flashing their big buck teeth at us. People squatted in perfect comfort on their haunches in positions impossible for a westerner to assume. Conversation shifted to footgear, always of interest to an infantry soldier. In those days the GI issue of boots were crude looking. Sgt Jones recommended I get a pair of those wonderful paratroop style boots made by the Corcoran Company. They were of a lighter shade of brown than GI boots and had a pronounced bulbous toe. The next day Jones ordered a pair of Corcoran boots for each of us. As far as I can recall we were the only two in the unit to wear them. Jones and I were not destined to stay together for long. I was selected as 'cadre' for Able Company in the newly activated 1st Bn which fleshed out the regiment to its TO strength of 3 Bns. The next time I saw Jones I recognized him by his boots. They were exposed at the bottom of a poncho covering his face and body as he lay dead at the foot of Hill 113. He and his twin brother William of George Company were both killed in the attack on Hill 113.

I was wearing my Corcoran boots when injured in a jeep accident New Years Day. The regiment was regrouping from evacuation at Hungnam. Luckily, they were returned to me on release from hospital in late March. Those boots carried me, marching and countermarching, forward in attacks, on patrols, and back on withdrawals. There were many 24 hour days when they never left my feet. To an infantryman, next to his weapon, boots are his most prized possession. I wore them in comfort as we drove north in a series of counterattacks which threw the Chinese back behind the 38th parallel. They were on my feet when my luck ran out on 5 June '51. Shrapnel from a 155mm shell tore into my shoulder, fired, I suspect, most probably by the 555th 'Triple Nickle' FA Bn which had a reputation for firing short rounds. The blood gushed down my arm from a wound which looked as if a sharp ice cream scoop had gouged out flesh down to the bone. A medic bandaged me and asked, "Can you walk?" "Yes." In a haze I wandered down hill. after an hour or so found the Bn Aid Station. I was attended by a medic from my home town, St Clair, PA. I was soon in an ambulance. My boots were stripped off en route to a MASH hospital. The surgeons did a good job. I recovered full use of arm and shoulder.

WITH GOOD INTENTIONS
by
Major Arthur F. Dorie, U.S. Army (Retired)

GENESIS

Military theorist Karl von Clausewitz has described war as a political act, a continuation of diplomacy by other means. Accepting von Clausewitz's doctrine, it is reasonable to expect that if policy is flawed and diplomacy fails to settle differences, the armed forces of disputing nations will be called upon to resolve issues. Unfortunately, resolution by force, costly in blood and treasure, is often indecisive. War represents the failure of leaders to adopt reasonable and workable policies and of diplomats to resolve differences by statesmanship. All too often wars are fought and won only to be lost at the peace table by leaders and diplomats who, without vision, enter into agreements that sow the seeds of future wars. The war in Korea was such a war—a civil war, the consequence of faulty vision, complacency, and failed judgments that led to a joint occupation by ideologically opposed powers.

GEOGRAPHY, CLIMATE & PEOPLE.

To understand Korea and why war came to that nation, one must begin with some fundamental knowledge of the country, its people, and its history as it appeared to the U.S. Army during its occupation. Korea (Chosun) was a 600-mile-long mountainous peninsula jutting from the Asian continent. Shaped somewhat like a larger state of Florida, it averaged approximately 150 miles across and was bounded on the east by the deep-water Sea of Japan; on the south by the 120-mile-wide Korea Strait separating it from the Japanese island of Kyushu; on the west by the shallow Yellow Sea; and in the north by the great Yalu and Tumen Rivers which arose on the slopes of 9,000-foot Mt. Paektu but flowed in opposite directions to define clearly Korea's borders with Manchuria and Siberia.

It has been said in jest that Korea would be the largest country in the world if its mountains were hammered flat. That might best be said of the industrial north, where impressive mountain ranges and high-elevation plateaus and valleys mark its rugged beauty. The Taebaek Range extends spine-like down the east coast, decreasing in elevation farther south. The west coastal is flatter, more irregular than the east coastal area, where mountains came closer to the water's edge. Rice paddies are extensive on the coastal plains and terraced on the hills, especially in the agricultural south.

The tidal reach on the west coast was the second highest in the world—up to 32 feet at Inchon and Chinanpo. The lie of the land dictated the flow of the rivers, most of which drained southwest or west into the Yellow Sea. A notable exception was the Naktong River, flowing south. Most were wide, some were deep, and many were fordable on underwater bridges built by depositing layers of rocks on the riverbed. Most of the trails, roads, and railroads were located along the coastal plains, with only an occasional one cut through the mountains to connect both coasts. A road and railroad connected Pyongyang with Wonsan at the waist of the peninsula. Some trails had been improved into stable dirt roads by an accumulation of rubble and clay and rose a few feet above adjacent paddies. Such roads were often tree lined. Some roads and trails shown on 1917 Japanese-surveyed maps were nonexistent, and bridges were mostly narrow and poor. Korean winters were cold, especially at higher elevations in the north, where the arctic weather resembled that of Siberia and Manchuria. Summers were hot and dusty, or hot and rainy, depending upon the frequency of the monsoons. The stench of country air was almost unbearable. Human excrement was used to fertilize the paddies. Ox-drawn honey wagons added to the stench. Drinking water had to be treated to avoid dysentery.

Nomad tribes from Manchuria emigrating to a new country called it Chosun, "Land of the Morning Calm." In 2333 B.C. Pyongyang became its capital its capital. A poor people with a separate culture and a distinct language and literature, they suffered over the centuries through wars and invasions by Manchus, Chinese, and Japanese. Most Koreans were followers of Confucius or Buddha, although many Christians lived in the south. One-third of its thirty million people ived in the north, two-thirds in the south.

GEOPOLITICAL POWER STRUGGLES.

Historically, Korea was an invasion route. For the past century it had been more of a buffer state in the vortex of a Japanese, Russian and Chinese power struggle. The resources of Manchuria (iron, timber, coal, food, and water power) and of mineral-rich Korea (iron, coal, tungsten, gold, and graphite) were tempting, especially to resource-poor Japan. The First Sino-Japanese War (1894–1895) and the Russo-Japanese War (1904–1905) were fought over issues as to who controlled Korea. The question was answered by the Treaty of Portsmouth in 1905 when Teddy Roosevelt, the mediator, reportedly said, "Korea is in the Japanese sphere of influence."

Japan occupied Korea in 1905, annexed it in 1910, and held it until 1945—a period of sorrow for the Korean people. Japan abolished many of their customs, made Japanese their national language and drafted the men for military and labor service. Japanese nationals were placed in all key positions in industry and government. Many fled the country, including Syngman Rhee, an activist who went to the U.S., where he received a Ph.D. from Princeton. Living in Hawaii, he lobbied for his country's independence. While there he was elected president of the Korean Provisional Government-in-exile. After Japan's defeat Rhee returned to Korea. He was very critical of the U.S. for sanctioning the de facto partition of his country at the 38th parallel . In philosophy, he was an extreme rightist and a bitter critic of the occupation. He was also an outspoken critic of General Hodge, commander of American occupation forces.

ORIGINS OF THE KOREAN WAR

The postwar fate of Japanese-held Korea was discussed at World War II conferences, first at Cairo and Tehran in 1943, then at Yalta and Potsdam in 1945. It was agreed in principle Korea would become free and independent in due course after the defeat of Japan. *In due course* referred to some temporary form of trusteeship until Korea recovered from four decades of Japanese oppression. Stalin did not play his cards straight, for *free and independent* meant one thing to him and another to the British and Americans.

In November 1944, six months before Germany's surrendered, the JCS estimated an Allied amphibious force invading Japan could suffer a million casualties if Japan recalled its crack 875,000-man Kwantung Army from Manchuria to bolster home island defenses. Aware Stalin had told FDR at Tehran Russia would go to war against Japan after Germany surrendered, the JCS strongly suggested the president convince Stalin to declare war against Japan three months before the planned invasion of Japan. To the planners this meant a Soviet declaration of war in August 1945. The date planned for the Kyushu invasion was 1 November 1945. Kyushu was defended by an estimated 300,000 Japanese. Stalin's declaration of war would hold the Kwantung Army in place in Manchuria.

Since his agricultural and industrial sectors in Russian Europe had been largely destroyed, Stalin, who in the 1930s had already begun to develop heavy industry in Siberia, saw an opportunity to build a single economic system in Siberia, Manchuria, and Korea. To get warm-water ports and other spoils from a defeated Japanese empire was his ambition. And so it was in February 1945 at Yalta that Stalin agreed to enter the war against Japan within three months of Germany's surrender. His unspecified quid pro quo payoff would be Manchuria, Korea, and part of northern China. Stalin also had designs on Hokkaido, Sakhalin and the Kurile Islands. But it was at Potsdam during 17 July–2 August that Korea was conceded by default to the Soviets.

By mid-1945 strategic Allied bombing and naval blockade had forced Japan to the point of unconditional surrender. A surrender offer was made by the Japanese ambassador in Moscow through Stalin who relayed it to Truman and Churchill at Potsdam. On 27 July Truman and Clement Attlee, Churchill's successor, sent an immediate surrender ultimatum to Japan through Stalin. Stalin did not relay it. He wanted to end the war in Asia as a partner in victory. His Korean troops of the Red Army would act as a police force to incorporate another nation into the Communist list of allied countries under the heel of Red Russia.

However, with an unconditional surrender by Japan, neither the bomb invasion or the Red Army was needed to conclude the war. Months earlier General Douglas MacArthur had recognized the need to tie down the Kwangtung Army in Manchuria before launching an invasion of Japan. He is reported to have stated that in any quid pro quo it was inevitable that Russia would eventually get all of Manchuria and Korea and possibly part of northern China. MacArthur was completely surprised when an atomic bomb was dropped on Hiroshima on 6 August 1945 and by the rapidity of events that followed. Stalin declared war on Japan on 8 August, a second bomb was dropped on Nagasaki on 9 August. Japan offered to surrender unconditionally on 10 August. The Soviet leader wasted no time collecting his spoils of victory. Russian forces quickly occupied Manchuria and northern Korea and their warm water ports. Only MacArthur's determination kept the Russians out of Japan; and an off-hand policy decision by the State-War-Navy Coordinating Committee (SWNCC) during a night-long session on 10–11 August limited the Red Army's move into Korea to the 38th parallel. With approval by Washington, London, and Moscow, the line became part of the Japanese surrender protocol.

Bringing Russia into the war against Japan was a blunder by the U.S. and Britain. In so doing the seed for a divided Korea and the Korean War was sewn. Who among the planners knew of the atomic bomb or that it would end the war without need for Russian involvement? Truman did. At Potsdam in July 1945 he already knew of the successful test of the atomic bomb at Alamogordo. He could have taken steps to neutralize Russia's entry into the war. Who in SWNCC could foresee a line drawn for the disarmament of Japanese forces in Korea would result in the de facto political division of a nation intended to be made free and independent? Stalin alone knew of his intention to sieze as much Korean territory as possible before the Allies could land in Korea.

DEPLOYMENT TO KOREA.

The atomic bomb was a welcome addition to the U.S. Army's arsenal in 1945. It was credited with ending the war and saving a million Allied casualties. It also changed the future of the battle-hardened XXIV Corps of Lt. Gen. John R. Hodge on Okinawa. General MacArthur appointed Hodge, a soldier's soldier with the reputation of being the "Patton of the Pacific," as commanding general of all U.S. Armed Forces in Korea (USAFIK). On 1 September Japanese Maj. Gen. Kozuki Yoshio radioed Hodge from Seoul that there many Communists among the Korean people and the Red labor unions were planning to disturb 'peace and order' when the Americans arrived. He also reported that the Russians had arrived at the 38th parallel on 26 August. The American general took advantage of the information and utilized the help Japanese could give him during the early occupation.

Under new orders, the XXIV Corps shipped to Korea after the official 2 September surrender of Japan. The Corps 3 infantry divisions, 6th, 7th 40th and supporting units occupied the peninsula up to the 38th parallel. It accepted the Japanese surrender in Seoul on 9 September and began disarming and repatriating Japanese soldiers and civilian nationals in its zone. Within weeks the American force of 72,000 troops declined to 45,000 as the 40th ID embarked for California, and Washington's demobilization plan took hold.

The history of XXIV Corps's military occupation presence of the U.S. Army in Korea during 1945–1949 can best be described through that of the 7th ID, which covered the northern sector of the American zone. The 6th ID, which was based in Pusan, occupied the southern half of the peninsula. The 7th ID served in the as an American trip wire in the Cold War. It would be the first American force hit by invasion. Only an atomic bomb could have saved the division. Only the president had the power to authorize its use.

The bloody battles at Attu, Kwajalein, Leyte, and Okinawa had honed the 7th ID for the expected invasion of Japan. The atomic bomb, the sudden surrender of Japan, and the rapid advance of the Red Army into Manchuria and Korea changed that scenario. The division found itself under new orders on a multifaceted, unprepared mission to Korea. The major elements of its new occupation assignment included landing at Inchon, disarming and repatriating the Japanese Army and other Japanese nationals in its zone, assisting military government, occupying the peninsula up to the 38th parallel and guarding the parallel to prevent unauthorized crossings.

The division sailed from Okinawa 5 September 1945 landing at Inchon on 8 September. Welcomed by poverty-stricken Koreans as liberators, received with pomp and ceremony by the yet armed Japanese Army and Korean National Police (KNP), the division established its HQ in Seoul, and unlike the occupation of Japan entered upon a military control both difficult and dangerous.

It had already been agreed in August the 38th north parallel would be the demarcation line for the disarmament and repatriation of the Japanese in Korea. This was a task estimated by the Americans to take between two and three months. The 38th parallel now divided the Koreans and their country into two economic spheres, one industrial and the other agricultural. Within weeks, Hodge advised MacArthur that he was dissatisfied with the division of Korea, stating it had absolutely nothing to commend it.

After landing, the division quickly deployed its three regiments and support units. The 32d Infantry was designated border guard and sent to the 38th parallel, where it met up with Soviet troops. The 17th Infantry was sent into the large area south of Seoul, and the 184th Infantry (National Guard) was stationed in Seoul, the capital. In January 1946 the 31st Infantry was reactivated and replaced the 184th, which was deactivated and reverted to the California National Guard. The 31st Infantry would later send a battalion to guard the eastern end of the parallel. Disarmament of the Japanese Army began immediately and went well. Repatriation proceeded slowly.

Koreans had to be located to replace Japanese nationals who for decades had held key positions in industry, commerce, government and the infrastructure. As a consequence many Japanese continued in their positions until suitable replacements could be found and or trained from the Korean national populace. This was another source of irritation and outright anger to the populace of South Korea. It was also a major string to the bow of the DPRK aiming its propaganda arrows at the village peasantry of South Korea.

OCCUPATION AND OUTPOSTS.

Relations with the Russians along the 38th parallel started out friendly. Some slight border adjustments were made in the field to satisfy both sides. At the onset of the Cold War in early 1946, the border took on the appearance of a static battle front. The 32d Infantry and one battalion of the 31st Infantry deployed on one side of the parallel, the Soviet 25th Army of 40,000 men on the other. Raids, kidnaping, sniping, and "accidental" firing of mortars at American outposts, patrols, and listening posts were daily occurrences. United States aircraft were regularly fired upon while in friendly air space near the border. Outpost duty along the 38th parallel, included the lower Ongjin Peninsula, was a no-nonsense and a play-for-keeps border war.

An artificial east–west line 210 miles long over hills, valleys and waterways was too extensive a border to occupy in a conventional regimental defensive front. In consequence it was manned by a series of outguards posted near border crossing points. These isolated units were usually located miles from parent company or battalion CP. These outposts were supplied by truck, except for the Ongjin Peninsula, which was ship supplied. A typical outguard consisted a reinforced squad of fourteen men, including cook and radio operator. They lived in Quonset huts equipped with a generator. Commanded by a sergeant, each outguard patrolled its sector of the border, maintaining observation and listening posts and controlling border crossings, alert for infiltrators and raiders.

A virtual state of war intensified along the parallel. Large demonstrations by politically diverse factions fanned the flames of growing discontent among the civilian populace in general and student bodies in particular. Americans had initially been welcomed as liberators. They were soon viewed by many Koreans as unwanted occupiers dividing their country and splitting their in families. Some insensitive American soldiers looked upon the Korean people as a lower class of humanity, calling them "gooks." Communist guerrilla bands organized in mountains and countryside, were the tools used by Communists and their sympathizers in the struggle to gain power in the cities and provinces. Guerrillas occasionally raided police stations, creating chaos wherever they struck.

Army warehouses, supply trucks, boxcars, and POL dumps were frequently entered and looted, aggravating the division's supply problems. Some of the other frustrating problems were ater in gasoline jerry cans, oil drums, vapor lock in tank engines, certain TE weapons and spare parts shortages, short rations, and bartering by supply sergeants—the soldiers were right when they spoke of being at the end of the army's supply line. Korean mama-sans washed GI laundry in streams, while papa-sans cut hair and performed odd jobs for soldiers. The black marke flourished. Many such transactions were paid for with cigarettes. Electricity generated in the Russian zone was turned off by the Reds every night. Generators were in short supply, refrigeration was a continuing problem. American troops lived in former Japanese barracks or engineer-built Quonset huts. The ARC, librarians, hostesses, and eventually the special services branch operated several service clubs and facilities. The army sold a limited number of Okinawa-tested jeeps and command cars to a few fortunate soldiers to boost morale. There was no R&R, however, and very few dependents went to Korea.

Spit-and-polish formal guard mounts were held daily in and around Seoul, where XXIV Corps, 7th ID, and the 31st and 32d Infantry Regiments were headquartered. Many permanent guard posts were manned by the 31st Infantry and included the Russian embassy (caretaker status), the French embassy, and the railroad marshaling yard, where an occasional detachment of Russian soldiers on special detail was restricted to living in the cars. POL dumps, the Class VI warehouse, and various other facilities at Kimpo, Ascom City, and Yongdungpo were also posted. They were so spread out that an officer of the guard had to drive more than 125 miles a night just to check them. The smell of burning carbide lamps and other foul odors in a dark and dingy city with an occasional dead or drunk Korean lying in the gutter or on the sidewalk was an unforgettable experience. It was as if the Korean people were living two or three centuries in the past in a time that life had little meaning.

The 31st Infantry, less one battalion along the parallel, was billeted in a former Japanese compound. A full military schedule of training, guard duty, parades, ceremonies and inspections was maintained. Many of these garrison functions were at the expense of combat readiness in an attempt to maintain civilian respect. Soldiering was hard in Korea. This regiment was the army's "Foreign Legion, 'La Legion Etrangiere, des Etats Unis,'" a regiment which had never been stationed in the continental U.S. Activated in the Phillipines in 1916, it had served in Siberia, the International Settlement in Shanghai, and in Japan, decades before, on an earthquake relief mission. It had fought, then surrendered to the Japanese on Bataan, suffering the barbarities of the infamous Death March. Officers and men of the "Thirsty-first," were proud of their battle streamers and their Shanghai Bowl Ceremony. MacArthur wrote: "There is no unit in the American Army which has served with greater distinction, both in peace and in war, than the 31st Infantry."

The 17th Inf was posted in the south of the 7th Division's zone during the occupation. Taejon, Chongju, and Ongyang were three of the larger population centers. Cities and villages were subject to political unrest, usually Communist inspired. Most farmers were tenants demanding land reform, easy prey for Communist agitators. Guerrillas were a daily concern. On 15 August 1948 the regiment was reduced to record status to facilitate the planned evacuation of the 7th ID from Korea to Japan. From a soldier's perspective, occupation duty in Korea was a duty station to be endured. Life was spartan, unforgiving, often depressing. General Hodge considered Korea his worst assignment. Japan was the land of the Big PX. According to historian Patrick C. Roe, one company commander in Japan was known to have advised his troops they had only three things to fear—diarrhea, gonorrhea, and Korea!

DISCIPLINE GOES SOUTH.
The U.S. Army, in common with all armies from the time of Caesar's legions, follow a caste system in which discipline, rank, and privilege function together like a three-legged stool. It is accepted that rank hath its privilege. RHIP differentiates status between the leaders who impose discipline, and the led, who accept it in accordance with the military oath of enlistment. In a military unit, it is a given that discipline is necessary if orders are to be obeyed. The tremendous, rapid expansion of the army during WW II led to the appointment of some officers and to selection of some NCOs who seriously abused their authority. In consequence, complaints erupted that required congressional investigation at wars' end.

The Doolittle Board convened in 1945–1946 to inquire into the caste system and abuse of power. It interviewed forty-two former soldiers and read a thousand letters of complaint, some of which were meritorious. The abuses charged were usually attributed to a few wartime misfits rather than to professional officers. Instead of taking action against the few, the board recommended that *all officers* have less power. The tried-and-proven caste system developed over the centuries was modified by Congress.

The recommendations of the Doolittle Board were implemented. For several years, NCOs and company grade officers lost much of their authority. Discipline declined. Courts-martial and boards replaced many corrective measures that had formerly been handled at squad, platoon, and company level. The Far East was not immune to these changes. Beginning in 1946 discipline fell victim to defense appropriation cutbacks and ultra-rapid demobilization that roiled the army. Much stability and unit cohesiveness was lost. The war was over. Veterans wanted release from duty, especially those in undesirable duty posts such as Korea. Under these worst conditions, the officer corps became more professional as many WW II reservists elected to make the military their life career, About 25,000 who met world wide specific requirements were integrated into the regular army. They became the backbone of the US Army.

Be fair, be firm, be friendly" became the guiding philosophy of NCOs and company-grade officers, who were severely tested as rotation to the ZI (Zone of thge Interior) depleted the ranks in Korea. The shortage of commissioned officfrom the ranks were appointed as acting squad leaders and platoon sergeants . Newly assigned men from the States returning to service after a taste of civilian life stiffened the backbone of the new corps of NCOs. A few newly enlisted men had taken the suggestion of judges to join the army or go to jail. Overall, the average age of the enlisted ranks which became more of a volunteer army, declined from that of the citizen-soldiers of WW II. The old Army was on its death bed while the new Army was yet in swaddling clothes.

U.S. POLICY EVOLVES.

Confronted by the Cold War, General Hodge, and staff officers became increasingly concerned about a possible invasion. American forces stood in harm's way, and could be destroyed if the Russians were to cross the parallel in force. American forces could not be reinforced in time to be saved from destruction. Nor would they have much chance in a withdrawal. Only use of atomic weapons could have saved them. By the summer of 1947 Washington became aware of that concern. The president's manpower restraints and anemic defense budgets were forcing the armed forces to design military policy giving them a bigger bang for the buck. So serious were matters that Truman's military advisors forced a major decision. The brass bit the bullet and backed a plan to transfer combat forces from Korea to more strategically important Japan. The State Department opposed the move for its own reasons

Seeking to develop future policy toward Korea, SWNCC requested that the JCS comment on the relationship of Korea to U.S. security. In a 29 September 1947 Report on Korea's Strategic Significance, the JCS replied, "...from the standpoint of military security, the United States has little strategic interest in maintaining present troops and bases in Korea." The generals believed the Korean occupation forces would be better used in areas of greater strategic importance in Japan or Germany. Truman was not ready to yield Korea to the Communists. The JCS report was influential in the drafting of NSC-8 on 2 April 1948, calling for the U.S. to withdraw its forces from Korea at an early date. It recognized that American military leaders wanted to pull troops out of Korea without abandoning the country. The conundrum to be solved was how to do it.

The State Department did not want the US to abandon Korea to the Soviet Empire. Truman approved NSC-8 which offered a withdrawal plan to clear Korea not later than 31 December 1948. A small constabulary capable of handling domestic problems was created. It would not have the capability to resist a North Korean invasion. The date was extended to 30 June 1949 because of State Department opposition and the eruption of the October Yosu rebellion. The South Korean constabulary force was increased to 100,000 men. It was an unbalanced, inadequate force unable to cope with potential invasion and North Korean guerilla activity.

After the 7th ID withdrawal from Korea and relocation to Japan, only the 5th RCT covering force remained in place on the peninsula. Another SWNCC paper on 23 March 1949 warned the U.S. should "not become irrevocably involved in the Korean situation lest any action taken by any faction in Korea or by any other power in Korea be considered a *casus belli* [cause to declare war] for the U.S."

A NATION DIVIDED.

With the American trip wire disarmed, the decision to make Korea a free and independent nation became difficult. The 38th parallel, originally a *surrender line*, became a frontier dividing the peninsula into two sectors, splitting families and the economy. Stalin saw it as a *political division*. When American and Soviet occupation commanders failed to agree on Korean reunification, the American Commander referred the matter to the American government. The Moscow Agreement of 21 December 1945 and subsequent joint conferences in 1946 and 1947 failed to resolve the reunification problem. The Korean people became increasingly frustrated.

Convinced that it could not reach agreement with the USSR, the U.S. placed the matter before the UN General Assembly on 17 September 1947. That body adopted a resolution on 14 November calling for the election of a national assembly and a national government for all of Korea. It also established the UN Temporary Commission on Korea (UNTCOK) to facilitate the movement toward reunification and independence. It called for American and Russian troop withdrawals from Korea ninety days after the establishment of a national government, or as soon thereafter as possible. The USSR took the position that the UN did not have jurisdiction over the Korea boundary question. In UN debate, Russia refused further consideration of the matter.

UNTCOK set 10 May 1948 set as election day for all of Korea, or in that part of Korea accessible to the UN. Prevented by Soviet Russia from crossing the 38th parallel, the commission set up an observation program for registration days and election south of the 38th American military patrols stood guard and prevented interfering guerilla activities. Those elected to the national assembly met on 31 May 1948. One third of the assembly seats were reserved for North Korea. In a three month period the assembly convened, adopted a constitution, and elected Syngman Rhee president. In honor of President-elect Syngman Rhee, General Douglas MacArthur, Supreme Commander Allied Powers (SCAP) and Commander in Chief Far East Command (FECOM), flew from Tokyo to Kimpo to honor the founding of the Republic of South Korea. He was met by an honor guard of the 31st Infantry, his old Bataan regiment. The entire 15 route to the capital was flanked by Korean guards standing at attention on both sides of the road.

At about the same time the Republic of Korea was established, Russians created the Democratic People's Republic of Korea (DPRK). Following unobserved elections to a Supreme People's Council on 25 August 1948, the council proclaimed the DPRK on 9 September 1948 with Kim Il Sung, a former Soviet Army major, as its premier. On 18 September Moscow announced that all Soviet forces would be withdrawn from Korea by the end of December 1948. Tacitly, the USSR would still dominate the new communist puppet regime. In October the DPRK assumed responsibility for the 38th parallel, allowing the Russian Army withdrawal. A select advisory group would remain. A General Assembly resolution on 12 December 1948 recognized the ROK as the only lawful Korean government.

TOWARD TOTAL WAR.

Communist guerrillas were a continuing concern of the U.S. Army in Korea. They steadily infiltrated the South by land and by sea and joined bands already in the hills and mountains. For more than two years, little progress had been made in land reform, inequalities of wealth, or of reunification. Frustration and discontent ran high, especially among tenant farmers. In 1947, demonstrations and raids on police stations of the anti-Communist Korean National Police were almost daily occurrences. Communists and their sympathizers became more active in 1948, gaining considerable support. Rebellion and guerrilla activity threatened to ignite a civil war in the American zone. A rebellion did begin suddenly on 3 April 1948. Guerrilla bands attacked police stations and villages on Cheju-do, a large island off the southern tip of Korea. This inaugurated the campaign of North Korea's armed guerrilla struggle for control of the South. As the rebellion gained followers, it appeared to be a premature popular uprising a month in advance of the upcoming UN-sponsored national elections. The South Korean Labor Party (SKLP), a leftist organization, played some part in setting the stage, but the situation quickly got out of control as whole villages were torched and their inhabitants massacred. Taking on the character of an organized partisan movement, the uprising spread to the mainland and wasn't suppressed on Cheju until a year later after claiming 60,000 lives, 20 percent of the island's population. Another 40,000 fled to Japan.

Although it was never proven, strong evidence existed that guerrillas sabotaged a troop train on 14 September 1948 at Napan, killing 36 GIs and injuring another 60. These were American soldiers on their way home. It was the largest number of American casualties suffered in Korea at any one time prior to the the 1950 Korean War. Only two months after taking office as president of the newly proclaimed ROK, Syngman Rhee was faced with the Cheju rebellion that put the survivability of his government to the test. It began on 19 October 1948 when the ROK 14th Regiment at the southern port city of Yosu rebelled. Led by Communists among its NCOs, the rebellion was triggered by an order for part of the regiment to go to Cheju-do to help suppress the rebellion. Beginning at regimental headquarters while troops were boarding for the move, the insurrection was joined by SKLP leftist supporters. The rebels seized Yosu, then Sunchon (not to be confused with a village by the same name in North Korea), and prepared to seize other towns. Almost two hundred soldiers from the ROK 4th Regiment went over to the rebels, who by then numbered several thousand.

The Yosu rebellion fanned fires of public insecurity. The American 31st Infantry (−) in Seoul was put on alert in preparation to move to Yosu to engage the rebels. "Take no prisoners," was part of the field order issued by the regimental commander to his officers. However, the need for the 7th ID regiment was lifted when American C-47s ferried Korean troops into the area. Fortunately, Rhee's security forces got the situation in hand. By 25 October the rebellion had been suppressed. 1,200 police, soldiers and government officials had perished. Some 1,500 rebels were also killed, thousands of others escaped into the mountains to fight on as guerrillas.

As if the Cheju and the Yosu rebellions and other incidents did not represent enough of a challenge for the new republic, Rhee chose to rattle ROK sabers with talk of a "March North." Kim Il Sung rattled his own saber and spoke of reuniting Korea under North Korean control. Kim Il Sung turned his border commanders loose in May 1949, one month before the American 5th RCT covering force withdrew from Korea. The three most serious border actions that followed took place near Chunchon, at Kaesong, and on the Ongjin Peninsula. Any gains either side made during the heavy fighting were eventually erased. While Korean fought Korean during May 1949 for commanding ground near the border, the bulk of two ROK battalions defected to the North. Each side infiltrated guerrillas across the border. The DPRK was more successful than the ROK in supporting a revolutionary guerrilla base.

In late July 1949 the fledgling ROK Navy, trained by the U.S. Coast Guard, took advantage of Rhee's summit meeting at Chinhai (a ROK naval port) with Chiang Kai-shek to make itself known. ROK ships engaged the DPRK west-coast fleet and sank most of it at the mouth of the Taedong River in North Korean waters. There were brief eruptions of fighting on the Ongjin Peninsula later that year, and the number of guerrillas operating in the South during October grew to some 90,000. These incidents totaled almost 1,300.

GOODBYE, GOOD LUCK! WE WILL RETURN!

Under the command of Maj. Gen. William F. Dean, military governor and deputy to General Hodge, the 7th ID sailed from Korea at the end of 1948 and closed on Hokkaido and northern Honshu in January 1949. Before departing, some of its line officers advised their men to study the terrain, for they would return someday to fight for it. In Japan the division relieved the homeward bound 11th A/B Division on occupation duty that was as plush as Korea was hard. The under strength and under equipped division also gained officers and men from the airborne division, the 12th Cavalry Regiment, and from state side shipment of recruits to Japan.

Although Ambassador Muccio and President Rhee opposed the total withdrawal of American combat forces from Korea, the 5th RCT covering force was withdrawn on 29 June 1949 and transferred to Hawaii. Muccio was concerned that the ROK Army was neither sufficiently well trained or equipped. Total withdrawal would give the appearance of an American abandonment of Korea. The only American military presence left after June was the 500-man Korean Military Advisory Group (KMAG) under the command of Brig. Gen William L. Roberts and a detachment of 150 airmen who maintained USAF operations at Kimpo. MacArthur was free at last of responsibility for Korean matters. General Roberts reported directly to Ambassador Muccio, acting also as his advisor. Other members of KMAG acted as advisors to the eight under equipped ROK Army divisions that evolved from the former constabulary.

A speech delivered by Secretary of State Dean Acheson on 12 January 1950 before the National Press Club in Washington wrongfully implied that South Korea was outside the defensive perimeter of the U.S., the green lights flashed in Pyongyang and Moscow. Ambassador Muccio saw the possibility of invasion. He made forceful but unsuccessful recommendations to provide the ROKs with the weapons they had been denied. He wanted the ROK Army to be prepared to defend itself without the need for a guarantee of U.S. military protection. Time had run out. The DPRK and the USSR had been planning a North Korean invasion of the South since 6 March 1949, intent on reuniting Korea on Soviet terms. The honorable undertaking the U.S. had entered into with good intentions was marred by faulty vision, complacency, poor diplomatic and military judgments and inadequate determination. The United States withdrew American military forces from a divided nation soon to erupt into a civil war that could have been avoided.

U. S. Marines hold a memorial ceremony for their fallen comrades. June 21, 1951.

RED DRAGON
The SECOND ROUND
FACES OF WAR II

465 28 5242

Pat	N.	Westfall	38 607 374 (Korea)
First Name	MI	Last Name	Serial Number
None	3745	6 Sept 1925	M/Sgt, then S/Sgt
Nickname	MOS	Birthday	Grade / Rank
HM/31/7 & F/31/7		17 Sept '50- 15 June 1951	Temple Texas
Unit (s)		Duty Tour (s)	Home Town

Silver Star   Bronze Star, V Device   Combat Infantry Badge w/star   Purple Heart   UN Medal

Medals & Awards

Korean Campaign Service Medal, 6 stars   Natl Defense Service Medal, Oak Leaf Cluster   KWSM

'TRUMAN TROOPER' AND HIS SECOND WAR

In early July when the Korean war began, I was stateside in an 81 mm plat of the 42nd AIB at Ft Hood, TX. In common with other 'Truman Troopers' having WWI II service, I received orders for FECOM. On 20 July I was assigned to 31st Inf Regt, 7th Inf Div. Experienced on both 60mm and 81mm mortars in WW II, I was not surprised by assignment to 1st Plt, Hvy Mortar Co, 31st Regiment. I found all mortar principles were the same. The 4.2 mortar was just bigger, heavier and had greater range. Lt Wilson was plt ldr, SFC Courtney was plt sgt, I was 2d sqd ldr. I made both the Inchon west coast landing, and the second Iwon landing on the east coast in Oct with this group. Thanksgiving Day we were in a blocking position at the Fusen Reservoir. Receiving orders to move east of the Chosin Reservoir to replace the 5th Marines, we attempted to cross an intervening mountain range. The Japanese maps we used showed a passable road. Nearing the crest, the road which was gradually narrowing, almost disappeared. Our jeeps and 3/4 ton weapon carriers could back down what was now less than an oxcart trail, our heavy 6x6 ammo trucks with their trailers could not.

I was elected to round up all snow sleds, oxen and Korean papa-sans I could find. My squad supervised and guarded unloading of all our 4.2 ammo onto sleds and oxcarts. It was a slow process. We saved all the ammo and eventually got all vehicles back to a location where trucks could be turned around and reloaded. On arrival at the MSR, we were assigned to support the 2d Bn of the 31st. We brought up the rear of the column, eventually fighting our way into Koto-ri where we and 2d Bn / 31 were attached to "Chesty" Puller's 1st Marine Regt. While we waited for the 2d Bn to arrive my friend, Sgt Morris Haley sqd ldr 4th sqd, found a bathtub. He asked if I wanted a good hot bath. Deluxe luxury! Both our squads and others in the platoon as used that bath tub. Next morning at chow, Morris told me he dreamed our convoy was ambushed, but we made it out OK. I noticed his shoe pacs were on the wrong feet. I told him, "Some people think that's bad luck. "He remarked jokingly, "Nothing can happen, I would be out of uniform!"

As last unit in the column we had an ambush plan, odd number trucks took the left side of the road, even numbers, the right. Riding along that afternoon, rolled up in my sleeping bag, I was awakened by MG fire. We were pinned down until Lt Wilson had our bazooka gunner, Cpl Uhlrich, fire his 3.5 bazooka at the MG. He knocked it out with his 2d rocket. Word came to me that my friend Morris Haley had been hit and wanted to talk to me. He was dead by the time I got there. I knew people in WW II and later in Korea who were killed, but Haley's death hit me really hard. We made it into Koto-ri and joined the Marines, making the "March Back to the Sea." with them 12 December. We loaded aboard barges and put aboard ships in Hungnam harbor. We sailed back to Pusan, arriving on 20 December for an extensive period of reorganization and training of 120 replacements, bringing us up close to former strength. Lt Wilson was the surviving company officer. He acted as company commander until Major Walter Johnston took over. The major was with us for 6 weeks waiting for his rotation orders. He had been with KMAG for two years, in 1949 and '50. He rotated in mid March. Lt Wilson again became CO. It was still winter when we started north to retake South Korea from the Chinese who had driven us out of North Korea. I served with some very good men in Heavy Mortar Company, making lifetime friends who have never been forgotten.

Near the end of March I asked for a transfer. I had never seen eye to eye with Lt Wilson. Now he was permanent CO, I preferred to serve elsewhere. He forwarded my request to Reg't. It was approved. I went to F Co, known as "The Fighting Foxes," in my opinion, the best rifle company in the regiment. Company Commander was Lt Abbott. He was a leader that caused men to give that extra effort. There were 3 young sqd leaders, Nizack, Rosner and Paige, the 4th was William Guy, an AF officer in WW II. He had reenlisted as an NCO. He wanted nothing more than to be a sqd ldr. He was one of the best. I could write a book about this group. They had the courage and the knowledge which made my job as platoon sergeant an easy one. I was wounded in May '51 on Hill 300 by a hand grenade. The concussion ruptured my eardrums. I still have a hunk of that grenade above my left knee. The medic put a big bandage on the scratch above my knee. Carried on a stretcher to the aid station, I remember little except my head felt if someone was beating it with a stick. The doctor took off the knee bandage. He then chewed me out for coming to the aid station. He paid no heed to my head. Lucky I did not have a weapon! I climbed back up the hill, my head throbbing as if it would burst. I arrived just as the company was starting an 8 mile march to a rear reserve area. So much for the care I received. I hope it is better in today's army.

Above Left. Chinese soldiers cross the Soyang River under fire during their 5th phase offensive, May 1951. Photo from the Internet. Above Right. GIs of the 5th Regiment, 24th Division take another hill, March 1951. Photo from National Archives. Below. Lt. Gen. Mathew Ridgeway and Maj. Gen. Charles Palmer hold conference at Chipyong-ni, March 1951. shortly after the 1st Cav. broke through to the 23rd Regt. of the 2nd Division. Photo from the National Archives.

RED DRAGON
The SECOND ROUND
FACES OF WAR II

Donald	A.	Chase	RA 31 467 752
First Name	MI	Last Name	Serial Number
Don	1745	11 January 1926	Cpl
Nickname	MOS	Birthday	Grade / Rank
B Co 19th Inf Regt 24th Div		January 1951-June 1951	Natick, MA
Unit (s)		Duty Tour (s)	Home Town

Combat Inf Badge w/ star Bronze star w/ V,OLC Purple Heart,2 OLC GCM,2 Knots EAME, 2stars

Medals & Awards

WW II VM ACSM NDSM KCSM 5 stars UN Medal ROK PUC Korean War Service Medal

WOUNDED IN ACTION

We had been in the attack for 6 weeks, day after day, moving north in recovery of terrain lost to the Chinese and North Koreans after the Chinese intervened in November. The day of 13 March started in the usual way. My squad was in the lead as we made our way up a winding ridge line. We had not gone far when bullets spattered amongst us. Everyone hit the dirt, at the same time trying to locate the enemy. As in most of these previous encounters, there was not a heavy volume of fire, just enough to make everyone seek cover. It was obvious the enemy was leaving men behind in a delaying action. Even though we were pinned down, I had noticed a rocky ledge a short distance away. I received permission from our Lt to move there for a better look. I crawled up to the ledge and placed my BAR on it while I clambered up for a better look. I now had a clear view of the overall area. A short distance away was another ridge. I was looking it over, when an enemy soldier stepped out from behind a large rock. I didn't think he had seen me. Wrong. While turning to lay hands on my BAR, he shot me twice. One bullet went through my upper left thigh, leaving a hole as big as a baseball. The second splattered on a rock, 6 pieces of it went into my lower back. The effect was like being hit with a giant club.

I crawled off the ledge to get better cover and have my wounds attended. For a short time shock kept away pain, but soon agony set in. I was wounded high in the mountains and the aid station was far below, presenting an evacuation problem. Luckily, a group of Korean 'Chioggi' bearers had just dropped off a load of C-rations to the company. Led by a GI guide, four of these men carried my litter down to the aid station. I was bandaged, given a morphine shot and placed on a litter. Morphine dulled the pain so I was in pretty good spirits. I knew my wounds were not life threatening, yet would call for hospitalization and time for healing. To an infantryman it was almost like a paid vacation. We started mid morning, but darkness had now set in. I began to wonder if we would ever reach the aid station. The morphine wore off, my leg began throbbing. We reached the aid station about eleven PM. I had tears in my eyes from pain and joy. We had made it. I have never forgotten that trip, or figured out how my GI guide located the aid station.

Next stop was the Swedish Red Cross Hospital in Pusan. I don't know what circumstances sent me there, but it turned out to be a very pleasant hospital stay. In addition to Americans, there were Turks, British, Australian and French. There was no friction between the different nationalities. Those who could walk assisted those who could not. The special camaraderie that exists among soldiers was highly evident, regardless of nationality. The doctors, nurses and staff personnel were wonderful and the care we received was outstanding. Generally speaking, the atmosphere of most military hospitals is rather dark and gloomy but at the Swedish Hospital it was just the opposite. Even though every man there was suffering from wounds of different type and severity, and the daily change of dressings was painful, a certain level of lighthearted cheerfulness always prevailed. Much good natured bantering went on. This was especially true each morning when the nurse would give each man a penicillin shot. I think the general atmosphere of the hospital was set by the nurses, encouraged and abetted by the doctors and surgeons who staffed the hospital. A great bunch.

A very pleasant experience at this hospital was due to the kindness of a young Korean girl in the mess hall. One of her jobs was to serve the coffee, tea and cocoa. Americans preferred coffee, but the British preference was for tea, as was mine. The tea was usually gone by the time I reached the mess hall. Noticing my disappointment one day when the tea urn was empty, this young lady asked if I was British. I told her, "No, American, but tea is my favorite drink." In the days that followed, no matter when I showed up, there was always a mug of tea. She did this unobtrusively so it was not obvious I was getting special consideration. I was so touched that a friendship developed. When her work day was over, and when I could hobble, we would walk around the compound and watch the nightly movie together. She was a great companion and good friend. I have often wondered about her life after the war.

My thigh wound was healing but not enough skin was left to cover the area. To correct this, a chunk of muscle was cut out and wire stitches used to stretch the skin to cover the area. I had been in the hospital about six weeks and was anxious to rejoin my company. If a hospital stay is too prolonged, a soldier might be sent to a different outfit rather than back to his own unit. I didn't want to again be the "new guy." I asked my doctor to release me. He was reluctant, but finally did so. I guess the shortage of infantry helped.

Members of the 10th Combat Engineers of the 3rd Division operate this ferry on the Han River. March 16, 1951.

13th Combat Engineers of the 7th Division get ambushed while working on road near Ami-dong, Korea.
March 1, 1951.   Both photos from National Archives

RED DRAGON
The SECOND ROUND
FACES OF WAR II

Levi	O.	Haire	RA 14 285 585
First Name	MI	Last Name	Serial Number
Rabbit	3064	26 Dec 1930	Sgt
Nickname	MOS	Birthday	Grade / Rank
H&S Co 13th Engineer (C)Bn 7th Div		16 Sep '50- Jul '51	Morrow, GA
Unit (s)		Duty Tour (s)	Home Town
Good Conduct Medal	Korean Campaign Service Medal, 5 stars		Occupation Medal, Japan
Medals & Awards			
National Defense Service Medal	United Nations Service Medal		Korean War Service Medal

NO PURPLE HEART!

In May of '51 we were somewhere just above the 38th parallel awaiting rotation. We had been relieved of duty, our replacements had arrived. We had it easy, catching up on sleep, taking showers and eating warm food. One morning while at breakfast with Sgt Acey Lee Salyers, known to us all as "Wahoo," the subject of Seoul came up. We had never been to Seoul. Every time we came close we bypassed the city. We looked at each other, "What the hell, let's go take a look." We got up, rinsed our mess kits and stowed them away. We walked over to the truck park and started looking into gas tanks. I found one full of gas, we climbed in and off we went. We drove for some time. At times traffic going in our direction moved. At times we halted for traffic moving in the opposite direction.

We came to a long timber trestle bridge. Seemed as if half the engineers in Korea were working on it. The MPs directing traffic stopped us to let traffic move in the opposite direction. As we sat I said to Wahoo, "Someone's calling me." "Who the hell would be calling you way out here?" "Don't know, but somebody knows my name!" Up from the near end of the bridge came CWO Francis Luther. He had been our Bn Motor Officer in Japan. He returned stateside in 1949. His first question was, "Have you two made sergeant yet?" "Yes, we both have." We talked most of the afternoon about old times, who was still with the Bn and what we had done since he left. Late that afternoon, he said, "You two better get started back, you don't want to be caught out after dark." We returned to camp, parked the truck and, as chow was about over, rushed to retrieve our mess gear for supper. No one had missed the truck, or us either. No one asked where we had been. We never did get to see Seoul. CWO Luther was one of the VERY BEST!

A day or so later we were lying on our cots, still waiting for rotation orders to come in. Two excited Lts came running in to the tent. One of the motor road graders had broken something in the steering. Mechanics had determined a small part was broken, no spare part available. The grader was blocking the small "goat trail" the equipment had been working on. "The Chinese offensive is getting closer and closer. The Bn will lose the grader unless something can be done quickly." This all came tumbling out. They had been told "Wahoo," who was about to rotate, could probably figure a way to handle the problem. Wahoo was a legend in his own time in our 13th Engr Bn. He had an innate ability to cobble up repairs on engineer equipment, coupled with a knack for "field expedients" that set him apart from the rest of us. Wahoo told the Lts, "No problem, just drive it out." That grader operator and Wahoo had served together in Hawaii several years before. They hated each others guts. Lt said , "OK, come with us." Wahoo said "If he comes, I ain't goin'." He wanted Sgt Jewel White and me to go with him. "OK." We gathered up what we needed, loaded onto a truck and took off. The other operator jumped on the truck. Wahoo stopped and told the two Lts he wasn't going. After some hot words, I said to Wahoo, "Let the 'so and so' come. You don't have to use him." I was wrong. There were more harsh words, then away we went.

As we located the disabled grader we could hear fighting slowly moving toward us from across a small valley. Wahoo tied a chain from the right Pitman arm to the left side of the scarifier, same to the other side. He put me on the left, White on the right. We kept the chains tight until he came to sharp curve. One of us would pay out the chain, the other took up slack. We got to be pretty good at it, until we came to a sharp right hand curve where I lost my balance. I caught the leaning wheel shaft running down the side of the frame. Just then, Wahoo leaned the wheels in the opposite direction. This put the ring finger of my right hand between the U-joint and the frame, cutting it off at the first joint. I screamed. Wahoo stopped. With my left thumb on the pressure point of my right hand I managed to stop the bleeding, but boy, did it bleed! Our truck was behind us being driven by the first black replacement to our Bn. He sure was a no.1 driver. How he managed to get his truck around the grader on that "goat trail" was a miracle. He performed another miracle of speed in getting us alive to the Bn Aid Post. Scared the crap out of me. I was patched up, pieces of shattered bone were removed. Next morning 23 of us were placed in a C-47 and flown to Pusan. I was told I would have to go to Japan. I said, "No way, my orders for rotation are being cut back at my Bn!" I conned the Doc into fixing me up and letting me return to Bn before I should have been released. The finger was infected. It looked real bad. Finally the Doc gave me some ointment to dress the finger. He let me go so I could return to my company. I had been gone 33 days. A few days later, the same to Pusan but now on my way home. My finger took several months to heal. I now give only a crippled one finger salute of V for Victory!

Above. An enemy soldier hit with napalm makes an ugly 'face of war'. Photo by Roy Wilson. Upper Right. The 3ʳᵈ Ranger Co. 3ʳᵈ Division supported by armor, attacks north of the Imjin River, 11 April 1951. Photo, National Archives. Lower Left. Chinese POW's are transported to the rear. Photo by Roy Wilson. Below Right. Helicopters for evacuating the wounded was a new concept that proved invaluable. Many GIs are alive today because of a rapid trip to a Mobile Army Surgical Hospital (MASH) or a Navy Hospital Ship offshore. Photo from the National Archives.

RED DRAGON
The SECOND ROUND
FACES OF WAR II

James	H.	Appleton	115 8912 USMC
First Name	MI	Last Name	Serial Number
Appy	0311	26 August 1931	Cpl
Nickname	MOS	Birthday	Grade / Rank
Item Co 5th Marine Regt 1st MarDiv		Apr '51-Apr '52	Nashville, TN
Unit (s)		Duty Tour (s)	Home Town

Silver Star Commendation Medal w/ Combat V   Navy PUC, 1 star   USMC Good Conduct Medal

Medals & Awards

USN Occpn Medal, Eur clasp   NDSM   KCMS,3 battle stars   KSM   UN Medal   ROKPUC   KWSM

THE HORSESHOE AMBUSH

It was now mid June. I had been in Korea for two months and had adapted to my role as a fighting Marine in the mountainous terrain. We had been moving forward everyday for a month, right on the North Korean Army's ass, pushing him, hoping to get him in the open where we could really clobber him with artillery or close air support. It didn't happen, it became a dirty kind of war where we hurt him; he would sometimes turn, and on occasion, hurt us. We knew we were close on his heels because we would find warm coals from his fires of the night before, and other evidence of a hasty retreat. This morning we left our ridge positions and walked across the rice fields on the valley floor to begin climbing toward one of the major peaks in the 'Punch Bowl.' Our objective was the "Kansas Line." We were to consolidate there before resuming the advance. The climb was steep but we maintained a fast pace because the terrain we were in afforded excellent opportunities for ambush. However, we were a bit careless. We had not sent scouts to our front to check the trail. We had climbed about 500 meters when the point element topped a little landing in the trail, stopping for a short breather before resuming the climb. The North Koreans were waiting for us. They welcomed us with a classic horseshoe ambush.

The horseshoe ambush worked just dandy on us in Korea. It demonstrated again an age-old axiom, scouts must precede the advance of the main body to prevent surprise. The horseshoe ambush concept is simple. Men hidden in line on both sides of a trail, or road which the enemy will use in his advance. The rear arc or base of the horseshoe is a prepared position, bristling with weaponry, waiting for the enemy to move into the trap. When "the whites of his eyes" are visible, the trap is sprung. The men in ambush open fire from both sides, or in mountainous terrain perhaps one side only, while the base of fire at the back of the horseshoe hammers the approaching enemy from the front. As deadly in its effect today as in the bygone past. The only difference, guns are used, not arrows or spears. In war, only men change. Some tactics are as immutable as the sands of time. We live and learn anew.

I was seventh man back from point when all hell broke loose. The trail was filled with enemy fire from ahead and each side. We could hear on both sides of the trail the unmistakable sound of Russian made 'Burp Guns.' These weapons could dump 1200 rounds per minute at you, literally throwing up a wall of bullets if a number of guns fired simultaneously. Up ahead I could hear the deep throated chatter of a Russian made Maxim heavy machine gun chewing away at any target its bullets could find. In my mind, the noise and fury lasted an hour, in actuality it was a brief 30 to 45 seconds. In that short expanse of time and in a short killing stretch of 10 to 15 yards, the first six men were hit. Two died instantly. The next four were repeatedly hit by burp gunfire. Some of their wounds were from the big machine gun at the head of the horseshoe. I was the seventh man and did not get a scratch. I could not help but think of the phrase, "Fate is the Hunter." I crawled back down the trail to meet the plt sgt who asked, "How many have been hit?" I told him, "All of them but me. The first two guys on point are dead. The rest of them up there are wounded." The plt sgt told the next few guys to accompany me to get the wounded back down trail to cover of some rocks where the Navy Corpsman could work on them.

Our plt sgt sent me back to recover all rifles I could find. By my third 'visit' to the ambush point, the enemy had probably pulled back. However, taking no chances, I crawled up to where the point had been hit. A few minutes later I crept back, dragging six M-1 rifles. Sixty lbs is quite a load to drag. The Skipper sent a party to scout out an area where a chopper could come in to pick up our wounded. Litter parties were selected while the Corpsman tended the wounded. In about half an hour the scout party radioed to tell us they had found a nearby spot suitable for a Medevac chopper to land. A fire team was sent to secure the area to make sure that a nearby enemy would not be able to interfere with the pickup of our ambush casualties. One of the men in the security party threw a smoke grenade to let the chopper pilot know the area was safe for him to come in. The chopper set down safely. The wounded were soon on their way either to an Navy Aid Station (equivalent an Army MASH hospital), or a hospital ship off the coast of Japan.

Our company had "stepped in shit." We were way out on a limb in the position where we had been ambushed. No other outfit was in the immediate area close enough to support us. We dug in, made perimeter for the night, filled with trepidation, not knowing what was coming next. During the night grenades were lobbed down at us from above, but nothing serious. We lived to fight another day.

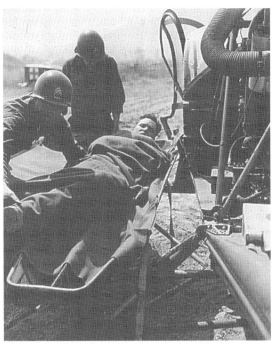

A wounded G.I. from the 24th Regiment awaits evacuation to the aid station. This photo seems to say 'ammo up and wounded to the rear'. Feb. 16, 1951.

A wounded G.I. is loaded on a helicopter at the 21st Regt. collection station near the 38th parallel for evacuation to a base hospital, April 3, 1951.

The personnel and equipment used to save lives is shown here at the Headquarters of the 8225th MASH. Oct. 14, 1951. Use of the helicopter for quick evacuation of casualties was truly a blessing.   All photos from the National Archives

RED DRAGON
The SECOND ROUND
FACES OF WAR II

Lulan	E.	Gregg	RA 16 232 446
First Name	MI	Last Name	Serial Number
Lue	014	5 June 1929	M/Sgt then S/Sgt
Nickname	MOS	Birthday	Grade / Rank
8076Mobile Army Surgical Hospital		21July '50- 18 June '51	Omer, MI
Unit (s)		Duty Tour (s)	Home Town
Korean Campaign Service Medal, 5 Stars		Good Conduct Medal	Occupation Medal, Japan
Medals & Awards			
National Defense Service Medal		United Nations Service Medal	Korean War Service Med

MASH

Mash! Now a part of Americana as the title of one of the most popular TV shows of all time. It was the unit in which I served during the Korean War. My story is intertwined with the 8076th Army Mobile Surgical Hospital from which many episodes of the TV show were taken. The reader will recognize some of them from the real life occurrences described during my tour of Korean duty. I was a young Regular Army soldier, enlisting shortly after my 17th birthday. I had dropped out of school at age 15. At enlistment, I had a two year work history as a deck hand on the US Army Engineer hopper dredge, General George G. Meade. One of my reasons for enlisting was the realization that quitting school was a big mistake. I knew I could get my high school equivalency through the Univ. of Maryland extension school and then pursue a college degree through the same extension school at the Univ. of Maryland.

I enlisted 5 Oct 1946. Over the next 18 months, after graduation from Wheel & Track Electricians School, I served as a mechanic, then as an instructor in 1st & 2d echelon mechanics for OCS candidates at the Ft Benning Infantry Center. In April '48 I transferred as mechanic to 49th General hospital in Tokyo. While there I continued my college curricula at the Univ. of Maryland extension school and attended Army Translator & Interpreter School. In late June after outbreak of war, I was transferred to the 155th Station Hospital in Yokokama where the fabled 8076th MASH organized for Korea. Two Medical Service Officers, 12 doctors, 12 nurses and 58 EM made up the personnel roster. I was the Motor Sergeant. We sailed for Pusan 21 July on USNS Sgt George D. Keathly. A typhoon caused 2 vehicles to break loose. It took a couple of hair raising hours to tie them down again. In Pusan we uncrated equipment and traded items we did not need for stretchers which we knew we would need. That same night we loaded aboard flat cars, arriving at Kumchon the next day. We found ourselves on a siding next to a fully loaded ammo train. Our engine had ben taken off our train for reasons unknown to us. Fighting was going on. We were drawing small arms fire. We located an engineer, threatening him with dire harm if he did not hook up our cars and haul us out of there. Corps HQ did not know what to do with us, but finally sent us south to Taegu. Fighting was going on there also. We went south to Miryang to set up the hospital to receive patients.

Once, while transporting supplies from Pusan to Miryang, we were ambushed on a hair pin curve, MGs firing at us both front and rear. Unable to move, my guard had a bright idea to use one of the oxygen bottles as a missile. I turned the truck so the rear faced the direction we were headed. We placed the tank between some cases, I knocked off the head with my rifle butt. The tank zoomed, skittering straight at the machine gun, scattering the gun crew in panic. Turning the truck around, we hightailed it out of there while I fired my M-1 at the regrouping gun crew. At Miryang, we furnished forward hospital support for all Naktong perimeter troops except the 25th Div which was supported by 8063rd MASH. I don't recall where, but one day a helicopter trying to land created a spiral wind collapsing the nurses' shower tent. That gave rise to the scene in "MASH" where everyone saw a naked "Hot Lips" trying frantically to locate her clothing. On average, we could set up sixteen, 100 foot long sectional tents and be operating in less than 2 hours, and have the entire hospital functioning in 4 hours. Once we tore down the entire hospital and had it on trucks in an hour and 15 minutes.

As the North Koreans fled north, 8076 Mash followed our pursuing troops. 28 Oct we set up at Haeju in what had been a Russian Red Cross Hospital. All personnel must have left by the back door as we came in the front. They fled in a motor launch. Women were still strapped in OB chairs in the act of giving birth! In Pyongyang while searching the premises of the Univ of North Korea's Teaching Hospital, we found human cadavers. The formaldehyde had not been changed recently, flesh was falling from the bones. Day before Thanksgiving we moved to Kunu-ri and located a big field to handle C-47s. As one C-47 took off, another landed to be packed with wounded GIs. We had evacuated all but 50 patients. Doctors were still operating while all this went on. The last 50 GIs and the rest of MASH personnel were evacuated under care of one doctor, two corpsmen and myself. We lost no one in that move. Leaving the site, we were cut off by Chinese forces on horseback, some blowing bugles. We were saved by men of the 2d Div Reconn company and the 2d Military Police company. If not for them, we would not have evacuated Kunu-ri alive. Several of them gave their lives to save ours. Reaching Pyongyang, nurses were evacuated by air to Taegu. They rejoined us 7 Dec when we set up at Kaesong.

Above Left. Corsairs circle the carrier USS Valley Forge waiting for a flight to take off. Above. Panther jets with folded wings crouch on the snow covered deck of the USS Princeton. Left. The Marines unload at Wonsan from LCVPs. October 26, 1950. Below, Bottom. The USS Missouri fires its 16 inch guns at Chongjin, North Korea, only 39 miles from the Manchurian border, October 21, 1950.

All photos from the National Archives.

RED DRAGON
The SECOND ROUND
FACES OF WAR II

Charles	L.	Grove	568 36 26 USN
First Name	MI	Last Name	Serial Number
Chuck	Electrician	11 Jan 1930	EMP 3
Nickname	MOS	Birthday	Grade / Rank
USS Ajax (AR6)		Sept 1950-Dec 1951	Long Beach, CA
Unit (s)		Duty Tour (s)	Home Town
Korean Campaign Service Medal		Navy Occupation Medal	National Defense Service Medal
Medals & Awards			
United Nations Service Medal		Republic of Korea, Korean War Service Medal	

THE SHIP THAT HIT A MINE

I suppose war may be a glorious pursuit if you are a soldier of fortune. But for normal folks, the horrors of war eclipse the glory. And the horrors of war are a subjective phenomena. For each individual, it depends on the intensity and duration of his exposure and, of course, to whomever and whatever it happens. Okay, let me try to recapture your attention. I'm just an average guy who joined the US Naval Reserve as a teenager, mainly for the fun and games and the annual cruise we eagerly anticipated each year. A couple of years into my hitch something happened. In late June of 1950 came the Korean "police action." I was called up for active duty.

I was activated, but not motivated. In September of 1950 I was assigned to the *USS Ajax (AR6)*. The Ajax was a repair ship, a floating machine shop whose mission was to drop anchor in a safe harbors and administer repairs to tired and wounded fighting ships. This meant, for the duration of my enlistment, alternating between Yokosuka and Sasebo, Japan. So, for the most part, my active duty for which I 'earned' my medals was a virtual extension of the fun and games I enjoyed stateside, but with an exotic oriental twist. Indeed, the only time I ever engaged the enemy in combat was the time I had to duke it out with an obnoxious sailor in a Yokosuka pub. The closest I came to being a casualty, wounded or killed in action was after a night of merrymaking in another pub in Sasebo. I was queuing up with dozens of happy sailors, waiting to pass through the gate to the boat dock. Everybody was laughing and joking as they waited. I spotted another open gate that was closer. I broke ranks and went for it.

"Hey, you,!" someone hollered, "Go through this gate." It was the Marine guard at the gate.
"This one's closer," I said, staying on my course. Whereupon the guard pulled his .45 and showed me the big hole in it.
"I said, go through THIS gate!"

I remembered President Truman's celebrated remark about the Marines being "the US Navy's police force." Seeing no point in letting this war weary jar-head earn another medal at my expense, I said, "Yes, sir!" and graciously complied with his request.

On 12 June 1951 I finally had my glimpse at the reality of war. The destroyer *Walke (DD723)* was steaming along in the Sea of Japan, part of a carrier task-force screen. She hit a drifting Russian built mine inflicting extensive damage to the ship, portside aft, killing 25 men and injuring 36. The stricken vessel was brought to Sasebo and placed in dry dock. Some of the crew were still aboard, although the wounded had been evacuated for medical care earlier in the day. I was one of the men drafted as a working party to go on board the Walke to unload ammunition from its magazines for storage in an ammo dump about a quarter of a mile away.

But first, I had to view the damage, just to satisfy my own curiosity. I found the compartments which had been damaged by the mine explosion. I frankly was not prepared for what I saw. There was a huge gaping hole in the hull, and much of the deck area in the compartment where I stood was gone. A sailor was sitting on a bunk by the bulkhead opposite the hole, just staring into space, a dazed, almost vacuous look on his face. I said to him, "What are you doing here, Mac? You should be topside, you're in Sasebo at dockside." He answered me as if I were not there, "I was just lying here, off watch, talking to my buddy over there, then a blast, my buddy, the other guys, bunks and all, all gone. He looked at me, now recognizing my presence, "I don't know how or why I survived."

A corpsman came in, wearing rubber gloves. Whistling nervously, he carried a white canvas bucket. He inspected the overhead, tops of lockers and bunks, picking little stringy things up and dropping them into his bucket. When he finished in that compartment, he took his grisly harvest and went on to the next compartment to resume his ghoulish task, still whistling in his own personal graveyard. I went out and joined the working party which is what I should have done in the first place. I fully realized for the first time that war was not fun, games and fellowship of an annual cruise with one's buddies. It was death, with not even a body to bury at sea.

As I write this memoir, over fifty years later, the profound sense of desolation I felt then still remains a palpable thing within me.

Above. This classic picture shows some serious Marines involved in 'house cleaning' in Seoul, Korea.   A very hazardous chore. September 20, 1950.   Photo from the National Archives.

It was always 'open season' in Korea and this Marine has just bagged a North Korean soldier.   Photo Mel Boland.

Not quite all the comforts of home but he looks like he is 'coping' pretty well. In the Chunchon area. After Chinese spring offensive.   Photo from Melvin Boland.

RED DRAGON
The SECOND ROUND
FACES OF WAR II

Melvin	James	Boland	1066294 USMC
First Name	MI	Last Name	Serial Number
Mel	0311	25 April 1930	Pfc
Nickname	MOS	Birthday	Grade / Rank
B/1/1/1st Mar Div		April 1951-May 1952	St Louis, MO
Unit (s)		Duty Tour (s)	Home Town

Korean Campaign Service Medal,3stars   Nat'l Defense Service Medal   Korean Peace Medal

Medals & Awards

Navy Presidential Unit Citation   United Nations Service Medal   ROK Presidential Unit Citation

WHEN YA GOTTA GO, YA GOTTA GO

It was in late June or early July 1951. I'm not sure, dates are a bit hazy in my mind after 50 years. I and my foxhole buddy, Dale Cook, were dug in on near the crest of a large hill east of Chunchon Korea, near the 38th parallel. It was about 5 miles across the valley to the next range of hills where the Chinese positions were located. Shortly after daylight, the Chinese began 'sniping' at us with what sounded like a 76mm recoilless rifle. For sure, it was a flat trajectory "Whiz-Bang." When the round went by, we knew it was a high velocity weapon. You could tell by the "whistle." The rounds either hit the side of the hill where we were dug in, or kept on going to give some of those in the rear areas a taste of what it was like on the line. Everything was quiet the second morning we were on the hill. I told Dale I felt like a cup of cocoa. "Even the Queen's men don't have cocoa," I remarked, "They have to be satisfied with tea." I mashed the round block of cocoa from my breakfast C-ration, poured it into my canteen cup, filled it with water and began to warm it up over a small can of 'liquid heat.' It was soon hot, almost too hot to drink. I lifted it gingerly to my lips. As I did so, the first 76mm round of the day came in, right at us. In a mad dash, I scrambled back into our foxhole, spilling hot cocoa all over Dale.

When the Chinese gunner finally decided to halt his daily pot shots, we had a chance to dig our shoulders out of our helmets. Dale looked over at me and said very seriously, "Boland, they saw the steam from your cocoa." I spent the rest of the day trying to convince him that it was impossible for the gunner, or anyone for that matter who was five miles away, even using binoculars, to see the small amount of steam from my cup of cocoa. Even though I did not fully convince him, he put up no argument the next morning when I tried again to start my foxhole day with a bracing cup of hot cocoa. You guessed it, I don't have to tell you what happened! My cup of hot cocoa gave Dale another hot bath of sticky cocoa. After that, all the talking in the world could not have convinced him, even if our Division Commander, MGen Thomas, had passed the word! He was firmly convinced that the Chinese had spotted the steam from a distance of 5 miles away. I tried to tell him that it was me, out in the open warming my cocoa, not the steam from the cocoa that the gunner had spotted. It was a useless. Dale and I were foxhole buddies for many months after that. He carried the conviction that steam from cocoa was a dead give-away. Anytime I fired up a cup of cocoa, Dale left our foxhole to go elsewhere.

While in that same position, the Chinese gunner persisted. He seemed to take a vindictive delight in taking shots in our vicinity. After I had spilled the second cup of hot cocoa over Dale, I stayed in our foxhole in daylight. That gunner was too damned good. I didn't care to risk my hide further to his accuracy and unlimited supply of ammo. We had now been in the same position for three days. As with most of humanity, my body had long ago reached a state of regularity with the elimination function common to all mammals. Every morning my "urge" was as regular as clockwork. My problem in taking care of the "urge" over the past three days was an alert Chinese gunner. He was active from daylight to dusk. I had gained great respect for his abilities. I no longer challenged him by leaving our foxhole. The third morning at my usual time, I had reached a point of desperation. I told Dale, "I gotta go! I'll have to stay in our foxhole while I attend to the call of nature." Dale said to me in all seriousness, "Boland, you'll just have to get yourself killed. You are not going to use this hole to relieve yourself." He damn well meant it, too. I began timing the interval between rounds.

There seemed to be 8 seconds between each round. I had a huge wad of paper in my hand. I knew I would have little time for delicacy of manners. I worked my fatigues down around my ankles, ready to spring out of our foxhole. When I heard the next round, I was out of that foxhole with the speed of a cheetah and the leap of a gazelle. I moved about five feet away from our foxhole, stuck my behind down hill and let fly. It sounded like a small explosion. I used one hand to pull my fatigues part way up my legs. The other hand with the wad of paper was busy doing what I told it to do. Finished with my wad of paper, I tossed it downhill. I used that hand, now free of encumbrance, to pull the other leg of my fatigues around my waist while simultaneously emulating a base runner sliding home, just in time to escape the gunner's next round. I sang the Hallelujah Chorus with deep feeling! Handel would have been proud.

Dale was laughing. I had to join in. Even then it was funny, but also damn serious. Literally, my butt was on the line! We talked about entering "Boland's Eight Second Bowel Movement" into the Guiness Book of World Records but decided there was no apt category.

Above. A grenade battle by members of the 15th Regiment of the 3rd Division near Uijong-bu, 23 March 1951. Below. A machine gun position south of the Imjin River, 26 April 1951. Both photos courtesy Roy Wilson Top Right Another hill is taken with an ever increasing body count.. Right. A G.I. collects a live one. Lower Right. A wounded soldier is placed on a litter, then begins the race against time to get him to an aid station.

Three Photos from National Archives.

RED DRAGON
The SECOND ROUND
FACES OF WAR II

Donald	A.	Chase	RA 31 467 752
First Name	MI	Last Name	Serial Number
Don	2745	11 January 1926	Sgt
Nickname	MOS	Birthday	Grade / Rank
B Co 19th Inf Regt 24th Inf Div		January 1951-June 1951	Natick, MA
Unit (s)		Duty Tour (s)	Home Town
Combat Inf Badge w/star	Bronze Star w/ V,OLC	Purple Heart, 2 OLC	GCM 2 knots NDSM
Medals & Awards			
EAME,2stars	WWII VM ACSM KCMS,5stars	UN Medal	ROK PUC KWSM

PURPLE HEART TWO

19 April 1951, I reported back to my company. What immediately struck me was the number of men I did not recognize. The routine had not changed. We were still in the advance, so it was easy for me to pick up where I had left off. Thankfully, someone else was lugging that heavy BAR. After a few days, the routine changed. We were ordered to fall back quickly. The enemy had launched a major offensive. We retreated hurriedly, yet in an orderly manner. Still weak from my hospital stay, the first day was at such a fast pace I could not keep up. I and two other men were told, "Do the best you can. Try to catch up before nightfall." As we were all scared of capture, we had incentive to keep moving. We met another straggler carrying his .45 Colt in hand, the only survivor of his tank crew. He told us he would shoot himself before being captured. Fate that day was with us. Just before dark we came on to my squad digging in across a ridge line. They had been designated as a blocking force. The others continued on to find their units.

The squad was spread out across a ridge line. Our orders were not to leave our position until notified. Tension built. As the enemy drew near we heard the clank, rattle of equipment and sing song voices. The scent of garlic wafted to us on the night air. They were nearby. A shot rang out to our rear. Within seconds, the platoon runner crouched down and whispered "It's time to leave." He led us to the platoon, but our sqd ldr did not join us. We never heard from him again. I don't remember how long the retreat lasted. Days and nights blended together. We reached an area where we dug deep foxholes and connecting trenches. All foxholes soon had overhead cover. Barbed wire was strung. C-ration cans with small pebbles were hung on it to rattle if disturbed. Every day our P-51 Mustangs bombed, strafed and napalmed the enemy, keeping them at bay during the day. At night enemy attacks were repelled by the light of flares from our mortars. We began to feel we could handle anything the Chinese threw at us. Replacements came to fill our depleted ranks. Most of the men were solid, but one new guy in my squad was a 'Nervous Nellie.' He should not have been sent to a line outfit. One night his fear caused him to shoot at a noise. The noise was from a nearby foxhole, one of our own men. Daylight revealed him slumped in his foxhole, dead, his brains leaking onto his chest. It was a dreary, grisly sight in the midst of pouring rain.

After a couple of weeks we took up the offensive. The grinding march over mountain ridges started anew. We would drive the enemy off the high ground during the day, at night dig a defensive perimeter to repel counter attack. Next day, do it all over again. It was a relentless grind, punishing us almost as much as the enemy. One day lying on the ground under mortar fire, a shell exploded nearby, slamming a chunk of rock onto my left hand. It swelled twice normal size. I lost the use of it for several days. We had now been in continuous offensive action for a month. Eyeing men around me, I saw emaciated, ragged, bearded, dirty, smelly zombies, operating on will power alone. Nevertheless, the day would brighten and spirits lift when the Chioggi bearers arrived with mail and hot coffee. It was now early June. The weather had turned broiling hot. Drinking water was short, a miserable time. Our attack this day was up a ridge that had been napalmed that morning. Everywhere in sight, scattered, were dead Chinese looking like over grilled hot dogs, seared, charred bodies with body juices leaking out. It was a stomach churner, even to combat hardened infantry veterans.

The squad was down to four men. I saw my sqd ldr go down. He had been hit in the knee. I called, "Medic." We three resumed the attack. Reaching the crest, I crouched behind a blasted tree stump wondering what to do next, when something slammed into my neck with terrific force. My mouth flew open, a sheet of blood sprayed out. Momentarily stunned and paralyzed, I could not move arms or legs but did not lose consciousness. When the Medic reached me I refused morphine, feeling I had a better chance if I could, to a degree, control how I was handled. I was loaded onto a poncho stretched over two poles as a makeshift litter. I don't know how long it took to get me to the aid station. The examining doctor knew right away my neck was broken. Sand bags were placed on each side of my head to prevent movement. He told me I was lucky to be alive. In Japan I was put in a head to waist cast which eventually allowed restoration of feeling in arms and legs. Doctors gathered at my bedside in hospitals in Korea, Japan, Hawaii, Texas and Massachusetts to discuss the best way to remove the bullet from my neck. After many bedside consultations at Massachusetts Murphy General Hospital, the bullet which had gone in below my chin was taken out through my neck. I keep it today as a souvenir. I recovered full use of all my faculties and returned to active duty. God Bless those wonderful army surgeons who cared for me.

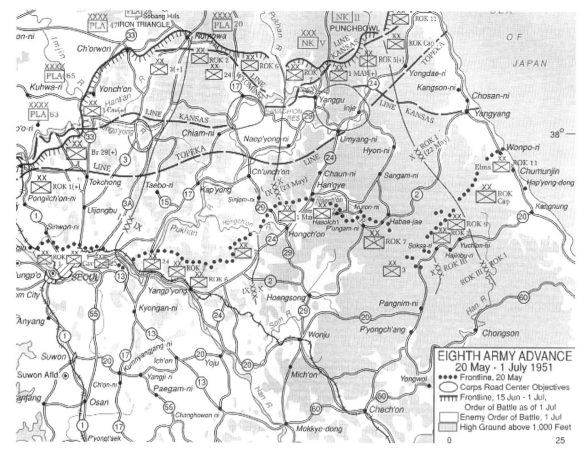

The 8th Army battle lines from May to July 1951.   Map from Ebb and Flow.

3rd Division troops in the attack in the Sobang Hills. This was a hot corner of the Iron Triangle. July 3-5, 1951.
Photo from the National Archives.

F9F-2 s Panthers take off from the USS Valley Forge for a ground support mission. Photo from National Archives.

RED DRAGON
The SECOND ROUND
FACES OF WAR II

James	H.	Appleton	115 8912 USMC
First Name	MI	Last Name	Serial Number
Appy	0311	28 August 1931	Cpl
Nickname	MOS	Birthday	Grade / Rank
Item Co 5th Marine Regt 1st MarDiv		Apr '51-Apr '52	Nashville, TN
Unit (s)		Duty Tour (s)	Home Town

Silver Star Commendation Medal w Combat V   Navy PUC,1star   USMC Good Conduct Medal

Medals & Awards

USN Occpn Medal w/Eur clasp NDSM KCMS,3 battle stars KSM UN Medal ROKPUC KWSM

IN LINE OF FIRE

Judeo-Christian philosophy teaches of a life after death. The concepts of "Heaven," an Eden-like savannah where the 'good' dwell in a land of "milk and honey," and "Hell," where the 'bad' abide in the depths of a fiery, eternal furnace. Which abode one will abide in an 'after life' is pre-determined by one's moral conduct during life. Any combat veteran who has survived the crucible of a close up, intense firefight with an enemy intent on killing you, will maintain he has seen the face of hell while alive. War is a surprising experience for a citizen soldier at age 19, a few short months before was a naive American teenager. Boys became men overnight.

North Korea, just north of the 38th on a hot July afternoon in 1951. We had just gained the summit of a ridge on the south rim of the Punchbowl. This was a ring of hills, the lips of an ancient volcano. Held in the cradle of the old crater was a vista of beautiful gardens and small straw-thatched huts, as yet unscathed by war. With no enemy contact, we figured when we reached the crest we would dig in a defensive perimeter and relax for a day or so. No such luck. Our Skipper, Capt Neil Dimond, radioed Bn for instructions. The Skipper was ordered to bear east on the ridge and take position about 500 yards from where we were. Our mood was jovial.

We had dropped our outguard, a very dangerous thing to do in a combat area. We had gone about 200 yards, reaching the summit. We came upon a small ridge lowering into a long saddle toward another knoll about 100 yards away. As our point group of 15 marines came off the knoll onto the saddle, Eden turned in to Hell. Transformation was instantaneous. One minute a peaceful cake walk; the next, Satan's trident was stabbing us with noise, smoke, smell of cordite and sulfur, the zing of bullets several feet away. Closer to my ears, bullets snapped like cracking whips and buzzed like angry hornets. Rifle and burpgun fire reach a crescendo, the chattering roar of a Russian Maxim 7.62mm MG spouts bullets kicking up clods of dirt. The thud and crashing bang of exploding grenades make for a cacophony of destruction. This must be what hell sounds, smells and feels like. I dove for cover, off the ridge.

Suddenly it stopped. The Skipper ordered Sgt Pattillo, a Texas marine, to bring up his MG section and return fire. As he started to set up his gun, the enemy gunner with his Maxim MG stitched a pattern in Pattillo's chest, killing him and mortally wounding the ass't gunner. The rest of the section finally got the MG set up to return fire at the enemy across the saddle. Our three tube 60mm mortar section lobbed shells into the enemy position. In a few minutes all was quiet. We figured the enemy had been knocked out. The Skipper sent out a small probe patrol to check out the situation. Twenty yards out they came under heavy fire, one man was hit. With help he made it back to our position. Our Arty(Artillery FO) called an artillery strike. As we were within 100 yards of the enemy it was a chancy proposition. When the shells came crashing in I curled into a small ball. It is amazing how the human body can shrink in size when under fire! He zeroed in and calling for "Fire for Effect." They were very accurate. All fire hit on enemy positions. Another probe patrol was sent out. Same heavy fire greeted them. A nearby Forward Air Controller, himself a Navy pilot, agreed to call in an air strike. He warned it would be a tight fit. A 500 yard margin was usually stipulated as a safety zone. We put out 'Air Panels' of red plasticized canvas ahead of our position. In they came, a flight of Navy-Marine Grumman F-9-F Panther jets, loaded for bear.

First making a verification pass, they howled in across the enemy ridge like Irish Banshees, MGs guns blazing, 20mm cannons firing, their 2.5" rockets scorching down at enemy positions. They finished with a friendly 'Wing Wave' at us before returning to their carrier. Another probe patrol met with heavy fire. It was now almost dark. The Skipper checked with Bn who advised we button up for the night. Tomorrow ,"How" Company would pass through us and try to root out this bunch of die hard gooks we couldn't seem to touch.

We spent a sleepless, watchful night on alert for an attack that did not materialize. In the morning "How" Company walked up the ridge without firing a shot. The enemy had steamed his breakfast rice in fire pits before making his leisurely departure, leaving the hot coals behind to tell us he had not been long gone. That morning on patrol, I scouted the area where they had been dug in. It was no wonder they had not been hurt. They were dug in deep, in little 'spider holes,' tunneled down and under. There were numerous small bunkers covered with heavy timbers, several feet of dirt on top, all well camouflaged. The next day I went on a long patrol, down into the Punchbowl and across to the hills on the other side. We ran into no enemy activity and were not shot at. It was a nice day.

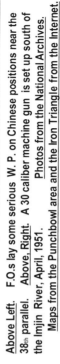

Above Left.   F.O.s lay some serious W. P. on Chinese positions near the
38th parallel.   Above, Right.   A 30 caliber machine gun is set up south of
the Imjin River, April, 1951.   Photos from the National Archives.
Maps from the Punchbowl area and the Iron Triangle from the Internet.

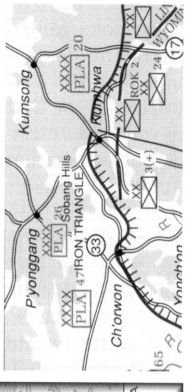

RED DRAGON
The SECOND ROUND
FACES OF WAR II

James	H.	Appleton	115 8912 USMC
First Name	MI	Last Name	Serial Number
Appy	0311	28 August 1931	Cpl
Nickname	MOS	Birthday	Grade / Rank
Item Co 5th Marine Regt 1st MarDiv		Apr '51-Apr '52	Nashville, TN
Unit (s)		Duty Tour (s)	Home Town

Silver Star   Commendation Medal w Combat V   Navy PUC,1star   USMC Good Conduct Medal

Medals & Awards

USN Occpn Medal w/Eur clasp   NDSM   KCMS,3 battle stars   KSM   UN Medal   ROKPUC   KWSM

THE MEAT GRINDER

Early July 1951. For 60 days we had been in hot pursuit of the elusive 'ragtag' remnants of a once proud North Korean Peoples Army. Item Company had been hard on their tail for two weeks. However, they still had fangs. They taught us a salutary lesson two days before we pulled in to dig defensive positions here on the south rim of "The Punch Bowl." In the push north we and the 7th Division of X Corps had successfully retaken all of the real estate in South Korea in our sector. We were again fighting Chinese and North Korean Communist Armies in North Korea. This new position was part of the "Kansas Line," a phase line stretching across most of the Korean Peninsula which, depending partly on the tactical situation, but more consequentially on the political situation, could either be a fall back defensive line, or a consolidation line for regrouping prior to a continued attack northward. Politicians and generals would decide the issue shortly. In the meantime we dug in, patrolled and waited. We waited about 30 days before receiving word that our Bn would be relieved by a ROK Infantry Division. Next day we walked off, away from those hills we had struggled so hard for in many small battles and fire fights in the push north. Trucks took us to a wide valley near the little town of Wontong- ni.

We arrived about noon filled with joy, anticipating of 30 days peaceful R&R. Before we had a chance to even dig a ditch around our pup tents, a line of MTS Bn trucks rolled in. We were given 30 minutes to roll packs and climb aboard. We learned we were headed back to the MSR to "plug a hole" in the line. As we climbed aboard, each man was handed two Mark 2 Fragmentation hand grenades. The .50 cal MG ring mount on each truck was manned by a gunner at the ready. This was obviously going to be a very serious business. The trucks took off like a turpentined cat on a dusty narrow dirt road headed northward. After a short ride of less than 15 miles, the trucks stopped. We piled out to be greeted by our new Bn CO, Major Morse Holiday. He was a diminutive, stocky little Mormon in perfect physical shape, 'Gung Ho' to the core. He set a blistering pace as he led us to the base of a low ridge shaped like an L. The base of the L hung down to the south, while the long stem ran east to west. The Major deployed How Co on the left of the stem of the 'L', George Co on the right of the stem of the 'L,' while Item Co was strung out on the base of the 'L.' The 'L' shape was in a perfect position to block off a long road coming from the north. The road for about a quarter of a mile was a straight shot, not a curve in it, as it headed right at us. For that quarter mile, the road was an infantry officer's nightmare. On the east side of the road was a perpendicular drop off, the west side rose up in a sheer bluff. It turned out to be a nightmare for an entire North Korean Bn.

All six Bn Heavy MGs were set to fire directly up the road. Our 12 LMGs were set up to supplement fire of the Heavy MGs. Wpns Co set their 81mm mortars to fire anyplace on the road. Our Arty FO set his fire concentrations to seal off the far end of the road, denying the enemy any possibility of retreat. We sat back to wait. Waiting, we learned what had happened. The North Koreans had broken through an Army 2d Division position. Unless stopped, North Koreans would have an open road southward to disrupt supply and communications lines, and to destroy supply depots and POL centers. They had to be stopped. We had been selected because we were immediately available in our "R&R" rest area to be "stoppers." By 1900 hours we were dug in, all set, and ready for action.

About 2200 hours the North Koreans appeared, marching in column of twos on both sides of the road. Gunners of our Heavy MGs held fire until the enemy was about 50 feet in front of them. When the 6 heavies and 12 lights opened up, firing straight up the road, the roar was deafening. Tracer rounds, one bullet out of five, made an eerie half light, bouncing off the bluff, ricochetting off the road and enemy equipment. I was around the corner of the L and could hear the mayhem going on. Artillery rounds came in, sealing off the back door. The MGs in awesome ambush had set up a killing field, chewing up bodies, tearing flesh, ending life. The carnage went on most of the night. Any movement set the guns to roaring again. About 0400 in the morning it seemed to be over. As the sun broke through trees to the east we saw the grisly effect of our murderous ambush. We were ordered to saddle up and move north up "Butcher's Alley" to scout and reconn the Army position to the north which had been overrun. As we moved through the abbatoir I could not help but recall the blood and gore of a slaughter house I had once seen when I accompanied my uncle to a place where he took pigs from his farm to be killed. We were later told we had 'eliminated' to the last man, a NK Bn of 454 soldiers. The sight I saw when I came to the scene of the breakthrough was also a slaughter house, but that is another story of my year in Korea.

Above. Gen. MacArthur and Gen. Ridgeway visit the troops near the 38th parallel. Apr. 3, 1951. Right. 7th Division troops prepare to assault another hill, near Chunchon, June 1951. Photos from Archives.

Lower Right. Proudly showing the 2nd Bn., 17th Regt. Hqs. 'Home of the Buffalos.' Photo from David Link.   Below. Some frozen 'faces of war'.   Photo by Ben Luci.

RED DRAGON
The SECOND ROUND
FACES OF WAR II

David	F.	Link	RA 16 300 474
First Name	MI	Last Name	Serial Number
Davey	1745	14 April 1931	Cpl
Nickname	MOS	Birthday	Grade / Rank
HQCo 2d Bn 17th Inf 7th Inf Div		Sept 1950- Aug 1951	Burr Oak, MI
Unit (s)		Duty Tour (s)	Home Town

Combat Infantry Badge   Bronze Star   Korean Campaign Service Medal, 5 stars   UN Svc Medal

Medals & Awards

Presidential Unit Citation Occpn Medal-Japan Nat'l Defense Svc Medal Meritorious Unit Citation

A TRIBUTE TO DAVEY

Davey was a good buddy who passed on 20 years ago at too young an age and too soon for one who eked out survival in that bloody war fought in Korea in the early 1950's. His story is not unique, it is typical of thousands of young Americans who lived through some of the most important times in our nation's history. Davey left home in Burr Oak, MI on graduation from high school. Like most young men he was looking for adventure, excitement and an escape from the dull life of a small town. He processed through Ft Knox, KY in Sept 1948. Due to a sudden surge in enlistments, one troop train was sent to Ft Lewis, WA while another train of recruits ended up at Ft Sill, OK. A popular saying a couple of years later was, "We enlisted when they were feeding us instead of needing us."

We opened a section of Ft Sill closed since WW II. Conditions were spartan, to say the least. Basic training in the reactivated 37th RCT began. Davey, with 29 more wide eyed recruits, was selected for the Regtl I & R platoon. Being a 'hand picked' group was great for our ego, but it got us into more than one brawl with other GIs who didn't share the same opinion. "Basic" was not hard. This was 'peace time.' Blessed with an excellent cadre, all WW II combat veterans, we absorbed like a sponge every combat lesson passed on to us. Although much of the training took on a 'game like' atmosphere, the hard lessons were there. The words of those combat veterans had a tremendous impact on young recruits. When basic ended we were disappointed to learn the 37th RCT was again being deactivated. We were parceled out all over the world as replacements. Davey was in a group from the I & R plt sent to Ft Benning, GA to reactivate the 3d Infantry Division. Most of us were jeep drivers for a time. Davey drove for the Light Aviation Section where he developed a burning desire to be a pilot. Boredom got the better of most of us. Davey put in for a transfer to FECOM. Summer found him in Sendai, Japan assigned to 2d Bn, 17th Inf Regt, 7th Inf Div. Early in 1950 I too went to FECOM, but was assigned to Camp Crawford in Hokkaido. Close enough for friends to keep in touch by phone. Davey wangled a job at the Tagajo Dependents School.

June 25th, 1950 ended an easy life for occupation troops. In August we were at Camp Fuji getting ready for our 'baptism of fire.' I was able to get together with Davey several times before we landed at Inchon. Small and baby faced, he could have passed for Audie Murphy's younger brother. He thought the war would be just one big adventure. I did not see Davey at any time during the entire Inchon operation. After our landings at Iwon and the drive north by the 17th Infantry to the Yalu, I saw him twice for brief moments. In late January ,as we started our drive to throw the Communists out of South Korea for the second time, I ran into Davey. I was happy to see he had made it out of north Korea alive. He was driving a jeep for a Bn officer. Noticing several bullet holes in his windshield, I said, "Davey, you better put in for a new windshield or you'll catch your death of cold from all that ventilation." His reply was "Can't get a new windshield unless there are at least a dozen holes in it." When Col "Buffalo" Bill Quinn took over as CO of the 17th Infantry, he circulated an order designed to raise regimental morale by giving each man in the 17th a distinctive appearance. "Every man will grow a handle bar mustache." This of course, for Davey, was impossible. Several of Davey's officers threatened to have him transferred if he didn't grow whiskers. Still impossible for Davey. The last time I saw him before , he had me examine him closely to see if I could see any sign of whiskers. Whiskers do not a soldier make. Witness the 1951 article from Stars & Stripes:

With the 7th Division in Korea------ WHILE UNDER FIRE, DRIVER REPAIRS JEEP, SAVES CONVOY

The lead jeep in the 17th RCT convoy was stalled on the narrow mountain road but that wasn't all the trouble. Enemy ambushers were raking the line of vehicles with blistering small arms fire. When the attack broke out, everyone leaped from the sitting- duck vehicles and dove for cover, unlimbering their weapons for return fire. Everyone---that is---except the leading jeep driver, PFC David F. Link. Link simply eased himself out from behind the wheel, strode around to the front end of his jeep, and lifted the hood. While bullets hissed through the air around him, the young driver made his "first echelon" maintenance repair on the engine. His work completed, Link clambered back behind the wheel, leading his convoy through the road block to safety. He was unhurt. Hours later men of the convoy were still talking about Link's levelheaded bravery. One of his buddies summed it with, "How cool can you be?"

After discharge, Davey married and had two children. He achieved one of his dreams before his early death. He became a pilot, taking his family on vacations to Florida, Alaska, and Central America. His motto,"Live fast, die young," left a beautiful memory."

An M.P. from the X corps sets up a 30 caliber machine gun to return fire on a Commie ambush. North Korea. 1950.

An M-16 from the 7th Division takes the enemy under fire. December 1950.   <u>Both photos from the National Archives.</u>

RED DRAGON
The SECOND ROUND
FACES OF WAR II

James	A.	Jones	1177233 USMC
First Name	MI	Last Name	Serial Number
"Okie"	0331	3 March 1933	PFC
Nickname	MOS	Birthday	Grade / Rank
Item/3/7/1st MarDiv		July '51-July '52	Retrop, OK
Unit (s)		Duty Tour (s)	Home Town
Purple Heart		Korean Campaign Service Medal w/3 stars	Navy PUC
Medals & Awards			
National Defense Service Medal		Korean Combat Service Medal	ROK PUC

TWO MARINES SHARE A 50 YEAR MEMORY

Although they had kept in touch by mail and 'phone, it was 50 years before two USMC Korean War survivors again met in person. Siamese twins in Korea, not joined at the hip, but rather by a common bond of combat comradeship and a fervent desire to live. In combat, two men cooperating in all things stand a better chance of surviving the rigors of war. Jim "Okie" Jones and Clarence "Red" Roberts in mutual support, each for the other, shared a comradeship impossible to attain, or even visualize unless experienced. Words can't describe it. It is a visceral emotion derived from battle, exemplified by men willing to die in tight combat situations to save comrades. Combat veterans seldom discuss it amongst themselves. In trying, language becomes mawkish. The only words close in meaning are reserved for emotions of the love of man for woman, minus sexual overtones. However, it is easily recognized if one overhears conversation between two foxhole buddies as they discuss their passage between the grinding millstones of war.

Helen Jones and Waneme Roberts, wives of fifty years, were privy to this relationship as "Okie" and "Red" met in retirement to reminisce battlefield comradeship. In Jan 1951, Jim Jones enlisted in the Marines at age 17, 2 months shy of 18. Six months after completing boot camp, he was in Korea, assigned to a MG platoon. He received a leg wound in his first month of combat, was hospitalized for 6 days, then reassigned to combat duty with "I" Co where he was paired with 21 year old Clarence Roberts Jr. of Follansbee, W VA. Item company was then battling for Inje, just north of the 38th parallel, near the eastern seacoast. The two became inseparable friends in their 11 months together as a two-man machine gun team, sharing innumerable foxholes, sweating as they dug into rocky soil, even in the bitter cold of winter. They alternated as gunner to share equally the more hazardous gunner's duty. The gunner is more exposed to enemy fire than the loader who lies flat and keeps the feed belt from tangling during rapid fire. "Red" soon learned that "Okie" also had a sweetheart back home. Mail call was a time to celebrate bringing letters, news and packages from home. "Okie" and "Red" regularly returned letters to their sweethearts telling them of their lives as Marines in Korea.

Helen and Wanema listened as old comrades recalled hundreds of memories of their wartime experience. In private, they agreed they now better understood their husbands than ever before. The two aging Marines talked of the bitterly cold weather of 30 and 35 below zero, the four layers of clothing which allowed survival, but left them as cold as if living in a freezer. They remembered the quilted cotton uniforms of the Chinese, the bugle calls heralding attack, the tennis shoes they wore, their concussion grenades, their bravery as they walked into the slaughter house of Marine gunfire, their unlimited numbers which often allowed them to penetrate Marine positions, the close air support by Marine pilots, the support of naval gunfire when the 1st MarDiv fought near the eastern seacoast. They recalled stinking rice paddies fertilized with human waste, the mountains, which when climbed, led only to more mountains, the innumerable rivers in every valley between mountain ridges, the pitiful refugees, the hungry children, the summer heat which was almost as bad as the cruel winter weather. They recalled the use of WW II ammo, equipment, clothing and K rations still in use in this new war. They wondered at the American equipment found on Chinese dead, at that time unaware it was WW II lend-lease.

Their voices grew husky as memories recalled friends, other youthful marines, who died before they barely had lived as young men. They remembered the Marine Corps creed that no dead or wounded man is ever left behind on patrol or in strategic retreat. They recalled the wounded Marine they and two others were carrying on a stretcher when a Chinese grenade was tossed in their path. How the wounded Marine rolled off the stretcher and onto the grenade in a heroically selfless act to protect his litter bearers. "Okie" remembered the sight of his first combat casualty, a man blinded by shrapnel. They recalled the dead, Chinese and Marines, inextricably mixed in death just as in life they had been tangled in the midst of close combat. They wondered why their friends died and they had not. About the can of beans that "Red" was eating, held in front of him, taking the bullet that would otherwise probably have killed him. They agreed their daily Bible reading gave true solace to their spirits, and that they had never met an atheist among their fellow foxhole 'grunts'. Anger, sorrow, fear and confusion were vivid in their memories, as were the times when humor lifted spirits, allowing them to go on. They agreed that they went to war as youths, but came out as men aged beyond their years. Most of all they thanked their Maker for bringing them home safely, in full pride of their service to the country that gave them birth.

Navy Sky Raiders from the USS Valley Forge furnish close support. Their rockets were devastating, October 24, 1950.

<u>Left.</u> A 105mm howitzer at work in the Pusan Perimeter. The firing angle indicates that the enemy is ' too close for comfort.'   <u>Below</u>. A happy Marine has just drawn his beer ration. July 25, 1951.   <u>Photos from the National Archives.</u>

RED DRAGON
The SECOND ROUND
FACES OF WAR II

James	H.	Appleton	115 8912 USMC
First Name	MI	Last Name	Serial Number
Appy	0311	28 August 1931	Cpl
Nickname	MOS	Birthday	Grade / Rank
Item Co 5th Marine Regt 1st MarDiv		Apr '51-Apr '52	Nashville, TN
Unit (s)		Duty Tour(s) in Korea	Home Town

Silver Star   Commendation Medal w Combat V   Navy PUC,1star   USMC Good Conduct Medal

Medals & Awards

USN Occpn Medal w/Eur clasp   NDSM   KCMS,3 battle stars   KSM   UN Medal   ROKPUC   KWSM

PLUGGING THE HOLE

In the past 48 hours we had a full plate to chew on. On 2 July 1951, our 3d Bn 5th Marines had been pulled off line for an 'R&R' rest back in reserve. We were tired after a 45 day hard chase, punctuated by many small battles, as the retreating North Korean Peoples Army turned to fight us off. We had barely gotten our gear unrolled and pup tents set up when we ordered to load aboard trucks. After a short, hurried 15 mile trip we set up an interception road block. Our job was to halt an enemy force that had broken through an Army position. If not halted, they could destroy supply points and POL dumps, and ravage communications and rear area support units. We moved into a quick defensive position where shortly after nightfall the enemy walked two abreast into our trap. They had no place to run, we caught them on the road with a vertical drop off on one side, and a sheer bluff on the other. Artillery fire closed the road at their back door, we slaughtered them with direct fire of 18 MGS at the front door. In our advance the next morning we walked down "Butcher's Alley" through a body count of 454 dead North Koreans. Our objective now was to fill the hole where the enemy had punched through. We were a reinforced Bn of Marines, off the line after 45 days of rough and tumble combat, a proven tough fighting force, a bit haughty and arrogant perhaps, but able to kick any enemy's ass if they chose to tangle with us.

We moved up the road the enemy had used walking down into our 'meat grinder.' We were much more cautious, putting out scouts before moving forward. Passing through the far end of the trap our artillery had so effectively blocked, we saw a few bodies, but mostly just torn pieces of flesh. We climbed up hill to the position where the enemy had broken through our Army buddies' position. It was not a pretty sight, the North Koreans had left their own version of an oriental butcher shop. What had happened was obvious. The Army had received a beer ration on line, something that the Marines never, ever do. We never drink or get a beer ration while in combat. All evidence in this case pointed to a distribution of beer to these troops. There were great numbers of empty beer cans scattered around, some full ones never opened. Around the foxholes there were one or two, sometimes three or four dead American soldiers, their bodies baking and beginning to fly bloat in the hot July sun. Some had their throats cut. Several were impaled by a bayonet on an American M-1 rifle sticking in their bodies, others gun shot or stabbed, bodies contorted in the agony of death.

There was ammunition everywhere, belts of machine gun ammo, bandoleers of .30 cal M-1, carbine clips, frag grenades, C-rations, mess gear and canteen cups, a couple of cups still sitting on the little 'Heat Tab' coffee warmers. Near a clump of trees at a Medical Aid Station was the saddest sight of all. Three stretchers held burned bodies of three GIs in contorted and grotesque positions, clothing burned off, stretcher handles barely charred. Gasoline had been doused on those wounded men, then set on fire. Marines kill in war, but this was not war. It was murderous torture. Moving along the main trail we found a GI, face down, a pick-axe buried in his back, drying blood had streamed from the wound. Word had been passed back from scouts ahead, "Don't move the man in the trail; he's booby trapped." Sure enough, when a rope tied to his leg was pulled, a grenade exploded as his body was tugged aside. Our Bn CO called a halt in the column as each platoon passed so we could contemplate the meaning of "alert and vigilant at all times" The experience was worth a 1000 training sessions. The Bn Skipper then got on his radio, advising regiment and division what had occurred here, and further, a troop detail was needed to police up useable supplies, weapons and ammo lying around.

As we saddled up preparatory to making the final ascent to the main ridge, shots rang out from the column point already in motion. We heard the wailing cry of a wounded man, "Don't shoot, don't shoot, I'm an American!" Out of the underbrush came a sorry looking excuse for an American soldier, half dressed, tattered, blood running from his hand, his wound inflicted by Marine rifle fire. He was the sole survivor of the massacre. His wound treated, he was debriefed as to the occurrences two nights ago. Our assumptions were correct as to beer, lack of alertness, slack discipline and breakdown of defensive integrity. The soldier fell into our ranks and was evacuated next day by Medi-Evac copter. Arriving in pitch black darkness at our objective, we hastily dug in expecting a night attack. Next morning we began taking sporadic small arms fire from a ridge to our front. Our Forward Air Controller soon had the situation in hand, calling for an air strike which, with rockets, napalm and 20mm cannon fire, soon cooled the enemies' martial ardor. Shortly a ROK outfit relieved us to give us time for another go at "R &R" in a reserve area. I was 2 weeks shy of my twentieth birthday.

Above. Korean laborers unload another truck load of artillery brass at a collection point. Just part of the cost of fighting a war.

Left. Early in the war this battery of 90MM anti-aircraft artillery was used to support ROK troops.
Both photos from the National Archives

Below. At the start of the Chinese 5th phase offensive the CCF 40th Corps tried to trap the American 24th Division east of Kapyong, April 24, 1951.   CCF photo taken from the Internet.

RED DRAGON
The SECOND ROUND
FACES OF WAR II

John	NMI	Covach	O-61893
First Name	MI	Last Name	Serial Number
None	1542	17 March 1929	Col USA Ret, Then Lt
Nickname	MOS	Birthday	Grade / Rank
Co A 31st Inf Regt 7th Inf Div		17 Sept 1950-Feb 1952	St Clair, PA
Unit (s)		Duty Tour (s)	Home Town
Combat Infantry Badge		Bronze Star w/ V for Valor 2 OLC	Purple Heart Medal with OLC
Medals & Awards			

Numerous other Medals & Awards for the Korean War and for the Vietnam War.

THE CAPTAIN WHO FLUNKED MAP READING

My hospital stint at the 272d Station Hospital in Sendai, Japan ended mid March '51. The surgeons wired my broken jaw and gave me a plastic splint enabling me to eat solid food while it healed. The dental team had repaired my fractured and broken teeth. I returned to A Company to find a new company commander, a Capt Wilkie, and my 1st platoon now led by my friend, Lt Walker. I was assigned 2d platoon. The company was now pushing north. I soon learned that Capt Wilkie, while a brave soldier, was an ignoramus when it came to reading a map. He could not find his way around on the terrain. Apparently he never learned to "Read Right and Up," or fathom the procedures to interpret magnetic declination. This failing, combined with a stubborn streak to either acknowledge ignorance or allow help from his subordinates, ultimately led to serious disaster and later, in a way, to his untimely death.

On the 3d of April we went by foot to Songsan-ni. We were running screening patrols over the countryside to locate the disorganized Chinese. Weather was miserable. We occasionally overran small Chinese units. Typically, the Chinese at this time either ran or surrendered, seldom putting up a fight. The screening action went on for five days. We were always on the move in a continuous cold rain. We slept in our ponchos, never under cover. Killer weather for infantrymen. Whenever possible, we just squatted and let the rain drip off. Skies were wet, food soggy, clothing sodden, we were chilled to the bone. A break put us into Division reserve.

Under tents at last for a week of rest. On the 15th we crossed the Soyang River against light resistance. Simultaneously we set road blocks to stop the fleeing 3d and 5th Divisions of the South Korean Army that had broken under Chinese attack. Through early May we continued to run strong patrols to come to grips with the Chinese Army. The rains continued. The roads were impassable. Food and ammo was received by airdrop. We moved over such brutal mountainous terrain that I marveled it could physically be done. In one instance after reaching a mountain top we were too exhausted to dig in. The Chinese shelled us. We ignored the incoming rounds, inconceivable to man of my training. We felt that it was God's will whether we lived or not. His Hands on us, we survived.

The Chinese were in far worse shape. A Chinese division, perhaps two, had been caught by our Air Force as they moved through a defile on the Pukhan River. A river blocked one side, high bluffs the other. The Chinese were simply exterminated. The havoc wrought by napalm was devastating. Roasted bodies were everywhere, one Chinese I will never forget had his back against the steep bluff, leaning forward, as if in supplication, his black, charred hand held a cigarette placed by a passing GI. Macabre humor of war.

Bodies on the road and in paddies below were bulldozed into mass graves. The site was known both as Massacre Valley and Maggot Valley. The Chinese formed a defensive line north of the Pukhan River. On May 21 I was ordered by Capt Wilkie to move north to secure a ridge leading directly to our objective, Hill 327. My platoon secured the ridge without resistance. Knowing Wilkie's map reading difficulties, I studied the terrain in great detail. Now certain where the objective lay, I ran into a staff officer who told me the company would soon join us. He concurred in my assessment of the objective location, taking a compass reading in verification.

As the company moved up, Wilkie told me to tack on the end of the column. Reaching the forward edge of the ridge, all platoon leaders were called forward to join him and an accompanying Artillery FO. A ridge lay about 400 meters to our front. Wilkie announced it as our objective. I dissented, saying our objective was further to the right, citing the staff officer as in agreement with my observations. Wilkie would have none of it. The FO was ordered to fire on the ridge. The rounds fell out of sight off to the right. Wilkie stubbornly held to his plan and had the FO march the rounds to "his" ridge. We 'assaulted' the ridge. No enemy. Wilkie called Bn saying we had taken the objective. This set up a disaster. The Chinese had repulsed Charlie Company which had attacked the same hill from another direction. 'Charlie' was ordered to move back up the hill and tie in with us. Of course, we were hundreds of meters away. 'Charlie' was greeted by a rain of fire and a hail of grenades. As a result of Wilkie's error, preparatory artillery fires were wasted, lives of precious GI infantrymen squandered. Capt Wilkie was killed a few weeks later. Cautioned that enemy bunkers we had taken were not yet cleared of the foe, he ignored the advice, stuck his head into a bunker, and was shot by a Chinese soldier.

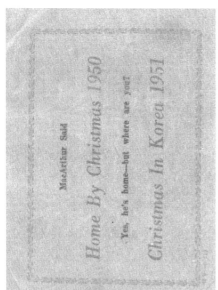

MacArthur Said

Home By Christmas 1950

Yes, he's home—but where are you?

Christmas In Korea 1951

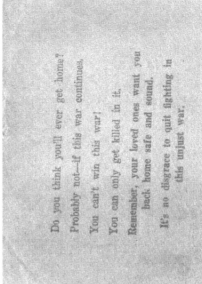

Do you think you'll ever get home?

Probably not—if this war continues.

You can't win this war!

You can only get killed in it.

Remember, your loved ones want you back home safe and sound.

It's no disgrace to quit fighting in this unjust war.

<u>Upper Left.</u>   A quad .50, M-16 of the 45th Division is dug in and ready for business. [Deadly business]. February 1952. <u>Lower Left.</u> Flares light up 'Old Baldy' for the 45th Division during a fire fight, June, 1952. Both photos by Glenn Ed White. <u>Above Right.</u>   A Chinese propaganda leaflet found while on patrol on 'Old Baldy', by Jack Doyle of the 45th Division.

Jacques	K	Doyle	US 51 048 085
First Name	MI	Last Name	Serial Number
Jack	1745	25 Feb 1928	Sgt (T) 15 May 1952
Nickname	MOS	Birthday	Grade / Rank
179th Inf Regt 45th Inf Div NG		Dec 1951-Aug 1952	Binghampton, NY
Unit (s)		Duty Tour (s)	Home Town

Combat Infantry Badge   Purple Heart   KCSM w/3 stars   United Nations Service Medal

Medals & Awards

Occupation Medal(Japan)   New York State Medal for Korean Svc   ROK 50th Anniversary Medal

THE INVINCIBLE REBEL

I was one of the many men who were 'fillers' in the Oklahoma National Guard 45th Division when it was federalized and called to active duty in the Korean War. Our basic training was conducted at Camp Polk before the division was sent to Japan. We were given advanced training in Japan for seven months and then spent 8 months as a front line division in Korea before we began as individual soldiers to rotate back home to the states. The 45th Division remained as fighting division in Korea until the truce was signed in 1953.

Most of my memories of Korean War service are of the men I served with. The man I will never forget was an Oklahoma National Guard soldier by name of Raymond Crawford. Ray was a very capable soldier as long as it suited him. His outstanding character trait was a total lack of respect for authority. James Farr, a veteran of WW II, was our 1st Sgt in basic training. Ray was the bane of Sgt Farr's existence. Ray insisted on calling him "Jim." Sgt Farr would say, " Private Crawford, you must call me Sergeant." "Yes, Jim, I will." "I mean now, Private." "OK, Jim, I will from now on, Jim, I will." Ray never did, not once, ever call him Sergeant.

Farr would get so mad he would send Ray over to the mess hall for KP duty. On one occasion Ray was ordered to clean the field service stoves. Ray cleaned the corner of one stove, over and over. The cook yelled at him, "Clean the damn stoves, Ray." "I am, I am." He just kept cleaning the same one foot area over and over. He was the only soldier I ever heard of who was kicked off KP!

We were sent to Japan on one of the 'General' class troop transports, the men of the regiment all on the same ship. The highest ranking officer aboard was our Regimental Colonel, Fred A. Daugherty. One day, Ray and I were on KP duty, serving food in the mess line. The troops, holding their mess trays would file by. From the steam heated pans we would place a spoonful of food on each tray. I served green beans. Ray sat on a stool at the end of the line doling out spoonfuls of chocolate pudding, considered to be the most desirable part of the meal. Everyone got one spoonful unless Ray knew him as a friend. Ray would the hold the tray with one hand while he dolloped out three or four spoonfuls of pudding. Col Daugherty came into the ships compartment to check the mess line.

As is the army custom with a ranking officer, he was accompanied by several junior officers. Everyone tried to look and act more efficiently under the eye of the Regimental Commander. The sergeants checked quickly to make sure that every detail was correct. Ray looked up from his spooning to see who was standing behind him. A friend of Ray was next in line. I held my breath to see if Ray would be impartial. Not to worry, Ray held his tray and gave him four big spoonfuls. The soldier looked sheepish, but continued on. The next man got one scoop and began to complain. "Move on, move on," Ray told him. All the officers eyes lit up. They all looked expectantly at the Colonel. He just shook his head, smiled, and the inspection party moved on. We had a wise Colonel who in civilian life was a judge. The incident was typical of Ray's one man war with army authority reflecting, "I'll do it my way, not yours!"

In Japan we lived for a time in tents doing field problems, then went to an army camp where we lived in brick barracks. We luxuriated in hot water, but better quarters carried a penalty of maintaining spotless barracks, shining brass and strict inspections. More attention was paid to standard army drill. Our platoon sergeant was checking us prior to a officer's inspection. At attention, only eyes were allowed to move. Our rifles rested on small rocks to keep the butt plates clean. Our platoon sergeant was in front of me when he heard a sound from the rear rank. "Crawford," he yelled," What are you doing?" "I'm eating an apple. "Front and center," he ordered. Ray appeared, a half eaten apple in one hand, rifle in the other. "Ray, go to the barracks, pick up a BAR, your pack and helmet, return here!" Ray did so. The sergeant placed a painted rock about the size of a basketball in his pack, then told him, "Double time around the parade ground until I tell you to stop. Ray was a wiry, muscular soldier, he could have double timed all day had he wanted. The sergeant continued his inspection, glancing in satisfaction at Ray as he ran each lap. The last interval seemed to take a bit longer. Ray ran by in a cloth cap, a carbine, and an empty pack. "Private Crawford, get over here. Where is the rock I put in your pack?" "It's in there." "Show me." Ray dumped his pack. A small rock rolled out. Everyone broke out in hilarious laughter, including the sergeant. Composing himself, the sergeant sighed and said, "OK Ray, get back in ranks." Ray was truly one of a kind.

Above. An M-24 Chaffee light tank in action. Upper Right. Tankers of Co. D, 89th Tk. Bn. give first aid to wounded GI, north east of Seoul, May 1, 1951. Below AD Skyraiders from USS Princeton use torpedoes to destroy the Hwachon Dam. May 1951. Lower Right. A Chaplain holds prayer services for members of the 31st Regt. near the Hwachon Dam. All photos from the National Archives.

The formidable face of Heartbreak Ridge. One of the bloodiest and hardest battles of the war.

High angle fire capabilities made the mortar an ideal weapon for the mountainous terrain of Korea. They were in constant demand.

A wounded G.I. from the 24th Regt. is helped to the rear by his buddies. Near Chorwon. Apr. 22, 1951.
All photos from National Archives.

149

RED DRAGON
The SECOND ROUND
FACES OF WAR II

Ronald	C.	Feldkamp	US 560 74 989
First Name	MI	Last Name	Serial Number
Ron	3577	13 Feb 1930	S/Sgt
Nickname	MOS	Birthday	Grade / Rank
HM/31/7		Aug 1951- June 1952	Whittier, CA
Unit (s)		Duty Tour (s)	Home Town

Combat Infantry Badge   Bronze Star   Korean Campaign Service Medal with 2 Bronze stars

Medals & Awards

National Defense Service Medal   UNSM   KWSM   ROK PUC   Korean Peace Medal

HIGH ANGLE FIRE

Drafted 10 Jan '51, I trained 14 weeks at Camp Roberts, CA then spent several additional weeks in leadership school. Aug of '51 I was sent to Korea, and assigned to 31st Inf Regt/7th Inf Div, then to Heavy Mortar Company of the 31st Infantry . HM was equipped with twelve 4.2" mortars, a high angle fire weapon lobbing a 25 lb shell, a bit larger than a 105mm howitzer. I spent several days in a 1st plt, 4 tube mortar squad but was soon assigned to the FO section as radio man for LaMar (Shorty) Jennings,1st plat FO. We were in support of the 17th Inf Regt. My job was to lug the 44 lb SCR 300 radio up and down the steep Korean hills. I had 'graduated' to FO when Capt Marvin H. Campbell took command of the company in late Oct. Capt Campbell was an exemplary commander, in many respects, I was told, much like Capt Wilson who commanded HM after the Chosin Reservoir, until mid June when he was transferred to Regt HQ. Both were "mustang" officers who recognized men respond to pull better than push. Capt Campbell was an outstanding officer, a 'soldier's soldier.' His steady, resolute attitude brooked no nonsense, yet he carried an engaging air about him. Although his calm demeanor was that of a tutor, he was a stern disciplinarian. He was respected by every man in HM Co.

Capt Campbell had served as a private in Co A, 31st Inf in the Phillipines. Captured at Corregidor, he escaped to spend the rest of WW II fighting alongside Filipino guerillas until Gen MacArthur's return in 1944. With Capt Campbell's arrival in late Oct., my education as a soldier and FO commenced. He was firm and fair. He gave me good advice, reprimanding me when I was wrong, encouraging me always to learn my trade as a soldier. Under him, company morale returned to its former high level. It had sagged disastrously under an interim commander who had been a "bunker commando." I make these comments because I have learned it is under the leadership of the company commander that officers and NCOs set the tone for performance, and survival, of soldiers in an infantry company. I learned my trade under tutelage of an officer who was one of the best troop leaders in the US Army.

In early Jan '52 I had learned my job well enough to be assigned as an FO on Hill 605 in the Mundung-ri valley sector, east central front. My OP was in the B/31 sector of the line. Early one morning in full daylight, a CCF relief column in battle array emerged into view from a treed area. They had to cross a long but narrow rice paddy. It was the beginning of a turkey shoot. My view at 2 o'clock covered their front and both flanks. As at most OPs, an artillery FO was present. In this case, it was a junior FA 2d Lt who drew the duty. He attempted to bring his 105s into action. The paddy was in defilade to his howitzers. After several futile ranging shots he reluctantly gave way to our 4.2s. My 4 gun HM 1st platoon was in perfect position. I quickly asked my FDC for a 'zeroing in' round, using map coordinates 200 yard left and add 200 yards from my intended target area. FDC plotted target, range and deflection. The confidant Chinese commander, knowing that he was in defilade to our artillery, sent 3 men across testing the situation. We waited.

Nothing happened. More waiting. The CCF column started across the paddy. FDC had sighted all four mortars to fire 200 right, drop 200 of my zero-in round. The column was now past the middle of the paddy. I recall the artillery Lt was engrossed and excited saying, "They're coming out into the open. Now more are coming." I called for mortar fire, "60 rounds, Fire for Effect." The effect was awesome. As smoke, dust and frozen clods settled to earth, the column was not to be seen. Bodies, parts of bodies, and a few running men were visible through binoculars. The rest of the Chinese column was still hidden in the treed area. I called to FDC, "Add 300, 40 rounds, Fire for Effect." We had no way of knowing the damage inflicted in the treed area, but 40 rounds, some of them tree bursts, must have badly hurt the enemy concealed there. In a way, it was payback for the 72 casualties suffered by "B"Co in an earlier combat patrol. The "Turkey Shoot" ended with the usual phone calls from 7th Div and X Corps, "What's going on?"

In mid Jan, lst platoon/HM was moved eastward in support of 2Bn/31. My new FO position was just north of 'Heartbreak Ridge'. It was very rugged, steep terrain. Positions were in much closer proximity to the enemy due to deep ravines and steep canyons. Previously, the greater hazard had been artillery and mortars. Now it was snipers with their deadly aimed telescopic rifle fire. One sniper played a major role in my education as a soldier. The OP bunker had a low entry opening. At 6'3" I, and other tall soldiers, had to stoop to enter, leaving our helmets outside the bunker. Coming out of the bunker, a man was exposed, head, neck, shoulders, before he could crouch into the protection of the trench. One day as I stepped up and out, something in my head, or a voice from the bunker(?) said, "Ron." I turned my head. A whiz-buzz by my left ear kicked dirt over my helmet. The luck of the draw was with me in that moment. After that, until I rotated from Korea in June of '52, I was always aware of my position in relation to the enemy.

One morning as I prepared to fire support for G/31, I was ordered out of the FO bunker by an artillery 1st Lt, "Too crowded in here. Wait in the Medic's bunker." I knew this to be wrong but he had bars, I wore stripes. I had barely gotten to the Medical bunker, when a runner came yelling, "4.2 FO, 4.2 FO!" I ran back to the OP where the 2d Bn CO on the phone proceeded to carve me a new anus. He ordered HE fire now! A "G" company patrol was in serious trouble. Minutes later we fired WP to give covering smoke for their withdrawal. It had been a bad day for "G" Co and myself. Capt Campbell at FDC heard the Bn CO chew me out on the Bn wire net. He jeeped to the hill and climbed up to arrive just as the patrol came in. He questioned me. I told him what had happened. He was upset. He also chewed me out, reiterating my duties as an FO. In no uncertain terms, I was told to never leave the OP on orders from anyone, stripes, bars or stars. Standing orders are: "Stay in the OP!" Later that day the LT Col commanding 2d Bn called to thank me for my FO performance. It helped my state of mind. It was also obvious that Capt Campbell had relayed to him the true story.

Near the end of Jan, we moved to the Punchbowl in support of the 27th Inf Regt/25th Div. We had two enemies, the North Koreans and the weather. It was sometimes hard to tell which was worse when the temperature dropped to 30 below. Marty Gascon was my radioman. He wanted some time off the hill. I asked for another man. Capt Campbell asked for names, but the 2d Plt Ldr spoke up saying he had a man. His name was Les Fault, a replacement, not happy in a mortar squad. He wanted real action on the line. The Capt confronted Les, telling him no transfer at this time but he could try out. He was ordered to accompany me to the top of Hill 1243, where he would find plenty of action available to him. I zipped him in with instructions on what to expect. We left for the hill. It was a difficult climb, steep and icy. Les soon lagged. I told him we had to be at the tramway to get our equipment before dark, then inquire our way to Baker Co CP. I told him," Hurry it up, Les, after dark only a dumbbell wanders into the position of a rifle company on the MLR." I went on ahead to relieve the FO who growled, "Where you been?" He handed me some maps and informed me, "This place is a living hell," then hurriedly left to get to the bottom of the hill before dark. Les got in at dark, exhausted. His lack of experience kept him out of preparations being made for an early AM patrol. He was along to learn the trade, "OJT," we called it.

At the ridge crest the NKs were infiltrating and harassing Baker Co positions. Each rifle platoon had several automatic weapons which often broke into a loud chattering. This was life on the line. NKs operated at night, we in daylight. Little sleep for the dogface soldier. The Baker CO wanted close in defensive fire concentrations plotted, too close for HE. We had FDC set WP shells to fire on call with proper charge, elevation and deflection set for each concentration. FDC recorded this data so fire could be placed on a specific map location at a minutes notice. Les and I hit the sack early, keeping warm. I was asleep, but was awakened by the hill in motion, rocking as if I were aboard ship. We were on the receiving end of a continuous barrage from enemy artillery and mortars. We lost wire communication, commo wires cut by shell bursts and shrapnel. We still had radio communication with Baker Co, not as reliable as telephone due to static. Bugles signaled, we expected an imminent attack. Baker CO told us to come to his CP to eliminate one leg of radio transmission. Before leaving, I called our FDC for 60 rounds on the plotted concentrations. I told Les, "Pack up, we gotta go." Between our own fire and that of the North Koreans, we had some anxious moments. However, our bunker and the rifle bunker in front of us held against the shelling. We had numerous close hits. Les had wanted action, he was getting it.

We had about 60 yards to go to reach Baker CP bunker. I went first, slipping, sliding on the icy trail, feet tangling in broken commo wire. Enemy fire walked the ridge line back toward me. Shrapnel whistled through the air. My only thought was COVER. I turned back to the bunker just as Les was leaving it. I hit him with a football block which sent us both tumbling back into the bunker. All my emotions and body parts were in high gear. I had to steady my nerves. Some relief was necessary. I grabbed an empty C-ration can. Filled two of them. It calmed me down. A thought came. The NK artillery was walking the ridge, back and forth, traversing and searching. I told Les, "When the shelling goes by, we'll make a dash for it. We did, making the CP just as the shelling started back. At the CP the Baker CO was preparing for an enemy assault. I checked in with FDC. In silence, we all awaited the expected attack.

It never came. Anxiety subsided after a long wait. The XO broke silence by saying he had tried to count shell bursts to keep his mind occupied, said he was past 900 when he lost count. Outside the bunker, a fog covered the ridge. Was that what stopped the attack? We'll never know. Les and I returned to our bunker, commo men restrung wire, all back to normal. Two days later Les was evacuated with frost bite. He returned to the company after several weeks. On a trip down to the FDC, I ran into him and asked if he wanted his old job back. He grunted, "No thanks, I've got a good job driving a '6 by' (6) troop carrier in 2d plat." Don Schoener from New York was my new radio man. He and I worked well in tandem until we were relieved near the end of Feb. There were many other OPs and situations too numerous to mention. The many friends I made while on line live in a special place in my mind, never forgotten.

My pinochle partner, Merle (Red) Turner and I rotated home in June '52. After 50 years, my hat is still off to the GI infantrymen, mostly draftees by now, who took all the Chinese and North Koreans could dish out, repelling assault after assault, in attack never wavering, taking objectives at the cost of their lives. Heroes all in my book. My duties were different, a half step removed. We all served.

<u>Top Left</u>. The 31st Hvy. Mortar Co. sets up for action. The photo below shows a firing pit in the foreground and living bunkers dug into the hillside in the background. <u>Lower Left</u>. A heavy .30 caliber machine gun is dug in for perimeter protection. <u>Upper Right</u> Approach road to the MLR with Heartbreak Ridge in background. <u>Above</u> A 4.2 heavy mortar is about to send a round on its way, winter 1952.

<u>All photos by Pete Aguilar.</u>

RED DRAGON
The SECOND ROUND
FACES OF WAR II

Peter	T.	Aguilar	US 56 146 160
First Name	MI	Last Name	Serial Number
Pete	1812	26 Feb 1930	Sgt
Nickname	MOS	Birthday	Grade / Rank
HM/31/7		August 1951-Sept 1952	Los Angeles, CA
Unit (s)		Duty Tour (s)	Home Town
Combat Infantry Badge		Korean Campaign Service Medal,2stars	ROK 50 Medal
Medals & Awards			
National Defense Service Medal		UN Service Medal with O/S bar ROK PUC KWS Medal	

CLOSE CALLS

I was inducted into the Army of the United States in my home town of Los Angeles March 14, 1951, less than a month after my 21st birthday. I spent 14 weeks in basic infantry training at Camp Roberts, CA. I went then to San Francisco where I, along with 7 other infantry soldiers, were fortunate to be listed on the passenger manifest of a MATS (Military Air Transport Service) plane to Tokyo. The plane was full, all other seats were occupied by Air Force personnel. We made stopovers in Hawaii and Wake Island. Stopovers for refueling and maintenance were too short to see much of anything, We were allowed out of the plane to stretch our legs.

From Tokyo we went to Pusan. There at the 'Repple-Depple' (Replacement Depot) I was assigned to Heavy Mortar Company, 31st Inf Regt, 7th Div. When I reported in, the platoon was firing from atop Hill 1073. All ammo for the 12 4.2 inch mortars in the company was sent up on a tramway powered from the rear wheel of a weapons carrier, tire removed. With the truck engine in reverse, the cable, wrapped around another truck wheel on top of the hill, cycled endlessly. The rope handle of a wooden box holding two mortar shells was hung from one of the many hooks on the cable. The box, holding two shells, weighed 66 lbs. The tram had been built by M/Sgt Gus Edson of the 13th Engineers. Prior to that time all ammo had to be carried up that steep hill on a man's back. As a result of the tram, our fire was limited only by the ability of the rear echelon to keep us supplied. My plat sgt was Bill Mathis. Don't recall my plat ldrs name. He was a Chosin Reservoir vet. For the first two weeks all was well. I had time to acclimate myself to the altitude and the very hot, humid weather. I also learned to dig mortar and ammo emplacements as well as a foxhole. A foxhole, I learned, to be a good shelter incoming artillery fire, had to be more than a hole in the ground. On Sept 5th, we left Hill 1073, never to return.

We moved to a new position. I still have no idea where we were. That night about 11 PM, we were attacked in a fight that went on all night. Attacks came in successive waves. It was my first experience in close infantry combat with the enemy. They were Chinese, and they were persistent, hitting us at 15 minute intervals. Our heavy mortars, firing shells larger than a 105 howitzer, were too much for them. Mortar fire, machine gun and rifle fire from our own company weapons plus fire from an adjacent rifle platoon kept them from breaking our positions. Even so, it was a close call. On several occasions, our mortar tubes were pointed almost straight up as we fired on minimum charge and maximum elevation. These shells landed about 50 yards ahead of our gun positions. Too close for comfort. A 4.2 shell has a 25 yard burst radius. The Chinese attacks quit about 5 AM. As daylight lit up the scene, it was difficult to see through the smoke. It was more smog than smoke. Much like Los Angeles on a hot, still day. We had fired so many rounds the smoke had not dissipated. It was actually hard to breathe, something I had not noticed during the night as we fed ammo to the gun. The Chinese had not been able to recover all their dead. Their bodies were strewn in the contorted positions in which they died.

Much of a mortar company's combat time is spent in relative safety of defilade positions, covering and protecting the infantrymen of the rifle companies. Our job is to deliver fire to assist the men of a rifle company in attack. In defense, our fire is concentrated on an advancing enemy. Our Fos (forward observers) however, shared the daily lot of men in the rifle company front line foxholes and bunkers. They constantly observed the enemy, acting as our eyes, aiming our mortar fire. There are a few occasions however, when men of a mortar company earn their Combat Infantry Badge in much the same fashion as does the front line dogface.

A day in May 1952 was such a day. We in the 7th Division were to have relieved the 24th Infantry Division under cover of darkness. Due to the glitches often occurring in the chaos of war, it was 8 AM before we reached the relief area. The Chinese had us under observation. They astutely waited until the 3 firing platoons of HM/31, all of HM/24 and Dog company, 24th Inf Regt were boxed in an area measuring about 100 yds by 75 yds. As we were sorting ourselves out in exchange of positions, the Chinese poured in well over 200 rounds of 76mm gun and mortar fire. It was devastating to our equipment. We lost clothing, blankets and many items carried in weapons carriers and Jeeps, not to mention a couple of 6x6 GI 2 ½ ton trucks and a lot of flat tires on trucks and trailers. One of our ROKs, Soo Chun Duk, at the risk of his own life set off WP rounds to cover us with smoke. By the Grace of God, none of the 75 men of our company in that impact area were killed or wounded. We all lived to tell the story. It was truly a miracle.

In the bitter fighting of late 1951 there was always an excuse to take another hill. ' To straighten out the line, or for better observation, or to deny the Chinese better observation, etc. etc.' Here GIs battle for another hill in the Heartbreak Ridge area. Soon it would be War '1918 style' with trenches, bunkers and much blood. Photo furnished by Ron Feldkamp.

Elements of the 15th Regiment of the 3rd Division get pinned down by the Chinese troops. Taken near the 38th parallel March 23, 1951. Photo from the National Archives.

RED DRAGON
The SECOND ROUND
FACES OF WAR II

James	H.	Appleton	115 8912 USMC
First Name	MI	Last Name	Serial Number
Appy	O311	28 August 1931	Corporal
Nickname	MOS	Birthday	Grade/Rank
Item Company 5th Marine Regt 1st MarDiv		Apr '51-Apr '52	Nashville, TN
Unit		Duty Tour(s) in Korea	Home Town

Silver Star Commendation Medal w/ Combat V Navy PUC 1 star USMC Good Conduct Medal

Medals & Awards

USN Occpn Medal w/ Eur clasp NDSM KCSM 3 battle stars KSM UN Medal ROK PUC KWSM

SCARED!

We had been driving forward all week long. walking 20 miles a day, pushing toward an objective called the "Kansas Line." Most days we just walked up and down hills. We didn't really get into any real fire fights, but once in a while ol' "Joe Gook" would turn and fight. Today we had pulled up on a 'finger ridge' which led all the way up to the grand-daddy of all hills, Hill 1052 in Kanmu-bong Province of North Korea. We had a good position near the base of the ridge as it meandered down to a little stream which ran alongside the trail which went from our position up through 'Indian Country' to big boy 1052. This was the eventual prize of our next operation. Whoever owned Hill 1052 looked down the throats of all enemy positions in the area. We knew without being told that it would be our job to take that 'big sucker.' It was a warm October afternoon. We had stopped for the day at 3 PM to dig in our company position which started from trail and stream at the bottom of the ridge, extending upward along the ridge about 1000 yards where we tied in with another Marine company. The trail was a natural avenue of approach the enemy could use to probe our positions. MGs were set to fire up the trail. Riflemen on the ridge above could fire down at the trail. The setup would make a good 'killing field.'

I had gotten to be pretty good at setting booby traps. So it was not unusual for our Skipper, Capt Neil Dimond, to tell me, "Go back down the trail about 50 yards or so and set up some 'Bouncing Betties, 'trip wire grenades and flares. 'Bouncing Betty' was a type of mine which, when triggered, flew up about six feet held there by a chain before going off. It was sometimes called the "Headless Horseman" as it often resulted in that effect. Trip wire grenades are regular frag grenades rigged with a trip wire stretched across the trail. A wire attached to the safety pin is pulled out by an unwary trespasser which results in a deadly blast in about 4½ seconds. Flares illuminate the scene so that riflemen can achieve better aim. My chore finished, I went to my foxhole to prepare my evening cuisine. It was a real delight; Meat & Limas, Dark Sweet Cherries and those abominable stale crackers, circa WW II. About 2100 hours, one of the company runners tells me, "Appy, the CO says go back down the trail and disarm your booby traps. A ROK Army patrol is going out at 2300 hours. He doesn't want any of them killed by your booby traps!" Talk about being placed between a rock and a hard place! Disarm 2 'Bouncing Betties,' 2 trip wire grenades and 2 flares in the dark? Hell, I wasn't exactly sure where I had placed them! I had visions of a North Korean patrol jumping my skinny litle ol' Tennessee ass and dragging me back to Pyongyang.

I tried to get some of my buddies to come with me, finally prevailing on my friend Keith Zimmerer. When within 20 yards of my booby traps he said, "Appy you're now on your own, I'll cover you from here." The big problem is things never look the same in the dark as in daylight. I didn't have a clue how I was to locate them. Finally, I decided to roll up my shirt sleeve and walk with my bare arm in front of me in hope I would feel the cold steel trip wire before I triggered my own booby traps. First I would encounter the trip flares. If they went off it gave me a chance to test my procedure before killing my fool self as they furnished light only. Worst hazard, I might get burned. As I groped down the trail, I could feel my heart pounding so hard inside my Marine Utility Jacket I expected it jump out of my chest. I located the first flare, then the second. I took a breather, I didn't want to get over confident and miss the first 'Bouncing Betty." All the time, I just knew the North Koreans were waiting for me to finish before pouncing on my sorry carcass to haul me back north. Heart pounding even harder, I kept on groping, finally locating the first "Bouncing Betty." One down and three to go! Figuratively speaking, I kept cramming my heart back down my throat as I located the second "Bouncing Betty." The worst was yet to come. It was a more treacherous and harder thing to locate the spot where I had rigged the grenades. With a combination of sheer luck and much prayer, I located the first grenade, disarming it. I then remembered where the other grenade was located in respect to the first. I quickly disarmed it also, bending the grenade pin so it would not easily pull out if I stumbled running back to our company positions. I don't know how fast professional runners do the mile, but I'll wager I ran a close second in the time it took to return to our lines. I was careful as I came close, since our own guys sometimes forget to yell out and ask for the password.

Back in my foxhole I sat a few minutes smoking a calming cigarette. The same runner returned to tell me, " Appy, Skipper says go back out and rearm your booby traps about 0300 after the ROK patrol returns." I told the runner to tell the Skipper, "Roger." To myself I said, "When it snows in Miami." I remembered FDR's "Nothing to Fear but Fear itself." FDR never disarmed 6 booby traps!

Above. Gunners from the 31st Regiment, 7th Infantry Division fire their 75mm recoilless rifle in support of the infantry. June 9, 1951. Below Right. Wounded GIs from the 7th Regiment of the 3rd Division are receiving first aid after their bloody fight for Hill 717. July 3, 1951. Both photos from the National Archives.

Below Left Chesley Yahtin stands by his ambulance. 7th Med. Bn. 7th Infantry Division Spring, 1951 Photo courtesy Chesley Yahtin.

RED DRAGON
The SECOND ROUND
FACES OF WAR II

Chesley	Q	Yahtin	RA 19 347 093
First Name	MI	Last Name	Serial Number
Chief" or "Doc"	Amb. Driver	8 Dec 1930	Pfc
Nickname	MOS	Birthday	Grade / Rank
Amb Co 7Med Bn/7th Div	Sept '50- Aug '51	Warm Springs, OR	
Unit (s)	Duty Tour (s)	Home Town	
Purple Heart w/OakLeaf Cluster	Combat Medical Badge	KCSM w/ 6 stars	
Medals & Awards			
OM,Japan NDSM Army PUC	Navy PUC ROK PUC	Korean War Service Medal	

INDIAN MEDIC ASKS, "WAS IT WORTH IT?"

I am an Indian of the Warm Springs tribe. Our 'reservation' is in central Oregon. Today I am more fiercely proud of my heritage as a Native American than I was in my youth. We learn as we travel the path of life. I enlisted in the Army to obtain a better understanding of the white man's world in which I was destined to live my destiny. I had the impression society's acceptance was gained easier among fighting men than in other areas of American society. During my military service I found this to be true among my enlisted comrades, but far less so by regular army NCO's and officers. To them I was stereotyped as "That Crazy Indian Kid."

11In 1949 I enlisted in the Regular Army at age 18. After basic training I was shipped to Japan and assigned to the 7th Div which was then on occupation duty. In preparation for the Inchon invasion I was trained in the 7th Med Bn Ambulance Company of the 7th Div. When we landed at Inchon, my group became entangled with a company of Marines. I was shoved into a line, handed a BAR and 8 grenades to carry. I had no idea of what to do or where to go. The Marines, learning that I was a Medic, put me to work collecting their wounded under fire. I suddenly realized, in addition to being almost scared to death, no one gave a damn about my life except me. I was taken across the Han River on a pontoon bridge. After another 2 days with the Marines, I managed to find my unit by asking questions of every GI I came across. Reporting in, I was immediately assigned duty with the 17th ROK Regt and again crossed the Han River to a large mountain east of Seoul. There was a tremendous battle going on. My job was to collect and evacuate the South Korean wounded. The battle slowed. After a few more hours no more wounded were being brought to the collecting point.

With no interpreter to tell me what was going on, I followed a couple of Marine Corps tanks up a broad irrigation ditch where fighting was still raging. Those wounded South Koreans were sure glad to see me. I dragged as many as I could out of the line of plunging fire. On my last day there, a North Korean came out of nowhere and began attacking the South Korean wounded awaiting evacuation. In trying to stop him we grappled, face to face. I was forced to kill him. After that, my mind seemed to go blank at times. In one of those episodes while under MG and mortar fire, I failed to see a sign, "MINES" in a paddy field as I took my ambulance through the paddy field to pick up a load of wounded. Miraculously, not one mine exploded. After that, I was for sure, "The Crazy Indian Kid."

To those officers and NCOs always in the rear, safe and sound from the agony of war, sleeping in dry tents on clean sheets, eating good food with pretty nurses nearby, my sobriquet, "Crazy Indian Kid," identified with the idea I was just another 'drink crazed Indian'. This characterization of Indian men lives in the minds of much of the white population in this nation we share. I suffered for that concept by permanent assignment to front line jobs, retrieving wounded while under fire, dragging KIAs to a collecting point and other duties of like hazard. I was routinely ordered to drive ambulances up heavily shelled roads, or on roads known to be mined where other drivers were reluctant to go. It seemed I was the only one in our company who never got a break from dangerous duty. June 1, at the Hwachon Reservoir while collecting KIAs, I was attacked by a North Korean soldier carrying a burp gun slung on his shoulder. He didn't use his gun. He hit me with a body slam. Scared! I thought I was going to die. I had no training in personal combat. We wrestled, somehow I came out on top. He became my prisoner. Like the battles at the Chosin Reservoir the previous winter, I could not get these new scenes out of my mind. A nightmare haunts me to this day. I hear cries of the wounded, the whispers of the dying trying to tell me something. In my dreams I never have answers for them, I can only hold them tight as they die, my mind wracked with their agony. To this day, I often awake in sadness from one of these dreams, my eyes wet with tears.

On return to the US, I was denied leave to see my family. I went AWOL. On my voluntary return to duty, I received a Dishonorable Discharge and booted out of the Army. Now in my old age, suffering from the effects of frostbite at the Chosin Reservoir and in recognition of my two Purple Hearts, I could use the psychiatric care available to ex-soldiers from the Veterans Administration. This is, of course denied me, as it is to all soldiers with a "Dishonorable." I blame my officers and senior NCOs of the "Old Guard" Regular Army. I believe they tried to get me killed and out of the way. Anyway, who cares about a "Damned Savage?" I ruined my life in saving white men. To this day I say to myself, "Was it worth it?" Paranoid? If you walked in my moccasins, what would you think?

An F4U Corsair takes off from a carrier to provide close air support for U.N. ground forces. <u>Photo from National Archives.</u>

Cpl. Appleton ready to go hunting for commies. Note his sniper rifle and 'camo' gear. Hill 854. Winter of 51 - 52.
<u>Bottom photos</u> <u>courtesy of James Appleton.</u>

'Appy' with his sniper rifle and PFC Dinkins just returned from patrol. Hill 854 just north of the Punchbowl. Oct. 51.

158

RED DRAGON
The SECOND ROUND
FACES OF WAR II

James	H.	Appleton	115 8912 USMC
First Name	MI	Last Name	Serial Number
Appy	0311	28 August 1931	Cpl
Nickname	MOS	Birthday	Grade / Rank
Item Co 5th Marine Regt 1st MarDiv		Apr '51-Apr '52	Nashville, TN
Unit (s)		Duty Tour (s)	Home Town

Silver Star Commendation Medal w Combat V   Navy PUC,1star   USMC Good Conduct Medal
Medals & Awards
USN Occpn Medal, Eur clasp NDSM KCMS,3 battle stars KSM UN Medal ROKPUC KWSM

IT WAS A LONG SHOT

In late August 1951 it was beginning to feel a bit like fall. After volunteering for sniper duty, I was put through an intensive sniper training course at Inje, a little village just over the 38th parallel in North Korea. My instructor was a tough Gunnery Sergeant of the Corps 'Old Breed.' I was given further training at a camp near Won Tong-ni, another small village in North Korea, then reassigned back to my old outfit, Item 3/5. During the early fall we had stayed relentlessly close on the tail of the remnants of rag tag North Korean Peoples Army. Every few days he would turn and fight like a cornered rat, only to turn tail and resume his retreat to the north. We came to a mountainous area with ridges splayed out like fingers on a hand. We were told we would probably stay here for a while. In the vicinity of Hill 812 we dug deep foxholes. After that we built bunkers. There was plenty of timber available. This part of south central North Korea is very rugged. Hills grow out of hills in never-ending parallel cascades of successive canyons and ridges.

On the offensive, we had pushed forward 18 to 20 miles each day to stay close on 'Joe'Gook's' tail. When we could make contact, we "would rough him up" a bit to encourage him to continue his retreat. On Hill 812 we had an unusual position. We occupied a long finger ridge opposite a ridge held by the North Koreans. To picture the terrain situation, place your two hands in front of you, next to each other, close to your belt, then close your hands into fists leaving only the "social finger" extended on each hand. By end of the third day we had built an OP at the extreme end of our ridge where the finger nail would be. "Joe Gook" had done the same on his ridge. Each OP kept close watch on his enemy's position. It was a "Mexican Standoff" lull in the fighting. Mornings and evenings, the North Koreans would stroll down their ridge to relieve their men in the OP. They might as well have been on New York's 42d Street. Their nonchalance was infuriating. After a couple of days, the Skipper told me, "'Appy', put that sniper training to some good use. See if you can't teach those relief guards a little respect!" A couple of my buddies borrowed field glasses while I took a couple of sandbags to use as a steady rest for my rifle. We set up about 200 yards down ridge using some brush for cover. I laid out my sand bag rests. My buddies took position above and back a bit to observe my fire, to triangulate and help me adjust my scope.

For gun buffs who may read this, my first sniper rifle was a Cal.30 M1-D with an 8 power Weaver Scope, fitted with a leather cheek piece and muzzle "Flash Hider." Later after I gaining some seniority whiskers, I traded the M1-D for the classic sniper's rifle, a Springfield Cal .30 Model 1903-A-1 with a 10 power Unertyl Scope, having mounts for external windage and elevation adjustments. It was a real beauty, coveted by all members of the Sniper Corps. This afternoon I registered in by trying to put a round through the NK OP bunker window. I used 30.06 tracer ammo so my buddies could follow my shots and tell me how to adjust my sights. After several adjustment shots, I put a round through the bunker window. My buddies watched me put a second round in the same place. We then sat back and waited. I added a little elevation to my sights as I would now be using AP or 'ball' ammo which is a bit heavier than the tracer round filled with magnesium powder, which as it burns, leaves a characteristic reddish color in wake of the bullet.

About an hour later, down the ridge, here came Abbott and Costello out for their evening exercise stroll to their OP bunker. As they got opposite me, I eased the "03" down on the sand bag, took a good fit of the stock tight into my shoulder, picked up my target in the scope, tracked hm for a few paces, took in a good breath, let out half of it and slowly squeezed the trigger while maintaining my sights on him. My buddies yelled, "'Appy',"you got him! His body rolled down the bushes on our side." His companion ducked over to the other side of the ridge. I inserted a fresh cartridge while we waited and watched, I through my scope, my buddies with their binoculars. Within a few minutes, the second North Korean made a dash across the ridge to rescue his buddy. I gave hm rapid fire, my buddies joined in with their M-1s. The real estate in that area must have gotten untenable because he hightailed it back across the ridge. He tried again with the same result. He gave it up as a bad idea. We waited until dark then returned to our line positions.

The next morning the body was gone, recovered in the night. After that episode, enemy replacement shifts were not so cavalier in walking down the ridge. We never saw them again. They must have used the reverse slope of their ridge to "change the guard!" After checking the Field Artillery Forward Observer's map, the distance was determined to be about 1200 yards. Truly a long shot!

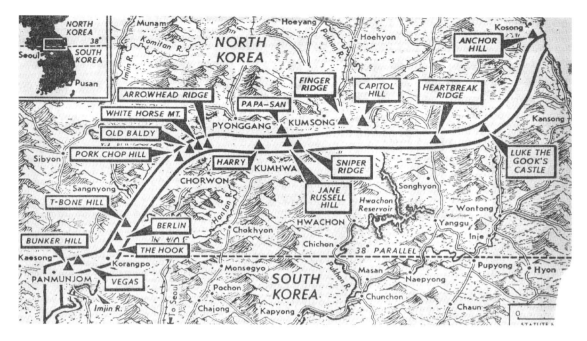

The above map shows the DMZ with names of all major battle sites.

A medic from the 3rd Bn, 23rd Regiment of the 2nd Infantry Division treats a wounded G.I. while a wounded ROK soldier is helped up the hill for medical treatment. Both were evacuated by helicopter.   Photo from National Archives.

RED DRAGON
The SECOND ROUND
FACES OF WAR II

Donald	M	Cohen	RA 16 348 977
First Name	MI	Last Name	Serial Number
Don	4812	25 November 1932	Sgt
Nickname	MOS	Birthday	Grade / Rank
"C" Co/ 1/38/ 2d Div		May 1951-April 1952	Chicago, IL
Unit (s)		Duty Tour (s)	Home Town

Combat Infantry Badge   Bronze Star w/ V device   Purple Heart Medal   Good Conduct Medal

Medals & Awards Presidential Unit Citation   Occupation Medal-Japan   Korean War Service Medal
Korean Campaign Service Medal, 4stars National Defense Service Medal United Nations Medal

WHAT HAPPENED TO RALPH KING ON HILL 1179?

I enlisted in the US Army in December 1950. Went through 8 weeks basic training at Ft Leonard Wood plus 2 additional weeks of engineer training. My orders were then cut for Camp Stoneman, CA. There I and my five buddies, the six of us had enlisted as a group, all boarded a WW II Victory ship for Japan. In processing at Camp Drake in Japan, we were all assigned to the 2d Division. Joining the division on line 14 May 1951, we six were assigned to the 38th Regt which was involved in the fighting on Hill 1051. On 18 May, 8 Chinese divisions hit us. I had never seen so many Chinese. They kept coming and coming. It took a whole week to drive them back in a battle which came to be called "The May Massacre." The next big battle was on Hill 1179, where two of my five buddies were killed, Lloyd Campbell and Adsem. Four of us survived to fight at Bloody Ridge, Heartbreak Ridge and "Operation Touchdown."

We had taken Hill 1179 and quickly began preparing defensive positions along what was called the 'Kansas Line.' Three other hills, 983, 940 and 773, overlooking the western portion of our line, were held by North Koreans observing our every activity. We had been probed on several nights by North Koreans. Orders came from division directing all 3 regiments to send out their own probing patrols to ascertain if these three Korean hill positions posed a threat. We had been briefed on what we were to do on the patrol. PFC Eddy's group would provide covering fire behind our patrol. We were waiting word to move out when Lt Dent showed up with a new replacement. He was a black guy, the first to be integrated into our platoon. Looked like a good soldier to me. We were always glad to see another warm body in the platoon to share the wealth. He was introduced as Pvt Ralph King from Arlington, VA. I was told to take King on patrol and indoctrinate him into our patrol procedures. I told Ralph to put his gear into our bunker and follow me. Moving down hill we came to a pile of big rocks. I placed Ralph on the highest one to give us covering fire in case we were chased back up hill. His position was between the two advancing rifle squads formed in a V shape, resembling a flock of geese flying south.

We moved to the hill bottom then around to our left where we ran into two Russian T-34 tanks. Close up, they were monstrous. One of the riflemen decided he could fire a bullet into the mouth of the tank cannon and detonate the shell in the breach. A boy genius! He fired, missed, and the situation exploded when that bullet clanged on the tank armor. The tanks opened up with machine gun and cannon fire while their infantry, riding shotgun, threw grenades at us. We climbed back up our hill, returning fire as best we could. One rifleman was hit in his upper leg, we helped him back up hill. Had it been the joker who fancied himself as Annie Oakley, I would have let him make his way back as best he could. A damn fool who thinks he can take on a tank with an M-1 doesn't need help.

When we approached the rock formation, King was nowhere to be seen. We decided he must have gone back with the retreating riflemen. We conked out when we got back to our bunker. Shortly after our return, Lt Dent showed up. He wanted to know what had happened to King. He seemed upset. He would have to make out a report to the company commander. Over the next few days I was interviewed by a Warrant Officer and a couple of guys from CIC (Civilian Intelligence Corps). After being interviewed several times, I finally had enough. I said, "You know everything I know. I'm not changing anything. Contact me again and I'll use this carbine on both of you." As I left, carbine in hand, I could see both the Warrant Officer and Lt Dent wink and smile. I was never asked again.

I belatedly recognized that the concern was whether we had hung King out to dry. Integration was then of prime concern in the Army. The brass wanted to make sure President Truman's order was being obeyed at all levels. Any racial discrimination would adversely affect the morale of young black soldiers thrust into close association with their white counter parts. The mystery was solved at the 1995 dedication of our National Korean War Memorial while I was standing at a unit muster with my old wartime buddies. I felt a hand on my arm, "You're Sgt Don Cohen, right?" I turned to see a black guy, bald and grey. I said, "Yes." "I'm Ralph Hodge, you put me on a big rock to give you covering fire." "No, that was Ralph King." "No, Ralph Hodge." How we ever mixed up his name we'll never know. He had been hit in the hip. Some guys from above helped him uphill. He was flown to Japan, then the States where he put a year in the hospital. Discharged, he finished college with a PhD in Civil Engineering. With his Purple Heart he decided to join the Air Force. He spent 33 years as an officer, retiring as a 'Bird Colonel.' We now keep in contact seeing each other at 2d Div. reunions.

<u>Above Left</u>. Heartbreak Ridge with ' Luke the Gook's Castle'— the pinnacle in the upper right of photo.   <u>Above.</u> Sgt. Proft proudly flies his Texas flag at his OP on Bloody Ridge, Hill 983, Sept. 1951.   <u>Both photos courtesy of Gene Proft.</u>
<u>Below</u>.   An 8 inch howitzer from the 720th F A Bn., X Corps, fires in support of the 5th ROK Division. Near Yang-gu, Aug 1951.
<u>Photo from the National Archives.</u>

Above Left. Whenever and wherever they could be useful the, Navy furnished gun fire support for the Infantry. Here the USS Helena adds her big guns to the fight. Above Right. Here the Ethiopian troops are given a welcome to Korea. They proved to be great fighters. Photos from National Archives.

Below Left. This W.P. was not hitting the Chinese positions. An accident in the 37th Field Artillery ammo dump creates this bit of excitement, October 1951.

Right. Lt. Barnes stands beside a sign that reads, "This is the M L R. The Reds direct traffic beyond this point." .... Mortar Valley.

Both lower photos courtesy of Fred Proft.

RED DRAGON
The SECOND ROUND
FACES OF WAR II

Fred	E.	Proft	US 54 028 960
First Name	MI	Last Name	Serial Number
Gene	1576	1 July 1928	SFC
Nickname	MOS	Birthday	Grade / Rank
1st FA Obsvn Bn, X Corps		3 Jul 1951-17 Apr 1952	Port Arthur, TX
Unit (s)		Duty Tour (s)	Home Town
Bronze Star w/ V device	Korean Campaign Service Medal w/ 4stars		United Nations Medal
Medals & Awards			
National Defense Service Medal	ROK Presidential Unit Citation		Korean War Service Medal

MEMORIES OF KOREA

I just missed the draft for WW II, but my number was called on 30 November 1950 for the Korean War. At Ft Sill, OK I was assigned to the 653d FA Obsvn Bn. I landed at Pusan on 1 July 1951. My orders were for Battery B of the 1st FA Obsvn Bn located in the X Corps sector. A Sgt met me. He asked, "Are you Proft?" When I answered, "Yes," he grabbed my arm to inform me I was not to leave the area unless he accompanied me. I was his replacement. He didn't want anything to happen to me! My radio call designation was to be "Nathan Hale Baker Flash." With that ID as my radio call sign, I was equipped for duty on my first front line 'Flash' FO assignment at an OP covering Bloody Ridge on the East Central Front. I was told the OP was on a hill. Where I came from we called them mountains! Loaded with a pack stuffed with all my personal gear and needed military equipment, I was laden like a Missouri mule. I didn't think I could make it to the top. My leg muscles and knees were killing me. The 'veterans' and the Korean "Chiogi" boys would slow down to let me catch up. A month later and I was keeping up with the best of them, but oh! man, that first hill climb!

In writing an essay in connection with the 50th Anniversary Commemoration of the Korean War, I reread letters I had sent home 50 years before. They were real memory joggers. I had encapsulated some of those wartime incidents in my letters home. My children and grandchildren thought them interesting and informative of events and happenings of that wartime period. Perhaps the readers of the book *Red Dragon*® will agree with the editor of this book who urged me to record them for his readers and for posterity.

ARTIFICIAL MOONLIGHT On moonless cloudy nights, giant searchlights in the rear would bounce their beams off clouds to light up the front as a full moon would do. Watching this procedure being set up was sometimes hilarious. An officer on the line would direct them up/down, right/left. Sometimes the beams would be set so low they lit up our positions as if in daylight. When that happened you could hear the howls of disapproval from the infantrymen all along the MSR. "Shine the damn thing on the Gooks, not on us!"

FIRE POWER On my 1st OP, the infantry on line with us were a jittery bunch. If a tin can were to rattle down hill,(either dislodged by an animal or thrown by a soldier) all hell would break loose. It sounded like a full scale war until an officer stood up and shouted "Cease Fire, Cease Fire, God Dammit, Cease Fire," firing then dribbled to a stop. Next morning, you'd see those guys going down hill for more ammo, only to repeat the scenario a few days later. Veteran outfits react differently. First a few shots, then a crescendo.

THE WORM One of the infantrymen began violently coughing and gagging. A minute or so later he yelled, "Look at that damn thing, it came out of me!" From his vomit, a roundworm about 4" long was crawling away. One of his buddies chased it down, killed it with an entrenching tool. The first thing I did when I returned home to Texas was to go to the drugstore and buy some worm medicine!

THE RIFLE Some guys from the same jittery outfit were going on patrol. One man tripped, digging the muzzle of his M-1 in the ground, plugging the muzzle. He stood up, pointed the rifle in the air and fired 2 shots. Two neat bulges made rings around the barrel. His patrol leader, after dressing him down, was going to make him go on patrol with the weapon until one of his buddies lent him his rifle.

THE MARINE Right after I checked into Baker Battery I was on my way one morning to my FO position. The Marines were in process of being relieved by an Army division. As I started up hill I saw this Marine who was crying. His pal was trying to comfort him. It made me realize that "those tough Marines" were just as human as the rest of us GIs. They had been through a rough ordeal.

TEA TIME! A British gun battery was firing a mission for me on enemy troops I had observed. We were getting on target when the British officer on the phone said, " We will suspend fire for 15 minutes." I asked," What's the problem?" His answer was, "It is tea time." He said they would get back to me after the break. I told him, "Forget it. The enemy will be long gone by that time!" I found it hard to believe this was a common occurrence until in later years I saw the movie, "A Bridge Too Far" where the British halted their relief column to have tea while their own men were being clobbered on a bridgehead. Strange things happen in a war.

THE TURKS When the Turks were on line with us, I felt safe and secure. I had heard tales about their tactics and fierceness in battle. For example, they would set up an ambush on the line by deploying a squad of men in a perimeter around a campfire where one or two men would sit as decoys. When the enemy came to investigate the open fire, they were allowed into the perimeter, then killed. While eating with two Turkish Officers one day, I asked them about their country and what they had heard about the United States. I learned they thought everybody from Chicago was a gangster, and everyone from Texas was a cowboy! These ideas came from American movies shown in Turkey. I had the unique experience of working with Turkish, French, British and Ethiopian troops. In talking with these UN forces, I found they knew more about Americans and our country than we did about their country or people.

THE SPIRIT OF BATTLE The French Bn, at one time were on line with us, sent out a probing patrol to Hill 651 across the Satari valley. They got across the valley and almost to the hill crest undetected. Nearing the crest they began shouting "Viva La France," yelling in French as they clambered upward. This awakened the enemy who began rolling grenades down hill ,subjecting the French to a heavy volume of small arms fire causing them to pull back. I later asked one French trooper whose eyeglasses had a missing lens, "Why do the French start yelling and lose the element of surprise?" His reply was, "Qui, Qui," that is the spirit of battle!" I enjoyed being on line with them. They were entertaining and interesting, having a completely different outlook of life than Americans.

THE TRADE One of the Frenchmen had a Thompson submachine gun. I traded my carbine for his TSMG. I lugged that heavy thing with its even heavier clips of .45 caliber ammo for a week, then looked him up and said I wanted to trade back. He laughed and said, "I knew you would be back." It may have been a good weapon for a gangster, but it was too heavy for a hill climbing FO in Korea.

FIREWORKS One afternoon we heard explosions, smoke was rising from an artillery unit on the other side of the valley. We assumed it was "incoming mail,"but soon realized it was their own ammo exploding. We stood watching the fireworks until something hit our water bag and sizzled to the ground. It was a piece of an exploding artillery shell. We stopped being spectators and took quick cover.

FRIENDLY FIRE One night we heard planes flying over followed by explosions, some pretty close. We figured an enemy air raid until we looked at one of the larger bomb fragments and saw US ordnance markings and letters. *Friendly Fire*, I believe it is called.

NAVAL SUPPORT A Marine spotter from the Battleship Iowa used our OP instrument bunker to fire the ship's 16 inch guns on an enemy position across the valley. The enemy had dug caves into the mountainside, bringing up artillery that would move out, fire, then pull back into a cave. The spotter was good. He was on target with his third round. Flight time of the shells was over 2½ minutes. Those big shells came roaring in like a freight train. He really worked those artillery caves over good. 30 minutes after the shelling stopped, we could see the enemy come staggering out of their caves as if they were drunk. I didn't think anything could stand that pounding.

THE SNIPER Another day looking through my scope, hunting for targets, scanning enemy trenches and bunkers on the ridge line nearest us I saw this guy in a brown uniform with red epaulets. His cap had a red band on it. I was sure I had spotted a Russian advisor. ecause the ridge line was so close, I thought I would try my hand at potting him with an M-1 rifle. One of my OP men looked through the scope to tell me where my rounds were hitting and what corrections to make. I did not hit him, but came close enough to make him take cover. Next day we all paid for my foolishness. They brought up an antitank gun and proceeded to work over every bunker on our ridge. They were good, too! When they got to our bunker, the first round was high, the second was low, we emptied the bunker before their third round hit right smack into the observation 'slit', tearing up all our maps, phones, instruments and personal gear. When it was over, one of the infantrymen came over to our OP to tell us, "Don't draw any more fire on our positions!"

HILLS AND MOUNTAINS- - Jagged peaks and ridges, swift mountain streams and small valleys were typical of terrain in the X Corps area of the East Central Front where I spent most of my time in Korea. A terrain map of Korea shows the western and southern parts have more flatland with hills of lower elevation than eastern and northern parts of Korea. I hated this aspect of my duty when we had to climb the high mountains, especially if loaded with water, rations, supplies and other military gear. With the exception of the bitter winter cold, the interminable, steep and arduously climbed mountains were the worst aspects of Korean service. When possible we utilized Korean "Chiogi" porters. They went up and down the mountains with a patient, side- wise, peasant plodding gait, carrying tremendous loads without stopping for breaks. I adopted their mode of climbing. It made the task easier. I envied the fellows on the Western front. On a visit to their sector, I climbed to their highest OP in 15 minutes. It was a gentle slope and an easy path.

THE FLAG A goodly number of Texans were in our Flash Platoon. The Texas flag flew on a pole near our forward CP. In one area, a column of tanks moved up each night to block the valley floor. As they passed the Texas flag, the officer in the lead tank would order 'Hand Salute.' Each tank in passing would render a snappy salute. The officer in the lead tank was a Texas Aggie.

AFTER THOUGHTS 10 months of Army service in Korea made me intensely aware of the blessings we have in the USA, blessings that many people take for granted. These are never appreciated until we are deprived of them. I pray that God may always bless America!

Above Left.   Map of the battle at the Imjin River,   April 1951.
Above.   Troops from the British 29th Brigade regroup after the battle at the Imjin River, Chinese 5th phase offensive, April 1951.
Lower Left: A British soldier is treated at India's Field Hospital. It looks like some of the treatment might be a cup of tea.
Map and photos from the Internet and Archives.

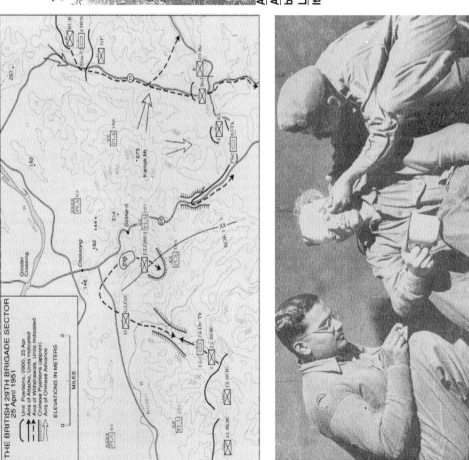

Photo at right of Lieut General A. Banerjee that was taken in June of 1983 while he was serving as Director General of Medical Services for the Indian Army.   Photo courtesy of General Banerjee.

RED DRAGON
The SECOND ROUND
FACES OF WAR II

Ashok	None	Banerjee	MR 381 Indian Army
First Name	MI	Last Name	Serial Number
None	Medical Officer	02 Jan 1926	Lt Gen (then Capt)
Nickname	MOS	Birthday	Grade / Rank
60 Indian Field Amb.	11 Nov '50-10 Jun'53	Dharbanga, India
Unit (s)	Duty Tour (s)	Home Town
Mentioned in Despatches	Param Vishist Seva Medal	Vir Chakra
Medals & Awards		
General Service medal w/ Korea Clasp		United Nations Service Medal

OPERATION COMMANDO

As a member of 60 Indian Field Ambulance I had been active in our medical role of tending battle casualties since arrival in Korea November 1950. Combat service tends to harden the sensibilities. It is nature's way of coping with the terrible sights and carnage of war. However, as a medical doctor in my chosen field of service to mankind, I was never able to overcome the mental anguish at the human devastation of the battlefield. After almost a year of caring for battle casualties, my heart constricted when, in late Sept '51, I heard the hush-hush rumor that a new offensive termed "Operation Commando" was in the near offing. I was then with a forward detachment of 60 Ind Amb assigned to give medical coverage to Commonwealth Division's 28th Brigade. Our CO, Lt Col Rangaraj, myself and a detachment from 60 Ind Amb crossed the Imjin river to prepare a Casualty Clearing Post for the wounded men of Operation Commando who were sure to begin arriving the next day. We also set up a Dressing Station on the banks of the Imjin.

We spent the night in the open, exhausted, with little sleep, anticipating and excited, knowing that the morrow would be a bloody day of reckoning for the British Infantry in the attack. Early on the morn of 3 Oct, we moved out in darkness to arrive at an area designated by Brigade as a site for our CCP. This was a re-enterent (foot of a ridge) of a hill feature just short of the road. We had hardly put up a squad tent for use as a dressing station when we were told to relocate. The site had been preempted by the 8th Hussars (Tank Regt) as their Regimental Aid Post. We moved up the re-enterant about 50 yards and set our CCP there.

We had barely settled in when we heard the shrill screech of a shell, followed by an explosion as the shell impacted nearby. Myself, the Padre of our Brigade, and Capt Subhu Krishnan were all in the Reception Tent. As one man, we hit the deck! The shell had landed at the exact same spot where we had earlier located, only to be displaced by the 8th Hussars Regimental Aid Post! One NCO was KIA. The Regt Med Officer took shrapnel in the spine, resulting in paralysis. One of the 8th Hussar tanks was demolished. We attended the two wounded men, evacuating them to the rear in our ambulance. The rest of the day was spent in ministering to the wounded who came pouring into our CCP. Enemy resistance stiffened. The attack came to a virtual standstill. The necessity for a change in tactical planning and need for an alternative attack procedure was apparent to those directing "Operation Commando."

The last of that wounded on that day's action were evacuated by late evening. We had a chance to get a nights sleep. I lay awake for a time in my foxhole(my first experience in such cramped quarters) thanking God repeatedly for my lucky escape that morning. On the morning of 4 Oct, The Royal Northumberland Fusiliers and Kings Own Scottish Borderers went all out in the attack to take Pt 355. 3Bn Royal Australian Regiment mounted a flank attack on the right to assist in the operation. Pt 355 was taken at 1130 hours. Next day, 5 Oct, a further attack was planned in which 3Bn RAR would take Pt 317. 1Bn RNF was tasked to capture Pt 217 whilst 1Bn KSLI was to exploit the area north of PT 217. The decision was made to have a modified CCP nearer the 3RAR sector as this Bn was expected to take heavy casualties in their attack on the Chinese enemy.

In the early morning of 5 Oct, I was ordered to take several ambulances and a detachment of men to establish an auxiliary CCP post near Myriyang-san. The slight hillside was heavily wooded. Fighting was severe and casualties were heavy. 3Bn RAR captured Pt 317 after a day long battle in which they suffered numerous casualties. Our auxiliary CCP was within mortar range. Shelling was intense from time to time. We had not had time to dig in so it was necessary to work out in the open to attend the casualties. The morale of the troops, medical and wounded alike, was excellent. I was impressed by the manner in which the casualties behaved under such stringent conditions. It was painful to see so many young soldiers in their late teens being disabled by the ravages of war. Fighting continued in a desultory way for the next three days. The total number of casualties for "Operation Commando," 3 Oct through 8 Oct was 348. 272 were Battle Casualties, 22 were due to Battle Exhaustion, and 54 were Medical.

War takes its toll in death and suffering, friend and foe alike. It is my fervent hope that mankind will learn to live without war.

Above. In the early days of the war, first aid was slow and crude. Here a Navy Corpsman is holding a plasma bottle while giving a transfusion to a wounded Marine. Below. With the advent of helicopters, quick evacuation from the battlefield saved many lives. Later still with the arrival of 'flack jackets' the GIs survivability was further improved. Archive Photos.

RED DRAGON
The SECOND ROUND
FACES OF WAR II

Joaquin	B.	Benitez	1152115 USMC
First Name	MI	Last Name	Serial Number
None	0311	14 July 1929	Sergeant
Nickname	MOS	Birthday	Grade / Rank
I/3/7 1st MarDiv		6th Draft Feb-11Sept 1951	Rescue, CA
Unit (s)		Duty Tour (s)	Home Town
Purple Heart Medal	American Campaign Service Medal		Asiatic Pacific Campaign Medal
Medals & Awards			
Victory Medal	NDSM	Korean Campaign Service Medal w/ 3Bronze stars	UN Medal

A MARINE HAS A HOSPITAL TOUR OF DUTY

It began on 10 Sept 1951 with the order to occupy Hill 749. We had spent most of day in truck convoy getting there. Disembarking, we walked across a small valley, crossed a river and began the climb. Hill 749 was steep and thinly wooded. It had rained that day, making for a slippery ascent. Ropes were tied, tree to tree, for use as hand holds to help us in climb. The first night was quiet, with only occasional light machine gun and sporadic rifle fire directed at us. I spent considerable time scouting the lay of the land, moving frequently so as not be a sitting target. 11 Sept was a warm, beautiful day. Out on the finger of one the hill's ridges, I could see Lt Ramer and several other marines firing across the ridge. Sometime later my squad leader ordered me to scout the area out to the end of the finger. As I crawled out on the finger, I passed the still figure of a marine whose head was pointed in the same direction I was moving. He was dead. About 10 feet further lay Lt Ramer, apparently dead. There were several large boulders and a few trees which I used as cover as I tried to go to the end of the finger to accomplish my mission. Two of the enemy below me in the ravine saw me. I could see the grenades arc through the air up toward my position. Grenade fragments hit me in the shoulder and helmet.

As they raised up to throw again, I fired my M-1. I began to move back up the finger as more grenades were thrown by enemies to my left. I threw all four of my grenades in retaliation. I spotted more of the enemy across the ravine. I fired several 8 round clips from my M-1 at them. I was reloading when a grenade landed an arms length to my left. Another grenade explosion nearly lifted me off the ground. I felt several sharp pains in my chest, left hip and in one leg. I managed to turn around and began the crawl back up the finger, dragging my rifle with me. I stopped to rest, yet realized I must get back or I would die. Halfway back up, I spotted two marines. They duck walked in low squatting profile, reached me and together dragged me back to the position I had left earlier.

A corpsman dusted my wounds with sulfa powder and bandaged me. Several times he gave me a morphine shot. Until shortly before dawn next day, mortar rounds kept everyone in his foxhole. Medical evacuation was not possible until daybreak when enemy fire ceased. I was carried down hill by Koreans of the ROK Service Corp. After their up hill climb with food and ammo, they carried wounded down. Going down it was steep and slippery. Bearers sometimes fell, throwing me off the stretcher. Other Koreans loaded us on to a DUKW which took us across the river. A helicopter lifted me to a rear area clearing station. A C-47 took a load of we wounded marines to the 121st Army Evac Hospital at YongDong-po. Two days later I was in recuperation on the hospital train, being helped in and out of bed by a former Japanese 'suicide pilot.' WW II had ended before he was assigned his Kamikaze mission. Next, I was flown stateside to Travis AF Base, thence to Mare Island Naval Hospital where I spent 4 months for several minor surgeries.

This hospital flat- on- my- back time gave me time for reflection. One memory haunted me as I recalled a prior incident. We had been ordered to take "at all costs" a hill needed to observe enemy positions. It was my first close look at the enemy. I shot one frightened enemy soldier in flight who turned his head to look behind him. Others of the fleeing enemy were shot in refusal to surrender. Just as it was getting dark, a figure ran from a Korean hut on the hillside to another hut lower down the hill. Four of us fired at the running figure. Next morning, a fire team with an interpreter made a reconn down the hill. The figure we had fired at was a ten year old girl. Miraculously, she had suffered only a bullet burn on one leg. There were three holes in the loose clothing she was wearing. The older persons were questioned and found to be "innocent bystanders," civilians caught in the midst of war. We left all the rations we had with us in slight recompense for the terror we inflicted. I have thanked my maker on many occasions that I did not have to shoulder the death guilt of this innocent girl and go to my grave with such a mortal sin on my conscience.

Released from Mare Island Naval Hospital I reported to Camp Pendleton as a troop handler. A surgical session at Santa Margarita Naval Hospital removed more grenade fragments. I returned to Camp Pendleton until released from active duty. I went on to college, obtained my degree working at McClellan AF Base, retiring after 32 years of service there. In tribute, I owe my life to those two marines who risked their lives to help a badly wounded marine. They honored the USMC code of never leaving a wounded man.

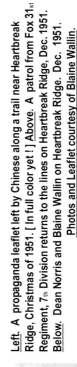

Left. A propaganda leaflet left by Chinese along a trail near Heartbreak Ridge, Christmas of 1951. [In full color yet !] Above. A patrol from Fox 31st Regiment, 7th Division returns to the lines on Heartbreak Ridge, Dec. 1951. Below. Dean Norris and Blaine Wallin on Heartbreak Ridge. Dec. 1951. Photos and Leaflet courtesy of Blaine Wallin.

Mr. Moneybags is in Florida this Christmas.

RED DRAGON
The SECOND ROUND
FACES OF WAR II

Blaine	B.	Wallin	US 55036678
First Name	MI	Last Name	Serial Number
None	1745	10 Sept 1928	Sgt First Class
Nickname	MOS	Birthday	Grade / Rank
Fox/31/7		April 1951-Mar 1952	Cambridge, MN
Unit (s)		Duty Tour (s)	Home Town
Combat Infantry Badge		Korean Campaign Service Medal w/bronze star	

Medals & Awards

National Defense Service Medal   United Nations Service Medal   Korean War Service Medal

ONE YEAR IN A RIFLE PLATOON

By the end of 1950, the 'police' action in Korea was chewing up men faster than voluntary enlistment could fill ranks. I was drafted in late November and given three months basic training at Fort Riley, KS, then home on a week's furlough. I shipped overseas on the Marine Phoenix to Pusan in Korea. Assigned to the 7th Inf Div and placed on a train, I was handed over to a Sgt on arrival at what was to me to me, an unknown destination. He shepherded 14 of us to Fox Company, 31st Inf Regt. This was to be my home for the next year. Looking back, it was a good home for making battle friends. My year of 'tutored education'- military on-the-job training-however educational it was, is not a course I would care to repeat. I was placed in the 4th sqd of the 2d plat. My sqd ldr was William Guy, a former AF officer, who after WW II, enlisted in the Army. Another WWII vet, Pat Westfall, was our plat sgt and also a HM/31/7 survivor of the Chosin Reservoir battles of the previous winter. Capt Abbot, another WWII vet, was Company Commander. He was a hard driver, not prone to sympathy. I watched actions of these men closely in a pragmatic effort to glean the lore of combat survival they had so obviously learned. While I know luck plays a significant role in a soldier's survival, soldierly skills also play a major role.

Other squad mates were Cpl Kenny Howard, Akron, OH, later 1st Sgt; Jessie Gonzalez, Los Angeles; Dean Norris, Ohio; Shokaskie from an Eastern state; Penrose; and Cannon O'Grady, Macomb, Ga. O'Grady was not sociable with Yanks. Two close friends were Donald Gagnon and Leo Kovar from Lincoln, NE. Kovar and I were both farm boys. Gagnon was a machine gunner. I was assigned as assistant gunner. My job was to lie to his left, slightly behind him to smooth out the ammo belt so it fed with out kinking into the LMG. Shortly after my arrival, I had my baptism of fire. In the attack on Hill 300, Capt Abbott sited our gun with a good field of fire on the objective. Unfortunately we had no cover, and were targets in a shooting gallery. We gave the attacking rifleman heavy covering fire. The Chinese turned every available weapon on us in an effort to wipe out our LMG. Enemy fire rained down on us, finally with success. I felt a sting on my neck. I reached up, wiped off blood, more blood than from my slight neck wound. Gagnon was running a river from his riddled left shoulder. He was taken off in a stretcher. I returned to the line after being patched up.

Later in an attack on 'No Name Hill', I was partnered with Leo Kovar. Leo was a WW II Reservist, married, with a daughter he had yet to see. He was a MG ammo bearer. In this attack we both carried two 500 round boxes of .30 caliber metal belted MG ammo plus a dozen grenades in addition to our own rifles, personal grenades and ammo. It makes for a heavy load, especially up hill, and Korea was all uphill. Pooped, we leaned against a shell torn tree stump to rest. Capt Abbot was with our group of 12 men. The two squads ahead of us had been pinned down. I told Kovar I was going to crawl up 15 or 20 feet to see what was going on. A few minutes later I heard Capt Abbott radio for supporting artillery fire. We got it, including a short round which hit smack dab on Kovar. All that I could see when the smoke and dirt cleared were some of Kovar's intestines looped over the jagged branch of a shell torn tree 40 feet away. I have thought of Leo Kovar many times over the years. If he had been as curious as I, would he be alive today? On 17 June we pulled back into reserve for rest and replacements. There were now 11 men in my platoon. We had numbered 40 when I arrived in early April. Sgt Guy and I were all that was left of the 4th squad. I had passed my first course in survival the hard way.

Back on line into the meat grinder. The start of a series of offensives designed to push the Reds completely out of South Korea. Our positions were on Hill 1073. Hill 1073 was noted for its tramway built by Sgt Gus Edson of the 13th Engineers. It supplied HM/31 with 4.2 mortar ammunition. HM had mounted its 12 guns near the top of that 3600 feet high hill a month or so earlier. Shards of shrapnel in my neck caused blood poisoning. A week of penicillin shots in a field hospital put me back in my company. At the bottom of the hill, I bummed a ride on the tram. While it was forbidden, I prevailed on the operator to overlook the SOP. Only free ride I ever had in Korea! With luck and careful attention to my 'soldier's bible for survival', I returned to the states as a Sgt First Class in April of 1952. The 'police' action continued for 15 bloody months before a cease fire was negotiated on 27 July 1953. I was a different young man than the callow youth of a year earlier. I spent the rest of my army career as a plat sgt in the "Dixie" Regt NG at Camp Atturbury, IN. I had a burning desire to pass on hard learned lessons of my year as a Combat Infantryman in Korea. Knowledge saves lives.

Top Photo. Trouble heading south ! This train load of Chinese tanks are on the move with an eye open for American aircraft. Late 1951. CCF photo from the Internet. Below. A Marine surveys the final results of another human wave attack. Right. Another dead enemy soldier adding to the many ugly ' faces of war.' Photos courtesy of Bill Palizzolo

RED DRAGON
The SECOND ROUND
FACES OF WAR II

William	V.	Palizzolo	10-602 277 USMC
First Name	MI	Last Name	Serial Number
Bill	O311	10 July 1931	Sgt
Nickname	MOS	Birthday	Grade / Rank
B/1/7/1MarDiv		14 Apr 1951-15 Mar 1952	Boston, MA
Unit (s)		Duty Tour (s)	Home Town

Purple Heart Medal Korean Campaign Service Medal, w/4 stars U N Medal ROK PUC

Medals & Awards

Navy Presidential Unit Citation National Defense Service Medal ROK War Service Medal

FATE FLIPS THE COIN

I was born in South Boston which had the highest number of combat deaths of any neighborhood area in the country during the Vietnam War. This has nothing to do with the Korean War except both were 'Generaled' by politicians. As youngsters, our major entertainment was tossing coins against a wall. The closest coin to the wall won all the coins. Starting at age 10 with pennies, at 18 we were pitching quarters. At 16 I joined the Marine Corps Reserve to have new clothes, shoes and underwear. I was 19 when the war began in Korea. Nov 6,1950 I was sent to Paris Island, on to Camp Pendleton, then boarded ship to Korea. My first day in Korea, 7 of us were helicoptered to the front lines. I stayed there one full year, April of '51 to April of '52 as a rifleman and bazooka gunner leader. One of my commanding officers was 2d Lt Eddy LeBaron called "Little All American" for his feats on the football field. He must have been a well known personality. Rear area officers, Captain to Colonel, would jeep to the front lines just to see and talk to him. I was not, and am not a football fan, so could not understand why these high ranking officers would risk the dangers of the front line just to shake hands and talk. He later went on to play professional football but I never kept track of his football career. I do remember he was a brave officer and a good guy. Maybe one reason I liked him is because he was shorter than I! I'm 5'7".

Getting off the helicopter that first day I noticed a canvas tent spread flat on the ground. Underneath it were 7 bodies. The Sgt told us that we were replacements for these 7 men. He also announced a typist was needed for Co HQ. I was tempted to volunteer but did not want to repeat the drudgery of my last job as a typist for a trucking company. My buddy, John Protevi, now deceased, did volunteer. I was momentarily concerned I might have made a mistake. As it turned out, I did not. The 6 of us trudged to the top of the hill to join our units. I had no sooner reported in, when in an effort to evade incoming mortar rounds, I hit the dirt. My canteen came loose, rolled over the cliff, never to be seen again. Our Medic, a black man named Hogan, saw what had happened and gave me one of his two canteens. That simple act of kindness has stayed with me over the years. I hope he reads this and contacts me. 'Doc' Hogan received several awards for bravery, risking his own life on numerous occasions as he treated front line casualties.

The Chinese would attack at night, bugles blowing, shouting, "Marine, you die!" More Chinese died than did Marines! Photos taken at the time attest the truth in graphic detail. I never thought I would leave Korea alive, or at least without a crippling wound. As it turned out I took my only wound in a mortar attack where a hunk of shrapnel gashed my upper thigh. I was one lucky guy! On Hill 673 I went down with an attack of malaria, fever of 105 degrees. Lt LeBaron saw the sweat on my face but could not evacuate me for 2 days due to the ferocity of battle at that time. When it was over, I turned myself in to a Mash Hospital. I suffered 3 more attacks while in Korea. Back in the states the VA gave me a "sure cure." Thankfully, I haven't had another attack these past 50 years.

I really was one lucky Marine. We changed positions to an area 15 miles away, moving out, full pack and weapons. It began to rain. It was September but felt like January, cold,cold. We had ponchos yet were soaked to the skin. 11 PM after a hard hike we arrived at the new position. Ordinarily we would have dug individual foxholes. Because it was so cold we decided to dig a bigger hole to sleep together to benefit from each other's warmth. We finished the hole, and crawled into our sleeping bags. Had just began to warm up when the Co Cmdr showed up with the other bazooka team leader. Chinese tanks had been spotted. One team had to move toward the road to guard it. Neither team wanted the duty. We flipped a coin. I lost. My team members screamed at me for losing. We moved a few hundred yards to a position overlooking the road. Again we dug in, sleeping two at a time with one man on lookout. A mortar attack began that lasted hours. At daybreak on order, we rejoined the company. The rain had stopped but it was still cold, muddy and miserable. On our way back to join our platoon, we passed by our original 3 man foxhole. It had taken a direct hit from a mortar shell. Had we not been posted to tank guard overlooking the nearby road, we would have been dead. With a direct hit, it would have been a tough call to link body parts with names. My comrades were now patting me on the back in congratulation for losing the toss! We were known as the "Lucky Bill Bazooka Team" for the next few weeks. 51 years ago, I remember it as if it were yesterday. Every time I go to Vegas I keep thinking I can't lose. I won the most important coin toss of my life in Korea!

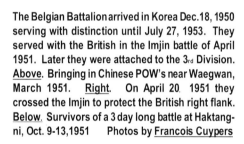

Above. Members of the Belgian Bn. in painted faces return from a night patrol near Waegwan, Korea, March 1951. Note burp gun on the left and 'man's best friend ' on the right. The Belgians were professional troops.

The Belgian Battalion arrived in Korea Dec.18, 1950 serving with distinction until July 27, 1953. They served with the British in the Imjin battle of April 1951. Later they were attached to the 3rd Division. Above. Bringing in Chinese POW's near Waegwan, March 1951. Right. On April 20, 1951 they crossed the Imjin to protect the British right flank. Below. Survivors of a 3 day long battle at Haktang-ni, Oct. 9-13,1951 Photos by Francois Cuypers

Below. The Chinese 'owned' a part of the Imjin River for a brief period after the battle. These were 'permanent- party', thanks to our Air Force and Artillery. The famous battle of the Imjin took place in April 1951.

Above. The Belgian Bn. retreats over the Imjin River, April 25, 1951. Right. Catholic Padre "Peter' and a Korean elder enjoy a 'smoke break together.' Lower Right. Some Belgian soldiers proudly display their Christmas dinner, December 1951. Lower Left. The Belgian Bn. C.O. Sept. 1950 to Aug. 1951 was Lt. Col. Albert Crahay. All photos by Francois Cuypers.

RED DRAGON
The SECOND ROUND
FACES OF WAR II

Billie	G.	Kanell	RA 17 317 531
First Name	MI	Last Name	Serial Number
None	1745	26 June 1931	Private
Nickname	MOS	Birthday	Grade / Rank
Item Co 35th Inf 25th Div		28 Aug---7 Sept 1951	Poplar Bluff, MO
Unit (s)		Duty Tour (s)	Home Town
MEDAL OF HONOR	Purple Heart	Combat Infantry Badge	National Defense Medal
Medals & Awards			
Korean Campaign Service Medal, one bronze star			United Nations Service Medal

GREATER LOVE HATH NO MAN THAN THIS

His life ended on 7 September 1951 in the far, far away country of Korea at Pyonggang a place with a strange and unfamiliar name thousands of miles from his place of birth in Poplar Bluff, MO. He was 20 years of age, just reaching maturity, too young to die. He sacrificed his life upon the altar of freedom to save the lives of his comrades. He had enlisted in early 1951 in answer to his country's call, not waiting for his draft board notice. He came from a military family. His father, a veteran of WW II, had retired after 20 years service in the US Army. One brother was currently serving in the Army, another in the Air Force. Military service was a proud tradition in his family. He took basic training at Schofield Barracks in Hawaii where a selected few of his class were further assigned to Advanced Infantry Training School. He graduated in late July 1951. From Hawaii he flew to Japan for processing military records and issue of new uniform clothing suitable for the Korean climate. He was also issued a Garand M-1 rifle, still in cosmoline. An old army custom required he memorize his rifle number before he left the depot. He already knew the old army adage: "This is your piece. Sleep with it, it is at your side as you eat, you take it with you everywhere you go. Take care of it and it will take care of you."

In a few days he took ship with other young soldiers to Korea where he was assigned to Item Company of the 35th("Cacti") Infantry Regiment of the 25th Infantry Division. His regiment was then engaged in the Pyonggang area at the apex of the 'Iron Triangle'. On 28 August 1951 he joined Item Company north of Pyonggang. Both Item and Love companies were dug in on Hill 717 several miles in front of the main battle line in alert position to warn of a major Chinese offensive attack. Billie Kanell joined his squad about 5 PM. He was there but an hour when his platoon was ordered to make a 5 day routine relief of another company platoon on Hill 717. Upon completion of the relief about 9 PM the new man, Billie Kanell, was assigned to a forward bunker with two other men, PFC Steve Mullan of Santa Clara, CA and PFC F. M. Rodriquez. Mullen and Rodriquez had only a nodding acquaintance. In the get-to-know-you stage, Billie showed Steve a pearl handled revolver his dad had given him for close-in protection. Mullen advised it be kept hidden., It was not "regulation" and might be confiscated. The three began exchanging confidences as soldiers are wont to do as they size each other up in the process of determining mutual combat dependability. Bille Kanell was Protestant, both Mullan and Rodriquez were Catholic. Their position was a 3 man machine gun bunker which meant they were more exposed to the enemy than a rifleman in his foxhole. About midnight, in soldier parlance, "All hell exploded." The Chinese launched a massive attack on Hill 717.

The Chinese attack made in brigade strength outnumbered the two American rifle companies 5 to 1. After several hours of tough, hard fighting American positions were overrun. The three men could see Chinese outlined against a background of flares and light from tracer bullets. One Chinese as he ran by tossed a concussion grenade into the bunker. Mullan saw Billie's hands go up. He clasped the grenade to his chest just as it exploded. The fighting continued. According to Steve Mullen, "Billie Kanell was still alive and conscious. Some time passed. "It could have been 5 minutes, or half an hour or so, I'm not sure. In any event I had only 2 rounds left and Rodriquez was almost out of ammo. We were completely surrounded by Chinese. Some time around 3 or 4 AM another concussion grenade was thrown in to the bunker. Rodriquez and I were kneeling. Billie Kanell grabbed that second grenade, held it to his chest as he squirmed around turning his back to us. That second grenade killed him. Rodriquez and I didn't get a scratch. The battle ended about 6 AM. Billie's body was placed on a poncho, his body was carried to the rear, placed on a stretcher then carried back to QM Graves Registration. "I was wounded in the left arm by mortar fire next day while in a bunker with 2 other wounded men and was evacuated 2 days later. American artillery pounded the Chinese incessantly, allowing us to be sent to a rear area hospital. While there, I received a Medal of Honor packet questionnaire asking that I give my version of Billie Kanell's actions. Rodriquez was a good Joe. He had gotten through to someone in HQ about Billie's heroic deed. All I had to do was verify."

The 3d Bn Situation Report (SitRep)states that I and L Companies on Hill 717 were hit by a brigade of Chinese making several "human sea attacks, wave after wave" between 2400 and 0600 hours 7 September. The Love Company platoon on Hill 682, 1000 yards to the right of Hill 717 was beset by 2 Chinese Bns girdling the hill, blocking reinforcements or supplies. 46 American soldiers died in these attacks. The Chinese left more than a hundred men tangled in the barbed wire, but managed to carry off the rest of their dead.

RED DRAGON
The Second Round
FACES OF WAR II

FREEDOM IS NEVER FREE
IT HAS NO MEASURE
IN WEALTH OR TREASURE
IT IS PAID IN LIVES OF OUR YOUNG
WHEN YOU GO HOME
TELL THEM FOR US AND SAY
FOR YOUR TOMORROW
WE GAVE OUR TODAY

Rank: Private RA 17 317 531
Organization: Company I, 35th Infantry Regiment
25th Infantry Division
Place and Date: Near Pyonggang, Korea September 7, 1951
Entered service at Poplar Bluff, Missouri
Birth: 26 June 1931
General Order: Number 57, June 13, 1952

CITATION

Private Billie G. Kanell, Infantry, United States Army, a member of Company I, 35th Infantry
Regiment 25th Infantry Division, distinguished himself by conspicuous **gallantry and**
outstanding courage above and beyond the call of duty in action against the enemy
near Pyonggang, Korea on 7 September 1951. A numerically superior hostile force had launched
a fanatical assault against friendly positions, supported by mortar and artillery fire. Private Kanell
stood in his emplacement exposed to enemy observation and action and delivered accurate fire
into the rank of assailants. An enemy grenade was hurled into his emplacement. Private Kanell
threw himself on the grenade, absorbing the blast with his body to protect two of his comrades
from serious injury and possible death. A few seconds later another grenade was thrown **into**
his emplacement and, although seriously wounded by the first missile, he summoned his waning
strength to roll toward the second grenade, using his body as a shield to protect his comrades.
He was mortally wounded as a result of his actions. His indomitable courage, sustained fortitude
against overwhelming odds and gallant self sacrifice reflect the highest credit upon himself and
the [citizen] Infantry of the United States and the United States Army

VALOR

There is a decoration
Which stands above the rest
To cite outstanding bravery
    Among our nation's best.
Thirteen stars are clustered
On a band of softened blue
And the medal it embraces
    Is held by very few.
    This honored Star of Valor
Speaks of peerless courage
And of selfless dedication.
    When hell and death drew near.
	Its mettle has been tested
	On the fiery field of war
	On jungle trails, in mountain vales
	    And on the ocean's floor.
	Its spirit has shown brightly
	Where eagles and hawks fly
	And where men who rode the thunder
	    Have gone to fight and die.
	    In many times, in many climes
	Engaged in mortal strife
	The act that gained the medal
	    Brought to an end a gallant life.
		And to those few who carry on
		Immortal, though they live,
		There is no tribute we can pay
		    Nor accolade we may give.
		    They did not seek worldly gain
		For honors, praise or laud
		But just to know they served
		    Their country and their God.
		
		From The Laughter and The Tears cc 1999
		............Robert A. Gannon
		United States Marine Corps

177

Above Billie Kanell gets all that cosmoline out of his rifle during basic. At left he nears completion of his advanced infantry training at Schofield Barracks in Hawaii. Photos Courtesy of Wanda Kanell Burkett.

New troops are transported from the port of Inchon in 'cattle' trucks to their respective replacement ['repo'] depot. There they will be quickly 'parceled out' to units whose needs and losses are the greatest. Photo from the Internet.

RED DRAGON
The SECOND ROUND
FACES OF WAR II

James	H.	Appleton	115 8912 USMC
First Name	MI	Last Name	Serial Number
Appy	0311	28 August 1931	Cpl
Nickname	MOS	Birthday	Grade / Rank
Item Co 5th Marine Regt 1st MarDiv		Apr '51-Apr '52	Nashville, TN
Unit (s)		Duty Tour (s)	Home Town

Silver Star Commendation Medal w Combat V Navy PUC,1star USMC Good Conduct Medal

Medals & Awards

USN Occpn Medal w/Eur clasp NDSM KCMS,3 battle stars KSM UN Medal ROKPUC KWSM

GROUND SQUIRRELS

In the fall of 1951 the Korean War had droned on into its second year. Whether it was geography or the time of the year, we suddenly faced a new adversary as we stood watch in "Indian Country." The first time I heard these furry little fellows, it scared the living hell out of me. One night standing watch, I heard a rustle and a flurry of movement in the underbrush which sounded to me like the whole North Korean army was rushing my position. The sound died away, but soon started up again. I woke up my buddy in the next foxhole and told him what I had heard. He raised up, all blurry eyed and opined, "'Appy', it's just those damn ground squirrels." I had not heard them before, having been away at sniper school. They began their quest for food about 2200, continuing nightly until around 0300 hours. Then we began to look upon them as an asset. We learned that as long as they roamed around out front, there were no 'bad guys' in the immediate area. The little critters would cease all activity whenever enemy patrols approached.

The dead silence was a giveaway that someone, or several someones, were crawling around to our front intent on something other than paying us a pleasant visit. The usual procedure when critter activity shut down was to wake your foxhole buddy on the premise that two pairs of eyes and ears were better than one. It was always amazing how deathly quiet it seemed to get when the ground squirrels ceased their activity. In that graveyard silence you could hear the beating of your own heart. You never knew whether the next thing you heard would be the sound of a grenade rolling toward your foxhole, or the chatter of a Burp Gun aimed at you. Worse, it could presage a good sized enemy patrol paying a decidedly hostile visit. Our furry little friends became valuable allies, just as effective in their warning as our best trip flares or trip grenades. In their silence out front, they alerted us to presence of the enemy.

On this particular night, my watch had turned into an eternity. I preferred the first watch from nightfall to about 0100 hours as I was prone to lie awake and fret about getting up to go on watch. Many times it did not make any difference since the Skipper would call for "100% All Night Alert." That meant that everyone was awake in every foxhole. This was generally the result of an indicated night attack. I could sometimes see my watch by moonlight, but this night was dark as pitch. In a case like this, the only way to ascertain the time is to burrow deep in a foxhole, snatch a quick peek using a lighter or flashlight covered by a poncho or blanket. This got to be an arduous chore, so I just had to estimate the time before calling my relief. I knew it must be close to the end of my watch because I had been deferring 'nature's call' and was about ready to burst. Then I heard the alarm! Or rather, the sudden silence.

Earlier I had heard a rustling in the brush down hill, followed by silence. I had mentally marked the spot, but that was an hour ago. These rustling sounds sounded a bit different. It suddenly dawned on me that it wasn't ground squirrels, but something else, something alien, something threatening, something that would kill me if I did not react quickly. Holding my M-1 in one hand, I picked up a Mark 2 Frag grenade with the other, while touching my buddy, Clarence Dinkins, with my toe. As he woke, I put my finger across his lips to signal silence. I pointed out front, holding up 2 fingers to let him know I heard 2 different sounds from 2 directions. Adrenalin from the ol' "Fight or Flight" system kicked in while fear made hair on the back of my neck stand at attention.

The rustling sounds I was now hearing were not our little furred friends! It dawned on me I was hearing a hand grenade rustling in the leaves and grass as it rolled toward our foxhole. I quickly fell to the bottom of our foxhole on top of Dinkins. As we hit bottom, I heard the grenade roll close to our foxhole, stop, then roll slightly away before it exploded. We rose up, ready to repel boarders, chucking grenades to our front, firing up a storm with our M-1s. The zing of an emptied M-1 clip signified we had fired a full clip. We ceased fire to listen. Not a sound. Soon the query from adjacent foxholes, "Appy, what the hell is going on?" I replied, "We had a night visitor but he didn't stay for supper." What had saved our hides and our lives was the raised berm of earth from our fox hole excavation piled in circular fashion around it. This slightly raised berm had preventing the grenade from dropping into our foxhole.

Oddly enough, Dinkins and I earlier debated if the hole was deep enough. We had decided to go another foot deeper! Later that night, the ground squirrels resumed their nightly food patrols. We maintained a tight watch. Everything was back to normal.

Above. Marine artillery at work. D Battery of the 11 Regt firing in May 1951.   Note homemade easy chair for spectators.
Below.   Two gunners from D Battery of the 11th are McLean and Galewick.   Photos courtesy of Barry McLean.

Above Right. A wounded G.I. is carried on a litter by Chinese P.O.W.'s in the 7th Regt, 3rd Division sector of the Chorwon Valley.
Below.   The wounded are quickly evacuated by this Bell Helicopter.   Photos by Tom Whitewater.

RED DRAGON
The SECOND ROUND
FACES OF WAR II

James	H.	Appleton	115 8912 USMC
First Name	MI	Last Name	Serial Number
Appy	0311	28 August 1931	Cpl
Nickname	MOS	Birthday	Grade / Rank
Item Co 5th Marine Regt 1st MarDiv		Apr '51-Apr '52	Nashville, TN
Unit (s)		Duty Tour (s)	Home Town

Silver Star Commendation Medal, Combat V   Navy PUC,1sta r USMC Good Conduct Medal

Medals & Awards

USN Occpn Medal,Eur clasp   NDS   KCMS,3 battle stars KSM   UN Medal ROK PUC KWSM

FRIENDLY FIRE

It was a beautiful sunny fall afternoon on a brisk autumn day. We had moved back up the lines to Hill 802 after a 3 week rest. We were back up to strength. I was functioning as the Executive Officer's runner, messenger, 'aide-de-camp', general flunky and 'gofer'. His job as XO carried the radio call sign Item 5. I was hanging around the company CP waiting to go on radio watch. Every one in the CP group manned the company radio for a 4 hour duty watch. After some experience in combat, we all developed a keen sense of hearing. We could detect the difference between incoming and outgoing artillery fire. The Division Artillery regiment, the 11th Marines, had placed a 2d Lt FO at the CP, registering artillery concentrations so he might direct fire at a moments notice to the most likely areas of enemy attack. Both the FO and the FDC kept these map grid coordinates on their map overlays for ready reference.

Having been in Korea for close to 7 months, you can bet a bundle I could tell in an instant whether the shell I heard was meant for the enemy or for us. This afternoon, in an instant I knew the shell I heard was an incoming round. But it was coming from the wrong direction! The shells were being fired from our rear where our artillery was located. As it whined in, it seemed to come directly at me. In a second, those rounds slammed into our lines, to my left, where our 1st platoon was located. As the smoke billowed up, the Skipper came out of the CP bunker and spoke directly to me, "Appy, take a 536 (walkie-talkie radio), run down there and see what the hell happened. Report back ASAP." I grabbed a radio and away I went, not in the least prepared for what I was about to see. At the scene, one squad of our LMG section had been cleaning their weapons, sitting on top of their bunker. The carnage was dreadful. It looked as if someone on a gigantic ladder had carefully zeroed in on that particular bunker and dropped a huge bomb, dead center.

There was blood and body parts strewn around. Some men were severely wounded, unconscious. Others were wounded less severely. They lay there, moaning in agony. I got on the horn (radio) and radioed the CP, "Item 6, Item 6, this is Appy. We've just taken a short round right on top of a LMG squad sitting on top of their bunker, cleaning their weapons. We need all the Corpsmen you can spare, and a Medivac Chopper, maybe two of 'em, ASAP. Over." The Skipper rogered my transmission with, "They're on the way, son. Keep it cool. Help in any way you can." Choggie Bearers (Korean Service Corps laborers) soon showed up with several litters, about the time the first Navy Corpsman arrived. Of six men in the squad, two were already dead. The other four were badly wounded, near death. It was the most gruesome scene I had yet seen in my tour of duty. One of the wounded, an ammo bearer, looked as if some surgical procedure had cut his skull off above the ears. It was hanging by a strip of tissue on one side of his head. Looking into the bottom half of his skull, the brain matter could be seen. I could not help but see it when I helped move his body. Another Marine had been hit in the torso. His chest looked like some grotesque instrument the size of a paint bucket had been used to scoop out a hole under his left arm. The arm, still attached to his body, hung only by the flesh on the back of the shoulder. Looking into his chest cavity, some vital organs were visible. Both men were in extreme shock, drained white from loss of blood.

Both were placed on stretchers with a bottle of plasma draining into them, trying hard to play catchup with the loss of blood The Marine with the head wound died almost immediately. The other was lifted by two Choggies who started toward the Medivac Chopper. It was apparent they had not been trained to moved a wounded man. I yelled "Eati-wah, bolly bolly" which, in Marine-Korean lingo, loosely translates as "Stop, come here quickly!" I motioned for them to get out of the way. Another Marine and I gently lifted him. We took but a few steps when he gave a great gasp and died. Both of us turned, our eyes locked , flooding with tears. A brave young man had just died before he had really begun to live. Neither of the other three wounded Marines made it to the Medivac which would have taken them to the hospital ship anchored off the coast in the Sea of Japan. I never knew any of their names. They were fairly new replacements who had been with us but a few short weeks. I never heard what cause the short round, whether it was a defective shell that fell short of its target, or whether it was a miscalculation of fire mission grid coordinates by the FDC or the FO. I had just passed my twentieth birthday. What I had just seen made me feel as old as Methuselah. Yet, life in the Corps went on.

The month long battle for Heartbreak Ridge was fought by the 2nd Infantry Division. This Division, bloodied at the Pusan Perimeter, and further decimated at Kunu-ri and Chipyong-ni would add greatly to its casualty list here. It suffered the most casualties of any division in the Korean War. <u>Above</u>. Exhausted troops are on Bloody Ridge. <u>Below</u> an aerial view of Heartbreak Ridge with hill numbers marked. <u>Photos from the National Archives.</u>

RED DRAGON
The SECOND ROUND
FACES OF WAR II

Anthony	NMI	Tavilla	US 51002305
First Name	MI	Last Name	Serial Number
"Tony"	3745	3 Nov 1927	Sgt First Class
Nickname	MOS	Birthday	Grade / Rank
Fox/2/1 23d Inf/2d Div		Sept 1951- June 1952	Boston, MA
Unit (s)		Duty Tour (s)	Home Town

Combat Infantry Badge Korean Campaign Service Medal, 2 stars United Nations Service Medal

Medals & Awards

National Defense Service Medal   Republic of Korea War Service Medal

HEARTBREAK RIDGE

When I arrived in Korea in September 1951, I was assigned to the 1st Sqd, 2d Plat, Fox Company, 23d Inf Regt. It was a proud regiment with a historic past. The regimental motto is "We Serve." Every man did his duty with the regimental motto in mind. The regiment was on 'Bloody Ridge' getting ready to attack Hill 931, the highest peak on Heartbreak Ridge.' 'Heartbreak Ridge' and its adjacent sister terrain feature, 'Bloody Ridge,' with its high peak of Hill 983 were critical to holding the 'Punchbowl,' an extinct volcanic caldera taken earlier with great loss of life. Taking, then holding, these two ridges in the two months mid August to mid October 1951, was to cost the 2d Division a horrendous 6,517 casualties: 609 KIA, 5,096 WIA and 498 MIA. The 23d Infantry casualty list for 'Heartbreak' alone was a staggering 1,832 men, one of every three man in the regiment. Hill 931 on 'Heartbreak' had been unsuccessfully assaulted by other American units, also by French and Turkish troops. The task was now handed to the 23d Infantry. Diversionary attacks by US Marines on one flank tied down some of the enemy reserves. The rest of the 2d Division feinted an attack in the mountains west of the Mundung valley. Tank thrusts into the Satae Valley east of 'Heartbreak' conned the North Koreans into believing we Americans had abandoned our 24 day attack to seize Hill 931 and attempts to take 'Heartbreak' Ridge. That ploy was successful in drawing some of the North Korean defenders off Hill 931 to defend adjacent areas menaced by the feint.

My fiery baptism into combat was a a night attack. Our objective was to capture the hilltop of Hill 931, the highest dominating terrain feature of 'Heartbreak Ridge.' Whoever held that hilltop looked down the throat of an attacking enemy as the 2d Division had learned to its sorrow. The assault began after intensive individual preparation and inspection of our gear. All riflemen carried four grenades. Every man began the hill climb with fixed bayonet and a full combat load of .30 caliber M-1 ammo including a bandolier of .30 caliber slung across his chest. Some men carried two bandoliers. Those men carrying flame throwers had .45 Colt Automatic Pistols as a side arm. Medics loaded their bags with extra morphine syrettes, a full kit of bandages and other items of the trade. With pounding heart, I lugged my BAR into battle that night of 5 Oct 1951. The Asst. BAR man, my partner, carried two extra clips, and an additional 40 rounds of ammo for my BAR. He lugged his M-1, by choice, rather than the lighter .30 caliber carbine. Our advance up the hill was covered by the fire of Quad .50 caliber machine guns from positions located near the bottom of the ridge. We advanced in an in-depth skirmish line. The rough terrain mocked any attempt to maintain contact with a man adjacent. It was slip, slide and struggle climbing that 40 degree slope, each man panting with the exhaustion of carrying his heavy load of ammo and individual gear. I could not help but think that this was the hardest job I would ever have to do in my life. And, I thought, quite possibly, the last job of my life.

I already knew that a half mile behind the line of combat, with the exception of a stray artillery round, I was about as safe as I would be back home in my church in Boston. Now, going into the maelstrom of infantry combat, I was going to learn how the other half lived. As we were about half way up, the artillery commenced firing on the hilltop and ridge line in the random pattern of harassing fire. The idea was to shell lightly, not to indicate by a massive artillery barrage that a determined assault was being made. Fire just heavy enough to cause the defenders to take cover in their bunkers except for those unlucky few on guard. We made our struggling way almost to the top without alerting the North Korean enemy. The signal was given for the artillery to "Give 'em Hell, Harry!" The 105 howitzers and the 155 howitzers opened up and pounded the hilltop. As we reached the ridge line, on signal, like a match being blown out, the shelling stopped. We hurtled over the top, every man firing at the surprised North Koreans on guard, and those emerging from their bunkers. We were in command of the situation, our organized and aimed fire was extremely heavy against the disorganized North Koreans. They fled in panic. From then on it was like swatting flies. Those that did not surrender were killed as they fled. I doubt many escaped. At 0600 hours 6 Oct 1951, Hill 931 was an American hill, bought and paid for in American blood.

We were surrounded not only by bodies of North Koreans just killed, but also by the bloated, unburied dead of several days past. It was a total victory for Fox company and the other 23d Infantry companies in the attack, but a sad victory, considering the price paid. I survived that attack and several others in my 10 month tour in Korea, as squad leader, then as plat sgt before coming home.

<u>Above</u>. By early fall of 1951 the war of 'rapid movement' was over and the lines were stabilizing. This meant trench and bunker warfare similar to WW I. Here classes in installing barb-wire and the use of bangalore torpedoes to breach it are being taught by the 13th Combat Engineers to the 17th Infantry Regiment, 7th Division. Photo by Norm Strickbine.

<u>Right</u>. Dale Kember is standing by proof that there was a 38th parallel. <u>Below Right</u>. Mine fields were clearly marked in both English and Korean. There was no warning in Chinese for their enlightenment. Laying and removing minefields was one of the more serious jobs of the Combat Engineers. 1951-1952. <u>Below</u>. Not exactly a cruise liner, the USNS Marine Phoenix was the mode of transportation for many G.I.'s going to and from Korea. <u>Photos courtesy of Dale Kember</u>.

RED DRAGON
The SECOND ROUND
FACES OF WAR II

Dale	W.	Kember	US 55 165 103
First Name	MI	Last Name	Serial Number
Tex	3729(mine planter)	21 June 1929	PFC
Nickname	MOS	Birthday	Grade / Rank
1092d Engineers(C)		18 Sept 1951- 10 July 1952	Serena, IL
Unit (s)		Duty Tour (s)	Home Town

Good Conduct Medal　Korean Campaign Service Medal with 3 stars　United Nations Medal

Medals & Awards

National Defense Service Medal　Korean War Service Medal　ROK Presidential Unit Citation

AN ARMY EDUCATION

I was farm raised in a good Christian family near Serena, IL. My Dad, a veteran of World War I, had taken me hunting at an early age and taught me safe weapons handling as well as how to fire and care for rifle, pistol and shotgun. It stood me in good stead when it was my turn to serve our country. I was a tall skinny kid, 6'1" and 135 lbs in high school. My high school basketball coach told me I did not have to worry about the draft as my bad knees and feet would make me a 4-F. I was drafted on 11 April 1951. My coach failed to pass the word to my local draft board. At the induction station in Chicago we lined up for physical exams. One big guy was bragging about how tough he was. Standing next to a man getting his shots, he gulped and passed out, knocking over a stand that held all the blood and urine samples. That held us up for a day. Bad feet, bad knees and skinny seemed to be what the Combat Engineers wanted. I was sent to Ft Leonard Wood for basic training. On 21 June I celebrated my 22d birthday. I was one of the old guys, "Pops." That's what happens when you wait to be drafted. One weekend just before I finished at Ft Wood, my brother-in-law came to visit me. He was an 11 year veteran and a Major in the Regular Army. I told the mess Sgt, "I have a guest." Sgt. says, "No way, no guests for trainees." I told my brother in law. He said, "You go back in there and tell him Major Franks will sit at the officer's table, and that you are my guest and will sit with me." I took a lot of ribbing over that incident, but the mess Sgt. kept quiet.

Korea was chewing up Combat Engineers. My bad feet put me aboard the Marine Phoenix for Japan. It was an uneventful trip, only one hurricane and two terrible storms. Our daily lecture sounded a peaceful note. I was assigned MOS 3729, and taught to be a mine planter. Figured I didn't need much instruction, I already knew how to plant. Our daily lecture emphasized, "Only about 1000 of you are coming home. Get used to the idea." Since the ship held close to 5000 men, I felt he was kidding. Funny thing, I developed a wart on my left index finger crossing the International Date line. Stayed with me while I was in Korea, but went away after crossing the date line coming home. God's truth! Processed at Camp Drake in Yokohama expecting my bad feet to keep me in Japan. Ha! A few days later a bunch of us were placed in a truck convoy. Paul Garber in my basic class at Wood was last in line. Sgt tells Paul, "No more room in the truck, stay here." Waved good by to Paul, vowing from now on to be last in line. Paul was from a neighboring town, slow, a bit handicapped. I figured I'd seen the last of him. In Korea I was assigned to the 1092 Combat Engineers, a National Guard unit from Kentucky. Most of the guys were 17,18 years old. One claimed he was 16. It was "Pops" all over again. On my way home, I missed my truck. Got on the next truck, and there was Paul. He had been assigned to the 3d Div as a rifleman and was on his way home, 9 months without a scratch. He paid for it later, dying at an early age from medical complications of war service.

Engineers have many jobs, building bunkers, foot and truck bridges, roads, you name it. If it was hard work while getting shot at, we got the 'church call' every time. My MOS was mine planter, so I built roads around mountains. We supported various divisions. Once, it was the Greek Brigade. I manned a .50 cal MG. Nobody at Ft Wood taught me that gig. It was on-the-job training. Guy by name of Banjo Eyes, our platoon guitar player, taught me those ropes. In Oct of '51, in support of the 1st Cav and near a battery of 105mm howitzers, I saw how the Chinese crossed barbed wire. First bunch of guys threw themselves on the barbed wire, the rest of them used their bodies as foot bridges. Those few that survived, must have been black and blue for weeks. Lucky the Chinks wore sneakers, not combat boots as we did. Their backs would have been broken. Don't remember many names, mostly nicknames.

One big guy, my best friend, Wells Bieble, was from Elwood City, PA, another was Henry Morvan. The three of us stuck together when we could. Every Sunday we got a quinine pill. Didn't need a calendar. Sunday was Quinine, Quinine was Sunday. We also got to see the Mongols in action or at least where they had been. On leaving a battlefield they would hang their enemies by making a cut through the neck, then hang the corpse in a tree. The decedents of Ghenghis Khan had inherited his cruelty. We did other jobs, loading wounded into helicopters to be sent to MASH units. Once we went north with 6x6 trucks to help another unit. Our job turned out to be loading dead bodies into the trucks. It was terrible. The smell of napalm, burnt bodies and human decay made a horrible stench. All in a days work for a combat engineer. Came home through the Golden Gate. Everybody was singing. Hard to describe the feeling, to be back home, see Old Glory waving, hear the Star Spangled Banner. Even today, the sight of our flag and the sound of our National Anthem make my eyes fill up. The tears are of happiness, to be alive and live in the United States as a free citizen in a free country.

A flight of B-29 bombers are seen on their way to bomb bridges over the Yalu River. Flying from as far away as Okinawa these 'beauties' were the work horse of the Air Force. Most of the factories, transportation centers, and troop staging areas in North Korea would know the wrath of what were then called 'giant' bombers. All photos from the National Archives.

The railroad marshaling yards at Pyongyang were a prime target for our bombers. This included the largest maintenance center in North Korea.

With a capability of moving over 40 trains a day this was a high priority target as this destroyed engine proves.

RED DRAGON
The SECOND ROUND
FACES OF WAR II

Daniel	NMI	Northup	RA 19 390 056
First Name	MI	Last Name	Serial Number
"LeRoy"	4745	28 Sept 1930	Pfc later SFC
Nickname	MOS	Birthday	Grade / Rank
A/31/7		2 Sept 1951-13 Aug 1952	San Bernardino, CA
Unit (s)		Duty Tour (s)	Home Town
Combat Infantry Badge		Korean Campaign Service Medal, 2 bronze stars	UN Medal
Medals & Awards			
National Defense Service Medal			Republic of Korea War Service Medal

GRENADE SPECIALIST

I arrived in Korea in late August 1951 and was assigned to Able company 31st Infantry as a replacement. I didn't know who I was replacing, a dead or wounded GI or a soldier rotating home. I suspected one of the former, considering the heavy casualties I heard of in the current Iron Triangle fighting. Arriving at the rear CP too late to go up on 'the line', I spent my first night in the "A" kitchen area. I had made a sleeping bag by sewing my two blankets into a mattress cover. The mattress cover had been liberated from a stopover barracks while en route from Yokohama to Sasebo. A light rain was falling. I saw a half dug hole that nobody seemed to be using. Next morning I learned it was a half dug grave. Covering the hole with my poncho, using sticks in a rafter formation to hold the poncho off the ground, I bedded down. It began to rain, but I was as snug as a bug in his proverbial rug, the water just rolled off.

I slept well until the North Koreans ruined my rest and the kitchen area with a mortar barrage of 25 or 30 shells. I stayed where I was. My hole offered good protection except from a direct hit. If that happened I wouldn't have any worries anyway. I could hear a bustle as GIs ran to get out of the impact area. At false dawn, still in my nest, I heard footsteps. I waited, but hearing American voices, I pushed up my poncho hut roof to look around. It scared the hell out of a few guys who knew why the hole had been dug!

After this auspicious beginning I went on to be a rifleman, a machine gunner, then a 3.5 bazooka gunner, and finally a rifle squad leader. It's easy to learn how to use all the weapons in a rifle company. Hang around long enough, manage to live and with the help of St Peter and a lot of good luck, a natural selection process caused by enemy fire takes over. We called it OJT. Our company was so badly shot up at Mung Dung-ni that the company commander appointed me a squad leader. When I told him, "Sir, I'm just a private, but I am 21, so I guess that makes me of legal size." He appointed me PFC on the spot. So much for never volunteering.

About the time we received replacements for our losses at Mung Dung-ni, we discovered fragmentation grenades were coming to us with 2½ second fuses instead of the old WW II standard 7 second fuse. That change had finally been made due to many complaints that a long burning fuse gave an enemy time to pick up a grenade and throw it back. For years the brass paid little attention. American grenade training protocol called for pulling the pin, count to four, hurl the grenade. Sadly, GI's learned that "Rosie the Fuse Setter" after a tiring night at the ordnance plant had, on occasion, cut some of the fuses a tad short. After a few GIs were killed following training protocol, the word went out, "Get rid of the damn thing before it decides you're the enemy!" Had the brass visited the line during an attack to toss a few grenades, the grenade would have been modified. Nothing gets to the brass quicker than having his own hide at risk. A soldier like General Dean, close to his troops, would have quickly solved the problem.

The problem still persisted. It was old in Napoleon's time, as old as armies themselves. With two different fuse settings and munitions plants shipping from stockpiled production, new and old grenades ended up being packed in the same box. If sufficient time was available before they were needed, grenades could be sorted. Opening a box of grenades at night was a different problem. The sense of feel in grimy, chapped hands is not acute. Some ordnance 'expert' devised a way to use a similar grenade handle on both types of frag grenade. The spoon handle on the 7 second grenade had a curled lip *cupped downward* which fitted *over* the hinge holding the spoon handle to the grenade. This same spoon handle also had a pin inserted in the handle encasing an arming lever. If the pin were pulled and the spoon handle held tightly, the grenade was safe, not armed. Loosen ones grip, the spoon handle drops, the arming lever flies off. The grenade, either 2½ or 7 second variety, is now armed, a deadly weapon of 35 fragments, each one potentially lethal in human flesh. The 2½ second grenade handle was similar except the curled lip was *cupped upward* and fitted *under* the hinge holding the spoon handle to the grenade. Easy to spot in daylight, but difficult to *feel* the difference at night. Needless to say, we adopted a field expedient of treating all grenades as having 2½ second fuses. The 2 ½ second fuse had one advantage. I had a good arm as a college javelin thrower before enlisting. I found I could now get a deadly 'air burst' on occasion.

Discharged at Ft. Lewis in Jan 1954 as a SFC, I stayed in the ER, putting in my reserve time as 1st Sgt of "G"company, 44th Division.

Above. The Commanding General of the 45th Infantry Division is congratulating PFC Henry Buelow on being awarded the Silver Star for action against the enemy on January 27, 1952. <u>Photo courtesy Henry Buelow</u>.

<u>Above</u>. Returning from a mission deep in North Korea these F9F fighters circle their carrier the USS Princeton and wait for landing instructions. Some of the first Navy jets to see action they were very efficient. <u>Photo National Archives</u>.

RED DRAGON
The SECOND ROUND
FACES OF WAR II

Henry	D.	Buelow	27 361 498 NG AUS
First Name	MI	Last Name	Serial Number
Hank	4745	11 Sept 1932	Cpl	Long Prairie, MN
Nickname	MOS	Birthday	Grade / Rank	Home Town
16th Reconn, 1st CavDiv & 45th Reconn, 45thDiv USN			25 Sept 1951-28 July 1952
Unit (s)			Duty Tour (s)
Silver Star Medal	Combat Infantry Badge		Korean Campaign Service Medal, 2 stars
Medals & Awards			
National Defense Service Medal	United Nations Medal		Korean War Service Medal, ROK

A VOLUNTEER'S REWARD

In 1947 at age 15 Hank Buelow joined the Minnesota National Guard. Large for his age at 6'2", well muscled and still growing, he was a star player on his high school football team. Not yet of 'legal catch size', he was discharged in 1948. At age 17 he reenlisted in a NG tank unit where he was awarded MOS of Tank Driver. He graduated in 1950, entering college on a football scholarship that fall at Colorado A&M. While home on Christmas vacation, Uncle Sam beckoned. His NG unit, activated for the Korean War, served as cadre at Camp Rucker, AL, training draftees under the provisions of Public Law 51, 82d Congress. While there he volunteered for Ranger training. While awaiting Ranger assignment he was given 10 days furlough in early Sept. This was an 'Army signal' he was on the alert list for Korean War duty. En route to Korea, the troop ship rolled and pitched as it encountered terrific ocean storms. Buelow, one of the few not laid up with seasickness, wore hip boots while working to keep the ships 'heads' clean and useable. Sick soldiers, in bunks racked five high heaved their guts out, often not making it to the 'head.' Buelow recalls this duty as a nauseating memory, necessary but unpleasant, which fell to his lot as one of the few soldiers on the ship not disabled by 'mal de mer.'

He arrived at Inchon, Korea late Sept. His Ranger pre-training came in handy as he clambered down the ship side cargo net in to an LSD taking them ashore. He and his records were brought up to date at the process center, should he become a Korean War KIA statistic. He was assigned to 16th Reconn Co, 1st Cav Div. Reconn Co was the G-2 intelligence point of the Division spear. On 30 Sept '51 he joined 16th Reconn on the MLR, in time to participate next day in an early AM attack on Old Baldy. This was a huge hill mass several thousand yards in width with a height of over 1200 feet. Treeless, the hillside had long ago been denuded by shell fire.

The barren hillside was pockmarked with foxholes, trenches, bunkers, caves and tunnels. In preparation for the assault next day, members of the squad to which he had been assigned were asked if anyone had been trained on a bazooka. He said that he had fired it a number of times in training. The squad leader directed him to take position on a small plateau 75 yards from the base of the hill. He was told to fire if a flare was tossed into an area, or if he spotted enemy troops advancing. His squad, under command of a RA sergeant, continued an advance as signaled by our artillery lifting fire from the hillside to the hilltop and reverse slope of Old Baldy.

He soon knew the pre-attack briefing which informed them there would be no opposition was flat out wrong. In his binoculars, when his squad was about a third of the way up the hill, he saw a group of Chinese soldiers pop up, waving white flags. He saw the squad leader motion 'do not fire' to his men. That was a mistake. No sooner had he done so than the "white flag" Chinese dropped back into their trench and opened fire. Within seconds Chinese mortar fire was dropping all around them, clear back to where he was positioned. His squad was massacred by Chinese perfidy in the treacherous misuse of the white flag of parley and truce..

In the midst of the heavy mortar barrage he heard a strangled cry for help. Leaving his foxhole he crawled about 30 yards to his left to find an American sergeant whose guts were spilling out on the ground. He yelled, "Medic" while cradling the sergeant in his arms, wetting his lips with water from his canteen. He tried to hold the man's intestines together while awaiting a medic. The sergeant told Buelow he was 23 years old, married, with two kids. He was afraid he was going to die and leave his family without means of support. The sergeant died in his arms. When he arrived, the medic confirmed the sergeant's death. That scene is a recurrent nightmare in Buelow's post war life. He headed back to his hole, retrieved his ammo and bazooka preparatory to making a retreat beyond the Imjin River. At the river bank he heard another soldier calling for help. The cry came from a soldier trying to swim the Imjin using only one arm. Buelow a strong swimmer, had no hesitancy in heeding the cry for help. He dove in and was able to help the soldier to the opposite bank held by friendly troops. He was a most grateful young American 2d Lt who had been badly wounded in one arm.

16th Reconn was in support of 70th Hvy Tk Bn when the attack took place about 1215 hours. Reconn Company casualties were 4 KIA, 6 MIA and 22 WIA. Lt Jones assumed command when Capt Woodson and Lt Coogan were wounded. Had he not volunteered to man a bazooka, Buelow likely would have been included in those statistics. A call for a volunteer had probably saved his life.

Above. Anther wounded G.I. is carried off of a hill in North Korea. 1951.
Below. One of the 'Mercy Ships' that provided hospital care to our troops in Korea.
Both photos courtesy of Bill Palizzola.

Above. Cpl. Joe Violette shortly before he was killed in action in the Heartbreak Ridge area of Korea. Joe was a medic with the 31st Medical Company serving with the 31st Tank Co. of the 7th Inf. Div. Nov. 1951. Photo courtesy Joe Russo.

RED DRAGON
The SECOND ROUND
FACES OF WAR II

Joseph	C.	Violette	RA 11 198 353
First Name	MI	Last Name	Serial Number
"Joe," "Doc"	03666	Unk 1931	Cpl
Nickname	MOS	Birthday	Grade / Rank
Tank Co/31st Inf/7		May '51-6 Nov '51	Aroostook Cty, ME
Unit (s)		Duty Tour (s)	Home Town

Korean Campaign Service Medal w/ 3Bronze stars   NDSM   UNSM   ROKPUC
Medals & Awards

Purple Heart HONORS: Bugler: "Taps"   Eight man firing squad   Folded American flag

BATTLEFIELD DESTINY

Somewhere in Korea, north of the 38th parallel, near "Heart Break Ridge" lies a narrow valley which runs deep into Chicom territory. It was the key to penetration of the Chinese MLR. In the late fall campaign of 1951, a northward push was made to interdict Chinese supply lines. It began a bitter battle continuing well into 1952. On 6 Nov, Tk Co, 31st Inf, led a patrol into the valley. Following the tanks was a pickup emergency squad riding in a lightly armored personnel carrier. In the carrier was the driver, Sgt Earl Morgan of Panora, IA; Cpl Earl Pasco, Rayland, OH who manned the .50 cal MG; Cpl James Byrd of Richmond, CA , radio operator and Joe Violette of Van Buren, MA, combat medic of the 31st Infantry Medical Co. It was a routine assignment for Joe, no different than 100 or so others he had pulled on his tour of duty in Korea. This day was to be different for Medic Joe Violette. It was his day of destiny.

The lead tank struck a mine for the first casualty of the day. Medic Joe bailed out of the personnel carrier and ran to the damaged tank. Sgt Morgan swerved the carrier around so that Cpl Pasco could bring his .50 caliber MG to bear on the enemy firing from the hillside. Before Joe Violette reached the tank it burst into flame. Other tanks in the column opened a heavy fire on the enemy. Joe entered the turret of the burning tank. He emerged carrying an unconscious wounded tanker. Enemy mortar fire doubled in intensity. With Morgan's help, Violette carried the wounded man back to the M-39. Violette returned to the burning tank. In response to Joe's urging, the three lightly wounded men emerged into the hail of bullets and mortar fire. With the aid of Pasco and Byrd they were helped into the personnel carrier. Violette had placed the wounded man on a stretcher at the rear of the carrier, holding it steady with his own body as he worked on the man. The tanker casualty had not regained conscienceness, probably due to severe concussion.

It was vital to get the open topped personnel carrier out of the torrent of fire before more casualties resulted from enemy plunging fire ripping into the valley floor. Morgan turned the vehicle on its tracks to get quickly out of there, back to the rear where the wounded could obtain better care. As the vehicle swiveled in the mud, it shuddered, then flipped over. The tanker Violette had been treating was catapulted onto another tank 15 yards away. The open top of the personnel carrier settled into the mud. Nearby tankers risked their lives to open the escape door in the bottom (now the top) of the carrier. All inside struggled out and clear of the vehicle. Then someone noticed Joe Violette was not among them. The others were being loaded into another tank when he was discovered. The impact of the overturn had thrown him forward. He had been pinned beneath the .50 caliber MG mount. His chest had been crushed. Joe Violette was dead, another KIA statistic of the Korean War. Capt Curt O'Reilly, 31st Regtl Surgeon gave him his epitaph, "In life he did a superb job as a Combat Medic, in death, he typifies the spirit of the Medical Corps on the field of battle."

The regiment set up a winter camp in the rear of Heartbreak Ridge. Friends of Joe Violette decided that the time had come to honor the memory of their friend. At the medical camp entrance a few miles from the scene of Joe's death, a simple sign commemorating his life and death was erected on the frozen ground. Men in passing by would pause for a moment of silence before going on. On 19 December 1951, Joe Violette was posthumously awarded the Silver Star.

CAMP JOE VIOLETTE
KILLED IN ACTION 6 NOV 1951
IN MEMORY OF A GUY
WHO MADE THE SUPREME SACRIFICE
R.I.P.

ED. This vignette reconstructed in part from *Pacific Stars & Stripes*, February 1952. Article and additional information furnished by his long time friend and comrade, Joe Russo, Combat Medic attached to 15th AAA AW Bn SP. The two men had been close friends since medical training at Fort Sam Houston before the Korean War. They volunteered together as combat medics for overseas duty.

Above Left. The battleship USS Wisconsin samples the snow and frigid weather of wintertime in Korea. 1952. Above. Another view of the USS Wisconsin shows off it's battery of 16 inch guns. Truly awesome and a great 'bunker buster'. Both photos from the National Archives. Left. This photo shows a typical day for the Infantry. Soaking wet and slogging through the mud these Marines get to replace equally miserable Marines in the line. Late fall of 1951.
Photo courtesy of William Palizzola.

RED DRAGON
The SECOND ROUND
FACES OF WAR II

James	H.	Appleton	115 8912 USMC
First Name	MI	Last Name	Serial Number
Appy	0311	28 August 1931	Corporal
Nickname	MOS	Birthday	Grade/Rank
Item Co 5th Marines 1st Mar Div		Apr '51-Apr '52	Nashville, TN
Unit		Duty Tour in Korea	Home Town

Silver Star   Commendation Medal w/ Combat V   Navy PUC 1 star   USMC Good Conduct Medal

Medals & Awards

USMC Occpn Medal ,Eur clasp NDSM KVSM, 3 battle stars   KSM UN Medal   ROK PUC KWSM

MOST POWERFUL CORPORAL IN THE USMC

Late in October I was serving in HQ of Item Company, 3d Bn, 5th Marine Regt, 1st MarDiv as the Company XO's runner, sort of a messenger, 'aide-de-camp', general flunky and gofer. On this night's mission I carried a SCR 500 backpack radio. Intelligence had ascertained that large numbers of North Korean troops were massing on a hill massif in the Division's immediate front. Division Operations had decided a tactical TOT operation was called for. TOT, meaning Time-On-Target, calls for every available artillery type unit to train all accessible guns on a given target. Each gun fires one round, or salvo, at a precise time. All rounds are timed to simultaneously strike the target. Such an operation is deadly in effect, and a tremendous blow to enemy morale. The Korean troops massing on that specific hill were to be hit with Item Company's three 60mm mortars, 3d Bn's six 81 mm mortars, 5th Regiment's twelve 4.2 mortars, 11th Regiment's 105 mm howitzers, 155 mm howitzers and 155 mm 'Long Toms." As a capper, the Navy would join with a salvo of 16 inch guns from the USS Battleship Wisconsin, steaming along in the Sea of Japan, some 15 miles off the coast.

As the mission swung into operation, it seemed the radio operator with the FOs of ANGLICO group (Air-Naval Gun Fire Liaison Company) who were on site with we infantry "grunts," was unable to communicate with the FDC aboard the USS Wisconsin. This was probably due to the rugged hill masses in eastern Korea which blocked certain types of radio transmission. In any event, they could not talk to each other. I could hear both of them loud and clear. So, neophyte as I was as a radio communicator, I offered my services as a go between to relay their messages back and forth. My offer was quickly accepted by both parties. I was given instructions by the Navy Lt of the ANGLICO group. I relayed these out to the USS Wisconsin. In due time the response came back from the USS Wisconsin, "On the way, Item 5."(Item 5 was my call sign, or rather that of the company XO. I was authorized to use it as his radio operator.) This meant that the three big guns in one of the Wisconsin's turrets had just salvoed, or fired. After "On the way," the sky lit up a bit off in the distance, even though it was a good way out. I knew those three huge missiles were shrieking through the air on their way to the enemy hill target. Joining in, depending on range to target and time of flight, I could hear other artillery weapons of Regiment and Division join the guns of the USS Wisconsin, all gun fire programmed to strike at the same time.

Almost in unison, back toward our rear, I could hear the other much closer contributors to this fire mission chime in with their donation to the fireworks. This ordnance was all bound for impact on that Korean hill top. Shortly, out in front, what had been the cone of a hill top in the North Korean topography was no longer there. It had disappeared in a violent dispay of fire and high explosives. Large chunks of rock and dirt were hurled high into the air. Clouds of dust, dirt and debris gradually cleared from the atmosphere. The area looked like a newly plowed field, but with boulders and shattered trees strewn around. I could see no activity through my binoculars. When the 16 inch projectiles of the USS Wisconsin came boring in toward the target, they sounded like three big oil drums hurtling through the air. Others said they sounded like a heavily loaded freight train going down grade. It was an awesome display of military destruction. Our company had been sent up to be in a blocking position in the event any of the enemy tried to take off southward after the TOT fire mission. None did. We saw no movement at all. While I feel sure not all North Koreans in that area were killed or wounded, those that were not had the good sense to lie low and wait for another day. While the North Korean was a barbaric, mean, treacherous and cruel enemy, he was also an intelligent, tough and persistent foe.

On this night in North Korea, while Harry S. Truman was the duly elected President of the United States and Commander in Chief of all American military forces, and General Matthew Ridgeway was the Commanding General of the Eighth US Army in Korea. I, James H. Appleton, was the most powerful Corporal in the entire United States Marine Corps. I had called in what must have sounded like Armageddon to those North Korean troops being massed in preparation for attack on positions of the First Marine Division.

The "Ole Girl," Battleship USS Wisconsin, was long ago decommissioned. Today her berth is a permanent moorage adjacent to Nauticus National Maritime center in Norfolk. Her day is past, but she contributed mightily to our nation in World War II and Korea.

Above. After giving shots to the G.I. s of A Btry., 15th AAA, 7th Division, Medic Joe Russo had one left over for their Korean mascot. He doesn't look like he appreciates it too much. Photo courtesy of Joe Russo.

Left. An elderly Korean woman and her grand daughter walk that long road to freedom. October 1951. Bottom. Helicopter pad and location of the 8055th MASH hospital. Late fall of 1951. Photos courtesy of Dale Kember .

RED DRAGON
The SECOND ROUND
FACES OF WAR II

Joseph	W.	Russo	RA 21 758 844
First Name	MI	Last Name	Serial Number
"Bud"	03666	10 May 1932	S/Sgt
Nickname	MOS	Birthday	Grade / Rank
A/15/AAA, 2d Ranger Co, 32d Inf		May '51-Mar '52	Trenton, NJ
Unit (s)		Duty Tour (s)	Home Town
Combat Medical Badge		Army Commendation Medal	Good Conduct w/Knot
Medals & Awards			
Korean Campaign Service Medal,3stars	NDSM	Army PUC	UNSM	ROKPUC

REFUGEES, THE FLOTSAM AND JETSAM OF WAR

It was foggy and cold, typical fall weather for Korea, I guess. I don't remember the date, except it had to be late Sept or early Oct. It was before my friend Joe Violette was killed. We were still in the Chuparu-ri valley area having yet to move to the Punchbowl. A number of us, rifle infantry and ack-ack, squatted around what we called a 'Smoke Pot', warming ourselves. 'Smoke Pot' was a name given to a GI field expedient which used a No. 10 GI ration can half filled with sand, then liberally laced with gasoline. From a distance it was carefully ignited by tossing a match into the can. After an initial flare up, the 'Smoke Pot' would burn for an hour or so, giving off little light but an astonishing amount of heat. Somebody said it was an old 'depression' trick hobos used when riding the rails.

The MLR had been quite for several hours. The Chinese then opened a continuous rifle fire, joined by light mortars. It wasn't aimed at us but into the area between our lines. We knew what it was. We called it 'Chinese firefighting'. Refugees were trying to come to South Korea. The Communists considered these people traitors and showed no mercy, women and children included. Shortly, through the fog came some GIs with several refugees. One of them, a beautiful young Korean women was dressed in what to me, as a Catholic, was a nun's robe. She could have been Buddhist. What startled us was her actions. She knelt at a mud puddle, and ever so delicately touched a cloth to the water. She then tried to cleanse her face, hands and arms. In the fog, mud and hell of war she was a vision from heaven. Such beauty did not belong among rough soldiers. I have carried her image in my mind for 50 years.

That same night a young Korean mother came through the Chinese lines carrying her baby in the conventional way, in a pack on her back. She, and by now quite a number of refugees, had gathered awaiting escort to the rear. I had attended to several of their walking wounded and had returned to warm my hands at the 'Smoke Pot' when I noticed this very young child looking at me from across her shoulder. His dark watery eyes had tear streaks down his face, etched in the grime of his face. He looked so forlorn that I rose to my feet to pat him on the back. When I did so, reaching behind his mother's back, I felt something wet. It was blood.

I checked the child over. To this day I do not remember whether it was a boy or a girl. The child had caught two small pieces of Communist shrapnel in the area of the buttocks. Taking those metal shards in the butt most probably saved his mother's life. Back wounds near the spinal area are usually incapacitating, if not deadly. I treated the wounds as best I could and tagged the child for a immediate care after evacuation. Not once did the child cry or whimper while I tended him. I chipped off a piece of that hard chocolate bar, Emergency Ration of WW II vintage, so old that it had effloresced to a white surface. I gave him the piece to suck on, although the child did not need pacifying. He was as calm as his patron Buddha. I broke up the rest of the 5 sections of the chocolate bar into manageable bites and gave it to the mother. She wrapped it in a cloth and placed it inside her robe. I then took her and several other 'walking wounded' to our aid station in the rear. They were treated and sent on to a rear area clearing station.

I have never ceased to marvel at the fortitude of the Korean people. They must teach their children in a similar manner as I am told American Indian children were raised. They are quiet and well behaved, responsive to their mother's behest. Likewise with Korean adults, their pain threshold as human beings must be the same as for all races. For all that, they outwardly react differently to pain, seemingly accepting it as part of an existence over which they have no control, hence to be born in comparative silence. Another thing that always astonished me about Korea and Koreans was the "A Frame brigade." These were labor units composed of elderly men past fighting age who had been drafted by the Korean government into labor service units. They were organized into groups to bring supplies up the mountainous hillsides to front line positions. Each elderly man, some with long white beards, carried an 'A frame' on his back. These labor brigades brought up water, chow, ammo, radio batteries, all kinds of supplies. I asked once what the average weight might be for each man and was told it would vary from 90 to 150 pounds. I saw one rice-powered human mule train carrying 40 gallon gasoline drums. Those drums, if filled with gasoline, weighed in excess of 300 lbs! Without them we would have been hard pressed for food or ammo. Those old Korean men had leg muscles like cables of steel! Asiatic Atlas personified!.

Above. The USS Juneau takes on supplies and prepares to return to Korea for more action. 1950.

Left. On board the hospital ship USS Consolation this sailor is taking a break with his ' feathered friend.' The Consolation served with distinction during the Korean War.
Below. The frigate Prasac from Thailand ran aground in North Korea. Helicopters were used to rescue the stranded crew. Early 1951.

All photos from the National Archives.

RED DRAGON
The SECOND ROUND
FACES OF WAR II

Melvin	W.	Bromby	569-01-61 USN
First Name	MI	Last Name	Serial Number
Bill	Small arms-Small craft	27 June 1929	Gunner's Mate 2d class
Nickname	MOS	Birthday	Grade / Rank
MTB Sqdn1 & MB Sqdn 2.	Jul 1950-Mch 1951 & Jun 1951-Jan 1952		Whittier, CA
Unit (s)		Duty Tour (s)	Home Town
Navy Presidential Unit Citation	Korean Campaign Service Medal, 2 stars		USN GCM, 1 star
Medals & Awards			
National Defense Service Medal	Korean War Service Medal	United Nations Service Medal	

THE LAST PT BOAT

Too young for WWII, but with a reactivated draft act swinging into gear, I enlisted in the US Navy in June 1948. Who would then have thought in 2 years we would again be at war! After completion of boot camp training in San Diego, I was assigned for further training in "small arms & small craft" with the US Marines. My fleet assignment following that training was a pleasant tour of duty aboard an AF-10 (Auxiliary Refrigerator Ship) supplying the 6th Fleet in the Mediterranean Sea. Immediately after the NKPA crossed the 38th parallel 25 June 1950, I was transferred to MTB (Motor Torpedo Boat) Squadron 1, Boat 619 at Norfolk, VA. The 619 had been commissioned in March 1942. She was a wood hull boat, 87 foot long and 32 foot beam, a top speed of 70 knots, manned by a crew of 16 men, including officers. Armament consisted of two torpedo tubes, two .50 cal MGs forward and a 40mm rapid fire gun aft.

After muster at Norfolk Navy Base we flew by plane to Pusan, Korea. Our MTBs were transported by APAs and AKAs to Korea. While awaiting arrival of our boats we joined a squadron off the west coast of Korea where Task Force 77 was maintaining a blockade. In that 6 week period before the Inchon landing, the NK Navy in the form of 4 patrol boats attacked the USS Juneau on 22 July 1950, the only 'naval battle' of the Korean War. The Juneau's 8" guns quickly ended the 'battle' by sinking all four. We all thought it was a sterling example of North Korean idiocy. Duties at this time consisted of patrolling and training of ROK personnel to handle MTB's.

The squadron moved with the invasion fleet to support the landing of Marines and Army men at Inchon. As we patrolled for survivors from disabled LCP's and LCM's during those unbelievable fast changing high and low tides, we almost lost our boat. Only the quick thinking of our skipper, Lt jg Sam Gildard, saved us. Quickly and adroitly he made a hard aport in a receding tide. We barely escaped grounding a quarter mile off shore. We continued screening cover for auxiliary ships supplying arms and equipment to our forces ashore. In other patrol assignments we cruised northward along the western Korean coastline where we would land special forces for reconns and raids on military targets inland. When we were spotted by the North Korean Peoples Army observers, their shore artillery would of course open fire on us. Our speed and maneuverability allowed us to escape without taking a hit. It must have been frustrating for the NKPA gunners. We continued our harassing raid tactics and fleet personnel recovery roles. During a break in the action, two boats of the squadron at a time would tie up along side the hospital ship USS Consolation while the other two boats remained on duty. Hot food, hot showers, and a chance to relax with a few laughs made a world of difference in our morale. For the remaining time of my first Korean tour we remained on west coast duty. In March 1951, we transferred our MTB boats to the ROK Navy. This ended the active duty status of the MTB boats commissioned in the United States Navy during World War II.

My second tour in Korea began at the Philadelphia Navy Yard where the new MB Squadron 2 was activated. These were new boats, commissioned in February 1951. Numerous changes had been made in their construction. The hull was all aluminum, impervious to attraction by magnetic mines. The boats were larger, 105 ft in length, 36 feet in beam and ran at a top speed of 105 knots. The crew strength had been increased by one man, to 17. Armament was heavier and of greater effect. The new MB boat mounted two rapid fire 40mm guns forward, nine 5" rockets and an 81mm mortar amidship, and a second battery of two 40 mm rapid fire guns aft. The two torpedo tubes of the older boats were eliminated. We were no longer "PT" boats but had a greatly changed role in the United States Navy. Our armament could now support deep reconnaissance, landing parties, sorties into enemy coastal defenses, harassing raids and scouting operations into inland waters for the fleet. The "PT" boat had grown up. Its torpedo boat function was in the process of being taken over by rockets fitted for guidance onto enemy ship targets. The MB was a new child of the modern US Navy.

In June of 1951 I returned to Korea as a member of MB Squadron 2 operating out of the east coast port of Yangyang. During that 2d tour we patrolled as far north as Hongwan above the 40th parallel, north of the port of Hungnam, site of the December 1950 evacuation by our Marine and Army forces after the Chosin Reservoir battles. At times we landed and later picked up South Korean espionage agents, also supplying these agents with food and ammunition. We raided enemy barge movement above the MLR in both day and night sorties. We also made several sea rescues of UN personnel. I returned stateside in January 1952, my duty completed.

Marine tankers give the Infantry a ride. This was probably greatly appreciated by the guys carrying the radio and the flame thrower. This photo was taken in 1953. All the troops are wearing 'flak jackets.'   <u>Photo from Archives</u>.

F4U - 4Bs are preparing to launch from the carrier USS Philippine Sea for another close air support mission. The 5 inch rockets under their folded wings will be a great help to weary Infantry in taking another hill.   <u>Photo from Archives.</u>

RED DRAGON
The SECOND ROUND
FACES OF WAR II

Dennis	D.	Strickbine	1018997 USMC
First Name	MI	Last Name	Serial Number
None	0311	11 July 1927	Cpl
Nickname	MOS	Birthday	Grade / Rank
C Co 1st Mtr Trnspt Bn 1st MarDiv		Jan 1951-Jan 1952	Herington, KS
Unit (s)		Duty Tour (s)	Home Town
Korean Campaign Service Medal, 3stars		Republic of Korea Presidential Unit Citation	
Medals & Awards			
Army of Occupation Medal-Japan		National Defense Service Medal	United Nations Medal

GUNG HO!

My first view of Korea was anything but reassuring. It was early in January of 1951 as we approached the coastline of Korea at Pohang after a very short stop over in Japan. We were replacements for the First MarDiv and were aware of how badly the Division had been mauled at the battle of the Chosin Reservoir. A chill ran through me, not entirely due to freezing weather or the sight of snow capped mountains. I had joined the Corps right out of high school in 1945. All through boot camp I had 'psyched' myself up to kill 'Japs.' Thanks be to God and Harry Truman, the Pacific war ended before I shipped to the war zone. I finished an uneventful hitch at the Marine Supply Depot in Barstow, CA, returning to Kansas to work for the railroad and begin a hasty, ill advised marriage.

When the Korean War began, I quickly volunteered for recall to duty, spurred by a boring job and a nagging wife. I had a younger brother already serving in Korea; I was sure he could use my help. After a hurry up refresher course at Camp Pendleton I was again instilled with the "Gung Ho' spirit. I soon found myself on the way to the "Land of the Morning Calm." With an added 5 years of maturity under my belt following my first hitch, I was more apprehensive of what lay in my future. This apprehension was bolstered during the retraining period where I carried a flame thrower hung on my 6'2" frame for most of the refresher course. Once ashore, in process of being parceled out to various units, call went out for anyone who could drive truck. I had plenty of experience during my first hitch, not only with trucks, but with fork lifts and other heavy equipment. I was assigned to C Co, 1st Mtr Trnspt Bn and given a truck which became my permanent home for the next year. I congratulated myself on not having to 'hump' that heavy flame thrower up and down the slopes of those forbidding, endless mountains, cascading down and across Korea like folds in a rumpled blanket. I was later to wonder if my judgement had been that good in admitting I could handle a truck and if fate was treating me all that well.

We were put to work immediately hauling the Division from the "Bean Patch" near Mason to the Eastern Front. The division had been assigned the task of eradicating thousands of North Korean guerillas bypassed in earlier efforts to 'end the war by Christmas.' My first trip to the area was one I will never forget. I was loaded with troops, driving fast over an ox cart trail mislabeled as an MSR. Driving under blackout conditions caused a great strain on my mind and body. Remarks from Marines in the back about my driving skills and ancestry didn't help. Keeping as close to the truck ahead as I could so not to get lost, we hit a small ford over a river. The truck ahead suddenly hit an object which sailed through the air right at me. All I could see was a dead body with outstretched arms. It hit my windshield and draped itself over the hood of my truck. A few violent moves of the steering wheel dislodged it. It didn't slow us down, but did bring a lot of remarks from the back about lousy drivers. I'll admit I was badly shaken for the rest of the trip.

We were not attached to an individual regiment, but rather were used wherever needed in the division sector. Sometimes, for days on end we lived in the cabs of our trucks, hauling troops, ammo and supplies forward and bringing back the bodies of dead Marines. It didn't take much of the 'brain-jarring' road punishment to reduce a driver to a zombie like trance so that he drove like a robot. We developed an efficient routine by happenstance while waiting at an a mountain pass checkpoint for MP in a guerrilla infested area to authorize road clearance. Drivers would park within a couple feet of the truck ahead and immediately fall into a sleep of total exhaustion. When the MP gave the lead truck the OK to move forward, the awakened driver would crank up and go into reverse to give a sharp jolt to the truck behind. The process would be repeated until all drivers were awake. The convoy would then move out.

We had a good unit and good men, but I never got the chance to know any of them well due to the nature of our duty, always on the go. One of my better memories occurred while moving troops up front. Corsairs were softening up the enemy on a ridge line across the paddies from our troops. One Corsair in the attack was hit and began spewing smoke. He was too low and too far out to make it. He bailed out anyway. The Chinese came running down the hillside to bag him. A great roar of sound came from our Marines. They rushed forward to rescue the pilot before the Chinese could get to him. I'm sure that was not in the original plan of attack. Marines got there first. The Chinese left many dead bodies in those paddy fields. My hitch was over at the end of Dec 1951. After enduring a better part of two winters, I was more than ready to come home. It was great to be back in the US of A, boring job or no.

<u>Right</u>. Troops of C Company, 31st Regt, 7th Division getting ready to make the attack on 'Jane Russell,' part of the Triangle Hill complex. Several of them are wearing air- marker panels.

<u>Center</u>. They are shown on 'Jane' with Hill 598 in the background.

<u>Bottom</u>. After taking the hill and fighting Chinese counter attacks all night, a few survivors gather in the rain at the base of the hill and get ready to go up again. October 14-15, 1952.

<u>Photos courtesy of D. E Schoenwetter</u>

RED DRAGON
The SECOND ROUND
FACES OF WAR II

Richard	E.	Fordyce	RA 16 38 5834
First Name	MI	Last Name	Serial Number
Dick	1745	10 June 1934	Sgt 1st Class
Nickname	MOS	Birthday	Grade / Rank
C Co 31st Inf Regt 7Inf Div		May 1952-Mar 1953	Indianapolis, IN
Unit (s)		Duty Tour (s)	Home Town
Combat Infantry Badge	Purple Heart Medal	Good Conduct Medal	National Defense Medal
Medals & Awards			
Korean Campaign Service Medal, 2 stars	UN Medal	ROK PUC	Korean War Service Medal

JANE RUSSELL'S TWIN HILLS

Growing up in the atmosphere of WW II with my dad serving as a Navy Seabee, it was not surprising that I was a gung-ho young patriot. I joined the service as soon as I was legal, at age 17. I thought of the Marines, but my dad and several others I respected suggested the army was where I would get my fill. No cameras or puff reporting, no frills or glory, just hard fighting. My 16 weeks of basic training at Ft Riley, Kansas was under the best field training Sgt in the US Army, SFC Keith Covey, 6' 4" of whipcord tough soldier. While in training I heard the 7th Division was considered one the best divisions fighting in Korea. When I reached Korea, I was absolutely delighted with my assignment to Charlie Co., 31st Inf Regt of the 7th Inf Div, known also as the Bayonet Division.

Early Oct 1952, a few months after my 18th birthday, we pulled off the MLR and went into intensive training for a major attack on what proved to be the Triangle Hill complex in the Iron Triangle. Heavy shelling of enemy held terrain by our artillery preceded our attack. We jumped off in early predawn of 14 October. Our objective was "Jane Russell," a section of Triangle Hill named after two of her most prominent endowments. We secured the twin hills by mid afternoon and set about re-digging the trenches which had been leveled by artillery and air bombing. Under Chinese sniper fire we continued preparation of new positions for the counter attack that was inevitable. An hour after dark set in our flares revealed black masses of bodies moving toward us. Chinese artillery began an intensive shelling. Almost as many rounds burst in their own ranks as hit us. Shells were exploding in our trenches, it seemed like in every square foot around us. Time after time we beat them off. They kept coming back. I lost track of time, but at some point, we were nearly out of ammo and were searching bodies for ammo and grenades. Our MG barrels were burnt out, guns were useless and out of ammo. We ended up passing single rounds of ammo up and down the trench to men in the critical areas under assault.

It was now about 2 AM. The Chinese had broken through in a number of places, creating large gaps in our line. Frontal attacks had ceased, but small bands of Chinese hit us from the rear. These attacks were weak, easily driven off. Those of us on the left of the line were completely out of ammo. We used the rifle bayonet and empty M-1s as clubs. The Chinese were out of ammo also; it was a stone-age clubbing brawl. A few weaponless Chinese ran down hill toward their lines. The rest were clubbed or bayoneted. There were now no Chinese in sight. There had been a lot of yelling and screaming, but suddenly it was very quiet. No one spoke or moved. It was merely a prelude to intensive shelling of our positions from the rear. We were being clobbered by our own artillery! I had blood all over my face. It was pouring, for some unknown reason, from my nose. When we could get our heads up again we saw a few Chinese. They appeared totally disoriented, stunned, confused, unable to organize themselves after gaining their objective.

Checking up, there were only four of us still standing to hold the hill. We went both directions of the trench, but found no one except several of our wounded and a few Chinese. Movement was slow and dangerous due to the continued shelling. We looked for a radio to call off the fire, found only one, smashed beyond use. I knew none of the other three. One of them said emphatically, "Let's get off this damn hill." I could not agree with him. I wasn't thinking clearly. All I could focus on was that we had been told to take and hold this hill. It was not bravery, it was imbedded training. I learned later the Regtl CO had ordered a pullback so the twin hills could be shelled and retaken on the morning of 15 Oct. In the confusion, we had been left behind. We finally left the hill, taking with us the few of our wounded we could find. It was nearly as tough going down as it had been going up. The hill was retaken that morning. I'll always believe we could have held it if we could have been resupplied with ammo and grenades. To this day, I do not believe that the regimental and division leadership were aware that a few of us were still in command of the hill, that the Chinese attack had failed.

I should mention that the shelling by our own artillery is just a part of war. No one made any glaring errors by failing to notify us. At the time the decision was made there were tremendous gaps in our line, plainly visible to the regimental CO. With the swarm of Chinese running around in confusion of battle, it must have seemed obvious none of us were still alive. I am extremely proud of the successful fight we put up to retain that hill complex. Everyone there fought the superb fight, one that American soldiers of any era of our nation's history would have been proud of. I still have great admiration for my 31st Infantry Regiment and the 7th Division.

Marine Corps tanks from A Company, 1st Tk Bn 1st Marine Division, support Infantry from the 7th Regiment in this attack on the east central front in mid October 1951. The tank on the left has already reached the ridge line. The middle tank is putting it's .50 MG to work. The tanks couldn't climb the mountains but their fire support was very comforting to have.

A Tanker's view of combat. The 90 mm main gun is firing on enemy targets on the ridge line and the handles of the .50 MG is within easy reach on the right, if needed. Oct..'51

The ready rack is full of 90 mm ammo at the start of an assault. Tankers very rarely brought much ammo back.
These photos courtesy of Roger G. Baker.

RED DRAGON
The SECOND ROUND
FACES OF WAR II

Roger	G.	Baker	11 71 148 USMC
First Name	MI	Last Name	Serial Number
Rog	1800	2 December 1932	Cpl
Nickname	MOS	Birthday	Grade / Rank
3d Plt A Co 1st Tk Bn 1stMarDiv		July 1951-July 1952	Culver City, CA
Unit (s)		Duty Tour (s)	Home Town

Korean Campaign Service Medal w/3stars   Navy Presidential Unit Citation   United Nations Medal

Medals & Awards

National Defense Service Medal   ROK Presidential Unit Citation   ROK Korean War Service Medal

TANK GUNNER

16 Oct 1951, 0400 hours we will head north over the MLR and into enemy territory in support of the 7th Marines. The mission is to take strategic terrain held by Communist North Koreans and Chinese. We do not expect a 'cake walk.' We were up late, arming, fueling and tightening tank treads. There was little talk, too much to think about. Sleep was slow to come as thoughts churned about in everyone's mind. A few days earlier I had been assigned as gunner on tank A-34. I had been taught how to zero in on a target, how to traverse the turret, raise and lower the 90mm gun, and how to trigger it. Heading north under an inky morning sky, our column halted. Peering out of the turret to my left I could see hundreds of screaming rockets take wing on tails of fire. The sight and sound sent chills up my spine. Those rockets were headed into the enemy heartland preparing the approach for our attack.

Dawn broke as we rumbled forward. We stopped again a few hundred yards forward of the MLR. Engineers ahead of us located and disarmed enemy antipersonnel and antitank mines buried in the path of our advance. Every few minutes corpsmen carried a wounded or dead marine on a litter back to the rear. Robert, "Red" Wheeler, our gunny sergeant, left his tank to talk to us. That did a lot to calm us. "Red" was a tall, lean and angular man with a wide toothy grin beneath a broad red moustache. His blue eyes twinkling, he offered me a lifesaver breath mint to soothe my dry mouth. He had served in the South Pacific in WW II and had been wounded at the battle of Iwo Jima. This was his last combat mission in Korea, he had only days to go before rotation. My buddy, Ernie Crawford who was a crewman in "Red's" tank, later told me that his last words of advice were, "Tell Ernie to keep his head down." He was fatally wounded moments later. We received the signal to advance. The tank ahead of us hit an anti-tank mine. My ears rang with the force of the blast. Through my periscope I could see four men trying to escape, two of them obviously badly wounded. Then both tanks behind us hit mines, leaving two tanks in the platoon, ours and platoon leader Joe Muser's command tank.

We edged around the disabled tanks, avoiding the corpsmen attending to the wounded from the damaged tanks. Five hundred yards into enemy territory we positioned our two tanks one hundred yards apart in a rice paddy. We fired round after round, as fast as we could load at a fortified ridge where we could see hundreds of the enemy. On our left flank, the 7th Marines were slowly advancing upon the ridge where we were directing our fire. The enemy was retaliating with mortar, artillery and rocket fire. We used armor piercing shells with delay fuses to penetrate deep into enemy bunkers. Most of the enemy fire was directed at our advancing infantry who were suffering heavy casualties. We could see dozens of our infantry being carried off the scene of action by our corpsmen.

It was now 1600 hours late in the afternoon. Smitty, our tank commander, radioed Lt Muser we were running low on ammo for the 90mm gun. Lt Muser's return message was, "Get the hell out of there!" The tank driver started his engine and began turning the tank around. A tank tread, stuck firmly in the muck of the paddy field, came completely off. The platoon leader radioed for a tank retriever to pull us out. I traversed the turret and used our last 90mm gun rounds to help cover our infantry as they withdrew. By the time the tank retriever reached the MLR we were under extremely heavy incoming artillery directed at our tank. The tank retriever was ordered to stay put. We were told to remove the 90mm percussion device and several other important instruments, bring them with us, and abandon our damaged tank. Lt Muser radioed he would pick us up. The turret was buttoned down after I traversed the gun.

One by one, the driver, the assistant driver, our tank commander, my loader and I crawled out the escape hatches in and below our driver and assistant driver compartments. The communist enemy knew we were in deep trouble. A sniper's bullet barely missed my head, I could feel its close passage and hear the 'zing!' as it barely missed me. It seemed as if the enemy artillery shells were falling like a heavy rain around us as Lt Muser worked his tank slowly toward us. As he reached us, and before we could climb aboard, a squadron of Marine fighter planes flew over the enemy ridge line. Dropping bombs and laying down a smoke screen, they took the heat off us. It was a long quiet ride back to our operations base. Lt Muser told us that a search light would be trained on my tank throughout the night. We would accompany the tank retriever next morning to bring our tank in to our base of operations for repair.

Roger G. Baker is the author of *USMC Tanker's Korea*. His memoirs of 3d Plt Able Co 1st Tank Bn 1st Mar Div were published in 2001.

Upper Left. On the MLR near the Punchbowl Marine tanks are dug in to give fire support to the Korean Marine Corps. Above. The mountain roads were always hazardous but a coating of ice made it really 'interesting.' Below Left. A load of Korean Marines are getting a ride on an A Company tank to a jump-off position for another attack Below Right. A tank-infantry patrol searching for the enemy. [East coast late 1951. West coast, 1952.] All photos courtesy Roger G. Baker.

RED DRAGON
The SECOND ROUND
FACES OF WAR II

Roger	G.	Baker	11 71 148 USMC
First Name	MI	Last Name	Serial Number
Rog	1800	2 December 1932	Corporal
Nickname	MOS	Birthday	Grade / Rank
3Plt ACo 1st Tk Bn 1stMarDiv		July 1951-July 1952	Culver City, CA
Unit (s)		Duty Tour (s)	Home Town

Korean Campaign Service Medal,3stars   Navy Presidential Unit Citation   United Nations Medal

Medals & Awards

National Defense Service Medal ROK Presidential Unit Citation ROK Korean War Service Medal

BASE OF OPERATIONS

Next morning we were up early, eager to retrieve our tank abandoned in 'No-Mans Land' the night before. Three of us in the tank crew were disappointed when we were told to stay in camp and clean up the instruments we had removed from our tank when we temporarily abandoned it. About 1030 hours as a bunch of us were discussing yesterday's events, a n artillery shell impacted about 50 yards away. Mondal Ammons of Sweetwater, Texas was severely wounded. A helicopter soon landed and lifted him in a litter off to a Med unit in our rear. It was a blow to me. Ammons had been one of my best friends while we were in training at Camp Pendleton. While Ernie Crawford and I were talking about Ammons being wounded, perhaps killed, Vernon Todd of Austin, Texas rushed down from a paddy several terraces above us. He wanted to know if the incoming shell burst had cost us any casualties. We filled him in. He said he had to get back, but invited us to join him in sharing a food package which he had just received at mail call.

We started to climb up the terraced rice paddy, heading for his tank platoon. The last thing I remember is the ground heaving in front of me as if in slow motion. I was thrown, unconscious, about 20 feet away. I came to, aware of the sound of incoming artillery shells exploding. I could hear cries of agony all around me. Fading in and out of consciousness, I could feel the ground shake and hear the massive crump of the big 122mm shells of the Russian built mortars that hit us with little warning. I called out to Ernie and Todd. Ernie called back that he had been hit. I said a silent prayer as the shells walked closer to our ammo dump. I knew a direct hit would be the end of all of us. The barrage ceased. All was silence for a moment except for groans of the wounded, and the bustle of corpsmen who had rushed up to tend them. I crawled out from under the tank where I had taken shelter after coming to. Still dazed and unaware of my own injuries, I lifted myself to my feet, wondering at my ability to stand. Taking a few steps, I stooped to pick up a strange object. It was a piece of a human skull. Glancing around, I saw the headless body of my friend, Vernon Todd.

That evening a smiling recovery crew, came in with our retreaded and repaired tank. They asked how the day had gone with us. I couldn't answer. I was still shaken on learning Mondal Ammons had died en route to the Med Hospital. Coupled with the deaths of "Red" Wheeler and Todd Vernon, I didn't feel I could answer without losing composure. In 2 days, of five tanks in our platoon, two remained. Of the 25 men in the platoon, 13 were still in fighting trim. We had 2 KIA and 11 WIA plus the death of my friend Todd Vernon of the 2d plat who had been standing next to me. Alive, in one piece, recovering from shock, I knew I was one lucky Marine.

CHRISTMAS MESSAGE FROM THE PUNCHBOWL

Better than two months had gone by since the death of my friend Todd. It was Christmas morning. Early in the day we had pulled out and headed for the 'Punchbowl', that infamous area that had been, and was still, a bloody battleground. On a steep mountain pass, tank A-34 threw its transmission. A retriever tank towed it back to the CP. Tanks had not been through this pass before. The crude dirt road was iced over. Many times our tank lost traction and started slipping towards the verge of the road cut into the steep mountainside. Our skillful driver was able to recover each time. At the top of the pass, I spotted a crude sign jutting out of the snow,

SCENIC VIEW OF PUNCHBOWL.

PARKING 25 CENTS

We all laughed. Reaching the valley below after hours of careful maneuvering, our four tank column pulled off to the side to allow passage of a small convoy of tarp covered Army trucks. We jumped out of our tanks to stretch our legs and talk to the Army drivers who had stopped once they had edged past us. They were a solemn group of soldiers. My curiosity getting the better of me, I lifted a tarpaulin to peer in back of one of the trucks. I was overwhelmed by what I saw. Dozens of dead soldiers, frozen stiff in death were stacked inside, alternating head to toe like sardines. It was Christmas, a grimly sad day for them to begin the long voyage home.

Our mission was to place a tank and crew atop each mountain above the Punchbowl to direct fire in support of the KMC (Korean Marine Corps). Twenty inches of snow had fallen, temperature dropping to 30 degrees below. The sight of the dead soldiers made us aware this could be our graveyard as well. It was a sobering thought as our tanks continued toward our designated positions.

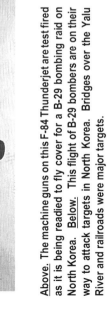

Above. The machine guns on this F-84 Thunderjet are test fired as it is being readied to fly cover for a B-29 bombing raid on North Korea. Below. This flight of B-29 bombers are on their way to attack targets in North Korea. Bridges over the Yalu River and railroads were major targets.

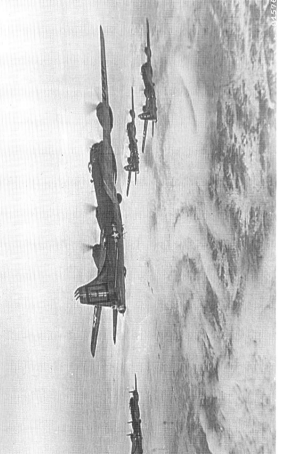

RED DRAGON
The SECOND ROUND
FACES OF WAR II

Lynn	W.	Dorsey	16 197 468 USAF
First Name	MI	Last Name	Serial Number
None	32331	28 March 1926	S/Sgt
Nickname	MOS	Birthday	Grade / Rank
343d Sqdrn 98th Bombardment Wing		26 Jul '51-16 Nov '51	Parson, KS
Unit (s)		Duty Tour (s)	Home Town

Good Conduct Medal   Air Medal   American Campaign & Victory Medals, WW II   Occp'n Medal, J

Medals & Awards

Korean Campaign Service Medal, 2stars National Defense Service Medal UN Medal ROK KWSM

SHOT DOWN

I was a Sperry lower ball gunner on B-17s and a G.E. blister turret gunner on B-29s in 1944-46, during and after WW II. As a member of the AF Reserve, I volunteered for recall to duty when the Korean War began. After my recall, volunteering for overseas duty, I was assigned to 343d Squadron, serving as left blister gunner in the B-29 "Our Gal," No. 1932, piloted by Captain Melvin C. Manley. There were 12 crew members. The others were 1st Lt Luke C. Fyffe, co-pilot; 1st Lt Wm. J. Haberle, radio operator; 1st Lt Al Zierler, bombardier; 1st Lt James Harig, navigator; M/Sgt Wilburn W. Foster, flight engineer; Sgt James A. Johnson, radio operator; Sgt Robt Abplanalp, Central Fire Control gunner; Cpl Harvey Simon, tail gunner; Cpl Ray Singleton, right blister gunner; and myself, Sgt Lynn Dorsey, left blister gunner. Our armament consisted of 12 .50 cal machine guns, 6 fired from the blisters, and 6 from CFC. Taking off from Yokoto, 33 miles from Tokyo, we bombed RR marshaling yards at Sandong-ni; military supply centers at Pyongyang, enemy airfields at Sandong-ni and many other targets. The most critical RR targets bombed were the RR marshaling yards at Rashin, just 17 miles from Russian Siberia, in the far northeast corner of Korea. In these raids each B-29 carried 400 bombs, each was a 100 'pounder.' Bridges and other point type targets were hit with 500 lb bombs. B-29s carried 40 of these 500 lb bombs.

On the 24th of October 1951, 98th Bomber Wing assigned two B-29 squadrons, our 343d Squadron and sister Squadron, the 344th, each flying four B-29s. We were given the mission of destroying the RR bridge at Sunchon. The 343d was the second element in the flight, with "Our Gal" as the last plane in our flight, flying the 'coffin corner' position. En route to target, while flying over the Sea of Japan, pilots commented on the rough seas as viewed from our altitude over the radar scope. After our bomb run, Captain Manley kept the radio open so all crew members could hear the flight leader's broadcast calling the 12 F-84s up from their near ground level positions where they had been attacking enemy AA batteries. Above us at an altitude of at least 35,000 feet, some 14,000 feet above where we were flying, I observed two planes, flying nose-to-nose at each other, guns blazing. One was a MIG 15, the other a British Meteor, one of 12 Meteors also flying cover. The Meteor suddenly blew up, wreckage spiraling down in flames. We were under heavy attack by a huge flight of MIGS, estimated then as close to 300 planes, but officially numbered later as 170 enemy airplanes.

From directly astern, one MIG flew through our 4 plane formation, his single 37mm and two 23 mm cannons blazing. His fire succeeded in knocking off half our vertical empennage, leaving it hanging over the tail gunner's position. He also blew a hole in our right wing, big enough to throw a chair through. Looking down, those in the forward part of the plane could see the sea below. The MIG was damaged by our CFC gunner. It was shot down as it continued in attack of our first element. There were a number of MIGs downed, but only one plane of our 4 plane flight returned safely to Yokoto. A second plane managed to limp back to base. The third plane in the flight was forced to land at the K-2 strip at Taegu, South Korea. It was so badly battle damaged that it was junked.

Although our wing was on fire, Capt Manley kept us in the air until we were off the east coast of Korea, near Wonsan. The US Navy maintained picket boats off Wonsan to interdict supplies and to assist in rescue of air crews, like ourselves, who were forced to bail out. I was preparing to jump over land as was the rest of the crew in the aft section. We were notified to wait until we had made it out to sea. I parachuted at about 15,000 feet, near the entrance to Wonsan Harbor where I spotted two islands. I missed them by miles! I later learned one was a leper colony, the other, a base for British Marines. Johnson and Foster drowned. Their bodies were picked up the USS Storms, DD 780, the same ship that picked up the rest of us who survived. Haberle and Fyffe were never found. A whale boat from the Destroyer USS Storms picked me up when I was about gone. The navy guys stripped me of my clothing as soon as I was aboard ship. Placing me in a cold shower, I was lightly slapped all over the body with bare hands. I was then wrapped in blankets and put in the Chief Petty Officer's bunk for the night. One of the things I remember, the cold shower felt warm! While aboard the USS Storms, the ship engaged in a gun battle with shore batteries. Fortunately, all enemy shells were near misses!

We were flown to Tokyo where we 7 survivors were debriefed at House No 513. There, we talked to fighter pilots who were in that air battle. They told us one man's chute had not opened. I don't remember how we arrived at the consensus it was Lt Fyffe's chute.

Above. Infantry troops in reserve are being taught new skills by a Lieutenant of the 13th Engineers. He is holding an AT mine and to the right of the blackboard is a display of cratering charges, AP mines and other deadly items. To the right of the instructor is a double-apron barb wire entanglement. Homemade 'napalm' and 'frag' goodies to hang in the wire were also demonstrated. Near the Iron Triangle, August 1951.

Photo by Norm Strickbine

Above. A wounded G.I. is loaded aboard a helicopter for a quick trip to a rear area hospital and some top medical care. He has already received first aid, is receiving plasma, and his chances for survival look good. Photo from the Archives.

RED DRAGON
The SECOND ROUND
FACES OF WAR II

Emery	A.	Vallier	RA 16 252 664
First Name	MI	Last Name	Serial Number
Em	3745	5 Sept 1931	Sgt
Nickname	MOS	Birthday	Grade / Rank
E/ 7th/ 1stCavDiv		10 Jan 1951- 18 Dec 1951	Detroit, MI
Unit (s)		Duty Tour (s)	Home Town

Combat Infantry Badge   Army Commendation Medal   Good Conduct Medal, Clasp & 3 loops

Medals & Awards

KWSM,4stars   Occpn Medal-J&G   AFEM-Berlin   NDSM, 1star   UN Medal   KWSM   Drill Sgt Badge

THE PRICE OF IGNORANCE

I enlisted in the Regular Army 28 July 1947. My mother died when I was a 3½. My younger sister, my new born brother and I were raised by my widowed grandmother who had five children of her own. We all learned to pitch in and help to the best of our ability, doing anything to help fill the larder during the depression. I attended Annnunciation School, quitting after finishing 8th grade when my grandmother died in 1946. Luckily was able to find jobs in a gas station daytime and at night setting pins in a bowling alley. The post war recession in 1947 caused me to lose both jobs. In the Army I was able to earn my GED in May 1950 before the start of the Korean War. I arrived in Korea January 1951 with the 339th Com Bn, but was immediately assigned TDY to the 532d Engr Bn in Pusan. I served there until Aug 1951 as a cox'n in LCPs bringing troops ashore, then was transferred to the 1st Cavalry Division.

The army when I enlisted was in transition from its WW II role of a global killing machine into a peaceful guardian of the emerging democracies of Japan and Germany. These countries, following defeat of their tyrannical governments in WW II, were being coached in the ethics of democracy by the United States. The American Regular Army had, in essence, been charged by Congress as the guardian of those ideals. Many of the officers and NCOs who gave me military training, acting as mentors on my progress as a soldier were veterans who remained in the service after WW II. Their knowledge of war and ability to lead transformed recruits into soldiers. We learned acceptable solutions to problems came from military skills, integrity, responsibility and respect for others. Not every soldier, officer and noncommissioned officer grasped those precepts as the following Korean War patrol incident reveals.

It was mid-November 1951 in Korea. At that time I was assigned to 1st Plt E Co, 7th Cav Regt, 1st Cav Div. We were about a half mile WNW of Hill 262 on OPLR on the Yokkok River, laying barbed wire and improving defensive positions. We heard, muted by distance, a weak call for help. We spotted a soldier, laying prone on a road paralleling our front, about 800 yards out. Moving to investigate, we stopped 150 yards from him, suspecting a trap or a decoy. I was told by Sgt Adkins or Arendt, I'm no longer sure which, to stay there, set up a base of fire with my BAR and two riflemen in event it was a trap or a decoy ambush. The Sgt and one other man approached the prone soldier. He was an American, not our outfit, who had suffered three wounds in a mine explosion and yet had crawled over a mile to get help for the other wounded men in his patrol. His story was radioed to our CP. Litters and men were sent out to assist us with the wounded. This patrol, half GI and half KATUSA, had been sent to check on one of our mine fields to see if any Chinese had stumbled into it. Grid coordinates of the mine field were plainly marked on the patrol leader's map.

The patrol had taken a chow break in the mine field. Starting to move out, they set off mines arranged in a daisy chain. If one mine went off, it triggered the rest. The count was 4 KIA and 7 WIA. We had recovered all the dead and wounded by the time the other men from E Co arrived. Returning to our lines, most of the men in the patrol and those sent to help were carrying wounded on litters or a dead GI over a shoulder. I was glad when we reached our lines, not only for the sake of the wounded, but also because I was loaded down with the patrol's riddled SCR 300 radio and two BARs damaged in the explosions. We were lucky that the detonations did not arouse the curiosity of the Chinese causing them to send out a patrol to investigate. We made it back without an incident.

Obviously, the patrol leader was deficient in his ability to read a map. He should have been thoroughly checked out before being allowed to lead any patrol. I have no idea which unit originated the patrol. I have often wondered how it was written up in the company morning report, the battalion and regimental daily situation reports. Was it a lesson learned so that every patrol leader was checked for map reading ability? Or was it whitewashed and swept under rug lest some officer, or officers, be charged with negligence? I will never know nor will the loved ones of those 4 KIAs on the patrol. The anguish and pain of the 7 wounded survivors was completely unnecessary. In my opinion, it was probably another case of an officer, platoon leader or company commander, assuming the patrol leader was proficient in his job. The plat sgt and plat guide, both of them in command above the patrol leader, bore a very heavy responsibility also. Both these NCOs should know their men and their abilities even better than the company officers. I hope similar situations never arise in our military today, but human nature being what it is, I can only hope.

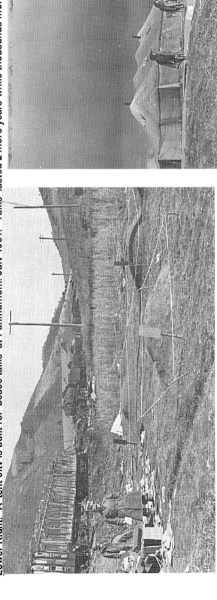

<u>Above.</u> An F-51 drops its napalm tank on a North Korean industrial complex while above right a B-26 has just dropped its napalm on an enemy held ridge line. Napalm and WP were greatly feared by enemy troops. <u>Lower Left.</u> A failed rescue attempt by the 187th Abn. Trying to save American POWs, the troopers arrived too late. 75 POWs were taken from a train and murdered at Sunchon, North Korea on Oct. 20, 1950. Three days later at Kunsang, N.K. 128 more executed G.I.s were found. Photos from National Archives.

<u>Lower Right.</u> A tent city is built for 'peace talks' at Panmuniom. July 1951. 'Talks' lasted 2 more years while thousands more died.

RED DRAGON
The SECOND ROUND
FACES OF WAR II

James	J.	Hon	US 55062090
First Name	MI	Last Name	Serial Number
Honcho		22 Jun 1928	S/Sgt
Nickname	MOS	Birthday	Grade / Rank
H&S 1092 Engrs© Bn I Corps		Mar 1951-Feb 1952	Nixa, MO
Unit (s)		Duty Tour (s)	Home Town
Korean Campaign Service Medal w/1 star			National Defense Service Medal
Medals & Awards			
Republic of Korea Presidential Unit Citation			United Nations Service Medal

COMBAT ENGINEER

I was drafted in Nov 1950. I knew how to drive, repair cars and trucks and had trained as a diesel mechanic. As a boy I learned to hunt and was a good shot. These skills which the enemy did not have, gave me a big advantage as an American soldier. It also qualified me for assignment to Engineer training at Ft Leonard Wood! The Corps of Engineers had refined the training process to a fine art. We organized in lines of two, marching or running from here to there for uniforms and tests: medical, psychological, dental, indoctrination and others long forgotten, plus short, short haircuts. A 14 week training cycle included instruction on the M-1 rifle, machine guns as well as 60 and 81 mm mortars. We received no specialized training in map reading, use of the compass, sniper's scope or the bazooka. These skills were vital as war service in Korea soon taught us. My class went to Korea by plane, 12 hours, and by ship, 14 days. Arriving by ship, I found many of my training group had died in battle during the big Chinese spring offensive.

My introduction to Korea was the horrible fecal odor of the paddy fields. The army food we received was equally horrible. My spirits were low, I was not optimistic about survival. Arriving at Suwon, 20 miles south of Seoul, my company commander explained the Chinese were trying to break through on our right. We ate, received ammo and hand grenades, loaded into trucks, went about 4 miles, then made a half hour climb up a hill and dug in. We could hear artillery pounding away. Several B-29s dropped bombs near Seoul. We could hear the explosions. There were a lot of flashing lights but we were not involved in any action. The next night was different. We began receiving machine gun and mortar fire. 3 P-51s dropped napalm on the hill facing us. One pilot let loose too soon, killing 2 of our men, badly burning 4 or 5 others. There were a lot of angry engineer soldiers! After 4 nights we returned to camp. We stayed at Suwon for a month, then in April moved north to Uijong-bu. Cold driving rain made roads muddy and slippery.

Arriving at the new camp, three of us were sent back to retrieve a lost trailer. Going south at about 2000 hours, the guy sitting next to me was shot in the back by a guerilla sniper. A Canadian ambulance behind us took him aboard and rushed him to a MASH hospital. He lived. I grabbed my M-1 and ran across a paddy field and up a small hill where I thought the shot came from. Too late, gathering darkness shielded him. Returning, I noticed I was in a mine field. Very, very carefully I picked my way back. Only God knew how I made it. Snipers were a constant traffic problem on the MSR roads that spring. It took a full year to root out all the North Korean stragglers left behind by their retreating army. These soldiers had turned to guerilla warfare after the Naktong Breakout and Inchon landings the previous fall. Snipers occasionally hit a truck carrying 42 gallon gasoline drums. That truck usually became a fireball. Several times while building or repairing bridges we were hit by rifle and mortar fire from North Korean guerillas.

In June we moved to Yonchon, near the Iron Triangle. We stayed there the rest of my tour in Korea. My unit was responsible for building temporary roads and maintaining primary roads. Main roads were like our local country roads but without paving. Dusty when hot; mud, axle deep in the rain. We built bridges of rocks, logs, dirt, any material available. I recall a special job we did on the north bank of the Imjin River. Approximately 120 Chinese, pack mules, oxen, jeeps and trucks hid in a rail tunnel from strafing planes.

A P-51 Mustang pilot scooted a napalm canister into the tunnel. It was an inferno. In a few days, the front advanced north. We were elected to clear the tunnel. We pulled everything out with chains attached to a bulldozer. We drew straws to see who would go next into the tunnel to attach chains. The smell was sickening. The debris was shoved over the cliff and the tunnel put back into service. A Stars & Stripes story verified the pilot's report. We needed no verification. Our noses were verification enough.

We did other jobs. We set up tents at Munsan for truce negotiation teams and a prefab camp at Panmumjon. On the American side of the DMZ we built many miles of the area separating the opposing armies. The truce talks began 10 July 1951. A truce was signed 27 July 1953. In the first 5 months of discussions there were 60,000 UN casualties. 22,000 of these were American. After a few months I was promoted to Bn Motor Sgt. In that job I dismantled captured Chinese trucks. They had wheel bearings made by Timken Bearings in Canton, Ohio! I spent 11 months in combat areas before return to the States to complete my term of service at Fort Dix.

The story of Korea told in one picture. Either rice paddies or mountains, and the Infantry became intimately familiar with every square foot of it. Climbing this mountain, these Marines seem to stretch back into infinity. Photo by Bill Palizzola.

RED DRAGON
The SECOND ROUND
FACES OF WAR II

Esper	K	Chandler	O-748 379
First Name	MI	Last Name	Serial Number
Chan	1542	16 July 1926	1st Lt Infantry
Nickname	MOS	Birthday	Grade / Rank
Able Co 2d Plt 27th Inf Regt 25th Div		Oct 1951-July 1952	Cotton Valley, LA
Unit (s)		Duty Tour (s)	Home Town

Purple Heart Medal Combat Infantry Badge Korean Campaign Service Medal,3 stars UN Medal

Medals & Awards

American Campaign Service Medal   WW II Victory Medal   National Defense Service Medal

"FOLLOW ME"

My military service career began in 1943 at age 17. I volunteered for the Naval Aviation V-5 Cadet program at LSU. My service was diverted to ROTC V-12 program with duty stations at Southwest Louisiana Institute, Tulane, and NAS, Corpus Christi and Iowa U. The war ended before flight training began. I returned to LSU in the ROTC program, graduating in 1948 as a 2d Lt in the US Army Reserve. My ROTC instructors, mostly WW II veterans, taught me three principles that guided my path as an infantry combat officer in the Korean War. "Follow Me," "Lead, don't push." "Take care of your men, they will take care of you." "Be fair, no pets, no favorites." "In war, casualties occur, be prepared to assume leadership." "Act decisively." "Take heed of the terrain." "Never ask your men to do something you would not do yourself." "If you are self-motivated, men will follow your lead." With these battle tested military maxims in mind, I felt no qualms when I was activated for the Korean War. I reported for duty at Camp Chafee, AR July 1950.

I was serving with the 180th Inf 45th Div in Japan when the Regiment was asked to ship 3 officers to Korea. I volunteered. In Korea I asked for the 25th Division knowing I would probably be allowed to choose my regiment. My assumption was correct. I opted for the 27th Infantry Wolfhounds, a proud regiment whose exploits I had followed while in Japan. The war was on slow bell. Washington politicians micro managing a war had curtailed ammunition supplies, frozen ranks and promotions, and issued orders to halt combat activities that might irritate the Chinese in a sensitive stage of the peace talks. Politicians never understand that peace is obtained when an enemy is beaten. Given a breather, he re-supplies, digs in and gets ready to renew the attack. Too bad politicians do not make a study of history, specifically the military history of past wars. Our country would suffer less loss of blood and men.

December 1951, we were on reconn patrol 3 miles in front of our sector of the MLR, near Kumwha at the base of the Iron Triangle. We ran into an ambush during this period of "no combat action." I started to jump up from the level of one rice paddy to the next when something slammed into my right leg. I thought I had tripped a mine. My leg felt as if it had been jerked out of its socket. My jump would have landed me on top of a camouflaged Chinese! I could now see the barrel of his weapon just above my head. Managing to stand on my good leg, and leaning against the wall of the rice paddy, I shot my ambusher who was so busy firing at my RTO, Pfc Donald Elm, and messenger, George Lovas, he failed to notice me. George Lovas yelled, "To your left!" Another Red soldier was pointing his burp gun at me. His burp gun lost the argument to my M-2 carbine. George, still standing up in full sight while loosening a jam in his M-1, again yelled, "On your right!" Inserting another clip, I swung my carbine toward a third Chinese coming out of a shallow trench. He was camouflaged in rice stubble. American carbine vs Russian burp gun, burp gun again lost the match.

Looking again back down that hill, what it meant to be a Wolfhound was vividly apparent. A rescue group were on their way up to help me. With the group, organized by Asst Plat Sgt John Matlock, was a medic and a litter. A hail of small arms fire and incoming mortar rounds did not deter them. As they made their ascent to where I lay, I could not help but recall the words of our Regt'l CO as he welcomed us to the regiment a few weeks past. "Wolfhounds leave no one on the field of battle. Your job is to carry out your mission. If you are on point, wounded and pinned down, have no fear. If a squad can not get to you, a platoon will come. If the platoon is not sufficient force, then the company, or the battalion, and if need be, the whole damn regiment. We take care of our own."

After a 3 month all expense paid vacation at the Tokyo Army General Hospital I returned to duty. At every level of rank, a wounded man returning to duty was offered a choice of rear echelon duty or return to his unit. I chose to return to Able Company whose loyalty and dedication to the honored traditions of the regiment had saved me on that hillside. I also wanted to talk to several men and explain their awards for valor I had initiated were in abeyance. Medals still were not being awarded due to ongoing 'peace talks.'

My service was mostly 'bunker duty' in contrast to the brutal battles fought by men that served in Korea before and after me. They have my utmost respect, particularly those Wolfhounds of Able Company who fought the ferocious battles of Sandbag Castle about six weeks after I rotated home. Today, I am still trying to have the medals for valor initiated so long ago be awarded to those men.

213

Above. More 'faces of war' the result of a Chinese human wave attack.
Photo by Bill Palizzola.　　　　　Right. Jim Kennicutt stands in
the doorway of his 'home away from home.' Below. These members of
the 45th Division show pride in their construction efforts and hope that the
Chinese artillery doesn't object to it.　　　　Photographer Unknown.

RED DRAGON
The SECOND ROUND
FACES OF WAR II

James	D.	Kennicutt	NG 25749186
First Name	MI	Last Name	Serial Number
"Kenny"	Machine Gunner	2 Feb 1932	PFC
Nickname	MOS	Birthday	Grade / Rank
M/279/45		Dec '51-May '52	Talhequah, OK
Unit (s)		Duty Tour (s)	Home Town
Combat Infantry Badge		Good Conduct Medal	National Defense Service Medal
Medals & Awards			

Korean Campaign Service Medal,one star   Japan Occp. Medal   UN Svc Medal

THE CALM BEFORE THE STORM

I was an 18 year old high school graduate in May 1950, no prospects of a job in Tallequah, OK or any ambition to go to college, having neither desire or funds. While talking to friends who joined the National Guard in high school, I learned the 45th Division was to be activated 1 Sept 1950. This brought back childhood memories of the 4th grade. I had attended a rural school about one half mile from Camp Gruber where the 42d Rainbow Division trained during WW II. On my way to and from school I would watch the men and Army vehicles. To my young eyes it was a grand sight. I decided some day I would be a soldier. On 23 Aug, one week before the 45th Division was activated, I was sworn into the National Guard. I pledged allegiance to the United States of America and gave my oath to defend her from all enemies, foreign and domestic. We went to Camp Polk, LA for basic training. In Dec 1950 we were assigned to FECOM in Hokkaido, Japan for advanced infantry training. Ten months of intensive training fitted us to relieve the 1st Cavalry Division which had been heavily engaged in Korea since early July 1950. They would replace us in Japan occupation duty.

We landed at the port of Inchon sometime around Christmas 1951. We sat in railroad coaches with the hardest bench seats I ever encountered. There were not enough seats for everyone, cars were unheated, drafty. We huddled for warmth, but were numb with cold by the time we arrived at the staging area. Arriving at night we were shown to unheated tents, no beds, cots or anything else. We slept on frozen ground. It was a fit initiation for service on the MLR which was our destination. We arrived at the MLR sometime around New Years Day 1952. At that time I had no idea where we were. In later years I learned to locate myself on the map of Korea by placing on the map the sites of "T-Bone," "Pork Chop," and "Old Baldy," names given to terrain features by GIs who preceded us in this area. These were battle sites with which I soon became familiar, even though I did not then know where I was. Luckily for me, my six months service in Korea occurred when the war was being waged at slow bell. It was a period of relative calm, a lull stemming from the peace talks at Panmunjom. The North Koreans, China and silent partner Soviet Russia sat on one side of the conference table, while South Korea and the United States, representing the United Nations, sat across the table as adversaries.

The end result of the vicious actions of the six months previous to my tour resulted in both sides digging in. Each side held strong points on the terrain, heavily fortified with barbed wire and mines laid in front of their positions. Two opposing jagged lines now stretched east to west across Korea, mostly above the 38th parallel. A small coastal area west of Seoul remained in Communist hands. Artillery units of both sides had registered fire concentrations on the enemy MLR. In GI vernacular, an artillery concentration designated by specific map coordinates meant that every position, on either side was "taped" for immediate artillery fire. Tremendous fire power could be brought to bear on the enemy at a minute's notice. It made for a war similar to the trench warfare of World War One. American GIs called it the "Rats and Bunker War," in obvious allusion to the horde of rats that lived as unwelcome company with them in their fortified bunkers. Bunker is a military term given to an earthen dugout which in Korea, due to the mountainous terrain, was generally dug into a hillside, roofed with logs, and covered with several layers of sand bags. The sides were buttressed with sand bags and any other junk available. Firing slits were built into a bunker by leaving spaces between sandbags or using the space between two logs laid on sand bags at different levels, allowing for placement of a firing embrasure. A bunker was generally proof against shrapnel. It gave cover for sniper fire, but was of little protection from a direct shell hit. But it was a haven for rats!

I did not take part in patrols which were the major combat activities during my period of service. It was my job as machine gunner to cover patrol advances and withdrawals. Recon and combat patrols into no-mans land were the chief causes of casualties during my time. Sporadic artillery fire added to the body count. On several occasions we were stationed on an exposed ridge finger which in case of enemy attack gave us little chance of escape. My hazards were tame compared to the men in the rifle companies. I rotated home in May 1952 after 6 months in Korea. The 10 months spent in Japan equated to 6 months in Korea which in total amounted to a year's combat tour. Today, I am still proud to have done my duty as an American citizen and to have played a small part in the noble cause of South Korean freedom. Every year at "M"/279 company reunions I meet comrades who are still as close to me as brothers.

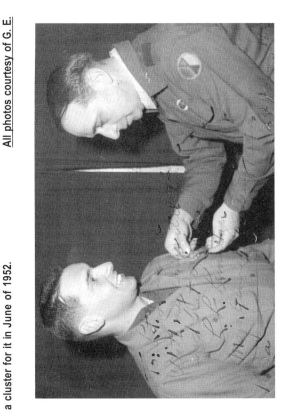

Above. It's S.R.O. for 7th Division troops at the Betty Hutton USO show near Kapyong, March 1952.   Below. Lt. Gerald E. Lawrence receives his first Bronze Star from Gen. Lemnitzer, C.G. of the 7th Infantry Division January 24, 1952. He was to receive a cluster for it in June of 1952.   All photos courtesy of G. E.

Gen. L. L. Lemnitzer, C.G. of the 7th Infantry Division, and Betty Hutton pose after her USO show performs near Kapyong, Korea, March 1952.

RED DRAGON
The SECOND ROUND
FACES OF WAR II

Gerald	E.	Lawrence	O-22 094 403
First Name	MI	Last Name	Serial Number
Jerry	1542	15 Apr 1929	1st Lt
Nickname	MOS	Birthday	Grade / Rank
Item Co/ 3d Bn/ 31st Inf,7th Inf Div		Aug 1951-July 1952	Winfield, KS
Unit (s)		Duty Tour (s)	Home Town

Combat Infantry Badge   Bronze Star Medal ,OLC   Korean Campaign Service Medal, 4stars

Medals & Awards
National Defense Service Medal   United Nations Service Medal   Korean War Service Medal

AIDE-DE-CAMP

Thirty days before the Korean War broke, I graduated from Kansas State University, concurrently receiving my commission as a 2d Lt of Infantry. Although I knew I might soon be called to active duty, I applied for a teaching job. Before school started, 1 Sept 1950, I received orders to report to Ft Leonard Wood, MO. The post had been closed following the end of WW II. We opened it. I acted as a basic training instructor in the winter months of 1950-'51. After a month at Ft Benning, GA, and a short leave home I made a sea voyage to Japan in a Liberty ship. Trained for a month at Camp Gifu before boarding an LST for Pusan. There I loaded into a train of 'cattle cars' for the front line. I don't remember where we were put into trucks, but I vividly remember my first sight of war, dead Chinese on both sides of the road leading to the Hwachon Reservoir. At HQ 7th Div I was assigned to Item Co, 31st Infantry Reg't.

Beginning the first week in August I spent several months on the MLR, frequently leading patrols out in front of the line. However, I always felt my primary job was to tend to the multitude of duties of an infantry platoon leader responsible for the well being and combat effectiveness of 40 young American fighting men. On a later patrol, one particular incident stands out in my mind. I had taken a squad of my platoon out about 1000 yards in front of our line. The day before, our artillery targeted an area to the right and in front of our ambush patrol location. Just after we settled into position, we spotted tiny lights directly ahead of us. I radioed the artillery FO who was familiar with the area, and whispered softly into the mike, "Swing left about 500 yards and down 50 from where you were firing during the day." He fired one round, right on the targeted lights, so I again whispered. "Continue firing." The flickering lights disappeared, not to return that night. The next day the FO kidded me about whispering into the radio mike. I told him if he had been with us, and as close to the Chinese as we were, he would have damn well whispered too. That night it turned very cold. We had not yet received winter uniforms or footgear. One of my men suffered the first case of frostbite of the 1951-'52 Korean winter.

Shortly after Thanksgiving, back in reserve, we were alerted to replace another Division in the first week in December. This Division had suffered heavy casualties taking Heartbreak Ridge. I was one of 3 officers told to make a reconn of the area prior to the relief. We had to cross an open valley which was under Chinese observation. Going out, we had no problem, but on return as we crossed the valley we heard a shell explode up ahead. As we passed behind the ridge line shielding us from observation, we saw a jeep that had just been struck by a mortar round. All 4 men were dead. There was a tank and a large bunker nearby. Someone in the bunker yelled, "Get the hell out of here, you're drawing fire!" We were only too glad to oblige. We later learned one of the four men was the tank company commander who was due to rotate home the next day. He had come to say goodby to one of his tank crews.

Our division commander was Maj Gen Lemnitzer. His aide, a West Point graduate and Regular Army captain, was up for promotion to Major. He was not eligible until he him person came up on Heartbreak Ridge to interview me. Again, I never knew why, but he chose me from the ten names submitted. It was the most interesting job I ever had, in or out of the Army. Serving as his aide, I traveled all over Korea. He always treated me with the utmost respect. It was characteristic of the man in his dealings with others.

By virtue of my position as his aide, I was privileged to meet General Van Fleet on many occasions. I was an interested listener in meetings with General Ridgeway, and General Mark Clark, a WW II friend. I was privy to high level conversations with Singman Rhea, President of South Korea and John Musio, U.S. Ambassador to South Korea. I became aware of the close associations, as well as the strictures, between diplomats and the military in a functioning democracy. I had enough points to rotate home in March of 1952, but when he asked me to stay until July when he expected to return to the US, I said, "Yes sir, General, I will." We came home July 1952, flying direct to Washington, DC, a place I had never been. He took me in a staff car to see many of the major sights in our capitol before I returned to Kansas and my wife. He asked me to keep in touch which I did. I had the privilege and honor of visiting him at the Pentagon in 1962 while he was serving as Chairman of the Joint Chiefs of Staff. He was one of America's great generals.

Above Left. Combat Engineers search for those elusive wooden box mines on the MSR. The passing G.I. is hoping they don't find one. Photo by Roy Wilson. Below Left. Thousands of feet of camouflage were erected to hide sectons of the MSR from the prying eyes of the Chinese. National Archive Photo.
Above. A Chinese POW checks his tired feet, Chorwon Valley, 1951. Below. Stars and Stripes humour. Courtesy of Tom Whitewater.

A GI Cartoonist in Korea

"I see our replacements got here, Pasquale."

RED DRAGON
The SECOND ROUND
FACES OF WAR II

Lawrence	NMI	Hochfeld	RA 12 334 98
First Name	MI	Last Name	Serial Number
Larry	1816	11 Aug 1932	Pfc
Nickname	MOS	Birthday	Grade / Rank
504th Trans Truck Co		22 Nov 1951- Jan 1953	Brooklyn, NY
Unit (s)		Duty Tour (s)	Home Town

Good Conduct Medal   Meritorious Unit Emblem   Korean Campaign Service Medal,4stars

Medals & Awards

National Defense Service Medal   United Nations Service Medal   Korean War Service Medal

ESPRIT DE TRANSPORTATION CORPS

It was a beautiful sunny morning in November 1951 when the troop ship from Yokohama dropped anchor at Inchon. After an all day wait, near sunset we scrambled down cargo netting hung over the ship's side into LCVPs (Landing Craft Vehicle Personnel) waiting alongside to take us ashore. When the LCVP ramp went down, the fecal aroma of 'night soil' hit our nostrils. It was the pervasive, overwhelming, nasal assaulting odor then characteristic of the peasant agricultural economy of Korea. We were trucked to Chunchon for processing. I was assigned to 504th Transportation Truck Company in Wonju, one of the five companies of the 70th Truck Bn.

After a week of instruction in vehicle maintenance, I was selected as one of ten soldiers sent to Seoul for the 351st Transportation Highway Transport Group Truck Driving school. Here I learned the 'ABCs' of truck driving including the mystery of "double clutching." We were also given extensive instruction in vehicle maintenance and emergency repairs. A month I returned to fulfill my role in the mission of the 504th, to freight supplies of all kinds, in any weather, and under all conditions, no matter how dangerous, to front line units. Our record was so outstanding in overcoming difficulties in these sometimes very dangerous supply deliveries that in late 1952 we were awarded a Meritorious Unit Commendation, setting us above and apart from other truck units with similar missions. While it puffed out our chests for a time, it meant that we were often singled out for the tougher jobs. Such is the price of military fame!

The outstanding record of the 504th was due to two outstanding officers, our Company Commander, Captain Clarence Walk and Chief Warrant Officer Goggins, our motor pool officer. These two men with their hands on attitude, their ability to educate, their knowledge of the military aspects of the US Army as applied to the trucking business of getting supplies to front line units, knowledge of human nature, a fatherly attitude in combination with a strict military discipline, fostered an attitude among men of the company which I have never encountered in civilian life. We were motivated to do our best, to never hang back from a difficulty, and always give our utmost to the task at hand. In the years since Korea I have yet to see an American company with employees as motivated in performance as were the men of my Korean war outfit. It is, I think, as I look back over the years, a tribute to American style leadership.

Captain Walk was a real southern gentleman. On many an occasion he came to the motor pool to work with the men whose job it was to see to it that trucks were kept running 24 hours each day. If he thought it would be of help, he would explain to those working on the vehicle the nature of the mechanical problem, On the other hand he would listen intently when one of the maintenance crew explained a complex problem he had not encountered before. With such an attitude in command of the company, trucks were always available for convoy duty. Captain Falk made numerous trips with us in convoy, always driving the lead truck on a dangerous delivery.

CWO Goggins was always on the spot when a convoy returned from a front line delivery. His invariable first question to each individual driver was, "Anything wrong with this truck?" If so, the truck would immediately be 'redlined' and a maintenance crew put on to correct the mechanical difficulty, change a tire, whatever, to ready the truck for its next trip. When a driver took his truck out of CWO Goggins motor pool, he knew that truck was in the best possible condition a dedicated maintenance crew could effect. CWO Goggins was always on hand to help gas up the vehicles and listen to stories of his drivers. He made sure each man, no matter how late his arrival back from a convoy, had a hot meal before he hit the sack. Other company officers were always on hand if men needed advice. The company XO was the 'disciplinary' officer a driver encountered if he got off base or out of line, needing to be dressed down or admonished to clean up his act and "get with it." The GI's in the 504th were from all over the United States, a polytypic mixture of men found only in this country. They worked together to make the 504th the best company in the Transportation Corp.

After we moved to Sokchori on the Sea of Japan, we made our pick ups from LSTs that dropped their ramps on the beach. We would back up to the ramp and load direct from the LST. It was an interesting way to handle a problem, a tribute to a unique concept in American marine engineering. For the last seven months I was with the 504th, my job was company clerk and mail clerk. It gave me the opportunity to become acquainted with every man in the company. I keep the memories of this great group of men deep in my heart. I have never forgotten them or my days in the United States Army. I went in an 18 year old kid and came out a 20 year old man.

Above. An 81 mm mortar team from the 5th Regiment are earning their pay. Punchbowl area. August 1952. Below. Another bridge utilizing assault boats is constructed by hard working engineers. South Korea - 1950.

Above. No, it's not a crap game but these G.I.s from the 3rd Infantry Division are cooking up something special. North Korea - December 1950. Archive Photos.

220

RED DRAGON
The SECOND ROUND
FACES OF WAR II

Paul	Z.	Hinson	US 53 010 963
First Name	MI	Last Name	Serial Number
PZ	1745	14 Aug 1928	M/Sgt
Nickname	MOS	Birthday	Grade / Rank
3dPlt Fox Co 279th Inf 45th Div		Jan 1952-Aug 1952	Greenville, AL
Unit (s)		Duty Tour (s)	Home Town

Silver Star Medal   Combat Infantry Badge   Korean Campaign Service Medal, 1 star   UN Medal

Medals & Awards

Occupation Medal-Japan   National Defense Service Medal   Korean War Service Medal

PLATOON SERGEANT

In 1950 I was in college. I took summer and fall quarters off to work for the US DA to recoup funds enabling me to attend classes next year. Unfortunatly, I was drafted and entered service 9 Nov 1950 to begin basic training at Fort Jackson, SC at $50 per month, the pay scale of a recruit. Later promotions topped out at $205 per month plus combat pay. I then went to Camp Polk, LA where I was assigned as a 'filler' into the recently activated 45th Oklahoma NG Division, not at full strength when activated. In April 1951 we sailed from new Orleans aboard the troop ship "John Polk" via the Panama Canal, a stop in San Francisco, city of the Golden Gate, a detour to skirt a mid-Pacific typhoon, then on to Otaru, Japan. Advanced training began immediately on the island of Hokkaido. Training was difficult, the terrain was terrible, the weather ranged from one extreme to the other, plus we were in a new environment.

In late December I received an assignment to the "Land of Morning Calm," as Korea is often described in travel brochures. My first combat assignment was 16 January 1951 on the Main Line of Resistance. The MLR was a military line set up to prevent infiltration into South Korea by North Koreans and Chinese across "No-Man's Land." We spent the next eight months resisting North Korean and Chinese probes and attacks as well as attacking and probing their positions. We gained no ground in the whole time our unit was there. The end result of our 8 month tour of duty was many casualties and KIAs. The men in our sector of the MLR were basically of two groups; original National Guard troops, now in the minority, and we draftees and Regular Army men. While we learned much from these guardsmen, both noncoms and officers, it was not until they began to return to the United States in late 1951 that we began to function as a composite whole. The clannishness, which had split us to some degree, no longer existed. Promotions opened up. Men could now be paid in accordance with the army pay scale of the job they were doing. It was a big morale boost.

On our first patrol mission, one No-Man's land crossing incident almost ended in tragedy. We had been alerted that a South Korean counterspy returning from a North Korean spy mission might be encountered trying to come across No-Man's land. He was to be taken prisoner. Jay Hibberts, acting as point man on our daylight patrol was deadly with a rifle, having learned to shoot as a young boy in the hills of North Carolina. An enemy soldier was spotted making a solo crossing. Frantically, I passed the word to Jay, "Don't shoot, don't shoot." Our prisoner was a colonel in the ROK Army, returning from a spy mission in the north. He was "captured," which led to a lot of laughter later, but at the time was not funny at all, particularly to the ROK colonel. Another incident almost caused me to be demoted from my job as squad leader. The Chinese and North Koreans had been quiet for several days as the "peace talks" swung into high gear. We had a man on LP (Listening Post) duty near the foot of a long ridge finger, downhill from our position. He used his M-1 to bag several Korean pheasants. His shots broke the morning stillness, causing queries to ripple down from Division HQ to Regt, Bn and Co, all the way down to me. When the facts came out, I almost lost my stripes. The only persons benefitting from the incident were the pheasant shooter and the company cooks who shared his roasted pheasant.

Comer Kelly, a man from my home town, was a man who never missed a meal. We met in Camp Polk for the first time. Were it not for all the hills we climbed, Comer would have weighed 400 pounds. Comer was also a dead shot with a 3.5 bazooka. Once he was ordered to fire into a cave the Chinese and North Koreans had been using. After he fired, I saw no result. "Damn it, Comer, you either missed or fired a dud!" "No, I didn't," he replied in his high pitched voice. Just then I heard a low explosion and saw a tremendous whoosh of dirt and dust erupt from the opening. What his rocket hit we don't know, but it caused one hell of an explosion in that cave. We were able to recover all our dead and wounded but for one man. Just recently, our platoon members sent to Washington the approximate location where his remains might be found. Fifty one years late, but it may help relieve his immediate family. We were blessed with a lot of good officers, best of all a top notch platoon leader in 1st Lieutenant Darrell Irvin and in Company Commander Captain Dick Gavin. Respect ran both ways in our company, men to officers and officers to men. I personally say "thanks" to all my fellow soldiers in the 3d platoon for their respect. My opinion is we 'fillers' did not let the 45th Division down in any way. The 45th had a good record. We strove to maintain the hard won reputation earned in two wars before our time of service in Korea.

Above G.I.s travel in style from the Port of Inchon to their new units on the MLR. Upper Right. Captured weapons include the Burp Gun, the Thompson Sub machine gun, and the standard issue Russian rifle. Right. A 'hot chow chogie train' brings up rations during a lull in the action. Below. The spring thaw of 1952 creates a lot of exercise for these lucky G.I.s. All photos courtesy of Roger Lueckenhoff.

RED DRAGON
The SECOND ROUND
FACES OF WAR II

Roger	J.	Lueckenhoff	US 55 026 642
First Name	MI	Last Name	Serial Number
Lucky	1745	29 Feb 1928	M/Sgt
Nickname	MOS	Birthday	Grade / Rank
A Co 160th Inf Regt 40th Div		Jan 1952-Aug 1952	St. Thomas, MO
Unit (s)		Duty Tour (s)	Home Town

Combat Infantry Badge   Occupation Medal, Japan   Korean Campaign Service Medal, 2 stars

Medals & Awards

National Defense Service Medal   United Nations Service Medal   Korean War Service Medal

READY, AIM, FIRE EVERYWHERE

Drafted in October 1950, I was assigned to the 40th Infantry Division, Camp Cooke, California. After completing basic and advanced training in April 1951, we shipped out of Oakland, CA for locations in Japan which the 24th Inf Div had vacated when that division was sent to Korea in the first days of the Korean War. In Japan another period of intensive training which included amphibious landings and airlift unit transfers was begun. We completed a year of repetitive training exercises creating for many of us a desire for change. On 22 December 1951 the division was alerted for duty in Korea. It was not the Merry Christmas greeting we expected, but we were well prepared and confident we were ready to cope with any combat problems we might encounter. A number of the incidents that lay ahead were of a type we had not experienced in training. We were the "Sunburst" Division, exposed to live fire throughout our training, responding to the commands, 'ready, aim, fire, 'fire when ready,' 'fire in the hole' plus constant reminders we were headed for Korea where facing enemy fire was a certainty. A couple of days after our "Korea" alert, our barracks in Camp Zama, along with six others burned to the ground. We lost most of our equipment and some of our personal possessions, but no loss of personnel. On 7 January we boarded ship for Inchon, landing early AM of 11 January on our way to where 'fire' became reality.

We were greeted by bitter cold and the whistle of a locomotive waiting at dockside to transport us inland. It was the start of a deep freeze we were to abide until spring. Crammed into box cars, warmed only by GI bodies fueled by icy Crations, the ice box experience foretold the next three months. At railhead we were assigned to positions in the Iron Triangle sector, but to the rear of MLR positions. We bunked in a squad tent heated by a small pot bellied stove, gravity fed by fuel oil from a container on the hillside above. It was 15 degrees below. We slept on cardboard, ponchos, anything available, to keep our sleeping bags off the frozen ground. There wasn't much to find. The area had been swept clean by previous GIs. Sleeping on an ice block would have been as comfortable. Around midnight, while two of us were on "stove tending" detail, the fire went out. My buddy grabbed a tin of gasoline and poured some into the hot stove before I could yell, "DONT!" As he reacted to the explosion he sprayed burning gasoline in a semi-circle over sleeping bags and the back of my parka. Bodies rocketed out of sleeping bags, pounding away at the flames. I headed for the exit to roll in snow. Didn't occur to me shedding the parka should have been priority one. Luck, and the patron saints who protect young soldiers prevented serious injuries. Men and tent survived, a new issue of sleeping bags and a parka re-equipped us.

The business was combat. On 19 January '52 we relieved the 19th Inf Regt 24th Div in MSR positions near Kumsong. The first 10 man patrol sent out from my A Company, was led by SFC Knepp who was wounded in a contact with an enemy patrol. The enemy had two men KIA and several wounded. Our Baptism of Fire. In early April we moved to positions in the Kumwha-Kumsong sector. Some of my old buddies in the 3d plat were in a LP in front of the MLR. About 100 feet in front lay a napalm barrel rigged with a WP grenade as an igniter. In the dark of night a beer ration bet was made by one man he could get an air burst with a flare grenade, and the other could not. Neither won. Both got air bursts starting a fire that burned two days down hill to a ROK outpost, then up hill to our positions. The fires provided more night light than moon, search lights and flares combined. A trail used by patrols acted as a fire break, preventing the napalm barrel from exploding. Flares and grenades were taken from mischievous boys. Lesson learned.

June '52. General Cleland succeeded General Huddleson in command of the division. Shortly thereafter, he changed the division nickname from "Sunburst" to "Ball of Fire" and redesigned the shoulder patch. A number of division veterans complained, derisively referring to the new patch as the "Flaming Asshole." Somebody upstairs must have agreed. We returned to use of the old patch. Fire was everywhere in our war tour of duty in Korea. We were exposed to sights and sounds which have no parallel in civilian life. These audio and visuals of war are forever etched in our memories. As soldiers we engaged and destroyed the enemy, looked after our buddies, always with the objective of returning home. We fought "The Forgotten War," but those of us who were there will never forget those giving their lives in freedom's cause, never to return home to their loved ones. Aptly, it is termed the Supreme Sacrifice. I departed Korea late August '52 and was discharged shortly thereafter, returning to the warmth of family and friends in civilian life.

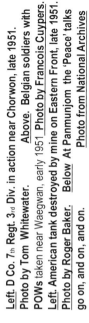

Left. D Co. 7th Regt. 3rd Div. in action near Chorwon, late 1951. Photo by Tom Whitewater.   Above. Belgian soldiers with POWs taken near Waegwan, early 1951 Photo by Francois Cuypers. Left. American tank destroyed by mine on Eastern Front, late 1951. Photo by Roger Baker.   Below At Panmunjom the 'Peace' talks go on, and on, and on.

Photo from National Archives

RED DRAGON
The SECOND ROUND
FACES OF WAR II

John	W.	Hill	RA 14367409
First Name	MI	Last Name	Serial Number
None	1745	6 Oct 1930	1st Sgt E-8
Nickname	MOS	Birthday	Grade / Rank
Fox Co 279th Inf 45th Div		Dec 1951- June 1952	Kinston, NC
Unit (s)		Duty Tour (s)	Home Town

Bronze Star Commendation Ribbon Purple Heart Good Conduct Medal Combat Infantry Badge

Medals & Awards

Korean Campaign SM,3 stars Meritorious Svc Medal Vietnam Svc Medal&Ribbon NDSM UNSM

TOP SOLDIER

I was a RA soldier assigned to the 45th Infantry Division before the division arrived in Japan. I was later assigned as a BAR man in Fox Co, 279th Inf Reg't. After a further period of training in Japan, supplementing stateside training before shipment to Japan, we were ready for a combat assignment in Korea. That took place in the dead of winter, 23 December 1951. We arrived in Inchon at night and boarded a troop train for movement toward the front. The Army had picked an ideal time to illustrate in miniature what we would soon know as the reality of combat conditions in Korea. It was snowing. The temperature was below zero. Men were hungry. At the railhead we off loaded into deuce- and- a- half Army 6x6 trucks. The trucks were open, no canvas covers. When we arrived at the bivouac area we were shown to squad tents. The snow was 2 feet deep, deep enough that it kept the wind from whistling beneath the bottom of the tent and the ground! That was the only benefit I could perceive in anything that had happened since we debarked from the ship! The next morning we test fired all weapons prior to moving to the MLR where we were to relieve the 1st Cavalry Division. The 1st Cav was returning to Japan to resume their former role as occupation troops. They had been in combat since July of 1950. They were due! Essentially we swapped places, they returned to occupation duty. We took over their combat role in Korea.

Our sector of responsibility was the Chorwon valley area of the MLR. We were near Old Baldy, the infamous hill which had cost so many American lives. Infantry operations in mid winter consisted of patrolling no man's land, the area in between the two sides. Chinese and North Korean fought on one side of that line. Americans, South Koreans and Bn sized UN contingents from 14 different UN nations opposed them. The United States, South Korea and British Commonwealth fielded divisions, other nations furnished Bns. Turkey furnished a hard fighting Brigade. As a side note, Denmark, India, Italy Norway and Sweden operated medical units under the UN banner. Winter patrolling was doubly hazardous, the weather was as much an enemy as the Chinese or North Koreans.

A man wounded on patrol needed a lot of TLC in the way of warmth and attention to insure that he did not die of shock in the sub-zero cold. Thankfully, our Medics were well trained and usually were able to get the man back to surgical care, but it was a tough job for the Aidmen and the stretcher bearers. Patrols were a nightly affair by both sides. Ambush patrols, reconn patrols and combat patrols kept everyone on his toes while he awaited his next 'turn in the barrel.' As far as we soldiers could tell, these patrols meant hazardous duty with little to gain. Being under small arms fire when on patrol was not nearly as bad as being caught in an artillery or mortar barrage. That was downright scary in the personal attention we were privileged to receive from the enemies big guns.

Guard duty in the MLR trenches had its periods of tension. One night our Regimental S-2 told us to be alert for Chinese infiltrators. They were to be allowed into our lines, but not allowed to leave. We were not to fire or otherwise alert them but to maintain close observation and take at least one prisoner. We went on full alert. From my position, everything that moved I saw as the enemy! I spotted movement up hill. I cautiously closed in on it, scared to the tips of my toes, only to find it was an empty sandbag blowing in the wind! I was mightily relieved. There was no contact with an infiltrator, let alone a group of them. It was all a false alarm! Shortly, I transferred to HQ & HQ Svc Co as NCO in charge of a half- track section, each 'track' armed with Quad .50 cal heavy MGs.

On another occasion we were on a daylight support mission in the Chorwon valley area near Pork Chop. My half track broke a tread. We were told to stay with the 'track' until a tank retriever could pick it up. Another 'track' would be despatched to allow us to continue our patrol mission once the disabled 'track' had been towed away. Of course, the Chinese spotted us and began shelling us with artillery and mortars. It turned out to be a very hairy afternoon on a daylight patrol that begun as a quiet walk in the park. We couldn't leave the tank, and the Chinese mortars wouldn't leave us alone. The 'track' gunner had expended all the ammunition he carried. Once that was gone, we were sitting ducks. We did call in our own artillery in support. We were a bunch of digging fools until the retriever showed up and hooked on the disabled 'track'. It now had some new battle scars that shrapnel had dinged into the armor. We made haste to leave the area. It was getting dark which gave us some cover from observation. We made it back without casualties, thanks to a Chinese observer who was not up to his usual standard of excellence. We were mighty grateful!

225

Left. Marines begin to use their 4.5 multiple rocket launcher to good effect in this 1951 photo. _____ **National Archives.**

Lower Left. The Chinese reply with their own multiple rocket launchers in this photo from the Internet. By 1953 the CCF artillery was equal in numbers to ours and artillery duels equaled any of the massive artillery battles of World War I.

Below. Maj. General Frank Lowe, a Presidential representative, examines a 'flash range' instrument on the MLR. A Marine Sgt explains its operation, 1951. Photo from the National Archives

RED DRAGON
The SECOND ROUND
FACES OF WAR II

Jacques	K.	Doyle	US 51 048 085
First Name	MI	Last Name	Serial Number
Jack	2745	25 February 1928	Sgt(T)
Nickname	MOS	Birthday	Grade / Rank
179th Inf 45th Division, NG		Dec 1951-Aug	1952 Binghampton, NY
Unit (s)		Duty Tour (s)	Home Town
Combat Infantry Badge	Purple Heart	KCSM, 3 stars	United Nations Service Medal

Medals & Awards

Occupation Medal, Japan   New York State Medal for Korean Svc   ROK 50th Anniversary Medal

SOLDIER, ASK NOT FOR WHOM THE BELL TOLLS. IT TOLLS FOR THEE.

Soldiers often refer to the first half of the Korean War as the yo-yo war since it was characterized by rapid movement, north and south from the tip of the Korean Peninsula to the border of Chinese Manchuria. By fall 1951, with most of the fighting front stabilized slightly north of the 38th parallel, the war became one of stalemate. Neither side could obtain their objective. China, because she could not match, even with Russian assistance, the war materiel needed for a win. The US-UN side could not win, because they were not prepared to spend the lives of enough soldiers to liberate all of Korea, nor use the atom bomb to reduce China to rubble. The second half of the war, to soldiers, became the "rats and bunker war." Both sides dug in for a prolonged siege of trench warfare.

The static war meant any large ground offensive was out of the question for either side. Little to gain and much to lose. The Chinese had "won" their war by pushing the US-UN out of North Korea, rescuing little brother North Korea. The UN and the US had decided the war would not be escalated so the Chinese knew their mainland was safe from attack. The Chinese also knew they could not "win" because UN Forces were far too strong in the air. They also exercised control of the seas. UN Forces also had "won" their war. The Communists had been pushed back over the 38th parallel and the world placed on notice that aggression would not be tolerated. Unfortunately, the US military with its tactical philosophy based on attack as taught at West Point, did not know how to "defend and wait." American military doctrine is aggressive, American armies are trained to fight. There are only 'Hawks' in the US military, 'Doves' are not tolerated. In consequence, our military genius and common sense came to an abrupt halt in November 1951.

US military leaders in command saw only part of the overall picture. Our casualties of 21,329 KIA and 52,384 WIA up to November 1951 could be justified by results. Afterward, the scenario changed. If our doctrine had been defensive, it is not conceivable that our casualties would have been even close to what they were. After Nov of '51, our casualties were 12,300 KIA and 50,900 WIA, 36.5% of our dead and 49% of our wounded took place in this period. Had we hunkered down and merely kept continually turning the crank of the hamburger machine, it is inconceivable that even the 'inexhaustible' manpower of the Chinese Armies could have inflicted that number of casualties on well dug in American soldiers, manning fortifications suited to the terrain. American engineering ingenuity was called for at this stage of the war, not the tactics practiced by generals tutored in the West Point doctrine of attack.

Two specific examples will illustrate. Chinese and American MLRs in 1952 and '53 on this front were about 1500 yards apart. Both held well dug in, fortified positions on high ground separated by the terrain of No Man's land. Two hills, Old Baldy, Hill 266, and Pork Chop, Hill 255, butted up against the Chinese MLR. General Van Fleet, concerned that "a static army is a soft army," approved the attack on these Chinese positions. The result was disaster. No damage to a well dug in enemy, and by our own estimate, only 10 Chinese casualties. Dissatisfied with this first repulse, attacks continued for months with no appreciable gain. The price paid was in blood of dead American soldiers. Smarter generals would have patiently waited for the Chinese to attack our fortifications. In the mind of this infantry soldier and others as well, patience would not have made us into a bunch of 'softies' as the General opined.

As a second example, "Operation Smack" staged 25 January 1953 used the 7th Division as a sacrificial lamb on Van Vleet's altar of 'Hollywood' war. A staged scenario, issued as a 6 page, 3 column document, inviting press and assorted dignitaries to witness, in safety, the useless deaths of American infantrymen. Shades of the Roman Coliseum! The show consumed 224,000 lbs of air bombs, 12,000 rounds of artillery, 100,000 rounds of .50 ammo, 2000 rounds of 90mm tank gun ammo, and 4500 rounds of mortar shells. The infantry fired 50,000 rounds of small arms, tossed 650 hand grenades and suffered 77 casualties. Not a dent was made in Chinese positions. No prisoners were taken, Chinese casualties estimated as 50 men. The Chinese used a fraction of their ordnance and inflicted far greater losses. The question is not what did we gain, but why was the fiasco staged at all? Why were we trying to occupy hills of no value? Why were we losing men in a ground war that had no purpose except preventing 'softness' in soldiers? The big break came when General Maxwell Taylor assumed command 11 February 1953. He visited the 7th Inf Div in March after the 7th took over 300 casualties in 2 days of fighting. General Taylor called off further attacks "as not essential to defense of the sector."

Above. A 45th Division G.I. gazes at 'Chink' territory from the MLR near Chorwon. March 1952. Below. Glenn Ed White shows American weapons destroyed by 'friendly' napalm. June 27, 1952 Photos by Glenn Ed White.

Above. Members of Love Co., 279th Regt, 45th Division prepare to move back into the line. West central front, early 1952. Below. Outpost No 6 in front of T-Bone Hill complex, L Co. of the 279th Regt. Photos by Glenn Ed White.

Above Left. While in reserve on the Eastern Front troops from L Co. 279th take a break from a forced march. Above. Crossing a pontoon bridge over the Soyang River the L Co. men get very little rest in their 'rest area.   Below Left.   Back in the lines near Inje these troops enjoy some sunshine during a lull in the action.

All photos courtesy of Glenn Ed White.

Below Right.   While in reserve Ed White gets to ride in a jeep. Always a treat for a 'ground-pounder.'

RED DRAGON
The SECOND ROUND
FACES OF WAR II

Glenn	E.	White	US 54 052 949
First Name	MI	Last Name	Serial Number
Ed	1745	7 Dec 1930	Pfc
Nickname	MOS	Birthday	Grade / Rank
L\279\45		Nov 1951-Oct 1952	Shreveport, LA
Unit (s)		Duty Tour (s)	Home Town

Combat Infantry Badge   Korean Campaign Service Medal w/2 stars   National Defense Medal

Medals & Awards

United Nations Medal Korean War Service Medal   Republic of Korea Presidential Unit Citation

OJT LEARNING CURVE

After the Chinese intervened in the Korean War, the Selective Service System swung into high gear. Like several million other young Americans at that time, I was drafted into the military, destined for Korea. With 'Basic Training' behind me, Nov 1st 1951 found me placed in an "air packet" at Travis AFB, CA. I got off the at the Tokyo airport designated as a 'filler.' A 'filler' or 'casual' is the army designation for a soldier who will function as a replacement for another soldier killed or wounded in battle. It is a scary impersonal process, bereft of the usual comradeship found in a military unit. This is so because he has not yet been assigned to a unit, the military home of the soldier. He is a 'filler', a replacement, a warm body. He is, as yet, an unknown quantity in his ability to "soldier." Once assigned to a unit, he will undergo scrutiny as old hands try to figure out if he will measure up. His first encounter with the enemy will, in the minds of his peers, determine whether he is a 'soldier,' a term defying description, yet is the common denominator of acceptance in any military unit. His comrades rate a soldier by the pithy age-old military adage, "Every man carries his own pack."

I took ship from Japan to Inchon in early November 1951. I wended my way through the assignment process and was assigned to Love Company, 5th Cav Reg't, 1st Cavalry Division. The Army in its usual muddled fashion had sent me to a unit that was returning to Japan to resume its occupation role after a year and a half of almost continuous combat in Korea. As a 'newbie' I did not go with them. Instead I was first transferred to Love Co of the 180th Inf Reg't, then to the 279 Inf Reg't, both in the 45th Division. The 45th Division was an Oklahoma National Guard Division which had undergone extensive training in the States and Japan before replacing the 1st Cav in Korea. In mid December the 45th Division assumed a combat role on the Main Line of Resistance (MLR) at the "Iron Triangle" on the west central front. On my first day on line in the 180th Reg't, Lt Hancock stepped on one of our own mines in front of my bunker. He was killed instantly. A bad start. We were on line but for a short time when we were pulled off for "reorganization."

The "reorganization" resulted in transfer to the 279th Inf Reg't. I looked upon it as a good omen that each assignment in two divisions and three regiments had kept me in Love Company! In short order L/279 was back on line. I was no longer a "filler," I had a home! On 7 February, 2d Plat Love Co was sent into the Yokkok-chon valley to attack "Dark Baldy," an area on Hill 290, "The T-Bone." I was in the 1st plat, assigned as a field wireman. I laid wire well out into the valley. As the 2d plat neared the objective on Hill 260, Lt Lamb stepped on a box mine. Sgt Paul Elkins assumed command, Lt Lamb was tended by the aid man. The platoon continued for another 400 yards. About midnight as the 4.2 mortars were adjusting their safety shield around the platoon, a round hit in the center of first squad. It was case of 'friendly' fire causing havoc in our own ranks, 4KIA, 10 WIA and one MIA. From my position in the valley I passed word back on my wire to HQ. The mission was aborted. Dead and wounded were rounded up for the long trip back. I had weathered what older men euphemistically called the OJT school. By that they meant 'On the Job Training,' self taught instruction.

The war now stretched in a continuous trench line across Korea from the Sea of Japan on the east coast to the Yellow Sea on the west, a stretch of 150 miles as the crow flies, another 30 or so miles as the trench lines zigzagged around dominating hills and ridges. It took a lot on men of both sides to man these long battle lines. It was not an even match in manpower. The edge that gave us rough equality was our expertise in use of artillery and mortars. Fighting along the MLR was mostly at night with much patrol activity interspersed with battalion sized attacks by the CCF. Night patrols were always unnerving. We always hoped it would be "the other guy." When it was 'your time in the barrel,' it was just a matter of gritting teeth and doing one's best not to let the other guy down.

Late afternoon of 10 June we were sent on a 'prisoner snatch' patrol near T-Bone Hill, beyond Outpost 5 on Upper Alligator Jaw. Our broad sweep of the area put us under automatic weapons fire by Chinese firing from a deep ditch. Full dark had set in, the only light was from muzzle flash of weapons. My carbine jammed. I was soon able to clear it by "feel" and join in the fight. A MG placed atop the drainage ditch bridge, fortunately firing over our heads, was soon knocked out. Heavy fire to our front was still a menace. Sgt Richard Bohrman who was closest to the canal hollered for grenades. These were passed up to him. He used them to noticeably lower the intensity of enemy fire. By this time the Chinese in the canal had moved around to our right. We were now surrounded.

Fire to my flank zeroed in on me. In crawling over the berm of a rice paddy, a bullet from a Burp gun burst cut the sock on my left foot, but no wound, no blood, no Purple Heart. A potato masher grenade had earlier landed about a foot from me but did not explode. My platoon leader, Lt Charles Snowden, repeatedly exposed himself to enemy observation, enabling him to call in artillery fire on the Chinese. 'Incoming mail' was so close I was afraid it might hit us as well as Chicoms. In this action Pvt Leo Pepin, himself wounded, carried a buddy back from an exposed position. A King Co platoon sent to assist us was driven back to Outpost 5. We made it back to our lines with 2 KIA, a number of wounded, but no prisoners. Later that month on 27 June while in my bunker I heard the zoom of planes low overhead. Two Marine P-51s were mistakenly strafing and napalming Outpost 6 to our front. Six men were burned or cut by barbed wire while bugging out amid burning equipment and exploding ammo. No deaths. Another of war's sad little ironies.

3 July, Love Co was in position facing "Old Baldy,"Hill 266. My buddy Chrisman and I were out in front of the MLR occuping an LP (Listening Post) to observe and listen for enemy activity. Shortly after we took up position, the Chinks opened up with an artillery barrage. Our .30 caliber MGs firing over our heads added to the racket. I looked at Chrisman. His knees were shaking like Jell-O on a wobbly table. I looked down at my own, they were shaking in tune with his. Even at that moment, it was a strange and hilarious sight! When the call came to return to the MLR, shaking knees or no, we made it back in record time. The artillery fire to our front was merely a prelude to what was coming that night, 3-4 July. We had been in the middle of the Chinese registration fire preparing for a battalion size attack on "Old Baldy." Item Company of the 179th Regiment was dug in atop Old Baldy in well prepared positions.

About dark mortar and artillery fire became intense on Old Baldy, and on us, on line to the rear. We were all manning our bunkers and fighting holes in expectation of an attack we felt was immanent. Looking up, the hill crest was an absolute inferno of exploding shells. The din was cataclysmic, increasing in ear shattering crescendo as the time neared for the Chinese to attack. Both sides were firing every gun, every battery, in every artillery battalion within reach of Baldy. Our fire was aimed at the flanks and rear of Old Baldy to stop the Chinese attack. The Chinese fire was directed at Item Co atop "Old Baldy." The hill crest on "Old Baldy" was covered in dust and debris. I saw body parts flying up into the air. It was horrible. I thought of the men of Item Co. Who could survive such an attack? One who is involved, or who is a witness, can never forget such terrible scenes. They are the cause of nightmares.

Hill 255, "Pork Chop," was about 2½ kilos northeast of Baldy. It was under simultaneous attack. The Chinese were going all out in this sector. Love Co was sent in to relieve the survivors of Item Co and reoccupy "Baldy." We found shell craters and collapsed bunkers. Most of the dead and wounded had been removed by the time I got there. Our losses were heavy, but much more so for the Chinese. There were seemingly hundreds of Chinese bodies strewn around, frozen in grotesque postures of death. There was much work needed before "Old Baldy" was again a defensible position. Our Company Commander, Captain Jack Rose was a tower of strength and leadership during these months. This was good as we began to show the stress of battle. During this time I did a lot of praying to our Lord that he would see me through this war. He heard me, as I am alive to attest. No amount of talking to God is too much. All soldiers need the faith and hope that God gives them so that they can do their best for their buddies and country.

On 14 July we were relieved by the 38th Reg't, 2d Division. They were pushed off Baldy, but retook the hill after a tough struggle. A series of see-saw battles ensued with high casualties on both sides. Our 45th Div was moved to eastern Korea, above the 38th parallel, near a town called Inje. We went into Army Reserve and a period of receiving replacements to bring our depleted ranks back to battle strength. I had a deep sympathy for these 'newbies,' recalling my own feelings of just six months earlier. I made it a point to talk to them whenever possible in a friendly way with no attempt to discuss combat situations unless asked. They would learn on their own soon enough, just as the rest of us had learned the hard lessons of OJT. Off line we went through another period of intensive training in which I and two of my buddies were wounded by 60mm mortar fire in a live fire infantry-tank training problem. Emphasis was also laid on familiarization with lessons learned by other units in fighting Chinese and North Koreans. We were given cross-training on *all* weapons used in a rifle company. We could then "double in brass" on any weapon as casualties occurred in battle. As a side benefit, replacements become acquainted with fellow soldiers in squad and platoon. Such acquaintanceship ripens into bonding comradeship and results in better combat performance, fewer casualties, and an esprit de corps that wins not only battles, but wars. These things were now crystal clear to me. It had taken me only 6 short months to learn these hard military truths.

We moved back to the line in September. This time we faced North Koreans. They were a different breed of cat from the Chinese. More cautious, not prone to mass attack in emulation of the "human sea" tactics of the Chinese. I missed a bad fire fight on 18 October, I was just to the rear of the MLR, awaiting rotation. An enemy platoon penetrated our trenches but were soon thrown out. On 25 October, while building a bunker, I suffered a painful back injury which took me off the line. A day later I received my rotation orders. Back injury or no, I was ready to go! While in Korea I took over 500 photos and made about 800 feet of 8mm movies. In retirement, my hobby has been to develop these for viewing by other veterans of the Korean War. It is one of life's rewards to me.

Looking back, I can not forget those who suffered or died from "friendly fire." They also served and paid doubly the price for freedom. The impersonal messenger of death in an artillery shell or a napalm bomb does not distinguish friend from foe, by gender or uniform.

Right.   Orphaned by the war these two young children search the railroad yards in Seoul for scraps of food. Did they survive? Only God knows...... Below. Sitting in the rubble of his home this Korean patriarch can still manage a smile for passing G.I.'s. Both photos courtesy of the National Archives.   Bottom Right. This Korean farmer has a load of wood on his A-frame to help fight off the frigid Arctic weather. Hopefully there are not too many shell holes in his house to let the heat out.   Photo courtesy Roger Lueckenhoff.

RED DRAGON
The SECOND ROUND
FACES OF WAR II

Chae Soo		Han	Civilian
First Name	MI	Last Name	Serial Number
None	War Correspondent	27 July 1926	Journalist
Nickname	MOS	Birthday	Grade / Rank
None		1940-1954	Hamhung, North Korea
Unit (s)		Duty Tour (s)	Home Town

Worked as a journalist and war correspondent for the Pusan newspaper Kuk-Jeh. Emigrated to the United States in 1982, US citizen in 1987. In Korea he was a playwright, screen actor and director. He has continued these activities in the US, adding to his repertoire the f roles of movie critic and radio commentator. He is an accredited film critic of Motion Picture (West) and a member of the The International Press Club of Los Angeles

HIDDEN ANGER- A PATRIOTIC KOREAN TONE POEM

PINE TREES WEEP PLAINTIVELY ATT HE FOOT OF A WINTRY MOUNTAIN
WHERE A RIVER RUNS COMPULSIVELY IN HIDDEN ANGER.
BRIDGE RAILS ON BOTH SIDES OF BRIDGE HAVE BEEN TAKEN AWAY
THROWN INTO A FIERY FURNACE, TRANSFORMING PEACE INTO DEATH
YET RIVER RUNS RELENTLESSLY, UNAWARE OF DEMONIC INTRUSION

ON A MURDEROUS STORM NIGHT, A LITTLE BOY WITH QUIVERING FEET
WALKS THE FLOOR OF BRIDGE TREMBLING AND QUAKING IN FEAR
WHILE A SHADOW OF KIMONOS IN RICKSHAWS DRIFT BY AND VANISH
HEARTLESS SOULS IN WOODEN SHOES STRUT IN HAUGHTY DISDAIN
FLAPPING THEIR SAMURAI GARB IN CRUEL AND BARBARIC TYRANNY.

OUT OF NOWHERE, A RAGING ANGRY MOB RUSHED ONTO BRIDGE
INDIGENOUS PEOPLE SING SONOROUSLY ON A DAY OF EMANCIPATION
OH, LONG LIVE BRIDGE, MAN SE KYO. A REFLECTION OF FACES
LOOK UPON A TRAIL OF DEAD SLAVES, a TIME OF TRIBULATION.
THE enemy conquered, imperialism has fallen to its knees
FURIOUSLY THE MOB BURIES THE FOE, ALIVE, MERCILESSLY IN SAND
AS THE WIND HISSED AND RAGED, BRIDGE WHISTLED AND WEPT

NUMBERLESS EYES THAT COULD NOT SEE MARCHED IN BLINDNESS
BANDS OF RED ON ARMS AND VOICES THAT SHOUTED HUMAN PARADISE
HUMAN PARADISE OVER AND OVER 'TIL THEIR THROATS WERE BLOODY.
RASPING SOUNDS OF "MASSACRE MERCILESSLY OUR CLASS ENEMY"

THE RED FANATICS STOMPED THE LAND OF SERENITY, OUR LAND OF
MORNING CALM BEQUEATHED TO US BY OUR ILLUSTRIOUS ANCESTORS.
THE TRAGEDY OF HUMAN HISTORY WEEPS TEARS MUTELY BENEATH
BRIDGE WHERE THE DEEP BLUE WATER IS IN MOURNING.

OH LAND OF MY ANCESTORS, FULL OF REFLECTING WAVES
AND THE SUBTLE WHISPER OF WIND IN PINE TREES. ONCE
A POET FAILED TO DEPICT DELICATE SHADES OF RUSTLING LEAVES
AND THE EXQUISITE SHIFTING OF BRANCHES ON PINE TREES
HE THEN CROSSED THE FIELDS AND RIVER OF N O RETURN
TO VANISH AND NEVERMORE BE SEEN.

OH, MY LAND, I WAS BORN TO SUFFER AND BE REARED IN SOIL AND MUD
NOW A DELUDED CIVILIZATION DEVOURS THE INDIGENOUS CULTURE OF
THE LAND OF MORNING CALM WHICH WAS SO FERVENTLY NURTURED.
THE WATER UNDER BRIDGE IS STILL, BUT BRIDGE IS FLOATING ON.

TRANSCENDING INTO ANOTHER DIMENSION OF DIVINE NATURE
A SHINING STAR APPEARS SUDDENLY BRIGHT IN THE DAYLIGHT SKY.
UPON BRIDGE CROWDS GATHER, POINTING IN DAYLIGHT TO THE STAR
SHINING HIGH IN THE SKY. AN HONORED ELDER PROPHESIES
THERE WILL BE INNUMERABLE DEATHS AMONG THE YOUNG MEN
WHEN THE SHINING STAR APPEARS SO BRIGHTLY IN THE DAYLIGHT SKY.

AS FORETOLD, THE KOREAN CONFLICT MASSACRED THE YOUNG MEN
AMONG THEM AN 18 YEAR OLD GI, YOUNG FACE RED WITH COLD.
HE TROTS TO THE WAR FRONT, THE "FROZEN CHOSIN RESERVOIR," ON
HIS SHOULDER A HEAVY M-1, IN DEFENSE OF THE INDIGENOUS PEOPLE

IDEOLOGY PLAYS ITS WRETCHED ROLE IN APPALLING SCENES OF WAR.
THE PROPHET DEPARTED FOREVER TO THE WEST. WHAT REMAINS
AFTER WAR? AN IDEE FIXE, AN AGGREGATION OF DETACHED SENSES
AND CONSCIOUSNESS IN AN ENDLESS AND EMPTY VOID.
EVERY MEANING IS BLOWN AWAY INTO THE VAULT OF THE FIRMAMENT
AS THE ARMY OF PEACE STEPS BACKWARDS INTO DARKNESS,
EMPTINESS OPENS HER WINGS, THE BEAM OF COMPASSION DISPERSES
NOW, BRIDGE AND RIVER I AM OUT OF YOUR BOUNDARY, HERE IN A
NEW CONTINENT ,AMERICA WHERE FREEDOM IS A BIRTHRIGHT OF ALL.

OH, MAN SE KYO, COME LIVE WITH ME ON EVERY STARLIT NIGHT AS THE
SACRIFICED SOULS SPREAD THEIR WINGS AGAINST THE SKY, PAINTING
A RAINBOW WITHOUT ANGER, HATRED OR IGNORANCE OF DELUSION.
THE RIVER CROOKS ITS WAY THROUGH VALLEYS TO VAULTED HEAVEN
A BEAM OF MERCY DESCENDS INVINCIBLE ON THE EARTH IN ETERNITY.

* MAN SE KYO-LONG LIVE BRIDGE-TRANSLATES AS "LONG LIVE KOREA!"
TO SAY THIS IN PUBLIC WAS PUNISHABLE BY ARREST AND TORTURE
DURING THE PERIOD OF JAPANESE OCCUPATION, 1905-1945.

Above. A 'scenic' view of the Iron Triangle near Kumwha, Jan. 1952 in G Co., 223 Inf. Regt. section of the MLR. Below. Medic Albert Manning on a march while training in Japan. He was killed on his first patrol in Korea. Both photos by Ted Perry. Above Right. Combat Engineers demonstrate the construction of 'instant napalm' to be installed in front line barbwire. Photo by Norm Strickbine. Below Right. 'Home Sweet Home.' Bunker in the 160th Regt. of the 40th Inf. Div. Jan. 1952. Photo courtesy of Roger Lueckhenhoff.

RED DRAGON
The SECOND ROUND
FACES OF WAR II

Theodore	S.	Perry	RA 17 289 236
First Name	MI	Last Name	Serial Number
'Ted'	1745	27 Aug 1931	Corporal
Nickname	MOS	Birthday	Grade/Rank
G/223/40thDiv		Jan '52-Apr '52	Nixa, MO
Unit (s)		Duty Tour (s)	Home Town

Combat Infantry Badge   Purple Heart   OM-Japan   National Defense Service Medal

Medals & Awards

Korean Campaign Service Medal w/ one star   United Nations Service Medal   ROK KWSM

LAND MINE SURVIVOR

Our 40th Division relieved the 24th Division during a blinding snowstorm the night of 17 January 1952. The 24th had suffered heavy casualties repelling Chinese "human sea" attacks and were glad to see us. It was a fitting introduction to war in the sub-zero realities of a Korean winter. Our regiment, the 223d Infantry, had trained continuously for 6 months in California prior to shipping overseas. We spent another 10 months training at the former Japanese Imperial Marine base at Ozo Jahara. Our training would now pay off, even though we were an 'ill equipped' fighting unit. Boots and uniforms were not suited to the rigors of the Korean climate. Our arms and ammunition were of WW II vintage. Even then, we were far better off in uniforms and military hardware than our Chinese foe.

Morale was excellent. My unit was determined to live up to the reputation of the American soldier, racked up by our forebearers at such great cost in national blood and treasure. Little did we realize, as we concluded relief of the 24th, that we would experience some of the most fierce fighting of the Korean War. These actions were little heralded then by the American press, or later recorded by the pens of academic historians who sadly neglect the ruthless struggle of trench warfare during the latter half of the Korean War.

My first patrol was 5 nights after we relieved the 24th. Our platoon was tagged for a night patrol deep into Chinese territory. Easy/223 was the point of the 40th Division spear aimed at the Chicoms. Easy was located on a hill at the base of the most northerly perimeter of the Iron Triangle. An ambush patrol moving out as darkness set in. was set up on a hill between our MLR and Easy Co., We trudged 5 miles in deep snow and sub-zero temperature to reach our ambush position, getting there shortly before midnight. Pfc Gonzales and I set up our BAR team at the base of the hill while Sgt Bill Dawson, Shields, Albers and other of my squad got into position. A large Chinese patrol passed near where Gonzales and I were buried in the snow in position set up to cover the rest of the squad until they got into their final ambush locations. Sgt Dawson returned to lead us to our new firing position. That's when all hell broke loose on the hill! Chinese had located us. A grenade landed in Earl Abler's lap. He threw it back. We sparred with the Chinese all night long, the darkness lit sporadically by flashes of fire from rifles and grenades. Our medic, Sgt Albert Manning, was killed. Every man was afflicted with frost bite to one degree or another. A fitting initiation into the brutalities of winter war in Korea.

We manned the MLR. for 60 days without respite. In 30 degrees below of winter cold, we slept in rat infested, unheated bunkers. Our weapons froze up. We learned not to oil them, oil froze. We had one hot meal per day until the mess tent burned. After that, it was dig frozen C- rations out of a can with knife or bayonet. I still think the reason rats were so active was they wanted to cuddle to keep warm! Night long combat, ambush and reconn patrols were our lot every third to fifth day. Thoughts of the next patrol kept us on our toes. Better, but not much, than thinking about lousy C- rations, numbness of toes and fingers and mounting casualties.

It was now April. After two weeks in reserve we made another night relief, this time of the 2nd ROK Division at Kumsong. Our squad was moved into a "suicide" outpost position with a 50 gallon barrel of Napalm laid below our squad location. It was rigged with an explosive device so it could be detonated in case of a massive Chinese night attack. Again, every third night, our squad began running 'all night' ambush patrols deep into Kumsong valley. We would lay in position along river banks and railroad bridges waiting for Chinese patrol movement. My squad was generally all alone. Sometimes we felt as if we were the only soldiers Uncle Sam could lay his hands on. On the night of 18 April Sgt Bill Dawson took us out as a reinforced squad on what was to be my last ambush patrol. Pfc Earl Albers said to me earlier, "Perry, if you can get us out of this patrol tonight, I'll kiss your ass in the middle of Times Square!"

Actually, I consider myself one lucky soldier. I survived stepping on a land mine. Carrying our squad BAR, I was last man in our squad file. The darkest night of my life, no starlight, nothing. I stepped, heard a click, then a loud explosion which threw me into the air. I came down on my face, hot blood running down my head, left foot 'on fire. Our medic, Sgt David Bleak who later was awarded the Medal of Honor, groped his way toward me and applied a tourniquet to my left leg. "C" company had a rough night, evacuating our wounded on stretchers. Morphine dulled my pain. I awakened next morning in 8076 MASH Hospital. Due to blood loss, I was not expected to live. Now, on morning examination, the surgeon thought my left foot could be saved. I was headed home!

Above. These aircraft mechanics try to 'keep em flying' but have a hard time trying to keep them from freezing. Everyone fought their own battles against the 'Siberian Express.' All photos courtesy of the National Archives.

This frozen G.I. has only the meager protection of a shelter half to protect him from the frigid winter weather.

Several Marines slip and slide their way to a hilltop outpost in the Chosin Reservoir area of North Korea.

RED DRAGON
The SECOND ROUND
FACES OF WAR II

James	H.	Appleton	1158912 USMC
First Name	MI	Last Name	Serial Number
"Appy"	0311	26 August 1931	Cpl
Nickname	MOS	Birthday	Grade / Rank
I Company/ 5th Marines/ 1stMarDiv		April '51-April '52	Nashville, TN
Unit (s)		Duty Tour (s)	Home Town

Silver Star   Commendation Medal w/ Combat V   Navy PUC 1 star   USMC Good Conduct Medal

Medals & Awards

USN Occpn Medal w/Eur clasp   NDSM   KCSM,3 battle stars   KSM   UN Medal   ROK PUC   KWSM

THE WORST ENEMY

The Korean War began on 25 June 1950 with Russian sponsored North Korean Armies invading South Korea. Initially successful in overcoming the poorly equipped South Korean Constabulary Force, the tide turned with American Marines landing at Inchon on 15 September 1950. That action threatened to cut off and demolish the North Korean Armies to the south. The NKs retreated. It was obvious to Dictator Kim Il Sung he had bitten off more than he could chew. In Nov 1950 the Chinese, supported by unlimited Russian war equipment, entered the war in support of their ally, North Korea, with nearly disastrous results to the South Korean-American Armies. So, in so far as military adversaries, the UN Forces had two enemies, the North Korean Peoples Army and the Red Chinese Peoples Army. The North Koreans were superior as fighting soldiers to the Chinese, but had limited military resources, while the Chinese with strong ties to the Soviet Union and Russian Dictator Joseph Stalin, had almost unlimited military resources on call.

But the most formidable of all forces in the Korean War was Old Man Weather. The first four years of the 1950 decade experienced the most severe winter weather in Korean history. Living out in the field for an army is very trying, emotionally and physically. Gen Washington wintered at Valley Forge. His troops nearly froze to death. Some of them did. Korea was a natural arena for bad weather to be a major factor in fighting a war. Korea sits astride the 38th parallel, going down to about the 32d parallel in the south and in the north, to about the 43d parallel. It is an extremely mountainous country in which the mountain ranges generally run from north to south. As such, these mountains act as giant air ducts for the flow of frigid air from north to south. Storms arise in the frigid plains and steppes of Manchuria and Siberia, and like some howling beast, roars down through the valleys, freezing everything in its path.

In this environment, everything freezes, blood and flesh, rations and water in one's canteen. Standing watch in a foxhole, facing into the wind, a man's nose freezes if unprotected. Reaching up to wipe it, a clumsy groping hand can break off the tip of a man's nose like breaking an icicle off a gutter. Temperatures that reach 15 to 20 degrees below zero during the day tumble to 30, 35 as low as 55 degrees below zero at night. Ammunition may not fire. Misfires have to be extracted. Try doing that wearing gloves or mittens! If a man is wounded, blood oozing out quickly freezes, stanching the bleeding, but leading to infection and gangrene if not properly treated. Drinking water frozen in the canteen must be thawed by placing in hot water if possible, or by placing it next to the muffler on a tank or a truck engine block if available. The alternative is melting snow in the mouth which freezes mouth and teeth. Corpsmen would parcel out morphine syrettes to be placed in men's mouths, keeping them thawed until needed for the wounded.

Clothing must be carefully layered. Start the first layer with regular cotton skivvie shorts and T shirt. The next layer is two piece cotton 'long johns', top and bottom, next goes wool pants and shirt, followed by heavy 'wind breaker' cloth outer trousers and jacket. Finally, field jacket and an alpaca lined parka. Some guys were lucky enough to have an Army khaki V-neck sweater which was worn over the top of the cotton 'long johns'. The head was generally covered with a 'jeep' cap, sometimes a stocking cap. Over that cap was pulled the parka hood, topped off with the ubiquitous steel helmet. If on a moving patrol and hit by nature's call it became as tortuous as an obstacle course to get out of the clothing before nature insisted on acting. Sometimes nature wins and one's inner clothing is soiled. Having answered the call of nature, one must hurriedly don clothing, layer by layer, and run to catch up with the moving patrol. No one wants to be left alone in "Indian Country." It is a scary feeling to be all by one's self in a combat area.

Baths are nonexistent. Such amenities belong in a civilized area far removed from the milieu of the combat soldier. After 60 days on the line, then to a reserve area for rest and regrouping, the smell of body odor, rancid sweat, old fecal matter caked on inner clothing from the times when "you didn't make it in time," the fetid breath from unbrushed teeth, all combine to make a man so filthy he wishes he were a cat and could give himself a bath with his tongue. That was life in the field in the frozen cold of Korea during those cold winters. Weather was the most insidious enemy of all. Old Man Weather didn't shoot at you with small arms fire, try to tear away your flesh with shrapnel or dismember you with explosives. He simply did his best to put you into a sleep from which you did not awaken. It happened to some men who had not yet learned the hard rules of survival in a bitterly cold land. Frozen Chosin!

Above. Usually a sign of 'welcome relief' this column of tanks and Infantry are moving south. The G.I. s of that period called it the 'Big Bugout', as the Chinese intervened in overwhelming numbers. This was later termed by higher headquarters as a 'retrograde' movement to 'more tenable positions'.   Photo from the Internet.

Left. Sgt. Joseph C. Rodriguez shortly after being awarded the Medal Of Honor for actions with the 17th Regt. of the 7th Inf. Div. May 21, 1951.   Photo from the Internet.
Below. PFC Joseph C. Rodriguez as radio-telephone operator for Lt. James J. Hill in Alaska, prior to his transfer to Korea.   Photo courtesy Lt. James J. Hill.

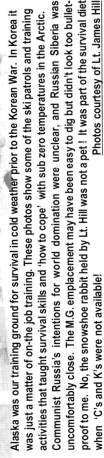

Alaska was our training ground for survival in cold weather prior to the Korean War. In Korea it was just a matter of on-the job training. These photos show some of the ski patrols and training activities that taught survival skills and 'how to cope' with sub zero temperatures in the Arctic. Communist Russia's intentions for world domination were unclear, and Russian Siberia was uncomfortably close. The M.G. emplacement may have been easy to dig but didn't look too bullet-proof to me. No, the snowshoe rabbit held by Lt. Hill was not a pet! It was part of the survival diet when 'C's and K's were not available!

Photos courtesy of Lt. James Hill

RED DRAGON
The SECOND ROUND
FACES OF WAR II

James	J.	Hill	O-947062
First Name	MI	Last Name	Serial Number
Jim	1542	25 Dec 1922	1st LT
Nickname	MOS	Birthday	Grade / Rank
Co H 2d Bn 196th RCT		1 Sept 1950- 31 Aug 1952	Watertown, SD
Unit (s)		Duty Tour (s)	Home Town
Not available.		All Medals & Awards lost in garage fire.	
Medals & Awards			

THE ALASKAN FRONT

Forgotten in the mists of our past history is the vigilant guard maintained by the United States to foil any attempt by the USSR to invade the Territory of Alaska during the Korean War. It was the concern of the American government that such an attack might be used to divert manpower and materiel from American forces supporting South Korea. In the Korean War years, the 196th Regimental Combat Team stood constant guard in Alaska functioning as a trigger fighting force should invasion occur. My unit, Heavy Weapons Company H of the 2d BN 196th RCT was called to active duty 1 September 1950. We were then stationed at Watertown, SD and sent to Camp Carson, CO where we were brought up to strength. Most officers and NCO's were WW II veterans who had elected to remain in the Ready Reserve. This activated cadre gave a 14 week course in basic training to the newly arrived filler personnel.

One trainee, PFC Joseph C. Rodriguez came direct to Company H from civil life with no prior military training. In my job as company training officer he stood out in his quick grasp of military essentials. His alert intelligence made an instant impression. Assigned as my radio-telephone operator, he did a superb job, keeping me abreast of everything going on in our training operation. When the Chinese entered the war in November, the casualty rate soared. He was one of those transferred by the Army to Korea as a replacement. In Korea he was assigned as asst squad leader in F Company 17th Infantry Regt, 7th Infantry Division. He had been in Korea but a couple of months when he was awarded the Congressional Medal of Honor. His total service was but seven months. He survived to receive the medal. I followed his career over the years. He retired as LtCol US Army. He now lives in El Paso, Texas.

After completion of training we boarded the troopship *Marine Adder* for Alaska, debarking at Haines to begin our 750 mile trek to Anchorage over the Alcan Highway, built during WW II. We rode in trucks for 10 miles and marched 15 miles each day to harden us up. We took daily baths in creek fed by glacial melt. Talk about cold baths! Salmon were running so thick they bumped our legs. They were big and ugly, but they didn't bite. We stayed alert for Kodiak grizzly bears. Moose crossed our trail but never challenged us. Anchorage was a town of many liquor bars but few conveniences. Electricity was furnished by the generator from a wrecked ship beached at Cook Inlet. We set up a tent city outside Anchorage ready for snow and cold weather. Cold weather survival training was very important for Alaska. I had been in the Air Corps during WW II and was among 3 others chosen to attend a cold weather survival training period for two weeks in minus 40 degree zero temperatures in a remote area near Ladd Field, Fairbanks, Alaska.

In theory we were the crew of a disabled plane from which we parachuted into this swampy marsh area outside Ladd Field. In addition to our 'chutes we had sleeping bags, parkas, warm boots, sox, a first aid kit with medical supplies, a knife, salt, pepper, and a .45 caliber US Army Colt revolver. We used the 'chutes for tents by draping them over willow bough hoops. We urinated on the hoops to freeze each leg in place where each arc was stuck into the snow. The 'chutes were draped over the hoops like a cocoon. Inside the tent, pine boughs were laid over the 4 foot deep snow. Sleeping bags were laid on the pine boughs making an insulated and soft mattress. The tents were arranged around a central atrium in the center where we kept a perpetual fire. The heat radiated from the fire entered the tent 'door' and kept the interiors quite warm. At 40 below zero there was no wind to blow flames which could cause the silk of the parachutes to catch fire, although it gave rise to caution. We did not build large fires which might get out of hand.

We lived off the land. In the swamp was a willow thicket, home to a large colony of snowshoe rabbits. We would locate a well used rabbit trail. One of us sat hidden on the trail while the others would beat the brush, driving the rabbits toward the 'trapper.' It was up to the trapper to capture the rabbit by whatever means he chose. We did not use the US Army Colt .45 but kept it handy with its 8 rounds in case of an encounter with a Kodiak grizzly. Thankfully, they all were in hibernation at that time of year. After cleaning the rabbits we built a rotisserie of willow boughs and baked them over the coals. An abundance of huckleberry bushes with clusters of frozen berries gave us frozen dessert after a meal of roasted rabbit. The food was adequate to maintain us all in good health. We returned in good shape to our unit in Anchorage to pass on to the troops what we had learned about survival in this frozen land.

240

Shortly after our return to Tent City all, our units moved into the recently completed permanent barracks at Fort Richardson. Orders came down from HQ detaching and assigning me to Big Delta for cross country ski training and instruction in military tactics developed for cold weather war in event of Russian invasion. Much of this doctrine was taken from lessons learned by the Finns in the course of their "Winter War" in 1940 when Russia failed in its first invasion of Finland. In this training we lived for up to two weeks in snow caves at a time when weather temperatures varied from 40 to 50 below zero. We were equipped with excellent arctic clothing suitable for the climate in which we were to operate. Our back packs, weighing about 45 lbs, were filled with dehydrated foods, enough to last for a two week period. Snow was melted on an alcohol stove for drinking and cooking water. Alaska in this area is very mountainous so we made our snow caves above timberline. Snow was hard packed from the blowing winds. We would dig an opening into the side of a huge drift, tunneling upward and back, hollowing out a cavern big enough for three men. Everything, including skis, went into the cave. Inflatable rubber mattresses kept our sleeping bags off the snow. All clothing was taken to bed with us to keep it dry. Candles were used to light the interior. They furnished enough light to read and also gave some warmth.

Daylight hours were short at this time of year. The crystal white snow and the Aurora Borealis made 'hours of darkness' quite bright! In the mornings we would break out of the top of the cave where snow was thinnest. We skied 25 to 30 miles every day from base camp, mapping the high ground and bush pilot air strips. A dogsled team was on standby in case of injury or sickness for transport back to base camp. Large equipment sleds pulled by tracked vehicles called "weasels" were kept at base. Tracked personnel carriers went by the name of "Otters." We spent considerable time testing military weapons under conditions of extreme cold. Machine guns, actually any weapon with moving parts, functioned best dry, no lubricants at all. The only exception was powdered graphite which worked well if used sparingly. At minus 50 degrees, the heat from a fired weapon generated water vapor which would condense and freeze the bolt and slide mechanisms causing weapons to jam. For example, a knife placed in a glass filled with No.10 motor oil would in an hour freeze so tight that the knife blade could not be moved. Our coldest day was minus 64 degrees at Big Delta. On the same day, just a few miles away in Yukon, it was minus 75 degrees. When the temperature rose to minus 20, the wind would blow constantly giving rise to a severe wind chill factor. We were most comfortable at minus 35 or 40 without a wind blowing.

I returned to Ft Richardson and passed on what I had learned to our troops in a series of lectures and demonstrations. Shortly thereafter, I was reassigned to Elmendorf AF Base as Asst G-1 in US Army and Air Force HQs. My term of duty was up in August 1952. I returned to Ft Lewis for separation. I then came to Portland, Oregon where I now make my home in a balmier climate.

AWARD OF THE CONGRESSIONAL MEDAL OF HONOR
JOSEPH C. RODRIGUEZ

Rank: Sergeant (then Private First Class). US 56-068-814
Organization: US Army Company F, 17th Infantry Regiment
7th Infantry Division.
Place and date: Near Munye-ri Korea 21 May 1951
Entered service: California
Birth date: 14 November 1928
General Order No.22 Department of the Army 5 February 1952

CITATION: Sergeant Joseph C. Rodriguez distinguished himself by conspicuous gallantry and intrepidity at the risk of his life above and beyond the call of duty in action against an armed enemy of the United Nations near Munye-ri, Korea on 21 May 1951. Sergeant Rodriguez, an assistant squad leader of the 2d Platoon was participating in an attack against a fanatical hostile force occupying well fortified positions on rugged commanding terrain, when his squad's advance was halted by a withering barrage of automatic weapons and small arms fire from five emplacements to the front and right and left flanks, together with grenades which the enemy rolled downhill toward the advancing troops. Fully aware of the odds against him, Sergeant Rodriguez leaped to his feet, dashed 60 yards up the fire swept slope, and, after lobbing grenades into the first foxhole with deadly accuracy, ran around the left flank, silenced an automatic weapon with two grenades, then continued his whirlwind assault to the top of the peak, wiping out two more foxholes, then reaching the right flank, he tossed grenades into the remaining emplacement, destroying the gun and annihilating its crew. Sergeant Rodriguez' intrepid actions exacted a total of 15 enemy dead, and as a result of his incredible display of valor the defense of the opposition was broken, the enemy routed and the strategic strong point secured. His unflinching courage under fire and inspirational devotion to duty reflect highest credit on himself and uphold the honored traditions of the military service.

Sergeant Rodriguez' feat of arms was memorialized in a 1952 and 1953 Korean War US Defense Bond Poster in these words: "Sixty yards to go. From atop the hill near Munye-ri, Korea, the enemy suddenly opened up with a withering barrage. Lieutenant Rodriguez, then a Pvt 1st Class with but seven months service, broke loose and dashed up the fire swept slope, throwing grenades. Disregarding fire concentrated on him, he wiped out three foxholes and two gun emplacements. Alone, he accounted for 15 enemy dead, led the rout of the enemy, saving the lives of his squad. 'Sometimes you have to take chances to reach an objective, he said.'"

Upper. Near the Manchurian border in Nov. of 1950 the
31st Regt. operated in areas where roads were nonexistent. The ever adaptable G.I.s were quick to put
the local oxen to work. Ox trains were the only way
to transport supplies and ammo to some troops.
Middle. These survivors of the Chosin Reservoir
battle load on landing craft to depart this miserable
land. Hungnam, December 1950.
Right. During November, 1951 the 31st Regt. was in the
Mundung Ni Valley, where 'chogie bearers' carry back
wounded from another ill-advised attack on a fortified
position.   All photos by Col. John Covach.

RED DRAGON
The SECOND ROUND
FACES OF WAR II

John	NMI	Covach	O-61893
First Name	MI	Last Name	Serial Number
None	1542	17 March 1929	Col USA Ret, then Capt
Nickname	MOS	Birthday	Grade / Rank
A Co 31st Inf Regt 7th Inf Div		17 Sept 1950- Feb 1952	Lt, Capt
Unit (s)		Duty Tour (s)	Home Town
Combat Infantry Badge		Bronze Star V for Valor, 2 OLC	Purple Heart with OLC
Medals & Awards			

Numerous other Medals & Awards for Korean War and Vietnam War service.

ASSUMPTION OF COMMAND

We returned to Mundung-ni in late Oct '51. It was a deja-vu scene for the 31st Inf. Regt. We relieved the 2d Div in Sept as the battle for Heartbreak Ridge was winding down. We were again occupying positions we held in Sept. It was the same devastated, surreal landscape as before, but now more settled and quieter. Both sides were taking a breather. The Mundung-ni valley ran along a north-south axis. "A" Company occupied the entire valley floor and extended up a ridge looking north. An OP on a ridge on the east side of the valley allowed observation looking many miles directly north into the valley proper. The Chinese were dug in on two ridges about 800 meters to our front and left. We received sporadic attention from the Chinese with occasional bursts of MG or artillery fire.

When this occurred we were quick to retaliate with equivalent punishment. If we saw any movement we took them under fire until they were killed or disappeared. The Chinese were not totally moribund. They ran small patrols down into the valley at night. We could spot them with an artillery BC scope, even at night. Our FO, Lt Rosencranz of A Btry 57th FA, was diligent in his pursuit of targets. He would let them get into open ground then open up with prearranged fire. On one occasion, they reached our barbed wire. They made no penetration, nor did any of them return alive to their own positions. They ran into a buzz saw. Between the fire of Lt Drenkhahn's heavy water cooled MG and Rosie's 105 howitzers, they were cut down, lying where they fell dead, tangled in the wire.

In late Oct, the situation changed. Orders came from Division to launch company sized attacks on Chinese positions on both sides of the valley. These orders bore the earmark of a staff officer who probably had never been involved in an attack on a heavily fortified position. No reason was ever given for what we all thought was an insane idea. "C" Co. on our left was first to suffer. Not only did they not overrun the Chinese fortifications, they never even came close. Many men, dead and wounded, incurred for an objective that had no tactical value. A classmate, "Red" Buchanan, also from my home town, took a 6 or 7 round MG burst that sent him back the states. Second Bn was next to be victimized. This attack took place about 1000 yards to the right of "A" Co. The terrain was so rugged that removal of dead and wounded was nigh impossible. The Korean stretcher bearers were forced to bring the casualties down into the valley by moving through our positions. It did nothing for our morale. The unspoken thought, 'when will it be our turn?'

Our turn came soon enough. On 4 Nov '51, Capt Freddy Height, our Co. Cmdr, received orders from Col Young Oak Kim to attack. Due to the restrictions of the terrain, he decided to attack in column of platoons. We waited while artillery and mortar fire rained down on the Chinese. Col Kim had arranged for tank, twin forties and quad fifties to fire from the valley below to assist us in our attack. This massive fire support was not enough to beat the Chinese into passivity. We sallied out of our defensive positions in the early morning of a clear fall day. Our objective was Hill 642. As Executive Officer I brought up the rear 200 yards behind the point of the leading platoon. Within 15 minutes of the start of the engagement, I received a radio message from Freddy Height to come forward to his position. I moved through a hail of mortar fire to see Lt Ogelsby and Sgt Morgan of the 1st platoon lying dead on the ridge as well as other men of the platoon. I got to Freddy. He was lying in a shallow ditch, bleeding profusely from a neck wound. He said, very simply, "You take command here." I took stock of the situation. It was not good. The Chinese had us bracketed with artillery and mortars in addition to the rain of small arms and machine gun fire that had already taken a heavy toll of the 1st and 2d platoons. I decide to get the hell out of there before the company was totally decimated. I contacted Col Kim on the SCR 300 and told him of our situation. He agreed that we should pull off the hill at once. We came off the hill in the reverse order we had gone up.

We brought out all our wounded and dead, no small feat in that terrain. In addition to our 4 dead there were 50 wounded, all in the space of 45 minutes. To what purpose? What was I to say in my letters to the next of kin? How did I explain this to the wounded men in my company? This was probably the most needless attack order of my military career. Because someone thought that a replay of WW I trench warfare was the way to go, we were set up for a fiasco. Now I had a company to rebuild. I assumed command there on Hill 642 and kept it until I rotated home in Feb '52. It took a long, long time for the effects of that 4th day in November to wear off. After over 50 years I still can not forget Lt Ogelsby, Sgt Morgan and others of A Company who died so unnecessarily on Hill 642.

Above. There were very few good sources of 'drinkable' water in Korea so these water points were quite important. They were usually at some distance from other units and had to supply their own security, so it could get 'hairy' at times. The top photo by Norm Strickbine was of a 13th Engr. 7th Div. water point, while the bottom photos furnished by Max Reynolds were of 2nd Engr. 2nd Division points.

RED DRAGON
The SECOND ROUND
FACES OF WAR II

Max	R.	Reynolds	ER 52 005 643
First Name	MI	Last Name	Serial Number
None	0427	15 May 1928	SP/5th
Nickname	MOS	Birthday	Grade / Rank
HQ Co 2d Engr Bn(C) 2d Division		March 1951-March 1952	Lima, OH
Unit (s)		Duty Tour(s) in Korea	Home Town

Korean Campaign Service Medal,3stars Presidential Unit Citation Expert BadgeRifle &Carbine

Medals & Awards

National Defense Service Medal United Nations Service Medal ROK Korean War Service Medal

WATER POINT

I took my basic training at Fort Knox, KY, then transferred to Fort Belvoir, VA for training at the Advanced Engineer School. I was given an 8 week course in water supply and purification, learning that potable water doesn't just ' happen.' It is a culmination of knowledge that civilization has been collecting since the time of the Roman Legions. As a result we no longer lose more soldiers to water borne diseases than to enemy action. In Japan my records were processed at the Assignment Center where I was placed with HQ Co of the 2d Engr Bn (C), 2d Inf Div. The 2d Div was then located in the Chorwon area of Korea. I was given a 3 man detail to operate a water point capable of putting out 50 gallons per minute. It was my job also to train my 3 man crew in the rudiments of water purification. Their only knowledge of water was that man needed water to stay alive! They were good men, quick learners.

The intake water from a source, usually a river or creek, was pumped into a filtration unit by a water cooled 1.5 HP motor. Liquid chlorine, released from a tank valve on a heavy, thick walled cylinder, gasified the chlorine for absorption into the effluent water taken from the filtration tanks. Chlorine added at this point could vary depending upon the dirt and organic content of the inflow. Another pump transferred the filtered water to portable 3000 gallon tanks for further treatment. If the water was dirty, silty and mud laden, it was necessary to back flush those 3000 gallon tanks after a settling period. After back flushing, the filter elements were coated with diatomaceous silica for the next run. A third pump was used to transfer the treated potable water---army term for drinkable, disease free water--- to 500 or 1000 gallons tanks which various units used to pick up water for delivery to the end users in their units.

Water was tested every 2 hours with a color comparator using rotatable discs to read the water pH. Water at the delivery point was required to have a chlorine content of 6 ppm. This was determined by adding phenolphthalein indicator to a test tube in which water was added up to a line etched on the test tube. The yellow color was checked in the color comparator to determine if the chlorine content was at the right level. Too much chlorine turned water red, indicating the water was basic instead of acidic as it should have been. A retreatment procedure was then used. The water had to settle for at least one hour and be rechecked for chlorine content before it was dispensed. My water point usually produced 15,000 gallons per day. By going all out we could push it to 20,000 gpd. This was our limit. We encountered our greatest difficulty when winter temperatures dropped below zero. As long as water was being pumped, it did not freeze in lines or hoses. Ergo, we pumped 24 hours per day. It meant little or no sleep for the four of us.

It was a real hassle to move all our equipment when it came time to move our water point forward or back as the changing front lines might dictate. It took hours and several trucks to knock down, move, and reassemble ready for renewed water delivery. Military necessity sometimes does not allow the usual timetable for moving the tons of equipment needed to operate a water point. During the Chinese Spring Offensive in April 1951, we were given one half hour to knock down, and load all equipment including the squad tent used for equipment storage and bunk space. We then waited in line for 6 hours in the midst of a traffic jam to get through a one way mountain pass. One tank was lost over the side of the narrow road, tumbling. It made a horrible clatter as it banged and bumped its way down the rocks cluttering that steep incline. I could not help but think of the tank crew that lost their lives in that accident.

Once while making an emergency move, I rode with a truck driver who ran out of gas. After bumming a couple of jerry cans of gas from passing traffic, we proceeded to get lost, ending up with Dog Company 2d Engineers. We were usually attached to the 38th Inf Regt providing their water, usually from a point a couple of miles behind the MLR. Not as safe as it sounds. The Chinese knew the military value of water points and mess kitchens. We were shelled a few times. Had to move. We kept a tripod Lyster Bag at roadside, available to any and all. We sometimes had 15 to 20 vehicles lined up, waiting for water. I returned home in March 1952, receiving my discharge at Camp Carson, CO. I reenlisted in rank of Sp/5 for 6 years in the active reserves in the 302d Special Services and later served as senior radio operator in a Field Artillery unit firing the 205mm howitzer. That cannon was so big it was towed by a 6 ton military truck. I was told the weapon had a range of 35 miles. We trained at Camp Pickett, VA and Ft Breckenridge, KY

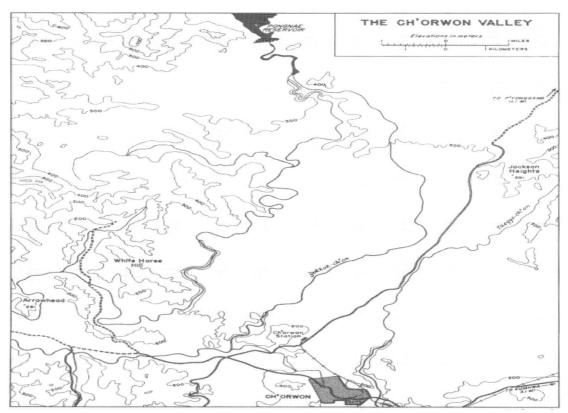

THE CH'ORWON VALLEY

Above. Map of the Chorwon Valley showing White Horse Hill and Jackson Heights.   Map from the Internet.
Below Left.   Troops of Company G, 223 Regt., 40th Inf. Division move back into the lines, Spring 1952.   Below Right.
Company G, 223rd Regt. gets close support from their 60mm mortar section.   Photos courtesy of Don Gardner.

RED DRAGON
The SECOND ROUND
FACES OF WAR II

Thomas	Riley	Bunner	NG 28 118 110
First Name	MI	Last Name	Serial Number
"Long Tom"	1745	4 March 1930	Corporal
Nickname	MOS	Birthday	Grade / Rank
"I" Co/223Inf/40Div		Dec 1951-May 1952	Apple Valley, CA
Unit (s)		Duty Tour (s)	Home Town
Combat Infantry Badge	Korean Campaign Service Medal w/ one bronze star		ROK WSM
Medals & Awards			
National Defense Service Medal	Occupation Medal, Japan		United Nations Medal

CITIZEN SOLDIER

The 40th Division of the California National Guard, was mobilized in Sept 1950 in response to the crisis on the Naktong perimeter. The 45th Division of the Oklahoma National Guard was called up about the same time. I trained stateside on the 60mm mortar, then served as an instructor in techniques of mortar gunnery. It has been said that mortars cause more casualties than any other weapon. This is undoubtedly due to the characteristics of the mortar which, in the American Army at that time, came in three sizes: 60mm, 81mm and the 4.2 inch(107mm)mortar. A mortar can be elevated to about 85 degrees from the horizontal. It has a high angle of fire, impossible to obtain with a howitzer. The 60mm is a 3 man, sometimes 2 men, crew served weapon which because of low weight and shell size is always handy for use in a rifle company. It is a deadly little weapon if used in close quarter combat. It has a rapid rate of fire, is almost noiseless in its passage from mortar to target. It has the capability to fire over a hill crest to seek out an enemy on the unseen reverse slope. In my own experience, I have fired 18 shells before the first one hit. This rate of fire is devastating to the enemy. He has no chance to hit the dirt before he is overwhelmed by rounds exploding within seconds of each other.

The 45th Div shipped to Japan 3 months before I completed my assignment as mortar instructor. I arrived in Japan in time to be involved in a rigorous combat training program. Its purpose was to train us to replace the battle hardened 24th Regular Army Division which for 16 months had been in the thick of the fighting. In essence we would switch places; we to Korea, they to return to Japan as occupation troops. I preceded the regiment, serving as advance enlisted liaison with the 21st Inf for two weeks in the Chorwon-Kumwha area. The 45th deployed to Korea in January '52. I rejoined my regiment, the 223d Inf Regt when it replaced the 21st Inf/24th Div on the MLR,, the front line where enemy faces enemy. I was on outpost duty in no-mans-land when "L" Co/ 223 Inf was pulled off the MLR to mount an attack supporting a group of Combat Engineers whose mission was to blow up two RR tunnels. They needed help toting 75mm ammo for their recoilless 75mm gun which was to cover them while working in the tunnel. On the way, Steve slipped going down the steep hillside. The 75 HE recoilless rounds came rolling down after him as he tumbled down hill!

While it was not funny to Steve, for some reason it hit my funny bone. Perhaps it is the way a man's brain deals with bad situations, or perhaps it was the simple Charlie Chaplin slapstick of his downhill tumble that made me laugh. Whatever, it relieved the potential grimness of the situation, none of the rounds exploded. Of course none should have, ammo prior to firing is set with devices which allow for rough handling. However, when dealing with live ammo one is never sure! Steve made his way back uphill after we retrieved the rounds he was carrying. We then moved past the 75 recoilless gun position and took up a forward position on a steep ridge where "L" Co had been engaged in a tough fire fight. Steve and I, about five feet apart, were providing small arms covering fire with our M-1s when a great roar of sound passed between us. The round, from a Chinese mountain gun, exploded about 60 yards behind us. The 76mm mountain gun has a flat trajectory which fires line-of-sight. After almost 'buying the farm' then and there, we decided to move back to the recoilless rifle position. We slithered out of there quick as we could, hopefully before the gunner zeroed in on us again. On the way there, the blast from another round blew our helmets off our heads. It was that close again. That Chinese gunner was one determined Chinaman. We were glad he had not qualified as 'Expert Gunner' during his boot camp basic training! In the valley below "L"Co was in trouble. I was witness to an action that makes me proud to this day to have been an infantryman.

Soldiers do their duty for love of country, but it is from the man next to him that he finds courage to continue. The men of L Co, under mortar and small arms fire, badly outnumbered, risked all to retrieve the wounded. Two man teams carried wounded back to the tanks giving fire support. 'Walking wounded' helped the more seriously wounded men. One tank lost a bogie wheel. A tank retriever cabled on to drag it back for repair. We began receiving heavy fire, guess we were doing some good. I learned that "L" had 60 casualties, 60% were walking wounded. The engineers had many casualties also. Not one man, dead or wounded, was left behind. Two and a half months later while the regiment was off line for a rest period, I received orders to return stateside. At home, it was if we were not at war. War news was buried in back pages. With open wounds of WW II still fresh in the national conscience, few were interested. The rotation system meant we came home as individuals. No parades or thanks of a grateful nation for us. Life went on.

Above. The business end of a heavy .30 MG is seen in the bunker above. Below. Its handiwork is shown on the forward slope of the MLR. This zone was in the 160th Regt. of the 40th Division area, Jan. 1952. Above Right. Back in the line in the spring of 1952. Shown is a 60mm mortar crew ready to fire. Below Right. An Armored 155 is brought up on the MLR for some serious 'bunker busting.' M Co., 160th Regt. 40th Div. Photos by Robert Riggs.

RED DRAGON
The SECOND ROUND
FACES OF WAR II

Robert	L.	Riggs	NG 19 240-375
First Name	MI	Last Name	Serial Number
Bob	1812	21 Jan 1929	S/Sgt
Nickname	MOS	Birthday	Grade / Rank
MCo 160th Inf 40th Division		7 Jan 1952-July 1952	Los Angeles, CA
Unit (s)		Duty Tour (s)	Home Town

Combat Infantry Badge Purple Heart Good Conduct Medal WW II Victory Medal ROK KWSM

Medals & Awards

Occpn Medal-J   Korean Campaign Service Medal,2stars   National Def Svc Medal   UN Medal

MACHINE GUNNER

I opted for National Guard service after finishing my 3 year hitch in the Regular Army. When the California 40th Division National Guard was called to active duty I was a S/Sgt squad leader of heavy MGs in Weapons Company 3d Bn 160th Inf Regt. These water cooled .30 caliber guns were capable of sustained fire for much longer periods of time than the lighter .30 caliber air cooled MG. Because the heavy tripod mounts could be sandbagged for stability, the water cooled MG was capable of sustained and more accurate fire than the .30 caliber light Browning air cooled MG. Water cooled MGs were battalion weapons whereas air cooled lights were organic to the rifle companies. Because warfare in Korea, when I got there, had stabilized into trench warfare similar to that of WW I, both light MGs and heavy MGs often worked in partnership to lay down interlocking covering fields of fire in front of the MLR.

I was luckier than most guys in my National Guard company. With prior military service I had a good idea of what life would be like when called to active duty. It was really hard on some men. They went through the paces of learning "The Army Way of Life," but all survived it. I am proud to have served with them. After a short period of training at Camp Cooke, CA we shipped to Japan in April 1951. Stationed at Camp Zama, we went through a rigorous nine months of strenuous live fire training exercises. In late December, just before leaving for Korea, a barracks fire consumed almost everything except what we had on our backs. It was at night, our individual weapons were stacked in rifle stands and ruined by fire. In rapid fire manner we were re-equipped with individual weapons and clothing and by mid January 1952, the 40th Division was on line, replacing the 24th Infantry Division. The 24th was redeployed to Japan to serve as occupation troops, and to lick their wounds after 18 months of continuous combat in the Korean War.

It was 27 below zero, lots of snow everywhere. For a guy from Southern California, that is damn cold. What was worse, we inherited the worn out machine guns used by the 24th Division. I was almost afraid to fire the damn things. I thought to myself, "This is one hell of a way to fight a war!" I soon found out that was the way I was going to do it. It took months to get new guns. In my 3d Bn, 160th Regt, we took over from the 24th somewhere around the Kumsong area of the Iron Triangle. Of course, our local neighbors, the Chinese from across the way, threw a big artillery welcoming party for us. They also sent out a lot of patrols to look us over, but they didn't act too friendly. So it was tit for tat as we settled into a state of ice box hostility. It sure wasn't like the war movies I saw back home, especially for us 'Machine Gunners.' We always seemed to be placed out in front of everyone else. I guess some one didn't like us! No wonder it is said 'Machine Gunners' don't last long in a good fight! Life on the front line was not a good way to live day in and day out. It was so damn cold that everybody hesitated to get out of the bunkers, yet all knew it was necessary, otherwise the Chinese would ring your doorbell. When you did go out, there was always some damn Chinaman shooting at you. At night little sleep was to be had. You stayed awake because you wanted to greet the next day with a head still on your shoulders. Those that slept in bunker or foxhole OP at night were likely to be "headless" by morning. The Chinese were very active with their night patrols.

You could sit and stare all day long out front, swear you had it memorized, yet as dark set in all the tree stumps sprouted legs and started an oriental dance. In my 5 months in Korea the only time we came off line was in mid Feb '52 on the move to central Korea. We were picked up last by a lone truck, as if we had almost been forgotten. At a crossroads we were shelled, taking a hit at the rear of the truck. Two men in my squad, Cpl Sharp and Pfc Gable were killed, myself and another man wounded. While I was on line, there was no great movement, forward or back. We took a lot of shelling and gave a lot back. We strove to stay alive, survive the freezing cold and the no-mans land patrols. Perhaps it wasn't a bad war as wars go, but it was enough for me. It was a hell of a way to live.

There is always humor somewhere around a bunch of GIS. One clear cold day I heard a lot of hollering outside the bunker. I stuck my head outside to see two guys in a snow ball fight. The Chinese joined the party by dropping some mortar rounds into the fracas. I guess the Chinese must not have much of a sense of humor. To sum it up, as I see it, I sure hope the people of South Korea appreciate their freedom because Americans and the other troops of the United Nations sure paid a high price for it. I am not bitter about my service in Korea. On the contrary, I am proud to have served my country. I have good memories of all the guys in my outfit.

Above. One of the most awesome weapons used in the Korean War, this 8 inch howitzer is mounted on a 155mm self propelled chassis. Undersized for the monster '8 incher', it usually needed bulldozers to help get it up on the MLR, where it destroyed Chinese bunkers by the hundreds. The 780th FA Bn. was equipped with 3 of these weapons but only 1 was used at a time. Two were destroyed by Chinese artillery fire. In nearly full recoil, the one above is firing in front of the Marine positions north of the Punchbowl, Feb. 1952. Below. One is being moved into place, Summer of 1952. Photos by George Ellis.

RED DRAGON
The SECOND ROUND
FACES OF WAR II

John	O.	Rem	RA 17-314-850
First Name	MI	Last Name	Serial Number
None	Disciplinary Barracks Guard	17 March 1931	Cpl
Nickname	MOS	Birthday	Grade / Rank
Battery B 780th FA Bn		Jan 1952- Mar 1953	Starbuck, MN
Unit (s)		Duty Tour (s)	Home Town
Commendation Medal	Korean Campaign Service Medal, 3 stars		United Nations Medal
Medals & Awards			
National Defense Service Medal	ROK Presidential Unit Citation		Korean War Service Medal

SANDBAG CASTLE OF 'LUKE THE GOOK' IS KAPUT

My father was an ordained minister of the Norwegian Lutheran Church of America. We moved often to a new parish as the church changed names, directions and philosophies. As a Regular Army soldier I felt right at home, comfortable in the midst of confusion, bewildering and inexplicable changes in assignment, in emphasis and direction with each new unit commander. Stateside, I trained as a Combat Engineer. En route to Korea I ended up in the US Army Small Arms Mechanics School at Eta Jima, Japan. Shipped on to Korea, my usual luck held. I was assigned to a Field Artillery unit. Not the usual red leg cannon cocker outfit, however. My assignment was to Baker Battery, 780th Field Artillery Bn, whose howitzers fired a monstrous eight inch shell. The SP, or as it was termed in the Bn, 'Sugar Pete,' laughingly stood for self propelled, meaning the howitzer was mounted on a motorized chassis. The chassis was designed for a 155mm howitzer, a much smaller artillery piece. Korea, with three times more mountains than flat country, was a poor choice of terrain for this underpowered cannon mover. But, just as in the church, you work with what you get.

When I joined the Bn in Jan '52, the 1st Sgt of B Battery told me 'Sugar Pete' had an opening on the gun crew firing from the hill above us. Not knowing what a 'Sugar Pete' was, I volunteered, since he told me it carried a bonus of no other duty. That night up hill I went, along with John Simon and Sullivan. The old crew had just come off Hill 1181, where gun cover protection had been provided by the Ethiopian Bn. The whole front was bathed in the light blue glow of search lights mounted in rear of the MLR. The effect was like a surrealist painting of a moonscape on snow. Next morning we moved the SP to a position about 80 yards in front of the MLR. The crew gathered in a small circle, listening to instructions from Lt Krafton. I heard a whistling sound of a shell coming at us. I dove under the chassis of 'Sugar Pete,' a couple of other new guys with me. The shells hit more than 100 yards away. When I crawled out, the rest of the group were still standing. Lt Krafton just smiled and said, "With a little more experience you'll be able to tell how close they're coming." Brand, the SP driver, told me that if I reacted that quickly in the future I would undoubtedly get home all in one piece!

We had been in a new position several days when Butler, the SP driver asst., took a sniper's bullet in his upper torso. Knocked him down. Cutting off his parka and layers of cold weather clothing, we found not a scratch on him. The bullet was found in the layers of cloth! The bullet had come from direction of "The Castle," hangout of "Luke the Gook." A granite pinnacle, it was located off our left flank about three quarters of a mile away. Commanding observation over the surrounding terrain, it had been a thorn in the side of every outfit manning that sector of the MLR. Dubbed "Sandbag Castle" by men of the 27th "Wolfhounds" Regiment, a bitter two week battle had been fought there the previous September. Their combat with the North Koreans was literally at a stone's throw distance. We suspended fire two days until a steel plate was welded to the rear of the chassis. March 2d, welding complete, 'Sugar Pete' maneuvered around 90 degrees to port. Ten rounds were fired point blank at 'Luke the Gook's Castle.' With the 3d round, the rock disintegrated. The 10th round completely obliterated it. It was no longer a sniper or observation threat to friendly units.

We quickly backed off our exposed firing position, expecting an artillery barrage in retaliation. It did not occur. During the next week the Gooks attempted several patrols up our hill, presumably with intent of wiping out our gun position. None of them made it even close. One morning I came out of the personnel bunker to witness a group of ROK soldiers practicing for the winter Olympics. Ten ROK soldiers were sledding down the steep hillside, using bodies of North Korean soldiers as toboggans. The Marines manning the MLR had ambushed the Gook patrol at the bottom of the hill the night before. The ROKs had been brought in to interrogate them.

'Sugar Pete,' designed as a 155mm howitzer mover, was woefully underpowered for the Korean terrain. A small incline required help of two D-7 bulldozers from the Engineers, one fore and one aft, one pulling, and one pushing. On those icy trails passing for roads, the bulldozers used winches and cables attached to trees or huge rocks to prevent both 'Sugar Pete' and the bulldozers from tumbling down a hillside. The Army now put my stateside Combat Engineer training to use. I doubled in brass at times like this! Returning home, the Army ran true to form. My 4th branch was Military Police! I became a disciplinary guard at a Detention Center.

251

Right. An F4U Corsair is being loaded with 5 inch rockets aboard the USS Philippine Sea, 1951. Lower Right. After a close air support mission this Corsair, minus rockets, makes landing aboard the USS Philippine Sea. Below. This Marine combats his constant enemy, the weather. Photo taken in the bitter winter of 1950 near the Chosin Reservoir.

All photos courtesy of the National Archives.

RED DRAGON
The SECOND ROUND
FACES OF WAR II

James	H.	Appleton	115 8912 USMC
First Name	MI	Last Name	Serial Number
Appy	0311	28 August 1931	Corporal
Nickname	MOS	Birthday	Grade / Rank
Item Co 5th Marine Regt 1st MarDiv		Apr '51-Apr '52	Nashville, TN
Unit (s)		Duty Tour	Home Town

Silver Star   Commendation Medal w Combat V   Navy PUC,1star   USMC Good Conduct Medal

Medals & Awards

USN Occpn Medal w/Eur clasp   NDSM   KCMS,3 battle stars   KSM   UN Medal   ROKPUC   KWSM

WALK IN THE SUN

The first Marine Division had moved from the east central front in X Corps area around the "Punchbowl" over to the western front, north of Seoul, near Panmunjom 'Peace Village.' This realignment was part of "Operation Mixmaster." The objective was to place 1st Marine Division in position to block any enemy thrust at Seoul, the South Korean. The war took on a whole new meaning and persona for the 'grunts' on the line (MLR). The old positions were located in a very mountainous area. Our tactics in that area had been to seize and defend the highest and most prominent hill masses in the area to give us observation of the enemies' movement. This allowed us to clobber him with our superior artillery and air support. The move to the western front in I Corps, often called 'Eye Corps,' put the division onto entirely different terrain. The MLR was set up in the western area, as in the former zone, in a continuous line of defensive positions. In this western zone, the main defenses consisted of a line of outposts set up out in front of the MLR. These positions were located on little knolls characteristic of the lower terrain elevations in this area. They were manned only at night, sometimes by a few men in a fire team, others perhaps occupied by a squad or a platoon. The size of the group depended on many factors; surrounding terrain, enemy activity, impending attack, to name a few. It was the job of the outpost to alert the MLR of enemy activity to our front. Outpost duty was extremely hazardous. These positions were frequently probed or attacked.

It was a warm, sunny afternoon in early April 1952. I was still working as runner for our XO, Lt Howard Feist, a really nice guy who had been a professor at Harvard before being called to active duty. Our Commanding Officer (CO) was Captain Neil Dimond, a great mountain of a man with a big grin all the time except when he was chewing your ass about some infraction of the military code. Then he was all teeth, no grin. I was hanging around the CP in case the XO needed me. I had nothing in particular to do since I was a 'short timer,' scheduled for rotation sometime later in the month. As a 'short timer,' in common with that breed, I had a tendency to keep my head down, take no unnecessary chances, or do something stupid, like volunteer for a patrol. I did not need any more medals.

Coming out of the CP, I noticed an old friend, 2d Lt John Fite who had been my 1st platoon leader before I got the 'exalted' position of the XO's runner. We had developed a mutually respectful personal relationship many months ago. I had survived nearly a year as a Marine combat infantryman. I guess in Lt Fite's eyes I qualified as a 'veteran.' Mr. Fite (we often addressed Lts in the Corps as Mister, a sign of respect) was one of those leaders men would follow on any mission, up any hill. He was 'Gung Ho' always up front, not pushing from behind. "Appy, what are you doing?" "Nothin' much. Just countin' the days. What's up," I replied. "Good. Get your pistol belt, take a walk with me." "Roger'" I said. " Wait a sec 'til I tell the XO that I will be with you." "OK."

We took off at a fast clip down a dirt road that headed out into "Indian Country," jealously guarded by the North Korean Peoples Army. The enemy positions were in a line of low hills a mile north of our lines. Half way out to the hill line was a small village which housed Koreans, men, women and children. They had no place else to go, I guess. They were boiling rice in a big black iron pot, oblivious to a war being fought on both sides of them. We chatted as we walked along. An "Odd Couple," for sure. He was an "Officer and a Gentleman," I was a Tennessee farm boy. We could chat about going home, not as Officer and NCO, but just man-to-man, hard to reconcile with civilian life considering our disparities, but not unusual here in the crucible of Korean war combat experiences.

We had walked so far, and gotten so close to the line of hills, I could damn near smell garlic on the breath of the North Koreans ahead. "Mr. Fite, where we goin?" We're damn near the outskirts of Pyongyang (capitol of North Korea)" He paused a minute, looked around, and said, "No, we're damn near there." Under my breath, I said, "Thank the Lord for that!" We each carried a 9 mm pistol. He, a German Walther, and I a German Luger I had swapped with a friend for my Colt Commander. We had about 15 rounds of pistol ammo as our whole defensive armament. Not enough in my book, let alone being outnumbered if we were jumped. We turned around. On the way back he explained he wanted to check the terrain in daylight before taking out a patrol that night. It showed why we all loved the guy, but who did he pick to accompany him on this walk in the sun but Ol' Appy, a 'short timer' with less than a week before I got aboard the 'Big Boat' for home. I momentarily considered volunteering for his patrol, but quickly thought better of it.

Above. At Camp Zama, Japan these troops load in a snowstorm, on their way to Korea to relieve the 24th Inf. Divison. Below. Members of H Company, 160th Regt. of the 40th Division. Destination Inchon, Korea January 1952, and their future is not too bright. Photos courtesy of Ed Marshall. Lower Right They will soon be manning positions like this .50 caliber Machine Gun pit, facing bitter weather and a merciless Chinese foe. Photo courtesy of Robert Riggs.

RED DRAGON
The SECOND ROUND
FACES OF WAR II

Edwin	E.	Marshall	28 106 035 (NG AUS)
First Name	MI	Last Name	Serial Number
Ed	1812, MG Section Ldr	18 Dec 1929	SFC
Nickname	MOS	Birthday	Grade / Rank
H Co 160 Inf Regtl Combat Team 40th Div		Jan 1952-April 1952	Los Angeles, CA
Unit (s)		Duty Tour (s)	Home Town
Good Conduct Medal	Korean Campaign Service Medal,1star		Occupation Medal-Japan

Medals & Awards

Presidential Unit Citation   National Defense Service Medal   UN Medal   Korean War Service Medal

THE REALITIES OF WAR

After 8 months hard infantry training in Japan, we shipped to Korea early January 1952 to relieve the 24th Inf Div. At Inchon we boarded a rattle trap train which took us to Chunchon. There we were issued full length parkas before boarding GI trucks bound for Kumwha on the east central front. It was the coldest ride of my life, 30 degrees below zero. The full length parkas we had been issued were a godsend. As it was, most of us experienced mild frost bite to our feet from the combination of 3 or 4 pairs of sox worn with rubber shoe pacs with no way for sweat to escape. The idiot who developed those cumbersome 'galoshes' for soldiers must have been AWOL when the Good Lord was working in the brains department. The next day, my feet hurt so bad it took an hour of walking before my feet felt normal. It was a hard lesson, "Never go to sleep with sweat soaked sox on your feet. Feet freeze!" That morning I accompanied an officer from the 24th to reconnoiter positions for the 2 HMG in my section. A jeep drove us across a stretch of No Man's land in full view of the Chinese. It must have been rice chow time, they did not mortar us. At the base of a hill near an Aid Station we began a steep climb of 200 yards before reaching the first bunkers. There I met the MG section leader I was to relieve.

After getting zeroed in, I returned to the base of the hill to await a ride back to Company Rear. I had my back propped against a huge rock about 50 yards from the Aid Station. A litter jeep with a soldier sitting in it was out in front. Out of nowhere, a giant explosion threw soldier and jeep into the air. Two more huge explosions demolished the Aid Station. I still remember my thought, "So this is what it's going to be like." Several days later we were on line. I had our guns set up to support Fox Co. Easy Co on our left sent our a night patrol that ran into trouble. Several men were killed. I could see at least one of them strung up by his heels in a tree to my front, evidently as bait. He hung there for some time. The whole Bn got involved in a fire fight when a patrol was finally able to retrieve his body. A few days later the Chinese attacked in Bn strength. They came over the small hills in front like a swarm of ants. We opened up immediately. Minutes later 2 P-51 Mustangs flew in to cut a tremendous swath through enemy ranks with their .50 cal MGs. The next pass they fired their wing rockets, and on the third, dropped napalm tanks. The few that escaped we draped over our wire in front. I don't think a single Chinese escaped. Patrols now became our main focus. One of my two MGs was always set up on a suspected Chinese LP or on a likely ambush spot to support our patrols. We would zero the gun in daylight. For night firing we removed all tracers from the ammo belt and erected a burlap screen in front to hide muzzle flash. Coordinating with a patrol, we would fire at preselected times during the patrol operation. Many times we saw debris at the target spot when day dawned.

Our routine procedure was to have one man awake on the gun, another on guard in the trench outside the bunker. I would stay awake with a sound power phone in my ear until 4 AM, listening in on the chatter to keep track of what was going on. Some nights Chinese bugles would blow. Then the cans hung on our wire would rattle. We would sweep the wire with MG gunfire. The rattle would stop. Dim light was supplied by searchlights shining up against the clouds. In the morning we would often see a dead Chinese soldier stuck on the wire that the enemy had not been able to retrieve. Sometime in March the Captain in charge of the Regtl Motor Pool came to our position on a sightseeing and picture taking tour. We warned him not to expose himself, to no avail. The Chinese saw him on the forward slope and cut loose with a mortar barrage. He took a hit in the middle of his back while diving into the entrance of our bunker. He served as a living shield, stopping shrapnel from hitting the rest of us. He was evacuated by helicopter with a sucking back and chest wound, but thanks to good medics and the Grace of Our Lord, he lived. So much for sightseeing spectators!

Thirty days later we were relieved. All except one man in my section made it safely to the trucks taking us to Kumwha. Two of my squad leaders, Bansmer and Anspach and myself were last out. I had just started to crawl out of the bunker carrying the extra rifles we had cached in the bunker when a mortar barrage hit. We waited until it let up. I started out again, but Anspach grabbed me and said, "You always go first, this time it's my turn." He was hit in the back. We tended him until the medics took him to the Aid Station. He lived, but I never saw him again. We left that hill for 5 days of heaven on earth. Showers, clean clothing, three hot meals a day, a hot stove in a dry tent to keep us warm, a daily can of beer. As a bonus, we never heard a mortar burst or a shot fired.

Above. This Marine tanker fires his 90 mm gun gun at the enemy, Spring 1952.   Above Right. The 1st Marine Division is moved from the north eastern sector to the western front. The 1st Tk Bn. requires 7 LSTs to haul their 105 tanks to Inchon, March 1952. Below. Some of the 1st Tk Bn's M-46 Patton tanks lined up, ready to go. Photos courtesy of Roger Baker.   Right. In December 1951, A Company of the 1st Tk Bn in the Punchbowl area have dug in some of their tanks along the MLR I don't think the tanker is carrying his skis.   Photo by Chris Sarno.

RED DRAGON
The SECOND ROUND
FACES OF WAR II

Christopher	E.	Sarno	11 61 183 USMC
First Name	MI	Last Name	Serial Number
"Lock & Load"	1814 (Tanks)	15 Jan 1932	S/Sgt
Nickname	MOS	Birthday	Grade / Rank
1st Tk Bn, 1st Mar Div FMF		Jul '51-Aug'52 & Sep '53-Nov'54	Medford, MA
Unit (s)		Duty Tour (s)	Home Town
Purple Heart	Navy Commendation Ribbon with sta r		Navy Presidential Unit Citation with star
Medals & Awards			
KCMS,3 stars	NDSM UNSM Occpn Medal-J	ROK Presidential Unit Citation	ROK KWSM

THE TURKEY SHOOT

Pulled back into reserve in mid March 1952, we were dirty, cruddy and tired. We had been on line since mid December '51 and were glad to get a chance to rest, clean up and eat a few hot meals. Scuttlebutt had it that the entire 1st Tank Battalion, all 105 tanks, were going to reassemble here, the first time together as a unit since leaving San Diego and landing at Inchon 19 months ago. My unit, Able Company, had 20 M-46 Patton Class tanks equipped with 90mm guns and a complement of 100 fighting, combat tested Marines. The scuttlebutt was correct. Four days later, 1st Tk Bn, with Able Company on point, headed east to the tiny fishing village of Soko-ri. There we met "Papa" in the form of ships of the United States Navy. We were loaded into 7 LSTs, escorted by 2 destroyers and a cruiser on the 5 day sea voyage around the Korean Peninsula to the battered port of Inchon on the west coast where we off loaded.

We had been briefed by our capable company CO, Capt Raphael. Able was to be in support of the 5th Marines. The entire 1st Marine Division had made the move to this vital sector near the Imjin River on the western front. It commanded the traditional invasion route to Seoul. The 1st Marine Division was moved from the mountainous eastern front to this hilly western sector to repel an expected Chinese offensive that intelligence had ascertained was aimed at taking Seoul for the third time. Rifle company Marines made the bumpy overland journey by truck over narrow mountain dirt roads, a most unpleasant trip for marines riding in the back of GI 6x6 trucks. We were now in a terrain of low hills and rolling terrain interspersed with rat infested rice paddies. A flatter countryside enabled better tank mobility. Our flat trajectory 90mm guns could be used much more effectively here in deadly point blank fire.

The higher mountains to the north were manned by CCF troops, not the bedraggled remnants of the North Korea Peoples Army. The CCF were redoubtable enemies, amply supplied with weapons and gear by their Russian allies. On the 2d of April, just to let the Chinese know that there was a new kid on the block, we were assigned to a combat patrol, one platoon of tanks to support various line companies of the 5th Marines. On this particular mission our tank commander was Lt Wilson, I was bow gunner, and Cpl Ray Kapinski was gunner. It was a nice sunny day. We were moving slowly behind the low hills. When we reached the hill crest line, below and to our front, was a Chinese infantry company. They soon spotted us and began a clumsy sprinting run, slowed by the gear they were carrying, as they scurried for the cover of a wooded area about 400 yards away. It was a dash for life, doomed to failure.

The Lt immediately gave the command to open fire with our .30 and .50 cal MGs,--but hold fire with the 90 until we get the order! The gunners on our five tanks could not believe the field day unfolding in front of them. Live enemy caught out in the open! Very shortly, Lt Wilson gave the order for the 90s to fire High Explosive shells with fuses set for air bursts. This setting meant that the shells exploded over the heads of the fleeing Chinese, showering them with deadly shrapnel. It was a turkey shoot. The Chinese enemy did not have even the most remote of chances. Not one survived. Those green Korean rice paddies ran red with Chinese blood.

That night I drew watch from 0200 to 0600 with Cpl Ray Kapinski. He told me what was in his mind when the order was given to fire the 90mm gun. The gunner's scope was the most modern instrument of its day, a product of quality German engineering. Ray said, "Chris, I saw this one Chinaman's face at 400 yards as close as if I could reach out and touch him. When I fired the gun, he wasn't there any more." Putting my arm on Ray's shoulder, I tried to reassure him. "Ray, I saw the entire thing from my post above the hatch. Bodies and parts of bodies were flying through the air. It's war, a real war. Don't let it get to you. If you do, you'll go off your rocker and end up in a psychiatric ward. Grit your teeth, know full well they would have done the same to you if they had the chance."

Silently I said to myself, welcome back to the Korean War. It was payback time in an ugly war in this forsaken country which was being totally blasted back into the earth from which it had sprung. Civilians never read battle accounts such as this. Coverage of the war was restricted by politicians dictating tactics to field commanders, amateurs micro managing a war they neither knew how to stop, or translate into victory. The latter days of the Korean War boded ominously for the new trend of war to come in Vietnam.

Some material in this vignette was extracted from an article by Chris Sarno, originally published in *Military* Magazine........Editor]

Above. The Navy destroyer USS Leonard F. Mason cruises the North Korean coastline looking for a target. Below. An Air Force B-26 prowls the sky over North Korea looking for trouble. All photos courtesy of the National Archives.

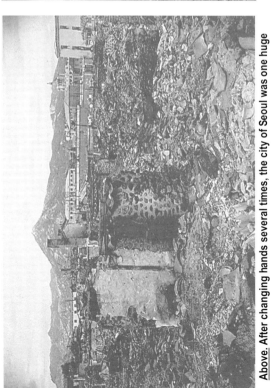

Above. After changing hands several times, the city of Seoul was one huge pile of rubble. Below. The North Korean port city of Wonsan became another pile of rubble due to Navy gunfire and constant Air Force bombardment.

Above. The Marine 1st Tk Bn loads up with ROK Marines for a little patrol action. The ride is a welcome change for the Infantry, particularly if they are going into a heavily mined area.   **Below** ROK Marines hang on while tankers from A Co. of the 1st Tk Bn. demonstrate a modern day cavalry charge,1952.   <u>All photos courtesy of Roger Baker</u>.

RED DRAGON
The SECOND ROUND
FACES OF WAR II

Ha-lyong	None	Hwang	Opr 08, G-2 8211
First Name	MI	Last Name	Serial Number
Gil-Lyong Hwang	Espionage	17 Dec 1929	Intelligence Agent
Nickname	MOS	Birthday	Grade / Rank

Served in 5 Guerilla Intelligence units: KLO G-2, KMC G-2, HID, SOU 105, AISS 6006-SAU 53

Unit (s)

1951 -1955   ******, Ham Kyung BukDo (Province), North Korea   Received seven medals for

Duty Tour (s)	Home Town	Medals & Awards

war time service. Five were traded for food while attending college. Two were lost in moving.

UNSUNG HEROISM OF A KOREAN NATHAN HALE

In the years following the 1905 Japanese invasion and occupation of our country, my father was one of the warriors that fought in losing battles to maintain our independence. In defeat, he fled to Manchuria, then under the weak government of the Manchu Dynasty. While of Chinese ancestry as our family name testifies, we have been Korean for almost 2000 years, coming to Korea about AD 28 during the Shilla Kingdom. The founder of our clan was Hwang Lak-he. He was for some reason on a sea journey to Kyo-Ji, now known as Vietnam. Blown off course, his ship wrecked, he settled in the Pong-he District in what is now Sean-la Province in the southeastern area of the North Korean Peninsula. With this ancestral background imbedded in my father's mind, his first thought in escape from the victorious Japanese was to flee to Manchuria where the Japanese then held no power, and would not until 1932.

There is a village in China, Yen-Bun, a suburb of Yanji City in Manchuria, inhabited mainly by people of Korean heritage, not far from the Korean-Manchurian border, where some of my father's relatives presumably still live. Other relatives may yet still live in ******* Hambuk Province, North Korea, where my grand uncle was born. It was this racial, cultural and geographic knowledge of my family clan which fitted me for the intelligence duties I performed during the Korean War. My father and I were bitterly hostile to the Russian sponsored dictatorial Communist regime that took over the government of North Korea following defeat of Japan and the 1945 partition of our country. We soon learned that life under the rigid Communist doctrine was worse than under the barbaric Japanese.

The Korean War broke out 25 June 1950. I was the oldest son, living in Gil-Ju, of an age most likely to be picked up for army service in the North Korean Army (In Min Gun). For months I hid, helped by my family and friends. We were absolutely elated when US and South Korean troops captured Hungnam and pushed northward. In December 1950, it was my father's decision for me to join the exodus from North Korea as one of the 97,000 refugees evacuated from Hungnam by ship to South Korea. The cold was dreadful, the worst in my memory. We accompanied US troops who had fought the battle of the Chosin(Jangjin) Reservoir after the Chinese intervened in the Korean War. When my father sent me away we expected it to be but for a short time. Everyone was sure that the Americans and the UN Army would return shortly. In the meantime I would be safe from the clutch of the In Min Gun. We were terribly wrong. The area of my birth is still held by Communists of North Korea, a nation where people today eat grass to prevent starvation.

Our ship took us to the South Korean east coast port of Pohang. The weather was warmer, although still very cold. The city swarmed with refugees, all looking for means of survival. A lucky few of the many thousands found shelter with relatives. I had no relatives in Pohang. I worked a few days unloading ships at the port, but realized that it was not a job with any degree of permanence. One day I noticed a South Korean Army recruiting poster placed on the wall of a building. I volunteered for army duty in late February 1951. After being interviewed by South Korean and American army officers, I was taken to an unknown island for training. Other young Korean men arrived until we had enough men for a training class. We shared a common bond, all of us were from North Korea, all had fled Communist tyranny. A South Korean soldier interpreted training information for us. Our unit was called KLO G-2 (Korean Liaison Office), also known as US 2d Intelligence Unit, Willowby Detachment. Our senior officer's name was Johnson.

Training consisted of reconnaissance methods in enemy territory, ways to capture North Korean officers for interrogation, and how to disguise ourselves to operate in enemy territory. We were given instruction in use of false documents and 'cover' stories to protect us if questioned. On the mainland, papers supported our cover story we were heading south to operate as guerillas. Training completed, we moved to Hongcheon by 1st Marine Division helicopter to begin our espionage duties. We carried out several operations. While recovering from an ankle injury, I was notified while in hospital we had so many men killed we were no longer an effective unit. After recovery, I was sent to Mukho, a small town on the east coast of King Won Province. I and a few others were taken on a US Navy ship to Yeo-do, an island in Young-Hung Mann, (Young Hung Bay) off the port of Wonson. Several small islands in Young-Hung Bay were held by South Korean Marines. The US 7th Fleet on constant patrol prevented enemy takeover, but could not permanently silence gunfire from coastal batteries. These guns were ineffective in their fire, both in range and accuracy.

US intelligence forces also operated out of these island bases. I was assigned to a group of guerillas headed by Ko- tak Lyong. He was a vigorous older man whose passion was the reunification of our country. He was a master sharpshooter, deadly with his rifle. Our group conducted many operations while we were based on Yeo-do. Our activity reports were sent to US Army G-2. I was wounded in a guerilla harassment raid on the enemy mainland. My comrades were able to bring me back to our base. I was sent to a rear area hospital until I recovered from my wound. Master Ko told me I did not have to return, he would adopt me as younger brother. I would not have to fight again, risking wounds or death, and perhaps not live to realize my dream of becoming a composer. I thought about this, but without money for food or a place to stay, I decided to return to Yeo-do. This time I was assigned as a guerilla in KMC (Korean Marine Corps)G-2. I stayed but a short time with this unit. After several operational raids, I was transferred to HID (Higher Intelligence Department) of the South Korean Army.

I became a member of the most artful and skillful guerilla group in the South Korean Army, the Yung Hung unit of HID Detachment, based on Ung-do, another island in Young-Hung Bay. There was another guerilla espionage unit based on Ung-Do island, designated as the Ko-Won group. Cells made up of dissident North Korean citizens who loathed the Communist government were organized. We spent many days in locating people whom we felt could be trusted in an internal operation of this kind. It was a ticklish, hazardous business. If we guessed wrong, and some did, a man could quickly be picked up, interrogated under severe stress, then executed by the In Mun Gun. Cells were generally composed of three people. Only a cell's leader knew the identity of the leader of a neighboring cell. This helped in preventing a wholesale wipe out of the network should a cell leader be tortured into divulging names.

Our operations involved many other types of activity. We conducted reconnaissance of military installations passing on information which was used in aircraft bombing raids by American and UN aircraft. We blew up rail lines and power lines as well as incited food riots and sabotaged fuel storage areas in quick hit-and-run raids. On several occasions we were given assassination orders to eliminate specific individuals. These were the most hazardous missions of all as these people of prominence were well guarded.

Our operations were about equally divided between orders from higher command and local operations we devised on our own. In carrying out orders from above we often ran across targets of opportunity. These went into our activity file to be executed at such time as we were not acting under higher orders. These hit-and-run raids were generally more successful than the ones on which we acted under orders. We had more freedom to improvise tactics using our own experience. We used SCR-300 radios to convey information to radio operators with the US Navy 7th Fleet. We would land on the East Sea coast line to reconnoiter In Min Gun coastal batteries which could then be taken under naval gun fire. We worked with both American and British naval units. I was always amazed at how quickly a coastal battery could be returned to firing status after it had been devastated by the big guns of the US Navy.

June 1953 I was involved in the capture of a North Korean officer taken from Ho-do Peninsula in Young-Hung Bay. My comrades got him back to our island base, carrying me with them. I had taken a severe wound in my right side during the "snatch" action. I was in a rear area hospital for the third time when the 'Cease Fire' took place in late July. In early 1954, recovering from my wounds, I again returned to duty. This time I was assigned to 6006th AISS (Air intelligence Squadron). Our American advisor was Donald Nicoles. I was designated team leader of 53d SAU (Special American Unit) and continued through early 1955 in reconnaissance and information operations in North Korea. By this time I had become adept in mingling with people of wartime North Korea. I adopted the guise of a wounded NK soldier. There were many such soldiers discharged due to wounds and left to shift for themselves. Using my background as a former North Korean citizen with wartime knowledge gained in military service, I could claim to have been discharged from a specific military unit. I was provided with plausible papers and a cover, continuing in this service until late 1955.

On receipt of my military discharge, I began my college studies in writing and music, taking up my interrupted dream of being a music composer. It was a hard time in my life. I received no pension of any kind for my four plus years of military service. As a means of making a living which would not interfere with my college studies at Sorabol Art College, I sold the magazine *"Readers Digest"* at the Dong Dae Moon RR station. Dong Dae Moon means "East Big Gate." There were four gates during the Yi Dynasty when Seoul was a walled city, today only three gates remain, North Gate has been demolished. The walls are long gone. In the mid 1950's it was a busy train and bus station, now replaced by a subway. Nearby was a huge market area. The huge crowds then thronging the area provided magazine sales to make my existence possible as a college student. I received my degree in music, but as with many other aspiring composers, I have lived a hand-to-mouth existence in the years since while I pursued my ambition as a composer.

My wife and family have been loyal and supportive of my musical aspirations. However, I have reconciled myself to the realization that I will never be known as a composer. In my old age I have a feeling of bitterness toward my government for lack of recognition for my wartime service or pension benefits. My writing activities about the Korean War have been suppressed as in violation of the 'Sunshine' policy which attempts a reconciliation with our 55 year old enemy even though it puts a heavy burden on South Korea. I do not understand such a policy toward North Korea with its brutal history of war and atrocity. Our people deserve better for their 50 years of hard work in making South Korea a free, prosperous and democratic nation.

<u>Above Left</u>. Still in shock, this Chinese POW is being held on the back side of Heartbreak Ridge.   <u>Photo by Gerald E. Lawrence</u>. <u>Above.</u> Another Chinese attack results in more of the terrible 'Faces of War'. <u>Below.</u> Those that suffer the most are the young and the old. 'Papa-san' with everything he owns on his back, and an orphaned baby in what remains of her home, 1952.

<u>Photos courtesy of Bill Palizzola</u>.

RED DRAGON
The SECOND ROUND
FACES OF WAR II

James	H.	Appleton	115 8912 USMC
First Name	MI	Last Name	Serial Number
Appy	0311	28 August 1931	Corporal
Nickname	MOS	Birthday	Grade / Rank
Item Co 5th Marine Regt 1st MarDiv		Apr '51-Apr '52	Nashville, TN
Unit (s)		Duty Tour (s)	Home Town
Silver Star Commendation Medal w/Combat V Navy PUC, 1star USMC Good Conduct Medal			
Medals & Awards			

USN Occpn Medal w/Eur clasp   NDSM   KCMS,3 battle stars   KSM   UN Medal   ROKPU   GOING

HOME PARTY

During WW II, servicemen served indefinite tours of duty in all theaters of a world wide war. "Duration plus six," was the term used by all in the services. It meant that every service person could expect his uniformed duty would extend, at a minimum, for six months following cessation of all hostilities. A "points" system favored combat veterans for a return to the states, but not to any release from duty. Many of those who rotated were sent after a short period stateside to the combat zone in the opposite hemisphere. Korea was a different kind of war, manpower was not as tight. The Department of Defense established a "Rotation System" in which troops would spend 12 months in Korea and then be eligible for stateside duty. No promises were made that the policy would be applicable to all troops. In practice, the policy favored combat veterans of the "Fighting" arms, Infantry, Artillery and Armor. Again, in practice, it included those of other services who were attached to the "Fighting" branches and who served side-by-side in combat zones.

I came to Korea in the 8th Replacement Draft, April 1951. It was now April 1952. I expected to rotate before month's end. The company bulletin board daily posted notices of promotion, change of duty status and stateside rotation lists. Whenever any one got "short" he checked the board. I was no exception. On 2 April, there I was, bigger than sin, Appleton, James H. Cpl 1158912 at top of the list. I had one more duty to fulfill before going home. I had to attend my "Going Home Party!" About half a mile in front of our lines was a Korean village housing about 70 Koreans of all ages. The village was a military hazard. It provided cover for an enemy who had previously shown he had no compunction about using civilians as shields to cover his attacks. American scruples prevented using artillery or air strikes to level the village. The Korean civilians must first be evacuated to safety before the village was razed.

Item Company had been ordered to burn this Korean village to the ground. We entered the village to evacuate the people. We were met by village elders wanting to know our purpose. When told, they understandably made vigorous objections. We knew the North Koreans had been using the village at night, crawling under the houses into the heating tunnels which underlaid every Korean house. These tunnels served as a base of operations for their partisan activity against us. They were told to gather everything they could carry, and given 30 minutes to prepare before we torched the village. At the half hour, the populace was gathered together. The North Koreans in the hills knew our purpose. They began to lob their mortars at us even before we began torching the village with our thermite grenades. They launched a weak attack while we were trying to evacuate this group of old men, women and children.

One Marine came upon a vegetable cellar concealing 5 women and a couple of children. They cowered in fear, refusing to join the others. After several minutes of exasperation, before anyone could stop him, he tossed a phosphorus grenade in their midst. The occupants came staggering out, covered with burns. The group was gathered and treatment began by our Corpsmen. We all glared in sheer contempt at the culprit Marine. His punishment would follow on return to our lines. As we started back many of the Marines carried a child in one arm, his rifle in the other. I had picked up a pretty little girl of 3 or 4 with a pitiful look of fear in her huge almond eyes. She was so frightened she would not respond to my few words of Korean. A tremendous explosion up ahead told us someone had stepped on a mine. I walked ahead in case my radio was needed to call for assistance. What I saw was horrible, but it could not have happened to a better man. The same Marine who had tossed the WP grenade had stepped on a American M-3 land mine. His leg was hanging by a shred. As he was being loaded into a litter while being given a shot of morphine, he said, "I guess it's payback time. Wonder if I'll qualify for one of those new cars for amputees?" He still had the insouciant attitude typical of some in the Corps.

We struggled back to our lines without further incident. The Korean nationals were loaded into trucks guarded by MPs for the trip back to the refugee camp. I gave my little Korean girl friend a great big hug and a candy bar to sustain her on the road to the camp. She had recovered enough to give me a little smile. I have often wondered what happened to her in later life. It was now 5 AM. I went over to get a strong cup of "Java" to fortify me for the coming day. In a few hours I would be saying goodby to my friends before boarding the little train headed for Munsan-ni, then on to Seoul, then westward through Yongdung Po to the port city of Inchon where I had a ticket on the "Big Boat" headed where I wanted to go. My Going Home Party was over. Now I was GOING HOME!

Above. A mortar crew from the 45th Infantry Division fires from a sandbag reinforced firing pit. 1952. <u>Photo from Archives.</u>

Above. A 'weasel' is used to bring in wounded from the 31st Regiment after the bloody battle for Jane Russell Hill in the Iron Triangle area. Battle took place on October 14-15, 1952 and casualties were heavy. <u>Photo from the National Archives.</u>

RED DRAGON
The SECOND ROUND
FACES OF WAR II

Denzil	NMI	Batson	RA 17 278 855
First Name	MI	Last Name	Serial Number
None	4745	19 March 1928	M/Sgt
Nickname	MOS	Birthday	Grade / Rank
2d Bn/3d Inf Div		Sept '51- '52	Republic, MO
Unit (s)		Duty Tour (s)	Home Town
Combat Infantry Badge Bronze Star Korean Campaign Service Medal w/2stars			ROK KWSM
Medals & Awards			
National Defense Service Medal		ROK Presidential Citation	United Nations Medal

HIGH TENSION-FALSE ALARM

It was late April 1952. We had been on line for 4 long months and were now dug in on "Little Gibralter." The hill had received the name probably because it was a key terrain feature, vital to holding the MLR. Every man had toiled to improve the strength of the bunkers we had inherited from previous occupants. The strength of a bunker, a soldier's home away from home in trench warfare, is directly proportional to size of the logs overhead and layers of sandbags piled on top and around the sides. Bunkers, if well built, gave protection from shell burst fragments, but not direct hits. That took concrete and steel, not local scrub timber and sandbag revetments. When possible, a bunker was always dug into a hillside. The back of a bunker was thus well protected, front, sides and overhead were the problem areas. "Daily bunker maintenance" was a routine front line duty. On the previous two nights there had been heavy enemy activity along our front. Last night, a unit to our east had been hard hit. The fight had raged all night long. We expected to be relieved in a few days. Men were eagerly awaiting a shower, clean underwear and some uninterrupted sleep.

Our Company Commander burst the bubble. We were informed that on the coming night no one was to sleep. An order for a 100% alert was given. Further, the all night alert, beginning tonight, was to continue in effect until otherwise notified. That meant sleep could be grabbed only in daylight hours. The CO said, "Sergeant, I want all men told of this order." I spent the next hour going from bunker to bunker in my platoon making sure every man had plenty of ammo and grenades. All 18 men who remained of our original 40 man platoon were now war-savvy vets. It was not necessary to tell them twice. Veterans who have been through the grindstones of war's grist mill are highly valued by commanders. Each man can be counted on because each man supports the other. Line sergeants, platoon leaders and company commanders take a pragmatic view: "One vet is worth 3 greenhorn replacements."

As I walked down the line, not a word was said. I could see the tension in the faces of the men. I was a bundle of nerves myself. This close to relief, now a major fight in the offing! I found a vacant foxhole in the middle of our line dug by a trooper no longer with us. I set myself for a long vigil. I walked the line a couple of times to check with each man. On my second pass as I walked by one of the LMG positions, the gunner said. "Sarge, you are going to get your ass shot off, walking around like you are." I recognized the wisdom of his remark and returned to my fighting hole. Out in front the frogs and insects were singing a deafening hallelujah chorus in praise of the warming spring season. Experience told me that as long as the chorus lasted, there was no movement to our front.

If the chorus went silent it meant slant eyed trouble was creeping up on us. A pale moon lit up the rice paddies. It promised to be a long night, night alerts always were. Knowing that adjacent units had been hit the last night added to the tension. I had a threatened feeling we were next. My foreboding was heightened by the fact that we had only 18 men in the reception party to welcome our Chinese guests. I was beginning to relax when an ominous stillness fell across the rice paddies. The frogs and crickets fell silent, like a chorus responding to a conductor's baton. You could have heard a pin drop. I stiffened, as I'm sure did every man in the platoon. My platoon sector had two Browning LMGs set in crossfire. Our machine guns, plus the frontal fire of 12 M-1s, and the rapid fire of our two 2-man BAR teams guaranteed the enemy would not get a cheap victory. His "Human Sea" tactics which ignored the cost in Chinese dead, might overwhelm us, but he would pay dearly in a ratio of at least ten to one by the time he finished us off.

The night dragged on at slow bell. The chorus did not resume, nor did the Chinese attack. Shortly before daylight the frog chorus resumed. We knew that another all night alert had turned into a false alarm. Shortly after daybreak, the Company Commander called to tell me the alert was over. We all gave a sigh of relief. With four men on guard, most of the platoon grabbed some shut eye. I was so busy with details I did not get a wink of sleep. By nightfall I was a walking zombie. It was times like this that caused me to ask myself the question, "Why did I ever become a platoon sergeant?" I made the mistake of airing my gripe out loud to some of the men. One of them, a draftee, said to me, "Sarge, didn't you enlist? Aren't you Regular Army? Anybody shove a bayonet up your butt to make you enlist?" My answer was a sheepish, "Nope." Once again the troops put me in my place. I couldn't argue with one word he had said. American soldiers, particularly combat veterans, are prone to speak their mind, to call a spade a spade.

<u>Above</u>.   Another war orphan ! This week old fawn was found and adopted by the 72nd Tk Bn of the 2nd Infantry Division.
<u>Below</u>.   Truce talks were still going on at Panmunjom.   The U.N. delegates were to get a two year course in semantics from the Chinese and North Korean delegates who were masters at 'doubletalk' and stalling techniques. Meanwhile on the MLR countless thousands more would die or be wounded.   <u>Photos from the National Archives.</u>

Edward	H.	Utley	O52196 USMC
First Name	MI	Last Name	Serial Number
O52196 USMC	0302	3 Nov 1929	Lt Col, then 2d LT
Nickname	MOS	Birthday	Grade / Rank
Wpns 1st Bn 1st Marines 1st MarDiv		Feb '52-Aug '52	Michigan City, IN
Unit (s)		Duty Tour (s)	Home Town

Medals & Awards

MISTAKEN IDENTIFICATION

In April 1952, shortly after the Division moved from the east coast of Korea to guard the approaches to Seoul, we were occupying positions on the Main Line of Resistance. My 1st Bn weapons platoon had completed digging in our support positions, laid out fields of fire for our MGs and identified crucial terrain targets and concentrations for our mortars. Enemy activity was comparatively light. After our tiring trip across the Korean Peninsula and labor of digging in our new positions we were glad the enemy was comparatively inactive. It gave us a chance to rest up a bit. The next night after settling in, we heard a noise out in front of our platoon.

One private, we'll call him Smith, fired four rounds from his M-1, threw out a hand grenade, fired four more rounds from his M-1, then threw another grenade. Apparently feeling that he had wiped out all Chinese Communist resistance in the area, he mounted the parapet of his foxhole and lit a cigarette. The flash of his match could be seen for a great distance. For some reason a Chinese sniper did not shoot him dead. We later came to the conclusion that the Good Lord takes care of fools, idiots and the mentally unbalanced.

The next morning, for penance and as a sweaty reminder not to repeat his stupidity, Smith's squad leader assigned him the job of digging a hole six feet by six feet by six feet deep. He was to do this while his buddies slept. Smith worked at digging his hole for a short time, then threw down his entrenching tool and stomped off. His squad leader, figuring it was of little use to chase him down since the platoon was on the MLR, vowed not only to watch him closer when he returned, but to ream him a larger opening in his rear end to remind him that the Corps did not put up with flagrant violation of orders. He intended to give Smith chapter and verse instruction from his NCO storehouse of disciplinary punishment to remind him he was a marine in the Marine Corps.

Sporadic fire erupted from both Chinese and Americans lines, centering in No-Mans land, drew his attention to the front. Someone was walking through the uncharted mine fields in front of our lines. Then the word was passed, "Cease firing, it's a Marine out there!" When the marine reentered our lines, it turned out to be Smith. When asked what he was doing out there, his reply, accompanied by a sickly grin was , "Huntin' deer." It stopped his squad leader and platoon leader cold. It was unbelievable from a rational marine.

Battalion Med was called and asked, "What should we do with this person?" We were instructed to disarm him, which we had already done, and to send him back to the Aid Station under guard. Under no circumstances were we tell him we thought he was crazy. They suggested we say that he had been called back for a routine physical exam. So, following that suggestion, a guard was appointed who marched Smith back to the Aid Station. In the meantime, a second lieutenant friend of mine had been notified he had been promoted to first lieutenant. My friend needed to go to the Aid Station for a physical as required by US Marine Corps regulations.

Because officers were preferred Chinese sniper targets, none of us wore insignia of rank. He departed for the Aid Station some ten or fifteen minutes before Smith and his guard. When he showed up at the Aid Station to announce he was there for his physical examination, the medics said, "Weeeee know." As they ran the him through a list of questions such as did he hate his mother, did he like boys or girls best and other questions in similar vein, he got very hot under the collar. The madder he got, the more convinced the medics became they had a dangerous psycho on their hands. The matter was not going well for either side of the discussion until Smith and his guard showed up. Fortunately for both, the situation was threatening to erupt into mayhem as my friend's anger grew by leaps and bound, while the medics on their side were beginning to consider a strait jacket.

Smith, propelled further and further up the chain of Marine Corps psychiatrists, finally told the shrinks he had been talking in his sleep and that I had been writing it all down and sending what he had said to his mother. That ended the Korean War for Smith. My friend passed a real physical and was promoted to first lieutenant. Even then, and after all these years the question remains, did we have a psycho or a shrewd country boy whose background contained information from someone of World War II who had told him stories about Section Eight discharges as a result of simulating mental unbalance? In either event, he did not belong in the US Marine Corps.

Left. Medics were very highly regarded most of the time. At other times they could be a real pain in the arm, as this soldier's expression shows. **Right.** Some of the best of the U.N. troops in Korea were the Turkish Brigade. Doc Hempen became good friends with them without being able to talk 'Turkey'. He is shown standing by their flag pole. *Photos courtesy of Carl L. Hempen.*

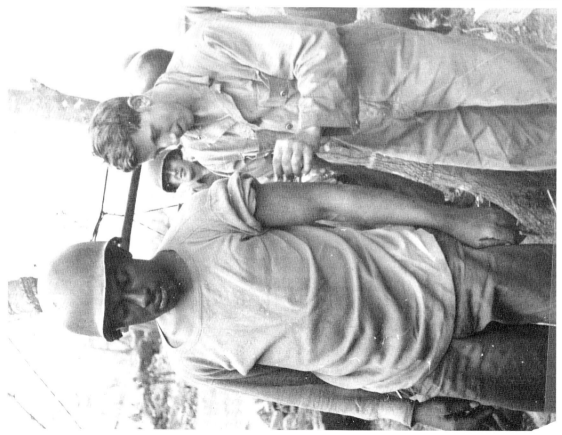

RED DRAGON
The SECOND ROUND
FACES OF WAR II

Carl	L.	Hempen	RA 17 306 862
First Name	MI	Last Name	Serial Number
"Doc"	Medic	29 Feb 1932	S/Sgt
Nickname	MOS	Birthday	Grade / Rank
2d Chem Mrtr Bn, 8th Army		Jun '51-Jun '52	Sandoval, IL
Unit (s)		Duty Tour (s)	Home Town
Bronze Star w/V	Good Conduct Medal	Combat Medic Badge	UN Svc Medal
Medals & Awards			
Korean Campaign Service Medal w/3 stars		National Defense Service Medal	KWSM

HEROIC BLACK SOLDIER----THE FEROCIOUS TURKS

A BLACK SOLDIER WAS THE HERO of this day in my life. All memory recalls is that he was a Pfc and his name was Jones. It was mid afternoon on a quiet day off line when I heard the shout every Medic learns to dread. The cry, "Medic, Medic," means that some soldier needs medical attention pronto. Panting and breathless, I arrived at the scene to be told what had happened. Two young Korean civilians saw some nubbins of corn in a field. The field had been mined. Even knowing this, hunger pangs overcame caution. They both paid dearly. I saw two bodies, the first was not moving, probably dead. I worked my way cautiously toward the first still form. Too late, he was gone. What had occurred was symptomatic of war. War and hunger march in lock step, hand-in-hand.

AS I MOVED TOWARD THE SECOND YOUNGSTER, stepping ever so carefully, looking for what might be an anti-personnel mine, scared to the tip of my toes, I found him alive. I called for a litter. A GI from the 1st Platoon picked his way in my footsteps, carrying the litter on his shoulder, watching every step as he came towards me. With his help the young Korean was loaded onto the litter. We started back, picking and choosing our way, looking carefully before we stepped again. As we worked our way back, I saw several mines that I had luckily missed on the way in. Needless to say, we both left the field with a sigh of relief, yet disappointed that one youngster had paid such an appalling price for a few grains of corn that he never got to eat. The other would live, but with the memory of his dead friend to haunt him over the years. This episode stood out in my memory because when I called for a litter, it was a black soldier from a different platoon who answered my call. Pfc Jones, God knows what you did that fateful day. On the Day of Judgement you will be first in line. In the Army, it is termed "Above and Beyond the Call of Duty." I have saluted you in my memory many times. And again, thanks for being there when the young Korean and I both needed you. I have thought many times over the years I should have moved heaven and earth to see that you were recognized with a medal for your valorous act of mercy.

A RED LETTER TURKISH-AMERICAN FRIENDSHIP DAY was the furthest thought from my mind as over the months I snapped pictures of combat areas, soldiers and the Korean scene. My last two rolls of film had been taken while the 4.2 mortar plat to which I was attached as Aid Man had been supporting the fire of a Turkish 81mm mortar unit. The language barrier it seemingly made it impossible to communicate. A camera broke that barrier. I went on R&R to Japan after a week or so with the Turks. When I returned from Japan, we were still in support of the Turks in that same long, narrow valley in Central Korea. While in Japan I had eleven rolls of film developed with 3 pictures of each exposure. I had intended to send these home to family and friends. I made gifts of a few pictures to one Turkish soldier with whom I had become friendly. When he showed other Turkish soldiers his pictures, it set off a flurry of excitement. Many Turkish soldiers crowded around me and offered to buy my pictures. They wanted to send them home.

I HAD A GREAT ADMIRATION FOR THE TURKS. They were real fighting soldiers. I gave away most of my photos. I could not pass a Turk after that without receiving a broad smile. A few days later just as I had finished chow, two Turks came by. With smiles and gestures, and a thumb point toward their camp indicated I should come with them. Surrendering without a struggle, I accompanied them to a tent that was filled with what was apparently top brass. There sure were a lot of stars on the shoulders of a number of the officers in that tent! In a moment I was served with a meal of a whole chicken, home made bread, and a soup concoction something like our pea soup. Although I had just eaten, I felt I could not insult their hospitality by declining, so I stuffed like I was starved. After a few bites of home made bread and delicious roast chicken, washed down with spoonfuls of pea soup, I was no longer pretending. It was the best meal in all my time in Korea. I had heard that a Turk never drew his knife without drawing blood. I found that did not hold true when bread loaves were cut in half! The Turks had a ferocious reputation but obviously had a most friendly side as well!

FROM THAT DAY until we moved from that position, one Turk, Aonan Ozyamanlar, and I became the best of friends, although neither of us could understand a word spoken by the other. He came from Izmir, Turkey. I had his address and wrote to him two years later. No reply. Was he killed later in the war? So many were, so many young lives were cut short in the prime of their youth. Was he one of those that paid with his life in the Korean War? I will never know. Yet, to this day, I vividly remember my Turkish friend which proves that friendship is possible between different races with different creeds. End of my story. It happened in a "Police Action!

Scenes from Tank Co of the 224th Regt, 40th Division are shown. Below. Sgt. Muniz from south Texas is enjoying[?]the 'winter wonderland' of Korea in February, 1952. Right. A chaplain holds church services at Kumsong, Korea. March 1952. Below Right. A minor problem gets roadside service for this tank. [A gun elevating mechanism problem.] May, 1952 in the Kumhwa area.

RED DRAGON
The SECOND ROUND
FACES OF WAR II

Arnoldo	A.	Muniz	US 54 024 587
First Name	MI	Last Name	Serial Number
Arnold	Track Vehicle Mechanic	11 Jan 1929	Sgt
Nickname	MOS	Birthday	Grade / Rank
Service& Tank Cos 224th Inf 40thDiv		Feb '52-Oct '52	San Antonio, TX
Unit (s)		Duty Tour (s)	Home Town

Combat Infantry Badge   Good Conduct Medal   Korean Campaign Service Medal, 2stars

Medals & Awards

WW II Occpn Medal-G   National Defense Medal   United Nations Medal   ROKPUC ROK KWSM

SHORT ROUNDS

February 1952 through October 1952 was probably the quietest and characterized by the least military activity of the whole Korean War. I feel lucky to have served during that time but it also gives me feelings of guilt because so many of my fellow veterans had it much worse than I did. My service was in a period of trench warfare, and although mild as measured by any military standard, it also had its deadly moments. Some of these were as funny as they were potentially fatal. While my 8 months were quiet by comparison, we were still involved in a war. People were being killed daily, some of whom I knew. I was a tank mechanic of Service Company, 224th Regiment assigned to the Regimental Tank Company. We were based at Kumwha on the Iron Triangle. It was the best base of operations of my service period in Korea. We had a good motor pool area, our supplies were fairly consistent and combat was practically nil. The ongoing peace talks created a much appreciated operations lull for our Tank Company.

Tanks in this mountainous country in a time of trench warfare were tactically employed as short range artillery pieces. The only problems we mechanics usually faced were those brought about when a mobile weapon is immobilized. Loose tracks, malfunctioning battery chargers, electrical failures, water in gas tanks are examples of problems requiring only one mechanic to answer a repair call. If possible, I would try to time my repair call with resupply of ammunition to a tank. In that way I would not be a 'one man army' if I ran into an enemy patrol. I could also lend a hand to the tank crew in loading or unloading ammo depending on the mechanical problem. These trips, usually made just before sundown, required spending the night at the site of the disabled tank. I always spelled the tank crew in night guard duty. By making myself useful, I was able to cultivate, and maintain, good relations with the tank crews.

My buddy, C.R. Walker and I were on a dual job in my 3/4ton Dodge utility vehicle. CR was taking a load of 76mm tank ammo to one tank, I was on my way to fix a dirty carburetor on another. The road was very bad. The Dodge was struggling to make it up the hill. The right side of the road was walled by a steep rocky slope, shallow drainage ditches on each side of the road. The left side still had a few splintered trees, survivors of recent shelling. We passed a group of grim faced, tired riflemen led by a 2d Lt also headed up hill. They barely acknowledged our hands waved in greeting. We were possibly 70 yards ahead of the soldiers when from our rear a shell whistled overhead. CR was driving, I was sitting beside him. We looked at each other, both realizing these were rounds from our own Long Toms. Brakes were slammed on, we bailed out. How it happened, I still don't know, but I ended up in the left ditch, CR in the right. The impact of the first shell made the Dodge bounce on its springs. A second round came screaming in. I was trying to dig myself deeper into the ditch, using my tongue as a shovel. The soldiers we had passed were also bellied out on the ground.

The Lt yelled, "Move that damn truck!" I was not about to get into a truck loaded with 76mm ammo while our 155 Long Toms were zeroing in on target. I pretended not to hear. He was still yelling when the 3d round hit. The earth shook, literally bouncing me in the air. Shock, vibration and fear loosened my bowels and bladder. When the 4th round came thundering in, all I could think of was, "Yea, though I walk through the valley of death...." The artillery must have finally got their bearings corrected because the firing ceased. The rest of the shelling went on overhead into enemy territory where the first 4 should have gone, hopefully causing a lot of Chinese to become acquainted with their ancestors. The Lt was highly pissed, still yelling, but I just pointed at my ears. He got the message, gathered his men and went back to hill climbing. CR dug his face out of the ditch and wobbled over to me. He wrinkled his nose and said, "Shit." "That's what it is," I replied, "And piss, too." "Shit," he repeated. I discarded my underwear, first wiping myself with it as clean as possible. I got in the driver's seat and drove the rest of way, CR keeping as far away from me as he could. To CR's credit he never mentioned my "accident" to anyone. A good buddy. Had he talked, I would never have lived it down!

Now in my seventies, I still swear it was the vibration that made my bowels empty themselves, not from a sense of fear! Not that I was never afraid. On the contrary, I was afraid every day I was in Korea. True, I was a mechanic and never in the same ball park in degree of danger as those riflemen on their way up hill. True, I served in a quiet period of the war. But in a war you never know from one day to the next if you will see another. The old man with his scythe doesn't choose his victims, he just wields it at random.

Above. This photo from the Chinese Archives shows a supply train headed south in 1951. The importance of supply and fear of air attacks is evident by the large number of anti-aircraft guns in the foreground.   Photo from the Internet.
Below Left. We also placed great importance on their supply trains. A train and a nearby storage area receive the undivided attention of the 452nd Bomb Group.   Below Right. This thoughtful pilot seems to be considering his future as he examines damage to his 4FU Corsair that he received on his 99th mission.   Bottom photos from National Archives

RED DRAGON
The SECOND ROUND
FACES OF WAR II

John.	A	Lynn	US 55 042 225
First Name	MI	Last Name	Serial Number
None	1745	23 Nov 1928	M/Sgt
Nickname	MOS	Birthday	Grade / Rank
Co K, 31st Inf 7th Div		19 Sept '51-4 May '52	Chicago, IL
Unit (s)		Duty Tour (s)	Home Town

Combat Infantry Badge   Korean Campaign Service Medal, 3 stars   Occupation Medal, Japan

Medals & Awards

National Defense Service Medal   United Nations Medal   Korean War Service Medal   ROK PUC

FIRE AND MANEUVER

I was not happy about receiving my draft notice. I was just getting set as an ironworker, a career I had begun as an apprentice at age 16. At age 22 I had been a job foreman for 2 years and was working on the bigger, more challenging construction jobs in my trade. While iron working is a very hard job, it provides excellent musculature for strength, agility and endurance, traits which certainly came in handy for a combat infantryman. I was sent to the 40th Division at Camp Cooke, CA where I was assigned to Co A, 1st Bn, 160th Inf Regt. The 40th Div was a Calif NG unit just called into federal service. The first fall in was haphazard, a few sgts and fewer privates. Looking around, I sensed opportunity. I told the other draftees to stand to my left, and assumed the position of a sqd ldr. I thus became an acting sgt and a start on the road to M/Sgt. Glancing at the plat sgt who had a slight smile on his face, I sensed we had an understanding. My reasons were simple. At the induction station, I noticed that NCOs did not stand in line at mess call. I hate standing in line. If stripes were the answer, I wanted stripes. The key was knowledge. The Army had a manual for everything. I read the manuals and learned my military ABCs. In the next 18 months I learned a great deal more, and in the process became a soldier.

The division was shipped to Japan where we trained hard and long. I was now a buck sgt, a 3 striper, drawing the pay of a sqd ldr. In one of the company commanders meetings for NCOs the subject of combat performance came up. The Capt stated no one really knew how he would react under direct fire. I voiced an opinion I should have kept to myself. In essence I volunteered for a transfer to Korea where I found myself in Co K, 31st Inf. In Japan our company had gone through basic training three times. As a squad we had worked out a method using men and fire control to maximum effect. Each sqd had 2 BAR teams, a BAR man and an Asst BAR man, and 3 fire teams, 2 men in each fire team, all armed with M-1s. The sqd ldr had to give only 4 signals to move the squad. Only one BAR would move at a time. The 3 rifle teams would increase their rate of fire while the BAR was moving. We had been taken off the MLR and moved into reserve where a training program was initiated. This particular session was a live fire exercise in which a squad on patrol was to ascend a hill (the one we were on), run into a large enemy unit, become engaged, then withdraw under fire.

We retreated downhill in our simulated short engagement, one BAR or the other firing in short bursts of 3 or 4 rounds. With the other two M-1 fire teams joining in, the noise was really deafening. However, with only 4 signals per move, it was really a simpler method of maneuver. For about 4 minutes it must have looked as if we had been completely routed, with men jumping up and running everywhere. It sounded like a small war, but every man knew exactly where he had to be and when to fire. When we returned to the platoon perimeter I gave my report, then handed over my ammo report prepared by the asst sqd ldr. When I looked outside the platoon perimeter, about a half mile away, I could see our other two company rifle platoons and the Hvy Weapons platoon running in our direction. Our plt ldr had called the CO and reported we had run into a Chinese guerilla outfit and exchanged fire with them! Our CO had heard the intense firing and came to the same conclusion. Closing on our perimeter, the CO quickly placed the company in a defensive position. I kept telling my plt ldr it was just my squad running the training problem as we had been ordered. He would have none of it, insisting to me and the CO that we must have run into the enemy. He could tell by the volume of fire!

The company commander heard me out. He was still skeptical, I think, because we ran the exercise again. It was as successful, noisy, and as spectacular as the first run. The Captain's only comment was he didn't think the Army wanted to change the way rifle squads were trained. A week later our plt ldr rotated. I became asst plat Sgt. We went back on the MLR and came off the line again 4 May 1952, a day that sticks in my memory. Our new position, about 1000 yards behind the MLR had very limited fields of fire. The AP mines that had been laid were clearly visible and could therefore be easily breached. There was no barbed or concertina wire to our front. The new plt ldr, I was now plt sgt--we were without a plt officer for 3 months--decided after talking to his NCOs, that we needed to upgrade our position with wire. While going down the steep hillside, I slipped and unfortunately tripped a 'Bouncing Betty' mine like one I had seen and bypassed. I spent the next 5½ months in Percy Jones Army Hospital in Lansing, MI. I was not awarded the Purple Heart, not the result of enemy action! I kept my wallet, none of my other personal belongings ever caught up with me.

Below. This picturesque [?] setting was the home of the 2nd Chemical Mortar Bn during 1951-1952. Photo courtesy of Carl 'Doc' Hempen.

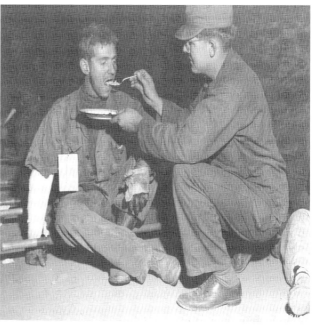

Above. With both hands damaged a G.I. gets special treatment from this medic. Below. With the increasing use of helicopters for medical evacuations, our wounded had a much better chance of survival. With a pod on each side, casualties could even be given in-flight IVs . Photos from the National Archives.

RED DRAGON
The SECOND ROUND
FACES OF WAR II

Carl	L.	Hempen	RA 17 306 862
First Name	MI	Last Name	Serial Number
Doc or Spade	Medic	29 February 1932	S/Sgt
Nickname	MOS	Birthday	Grade / Rank
2d Chemical Mortar Bn		June 1951-June 1952	Carlyle, IL
Unit (s)		Duty Tour (s)	Home Town

Bronze Star Medal with V   Combat Medical Badge   Good Conduct Medal   NDSM
Medals & Awards
Korean Campaign Service Medal, 3stars   United Nations Medal   Republic of Korea, KWSM

ONE OF GOD'S ANGELS*

Early May 1952. I was near the end of my year's tour of combat duty in Korea. The days were being marked off my pocket calendar in anticipation of going home. In the meantime I was still a medic 'on call'. The 4.2 mortar platoon to which I was attached as Aid Man had been pouring a heavy fire onto the enemy. Lt Turner was our platoon Forward Observer (FO). His accuracy in spotting the enemy drew retaliatory artillery fire which demolished his bunker with a direct hit. The call came in on the commo line that Lt Turner was badly wounded, "Send a medic!" I started out with no idea where Lt Turner had located his Forward Observation Post. Heading up the valley--in Korea, you were either in a valley or on a mountain--I approached a high ridge. There I ran into two tanks which were dug in for protection from artillery fire. The tankers provided me with directions to the FO's bunker. Reaching the area of the collapsed bunker, I found Lt Turner. He was in bad shape with a deep intestinal wound. I dressed his wound and gave him morphine to ease his pain. With the help of a three man litter crew from the rifle company manning that sector of the MLR, we loaded him on to a stretcher. The arduous task of getting him down the mountain to put his stretcher onto my med-evac jeep still lay ahead.

Bringing him down the mountain, all I could think of was, "Hold on Lt, we'll make it yet." For the four of us, taking that stretcher down the steep Korean mountainside was a tough proposition. The task was made more difficult by the care necessary to not drop the stretcher. That could have loosened the tight compress bandage which was keeping him alive, barely. In spite of our care, we lost control of our footing on one occasion but managed to hang on so he did not toboggan down the mountainside. At the bottom of the mountain we loaded him onto my med-evac jeep and took him to the evacuation area where a helicopter was waiting to take him to a MASH hospital. He was in a critical state. I did not expect that he would live. Certainly, I never expected to ever see him again.

War has strange twists and turns. One of these twists brought a deep sense of gratification. I rotated home shortly after Lt Turner was wounded, coming home on a slow ship, the U S Collins. Landing in San Francisco in June, I had a home furlough before returning to complete my enlistment duty at Valley Forge Hospital. I was assigned as Ward Master in Neurological Surgery. It was quite by chance that I went to the Officer's Ward for some reason, long forgotten. The first man I met in the ward was Lt Turner, very much alive and looking quite well. He had to tell every officer in the ward who I was and that I was responsible for him being alive. I felt he overdid the story a bit, but it sure made my day. It was a genuine joy that filled my heart, the satisfaction of having done my job. My reward was in seeing him again. I wrote a poem to express my feelings as a Medic for Lt Turner, but also for all the wounded soldiers of the Korean War. There were many, many of them, well over 100,000 men. The agony of their suffering still fills my soul.

MEDIC

It has been half a century
Seems like only yesterday
Time flies for those that survive
For the dead it does not work that way.

Man on F. O. duty badly hurt	Homeward bound to a new assignment
A man I hardly knew	To a hospital ward and a grand surprise
When the call came for 'medic'	There I met the man I hardly knew
I knew I had a job to do	Tears of joy filled our happy eyes
Find the man, bind his wound	I still pause to thank my god
Give morphine for his pain	That I was able to save a few
A rough shod ride to save his life	When on that Korean hill
Would I ever see this man again?	I heard the call, knew I had a job to do!

* One of God's Angels was a term often used to describe the role of an Aidman or 'Medic' in an infantry rifle company...Ed

Above. K Co. 31st Regt.'s sector of the MLR.   Below.
Sgt. Lynn stands near his bunker. Photos by John. Lynn.

Above. A 75 mm RR of D Co. 7th Regt in action in the Chorwon Valley. Photo by Tom Whitewater
Below A tank - infantry team on the move, 1951.   Photo from the National Archives.

RED DRAGON
The SECOND ROUND
FACES OF WAR II

John	A.	Lynn	US 55 042 225
First Name	MI	Last Name	Serial Number
None	1745	23 Nov 1928	M/Sgt
Nickname	MOS	Birthday	Grade / Rank
Co K, 31st Inf 7th Div		19 Sept '51-4 May '52	Chicago, IL
Unit (s)		Duty Tour (s)	Home Town
Combat Infantry Badge	Korean Campaign Service Medal, 3 stars		Occupation Medal, Japan
Medals & Awards			
National Defense Service Medal	United Nations Medal	Korean War Service Medal	ROK PUC

COMBAT BROWN

The probably apocryphal story about a company from another division who were just off line, in reserve status, hit the rumor mill just as we came off line. Supposedly this company had been ordered to lay out equipment for full field inspection. The story went they were hit by a band of NK guerillas and badly shot up as their weapons were field stripped. One Sgt fired a few rounds before he was killed. As a result, full field inspections were banned. Another consequence was posting of patrols around units in reserve. These patrols had two purposes: check for enemy activity and update map overlays to make sure there had been no change from the day before. In reserve, training classes were the order of the day. We had a very articulate Lt with a superior command of the English language. He was giving a class in map reading. I was proficient myself in this skill, but on a less erudite level. During his lecture, it seemed as if a number of men were not grasping his concepts. The second time I raised my hand and asked to present a less scholarly version to the men, the Lt turned the class over to me. I filed away for future use the lecture lesson I had just learned.

Later that day the CO gave orders I was to take two squads on a 20 mile security patrol around our reserve area. I was given a map overlay, told to draw rations, ammo, grenades, whatever else I thought necessary. The other sqd ldr was to be second in command. I knew I was going to have a bad day. In this other squad was a black soldier called "Combat Brown." He got his name by being as good a fighting soldier as one could find. He distinguished himself several times. As an example, on a patrol made just before I came to the company, the patrol came under fire from an enemy bunker. On his own, he worked around back of the bunker, emptying 2 BAR magazines into the rear entrance of the bunker. He let everyone know that somehow this last combat action upset him, causing anxiety and restlessness. He would awaken about 2 AM shouting what he would do to any "dirty Commies" he came across. He punctuated these cussing tirades by swinging his loaded BAR around our two squad tent. He would then lie down after 4 or 5 minutes and calmly go back to sleep. I resented not only my own loss of sleep but the effect on other men in my squad. After his 3d attack of "nerves," I asked his sqd ldr why he put up with such antics, saying I thought it was a call for attention, not a nightmare. He did not pull the trigger. In a real nightmare, he probably would have. I learned why, his squad leader was afraid of him.

We took off on our patrol, I figured about 10 hours to make the circuit. On our first break Brown broached the idea we were now far enough away, no one could see us. Take it easy and return just in time for supper? I flat told him no. The terrain made for a hard patrol. Again I heard from Brown. The BAR was too heavy, he could not go on. I traded weapons with him and continued making corrections on the map overlay. Brown wanted his weapon as we came in sight of our position. After chow, we were all tired, lying down on our bunks. Brown started more trouble. This time he didn't like sergeants, "They're all chicken shit and don't know their ass from a hole in the ground." He kept this up for several minutes. I expected his sqd ldr to rein him in. No such luck. Suddenly, Brown was standing directly over me. As most leaders know, personal space is a vital factor in leadership. The closer one is to a person, the more forceful he can be. Not knowing how violent or uncontrollable Brown might get, I erupted to my feet, placed my nose an inch from his forehead, a taut left finger prodding his chest, and with the other hand began a steady tap-tap on his chest. By touching him this way I could feel his body tense if he made a move. I then told Brown what he must do to survive in this platoon.

I would file charges and testify at his courts-martial. If you are acquitted, I will tend to you in a personal way which will make you wish we had never met. And, if he ever awakened us again with 'nightmares' or swung his BAR around the tent menacing us, I would figure him out of his mind, a danger to us all, and I would be forced to shoot him. Did he understand? He said he did. All he had to say was stop punching me with your finger. I told him he was a good soldier, but don't push it too far. That ended it. We got along fine after that. He later made Cpl as a BAR man. His sqd ldr was never promoted. I ended up as plt Sgt and finally as M/Sgt. It is said women like to gossip. They can't hold a candle to the men of a rifle company. It was all over the regiment by the next day. Later when I went to Rgmt'l HQ for promotion review, I was greeted by our CO, Col Noel Coxe who said, " Ah ha, Sgt Lynn. I know you. You're the plt Sgt. from K Company who has his own private woodshed. I have already approved your promotion. Keep up the good work."

Above. These three ROK squad leaders look 'rough and ready'. Their unit is unknown but they were in support of the 160th Regt. of the 40th Division during 1952. Photo by Roger Lueckenhoff.   Right. These G.I.s are viewing more 'Faces of War.' Another mass grave of murdered South Korean civilians.   Photo from the Internet.

Below After a battle for Hill 598 in the Kumwha area, these two G.I.s from the 31st Regt get patched up and enjoy a smoke. break. The ferocities of these battles were unbelievable, usually for land of little tactical value   National Archives.

Above. The 31st Tk Co. pulls in to Hudong-ni shortly before the Chinese attack, east of the Chosin Reservoir, Nov. 1950.   Photo by Beryl Williams.
Right. The port of Hungnam before evacuation and it's destruction by demolition and Navy gun fire.
Below. This LST load of 3rd Infantry Division troops were some of the last to leave Hungnam.
                Photos courtesy of the National Archives.

Chun Sun	None	Ma	K 1 116 319
First Name	MI	Last Name	Serial Number
None	Rifleman-1745	15 August 1925	Sergeant
Nickname	MOS	Birthday	Grade / Rank
HM/31/7		Aug 1948-Feb 1955	Kang Won Province, North Korea
Unit (s)		Duty Tour (s	Home Town
Navy Presidential Unit Citation with 2 stars			Presidential Unit Citation ROK
Medals & Awards			
Combat Infantry Badge(KATUSA)			ROK Equivalent of Purple Heart, 3 OLC

KATUSA

I was born in 1925 as third son to a small farmer in Kang Won Province. Our village, just east of Yang Yang, was in the mountainous coastal area of Korea near the East Sea. When Korea was divided at the 38th parallel after WW II, we became part of North Korea. Eighteen months of Communist rule convinced my father and mother they did not wish to live their lives or raise a family in a climate of fear and dogma. One night in January 1948 we packed, taking with us only what we could carry. We stole our way across the dividing line. Patrols in the area were spotty, not rigorous as they were later. We stayed with relatives for a time while my father determined how he would provide for his family. In Pusan, on my 23d birthday, I enlisted in the Army of the Republic of South Korea.

I served during the communist revolts in South Korea and the months after the Communist invasion. In 1950, I, with others of my division, was selected for transfer to KATUSA (Korean Army Troops with the United States Army). I was assigned to Heavy Mortar Company 31st Infantry. At first I was an ammo bearer. Then, at the battle of the Chosin Reservoir, we all became rifle soldiers as well as mortar men. In December, I was wounded and evacuated to 15th Army Hospital in Pusan. To my surprise, I was visited by Lt Wilson who took command after Capt Cody was killed. HM/31 was then near Taegu. The company was being rebuilt to combat strength after losses at Chosin Reservoir. When I rejoined the company in March, Captain Wilson told me I was to be his bodyguard. I later learned this duty was the result of commando raids by North Korean troops dressed in American uniforms, same as we of the Katusa. They knew the strength of American combat units in the war's early days was one third KATUSA. They used this knowledge to infiltrate HQs of several American units, selectively killing key officers in these attacks. The result was a HQ US Army decision that every American officer in a combat unit would have a Korean bodyguard assigned to him. I did my best for him as his bodyguard as I did for both Captain Campbell and Captain Goll later commanders of HM/31. I served 5 different company commanders of HM/31, I remember these three as they were good officers, highly respected by their men, American GIs and Katusa alike.

My job was to stay with, or close nearby, the company commander at all times, day or night. As a result, I learned to operate a radio as the company radio operator was also his constant companion. I did many things for all these company commanders as I was eager to make life easier for these men who had come so far from their homes to help us stay free of communist rule. I learned much also about American ways as did other Katusa soldiers, or ROKs as we were usually called. I think today as I look around and see the difference in our lives between 1950 and 2000, my countrymen and we as a nation, learned many things in that war from our American friends. Sometimes we had problems. R&R was set up for the American soldiers, giving them 5 days in Japan for rest and relaxation. At first we ROKs were not included. That did not last long. So many GIs complained that we were also given 5 days which we spent with our families in Korea. Another time 2 ROKS from HM/31 did not return from hospital after wounds. Big mistake. They were picked up by Korean MPs and assigned to a Korean Army punishment battalion. They lost honor and shamed the rest of us.

I was disheartened by the armistice talks in 1952. It would have been easier to negotiate peace with the communists if we held more "North" Korean territory. I was wounded again in summer 1952 but not as bad, returning to the company in October. Capt Goll was company commander. He spotted about 20 Chinese soldiers in a farmhouse. He asked for volunteers. I and several others took them prisoner. They were the remnants of a defeated unit. They were easy to capture. They put their hands up, glad to be prisoners. A little later I was wounded in the thigh. I pressed the wound together with my hands. I could barely climb but managed to get back to our trench. I returned to the company in February 1953. I was wounded again in the last battles of the war. I do not remember much about it. I regained consciousness in a hospital sometime in August of 1953. I was in convalescence until February 1955 when I was discharged from the Korean Army. I lost all records, letters, everything of a personal nature when I was wounded. My mortar company was gone. I could not remember my serial number, so was not eligible for service benefits. Capt Wilson came back to Korea in 1994 on a Revisit tour. He somehow located me from my serial number which he had kept. He gave it to me which has been of great help. We had written several times to each other. I lost his address when I was wounded. It was a long war for me.

RED DRAGON
The SECOND ROUND
FACES OF WAR II

Sung Sup	None	An	K1117168 Ret. 10 Dec 1955
First Name	MI	Last Name	Serial Number
None	Tank Rifleman	10 October 1922	S/Sgt, later M/Sgt
Nickname	MOS	Birthday	Grade / Rank
Tank Co 31st Inf 7th Div	16 Aug '50- May '54	Yeon Baek Gun Hwang Hae Do, No.Korea	
Unit (s)	Duty Tour (s)	Home Town	
Navy Presidential Unit Citation	Republic of Korea Presidential Unit Citation		
Medals & Awards			
Combat Infantry Badge(KATUSA)	ROK equivalent of Purple Heart, OLC		

KATUSA COMRADES IN WAR AND PEACE

I first met my friend and comrade Ma Chun Sun after enlisting in the Army of South Korea on 16 August 1950. He had already served two years in the South Korean Army. He enlisted about six months after fleeing the cruel dictatorship of Kim Il Sung in January 1948. I left North Korea on the advice of my father. "Go to South Korea before all trails at the 38th parallel are guarded!" I made the journey alone as young children and an ailing mother prevented my father from attempting an escape with all the family. When I came to Pusan ahead of the invading army of North Korea, I decided that honor, and a strong distaste for communism, required that I do my best to defend my new country. Unknowingly, I had enlisted just as men were being selected as KATUSAs to serve alongside American soldiers in US Regular Army units. These units were all one third under strength in manpower. We KATUSA were to furnish the one man of every three that brought these American fighting units up to combat strength. A number of men had been selected from Regular South Korean army units to be sent to American units as 'stiffeners' for the raw recruits. I was lucky enough to be in a group with one of these trained South Korean soldiers. His name was Ma Chun Sun. His accent was also North Korean. This common bond helped better acquaintance and strengthened as we learned we came from the same general area of North Korea. We hoped to be assigned together. That was not to be. While we were both posted to the US 7th Division's 31st Infantry Regiment, he went to Heavy Mortar Company. I was assigned as a rifleman to Tank Company. We were immediately taken to Japan for training.

We had three weeks of infantry training at Camp Gotemba on Mt Fuji. I learned to fire an American M-1 rifle. We landed at Inchon on Sept 15, 1950. My introduction to war as a rifleman was with 31st Tank Company in the taking of Suwon and Osan-ni. I learned much from the American soldiers of the Tank Company. At first, many GIs were cautious in their relationships but as they noticed I fired my M-1 at the enemy at every opportunity, they became more friendly and open. The North Koreans around Suwon and Osan fought from the vantage point of the low hills in the area. American infantry action plus point blank cannon fire of our tanks soon finished them off. This enemy force was the remnant of the highly trained NK 105th Armored Division which fought on the Naktong Perimeter. Returning to Pusan we took ship for landing at Ree Won, North Korea on the East Sea. We pushed northward, taking Poongsan, Cheolsan, Bukcheong and other towns in our northward drive. In late November we were sent to the Chang Jin Reservoir.

The terrible, frozen battles at Chang Jin lasted 17 days. It was my first experience with the human wave tactics of the Chinese Army. We were pushed back, and then back again. I was with the group that had to hold the enemy line for 2 weeks, surviving only because food and ammunition were dropped to us by airplane. We finally had to give up Changjin and retreat through the Hwang Cheol Ryung Pass under continuous attack by the Chinese Army. It took us five days of fighting to reach the outskirts of Heungnam. Troops of another American division were holding the Chinese away from the harbor. We were ordered to make a complete retreat from Heungnam the next day. I cried in despair as I watched the city go up in flames. The isolated Chang Jin area, breaking of the Chinese siege lines, the fighting retreat through the Hwang Cheol Ryung Pass while under continuous Chinese attack, the freezing cold, the death of so many fellow soldiers, all of these never leave my memories. Ma and I in our old age often think and talk of these things.

7th Division HQs was set up at Yeongcheon, Kyunbuk in January 1951. We went there. I spent the next two years in front line fighting barely surviving the shadow of death during those two and one half years of yo-yo war and trench battles that followed while the arguments went on at Panmunjom. Then on July 27,1953 the fighting stopped at the front line in accordance with the truce signed by both sides. North Korea now holds a small piece of South Korea. South Korea has a bigger chunk of mountainous North Korea. War deaths were over three million people. In contrast to the North, South Korea is well fed, happy and prosperous. Today, near the end of my life, I have no idea about my family members. My wife died during the war. I have only a daughter who I believe survived the war. I wish only to hear from them, particularly my daughter to wish her a very happy life. My parents are probably dead. I would like to bury the happy days of my childhood and the lost war days of my youth at my mother's and father's grave site if I could be allowed a visit to North Korea to mourn. For me the Korean War has not ended. The hurt is there. It will never end as long as I live.

Above. This sector of the MLR in the Kumwha-Kumsong area became painfully familiar to members of the 223rd Regt. of the 40th Inf. Div. The valley with its 2 bridges would be the site of numerous patrols and even more numerous casualties. Below. Don Gardner with G Co. 223rd Regt. of the 40th Inf Div adjusts his 60mm mortar. The 60mm mortar was available as close up 'artillery' support for the rifle infantry. It was in constant demand. Below Right. Even in reserve there was no escape from the weather. Even wading in a sea of mud beat life on the MLR.   All photos by Don Gardner.

RED DRAGON
The SECOND ROUND
FACES OF WAR II

Donald	F.	Gardner	RA 17 289 234
First Name	MI	Last Name	Serial Number
"Don"	745	27 Sep 1930	Sgt
Nickname	MOS	Birthday	Grade / Rank
G/223/40th Inf Div		Jan '52-Sept '52	Aurora, MO
Unit (s)		Duty Tour (s)	Home Town
Combat Infantry Badge	Good Conduct Medal	KCSM, oneBronze star	ROK PUC
Medals & Awards			
Japan Occupn Medal	Nat'l Defense Service Medal	UN Medal	ROK Peace Medal

PATROL ACTION ON THE MLR

G Company 223d Infantry 40th Div relieved elements of the 24th Division early January 1952. It was cold, temperatures well below 20 F, lots of snow. I served as gunner on a 60mm mortar team. We were north of Kumwha on the MLR. I was always cold during the two months we spent there. It was a position correspondents called a "Static Line," although the rifle companies involved in constant probing and ambush patrols did not agree. One night we were ordered to fire flares from our mortars. They illuminated an ongoing fire fight with a probing Chinese patrol. The next morning we retrieved the body of a young girl from that Chinese patrol. Papers found on her identified her as a member of the "Chinese Comfort Corps." Why she was with a Chinese patrol only Buddha knew.

We were relieved after 2 months on the line, first shower and clean clothing in 61 days. What a wonderful feeling to be clean again! It made me realize what treasures such simple amenities really are. After 2 weeks rest in reserve we hoofed it to new positions overlooking the Kumsong valley. The rifle squads resumed probing and ambush patrols which seemingly lead nowhere except to an increased casualty count of dead and wounded. One night we received orders to fire flares. We were located about 100 yards behind the 2d platoon point, fire orders were canceled within seconds before we could act on them. We then went on 100% alert as a Chinese patrol had broken through our lines. My buddy Shenton was killed by a WP grenade. Another friend was strangled. My friend White Wolf and his foxhole buddy were cornered in a bunker by heavy automatic weapons fire. They had been on the "northeast wall" and initially were not involved. Crawling out of the bunker, they dived into a foxhole. Their intense return fire stopped the Chinks cold. If they had not done so, our mortar squad was next on their shopping list. Next morning, just yards from us, I found a 9 mm pistol. It became a personal sidearm, supplementing a .30 cal carbine, my TO&E weapon. Shenton was scheduled to rotate that day. His orders had been cut. Another 12 hours would have seen him safely home. Such is the irony of war.

While in the Kumsong valley, my home town buddy Ted Perry was wounded as were several others during their 'ambush' patrol. He stepped on a mine laid by the Chinese during a 5 day "truce." A late April highlight was the assault made by the 140th Tank Bn on Chicom positions in the Kumsong Valley. The Chinese incoming artillery fire was heavy and accurate. One tank was knocked out. Sparks flew like a 4th of July pinwheel. G Company was pulled off the MLR in late May, or was it early June of '52? I've lost track. Our squad drew assignment of a combat patrol from our 'blocking' position. In late evening we set out. At 2 AM we came under artillery fire. We had been spotted, but escaped without casualties. 14 June a Fox company Reconn group trained for a prisoner of war 'snatch' mission by Major McCroy, our 2d Bn CO, raided on a hill near a 2d Bn outpost position. This stirred a Chinese hornets nest. Their artillery made it rough for us for several hours. I got so I could count the shells from a nearby Chinese mountain gun which had a distinctive sound when fired. With nothing better to do it kept my mind off the reason they were shooting at me! On another occasion, Carl Wiest and I were ordered to take up positions behind the OP to intercept 'possible friendly line crossers.' A very unpleasant duty. Wait, ask questions of 'possible friendly line crossers,' get shot for your pains! A difficult decision to make.

Anyway, we did as ordered. We were spotted and drew a barrage of mortar fire. Neither of us had a deed of ownership in that foxhole. We hightailed it out of there, hitting the dirt again and again as mortar shells exploded. The air was filled with shrapnel. Luckily we made it back to our squad. Nothing like fleet feet! We never did learn if the 'possible friendly line crossers' spoke English, or if they tried to cross the MLR. We broke it off at dawn. Before we reached the truck taking us back, a couple of rocket launcher jeeps arrived, launched their rockets and sped away. Those rockets made the Chinese go berserk. We heard the thump of distant mortars as they 'walked' their shells toward our truck. We made a dead run for the truck and got away. Another time, our plat ldr, plat sgt and myself went to the outpost to survey positions. We were all nervous wrecks by the time we finished. Thankfully, Bn scrapped those plans. The Bn moved further south. I rotated in September of '52. It was difficult to say goodby to the men I had soldiered with, good friends, comrades all. We had trained and fought together in the US, Japan and Korea since Oct 1950. But who could or would turn down a chance to go home? My hat is off to those magnificent young men of G Company, citizen soldiers of the USA.

Above. Tanks are assaulting Chinese positions in the Kumsong Valley area. Tank positions are marked just past the railroad bridge in the lower foreground in front of the 223rd Regt, Spring of 1952. Photo courtesy of Don Gardner.   Left. A Marine shows the value of the 'flak jacket' that began to be issued to troops in early 1952.

Archives Photo.

Below. Survivors of the Jane Russell and Triangle Hills battles of Oct. 14-15 gather in a reserve position to honor their fallen buddies. The 31st Regt. lost heavily in this battle.   Photo by D. E. Schoenwetter.

RED DRAGON
The SECOND ROUND
FACES OF WAR II

David	B.	Bleak	RA 19 344 416
First Name	MI	Last Name	Serial Number
Doc	Aidman	27 February 1932	Sergeant
Nickname	MOS	Birthday	Grade / Rank
Medical Co, 223d Inf 40th Div		Dec '51- June '52	Idaho Falls, ID
Unit (s)		Duty Tour (s)	Home Town

Congressional Medal of Honor   Purple Heart   Combat Medical Badge   Korean War Svc Medal

Medals & Awards

Korean Campaign Service Medal, 2 **   National Defense Service Medal   United Nations Medal

FIGHTING MEDIC IS AWARDED CONGRESSIONAL MEDAL OF HONOR

I enlisted at age 18 just prior to the start of the Korean War. We were to some degree, allowed to choose a duty assignment. It made sense to me to choose the Medical Department, both from a humanitarian viewpoint, and to learn skills useful in later civilian life as a meaningful occupation. After finishing my basic training, I was given additional instruction in advanced medical aid procedures. With my country now at war as a result of the North Korean invasion of South Korea, these studies were both appropriate and timely.

I was assigned as an Aid Man to the 223d Infantry Regiment, 40th Infantry Division, California National Guard when it was reactivated for service during the Korean War. The 223d Inf Regt was one of the three Inf Regts in the Division, the other two regiments were the 160th and the 224th. The Division trained in Japan for about 8 months before we were alerted for shipment to Korea. We arrived in Korea the first week of January 1952. For the next five months I had the usual duties of a medic assigned as an aid man to a rifle company. Some experiences were downright harrowing, particularly the night patrols under the glare of spotlights used to illuminate no mans land and the enemy positions. There were times when I was really scared, but that was usually after the action was finished.

Fear is what keeps men alive. But there are other kinds of fear, fear of being wounded, fear of blindness or paralysis. Probably the greatest fear of all is the fear of getting other soldiers killed by lack of knowledge, or if supplies and equipment are not available to properly care for our wounded. Not enough medics, not enough litters, not enough morphine, the list is endless in the mind of a combat medic. It all came together the night of 14 June 1952 near Minari-gol in North Korea. I was the aid man on a night patrol sent out to capture an enemy soldier for interrogation. We had gained a hill crest under intense enemy fire, suffering several casualties.

We then came under fire from several enemy hidden in a partially demolished trench. I was trying to evacuate a wounded GI when we were rushed by these men. In adrenalin driven desperation, I was able to kill two of them with my bare hands, finishing off the third man with my trench knife. Two other North Koreans with fixed bayonets ran at us. I grabbed them, knocked their heads together and continued down hill helping my wounded man. It was not a question of running, it was my job to get that wounded man back. I never stopped to think. At that point I was not a reasoning person. Had I been, I would probably be dead.

CITATION OF THE CONGRESSIONAL MEDAL OF HONOR

Rank and Organization: David B. Bleak Sergeant, US Army Medical Company 223d Infantry Regiment, 40th Infantry Division. Place and date: Vicinity of Minari-gol, Korea 14 June 1952. Entered service Shelley, ID. Born 27 February 1932, Idaho Falls, ID.

General Order No. 83 2 November 1953 Department of the Army

Sgt. Bleak, a member of the Medical Company, distinguished himself by conspicuous gallantry and indomitable courage above and beyond the call of duty in action against the enemy. As a medical aidman he volunteered to accompany a reconnaissance patrol committed to engage the enemy and capture a prisoner for interrogation. Forging up the rugged slope of the key terrain, the group was subjected to intense automatic weapons and small arms fire and suffered several casualties. After administering to the wounded he continued to advance with the patrol. Nearing the military crest of the hill, while attempting to cross the fire swept area, he came under fire from a small group concealed in a trench. Entering the trench he closed with the enemy, killed two with his bare hands and a third with his trench knife. Moving from the emplacement, he saw a concussion grenade fall in front of a companion and, quickly shifting his position, he shielded the man from the impact of the blast. Later, while administering to the wounded, he was struck by a hostile bullet but, despite the wound, he undertook to evacuate a wounded comrade. As he moved down hill with his heavy burden, he was attacked by 2 enemy soldiers with fixed bayonets. Closing with the aggressors, he grabbed them and smacked their heads together, then carried his helpless comrade down the hill to safety. Sgt. Bleak's dauntless courage and intrepid actions reflect utmost credit on himself and are in keeping with the honored traditions of the military service.

RED DRAGON
The SECOND ROUND
FACES OF WAR II

George	F.	Bray	RA 16 355 179
First Name	MI	Last Name	Serial Number
None	1745	11 April 1932	Cpl
Nickname	MOS	Birthday	Grade / Rank
/180/45		Dec '51-Sept '52	West Branch, MI
Unit (s)		Duty Tour (s)	Home Town

Combat Infantry Badge	Good Conduct Medal	OM-J	UN Medal	ROK PUC
Medals & Awards				

Korean Campaign Service Medal, 2stars   NDSM   Korean War Service Medal

TWO DAYS ON OLD BALDY

We had just received word that we were to replace "A" Company on 'Old Baldy'. "A" Co had spent the previous night there, suffering heavy casualties from intense mortar and artillery fire. Now it was our turn in the barrel. I was a BAR man in the 1st squad 2d plat, "B" Company, 180th Inf Regt, 45th Div. My good friend George Lampron was Asst BAR man. It was the morning of 8 June 1952. "A" was coming down the hill as we went up. There were more of us than of them. When we arrived at our area, our Lt assigned George and me to a position out on a finger on the front slope of 'Old Baldy'. Looking it over, I told George, "We have to dig this hole bigger and deeper. It looks like a good place for tanks to come up." We spent a lot of energy and sweat in the process. Our Lt came by a couple of times to check. As darkness covered the valley floor, Chinese flares lit up the darkening sky, signaling their artillery to open up. We not only got artillery and mortar fire, but insult added to injury. A Chinese captured US 75mm recoilless rifle started shooting at us. We could see the gun crew as they fired. Suddenly, it quieted. The Lt came by our new, deep hole and told us, "Fix bayonets. They will open up again, and their infantry will be right behind." George had broken his bayonet two days past and was quite worried.

The Lt was right. Chinese artillery resumed the barrage, artillery, mortars and tracers were flying everywhere. The Chinese infantry came up the slope in the midst of their own artillery! 1st and 3d platoons were hit hardest, their positions overrun by masses of Chinese infantry. A bunch of people came in behind us. We couldn't shoot because in the chaos of battle and darkness we could not tell if they were our men or Chinese. They got as close as 20 feet. We could see their outline against the skyline. We laid doggo until they left. Shelling continued most of the night. At daylight the Chinese artillery went silent. The Lt came to us and said, "We have to clear the hill." We formed a skirmish line and reached the crest. The Chinese were picking up rifles, ammo and anything else that was loose. They did not spot us until we opened up on them. There were eight Chinese running across the hill. I emptied a full magazine at each of them. Other GIs were firing as well. The Chinese, those that were able, ran off. "Old Baldy" was ours again. We found a man from the 1st plat, Cpl Elmer Scott of Nunica, MI. He was dead, hands tied with commo wire. He was a big man, well liked by his men. He had a real fighting spirit. His size was apparently too much for the Chinese to handle him as a prisoner. George Smrcina and I saw another body with hands tied with commo wire. It was T/Sgt Jerome F. Sears of Portland, OR. He was a platoon sergeant of either 1st or 3d platoon. He has been taken prisoner also, then shot in cold blood. We brought back his body.

I looked back and saw a Chinese soldier get out of hole and start to run. He was about 40 yards from us. Three of us with BARs opened up on him. The last we saw of him was his cap flying through the air. We backed off the top of 'Old Baldy" and tried to get some rest as we had to hold the hill for another night. Our Company was down to about 85 men. We had started the day before as a reinforced company of 205 men. The 3d Bn had assigned a squad from "I" Co and also a squad from "K" Co, another 20 men to beef us up. There were never a lot of men left to spend their retirement in an old soldier's home after a few days tour on 'Old Baldy'.

The Lt told us to go to the top of the hill so the Chinese could see us digging in on the forward slope. After dark as they opened up with artillery, we were to come back to the reverse slope where we were well dug in with plenty of ammo. After dark it began again. We faded back and let the Chinese plaster our vacated positions. The Chinese came over the crest, tossing grenades. Some of their English speakers yelled "Medic! Medic!", hoping to entice our medics into the killing ground. The shelling began anew. Mortars rained down, one so close I thought it would impact in our hole. I tried to curl up into my helmet, but it hit about 15 feet away. Dirt and fire came into the hole with us. Something hit me on the shoulder. I thought I was dead, but it was only a piece of a pack board used for carrying ammo that hit me. George Lampron said. "I saw fire and my eyes were closed! I must have seen it through my mouth!" Shelling all night long. When daylight came, we went back to the hilltop again. There were no Chinese on the hill that morning. Guess the Chinese thought we bugged out. They did not stay to receive American artillery fire on 'our' hilltop.

Editorial note: A National Guard Armory in Portland, Oregon is named in honor of Sergeant Jerome F. Sears, awarded the Distinguished Service Cross for valor. Elmer A. Scott of Nunica, Michigan was awarded the Silver Star in the same action.

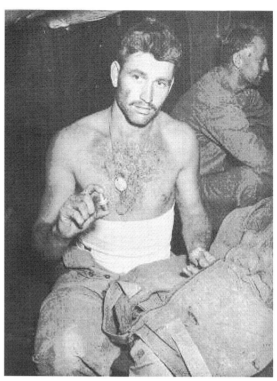

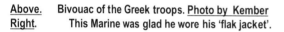

Above.   Bivouac of the Greek troops. <u>Photo by Kember</u>
Right.   This Marine was glad he wore his 'flak jacket'.

Bottom   Australian troops are treated for wounds after
returning from Operation Buffalo in the Samichon Valley,
14 August, 1952.   <u>Two photos fromNational Archives</u>.

RED DRAGON
The SECOND ROUND
FACES OF WAR II

Walter	NMI	Kosowan	SH 61 721
First Name	MI	Last Name	Serial Number
Wally	Rifleman, Admin Clerk, RT Opr	16 July 1930	PTE (Private)
Nickname	MOS	Birthday	Grade / Rank
54Tpt Coy, 2d Royal Cdn Regt 2 CAU		May'51-Aug'52	Kapuskasing,Ont., Canada
Unit (s)		Duty Tour (s)	Home Town
United Nations Service Medal		Korea Service Medal	Canadian Korea Service Medal
Medals & Awards			
125th Anniversary Medal, Canada		Republic of Korea War Service Medal	Korea 50 Medal

CAREER CANADIAN SOLDIER IN KOREA

In my early youth I decided to make the Canadian Regular Army my career. Accordingly, I enlisted in early 1950 and was assigned to 54 Transport Company as a clerk, administrative. Canadian forces destined for duty in the Korean War trained at Ft Lewis, WA. I was 'loaned', or as the Americans have it, placed on TDY with 2 Battalion Support Company, Royal Canadian Regiment as Company Clerk. We sailed out of Seattle in April, landing in Korea in May 1951. Korea was a foreign land to all of us, not only in geography but in the stench of the rice paddy fields and the sad sights of a war torn country. In the spring of the second year of the war, starving refugees were everywhere, uprooted from their homes on farms, in villages and cities, by the fury of battling armies surging to and fro over their pain wracked country. The worst sights were the starving children whose scrawny chests and protruding ribs were not concealed by their ragged garb. Most of us shared rations with these kids. Conscience would allow us to do no less.

My first war scare was as guard on an ammunition train passing through a guerilla infested area under black out conditions. The rail line for a short distance paralleled the fighting front. It was my first experience as a soldier. In June I was transferred to C Coy as a rifleman. On a tough 4 day patrol assignment, I found I was a quick learner, spurred by a spray of bullets kicking up at my feet. In one instance, while I was 2d on the Bren gun, we came under sudden fire. In primal urge to seek cover, I lost my footing, sending us tumbling down hill. Enemy bullets shot the pistol grip off the Bren and nicked the barrel. My next assignment was as C Company radio operator under the command of Capt Hayes. It was my duty to keep in contact with radio operators of night patrols, talking to them as their units were engaged by the enemy. I took reports of losses from other operators conveying their agony and fear as they spoke in the midst of hot combat. I became well acquainted with many of the men in the company over the radio, although I may not have recognized them in person. It was a harrowing experience receiving these messages from men, some of whom never returned. While it did not place me in personal danger it was nerve-racking just to experience their danger on a second-hand basis. At the Chorwon Reservoir on the Central Front we took high losses in A Company. Many refugees heading south came through our lines in that area. An American P-51 plane was shot down, ditching in the Chorwon Reservoir. He was rescued to fly another day.

In that area, some enemy shelling seemed to be fired on a time schedule. We could set our watches by Charlie Chan's morning salvo. He began his day firing from the vicinity of 'Old Smoky.' In September I was sent to Japan to be instructed as a senior radio operator. Instead of being returned to Korea, I was assigned to administrative clerk duties in the Canadian HQ in Japan. I remained in that job until March of 1952 at which time I was sent back to Korea and attached to US Eighth Army Headquarters in the Adjutant General's Casualty Section. My main duty was working in Pusan with the US Army Graves Registration Unit. It was a quite thrill to me as a Canadian Army private to be able to liaise with the staff from 8th Army HQ. I met many fine US soldiers, one I particularly recall as "Ron" from California. Would sure like to see him again. I returned home from Korea in August 1952, remaining in the Canadian Army, re-enlisting in 1953. Taking my release from the Canadian Forces in 1977, I enlisted in the Royal Canadian Mounted Police, serving 13 years as a Special Constable and telecommunications operator in Toronto. I finally attained a major goal in my life. I retired after 40 years of service, whole of limb, sound of sight, in good health ,looking forward to enjoy years of retirement still ahead.

I had the privilege of a "Korea Revisit" as a guest of South Korea in 2000. The most heart stopping moment was our tour of the Cemetery in Pusan. The sight of those graves recalled 1952 memories of buddies whose names I had registered in that cemetery. The memory brought tears to my eyes. Another vivid memory was the sight of classes of school children on tours of the memorials being told about the Korean War. They listened intently and were incredibly well behaved. Our final trip to Kapyong caused many of our group to relive their experiences of that brutal battle that cost the lives of many Canadian soldiers. I have also attended the US Korean War Memorial in Washington, DC. We Canadians were given a marvelous reception by our American veteran friends. Our Canadian Memorial in Brampton is also an impressive sight, truly a fine memorial to our fallen brothers-in-arms. I was young, well trained as a soldier. I have always thanked God for a safe return, and said a prayer for comrades left behind in the hills of Korea.

Above.. The value of the 71/2 pound armored vest is shown by this vest that stopped 78 grenade fragments. <u>Photo courtesy Jack Doyle</u>. <u>Right</u>. G.I. holds the vest that saved his life. He still received minor wounds to unprotected areas, but his life was undoubtedly saved by the new vests. <u>Photo from the National Archives</u>. <u>Below</u>. The use of helicopters to evacuate the wounded to rear area hospitals for quick attention to their wounds was another major factor in improving the soldiers chances for survival. <u>Photo courtesy of the National Archives</u>.

RED DRAGON
The SECOND ROUND
FACES OF WAR II

Jacques	K.	Doyle	US 51 048 085
First Name	MI	Last Name	Serial Number
Jack	1745	25 February 1928	Sgt(T)
Nickname	MOS	Birthday	Grade / Rank
179th Inf 45th Division, NG		Dec 1951-Aug 1952	Binghamton, NY
Unit (s)		Duty Tour (s)	Home Town

Combat Infantry Badge   Purple Heart   KCSM, 3 stars   United Nations Service Medal

Medals & Awards

Occupation Medal, Japan   New York State Medal for Korean Svc   ROK 50th Anniversary Medal

January 26, 2003 ARMORED VEST

Early June of 1952, the 179 Inf Regt was issued a number of the new armored vests. Twenty vests were issued to each rifle company to be tested under field combat conditions. We were then engaged in a dogged battle for an objective north of Chorwon. Despite the heat and the rugged terrain, the 7½ lb weight of the vest didn't seem to bother the men wearing them. The weight of the vest was evenly distributed. To men inured in carrying a heavy army pack for miles on end, 7½ lbs was a mere bagatelle. The designers of the vest had done a very good job. In the minds of the men chosen to test them, the likelihood that the vest gave a better chance of survival was probably the uppermost thought in their minds. Some men refused to give them up. Others gave them to a buddy for safekeeping, then claimed they had been lost. Some men wore them continuously for as long as 10 days, even while sleeping.

Their worth was soon proven. Pfc Albert LaPlante's life was saved. His vest took 78 metal grenade fragments which, in chest and abdomen, would undoubtedly have killed him. He suffered arm and leg wounds, but only one minor shard penetrated his vest. One man took a missile in the chest which penetrated the vest but lodged in a pocket Bible he carried over his heart. A nearby Signal Corps photographer was heard to remark, "The Good Lord helps those who help themselves." The GI: "Issue them to every man!"

My company was ordered to occupy Baldy in mid June. We had used this outlying outpost for patrols only up to this point. Hill 223, next to Baldy was a Chinese strong point. We had routinely set up a reverse slope defense on Baldy during the night, occupying the crest only during daylight hours. On 21 June the Chinese decided to stay on the hilltop. As squad ldr, I took my 2 BAR teams of 2 men each to accompany two rifle squads. We went back up to sweep the hilltop free of Chinese. I placed my 2 BAR teams in bunkers and made my way to the left of the hilltop to case the situation. I found a bunker manned by a Sgt Loiselle and Pvt Zakrzeski. Loiselle was on the phone talking to a Pvt Bennett who was acting as a lookout. "Some Chinese are walking toward me," radioed Bennett.

"Shoot a couple of rounds, comeback and join us," ordered Sgt Loiselle. We heard Bennett's M-1 bark a few rounds, shortly he tumbled down on top of us. A fourth man was sitting on a dirt shelf below the sandbagged roof of the bunker. They were the 4 man crew of a .30 cal LMG. The soldier on the shelf asked me my name and how long I had been in Korea. I told him, "Sgt Doyle, 2d plat, 7 months." He seemed frightened, responding in an unsteady voice, "Two months for me." He showed me a picture of his wife, two photos in a glass frame. "We were married two months before I came to Korea." I thought it risky to have glass in a breast pocket, but this was neither time or place for a safety lecture. He wore a protective vest. An extra vest lay on the sandbags. He asked me to pass it to him. He wrapped it around his upper legs and huddled as close to the dirt wall as his helmet and two vests would permit.

I was called to assemble my 2 BAR teams to line up with the 2 rifle squads on the right of Baldy. I reluctantly left the shelter of the machine gun bunker and collected my squad. We swept up toward the crest of the hill, pushing the Chinese before us. The Chinese retreated to manned positions along the crest and on their own side of Baldy. Chinese mortar fire now increased in tempo as well as direct small arms fire from the well fortified hill behind Baldy. Grenades from the entrenched Chinese above us wounded several men. Our small "sweep" unit of half platoon size broke up under this concentration of enemy fire. I was one of the men wounded as was one of my BAR men. With assistance from those in the "sweep" group, we made it back to an Aid Station. We were evacuated to a MASH hospital. While there, I learned from another wounded man the machine gun bunker had taken a direct hit that morning.

All four men died instantly. It was probably an 82 mm mortar. There were certainly enough of them being fired at us before we halted our attack sweep. When the bodies were carried out, it was noticed that one body had a second vest wrapped around its upper legs. The death of all four men was a tragedy to all of us, and more so to their families back home. The recently married man with the glass framed pictures of his new bride was in my mind the greatest tragedy of all. The hopes for the life they intended to build together were dashed almost as soon as they were born. War never fails to portion out a full supply of tragedy to its participants. Quoting John Milton, "They also serve who only stand and wait." Small solace to a young widow, but an oft repeated epitaph of war.

Above Left.   Wounded GIs of the 279th Regiment of the 45th Infantry Division are carried off of Old Baldy during the fierce battles of July 1952.   Above Right.   Sgt. Boyed Burnley by his foxhole near Old Baldy, June 1952. Below.   The site of some of the bloodiest fighting in Korea during 1952 took place here at Old Baldy.

All photos courtesy of Boyed H. Burnley.

RED DRAGON
The SECOND ROUND
FACES OF WAR II

Boyed	H.	Burnley	US 52 020 440
First Name	MI	Last Name	Serial Number
"Doc"	3666	11 March 1928	S/Sgt
Nickname	MOS	Birthday	Grade / Rank
Atchd L/279/45		28 Dec'51-7 Jul'52	Lynchburg, VA
Unit (s)		Duty Tour (s)	Home Town
Combat Medical Badge	Good Conduct Medal	KCSM with 2 stars	ROK PUC & KWSM
Medals & Awards			
Occupation Medal (Japan)		National Defense Service Medal	United Nations Svc Medal

MY LAST WEEK IN THE LAND OF THE MORNING CALM

The date was 30 June '52. After more than 30 days of intensive fighting, the 279th had been pulled off line for a much deserved rest. We bivouacked in a rice paddy 2 miles south of our old MLR position at Hill 324. The old army adage about "Being in reserve is not the safest place to be" was to be proven correct. At 0100, our first day of 'rest' was shattered by a phone call to Capt Rose, CO of Love company 279/45. We were to be attached to 1st Bn 179/45. He and the NCOs proceeded to our positions of late April where 1st Bn 279th had been on line. On arrival, he was greeted by the remnants of "A" and "C" companies, all that remained of 1st Bn 179th. The company sized outpost on "Old Baldy" had been chewing up rifle companies at a horrendous rate. L/3/279 left the rest area next morning after a night of 'rest.' It was late morning as we reached our designated MLR position. The rest of the Bn arrived shortly.

Item company under Lt Dennis J. Harrison took position on "Old Baldy" with the CP set on Hill 226. "K" was on the MLR to our left. A tank platoon was in a paddy just SE of "Old Baldy" to support us with cannon and MG fire. On 2 July, Capt Rose and the plat ldrs gathered to plan for relief of Item Co. 3 Jul, Capt Rose received orders to relieve "I" company at 0200 hours on 4 July. 2d Plat under Lt Herring was designated Bn reserve, in addition to holding the center of the Bn position on the MLR. That afternoon the Chinks began registration fire on the MLR, Hill 226 and "Old Baldy." Their objective was apparent. They planned to isolate "Old Baldy" by interdiction fire on our MLR supply routes. About 2200 hours 3 July, Chinese artillery opened up with TOT fire that literally shook the ground. "Time On Target" fire is an artillery term for cannon fire from all available guns hitting the target at the same time.

If you are on the receiving end, it makes you wish you were home, safe with the civilians! Very accurate 120mm cannon fire from Russian made tanks was aimed at MLR approach routes to prevent reinforcement from reaching Item company. Love company was firing all available weapons in continuous fusillade on the flanks of "Old Baldy" in support of Item company. Company cooks were swabbing down mortar tubes to prevent premature fire. Mortar bombs in continuous fire mode were rapidly dropped into the tubes. All units were firing everything they had. It was a cacophony of continuous noise. The Chinks were assaulting in continuous waves from the direction of Hill 228. Half carried weapons, others picked up weapons of the dead and wounded to continue the attack.

The radio antenna of "I" company radio was shot off. Love company could hear "I" transmissions and relayed them to 3d Bn. All wire phone lines had been cut by artillery. In spite of limited communication, we had 279th FA, 45th DivArty, and I Corps Artillery in fire support. Our planes dropped flares. At 2300, the 2d Plat under Lt Herring, reinforced Hill 226. On the way up, George Washington, the favorite Bn GI, fell into a hole, badly spraining his ankle. He refused to quit, insisted on lugging his BAR. At 0100 on 4 July, the 3 rifle squads of 2d plat moved up the back slope of "Old Baldy" proceeding to the right, keeping down slope 20 yards from the ridge crest to avoid intense incoming artillery fire. They arrived in the nick of time, as they crested the ridge top, all of "I" company on the forward slope was under heavy attack, about to be overrun. The Chinese attack was stopped cold. They withdrew at 0230.

The platoon of "I" company on the right flank had but one unwounded man among the few wounded men still able to fight. "I" company KIA's littered the fighting positions. The plat ldr was wounded but still capable of command. When the remainder of Love company arrived at 0500, the area was still under heavy mortar fire. All bunkers had collapsed. Love company men, in digging them out looking for wounded, found nothing but dead GIs. There were 30 dead Chinks in the perimeter, but in the saddle NW toward Hill 228 there was a virtual carpet of Chinese dead. Capt Rose said you could walk the entire 100 yard on bodies, and never step on dirt.

Love company was on "Old Baldy" for 4 more days. We were hit again, but their heart was not in it. They quit before we could weave their soldiers into a second gray uniformed carpet covering the Korean soil. This was a tough, hard battle, our losses were high. "I" company was almost kaput. We in Love company and Bn special troops suffered heavy casualties, but in sum, dealt far more death than we received. "K" company relieved Love company on 8 July. On 10 July, Love Co. was pulled off line to rest after 10 days fierce combat. My job as medic never let up in those 8 days before I was evacuated on 7 July as another of the many wounded men in that climactic battle for "Old Baldy," a Korean hill, useless, except as a political symbol. Another 10 days in the life of a soldier.

Above. The Chinese Armies enter the war with overwhelming numbers. After the initial shock these Marines at Yudam-ni re-group and start their epic battle to the sea. Nov.-Dec. 1950.　　　Photo courtesy of the National Archives.
Below.　The USS Valley Forge and the USS Leyte in Sasebo for supplies, 1950.　　　Photo from National Archives.

RED DRAGON
The SECOND ROUND
FACES OF WAR II

Robert	A.	Gannon	1194790 USMC
First Name	MI	Last Name	Serial Number
Presley	6511	7 Nov 1932	Sgt
Nickname	MOS	Birthday	Grade / Rank
VMA 132		June 1952-June 1953	Clinton, MA
Unit (s)		Duty Tour (s)	Home Town

Navy Presidential Unit Citation, Navy Unit Citation, Good Conduct Medal, UN Service Medal

Medals & Awards

Korean Service Medal, 3 stars   National Defense Medal   Korean War Service Medal   ROK PUC

MEMORY IS AN OCEAN

A single memory of war service for those who served in Korea would be like touching a single wave in the ocean. It is not one wave or one memory that make up the seas of experience. They must be taken as a whole to feel their power. Likewise, my memories are molded by all with whom I served. I came ashore in Korea over the beach at Inchon. Had I done so in the original invasion, I might have had justifiable bragging rights. However my June 1952 landing came much later, in stark contrast to that September day in 1950 when Lt Baldomero Lopez led his platoon over the seawall and down a road ending in a posthumous Medal of Honor. It was a gloomy day when I first stepped on Korean soil. The skies were weeping over a nation in conflict. My first impression of Korea was not a positive one when I saw a small mountain of seabags awaiting transport. Being a Marine, I thought of them as sea bags, but they could as well have been Army duffle bags. The terms are used interchangeably, just as marine and soldier are often interchangeable. Regardless of identity, those rain soaked canvas bags introduced me to the reality of fighting in Korea. This was a place where brave men died, where their meager worldly possessions were dumped into a ship's hold for return to their grieving families.

A few weeks later things got more personal. I ran into a boot camp buddy who told me another Marine from our old platoon had been killed. The three of us had enlisted together and spent our last day of freedom in Boston prior to departing for Parris Island. We wandered through the fabled Scollay Square, three small town boys in the big city. I was lucky, very lucky. I was in Korea but a few months before I was sent to sea aboard an aircraft carrier, the USS Sicily. I left Korea with nothing but a few scratches and a mild hearing loss. I was safely out of danger, but many friends were not. I lost another one in September 1952. Friends are lost in war.

The mood was almost festive on the day I left Japan for the last time. Two incidents brought me back to reality. I was surprised to find that members of all services and their dependents were also aboard the ship. A year earlier I had sailed from San Diego with a replacement draft of 3000 Marines. There were just 300 of us making the return trip. I couldn't help but wonder what had happened to the other 2700 men. Some of course, may have extended their tour of duty. Others may have gone home earlier or would leave later, a month or two either way was not uncommon. It depended on the casualty rates. A few may have been given early release for compassionate reasons such as a death in the family or other serious matter. Many others would have been wounded and returned by other ships or by airplane to stateside naval hospitals. Still, the difference was staggering. The mood was festive, but more so for some than others. Our ship was tied to the dock in Yokosuka. The main deck was level with a balcony running the length of a dockside building. Paper streamers ran from ship to shore. Messages flowed back and forth. The balcony was lined with young Japanese women, some were in tears. It was obvious that some returning from Japan had not endured a truly difficult tour of duty!

Shortly before the ship got underway, three rifle volleys cut the air. I looked down to see a smartly dressed Army detail rendering the traditional salute as a ship's crane lifted a pallet bearing six flag draped caskets aboard. The caskets were swiftly lowered into the hold. Instinctively, some but not all, had come to attention. Those at attention wore field uniforms. Others were busy with their 'ship-to-shore' communications. I confess to justifiable anger. The operation should have been performed with more dignity. The firing detail did well, but I was reminded of those sea bags at Inchon. The caskets went into the hold in the same manner as had the sea bags. The two week passage gave me time to study fellow passengers. For the pragmatic, Korea would be shuttled into a corner of their minds, neither totally forgotten or particularly remembered. For those who silently sat staring out to sea, it would never go away. In San Francisco, I anticipated the caskets would be first off the ship. It was an honor truly earned. It was too much to expect.

I soon learned most Americans were indifferent to the happenings in Korea. Long before the truce was signed, the hostilities were well on the way to becoming the "Forgotten War." That description gives me trouble. In order to be forgotten, it must first be known. Only those who fought there really knew Korea. A common myth is that soldiers do not talk of their war experiences. Only partially true. Soldiers talk to other soldiers. Many of them have talked to me. There is no medal or commendation I value higher. My poems, some of them elsewhere in this book, share stories of incredible courage of those who lost their youth and many, their lives, in Korea.

Above. Soldiers and Marines battle their way out of the Chinese entrapment at the Chosin Reservoir. Nov. - Dec. 1950.
Below . Aerial photo of the port city of Pusan. Photo taken in 1953. Both photos courtesy of the National Archives.

RED DRAGON
The SECOND ROUND
FACES OF WAR II

Marion	C.	Wheeler, Jr.	US 56 07 0511
First Name	MI	Last Name	Serial Number
'Chappie'	Military Police	23 Jan 1929	Cpl
Nickname	MOS	Birthday	Grade / Rank
C Co/728th MP Bn	28 Nov '51-19 Nov '52		Whittier, CA
Unit (s)	Duty Tour (s)		Home Town

Commendation Ribbon w/ Pendant   Good Conduct Medal   Meritorious Unit Citation   UN Medal

Medals & Awards

Korean Campaign Service Medal, 2stars   National Defense Medal   Korean War Service Medal

CAT HOUSE COP

I entered the Army 15 Nov 1950. After completing my 16 weeks of basic training at Fort Ord, CA, I was assigned to leadership school as an instructor. In early Oct of 1951 I shipped to Japan to attend a school for supply sergeants on the island of Iwo Jima. On 28 Dec '51 I was assigned to "C" Co of the 728th Military Police Battalion. Our HQ Company was located in Seoul. "C" Co. was based at Chunchon in the northeastern section of South Korea, a few miles south of the 38th parallel. Chunchon was the nexus of a road and rail network extending from the port of Pusan on the southeast coast of Korea to Seoul near the 38th parallel in the northwestern part of the Republic of South Korea. The road and rail network out of Chunchon supplied our troops fighting in the Iron Triangle area. It was a vital link in the supply network for all troops fighting north of Chunchon. One of our many jobs was to keep a close lookout for saboteurs and guerilas. Much of my time was spent in jeep patrols, directing traffic, and keeping our military out of harms way.

We were also charged with raiding "houses of ill repute" or as termed by most GIs, 'cat houses.' We would collect the women and take them to the medics to be checked for venereal disease. We were then charged with ushering them in GI trucks about 300 miles to the rear. It didn't do much good. Often they beat us back to Chunchon! I suspect they 'bribed' the train crews moving up on fast ammo trains from Pusan or 'hitchhiked' a truck or rail transport back to Chunchon. After a few raids, I began to remember faces!

The job of a military policeman is an odd mixture of the many police duties usually compartmentalized in today's civilian police force. In the Army, an MP fills many roles. He is sometimes the good cop, the old time patrolman who walked a beat. He is at the beck and call of all who need help. At others, he is the cop who raids the cat houses, the black market parlors, the drug dealers and other miscreants who bedevil a military society. He is a traffic cop, not so much a 'speed cop' but one who directs road traffic, unsnarls road tie-ups, and in general keeps traffic moving. He generally is a repository of unit locations. In this role he directs men, ammo and supply vehicles to their unit locations. A good MP has a rough map in his head of the various units in his sector of responsibility. He can then intelligently answer questions and direct men and vehicles to the correct destination.

As part time supply sergeant I was charged with responsibility of controlling all supplies the company needed for daily operation except for rations and medical supplies. It kept me busy scrounging and inventorying when I could get away from regular patrol duties. The Army held a conference in Chunchon to discuss the cease fire discussions that were being contemplated. Myself, and as many men as could be spared from other duties, were security guards for this conference. Never saw so much brass before or since! I had no idea there were that many generals in Korea. In early winter held by the 24th Infantry Division. The 40th Division was being deployed from Japan where they trained for a year after being sent over from the US. They were relieving troops of the 24th Infantry Division which was being returned to occupation duty in Japan. It seemed only fitting that these men of the 24th Division were to be given a rest as they were the first division sent from Japan to Korea in late June 1950 in an effort to halt the North Korean invasion of South Korea. The cold winter weather had now hit with a vengeance. I did not envy those infantrymen on the line.

For a four month period I made almost daily solo trips to Seoul by jeep to deliver and receive orders from our Bn Hqs. On this drive I became very familiar with the terrain along the road to Seoul. There was a 30 mile section that was a 'main highway' for "honey wagons" which was the GI term for the carts that collected night soil which was spread on the gardens and rice paddies as fertilizer. Whew, what a smell! I never got used to it, I often returned from one of these trips nauseated and green at the gills. I sometimes wondered whether I would ever again be able to smell anything except that horrible stench in my nostrils. How the Koreans lived with it day after day I will never fathom. I always wore a wet handkerchief over my nose. It seemed to help to some extent.

The one thing that stands out in my mind about my service in Korea was how proud I was to be an American. Seeing how the people of Korea lived was most debilitating and heart rending. I sincerely hope that our efforts in Korea were able to improve their lives.

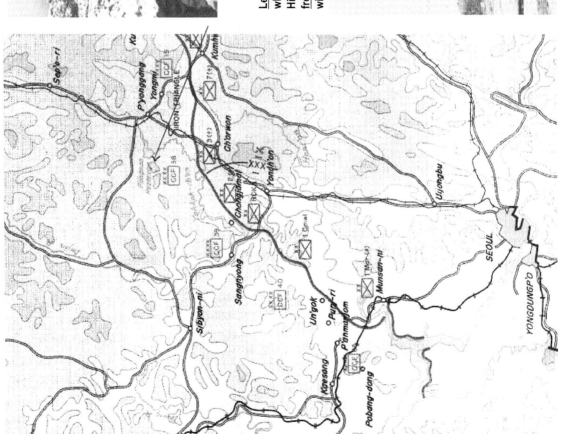

Left. Map shows the 3 hills above Chorwon, with arrow marking where Cpl. Hibberts received his 'early rotation'. Map from Jay Hibberts. Above. MLR bunkers during January of 1952. Photo from Don Gardner. Below. American tank destroyed by a mine with all aboard killed. Photo courtesy of Boyed Burnley.

RED DRAGON
The SECOND ROUND
FACES OF WAR II

Jay	E.	Hibberts	RA 14 379 329
First Name	MI	Last Name	Serial Number
None	4745	18 Sept 1931	S/Sgt, then Cpl
Nickname	MOS	Birthday	Grade / Rank
Fox Co,3dplat,1st sqd 279th RCT		24 Dec 1951- 10 July 1952	Murphy, NC
Unit (s)		Duty Tour (s)	Home Town

Combat Infantry Badge   Purple Heart Medal   Good Conduct Medal   Korean War Service Medal

Medals & Awards

Korean Campaign Service Medal, 2stars   Occp'n Medal-J   NDSM   UN Medal   Expert, Rifle

EARLY ROTATION DATE

I enlisted 10 Nov 1950 and went through 16 weeks basic training at Camp Polk, LA. Enjoyed a 14 days furlough before shipping out of New Orleans 25 March '51 on the Army Transport General John Pope. Arrived 27 April in Hokkaido, the big northern Japanese island. We stayed 3 weeks at Camp Crawford before moving to a sheep farm where we trained and maneuvered until late fall before heavy snow put us into barracks at Chitose. We were alerted for movement to Korea 5 December, and went on line the day before Christmas 1951. The thermometer registered 35 degrees below. Our coldest day that winter was 49 degrees below zero. We were wore those miserable shoe pacs which caused many men to suffer the disability of frozen feet. The National Guard boys rotated soon after we manned the MSR. January 30 we were issued the new 'Mickey Mouse' boots which eliminated most of the frost bite problem.

The Chinese were aware that a different outfit now manned the MSR. They worked us over pretty good with artillery and made a few probing attacks to get acquainted. Things quieted as they learned we would not be an 'easy mark.' We started out with disastrous daylight patrols in which we were silhouetted against white snow. Always point man on the newly initiated night patrols, the first prisoner captured was credited to my squad. I saw this Chinese soldier rise up out the snow, apparently trying to surrender. He had a cord across his chest supporting a burp gun behind his back. I almost shot him. My plat sgt yelled just in time, "Don't shoot him, we need prisoners." Two tanks accompanied us. Each tank lost a tread. We stayed with them under harassing mortar and artillery fire while tank retriever mechanics relaid treads on both tanks. We were lucky. We took no casualties in that fiasco. The weather was so cold our M-1s would fire only one round. We had to kick the bolts open. That taught us to stop oiling weapons. Oil froze.

My plat sgt told me to take care of our new plat ldr, Lt Irwin, on his first patrol. We were to take a Chinese OP. It was too strongly defended, we pulled back under heavy fire. I saw a hole nearby which offered protection. I grabbed Lt Irwin and shoved him into the hole, then jumped in on top of him, pushing him farther down. The smell let me know it was not a foxhole. Enemy fire be damned, I jumped out and pulled the Lt out after me. He was the maddest man I have ever seen. We crawled over to our CO to report. Before a word could be said, the captain hissed, "What the hell is that smell? Get away from me." I told him the Lt had fallen into a Chinese outhouse. The captain, cussing a storm, ordered us to the river in our rear to wash up. We crawled back, still under fire. I had only my boots to wash so I sat on the bank and watched Lt Irwin glare at me as he repeated over and over, "I'll make you pay for this if it takes me the rest of my life!" Today, it is an often repeated story at reunions. Lt Irwin joins in the laughter, but it was not funny then.

In late June '52, we had been on outpost duty for 30 days when we were pulled off line to go into reserve 12 miles to the rear. On 6 July I, learned my rotation date was 15 July. About 3 PM 9 July my plat sgt, Paul Hinson, told us we had to return and take 3 small hills, one hill for each platoon in F company, as well as grab prisoners for interrogation. Leaving at 2 AM, we reached the foot of the hill just before daybreak. We barely started our approach up the horseshoe shaped hill when the Chinese saw us. They fired on us from three sides, front, right and left flanks. Our Co Cmdr, Capt Gavin, radioed for the promised artillery support. Two lonely rounds came in. I was on the left flank and made it to the top of the hill. Looking down, I could see everybody pinned down by enemy fire.

I crawled into the Chinese trench, working my way along it, firing as I went. The enemy now focused his attention on me. I was scared, all alone, and not related to Audie Murphy. I started back. A Chinese soldier fired his burp gun at me from a brush covered bunker I had not seen going up. I answered with a clip from my M-2 carbine. The last thing I remember was black smoke from a grenade before it exploded. When I came to, I knew I was hit bad. A friend, George W. Carter, ran up hill and dragged me into a ditch. All he said was, "Where the hell are your clothes?" I had nothing on me but boots, armored vest, cartridge belt and shreds of uniform. I knew I would die if I stayed there, I crawled a half mile across the valley through a mine field I was not aware of. Lucky me! I made it without further harm, then passed out from loss of blood. A litter crew found me and took me to the aid station. From there, to a field hospital where 18 pieces of shrapnel were taken from my right leg and shattered thigh. It was 10 PM July 10. I was on my way to the USA, 5 days earlier than my expected date of rotation. Returned to my home 25 Sept 1952 after release from stateside hospital.

Above. Wounded from the 7th Regt., 3rd Division are collected for evacuation, July 1951   Photo from the Internet.
Above Right. After the battle some curiosities have to be settled. Two Marines are checking the Chinese KIAs. Photo courtesy of Bill Palizzola. Below. This totally destroyed hill was fittingly named Old Baldy. After the back and forth battles of 1952 it could have been on the moon. Nothing but death and destruction. Photo courtesy of Boyed Burnley.

RED DRAGON
The SECOND ROUND
FACES OF WAR II

Arthur	F.	Dorie	0-56572
First Name	MI	Last Name	Serial Number
"Art"	1542	12 Oct 1922	Major USA Ret
Nickname	MOS	Birthday	Grade / Rank
M Co 23 Inf 2Div		Dec 1951-July 1952	Long Island, NY
Unit (s)		Duty Tour (s)	Home Town

CIB w/star   PH   BSM w/OLC & "V"   GCM   Paratroop Badge   Glider Badge   ADSM

Medals & Awards

EAMECM ,3stars   WWIIVM   OM-J   KCSM, 2stars   NDSM   UNSM   ROK Peace Medal

AVE, IMPERATOR! WE WHO ARE ABOUT TO DIE SALUTE YOU!

Assigned to FECOM and the 7th Inf Div at end of 1951, I greeted my assignment with a great sense of loss. I could find no one with whom I had served in 1948-1950. I rotated 2 months before the start of the Korean War. So many of my old friends in 1/32/7 were dead, consumed in the fiery furnace of the tragic Chosin Reservoir campaign. I called the roll in my mind, Don Faith, Ed Scullion, Hank Moore, Dale Seever, Bob Wilson. Many other staff and line company officers of the 32d Inf were in unmarked graves east of the Chosin Reservoir. My feeling of loss was almost unbearable. I wangled an assignment switch placing me in 2d Division as CO of Mike Co. 3d Bn Heavy Weapons 23d Inf. My feeling for this company and its men grew on me during the winter of '51/'52 and the spring/summer campaigns of '52 as we fought Chicoms and the In Min Gun along Iron Triangle outposts from Chorwon to Kumhwa.

Our nickname of "Mighty Mike" fit well, but something was missing, the "esprit de corps" feeling I remembered so well from combat experience in WW II. That same spirit had prevailed in the 31st and 32d Regiments during my posting in Korea and Japan between wars. A system of rotation had begun, it was no longer "duration plus six"as in WW II. No one wanted to "die for a tie"as politicians wangled over terms in a limited war. Men performed well but lacked spirit, determination and camaraderie so essential to morale in a successful fighting regiment. Particularly noticeable were a man's actions as his time went "short," close to his date of rotation. Understandable, but it did not make for an outfit with the intense fighting spirit of the men of WW II.

Militarily, things went well until mid 1952 when action along the MLR increasingly reflected the lack of progress being made at the Panmunjom peace talks. The hangups between the two sides in most part related to forced repatriation of prisoners. Whenever negotiations went awry for either side it was reflected in violent action along the MLR where attrition was the name of the game. To spur talks along, the US 8th Army would increase artillery fire, "let guns do the talking." The Chinese, if they did not get their way, would assault our positions with absolute disregard of their casualties and kill as many of us as they could, their version of "Listen up!" This led to local engagements attracting the media, high command attention, politicians on tour and visiting celebrities, the likes of which had not been seen since the First Battle of Bull Run in 1861. Such masses of spectators interfered with combat operations. One incident which stands out in my memory reminds me of gladiators performing for Nero in the Roman Arena.

In July the 23d Inf held Old Baldy, Pork Chop, T-Bone and other hills on the MLR. The CCF attacked, knocking us off Old Baldy the night of 17 July. Lt Col Ralph Burns, Regtl XO, was given command of a provisional Bn of B, I, L and M companies of the 23d Inf Inf, plus a tank plat to counterattack at 1600 hours 18 July. Lt Col Burns had replaced Lt Col Chun, wounded earlier. The scarred hill had taken on political significance as did Pork Chop later. The order was, "Retake Old Baldy." To get final orders, Lt Col Burns and his COs reported to the 23nd CP, a sandbagged bunker dug on the reverse slope of a hill behind Old Baldy. What happened next was nigh unbelievable, but unforgettable. It was a travesty of American military ethics in blatant disregard of lives of American soldiers.

Arriving at the CP we were surprised to find the bunker packed wall-to-wall with people, others milling around unable to squeeze in. Media people, observers, staff people from all command echelons, including Commanding General James Van Fleet and his entourage, were part of the circus. It was a crowded theater. We, destined to play gladiator to Van Fleet's Nero, were unable to get our field orders. With the clock running, LtCol Burns saved the day. "Let's get the hell out of here. We know what we have to do."

We did not hesitate. Time was tight. Some troops had to pass through a friendly mine field to reach the LD. In absence of a Regt'l field order we crossed the LD on schedule and part way up the slope before all hell broke loose. My mortars and recoilless rifles were hammering the crest and beyond, HMGs were laying down covering fires while my LMGs were in direct support of the rifle companies. Yet, enemy fire overwhelmed us. The Chinese had learned. For the first time in this war we were on the receiving end of TOT fires, all his artillery and mortars hit us simultaneously. Perhaps we could have taken Old Baldy. We'll never know. The media had their news, the observers their stories, the spectators their spectacles. What we had was many dead, many wounded and a Regt'l CO relieved of his command. What Panmunjom thought of us did not enter our minds. Had we thought, we could have cared less!

Above Left and Right .Enemy territory in front of 31st Regt. positions, summer of 1952. Hill on right is receiving an air strike.

Right Troops from 31st Regt. draw rations before they attack Jane Russell Hill, Oct. 14, 1952.

Lower Right A weasel is used to haul off wounded after the battle, Oct. 15, 1952. All photos by D. E. Schoenwetter.

Lower Left, Col Lloyd R. Moses 31st Regt CO, mid 1952,   Courtesy of Clarence D. Beaver

RED DRAGON
The SECOND ROUND
FACES OF WAR II

Lloyd	R.	Moses	O-29362
First Name	MI	Last Name	Serial Number
None	1542	4 Sept 1904	MGen, then Col
Nickname	MOS	Birthday	Grade / Rank
31st Inf Regt/7Div		15Dec 51-10 Nov '52	Fairfax, SD
Unit (s)		Duty Tour (s)	Home Town

DSC   SS   BS   PH   LM   CIB w/star   ADSM   ACSM   EAME/3*   Paratrooper Badge

Medals & Awards

WW II VM   KCSM/2stsrd   NDSM   UN Medal   Croix de Guerre w/Palm

A REGIMENTAL COMMANDER COMMENTS ON THE AMERICAN SOLDIER

Col Lloyd Moses commanded 31st Inf Regt summer and fall of 1952, a period of some the most grueling trench warfare of the Korean conflict. He retired in Sept 1964 as Maj General after 33 years of military service. His autobiography, *Whatever It Takes*, contains many cogent comments extracted from his field journal. In tribute to the American soldier, some of them are quoted here......... ED.

"Soldiers up front live intimately with a few pieces of equipment, a rifle and a few comrades who contribute to each other's esprit. They have few other assets available. Their life is not a fire-and-fall-back-affair. If there is danger, they must bare their teeth and meet the enemy head on. Life expectancy is short, there is no money back guarantee they will live to see another day. Straying means becoming a casualty. It is safer to be with friends and in the hands of a cool, tactically skillful commander. A sense of humor helps."

"The Korean War changed American racial thinking. Army integration was quickly achieved on the fighting front. It became a matter of equal opportunity based on merit. In combat men learn to trust and depend on each other. They are not interested in your school, your speech, color or religion. They care only what each is worth to the team. Gen MacArthur's thoughts on the infantry soldier were recorded: "His is an old and honorable story. He carries his home with him, and often his grave, the whole paraphernalia of fighting is on his back. He must eat, fight and die on foot, in all weather, with or without shelter. Death has his finger on him always. It is a wonder that the morale of these uniformed gypsies never falters. His courage is legendary in the book of our nation's history.""

"My experience has been that when troops have to hurry-and-wait, it is because each echelon of command adds a time cushion so it will not be blamed. The proper procedure, learned here, was to reverse the process by delegating formation time to the NCOs. They thoughtfully considered each matter in the enlisted bunkers. No time at all was wasted waiting in formation for food, pay or sick call."

"In a democracy, all that can be done by discipline is to direct it. The American soldier's will to obey rests on reason, confidence and respect. He never seems to be conscious of being commanded. My experience with the 31st was of hard muscled, stubborn soldiers that would not be pushed around, worth cultivating by means other than force. Nor did they allow the enemy to push them around. There were no men courts-martialed, there were no desertions, even the men captured in the Kumwha sector found their way back in a short time. Combat quickly strips a fighting regiment of men unsuited for combat. Men of the most reliable principles in private life make the best and bravest soldiers in the field. They believed in the bayonet because as the saying went, "It is always loaded.""

"A good infantry officer possesses an appreciation of the terrain. In defense this means the study of counter-measures in event of enemy penetration with an eye to forcing his attack into some trap of the terrain where he can be carved into pockets and obliterated. There is a mystical power about the leader unnoticeable in the trappings of rank. His 'right of leadership' rests on mutual confidence to handle the mission, assignments, enemy, geography, climate, casualties and even monotony. Properly led, soldiers want to be employed to their full potential. Therefore they need faith that the leadership has the capacity to frame plans that will succeed."

"Command is a lonely duty, yet it is the most important ingredient for success in battle. It begins in the peculiar relationship between the commanding officer, staff and subordinate commanders. My rule was that a staff officer could not say "no" to a request from any of my subordinate commanders. That authority is reserved for the commander. The staff could say "yes" or refer recommendations to me. Such a procedure leads to better field rapport among subordinates and better battlefield communication."

"Service with men and officers of this old Regular Army regiment, highlighted an unusual history. Given the name 'Polar Bear' after occupation duty in Siberia in 1918/19, it was called the "Foreign Legion of the US Army," having never been stationed in the USA. Activated in the Philippines in 1916, it served in Siberia. It assisted earthquake stricken Japan in 1923, fought in China post WW I, and in WW II, on Bataan where survivors underwent the infamous "Death March. In my period of command we shared success, fear and icy foxholes, ever on watch for signals of personal defeat. Our working philosophy was a fixed resolve not to quit. These men were all of sound stock. They did not come into service looking for an easy life. They were seeking something strong and viable. In 2 wars and 19 infantry battles, I never served with more loyal, tenacious fighters than those in the 31st Infantry Polar Bear Regiment."

Below. A pilot climbs aboard his F4U Corsair for another close-air support mission of our troops on the MLR. Always welcomed! Photo from the National Archives. Right. A section of the MLR occupied by the 25th Infantry Div during the winter of 1952-1953. Everything possible was underground, as showing yourself could be hazardous to your health. Photo from the Internet.
Below Right Sherman tanks from B Co. 72nd Tk. Bn. support the 8th ROK Division on hill 812, near Nonjang-ni. Photo from Internet.

RED DRAGON
The SECOND ROUND
FACES OF WAR II

George	W.	Langdale	US 53 090 735
First Name	MI	Last Name	Serial Number
None	1745	14 Sept 1930	SFC
Nickname	MOS	Birthday	Grade / Rank
A2/1/27th Inf 25th Division		Dec 1951-Nov 1952	Walterboro, SC
Unit (s)		Duty Tour (s)	Home Town

Purple Heart   Combat Infantry Badge   Korean Campaign Service Medal w/2 stars

Medals & Awards

National Defense Service Medal   United Nations Service Medal   ROK Service Medal

BATTLE FOR SAND BAG CASTLE

In July 1952 Able company of the "Wolfhound" 27th Infantry Regiment was assigned positions in the Satae-ri valley. We often assisted in evacuation of casualties from Hill 1052 on our left flank. C/27, fighting for the crest of Hill 1052, was located considerably above our position. The hill crest had already acquired the name, "Sandbag Castle." The most depressing event in our role of litter bearers for C/27 was the evacuation of KATUSA Cpl Lee Yong Suk of Lt McLean's plat.. His wounds obviously would make him a quadruple amputee for the rest of his life. A few days later, one of the 89th Tank Bn's Sherman tanks laboriously being maneuvered down hill, came tumbling down the steep slope. Daylight was almost breaking when this occurred. The tank headed directly for the bunkers of HQ 1st Bn/27. No 0one was hurt, but Sgt Charles Rutledge and I agreed that speed records, in spite of darkness, were set by Bn personnel as they evacuated their bunkers. About that time rumors, circulated that we would relieve Charlie company.

We learned army scuttlebutt rumors are often well founded. Our 2d platoon was given the task of holding the near precipitous, almost needle like summit. This position was critical since possession gave observation over much of the terrain assigned to X Corps. Heart Break Ridge and the Punch Bowl were in view of this commanding terrain. It was also an "Achilles Heel" in that its loss would cripple X Corps defenses. As the cold monsoon rains began our morale sagged, wet bodies, wet clothing and no hot food. We were perhaps more resilient than other platoons. Our former Lt, Esper K. Chandler, had left behind him a highly motivated platoon when he rotated in mid 1952. That resilience was sorely tested on 5 Sept when we received an estimated 1200 rounds of mortar and artillery fire. We knew the fire we received was preliminary to an imminent attack on our position. The Chinese attack was launched soon after midnight, 6 Sept 1952. Our 2d plat held onto our MLR position, but lost, or in military jargon, conceded LP Agnes to the enemy.

This Listening Post was manned by the .30 cal MG crew of Cpl Benito Martinez, squad leader. There were 4 other men, 3 riflemen from C/27 and our replacement, Pfc Paul Myatt who had just joined us. We soon realized the prime reason we were able to hold on at the MLR was due to heavy and consistent fire from their machine gun. After the second attack on their position was repulsed, Cpl Benitez told us over his sound power phone line "If we are taken out, don't try to help us. There are too many of them. It would be useless. You would just be sacrificed." He undoubtedly realized that our lone platoon did not have the firepower to counterattack several hundred North Koreans. Near daylight, their MG fire ceased. Silence enveloped LP Agnes. F4U Marine Corsairs arrived to strafe and napalm the enemy. With Marine Corsair help, the momentum of battle changed to favor the 'Wolfhounds.' The platoon had been gravely weakened in the nights action, losing about 50% strength in WIA and KIA. Numbered among our losses were three squad leaders, the plat sgt and plat leader. Other platoons of A/27/ on our flank fared worse, losing 3 officers KIA and 3 WIA.

Artillery and mortar FOs began finding enemy targets after the Corsairs left. In early afternoon the experienced CO of L/27, Capt Ralph M. Hinman, reinforced us with the 3d plat of L Co from Regimental Reserve. He exuded confidence that said, "We would win any future firefight in this attack." He went on to say, "Sgt Langsdale, let us prepare to recapture LP Agnes." This was accomplished, but cost the life of a highly respected plat ldr, Lt Umlauf. At LP Agnes we found the body of Cpl Martinez and one riflemen surrounded by a piles of North Korean dead. Two riflemen escaped to the MLR. No one could recall the name of the replacement who assisted Cpl Martinez on the MG. He had been with us about 3 days. He was reported as MIA, then as KIA. After 46 years we learned at a Wolfhound reunion he had been captured semi conscious, sent to a POW camp, lived, and repatriated in Sept 1953. Cpl Martinez received the Medal of Honor posthumously. Four other men in the platoon were awarded the Silver Star. Our 25th Division CO, General "Hanging" Sam Williams complimented the Wolfhounds in these words, "Everyone [North Koreans] who came, stayed. They were all dead." Our next tough combat action took place a month later on a rainy dark night in late Oct, '52 as the 45th Div relieved us from our granite pinnacle at "Sandbag Castle." That's another story, never told, but one I will never forget.

A tremendously successful revenge raid was organized later that month. The leader in the raid, Lt Flanagan, was killed in the action. There is always a price to be paid in war. Quite often, it is the leaders, officers and NCOs of a line combat unit who pay most heavily.

Below Center. Sitting in the drivers seat of his trusty [rusty] 'iron horse,' Cpl. Stoyanoff gets ready to do the GI version of Casey Jones. Above. A couple of the Korean railheads that would have been challenge enough without a language difference. Below. Civilians were always a problem, cramming in to every spare inch with no regard for safety. Passengers could, and often, did include Chinese POWs on southbound runs. All photos courtesy of Stan Stoyanoff.

306

RED DRAGON
The SECOND ROUND
FACES OF WAR II

Stanley	None	Stoyanof	ER 16 292 100
First Name	MI	Last Name	Serial Number
Stan	Military Train Conductor	30 March 1929	Cpl
Nickname	MOS	Birthday	Grade / Rank
3dTMRS Transportation Corps		May 1951-June 1952	Detroit, MI
Unit(s)		Duty Tour(s)	Home Town
Korean Campaign Service Medal			National Defense Service Medal
Medals & Awards			
United Nations Service Medal			Korean War Service Medal

MILITARY TRAIN SERVICE

Recall of my Korean war experience after the passage of 50 years is like finding an old diary in a dusty attic. Many events over these years, marriage, raising a family and the blessings of peace have blotted out the many horrors of war which passed before my eyes. I use the term "passed in front of my eyes" advisedly because that is how the Korean War appeared to me. I was assigned to the military railroad service as a train conductor. My job was the transport of men and supplies from supply depots in southern Korea to the troops in the north, but never up to the actual fighting front. Trains stopped at a railhead where supplies were off loaded to trucks. My job of moving supplies and troops along the important main supply lines of the railroads afforded me an overall vantage point of war that few men experience. Every mile traveled was different. Devastated villages, burned out tanks, enemy bodies, MPs standing guard along the tracks were commonplace. Yet, I felt safe riding in my 'iron horse' steam locomotive, oblivious to the occasional danger of snipers or enemy guerillas engaged in train derailment. It was only when a trip ended and, if I noticed new bullet holes, would I again become aware of the importance that the enemy attached to a supply train. Thankfully, my job kept me busy.

New troops arriving in Korea had much curiosity to what lay ahead. Since this was a U N war, I had the opportunity of meeting soldiers of many nations. The Greeks, Turks, English and other countries that sent soldiers to Korea had a system of national military duty which reflected a difference in attitude because of national background. Most of these 'foreign' soldiers sang all the time and seemed to be excited about getting into the thick of things. Americans were curious, but brave, about going into an unknown conflict. American soldiers coming from the States were really civilian youths with three month basic training period as their only military background except what they heard as young teenagers during WW II. I can remember thinking, "How many of these young men would be returning to Pusan en route home to their loved ones?" Many on their feet, true, but many others would be in the mortuary trains brought back from the fighting front in the north. As the war progressed, south bound trains were sometimes fully loaded. Going north we carried fuel, food, ammo, supplies of all kinds to support the fighting soldiers. On the return trip south, cars might be loaded with scrap, vehicles to be salvaged, artillery for repair and refitting, wounded in hospital trains, and worst of all, the mortuary trains with the bodies of dead American soldiers to be taken to the United States for burial near their homes and relatives.

South Korea is a small country, a bit larger than South Carolina. Our rail operations covered about 40% of the Korean peninsula. Each trip took from 2 days to 2 weeks in either direction, north or south, due to limited rail trackage and priority given our particular train cargo. Food on these longer trips was sometimes a problem. However, we always seemed to find GIs who willingly shared rations with us. We were told to not eat Korean food due to danger of dysentery, which was endemic as human waste was used as an agricultural fertilizer. Cleanliness was not a problem. Our engines used water for steam. We always had plenty of hot water to wash. We almost always slept in the engine. It was always warm, though sooty and dirty. We seldom had a caboose or empty box car to sleep in, but if one was available in warm weather we utilized it in real luxury to stretch out and sleep in comfort. Each station had a military staff to operate and protect railroad trackage so we were always aware of what was going on as well as being in on the latest scuttlebutt. In one day we would pass from peaceful rice farmers in the south to sights of increasing havoc and destruction as the train proceeded northward. Every added mile gave an increasingly vivid view of the madness and ugliness of war.

Even though I was not shooting at anyone and was seldom shot at, I felt important to the war effort. At destination, I was greeted by soldiers, not in words, but in enthusiasm as they unloaded badly needed supplies. Returning south with an empty train was another luxury. We could wander about, sleep in empty cars and hold bull sessions with other returning conductors. An almost empty train gave a sense of security, it was not likely to attract guerilla action. We were aware that we were in the middle of a civil war in which vital information was sometimes relayed to North Koreans. My assignment to the Transportation Corps made me realize supply logistics are critical in military and civilian life. In America, such things are taken for granted. Getting food and supplies to the user, require functioning supply lines. The delivery routes for food supplies must be protected lest society degenerate into chaos.

Right. An 81 mm mortar crew of M Co. 15th Regt. 3rd Division. A few hours after this photo was taken, Cpl. O'Connor, seated, was KIA. Aug 14, 1952. Photo courtesy of William J. Dillon.
Below Left. A heavy MG from M Co. 15th Regt., 3rd Division fires in support of infantry attacking hill 717. [Operation Doughnut]. Action took place in July of 1951. Below Right. Troops of the 3rd Infantry Division were wounded in action await evacuation. Hill 717 action took place in July 1951. Both photos from Internet.

RED DRAGON
The SECOND ROUND
FACES OF WAR II

William	J.	Dillon	US 21 917 740
First Name	MI	Last Name	Serial Number
Bill	1745	6 June 1932	Cpl
Nickname	MOS	Birthday	Grade / Rank
Mike Co,15th Inf,3d Div & 5th Cav,1stCav Div		Mch 1952-Sept 1953	Sayville, Long Island, NY
Unit (s)		Duty Tour (s)	Home Town

Combat Infantry Badge Purple Heart Korean Campaign Svc Medal,4stars ROK PUC UN Medal

Medals & Awards

National Defense Service Medal   NYS Conspicuous Service Cross   Korean War Service Medal

LIVE AND LEARN

I was born in the early 1930's, raised as a teenager in a tough neighborhood in South Brooklyn. Another fellow, a fellow Irishman by name of Joe O'Connor, and I never saw eye to eye on anything. At that time, and in that place, every disagreement ended up with us dukeing it out. We remained enemies throughout our boyhood life. We fought often, almost every time we met on the street. In those days, it was all clean fighting, no guns, no knives. Even kicking was considered dirty fighting. Years went by. In 1951 I was drafted for the Korean War. I took my basic training at Ft Dix, NJ which meant I could, on occasion, get a week end pass to see the girl who became my wife. After completing my 16 weeks basic training at Ft Dix, I married the girl of my dreams. We spent our nuptial night in a New York City hotel. My bride went back to her parents home in the Bronx. I caught a bus back to Ft Dix. A week later we had a one week honeymoon at Williams Lake in New York. My bride spent a lot of time crying. Two weeks later I shipped out to Korea.

In Korea I was assigned to an 81mm mortar section Mike Co, 15th Inf Regt, 3d Div. While waiting outside a HQ bunker for orders, we could hear the sound of shells and artillery directly ahead. Two helicopters had set down and were loading dead and wounded men on stretchers. The wounded were placed in baskets on the sides of the landing skids, like they were later shown on the TV show "MASH." I wondered to myself whose place I was taking. Was it one of those dead or wounded men I could see being evacuated in front of my eyes? Several of us crowded into a jeep and were taken to our company assignments on the MLR. I reported to the plt Lt. He told me to report to Cpl O'Connor. I was dumbfounded to find myself facing my boyhood arch enemy, Joe O'Connor.

Neither of u could believe it. Halfway around the world, meeting face to face in a war torn bunker! We were both in shock, we said nothing for several minutes. Finally, Joe said, "Well, Bill, for once we are not going to fight each other. We're on the same side now, in the same uniform." We talked about our boyhood days. Joe and I became the best of friends, we lived, ate and slept in the same bunker, fighting a war together. I can remember saying several times when I was mired in the depths of gloom, "Joe, I don't think I'm going to make it out of this war alive." I had this funny feeling that I would not see my bride again or the good old USA. Joe always cheered me up by telling me that God has his hand on me and for sure I would come back alive. On the last day of Joe's life we were hit by a heavy barrage of artillery. Joe was acting as FO for our 81mm mortars. He was in an OP with two other observers.

He couldn't get through to us, the W-110 phone line had been cut by shell fire. I was told to take 2 men to trace and repair phone line from our 81 mortars to Joe on the OP. We found and repaired 8 breaks in the line caused by North Korean artillery shell fire. None of us were hit, but one guy sprained his ankle jumping into a shell hole when we heard an incoming round that hit close by. We made it safely to the OP. They were taking a tremendous pounding from a 76mm gun mounted on a Russian built tank. The shelling was so intense, the FO bunker had started to cave in. A South Korean officer in the bunker was hit. We got him out, an FO Lt from an artillery outfit came next. Joe was last to leave. Just as his head emerged from the demolished bunker, another round came in. Joe never knew what hit him. He was 18, too young to die. It took me a long time to get over Joe's death. Perhaps I never did.

There is a big difference between a garrison soldier and a combat soldier. The garrison soldier serves his time and returns to tell everyone what a great time he had serving his country. Combat soldiers never really come home. The body may, but the mind is back on the battlefield. Memories are bad and gruesome. I am 72, I still have nightmares. It hasn't been easy for my wife, either. I gave her my Purple Heart. She deserves it, living with me all these years. The only time I had a shower, trucks took us to a shower point. The hot water felt so good I almost passed out. Going back to the MLR was like putting a steak in front of a wolf, then taking it away. When I first came home, I took 4 showers a day to rid myself of the smell and stink that clung to my body. Of course, it was all in my head, but that didn't make it any easier. I'm better now, down to 2 a day. In Korea, I went 3 months without a shower. Non circumcised men had a real problem, but handled it by washing in a canteen cup. When I think of females in combat without water or a change of clothing for 3 months, wearing undergarments yellow in front and brown in back, I wonder why any woman would equate sexual equality to service in a combat unit. Shades of idiocy and the stupidity of a congresswoman who promotes such idiocy.

Above Left. A Marine sniper looks for a target in the Punchbowl area, 1951.

Above Right. A 155mm howitzer from the 936th FA Bn. fires it's 200,000th round, April 1952.

Left A 4.2 mm mortar crew.[unit unknown], earn their pay.

Photos from Internet.

Right. Cpl. Buschjost in a firing pit with his 4.2 mm mortar. Similar in bore size to the 105 mm howitzer, it was a most devastating weapon.

RED DRAGON
The SECOND ROUND
FACES OF WAR II

Ernest	L.	Buschjost	US 55 189 407
First Name	MI	Last Name	Serial Number
Ernie	Mortarman	4 July 1929	Cpl
Nickname	MOS	Birthday	Grade / Rank
2d Chem Mrtr Bn, atchd Co"C" 461st Inftry Bn	May '52-22 Jan '53		St Thomas, MO
Unit (s)	Duty Tour (s)		Home Town

Purple Heart Medal   Commendation Ribbon w/ Metal Pendent for Meritorious Service   UN Medal

Medals & Awards

Korean Campaign Service Medal, 2 stars   National Defense Service Medal   ROK KWSM

MISSOURI FARM TO KOREAN BATTLEFIELD

I was a Missouri farm boy, born on National Independence Day 4 July 1929. Raised in the small community of St Thomas, I graduated there in the eighth grade. There were 8 of us in the class and 7 in my 1947 graduating class from Meta High School. I helped on the family farm until I was drafted 11 September 1951, shortly after my 21st birthday. A next door neighbor was also drafted. He and I went together to Kansas City for induction. He was assigned to the US Marines, I to the US Army. I had 8 weeks of basic training at Fort Sill, Oklahoma, given a home furlough and after it ended, orders to report to the Port of Embarkation (POE) in Seattle, WA.

We left for Japan aboard the USS Phoenix. Two weeks later we arrived in Japan. Every day of that voyage was a day of misery. I was sea sick all the time. With no immediate assignment in sight, I volunteered for Cook's & Baker's School at Eta Jima. Accepted 10 March 1952, I finished 1 May 1952. This was a nice place and good duty. The course consisted of several weeks of school and on- job-training in actual cooking at an officer's mess hall. We were told that if we learned and did well we had a chance to stay as instructor and cook full time. I did well and scored high, but was rejected for assignment there as I did not have any college work. That one floored me! To be a cook in an officer's mess I had to be some sort of a college boy? Please spare me that sort of drivel!

I shipped to Korea May 1952. Another boat ride, another train. Aboard, I was handed an M-1 rifle, the first time I had ever seen one. With this weapon in my hand, I knew the gravy train was over. Off the train, several of us were trucked to a rear area of the MLR and assigned to the 2d Chemical Mortar Bn. I was assigned as jeep driver to the 4th sqd in A Co 1st plt, again a job for which I had not trained. I had seen jeeps before but had never driven one or knew anything about maintenance. More O-J-T, army style. The Bn had been in the same position for several months. Bunkers were well built, gun and ammo pits sandbagged in accordance with orders from Corps Commanders urging Heavy Mortar Companies "DIG IN" as outlined by Capt Arthur Wilson in an article published by The Infantry Journal, January 1952. It had been written while he commanded HM company, 31st Inf Regt. Perhaps the reason our Bn so quickly adopted the setup was because Capt Wilson took his WW II basic training in 1942 at the CWS School, Camp Sibert, AL.

This was the first time I had seen a 4.2 inch Mortar and the second time given a job for which I had not trained. That's the Army way! We were Corps troops, no Regimental Commander to look after us grandfather fashion as in the infantry regiment 4.2 mortar companies. We were parceled out and attached to various line units. My mortar platoon was attached to 'C' company, 461st Infantry Bn. We were regarded as an integral part of the battalion. On joining, I was told, "This is a '4 point' area. Wear your tin pot ALL the time. You can get killed around here." By "4 point" the Sgt meant we accumulated 4 points each month toward rotation. For combat troops, rotation was quicker than for the rear echelon where I had been up to now. There, 2 or 3 points per month, dependent on kind of duty, were awarded for less hazardous assignments. I learned to sleep fully clothed, boots on and tin pot handy.

From driver I worked up to ammo bearer, then charge setter. The 4.2 mortar used packets of five sheets of powder sewn together on one edge. A round hole in the center allowed the sheet to be placed over a steel tube at the base of the shell. Several of these packets gave it a maximum range of 4400 yards. The powder sheets were set off by a "shotgun" shell in the base. The number of sheets combined with elevation settings, set the range of the shell. Use only of the shotgun shell made it possible to fire at ranges less than 200 yards if under close in-enemy attack. I went to asst gunner, then gunner for most of my time. Made Cpl and squad leader before I rotated. I received my Purple Heart and Commendation Ribbon while with the 461st. One night we fired all night long.

Burned a hole in the bottom of the barrel. Changed to a new barrel and resumed firing. Shortly after that I went to Japan on R&R. While at the R&R center, I met a boy from a nearby town I knew before we were drafted into Army service. Took my boots off at night, too! Rotated in Jan '53 with enough points to come home. I was glad, but hard to leave my buddies. Married on 27 June '53 to the girl to whom I was engaged all my time in service. We raised a family of 4 boys and 3 girls on our dairy farm in St Thomas. I am in touch with four of my 4th squad buddies. We plan a get-together this year. We are all back on the gravy train. Isn't peace wonderful!

Left. A guard tower on Koji-Do Island. Too many POWs in one area made the uprisings almost inevitable. Above. Some of the thousands of Communist POWs that put a serious strain on the UN ability to control them.
Below. An aerial view of Heartbreak Ridge with W.P. being fired on enemy positions.

....................<u>All photos from the Internet</u>.

RED DRAGON
The SECOND ROUND
FACES OF WAR II

Benito	NMI	Martinez	US 54 055 424
First Name	MI	Last Name	Serial Number
Benny	Machine Gunner	April ? 1931	Corporal
Nickname	MOS	Birthday	Grade / Rank
Co A 27th Inf Regt 25th Inf Div		Nov 1951-6 Sept 1952	Ft Hancock, TX
Unit (s)		Duty Tour (s)	Home Town

MEDAL of HONOR Purple Heart Medal Combat Infantry Badge ROK Presidential Unit Citation
Medals & Awards
Korean War Campaign Medal, 3 stars   National Defense Service Medal   United Nations Medal

GREATER LOVE HATH NO MAN

The 27th Infantry known as "The Wolfhounds" moved into the Heartbreak Ridge sector after the regiment returned from suppressing prison camp riots in March 1952 at Koje-Do Island off the southeastern coast of Korea. The regiment stayed for an extended period to maintain order. Heartbreak Ridge on the MLR had been occupied by the Turkish Brigade. They had dug an extensive system of bunkers and connecting trenches. Two big bunkers flanked 'Listening Post Agnes' which was near the mouth of a tunnel that burrowed beneath the ridge pinnacle of 'Sandbag Castle.' Shortly after midnight 6 Sept 1952 an attack was launched on LP Agnes and the MLR. NK soldiers worked their way along the ridge finger toward LP Agnes. Cpl Martinez, manning a Light Machine Gun, was the NCO in a five man group defending LP Agnes. After several hours of intensive fire, he and his crew ran short of ammo.

Cpl Martinez told the other soldiers to withdraw to the MLR. He would cover them and continue to strafe the enemy with MG fire as long as his ammo held out. In response to a sound power phone call from his platoon leader, Lt Thomas McLean, urging him to withdraw, he replied he would remain at his post to delay as long as possible the North Korean attack. When the enemy crept forward with satchel charges, Martinez, now out of ammo for his LMG, took a BAR and withdrew to one of the bunkers flanking Sandbag Castle. As dawn broke, he reported he was firing his BAR at the onrushing enemy. Those were the last words heard from him.

Benito Martinez was born April ? at Ft Hancock TX, a town of about 800 population located on the banks of the Rio Grande 45 miles SE of El Paso. Ft Hancock, named after Maj Gen Winfield Scott Hancock, had a rich post Civil War history as stagecoach gave way to railroad. Ft Hancock and nearby Fort Quitman were satellite posts of Fort Davis. Troops posted there patrolled the border areas as well as the interior of Texas and Arizona where raids by Comanche and Apache Indians were then a part of daily life on the frontier. It is believed he carries in his veins the blood of the Yaqui Indians of Mexican Sonora and American Arizona. The Yaquis are a cross border tribe living on both sides of the boundary. They have as yet never been completely subdued by the government of Mexico. With this background, it is easier to understand the soldier and his decision which culminated in our nation's military highest award

THE MEDAL OF HONOR

Rank and Organization: Corporal, United States Army, Company A, 27th Infantry Regiment, 25th Infantry Division.
Place and Date: Near Satae-ri Korea 6 September 1952. Entered service at Fort Hancock, Texas Birth: Fort Hancock, Texas
Authority: General Order Number 96, United States Army.

Corporal Benito Martinez US 54 055 424, Infantry, United States Army, a machine gunner with Company A, 27th Infantry Regiment, 25th Infantry Division, distinguished himself by conspicuous gallantry and outstanding courage above and beyond the main line of resistance, his position was attacked by a hostile force of reinforced company strength. In the ensuing bitter fighting, the enemy infiltrated the defense perimeter and, realizing that encirclement was imminent, Corporal Martinez elected to remain at his post in an attempt to stem the onslaught. In a daring defense, he raked the enemy troops with crippling fire, inflicting numerous casualties. Although contacted by sound power phone several times, he insisted no attempt be made to rescue him. Soon thereafter, hostile forces rushed the emplacement, forcing him to make a limited withdrawal with only an automatic rifle and a pistol to defend himself. Shortly before dawn after a courageous six-hour stand , he called in for the last time, stating that the enemy was converging on his position. His magnificent stand enabled friendly elements to reorganize, attack, and regain key terrain. Corporal Martinez' incredible valor and supreme sacrifice reflect lasting glory upon himself and are in keeping with the honored traditions of the military service.

Information for this vignette furnished by members of A Co. 27 Inf. Regt. [Wolfhounds] in honor of Cpl Benito Martinez.....Editor

Above. This huge POW complex on Koji-Do Island would be the
scene of bitter riots and much anxiety for the UN command.
Below. This peaceful setting for an American bivouac was very rare.
Much too clean and neat. Both photos from the Internet.

Above. LeVern Sundet receives a nice surprise.
A visit from his brother Edwin, on the right in this
picture. Photo courtesy LeVern Sundet

RED DRAGON
The SECOND ROUND
FACES OF WAR II

LeVern	E.	Sundet	US 55142646
First Name	MI	Last Name	Serial Number
None	745	23 Sept 1930	Cpl
Nickname	MOS	Birthday	Grade / Rank
A/27"Wolfhounds"25th Div		Sept 1952-Aug 1953	New Rockford, ND
Unit (s)		Duty Tour (s)	Home Town
Bronze Star Medal	Combat Infantry Badge		Korean Campaign Service Medal w/3 stars
Medals & Awards			
National Defense Service Medal	United Nations Service Medal		ROK Korean Service Medal

MY YEAR OF WAR BEGAN AT SANDBAG CASTLE

Born and raised in North Dakota, I answered my Selective Service call on 16 January 1952. My basic training was at Fort Knox, KY in Battery B of the 509th Armored FA Bn, followed by a 8 week course in Leadership Training. After a home furlough, I shipped out of San Francisco for Japan. We were issued combat gear before going to Korea in early September. Leaving Inchon by train, we arrived next morning at an Army Replacement Depot. None of us knew where we were, or where we were going. Nor were we told. It gave us the feeling of being caught up in a robotic process where free will had no meaning. When we reached the 'Repple-Depple,' 6 of us were assigned to Co A 27th Infantry "Wolfhounds" Regiment. We were replacement troops for men killed or wounded.

We had the good luck to land in a famous regiment of proud traditions whose legacy we learned to up hold with a pride of our own. The evening chow truck took me to the bottom of a tramway where rations were sent uphill. Looking around as we went up, I could see the area had been really blasted by artillery and mortar fire. On arrival at the hilltop, I was assigned to my platoon. It was mid September. I had just missed a furious battle at "Sandbag Castle" in which a friend of basic training days who haled from Winona, TN had won his Combat Infantryman's spurs. "It was no picnic, he told me, "If it gets any worse, I want to be somewhere else!"

North Koreans had hit Sandbag Castle positions hard the week before the night of Sept 5/6. In an all night action, Cpl Benito Martinez of Fort Hancock, TX had tenaciously held Listening Post Agnes. It ended when he told the other 3 men of his MG team to move back to the MLR. bunkers. Two of those 3 men made it back. Cpl Martinez died at his post covering their withdrawal. His sacrifice was later honored by award of the Medal of Honor. As a replacement, I had a lot to learn. My education began that first night of my arrival on line. I took off my boots when I sacked out. About midnight, all hell broke loose. I scrambled around in the dark trying to find my boots and equipment. After that, I slept with my boots on and knew exactly where I had placed my gear. When I got out of the bunker, I was told to get behind a big rock and shoot anything that moved. It was a long night, I was sure glad when daylight came. Most squads were short of men, some had 5 instead of 9 or 10. New replacements arrived. Every one went to work to rebuild our positions. It was tiring, unrelenting work. Slipping and sliding, we carried logs up hill, built bunkers, filled sandbags. The ground was hard and rocky. We blasted with TNT to make new bunkers. The North Koreans could see smoke. They 'encouraged' us with a few mortar rounds. Their 120 mm mortar fired a shell twice the throw weight of our 4.2 mortars. We had to stay alert to stay alive.

Living conditions were very bad. Nonetheless, the guys all seemed to get along well with each other. Morale was good, our officers and NCOs knew their job. They looked after us, taught us the ropes. We went off line, replaced by another division. Our relief took place in a torrential downpour of rain on a night as dark as dark can get. Sgt Langdale was kept busy keeping us closed up and quiet so no one would get lost. We walked a long way that night. On arrival at the QM clean-up camp we found tents set up for us. Sheer luxury! I was amazed how quickly men found ways to celebrate their relief from rigors of combat. One guy had a guitar, another a harmonica, I played the spoons. Everyone joined in singing. The next day was my best in Korea. We showered, washed the filth of 3 months off our hides. Ah! Clean clothing! Something always taken for granted before combat service. We were then trucked to another rear area. We were 'off line', but still in reserve. In event of any major enemy action, we would be called back to the MLR.

Just after Thanksgiving a big medals awards ceremony was held for the regiment. It was a gala affair. The entire regiment participated with an honor guard. Troops passed in review paying tribute to the 97 veteran soldiers honored that day. There were 6 Silver Stars, 24 Bronze Stars and 67 Purple Hearts awarded for valor, bravery and wounds in the running battle for "Sandbag Castle." Those honored had their medals pinned by the hands of our Division Commander, Major General Samuel T. Williams, known as "Hanging Sam" to his troops. There were many other Purple Hearts awarded, but these were sent home to the next-of-kin as were 2 Silver Stars and several Bronze Stars. The rest of our time in reserve was spent in training, rehabilitation of equipment, and some relaxation. New gear was issued to men needing it prior to our return to the MLR. We all relished the respite from combat.

Above Left..   Be it ever so humble, these members of B Co. 72nd Tk Bn., 2nd Inf. Division at rest in their bunker, call it 'home,' 1952. Below. The occasion for the 'high priced' spectators is the firing of the battalion's 100,000th round. The 213 th FA Bn. [155's] reached this mark in Jan. 1952. Both photos from the Internet.   Above Right. John Stevenson with his KATUSA Kim Yon Ki in the Punchbowl area with the 223rd Regt. 1952.   Photo courtesy of John Stevenson.

RED DRAGON
The SECOND ROUND
FACES OF WAR II

John	J.	Stevenson	RA 11 222 736
First Name	MI	Last Name	Serial Number
Steve	4745	21 July 1933	Cpl
Nickname	MOS	Birthday	Grade / Rank
Item Co 223 Inf Regt 40th Div		Feb 1952-June 1953	Lawrence, MA
Unit (s)		Duty Tour (s)	Home Town

Combat Infantry Badge   Purple Heart Medal   Good Conduct   Navy Good Conduct Medal w/star

Medals & Awards

Occp'n Medal-Germany   Nat'l Def SvcMedal   KCSM w/4 stars   ROK PUC   KWSM   UN Medal

FOXHOLE DOGFACE 'GRADUATES' TO UNITED NATIONS HONOR GUARD

In the fall of 1951 at age 18 I was serving in Germany as a soldier in the 28th Division of the Occupation Army. I decided to volunteer for Korea. The US Army was quite happy to accommodate me. A few months later, with 20 days of combat under my belt and an additional 20 years of maturity on me, I wondered what kind of juvenile thought process had led me to volunteer for war. Yet, today, after long years in retirement, I am proud of my years of service to our country. And, in protection of my country I would again volunteer as I did more 50 years ago. But I would do so as a mature man without any youthful "derring-do" ideas of the glories of war. I was just 19 when I came to Korea, landing at Inchon February 1952. It was low tide. We anchored several miles out from the harbor, climbing down cargo nets to barges which took us ashore. At the replacement depot I was assigned to the 40th Division.

Assigned to I Co of the 223 Inf Regt, then in reserve at Kapyong,I got into an argument with a KATUSA soldier. I lost my temper and punched him in the mouth, only to find found myself on the ground with his pointed finger in my chest. He held me down until I cooled off. I learned later he had been a Karate instructor. He was one cool guy, never lost his composure. We became good friends. He had my respect also as a good soldier. At night we replaced the 5th RCT on the north ridge of the Punchbowl. Platoon Sgt McDonald and my squad ldr, Sgt Carter were given a rundown on the Chinese to our front. At daylight we saw the body of a dead American sergeant, lying in No-Mans land in front of us. He had been killed on patrol a couple of days earlier. We were cautioned not to attempt retrieval as his body had been booby trapped by the Chinese. The adjoining area on both sides was also heavily mined. There were no maps to aid in locating the mines. We were greeted that morning with the Chinese version of a daily alarm clock. They habitually lobbed in a few mortar rounds in the morning hours to keep us from getting too comfortable. They had several wheeled light artillery pieces which would fire a single round, then move to a new location to prevent our radar from locating them which would enable us to deliver counter battery fire. We stayed in the Punchbowl area for about five months before we were relieved.

In our static position, refinements in rudiments of civilization were soon introduced. One was the Army version of the sanitary facility we called an outhouse back home. Only back home, there was a roof to shelter an individual from the snow, rain and cold, also a door for privacy. The Army "12 holer" version was fitted with wooden seats and lids which could be closed. That was the sum of amenities. It was open to the elements, and as for privacy, two rows of 6 seats arranged back to back, meant 'company' was always present. Patrons using the facility had a view of the grandeur of open skies and the Korean countryside. More heavily manned areas were equipped with "24 holers," 12 seats, back to back. Otherwise, the larger model was just a big daddy version of the junior size. All versions were portable so they could be easily moved to a new location. The latrines were regularly given a heavy daily application of chloride of lime for both odor control and sanitary purposes. Our "twelver"overlooked a beautiful view of the Punchbowl.

I lost the first of my 9 lives using our "twelver." Mortar rounds impacted very near me. I could not dive for cover as my trousers bound my ankles in a noose. The second time it happened, I swore off. Thereafter I used my entrenching tool to make my own private "one holer" arrangements. Lost my second life from fright when during a bombardment a shell hit directly on the roof of my bunker. Came halfway through the roof, collapsing it. It was a dud, thank the Good Lord, but it was several minutes before my heart managed to migrate from mouth back to chest where it belonged. We were shelled so many times in that location we named it "The Shooting Gallery." We were finally relieved by a Philippine Army company. We moved to an area midway between "Heartbreak Ridge" and White Horse Mountain. Stayed there for a while then returned to the Punchbowl in time to watch the Navy bombard Chinese positions with an Army 2d Lt FO calling the shots. Made Cpl, was wounded and sent to hospital in Japan. Blessed with a healthy young body, recovery was uneventful. Instead of being returned to Korea, I was assigned to the United Nations Honor Guard in Tokyo. On my first day of guard, I was posted at the main entrance of a building where high ranking officers were assigned. The buzzer sounded 4 times to alert me that a Four Star General was leaving the building. I was prepared with a fancy salute as an aide emerged with a cocker spaniel. He opened the door of the 4 star limo telling the driver, "Take the dog home." To myself I said, "Welcome to Japan."

<u>Above.</u> After a grenade battle in the rain, these wounded GIs from the 17th Regt. of the 7th Division are gathered up for evacuation.   The battle was fought for Hill 657 in June, 1951.   <u>Below.</u>   Another aerial view of the backbreaking terrain in the Heartbreak Ridge area on the East - Central front.   <u>Both photos courtesy of the National Archives</u>.

RED DRAGON
The SECOND ROUND
FACES OF WAR II

Paul	G.	Myatt		US 53 097 106
First Name	MI	Last Name		Serial Number
None	1745	26 Dec 1930		Cpl, then Pfc
Nickname	MOS	Birthday		Grade / Rank
A/27"Wolfhounds"/25th Div		Sept 1952-29 Aug 1953		Nashville, TN
Unit (s)		Duty Tour (s)		Home Town

Purple Heart   Good Conduct Medal   POW Medal   Combat Infantry Badge   United Nations Medal
Medals & Awards
Korean Campaign Service Medal,1star   National Defense Service Medal   ROK 50th Anniv Medal

LOST AND FOUND HERO

Paul Myatt was a replacement, fresh over from Japan when he joined Co. A of the Wolfhounds in the first week of Sept 1952. It was a poor time for a new man to learn the tools of a soldiers's trade. Co A was then manning "Sandbag Castle" in the Heart Break ridge area. He came at a time when the regiment was battling a ferocious and sustained drive by the North Koreans to retake positions they had lost earlier in the war. "Sandbag Castle" was a redoubt perched atop a granite pinnacle which gave excellent observation over most of the central front assigned to X Corps. Its loss would be a disaster. It was a military prize the North Koreans coveted.

Myatt was assigned as assistant to Cpl Martinez who was manning a LMG at the LP located forty yards in front of the MLR. The 5 man fire team delivered flanking MG and rifle fire on the enemy attack which was of critical importance in preventing penetration of the MLR. When the night long battle was over, Martinez was dead as was one of the riflemen. Two men of the three riflemen made it back to the MLR when ordered to do so by Martinez. One man, the new replacement was missing. He remained missing for 46 years as far as his comrades were concerned. Cpl Benito Martinez received the Medal of Honor posthumously for his heroic role in the action. Myatt, carried as MIA on the regimental roster, turned up at a 1998 "Wolfhounds" reunion. He had been wounded and taken prisoner. He was repatriated as a POW, 27 August 1953. Myatt's story is best told in his own words, later in a notarized statement.

This statement is intended as a true and accurate account, under oath, of the events of Sept 5-6 1952 to the best of my knowledge. At that time I, Paul G. Myatt, was a Pfc in the United States Army assigned to Company A of the 27th Inf Reg't of the 25th Inf Division. "My US Army unit, 2d platoon A/27 was defending the summit positions of Hill 1052 [Sandbag Castle] near Satae-ri, Korea during late summer 1952. I accompanied my squad leader, Corporal Benito Martinez with a light machine gun to a forward listening post about forty yards forward of our company's main line of resistance and a stone's throw from the enemy. We assumed a position side by side in a small bunker at the post. Near midnight, heavy incoming mortar fire and artillery fire overwhelmed us. Martinez and I moved quickly into a tunnel entrance next to the bunker for protection. Then the North Korean infantry began their attack, rushing towards us and firing. We began returning fire immediately using a machine gun and a rifle. This fire fight continued for a considerable time. We stopped the first group of North Koreans with our fire. At this point enemy mortar and artillery fire began coming in heavy again.

The incoming shells began impacting at our position and then swept back behind us to the main line of resistance in the vicinity of the platoon and company command posts. North Korean infantry attacks resumed as the shelling moved towards our company's position. As Martinez and I talked together we realized the situation was very bad. We figured we might not get out alive, but we were convinced that the North Koreans would over run our whole company and the main line of resistance if they got by us. We felt we had to stay and try to stop them, or at least slow them down. We agreed to fight on in spite of the danger to our own lives. Martinez communicated this message to our platoon via sound power telephone. Shortly before dawn on September 6, the machine gun quit firing. Benny laid his .45 caliber pistol close by where he could reach it while he attempted to repair it. I was protecting his position by blocking the entrance to the bunker with rifle fire and grenades so he could keep on working on the machine gun.

Although many North Korean soldiers lay dead in the trenches there were still many others swarming everywhere. I had already sustained some superficial bullet wounds to my legs. When our bunker was hit with a barrage of fire, probably from mortars and/or concussion grenades, I was blown out of the bunker into the trench. I was stunned, barely conscious, and completely helpless. I had blood all over me from bleeding in my ears, nose, and other parts of my body. The next thing I knew, North Koreans were dragging me down a tunnel. They tied me up with wire. Later they told me they had killed everyone else, including Martinez. I was held for almost a year at POW Camp Number 3 near the Yalu River, enduring frostbite, malnutrition and torture. I made one attempt to escape. My punishment was torture and solitary confinement with very little food and water. In spite of being tortured, beaten and abused I never gave in to enemy demands for information." S/ Paul G. Myatt 22 March 2001 Notarized by Joyce Hargrove NotaryPublic of Tennessee

The "Wolfhounds" are in process of trying to obtain recognition of Myatt's role by urging a belated award of the DSC.............Ed.

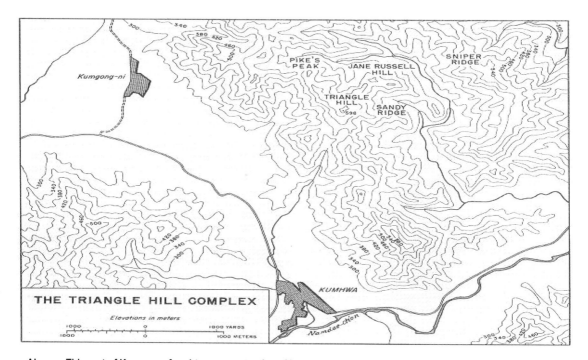

Above. This part of Korea was fought over constantly . Almost every hill had it's own name and sinister reputation. White Horse Mountain is located lower left of the map. The ROK 9th Division held off 23,000 Chinese there for over a week, more than 10,000 casualties were inflicted on the CCF 38th Army. Below. This soldier looks at White Horse with with trepidation, wondering what his future will be, or if he will even have one. Photo and Map from the Internet

RED DRAGON
The SECOND ROUND
FACES OF WAR II

Richard	E.	Fordyce	RA 16385834
First Name	MI	Last Name	Serial Number
Dick	1745	10 June 1934	Sgt 1st Class
Nickname	MOS	Birthday	Grade / Rank
C Co 31st Inf Regt 7Inf Div		May 1952-Mar 1953	Indianapolis, IN
Unit (s)		Duty Tour (s)	Home Town
Combat Infantry Badge Purple Heart Medal Good Conduct Medal National Defense Medal			
Medals & Awards			
Korean Campaign Service Medal, 2 stars UN Medal ROK PUC Korean War Service Medal			

MISSING IN ACTION

By mid afternoon 14 October '52, we had taken our objective on "Jane Russell, the twin hills named after the bosomy movie star, and dug in for the expected counterattack. It came about an hour after dark, preceded by a murderous hour-long artillery barrage. Shortly after 0200 hours we counted noses, there were only nine of us left. We still held the hill. John Dillon clutched his BAR although he had long been out of ammo. We all crouched in the ruins of a trench on the forward slope when another artillery barrage descended on us, killing five of our number. The trench literally disappeared, but thrown up and out, was the body of John Dillon, cut in two at mid section. Months later when I asked the Chaplain for help in responding to a letter from his parents, I was unable to give them all the facts as Army regulations required dog tags and a body as proof of death. Neither were available. It was not until my return home in 1953 when I could visit his parents was I able to tell them he died almost instantly, and, for certain, never knew what hit him. Today his name in the Korean War computer files in Washington, DC is listed as, "Died of Wounds while Missing in Action."

Fort Thomas, Kentucky   December 14, 1952   Cpl Richard Fordyce R.A. 16385834 Co C 31st InfRegt, APO 7, %PM San Francisco, Calif. Dear Richard, Our son John was reported missing in action since October 14,1952. A boy to whom John was assistant BAR man, James H. Donnerberg, recovering from wounds in a hospital in Japan, has written us you were one of the last from the company off Triangle Hill and assured us you would know that John was killed at the top of the hill. Will you please write us telling what you know, whether this is true, and, if so, how it happened; was it instant, do you know anything he said before and during the charge; etc. In his letter, the company commander said a thorough search was made, including the Graves Registration Offices of the 7th Division with negative results. Can you explain this in view of what you know. Donnenberg mentioned also that you knew others who could also tell us about our son. Will you ask them to write to us? We hope and pray for the safety of all you boys. We should like it if you are ever in our neighborhood to call on us. Sincerely, Mr and Mrs Carl I. Dillon.

WHY DID THEY FIGHT? CONDENSED FROM 1954 CBS BROADCAST BY ERIC SEVEREID

The greatest mystery in the Korean War was what made American youngsters fight so hard, so long and so well..in this kind of war. There have been armies that fought well for loot, there was none of that in Korea. Armies have fought well for glory and victory, there was little of that in Korea. Armies have fought well when their homeland was invaded; this was not true for Americans in Korea. There have been armies that fought well as crusaders out of burning moral or religious zeal, but thousands who fought so well had only the dimmest conception what the war was all about. They will fight again, automatically and instantly, should the armistice fail.

They did all this without the exhortations of political commissars. They bled and died in the mud of that bleak and inhospitable mountainous terrain and, in full knowledge that half their countrymen at home were too bored with it all to give the daily casualty lists a second glance. They had full knowledge that, while they were living the worst life they had ever known, millions of their countrymen were living the best life they had ever known. They gave liberally from their own paychecks to the emaciated Korean children while their prosperous countrymen showed little interest. And they felt no particular bitterness that all this was so. They fought right ahead at the time military authorities were publicly arguing they were being handled tragically wrong. And they fought right ahead knowing politicians divided their country about the very purpose of their fight, telling them that their wounds were all in vain. And they fought ahead knowing that, while Allied nations were cheering them on, Allied soldiers were not coming to help them in any great numbers. Whatever is responsible, these boy's behavior in this war outmatches, it seems to me, the behavior of those who fought our wars of certainty and victory. This is something new in the American story. This is something to be recorded with respect and humility.

Why have these youths behaved so magnificently? The answer lies deep in the heart and tissues of American life, none among us can unravel all its threads. It has to do with parents, teachers and ministers. With their 4-H clubs, scout troops, and neighborhood centers. It has to do with the sense of belonging to a team, with the honor of upholding it, the shame of letting it down. But it also has to do with their implicit, unreasoned belief in their country, and their natural belief in themselves as individual men on this earth.

One ' bone weary' mile after another our troops traversed Korea with only one reward. Climb another hill and fight another battle. If paid by the mile, they would all have been rich. <u>Photo courtesy of the Internet</u>.

RED DRAGON
The SECOND ROUND
FACES OF WAR II

Clarence	D.	Beaver	RA 17 287 626
First Name	MI	Last Name	Serial Number
Terry	Radioman(RT OPR)	14 March 1930	SFC, then Cpl or Sgt
Nickname	MOS	Birthday	Grade / Rank
HQ Co 31st Infantry Regt 7th Div		May 1951-Mch 1953	Tekamah, NE
Unit (s)		Duty Tour (s)	Home Town

Combat Infantry Badge   Bronze Star with V device   Good Conduct Medal   UN Service Medal

Medals & Awards

Korean Campaign Service Medal,2**   National Defense Service Medal   Korean War Svc Medal

THE HIGH PRICE OF REAL ESTATE

Summer in Korea can be hot and muddy, while in winter it is cold and buried in snow. I experienced both. I'll take summer every time. Autumn is probably the best time of year, if you are not dodging bullets, that is. During much of 1952 I served as radio operator for Col Lloyd R. Moses, Commanding Officer of the Seventh Division's 31st Infantry Regiment. October of that year is always in my memory and continues to contribute to some of my nightmares. Operation Showdown, the battle to take Triangle Hill (Hill 598) from the Chinese, kicked off on 14 Oct '52 and raged for several days. Col. Moses and I witnessed most of the first day's fighting from a forward observation post 600-800 yards from the battle itself. First and Third Bns of the 31st fought tenaciously to take the hill and despite vicious opposition succeeded in taking the crest. The enemy was determined to take it back and launched an overwhelming counterattack. As darkness fell, Moses conferred with the two Bn commanders and ordered a slow, measured, fighting withdrawal.

Next morning, 2d Bn/31 under command of Maj Warren B. Phillips and a Bn from the 32d Inf resumed the attack. By 1100 hours Hill 598 was again in our hands. The fight continued to take objectives Jane Russell and Sniper ridges. About that time Moses decided to join his men. He ordered me to put on a flak jacket, get my backpack PRC-10 radio and accompany him up the hill. We set out cross country from our OP on Hill 604, heading straight for Triangle Hill. We at once came under enemy observation and drew heavy mortar fire. I tried to ignore the incoming shell bursts. We finally reached the base of Triangle Hill about 3/4 mile from the OP where we had started. Col Moses chose the shortest route up hill, a 70 degree slope that our GIs had traversed only an hour or so ahead of us. As we labored upward, we glanced down (almost straight down!) and saw a group of soldiers attempting to lay a commo wire up the steep slope. Suddenly we were spotted, they began waving and shouting at us. "What are those guys saying?" Moses asked me. I replied, "Colonel, those guys are glad to see you up here with them." It was, I reflected later, a 1952 version of a high five.

At the crest, artillery and mortar fire was intense. Moses later estimated it at 10 rounds per minute, one round every 6 seconds. It seemed much more to me. One near miss knocked the mouthpiece off my radio, rendering it inoperable. Moses immediately ordered me to find another radio and contact his command post. Where the hell do you find a radio in the middle of a very hot war? I crawled along what was left of a commo trench, avoiding dead Chinese and a GI who had been fatally wounded. Incoming rounds impacted without let up, making for an interesting and potentially tenuous existence. Emerging at the crest of the hill, I saw a 2d Lt, a Forward Observer, sitting calmly out in the open facing the enemy. He had a radio! After some talk, he allowed me use it. I contacted our group at the forward OP and relayed Moses' orders to intensify our counter mortar fire. The OP in turn, told me to tell Moses to get to a 'hard wire' land line as soon as possible so he could talk on a 'secure line', not subject to being overheard by the Chinese.

Moses meanwhile had gone forward a few yards to toss a smoke grenade to let our people know the limit of our progress. When I told him of the message I was to relay to him, he said, "Let's go," and started back down the hill. We had hardly started when he spotted a wounded soldier lying unattended on a stretcher nearby. Without hesitation, he said, "Beaver, I'll take this end, you take the other. We carried that badly wounded soldier to the Bn Aid Station with artillery and mortar shells falling in close proximity on all sides of us. Arriving at the aid station about midnight, he said. "Beaver I have to get to a phone in a hurry. You can catch up with me later." He took off in a near run. I had no idea where he was going but figured Bn HQs would know. I hitched a ride on a half track that was returning from shuttling supplies up the hill. When I reached Bn HQs, he was emerging from the bunker. My next order was, "Find my jeep driver and interpreter. We have to get back to regiment." I went to a nearby tent crammed with sleeping GIs. It took a lot of knocking on heads and many profane responses before I located the two men. Finding them, we headed back to Regt'l Hqs.

Years later I learned that Operation Showdown was the costliest operation in terms of casualties endured by the 31st Regiment during the entire Korean conflict. Soldiers from the 31st Regiment were awarded two Medals of Honor, at least one DSC and handfuls of Silver and Bronze Stars. In my opinion, any GI who set foot on that worthless piece of real estate deserved a medal. Men of the 31st produced a lot of heroes in that battle. It was one hell of a costly piece of real estate. The high cost was paid in American blood.

Left. One of the most popular USO shows to tour Korea in 1952 was the Betty Hutton Show. Betty is enjoying a 'Kodak Moment' with hundreds of her G.I. fans. Right. Also on a later USO tour was this star of movies and later TV, Patricia Neal. Below. Several officers climb trees and use their field glasses to see over the crowd. Thousands of GIs are enjoying the show, in spite of the cold wet weather. These photos were in the 45th Division area but the shows played for most of the units in Korea. All photos by Glenn Ed White.

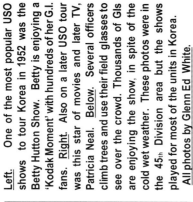

RED DRAGON
The SECOND ROUND
FACES OF WAR II

Robert	B.	Campbell	11 89 871 USMC
First Name	MI	Last Name	Serial Number
Soup-san	0333	21 May 1933	Sgt, then Cpl
Nickname	MOS	Birthday	Grade / Rank
Wpns 1st Bn lst Marines 1st MarDiv		Feb 1952-Feb 1953	Cleveland, OH
Unit (s)		Duty Tour (s)	Home Town

Navy Presidential Unit Citation   Combat Action Ribbon   Navy Unit Commendation   ROK PUC

Medals & Awards

Service Medal   Republic of Korea War Service Medal   United Nations Service Medal

GOOD NEWS & BAD NEWS

It was the late fall of 1952. My regiment, the First Marines, had just been withdrawn from the Main Line of Resistance and placed in reserve after a long period of bloody combat on the front lines. We were weary, cold, battered and looking forward to some of the amenities lacking on the MLR. Hot showers, hot chow and a daily beer ration cheered us up immensely. Of course, there were tradeoffs which did not give us the same measure of cheer--training exercises, inspections in ranks and layout of our gear, and work parties, the age old curse of all Marines trying to relax with a little 'bunk fatigue' to catch up on lost sleep. We consoled ourselves with the fact that we were not being shot at, nor were we having to duck artillery and mortar barrages. It could have been a lot worse.

We had returned from participation in a particularly grueling field exercise in the inclement cold weather of a Korean fall. We were sacked out on our cots, weary bodies recuperating from the travail posed by the formidable Korean hills in our tactical exercise. Everyone in our tent was bitching and moaning in the usual manner of troops after such an exercise. Our feet hurt, our backs ached. We were really beat. The tent flap burst open. The company clerk came busting in, waving a sheet of paper. "Lissen up, you guys. I got good news and bad news," he announced. He was greeted with hoots and derisive comments. He waited until the din died then continued his announcement. "Okay, wise guys, here's the good news. A USO troupe headed by Betty Hutton and a bunch of gorgeous Hollywood sweeties is coming here to entertain us big, bad Marines." He emphasized his words by outlining with his hands the form of a shapely female. His words elicited wolf whistles and cries of glee from marines long starved for female company. In 1952, Betty Hutton was known as the Blonde Bombshell. She was every bit as popular as Marilyn Monroe. We couldn't believe our luck! Betty Hutton and a bunch of Hollywood cuties to boot. We were ecstatic! It made all the chicken shit training easier to take.

"Okay? Ready for the bad news?" the clerk yelled over the hubbub. "You jokers have piss tube duty during the Betty Hutton show." We couldn't believe our ears. "What the hell is piss tube duty?" one of my tent mates asked angrily. "You guys are gonna stand guard over the piss tubes in the area to make sure no one uses them while the ladies are here," He answered smugly, "Wouldn't want to offend their delicate natures, would we?" The clerk had a wolfish grin on his face as he beat a hasty retreat out of the tent.

Piss tubes were empty artillery canisters that were half buried in the ground, set at a forward leaning angle of 30 degrees to accommodate the male urinary anatomy. In warm weather and several days of use piss tubes tended to be on the smelly side. Worse, when temperatures dropped below freezing, the footing around the piss tube became as slippery as a skating rink. The longer it was in use, the farther back the user stood so as to not lose his footing. In rear areas where more permanent installations were the norm, piss tubes reflected the more civilized attitudes of these areas. Large holes were dug with a ballooned hollow at the bottom, stones thrown in for drainage, earth tamped around the canister inserted into the pit. Chloride of Lime was used daily as an odor and sanitary disinfectant. The rough-and-ready improvisions used on the MLR and the slightly more refined versions found in a reserve area merely reflected the exigency of military life in the field. Anyway, there were dozens of these piss tubes scattered around camp.

The whole camp except our tent would watch the spectacular USO show and its ravishing Hollywood beauties. We had the dubious honor of guarding the odiferous piss tubes. The bitching in the tent was twice as loud and rancorous as it had been before the 'bad news' was unloaded on us by our jocular company clerk. We decided some clown must be having fun with us. The whole idea was too bizarre to be true. We checked it out. Bizarre or not, it was only too true. The brass in the rear with the gear had struck again! On the day of the big show we walked our guard posts in good Marine fashion, making sharp about faces as we reversed course and made squared corners on turns like the good Marines we were. While walking my post in the prescribed military manner, I strained my ears to hear Betty Hutton sing her bouncy songs, but all I could hear was distant applause and roars of approval of the lucky Marines attending the show. The Betty Hutton show was one of the best to play in Korea--or so I heard. I have many memories of my one year tour of duty in Korea, but recalling this incident to mind still rankles within me!

325

Above. Roy Zittle and his BAR at Sandbag Castle. Photo by Roy Zittle. GIs of the 40th Inf. Div. get hot chow on the backside of the MLR. Lower Right. A self-propelled 155 howitzer is put into firing position to 'take out' some Chinese bunkers for the 40th Infantry Division. Lower Left A couple of Two above photos courtesy of Robert L. Riggs. GI s are shown in the mountains of East-Central Korea. Photo from Internet.

Roy	E.	Zittle	US 52 135 892
First Name	MI	Last Name	Serial Number
"Petie"	2745	7 Sept 1931	Sgt
Nickname	MOS	Birthday	Grade / Rank
C 224th Inf 40thDiv		Oct 1952-Nov '53	Hagerstown, MD
Unit (s)		Duty Tour (s)	Home Town
Combat Infantry Badge		Good Conduct Medal	National Defense Service Medal
Medals & Awards			
Korean Campaign Service Medal w/3stars		United Nations Service Medal	ROK KWSM

ON THE JOB TRAINING

After I was drafted, I went through an eight week training course of something called basic infantry training. After 'graduating' and sent on furlough for a family visit before going to Korea, I had a chance to reflect on what I had been taught. Made me feel quite comfortable in my abilities as a soldier. Little did I know how little I knew. Further, how little did I know of what I needed to know! On sober contemplation 50 years later, I no longer blame the Army as I once did. I now know the blame lies at the feet of Congress and politicians of all stripes who gain favors with voters by dismantling armies whose victories have been won by the blood of the same breed of citizen that politicians pander for votes. I was one of those young American citizens drafted to fight a third rate enemy country. Just a few short years before it would have been quickly crushed by the victorious American WW II juggernaut army. My story is typical of thousands of draftees who served in the latter half of the Korean War. Armies need replacements for those killed or wounded. When we run out of veterans and reservists we resort to the draft. The need for men was so great the Army could not devote a year or two to train men as we did in WW II before committing them to combat. Hence the 8 week basic training period.

When I arrived in Japan en route to Korea, we were told any two buddies could stay together. My good friends, John Gdabo and Herm Holstman were always in front of me. The army operates alphabetically. Z for Zittle meant I was always last in line. When they were assigned to the 40th Division, they came back and told me. I asked for the same outfit. Next, at the 224th Inf Reg't, same story. At 224th Rear, they were assigned to 'C' Co. They told me to ask for "C." When I asked for 'C' company, the clerk said, "You're sure?" "Yes, I have a cousin there." " He still up there?" "Yes, as far as I know." He shook his head and said,"OK." Later an officer came out and asked what companies we were going to. To 5 men in 'A' he said, "A good company." Same for 4 men in 'B.' When he came to the 20 of us in 'C'" he stood for a few seconds, head down, then said, "Boys, I wish you luck. 'Sandbag Cast!e!' Charlie Company accounts for 85% of all our casualties. I didn't know what he meant. I was soon to learn. I thought, "What have I gotten myself into?"

We moved up to the foot of some mountain. I now know was Hill 1052, on "Heartbreak Ridge." Surveying it by moon light, it appeared to be a scene of desolation from the depths of hell. I could see the hillside was cratered and pitted, pockmarked like the face of a smallpox victim. There were splintered trees, stumps, barbed wire, wreckage of all kinds. As we waited for daylight to start our climb, a litter party came by carrying a wounded man. Again, I wondered, "What the hell have I gotten myself into!" In the tiring climb up this 3400 foot high mountain next day, lugging my gear, I could see more clearly in daylight the utterly barren and God forsaken landscape that was to be my home. When we reached our destination, I learned that Charlie Company was the defender of "Sandbag Castle" which had, until just a few weeks before in late October, been held by the 2d platoon of A Company, 27th Infantry, "The Wolfhounds." Now, late November 1952, 1st platoon "C "Company, 224th Infantry was charged with the defense of "Sandbag Castle."

Bob Aiken, an old paratrooper vet, greeted us. He became our lifesaver OJT mentor. The first thing he said was, "Welcome to 'Sandbag Castle.' What do you guys know about machine guns or BARs? We all confessed ignorance. He laughed, "I know you've been told to keep away from automatic weapons. Up here we have only two weapons, Browning Automatic Rifles and Light Machine Guns. I'll take you to the gunners. They'll teach you all you need to know, how to take 'em apart and put 'em back together, how to remove ruptured cartridges. You'll be first class gunners by sunset. You better be! The castle holds about 20 men. It's like 2 Vee's pushed almost together. The North Koreans are on higher ground 50 to 75 yards away and are dug in deep. They hit us often, and almost always at night. They play for keeps up here. Pay attention to your on-the-job training and get it right the first time. If you don't, there won't be a second time. You'll be on your way back to be fitted for a body bag." I sure paid attention, asking questions if I did not understand. Nor did I object to 7 hours of repetitive disassembly and assembly practice on the .30 cal L.G. and BAR. I listened very closely about how a ruptured cartridge is removed. He taught us other combat skills that enable survival. I guess I got it right. The North Koreans never broke through our defenses on Sandbag Castle. I lived to come home. But it was OJT, not basic training that gave me skills I needed to survive. Not all of us were lucky enough to be tutored by an veteran NCO like Sgt Bob Aiken.

<u>Above.</u> The 3rd Ranger Company prepares to make a night crossing of the Imjin River, April 1951.
<u>Below</u>. 5th RCT wounded are evacuated by tank at Kumcho, October 1950. <u>Both photos from the Internet.</u>

Paul	A.	Freeburger	RA 13 276 383
First Name	MI	Last Name	Serial Number
Sarge	1745	18 Nov 1929	T/Sgt E-6
Nickname	MOS	Birthday	Grade / Rank
I&R 14Inf Regt 25th Div		Dec 1950-Nov 1951	Palm Bay, FL
Unit (s)		Duty Tour (s)	Home Town
Bronze Star Medal w/V device		Purple Heart Medal Combat Infantry Badge	ROK PUC

Medals & Awards

Good Conduct Medal w/ 4 knots   Korean Campaign Service Medal w/ 3 stars   NDSM UN Medal

THE AIDMAN

Aidman, Corpsman, Medic, 'Doc,' 'Shanker Mechanic,' to name a few, he probably carries more sobriquets than any other soldier in the military. In combat his life is at more risk is at more risk than an infantryman. In heat of battle, he cares for wounded, exposing more of his hide to enemy fire than the recumbent soldier he is tending in his effort to save a life. He serves in one of the only two services, medic and combat engineer, that the combat infantryman allows into his select and hard won circle of battle comradeship. He has been given another name by many infantrymen, one almost of reverence, hard earned at risk of his life, "One of God's Angels."

In retrospect, war is too often portrayed as a time of glory and honor in lives of men. Tales of soldiers fill history books as they tell of days of triumph and despair. However, every war touches the lives of those who confront the enemy as well as those who watch with horror as events beyond their control change their very lives forever. No other fighting man deserves the respect and admiration of the Combat Infantryman more than does the Combat Medic. To be effective in battle, the Aidman must be physically and mentally tougher than his comrades in the combat forces. His job requires strength and endurance. He cannot be frail or overweight since he must be strong enough to carry survivors out of a rice paddy or a jungle environment. He helps at times to carry the litter of the wounded soldier, or to hoist him into an evacuation helicopter. When he has done all he can, and it is not enough, he has been seen with tears in his eyes. He is often a man who carries more of a religious ethic than the wounded man he is trying to save.

The Aidman must ask himself if he is able to establish an airway, dress a wound or administer a sedative under direct fire. He works under the well grounded supposition that more lives are saved in the initial few minutes of bodily injury than in the hospital. The combat medic must retrieve the wounded soldier. He administers the first medical attention to the wounded warrior. The wounded also benefit from recent advances in modern medical techniques. Helicopter pilots and their crews contribute to survival by quickly retrieving the wounded from the battlefield. In combination, these advances increase the chance for survival. Studies have shown that 92% of injured personnel who reached a military hospital alive actually survived their wounds. These adjuncts have worth only because the combat medic is there with his dedicated courage and the tools of his trade to initiate the process of medical care.

Combat medics must know what is in their medical kits down including the last Band-Aid. What he carries in That kit plus the emergency medical knowledge in his head, backed by his fortitude and commitment to his fellow soldiers, makes the combat medic kin to a saint in the military pantheon of heroes. Soldiers know he is the one who makes the difference whether many of the wounded live or die. After all, the first thought most soldiers have after being in combat is coming home alive to resume civilian life with family and loved ones. The combat medic in many, many cases raises the odds that the injured soldier will live to realize that hope.

Recognition of the Combat Medic is made by award of the Combat Medical Badge (CMB), established on 1 March 1945 by War Department Circular No 66. At that time the insignia was known as the Medical Badge. It quickly became known as the Combat Medical Badge since participation in combat was required as was case of its somewhat earlier cousin, the Combat Infantry Badge. The design is a caduceus [twin snakes twined around a winged staff] with a cross on the caduceus, all over a stretcher on a wreath. It would be another 20 years before the Expert Medical Badge would be approved in recognition of the skills possessed by the trained Aidman in peace time. The Korean War caused the creation of a second award of the Combat Medical Badge with the addition of a star above the cross. At the same time, in typical military foresight, badges with two stars indicating a third award and three stars for a fourth award were authorized. These badges were created for third and fourth awards for which no one was then eligible.

A little known fact about the CMB stems from the award of the CIB to the dogface infantryman of WW II. In late 1944 the CIB was authorized, granting in addition to the CIB, an extra $10 per month which raised the pay of an infantry buck private from $50 to $60 per month. Medics were not included. Infantrymen in all theaters deluged Congress and various military publications with letters denouncing the inequity involved, the gratuitous slight to the revered Aidman. WD Circular No 66 was issued soon thereafter.

Above. In the outskirts of Seoul this wounded Marine is helped to the rear for medical treatment. Sept. 1950.
Below. The 8063 MASH treats wounded from the 5th RCT and the 5th Cav. Regt. Nov., 1950. Photos from Internet

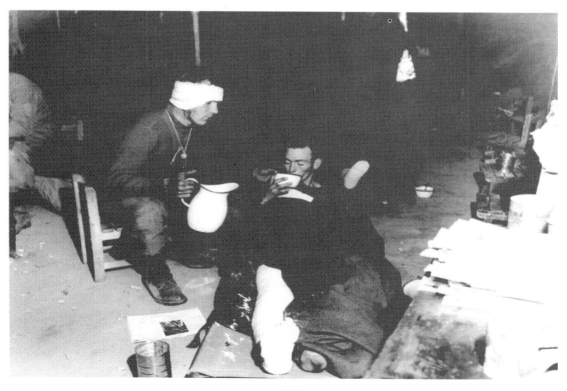

RED DRAGON
The SECOND ROUND
FACES OF WAR II

James	W.	Davis	784 66 43 USN
First Name	MI	Last Name	Serial Number
Doc	Corpsman	21 Dec 1926	HM0 later HM2
Nickname	MOS	Birthday	Grade / Rank
E Co 2d Bn 5th Marines 1st MarDiv		Jan 1952-Jan 1953	Portland, OR
Unit (s)		Duty Tour (s)	Home Town

Purple Heart Medal Commendation Medal w/V Good Conduct Medal ACSM WWII Victory Medal

Medals & Awards

Navy Presidential Unit Citation Korean Campaign Service Medal,3 stars UN Medal ROK KWSM

TWO WAR ANGEL OF MERCY

Back in 1945 when I was first assigned as a Navy Corpsman, I didn't cotton to the idea of being a Medic. I was not comfortable with the idea that my job could, and probably would, entail life or death responsibilities involving my own comrades. It was not that I felt my training was inadequate, it was more a sense that the duties violated some fundamental feeling I could not put a finger on. But, since one serving in a military role has little choice in a duty assignment, I finally decided that, if by doing my job well, I could help bring at least more one young man home that might otherwise have died, I would have done what I was being trained to do. That mental decision eased my mind and conscience no end. My training completed, World War II ended before I was sent overseas.

A refresher course at Camp Pendelton brushed up on medical procedures and skills I had been taught just five short years before. I was assigned to E Co 5th Marine Regiment. In this hard fighting regiment of the USMC I was called upon to utilize the medical skills I had learned. The gnawing feeling I had known since I was assigned as a medic was submerged by the almost daily need to attend to wounded men. Casualties were particularly heavy in the month of June. The high rate of casualties continued for several months as the regiment daily fought its way northward to eject the Chinese and North Korean armies south of the 38th parallel. In the dozens of instances where I was involved in taking care of a wounded Marine, some stand out more than others. Those that do usually had circumstances which were different than gunshot or shrapnel wounds incurred in the heat of an action. In November 1952 I was given a chance to use every medical technique I had been taught as well as those I had learned in practice over the preceding months.

This Marine had tripped on a mine. He could not be immediately evacuated because of the ongoing action and the difficulty of the terrain over which he would have to be carried on a stretcher. Four men upright, carrying the stretcher in the middle of a fire fight, exposes five men to gunfire and risks again wounding or killing an already wounded man. Poor odds. I told the CO I thought I could get to him and administer plasma which would give him a chance to live. I was able to work my way to the wounded Marine and give him the emergency medical treatment he needed for his chance at life. A message over the backpack radio promised a chopper at first light, but warned we would have to be quick as we were in a very exposed position which limited the time the chopper could stay at the evacuation scene. The Marines in the area set up a defense perimeter around the wounded man. Just before daylight using a flashlight hidden under a poncho I gave him another bag of plasma. At dawn the chopper showed up as promised having spotted our white smoke flare. We strapped a live Marine onto the chopper litter and gave him his chance at life.

We then ran back toward the MLR. "Charlie" must have still been asleep. We were not on the receiving end of mortar fire, or 76 mm whizbang flat trajectory shells. I do not know whether any of those I cared for lived or not. Not a day goes by I do not think of them in hope that others remember also the sacrifices they made for God, our country and the Corps. As the years have gone by, the gnawing I feel in my gut has never quit. The only difference is that today I now know, after VA counseling, that my feeling of guilt comes from wondering whether I could have done a better job. I am told I am not alone. Many, many veterans feel the same as I do

<table>
<tr><td>TAPS
American Civil War, 1863</td><td>INVOCATION FOR A FALLEN COMRADE
Ranger funeral ceremony, Bob Smyers,
Chaplain 2Bde, LRRP Rangers, 4th Inf Div, Vietnam,1973.</td><td></td></tr>
<tr><td>Day is done
Gone the sun
From the lakes
From the hills
From the sky
All is well, safely rest
God is nigh.</td><td>Fading light
Dims the sight
And a star
Gems the sky
Gleaming bright
From afar, drawing nigh
Falls the night</td><td>Thanks and praise
For our days
I end this tribute to our brother
With words from Taps
'Neath the sun, 'neath the stars,' neath the sky
As we go, this we know
God is nigh.</td></tr>
</table>

Left. The mighty carrier USS Leyte in Sasebo Harbor gets ready for a tour in Korea, 1950. Above. A large number of Chinese prisoners were taken as the result of the CCF April-May Fifth Offensives in 1951. Both photos from the National Archives. Below. After moving to the Western Front, these Marine Corps tanks ford a river looking for some action. Photo courtesy of Roger Baker.

RED DRAGON
The SECOND ROUND
FACES OF WAR II

James	W.	Newland	ER 56 114 613
First Name	MI	Last Name	Serial Number
Jim	Tank Vehicle Mechanic	12 Mar 1929	Cpl
Nickname	MOS	Birthday	Grade / Rank
Don't remember		10 Feb 1952- 14 Jan 1954	Monroe, WA
Unit (s)		Duty Tour (s)	Home Town
Good Conduct Medal	Korean Campaign Service Medal w/4 stars		National Defense Medal
Medals & Awards			
United Nations Service Medal	Republic of Korea War Service Medal		ROK Peace Medal

DRAFTED!

Like many young American males in 1951, I faced the draft. And, like many others, I elected to join the Naval Reserve to continue my schooling. As a bonus, I would not be drafted into the army. Little did I know! As the poet Robert Burns once noted in his poem, "*To a Mouse*," "The best laid schemes o'mice and men gang aft a-gley." It was a lesson I was in process of learning. I was a Construction Battalion Sea Bee, and like a good sailor attended my weekly drills. No draft notice for this boy. As the Korean struggle heated up, more and more of my comrades disappeared from drill sessions to become active navy members. I fully expected my call at any time. My sea bag was packed, ready. I was ready. There was an unexpected problem. The problem was employment.

As a recent college graduate I had encountered the same response from prospective employers, "Come back when you're out of the service." At last I found a job. It was a long way from those weekly reserve drills. Earning a living, supporting a new wife made reserve meetings a minor consideration. A month passed. A letter arrived from the CO of my reserve unit informing me that the Draft Board had checked the roster. "Suggest you make the next meeting." A day off work, a long trip to the city and this sailor was present at his drill. The CO told a couple of us that indeed the Draft Board had taken our names but not to worry, "The Navy takes care of its own." "Call me up now," I said. My shots are current. My bag is packed. My wife understands. I'm ready to go." The reply was, "These things take time. You'll get your call in due time. The Navy will take care of this matter." A few days later another letter arrived. This was from my Draft Board requesting my appearance. Like a good citizen I showed up waving my Navy Reserve card in explanation, "I am a sailor and not supposed to be drafted. Why is it so hard for everyone to understand such a simple truth?"

In a few days I found myself wearing olive drab, sniffing the air of Fort Ord. I kept telling everyone who seemed to be in charge of the situation that they were no longer just messing with me, but with the United States Navy. I mentioned several times that "press gangs" were outlawed after the War of 1812. They were making a huge mistake, and Oh Boy, would they ever be sorry. Several weeks of basic training had passed when one of the cadre came into the barracks saying that my discharge had arrived. I should get my ass pronto up to the Company Commander's office. Faster than a speeding bullet I was facing the top sergeant telling him, "It was about time!" To give flavor to my remarks I added a few choice words about the Army and Fort Ord. "That's alright son, go on in, the CO is expecting you." I should have known from the smiling face of the 1st Sgt that something was amiss. "Top" had never, in the history of his duty in a basic training company, been known to smile, ever. He ushered me into the Company Commander.

I reported to the Captain, snapping him my best salute. He was sitting behind his desk with the same grin that I had seen on the face of the top soldier. Looking back at the incident, it was much like the grin the cannibal chief must have worn as he welcomed the two explorers to his village. In his hand, the Captain had a rolled up piece of paper. He handed it to me, still rolled. Without thinking, while unrolling the precious document, I repeated to the Captain what I had said earlier to the First Sergeant. I read the document. My heart sank into my boots. It was not a transfer to the Navy. It was my discharge *from* the Navy! It was going to be a long war.

"Anything else you want to say, soldier?" The smile disappeared from the Captain's face. It was replaced by the same grim visage he had exhibited once before when I had been privileged to be in his august presence. 'Top' wants to see you now. Dismissed!" While the Captain's smile had vanished, the smile on the face of the 1st Sergeant now resembled that of a barracuda. He knew, they all knew, me and my big mouth and everything else I had belonged to the US Army, now and forever more. An old army saying puts it very well, "Your soul may belong to God, but your ass belongs to the United States Army, until death or discharge do you part!"

I was told to report to the mess hall and find out what wonders were in store for me. The cooks were waiting, having been clued in before I got there. Garbage cans and grease traps needed cleaning. Potatoes piled up waiting my attention. Floors, walls, mess tables needed scrubbing, windows were dirty and needed washing with GI soap, then rinsed and dried. Then for added flavor, there was latrine duty! My life as a sailor was over, my new life as a soldier had begun. As I said, it was going to be a long, long war!

Above. Originally a trainer for Air Force pilots this AT-6 was put to work in Korea spotting ground targets for our fighter bombers. Note smoke rockets under wings. Right. A flight of F-84 Thunderjets with their bombs still slung underneath are waiting for a call that targets are available. Below. A patrol of Australian infantry is getting ready to go out. This one went out from Little Gibralter on 13 May 1953. Of the 16 men who went out they suffered 3 KIA, 7 WIA, and 1 MIA.

Photos from the National Archives and Internet

RED DRAGON
The SECOND ROUND
FACES OF WAR II

Peter	J.	Worthington	ZC 9577
First Name	MI	Last Name	Serial Number
None	Platoon Leader	16 Feb 1927	Lt.
Nickname	MOS	Birthday	Grade / Rank
12Platoon Dog Co 3d Bn PPCLI		Mid '52-Mid '53	Vancouver, BC Canada
Unit (s)		Duty Tour (s)	Home Town
WWII Star	Canadian Vol O/S Medal	WWII Victory Medal	Korea Volunteer Medal
Medals & Awards			
Korea War Medal		Republic of Korea, War and Victory Medals	United Nations Medal

CANADIAN CAPERS

Korea was not my first war, but my first as an infantryman. At the age of 17 in WW II, I volunteered as a Telegraphist Air Gunner (TAG) in the RCN, flying coastal patrol in Fairy Swordfish aircraft. Promoted to sub-Lt in 1945, I was the youngest officer in the Canadian Navy. My conscience told me, also probably the least competent! However, a bit better pay kept conscience on short leash. On discharge I entered the U of BC, graduating after my return from Korea. Early in the Korean War I joined Princess Patricia's Canadian Light Infantry. In the summer of '52 I went to Korea as a Lieutenant in command of 12 Platoon, Dog Company. My first duty post was at 'The Hook' on the Eastern Front, north of Seoul. I later served as Bn Intelligence Officer. My final duty assignment was liaison with 6147 Tactical Squadron of the US 5th AF. I sat as observer in the rear seat of a T-6 aircraft, marking targets and directing Sabre Jets in attack on enemy targets. Deja-vu! I was back at the start of my 1944 WW II military career. Time to return to Canada!

Canadians of 25 Brigade were part of the First Commonwealth Division, probably the strongest division ever fielded by the Commonwealth. Australians, New Zealanders and Canadians outnumbered the British contingent. While I was there, the war was in a defensive mode. Initiative was confined to patrol activity. We sat in trenches and bunkers waiting for the inevitable Chinese attack under constant punishment by shelling and mortar attacks. 3d Bn PPCLI was ordered up into a counter attack role in Nov '52. The Black Watch, defending 'The Hook,' had been overrun in one of those 'human wave' attacks which were often successful, although tremendously costly in lives of Chinese soldiers. We could never figure out the Chinese objectives in these limited attacks. Was it to train their unlimited manpower in the offense? Or was it to show us who was boss? If so, they failed on both counts.

Relief of the Black Watch was our first serious enemy engagement. Everyone was nervous, including the platoon leader. Even for veteran troops, and we not yet blooded, counterattacks are always an uneasy assignment. All's well that ends well. This situation had a humorous side. Canadian forces in winter are issued a daily 2 oz tot of 90 proof rum to ease aspects of the cold. My style as rum ration issuer was not to measure, but rather give each man a swig from the rum canteen. Nondrinkers could pretend, imbibers could take a single huge gulp. Consequently we always had an emergency rum reserve, kept in separate canteens for crises such as getting shot, or coming in cold from patrol. I had a considerable reserve, independent of battalion. It worked well until...

On a midnight, in biting cold, we filed into position to counterattack, prepared to fight our way up a strange hill to restore a position we had never before seen. I could not help but wonder how my troops would behave. As the wait continued, my men became boisterous and aggressive. I decided my men were really gung-ho. I checked with my sergeant. He had noticed it also, adding, "The men must be dehydrated, they are drinking a lot of water." It then dawned on me. Instead of water we had brought the rum canteens! When the time came to move up hill, most of my lads were roaring drunk. God knows what would have happened if the Chinese had not already had enough. They had bugged out by the time my 'warriors' went into action. Hangovers were the only result. Mum was the word. The CO, unaware of what had happened, thought he had a bunch of loosely disciplined tigers in 12 platoon.

Christmas Eve 1952, I commanded the foremost platoon on 'The Hook,' closest to the Chinese on a terrain feature we called "The Pheasant." We were on full standby, ready for an assault on our great Christian holiday. All night long brisk activity went on in front of our wire, but no attack. No one got any sleep. At 'false dawn,' one sentry reported huge figures in front of our wire. They were so big we thought they must be Manchurians, never seen, but who had been reported on the front. I alerted Battalion which alerted Commonwealth artillery. At dawn, it was apparent these shapes were Christmas trees, not Manchurians! I reported to Bn who told me under no circumstances allow the men to go near the trees lest they be booby-trapped. Alas, too late. The men had already looted the trees of the gifts, propaganda leaflets, small glass figurines, North Korean Postcards, stamps and "Peace Diaries" urging we Canadians to desert "The American imperialist aggressors and "come over for good treatment." I informed the CO who told me to confiscate everything, it was "consorting with the enemy." I told the men the rear echelons wanted to share in the loot. Enough was turned in to satisfy intelligence. The men hid their souvenirs. No desertions. All was again well in 12 platoon.

Above. Lt. Worthington, Bn. Intelligence Officer of the 3rd PPCLI, gets a visit from Col. 'Cider Joe' Stillwell in the spring of 1953 His visit was after the Canadians had stopped a Chinese night attack. Photo courtesy of Peter Worthington.

Above. With good reason to smile are two of the top Mig Killers in the U.S. Air Force. With the 4th Fighter Interceptor Group, Jabara was first with 15 and Fernandez a close second with 14 ½ kills . Photo from the National Archives.

RED DRAGON
The SECOND ROUND
FACES OF WAR II

Thomas	M.	Nielson	AF 17290219 USAF
First Name	MI	Last Name	Serial Number
Tom	64150 & 64350	20 July 1933	A 1c,E4 then A 3c,E2
Nickname	MOS	Birthday	Grade / Rank
4th FI W		Apr 1952-Feb 1953	Monticello, UT
Unit (s)		Duty Tour (s)	Home Town
Korean Campaign Service Medal, 3 stars			National Defense Service Medal
Medals & Awards			
United Nations Service Medal		ROK PUC, OLC	ROK Korean War Service Medal

SWEET REVENGE

Shortly after my arrival in Korea, I was assigned to the POL Depot at Kimpo, K-14, 17 miles north of Seoul. Stateside, I had gone through AF Supply Technical School after basic, serving in a supply role in AC&W squadrons and a Bomb squadron. I was familiar with inventory control, record keeping and issue of supplies in support of flight units. However, in true AF tradition, I ended up in this POL outfit about which I knew absolutely nothing. I replaced an E-5 Staff Sgt, I was but a lowly E-2. Anyway, with a"PhD" in supply and a disciplinary mark on my stateside record, the A-1 apparently figured I was the card that fitted the job slot. I was of such low rank as to be expendable, yet possibly I could handle the POL supply problems. I soon learned that all inventory records were hand entered in a Cardex file. All this amounted to was that the Cardex records were whatever the file keeper said they were!

As my predecessor and I stood on the hill overlooking the railhead, watching Korean laborers unload fuel drums from boxcars to revetments, I was advised to record at least 10% of each shipment as "broken." I would need to account for losses due to pilferage and black market sales made by Korean soldiers. The emergency evacuation area which held fuel to gas all our vehicles and planes was about two miles from us. It was 'guarded' by ROK troops whose miserable, virtually nonexistent pay was supplemented by fuel stolen to sell on the black market, even to the Chinese, a few miles away. After looking into all aspects of inventory and supply, I decided that inventory levels left no room for contingencies. I set out to build up a back log to cover eventualities and to cut down on thefts for the black market. As it was, I did my best to stop losses by working with our 811th Engineers and local American MPs.

A TWX machine linked us to Inchon. All I had to do, based on inventory as shown on the Cardex file, was send a TWX specifying the quantity of drummed fuels needed, whether 80/87, 100/130 or 115/145 octane, JP-4, Diesel Fuel No. 2 or denatured alcohol for the 67th Recon's F-80s, and assorted lubricants. These would be on the way by rail in a few hours. My supply of "overages" of DF-2 turned out to be a logistic lifesaver in the winter of 1952/'53 when it was unobtainable elsewhere. A few months into my program, some mysterious and painful disease caused my gums to swell and bleed when I brushed my teeth. Went on sick call. Over a period of 7 weeks in August and September, all my teeth except three were pulled, a few on each dental visit. I could only gum soft food.

Midway in this de-toothing process, I passed up everything until I came to the reconstituted mashed potatoes. As lousy as they were it was the only thing in sight I could gum down. The Korean mess boy gave me a skimpy helping. The spuds were lumpy with undissolved powder, almost chewy. Even so, I asked for more. He refused. We wrangled. The Mess Sgt, an arrogant old RA from pre World War II, came to see what was going on. I explained my problem to him. He didn't care. Told me to shove off, or he would have me up for courts martial. I 'moved on,' hungry, and mad as hell. My tent mate was able to swipe 7 pound cans of Spam, applesauce in big No.10 cans, grapefruit juice and a few other items from 'Rations Breakdown' until I rotated in February of 1953.

When the DF-2 shortage hit that winter, I "opened up" our surplus storage to any and all, loading trucks from as far away as the Third Division in the Chorwon area. One morning, my old Mess Sergeant nemesis showed up at the depot to draw DF-2. I told him we had none. The Mess Sergeant was beet red, boiling mad. He needed DF-2 for his stoves! He had a general arriving for a mess dinner with the HQ officers! I told him, "I I have no DF-2, as I had already said." The Mess Sergeant erupted, "Everybody knows anyone can come here, and get all the DF-2 he needs!" He blustered, he threatened, "He would see my CO." I told him, "Cpt. Bonham is on the other side of this blanket. It separates his office from the supply office."

He stormed in to see him. Cpt. Bonham had heard every word,, "If Neilson says he has no fuel, he has no fuel. Best you talk to him." The Mess Sergeant was now in a permanent stage of purple. He had a hell of a time controlling his rage. I told him the only way I would be able to find DF-2 for him was for him to understand first, I would take no more crap from his help ,and, second I'd trade him one barrel of DF-2 for each case of C-rations. He didn't have any C-rations. Told him I had no DF-2. Only way I could find fuel was to see some C-rations. Half an hour later, his driver came back with 6 cases of C's. C's I could gum in my toothless state. I located 6 drums of DF-2. I think fondly of that episode. It was the only time I ever beat the 'Old Army/Air Force' sergeant combine!

<u>Above and Below</u>.   This line of Russian Mig-15 fighters enjoy their sanctuary in Manchuria.   The Mig was fast, maneuverable, and in control until we were able to put the F-86 Sabre jet. Flown by North Korean, Chinese and even Russian pilots, they proved to be no match for our pilots. In July of 1951, China had only 500 fighters of all types.   By July of 1952, they had <u>1500</u> Migs in Manchuria.   <u>These photos from the Chinese Archives and the Internet</u>.

RED DRAGON
The SECOND ROUND
FACES OF WAR II

Donald	A.	Chase	RA 31 467 752
First Name	MI	Last Name	Serial Number
Don	3745	11 January 1926	S/Sgt
Nickname	MOS	Birthday	Grade / Rank
I Company 15th Infantry 3d Div		November 1952-July 1953	Natick, MA
Unit (s)		Duty Tour (s)	Home Town
Combat Infantry Badge w/star	Bronze Star with V, OLC	Purple Heart, 2OLC	GCM,2knots

Medals & Awards

EAME,2stars   WW II VM   ACSM   KCMS,5stars   NDSM   UN Medal   ROK PUC   KWS Medal

STALEMATE WAR

After full recovery from my neck wound and its accompanying temporary paralysis, I was released from Murphy General Hospital and returned to full duty. My first assignment was the carpenter shop at Ft Benning followed by duty in the Psych Warfare School at Ft Bragg, NC. Bored, in late September, I asked for Korean duty. I processed for FECOM at Ft Lawton, WA and boarded the Marine Phoenix for the trip to Japan, docking in Yokohama early November 1952. Before being allowed to go to Korea I had to sign a waiver stipulating I had volunteered for this duty. That detail out of the way, I was allowed to choose my unit. I opted for the 3d Division and was assigned to I / 15 /3 as asst sqd ldr. Item Co was occupying an area of flat paddy land at the base of the Iron Triangle, north of the 38th parallel. During the 16 months I had been away, everything had changed except the weather. It was again bitterly cold.

It was no longer a war of movement but one of trench warfare, reminiscent of WW I. Spread out along the line were heavily fortified, partially underground bunkers, usually manned by 2 or 3 men. In a certain sense these were home. Much time was spent making them comfortable as possible. The ingenuity displayed was amazing. Stoves were devised to burn wood, straw, cardboard, anything flammable. Many had homemade bunks, tables and ottomans for seating. Considering conditions, these private 'castles' provided some comfort as well as safety, a life of luxury as it were. A major drawback was the bunkers were also home to hordes of rats which attracted poisonous 3 foot long, thick bodied snakes with wedge shaped heads. It was a squalid, 3 ring circus kind of existence.

Directly in front of the trench line was an apron of barbed wire. Beyond was the desolation of No-Mans Land. Two prominent hills, Outpost Tom and Jackson Heights, dominated No-Mans Land. The enemy controlled Jackson, we controlled Tom. Every night we sent two squads out to Tom, one squad worked on fortification, the other stood guard. The cold was intense. By the time we returned our hands and feet were so cold we had little feeling in them. Feet had so little sensation we stumbled as we walked. I do not recall any direct contact at this time, but constant night patrols and outpost duty were nerve wracking. Any movement in daylight brought a salvo of artillery or mortar shells. Consequently almost all action on either side was at night. Patrols, friendly and enemy, roamed No-Mans Land, resulting in frequent short but very deadly fire fights. On one occasion we were almost wiped out by a friendly 4.2 rocket barrage. Missed being in the target area by about five minutes. Bad communication at some level. Another hazard of war.

Adding to the difficulties was a communication problem within the squad. Each squad had two Korean soldiers and two Porto Ricans. These men were all good, willing soldiers but could neither speak or understand much English. I kept one Korean with me and partnered the other and the Porto Ricans with GIs. It made for a manageable combat unit on patrol. In one sense it was a quiet sector, but there was no possibilty of relaxation. Operating on patrol at night with vision hampered by darkness led to confusion in many instances. It took a high degree of alertness to survive. In daylight, the crack of a bullet from a sniper's rifle meted out death to the unwary. Day or night, there was no way to ease tension. Warmer spring weather brought a heartfelt, "Thank God" from the lips of many though it meant increased combat activity. Outpost Tom had been so heavily fortified that it was now manned day and night. We could clearly and loudly hear the enemy playing Chinese music on Jackson Heights. It was his way of letting us know he controlled that high ground. We witnessed a sad incident while on Outpost Tom. The pilot of a crippled jet fighter was trying to reach the safety of our lines. He kept dropping lower and lower as he approached, finally ejecting. He was too low for his parachute to fully open. He dropped straight down, out of sight into enemy held territory. There was no possibility of a rescue attempt.

In late April we pulled off the line and went into in reserve. What a relief, to get away from the 24 hour threat of death, to get a shower, eat a hot meal, have clean clothing, sleep on a cot inside a tent, not out in the cold rain. We had some refresher training, It was conducted in an easy going way by our plat ldr, Lt Francis Nester. He was a great officer, a real person, a gentleman. Always in command, yet he never harassed the troops. I never heard any one in the platoon speak of him in a negative way. He was one of the better officers. It was a privilege to serve under his command. After that rest we returned to the front line, a different sector but still in the Iron Triangle. The valley in front of us was ironically known as "Happy Valley." It did not live up to its name.

<u>Left</u>.   Wash day on the Han River, 1953.
<u>Photo by Bae Suk Lee</u>.

<u>Below Left</u>. Cpl Bogart with his 'understudy', 1953.   *Photo courtesy Harley Bogart*

<u>Below</u>. Early in the war a Korean house boy- KP seems to double also in brass as a laundry man, July or August 1950.

<u>Bottom</u>. A line company in reserve has a roof over their heads as a temporary comfort. This company street belongs to the 31st Regt. and was taken during winter of 1952 - 1953.

<u>Photos from the Archives.</u>

340

RED DRAGON
The SECOND ROUND
FACES IF WAR II

Harley	NMI	Bogart	US 55 220 883
First Name	MI	Last Name	Serial Number
None	3103	4 Feb 1931	Cpl
Nickname	MOS	Birthday	Grade / Rank
539 QM Laundry Co		Nov '52-Jan '54	Aurora, MO
Unit (s)		Duty Tour (s)	Home Town

Good Conduct Medal Korean Campaign Service Medal, 2** National Defense Service Medal

Medals & Awards

United Stations Medal   Republic of Korea War Service Medal   ROK Peace Medal

WE FEED, CLOTHE AND BATHE THE DOGFACE SOLDIER, THEN TRUCK HIS AMMO UP FRONT!

A Quartermaster soldier is a soldier with a multitude of duties, mostly of a housekeeping nature. All soldiers must eat. We in the QM are charged with the responsibility that he is fed. His clothing needs, winter and summer, for any climate from the arid desert to the freezing arctic is another one of the tasks shouldered by the QM. We set up Lyster Bags to chlorinate his drinking water, protecting him from disease and dysentery. QM shower points supply hot water for bathing when weather and combat situations will allow such an amenity. We bake fresh bread as a treat from home on those rare occasions when he is off the fighting line. We work to see that PX supplies get to the troops. We operate supply warehouses and often truck ordnance ammo to the front. These are just a few of the many housekeeping jobs assumed by the QM in routine course of supplying troops with the needs of existence. Yet we are, I believe, the recipient of more gripes than any other branch in the Army. The chow is always lousy; beans, C-Rations, K-Rations, none of it fit to feed a dog! Water from the Lyster Bag tastes terrible. Clothing doesn't fit. Shoes are the wrong size. Hot water always runs out before all those lined up can shower. "As for fresh bread, I've heard of it. None of it ever reached me!" As a QM soldier down in the ranks, I have concluded that the problems have no solution in armies numbering in the millions unless the Army appoints a QM soldier as a "dog robber" for every combat soldier as did the old Roman Legions, a slave for every soldier!

My tour in Korea was uneventful. I served in a safe rear area at Yong Dong Po. I had no intentions of going to Korea. The Army sent me to school, training me as a warehouse foreman. I had been assigned as Signal Corps permanent party at Camp Gordon, GA. I was as snug as a bug in a rug believing that the Army would not train me as a stateside warehouse foreman, then waste money so spent and ship me overseas. I had much to learn! In September 1952 orders came down that those that had not had foreign service were to be shipped overseas. 'Consternation Day' among the old timers, NCOs with rows of hash marks on their sleeves! When we shipped out there were more old time NCOs than there were PFCs like myself. In the pipeline we could be assigned to any outfit that needed warm bodies. We recognized too, although soft from stateside duty and untrained in combat techniques, we could be sent as fillers to any outfit short of men. While in the 'pipeline process', as luck would have it, I spent Thanksgiving as a Chemical Biological Radiological (CBR) trainee at Camp Gifu. In that school, we realized that if war involved CBR we were in for a bad time. We had little know-how. Equipment was lacking to protect our troops in that kind of war. The school kept us in Japan for 3 weeks.

We sailed from Sasebo to the hot war in Korea. We all wondered and feared what might lie ahead of us. There was six inches of snow on the ground at the repple-depple in 'San Mud,' and almost as much inside the tents where I was to sleep. I got to pull guard duty instead. Had never done that before. Didn't know what to look for. Next evening on the night train to Seoul I pulled guard duty again, this time with an M-1 handed to me instead of the carbine I had the night before. Lucky I didn't break my thumb when I loaded it with live ammo. Yong Dong Po was the end of the line for me. I stayed my whole time in a QM Laundry Company. The Koreans called us "Washee-Washee GI!" I had never heard of a Semi Mobile Laundry. It was mounted on trailers. When I was instructed to wash clothes, I said, "No, I was from the Signal Corps." That got me more guard duty and title of "Yard Bird." What caught my eye were new 3/4 ton Dodge trucks. I realized that the motor pool was the spot for this country gas station boy. I wangled my way in.

I got to see the sights in Korea, hauled mail to various PXs, once I made a delivery to the 5th Air Force and used their flush toilets. I decided if I was to ever be in another war, I'd enlist in the US Air Force! Our Base QM Depot supplied clean and well mended GI clothing. We patched "Mickey Mouse" boots, sorting them to insure the proper sizes could be furnished to front line troops. The warehouse stocked, literally, thousands of items. My warehouse training could have been put to good use there, but by this time I was classified as "yard bird" and motor pool driver. Our trucks got their worst wear in the last big battles in the summer of 1953 as we hauled ammo on a day and night schedule to the front lines. Most drivers had never been near the front. The first truck would carry someone who knew the way. Other drivers followed closely so as not to get lost. On return home, I knew I was no war hero, nor was I treated like one. Friends with scars and nightmares who gave their all were treated as was I. "Where ya been?"

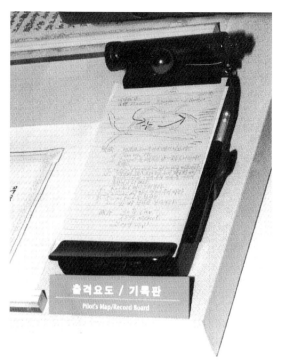

임택순(任宅淳)공군 대위
1930. 12. 31 ~ 1953. 3. 6

출격요도 / 기록판
Pilot's Map/Record Board

<u>Above</u>.　　!st Lt. Taek-soon Im.　　KIA, March 6, 1953.　　--　　Painting in Korean War Museum.　　--　　Seoul, Korea.
<u>Above Right</u>.　　Log book of Lt. Bae- sun Lee showing his 93 missions.　-　Korean War Museum.　--　　Seoul, Korea.
<u>Below</u>.　　　　Lt. Bae-sun Lee,　ROK Air Force stands by a F-51 Mustang fighter after one of his 93 combat mission.

RED DRAGON
The SECOND ROUND
FACES OF WAR II

BAE-Sun		Lee	0- 50839 ROK AF
First Name	MI	Last Name	Serial Number
None	Fighter Pilot	28 Jun 1931	Col, then Lt
Nickname	MOS	Birthday	Grade / Rank
10th Fighter Wing AF ROK		Dec '52- Aug '53	Hamhung, No. Korea
Unit (s)		Duty Tour (s)	Home Town
US Air Medal, USAF		UL CHI Military Medal of Merit,	KAF ROK
Medals & Awards			
93 Combat Missions in F-51 Mustangs			

FIGHTER PILOT

After my defection from North Korea in November 1948, I became a citizen of the Republic of South Korea. At age 18, to demonstrate my appreciation for the freedom in my new homeland, I enlisted in the Korean Air Force. Shortly, I was selected as a cadet for enrollment in the new Korean Air Force Academy. Our graduating class was in two groups, A and B. A group finished training 3 months earlier. B group joined the A group at Kangnung AF base in the fall of 1952. We operated in close air support in response to targets identified by T-6 Mosquito reconnaissance planes operating out of Chunchon KAFB. The T-6s would drop a smoke bomb and relay the map coordinates to our squadrons flying near that area. It is not easy for a fighter pilot to identify a target due to the speed at which he flies. The Mosquito T-6 would stay near the area and give us the result of our strafing runs and bomb attacks.

It was a well tuned partnership. The procedure had been devised and refined by the US Air Force and made a part of our training. My friend Im Taek-soon and I were part of the B group. We operated as members of a four plane squadron. Number 1 is the flight leader. He takes under his 'wing' the most junior member of the flight, generally the Number 2 plane in the squadron. Number 3 pilot takes his orders from Number One, and Number Four pilot receives his orders from Number 3. All in the flight of course immediately respond to orders from the Number One flight leader. The dual arrangement allows the flight to split into two mutually supporting flights which may hit different targets while in mutual support as well as cover each other in case of dogfights with enemy planes.

March 6, 1953, Im and I were flying in formation. Im flying his 15th mission, was in Number two slot. I was flying my 36th mission as Number 3 pilot in the flight. Our mission was to support our ground forces and knock out an enemy mortar position located near Kosong on the eastern seaboard. After targets had been identified, we began our bomb runs. Im, receiving updated instruction on his radio, attacked his target. I went after my target. In a bomb attack on a target, the plane is basically in a vertical dive. Immediately after the bomb is dropped, the pilot must reverse his dive almost 180 degrees, yet at a slant sufficient to get him away from the area of the target. Failure to do so can mean a crash into the target or being caught in the blast if a large munitions area explodes. In my dive, I glimpsed explosion and fire in front of me. I thought, "Im has hit a hidden arms depot!" I climbed to altitude to rejoin my flight.

However, I realized that I was now in number two position. Had we gotten mixed up in the chaos of combat? There was no time to ponder. We all finished our attack with rockets and strafing runs. When the flight regrouped, Im was missing. The flight leader and I circled back. Im's plane was on the ground in flames. My heart pounded. Im was my friend. He had been shot down by enemy AA guns. Im Taek-soon was truly a nice fellow, a mild personality and a great sense of humor. He had just met a girl while on leave and was enchanted with his new love. In deep sorrow I returned to base to collect Im's belongings to send to his family.

As the 'Peace Talks' drew to a close, the number of ROK Army support missions increased. We would get the USAF morning briefing and another from our flight commander before take-off. I was now a veteran fighter pilot with 90 sorties under my belt. I always felt fortunate I could return to base and relax, unlike our Army infantry soldiers who never had a chance to either rest or relax. On the 27th of July my morning began with target DT414741. We could see the orange flags separating our forces from the enemy. The T-6s identified the enemy bunkers. We made 8 strafe and bomb runs then returned to base. We had barely taxied off the runway when orders were received to strike target DT397747. The target location was not far from where my friend, 1st Lt Im Taek-soon was killed.

I thought of the tragic death of my friend with an indescribable anger in my heart. Perhaps he was with me in spirit as I successfully destroyed my assigned target. In early afternoon we were again in the air with orders to expend all munitions. As I climbed out of the cockpit, my mechanic congratulated me on my 93d mission and a job well done. Then and now, I am eternally grateful to the mechanics who serviced my planes. Without them, my successful missions would have been impossible. Every time I dived on target I knew it could be my last moment on earth. My dear God watched, guided and protected me, spreading his grace on me as I served my country and my people. Today we are a democratic, prosperous people, in a republic free of communist despotism.

Left. Flying a tight formation, these F-86 Sabre Jets own the skies of North Korea. In January of 1953 the South African Air Force [Cheetah Squadron] traded in their F-51 Mustangs for F-86 Sabres. Below. Although not an F-86, the Air Force jet here is laying a little napalm on a 'Commie' ground target. Both photos from the National Archives. Below Left. This F-86F Sabre Jet was flown by Lt. Ivan Holshausen of the South African Air Force Squadron in 1953. Notice the unique Cheetah insignia on the aft fuselage Photo courtesy of Lt. Holshausen.

344

RED DRAGON
The SECOND ROUND
FACES OF WAR II

Ivan	H.	Holshausen	PI-70221
First Name	MI	Last Name	Serial Number
None	Pilot	28 Mar 1930	Capt-then 2d Lt
Nickname	MOS	Birthday	Grade / Rank
2 Squadron S.A.A.F		6 Dec 52-20 Oct 53	Johannesburg, Union of S.A.
Unit (s)		Duty Tour (s)	Home Town

S.A.& British Korea Medals   US Air Medal   Zimbabwe Independence Medal   UN Medal

Medals & Awards

S.A. Gen'l Service Medal   Rhodesia Genl Svc & Exemplary Svc Medals   ROK Svc Mdl

THE FLYING CHEETAH POUNCES

In 1952 our 2 Squadron South African Air Force known as the "Flying Cheetahs" was integrated into the US Air Force 18th Fighter Bomber Wing. We were based at K55 Airstrip. In January 1953 we began flying F-86F Sabre Jets. Although on occasion we would fly the Yalu River boundary and along the Chong-Chong River on MIG patrol, our primary mission was ground attack. In the last few months of the war we did a fair number of armed recce's. These were armed reconnaissance missions in which a flight of four aircraft were assigned to a specific area. We were briefed to attack any military target we could find. Our usual armament was six fifty calibre .50 machine guns and two 500 pound bombs. We were equipped with supplementary fuel tanks which were dropped as they were emptied. This gave us an extended fighting range and additional time in the air. These missions were usually flown at much lower altitudes than a pre-briefed mission. It made for a busy pilot as he kept a sharp eye open for enemy ground targets of opportunity.

Targets were not easy to find. North Koreans and Chinese had developed excellent camouflage techniques. It was necessary to fly at low altitudes and look for signs of road traffic, and to scan road side areas that appeared to be of man made origin. These were closely scrutinized as possible supply dumps. Ox drawn carts were often used by the enemy in daylight hours as supply transport, so they were fair game. The pilots after a mission would compare notes as to any indication of new tricks the enemy might have developed since our last recce. Some missions were more effective than others, but it was desirable to maintain constant pressure on the North Koreans. We usually found worthwhile targets despite the enemy's excellent camouflage and dispersal tactics.

On one particular occasion we were operating in an area north of Panmunjom on the western Korean fighting front. The other three aircraft in our flight had attacked and destroyed targets of their choice. I had as yet not had a fruitful day. Careful scanning of my assigned area had yet to yield any results. With my armament still intact, I was now nearing the 'Bingo" fuel state where I would have to terminate my mission if I were to have fuel enough to return to K-55. Pilots do not like to return to base with a full bomb load. Yet, in this instance I was just about ready to call a "Bingo" return when I chanced on a railroad line crossing a small concrete bridge.

Next to the rail line was a typical Korean road which formed a "T" junction with the rail line. A closer look on the next pass showed the bridge to be more like a large culvert than a bridge. Destroying it would not entail more than a few hours labor for the industrious enemy to replace with the unlimited manpower he had at his disposal. We had learned that what we might knock out in daylight, the Chinese, working at night to avoid our aircraft, could overnight quite often improvise a makeshift but serviceable replacement. With my "Bingo" ticking away, I decided even a small irritant to their supply system was better than returning with a full bomb load.

I dived on the rail line, lined on the target, released my two 500 pound bombs, pulled up, then turned back to check for results. I could not believe my eyes! What I had hit was a fuel dump! The Chinese camouflage had been truly effective. I had not spotted anything out of the ordinary on either my first or second pass. My young eyes had been well trained to look for such things. The camouflage had been erected by some real military camouflage professionals. Only a lucky chance had sent it sky high. It was obviously a refueling point for their road transport that moved only at night. Fuel drums were exploding and going off like rockets. A column of black smoke was rapidly climbing thousands of feet into the clear sky. Chatter started on the radio telephone as other pilots spotted the high climbing column of smoke. Friendly aircraft began converging on the area to watch the great fireworks display. It was a great show as well as a possible invitation to get in on the action.

To this day I don't know if I also hit the rail line at which I aimed. The destruction of the fuel dump was a far more important and successful mission objective than a quickly rebuilt rail line. Certainly the visual effects were more spectacular. It was one of those crazy things that happen in a war. It was probably the most low key attack of my tour. No flak, but a really worthwhile result. I have always wondered whether some luckless soldier got into trouble for sloppy camouflage. It appealed to my sense of humor!

Above.   Bob Levulis and his BAR on the MLR with B Company of the 279th Regt. of the 45th Division.   Above Right.
In March of 1953 the 1st Bn. was pulled off the line to go to Cheju-do Island to put down riots at the POW Camp # 8.
Die-hard Communist POWs caused trouble to the very end of the war.   Both photos courtesy of Robert Levulis.
Below.   Photo of Seoul, Korea in front of the main train station in 1952.   Photo courtesy of Glenn Ed White.

RED DRAGON
The SECOND ROUND
FACES OF WAR II

Robert	E.	Levulis	US 51 127 618
First Name	MI	Last Name	Serial Number
Bob	1745	8 July 1928	Corporal
Nickname	MOS	Birthday	Grade / Rank
B/2 & HQ 1/279/45		Sept '52-Sept '53	Lackawanna, NY
Unit (s)		Duty Tour (s)	Home Town
Bronze Star	Combat Infantry Badge	Good Conduct Medal	ROK Service Medal
Medals & Awards			
Korean Campaign Svc Medal w/3stars		National Defense Service Medal	ROK PUC

ONE YEAR IN KOREA

September 2, 1952 was my red letter day of arrival at the port of Inchon, South Korea. I was greeted with a hard, driving rain followed by a soaking wet, long ride in a open GI deuce and a half. It rained hard for 24 hours, initiating me into Korean weather! Finally reaching my platoon in B Company, 279th Infantry Regiment, 45th Division, Lt Willey, of Macon, GA, assigned me to my squad. He was one helluva nice guy. Before going on line we lost Warrant Officer Wray in an accident. Capt Beatty, our company commander, was transferred. We had two weeks further training before going on line early Oct 1952. The company was assigned two replacement officers, Lt John Chauvin of Franklin County, NY as CO and Lt Harry Bradley of Don Ana County, NM as his Executive Officer. They came walking down the trench a couple of days after we first went on line. The CO asked me if I knew where the OP was located. I said, "No Sir, I don't." A few minutes later I heard a voice say "Here it is." That was followed by two quick blasts which killed both officers. They had trod into a mine field. It was a ghastly sight to see their torn bodies being carried to the rear for sacking into body bags. The gory sight swiftly initiated the process of turning me into a veteran. I muttered, " But for the Grace of God, there go I."

As darkness fell, the 'gook' loud speakers erupted into their new-to-us nightly broadcast. "Welcome to Col Bare and the 1st Bn of the 279th Infantry of the 45th Division." That really got to us. How did they know? No man had been taken prisoner. Still a mystery. In a matter of a few days we lost three officers. Christmas was spent on line. I had received from my girl friend Helen, later my wife, a box which contained a nicely trimmed artificial Christmas tree. It was a very nice gift to receive. The whole squad enjoyed it, not all at the same time, since some men were always on guard. A squad never assembled as a unit when on line unless in active combat. Months rolled by, punctuated by good byes to those rotating home after a year's service in Korea. While I was always happy for them, it also sent my mental calculator clicking on the number of days before it was my turn. In early February I received a surprise transfer to the Bn S-1 section where I had the job of "Safe Hand" courier. I was happy to get the job. It took me off the line for a time. A good friend, Ray Lawrence of Provo, Utah was also in the Bn S-1 section. We had been together in 2nd sqd, 2nd plat, Baker Company.

About a month later I was transferred back to the line. Shortly thereafter the Bn was sent to Cheju-do Island off the eastern tip of Korea. We left the MLR and loaded into Army 6x6's. We then trucked to the small South Korean port of Sokcho-ri. We lay on the beach the night of 17 March '53 waiting for LSTs to pick us up. We were not allowed to build fires for warmth. It was a miserable cold night. It was not much better aboard LST 758, "Duvall County." We loaded like cattle into the bowels of the LST for the voyage to Cheju-do. We arrived at the island 18 March. Our job was to guard North Korean and Chinese POWs imprisoned on the island.

Cheju-do had been selected because the island was practically escape proof. The POW camps had been plagued with a succession of communist inspired riots intended to support the Communist negotiators at Panmunjom. The riots had reached a point of severity which required combat troops to maintain control. It was a nasty business. The rioters, hard core North Korean and Chinese Communists, had taken over internal control of the camps. They used home made spears to prevent American MPs from entering the compounds to winnow out and remove those prisoners who were not in sympathy with communist doctrine. The only bright time of my duty on Cheju-do was the 5 days R&R furlough I spent in Osaka, Japan. Going and coming, I had a chance to see how the war affected the South Korean populace. It was a grim picture of near starvation for some Koreans, particularly the children..

After the riots were quelled we returned to the MLR. I was assigned chief switchboard operator. One rainy night as I sat on my helmet talking to men on guard, two friends Ray Lawrence and Ernest Nitsche, duties completed, turned in for the night. About an hour later I heard Ray's voice calling for help. We ran to his bunker. It had collapsed. Frantically, we dug with our hands. At night, no lights, all we had was feel. We pulled Nitsche out, but Lawrence was dead, smothered in mud. Nitsche was evacuated. For 40 years I thought he had made it home. I learned at a 1955 reunion that he had died the next day, 8 July 1953 on my birthday. 8 July 1955 was a sad birthday for me. July 9 ,'53 M/Sgt Henry J. Skinger, my platoon sergeant, was killed by an enemy mortar round while checking MLR positions of men in his platoon. Death had no respect for rank on the MLR. A lucky survivor, I came home late September 1953.

Left. Cpl. Roberts loads a 4.2 rocket into a tube of one of their launchers. 24 rockets could be fired in a 10 second period. The impact area must have been 'pure hell.'
                    Photo courtesy of Keith E. Roberts.
Above. A self propelled 105 mm howitzer of B Btry, 300th AFA Bn at work, July 1951.
Below Communist delegates to the peace talks in Kaesong take time out for dinner. This picture was taken at Kaesong in 1951. The 'talks' would go on for endless months while soldiers died. Photos from Archives.

RED DRAGON
The SECOND ROUND
FACES OF WAR II

Keith	E	Roberts	US 55 199 994
First Name	MI	Last Name	Serial Number
None	Chief of Sec. 4.2 Rockets	26 Dec 1930	Cpl
Nickname	MOS	Birthday	Grade / Rank
2d FA Bn, 4.2 Rockets		Feb 1952-Apr 1953	Indianapolis, IN
Unit (s)		Duty Tour (s)	Home Town

Army Meritorious Unit Award	Good Conduct Medal	National Defense Medal	UN Medal
Medals & Awards			
Korean Campaign Service Medal, 3stars	Army PUC, OLC		Korean War Service Medal

THE MEDIA CALLED IT A POLICE ACTION

My basic training at Camp Chafee, AK was as a field artilleryman, destined for service in President Truman's Korean 'Police Action.' I landed at Inchon in February 1952 and was loaded aboard a rickety coal burner train for Chorwon, then trucked on to Kumwha. When I was handed a .30 M-2 carbine there instead of a baton and a police badge, I knew I had been conned. To add insult to injury, I never saw a 'policeman' in all my 14 months in Korea. What I did see was wholesale death for American soldiers in a 'police action' where the casualty rate for number of men engaged was greater than any other war we have been involved in since our own Civil War.

I do not regret my service in Korea. It was a good cause, freedom of the South Korean people. What sticks in my craw is the manner in which the media portrayed the war, picking up the police action baloney handed out by politicians. If some of those lightweights in the media could have served a couple of weeks with the infantry before writing some of their condescending articles, the home front would have had a better understanding of the realities of the Korean War. Numerous newspaper clippings saved for my return showed me that the sacrifices of our many dead soldiers was never recognized. What I did note in those clippings was the glorification of Marines. My experience with the Marines at the battlefront was they often bit off more than they could chew, and then would call on the "inferior Army" for help. On more than one occasion, my outfit, the 2d FA Bn, would be rushed in support them.

We were not the usual artillery outfit, but a 'bastard' unit firing 4.2 inch rockets which were a tad larger than the shells of a 105mm howitzer. The Bn was equipped with six 105mm howitzer cannon and 12 rocket launchers firing anti personnel shells carrying a 2½ lb TNT warhead. When fired, the propellant left a fiery signature trail for about 80 feet. The rocket shell disintegrated into hundreds of shrapnel shards on impact. Each launcher could fire 24 rockets within a 10 second period of time. A good crew could reload and be ready to fire again within 90 seconds. Our crew, rated the best in the Bn, was composed of 5 rocket men and our truck driver who took care of ammo supply. He was a key man in our group. During a battle in which our rockets were a mainstay in resisting a six day Chinese attack, we radioed we were short of ammo. It was sent to us in several truckloads. As the trucks neared our firing position they were shelled by the Chinese. The drivers fled. Out of ammo, we all went to bring the trucks forward. We made it, but our section driver, a young soldier from South Bend, IN was seriously wounded. We heard he lived, but he never rejoined our unit.

It was early in March of '53 when we heard that some interrogated Chinese prisoners revealed a massive offensive was being planned later that month down through the Chorwon valley to retake Chorwon and Kumwha. These two devastated cities formed the base of the "Iron Triangle." We moved to Chorwon, waiting idly in position for a week before the enemy launched his assault. Their attacks continued for six days and nights. Shelled relentlessly all during this period, we maintained our positions at the same well dispersed location during the battle. The 105 howitzers in our Bn remained at our former fire base in support of units in that area. On the sixth day, the Chinese and North Koreans decided they had enough and ceased their attacks. It was conservatively estimated that they suffered more than 5000 dead. They accomplished none of their objectives. What a waste of human life, theirs and ours.

In the 14 months I soldiered in the Iron Triangle area before returning home, I learned that freedom is not ' for free' and, as I learn from a study of history in the years since, never has been free. Until man reaches a state of Utopia, we will continue to pay freedom's price with the lives of our young men. When I came home, I was as jumpy as a long tailed cat in a room full of rocking chairs. No wounds, just mental scars. I tried to heal with booze in the first seven years of marriage with my childhood sweetheart. The booze didn't work, the memories stayed with me. What I did get was a daily morning hangover. With my wife's help, I wised up and quit drinking over 42 years ago. The memories still bother me. Combat carries a strange psychological effect. People who have never been in a war, "Never been there, done that," do not understand, No mutual standard of reference exists which permits understanding. I am very thankful I came home in one piece. Many men died, others returned with missing body parts. Almost all veterans returned carrying mental scars of war. There has not been a day in 49 years that I have been able to forget. I wish I could. One of my school chums could not. He was killed by city police in his own back yard. He could not handle the rages his war experiences caused.

Above. Members of the 187th Abn. Regt. prepare to load up for a return to Korea. There were not very many opportunities for airborne operations in Korea, but the 187th did make two highly successful jumps in the first year of the war.
Below Maj. Gen. Lee Sang-Jo leaves peace talks after agreeing to exchange wounded and sick POWs. Archive Photos.

RED DRAGON
The SECOND ROUND
FACES OF WAR II

Gilbert	H.	Clausen	RA 17 252 151
First Name	MI	Last Name	Serial Number
Gil	7-1745 Abn Inf	6 January 1930	Sgt 1/c
Nickname	MOS	Birthday	Grade / Rank
HQ 187th Abn Regt		April 1953- August 1953	Askov, MN
Unit (s)		Duty Tour (s)	Home Town

Combat Infantry Badge Good Conduct w/loop ACM Vietnamese Star Pres Unit Citn UN Medal

Medals & Awards

KCSM,1* Am Exp Medal(Dom Repub) Air Medal w/V,16 clusters Sr Pilot Wings & Parachute Wing

MY FIRST WAR

After completion of basic training at Ft Sill, OK in 1948, I volunteered and was subsequently selected to attend Airborne Jump School at Ft Benning, GA. On completing this school I was assigned to the 82d Airborne Division at Fort Bragg, NC. In October of 1950 a battalion of the 82d was sent to Ft Benning to assist in teaching infantry tactics to troops destined for combat in the Korean War. In July of 1951 while at Ft Benning, I reenlisted for six years and was assigned as a tower training instructor. I also worked for a time in administration. End of the year 1952 found me and 5000 other troops on a ship bound for Japan and then on to the war in Korea.

At Sasebo, Japan we were sorted out for assignment to outfits in Korea. All GIs with an Airborne MOS were sent to the 187th Airborne Regiment in Beppu, Japan. The 187th was then redeployed to Korea by air for the third time during the Korean War. In March 1953 the regiment was inserted into the MLR, or as every GI called it, 'the line', in the Kumwha sector. The 187th had made its final combat jump at Munsan-ni on 23 March 1951 when it was dropped in an effort to trap retreating Chinese forces. We were now airborne troops fighting a ground war in the closing 'rats and bunker' phase of the Korean War. We served on line from March until the war ended, 27 July 1953. In August the regiment returned to Japan, remaining on duty there until 1955 when it returned to the US. I was assigned to the regimental commo section. The Regimental Commander at that time was Brig Gen Westmoreland. He was a real 'straight arrow,' smoking, drinking or swearing in his outfit was neither permitted or countenanced. The General was highly respected by his men who thought him a good guidance pattern for other officers to emulate. His photographic memory recalled birthdays and names of his NCO's wives. I was assigned as his enlisted aide, May 1953. This was to pay big dividends in my future military career.

With the war over we policed up all the ammo and other dangerous toys we had been allowed to play with while at war. The troops were to be flown back to Beppu, vehicles were returned to the US by LST. LST sounded like Navy, and Navy sounded like good food. Our chow had been less than gourmet. We were tired of powdered eggs, milk, potatoes and anything else that could be powdered, dried or dehydrated. Another sergeant and myself jumped at the chance to accompany the vehicles. We each had a jeep to deliver to Inchon. Each of us was given a case of 'C' rations for the trip. Being "Ambassadors of Good Will," we gave all our 'C' rations to the hungry little Korean kids hanging around the port of Inchon. After all, we would be eating good Navy chow for the next three days. After boarding our vehicles on the LST the ramp was pulled up. It was then we tumbled. The flag was US, but the crew was Japanese. The 'good Navy chow' was fish heads and rice. Half cheerfully, half grumpily they shared what little they had. They did give us as much tea as we could drink during our three day self inflicted diet. The weather didn't cooperate either. We rolled, pitched, tossed and yawed for three miserable days. In port at Moji, Japan we bee-lined to the Navy Exchange to eat up a storm.

My brief relationship with General Westmoreland paid off in 1955. I learned he was in charge of personnel at the Pentagon. In January I sent a letter requesting Flight School, OCS or CID. In May I was assigned to Flight School at Camp Rucker, Alabama. Six months later upon completing the school, I was promoted to Warrant Officer and assigned as a helicopter pilot. In March of 1966 I again earned my pay flying Huey 'copters' with the 1st CavDiv in Vietnam. Was shot down and rescued--bumps and bruises but no blood, so no Purple Heart. I did get 8 APCs and a canteen cup of gin. Then it was back to flying Hueys and another chance to let our brown brothers have a second chance at my fragile hide. I finished my military career as a fixed wing pilot for Military Intelligence. The fickle toss of the career dice by the assignment gods of war in the Pentagon did not see fit for me to serve with the 187th on their first Korean War jump at Sukchon, North Korea, 25 October 1950. I missed out also on their second and final jump at Munsan-ni, 23 March 1951. Korea did not offer many effective opportunities for deployment of Airborne troops or a chance to use the specialized skills developed for tactical warfare. Korea, after the first year, was a war of position, much like the trench warfare of WW I. Korea did give plenty of opportunity for airborne troopers to show off their combat skills and the esprit which make America's airborne soldier rank in the forefront of our elite troops. I am proud to have served in the Airborne and still consider them 'the best of the best.'

<u>Bottom.</u> Keeping his campaign promise, President-Elect General Dwight Eisenhower starts his inspection tour of Korea. In the chow line, Ike spends some time with the 15th Regiment of the 3rd Infantry Division. Sgt. Virgil Hutcherson, Sq. Ldr. with B Co. 15th Regiment is Ike's 'mess mate'. Gen. Eisenhower's son was assigned to the 15th Regiment also, December 4, 1952.

<u>Photos courtesy of the Eisenhower Library.</u>

RED DRAGON
The SECOND ROUND
FACES OF WAR II

Leroy	I.	Strope	US 55 308 093
First Name	MI	Last Name	Serial Number
Kilroy	3745	11 July 1932	S/ Sgt
Nickname	MOS	Birthday	Grade / Rank
Baker Company 15th Inf 3d Div		July 1953-Oct 1954	Jefferson City, MO
Unit (s)		Duty Tour (s)	Home Town
Combat Infantry Badge		Good Conduct Medal	Korean Campaign Service Medal,3 stars
Medals & Awards			
National Defense Service Medal		United Nations Service Medal	Korean War Service Medal

THE GUNS GO SILENT

I was drafted in November 1952 and discharged in October 1954. After I finished my basic training at Fort Riley, KS, I was sent to Fort Lewis, WA for a short period of further training, I then was processed for Korea. We sailed from Seattle, Washington and were told we would be sailing the "Great Circle" traveling a route along the Aleutian Islands. We were on a small ship, a "one stacker" and were packed in like sardines. Sleeping was in shifts, the bunks were never allowed to get cold! It was a scenic trip until we encountered a nasty storm a couple of days later. From then on, all of us were seasick and stayed that way. What had started as a scenic tour turned into a miserable voyage. We were very glad when we landed in Sasebo, Japan. We stayed there until we went to Korea.

A sizeable group of us shipped out of Sasebo, Japan as replacements destined to serve in the ranks of any of the several divisions fighting in Korea. We boarded an LST in Sasebo, the southern port on the island of Kyushu, for the short ocean voyage across the Sea of Japan to Pusan, near the tip of the Korean Peninsula. The primary topic of conversation during the trip amounted to a 'guessing game' as to which division we would be assigned. We knew we had little or no choice but it beat the alternative of staring at the steel wall of the LST. We knew all of us had a year to serve in Korea, and everyone recognized that some of us now assembled in the bowels of this WW II vessel would not answer roll call a year hence. Better to speculate as to which unit we would be assigned. Landing in Pusan, no time was wasted. We were placed aboard trucks and sent northwest to the rear area of the 3d Infantry Division sector. The memory of my first night in Korea has stuck in my mind for 50 years. We arrived at our destination late of an evening in early July. We were told to bed down. In the morning we would receive our company assignments. It was my introduction to war.

We bedded down in a heavy artillery area. Their guns were shooting up a storm. To sleep, I crawled under one of the trucks that had brought us there. All night long, guns fired in a sporadic pattern which I could not then fathom. As I later learned, the guns were being firing on request at specific targets, and also were being used in H & I (Harassing & Interdiction) fire. The effect was that none of us got any sleep. In the morning we were more tired than when we bedded down on the ground late the evening before. I was glad when morning came and we could move out. Later that morning I was assigned to Baker Company of the 15th Infantry Regiment. I was to spend the next 15 months of my life living, eating, sleeping in close proximity with the other infantrymen of that proud old regiment. We had many good people in our company. I felt fortunate to belong with them. Before the truce became effective, I went on a number of night patrols looking for the enemy. Knowing that Chinese contact could be made at any time kept every sense on high alert. The nights in Korea when I was on patrol were dark and scary. I was always glad to get back to our company area.

On 26 July the Chinese launched their final attack of the war on the 3d Division at Sniper Ridge. The last day of the war, 27 July, was a dinger. Our company was placed in front of a ROK unit to insure the cease fire was honored at 10 PM. I will always remember that night. Until the effective hour every gun on both sides fired continuously. The din was almost unbelievable. Both sides seemed to be firing every round they could get their hands on as a final message of hate and death at the other side. A man from another company standing about 10 feet from me apparently had more than he could stand. He shot himself in the arm. I felt very sorry for him when I saw what he had done to his arm and hand. He would have to face a court-martial when he got out of the hospital. That final evening as I was walking in a fairly deep trench where we were located in front of the ROKs, an incoming round hit the bank of the trench, knocking us down and spewing dirt all over us. If we had been in the open, not in the trench, we would probably have been dead. When the shooting stopped it became eerily quiet and remained that way for some time. We moved off the line a few days later.

For the next year we stayed in tent camps doing the usual things that occupy an army's time. It was not war, but not quite peace either. The threat of an outbreak, a renewal of the war, hung uneasily in the air. Fortunately it did not occur, although a number of incidents took place which could have reignited the conflict. The winter of 1953-54 was another cold year in Korea, but we were in tents with warm fires in stoves to mitigate the harsh cold of a Korean winter. Nor were we sleeping on the ground in a cold bunker, fighting off the rats. I was most happy when I received orders to come home for discharge. My army days ended in October 1954.

President-elect Eisenhower completes his Korean trip with a full inspection of the ROK Capitol Division, Dec. 1952

RED DRAGON
The SECOND ROUND
FACES OF WAR II

LeVern	E.	Sundet	US 55 142 646
First Name	MI	Last Name	Serial Number
None	745	23 Sept 1930	Cpl
Nickname	MOS	Birthday	Grade / Rank
A/27"Wolfhounds"25th Div		Sept 1952-Aug 1953	New Rockford, ND
Unit (s)		Duty Tour (s)	Home Town
Bronze Star Medal	Combat Infantry Badge	Korean Campaign Service Medal w/3 stars	
Medals & Awards			
National Defense Service Medal	United Nations Service Medal	ROK Korean Service Medal	

INTERLUDE

After our relief from the MLR late November of 1952 we were in reserve for several weeks. Shortly after we arrived, I had a wonderful surprise. My brother, who was serving in an Army Engineer outfit at one of the USAF Fighter bases, K-13, I think it was, came to visit me. He had found out where I was, and had gotten a three day pass to pay me a visit. We had a great three days recalling good memories of family and growing up together. It was so enjoyable to see him that after a week went by, I asked our company commander how much longer we would be at this camp. When he said it was indefinite, I asked if I could get a pass to go see my brother at his outfit. He gave his permission. The 1st Sgt fixed me up with a pass so that the MP's would leave me alone. I had looked over the map, and knowing from my brother's description of his trip where to go, I took off, hitchhiking rides on Army vehicles.

I remember crossing the Han River and going through Seoul on my way to the Fighter base where my brother was stationed. We had a great time together. I could not help but notice the difference in comfort level between his quarters and the way we lived in the infantry. The thing that really stuck out in my mind though was the food! They ate better, hot meals, on time, three times a day, just like back in the States. It was the same difference as in comparison of conditions on the line and back in reserve where things were much easier. I could understand it and why it was so, but couldn't help but be a bit jealous. We had another good visit. I enjoyed meeting his buddies as he had mine. When I left, they all crowded around, wished me well, and told me take care of myself. Going back, I caught a ride with a truck driver who said he knew where my outfit was camped. He was going right by there so could give me a lift all the way. I relaxed and didn't pay much attention where we were going. After a while, on looking around, where we were headed didn't seem right. I got off the truck and started walking back in the direction we had come from. I had no idea where I was.

It was getting along toward dark and I was beginning to worry. The nights were cold, I had no sleeping bag, nor a weapon in case guerillas were around. Just as I had really begun to sweat, a jeep came charging down the road and stopped. It was a bird colonel, all alone, driving himself. He said, "Soldier, what the hell are you doing out here?" I told him I was headed back to Co. A of my Regiment, the 27th Infantry. He told me to get in. He had a lead foot. No jeep I had ever been in before had been driven in such a reckless manner. I hung on for dear life. It wasn't long before we were back at Bn HQ of the 27th. When we stopped, he went into the BN HQ tent. The next thing I knew, somebody was assigned to go with me and get my ass back to my company. But it all worked out for the best. My brother and I were able to spend some time together. Also, I learned to be more aware of where I was at all times.

We went through several periods of duty on the MLR, rotating in and out of reserve. In one of those moves we changed from the eastern side of Korea to the west. The war settled into patrolling activity with its endless casualty tolls. The next time we were in reserve we worked with Korean civilians digging trenches and building bunkers for the 'Kansas"line fortification system. It was being built as a "fall back" position should it be needed. Long after the war I noticed the 40th parallel is the northern border of Kansas. Could that be where it got its name? We went back on line. About this time I lost a new friend, a replacement who had already been awarded a Bronze Star for valor. He had been issued a protective vest before going on night patrol. They got into a fire fight. The next morning at the ration pick area, I noticed a helmet and vest on the ground. I knew right away whose it was. A sad day for me. We had gone on a lot of patrols together. Sadder, after all these years, I can't remember his name.

We moved to an area on the MLR where I could see Panmunjom to our left flank. I went on a patrol in which a dog and his handler accompanied us. I didn't cotton to the idea. It seemed to me that the dog would be more apt to alert the enemy than to help us. But, what the hell, I was just a Cpl. I followed orders, I didn't make them. This was also the spot where a dumb action occurred in which a young guy from Porto Rico was injured and risked the lives of others who had to help pack him in. He shot a pheasant in front of the MLR. When he went to retrieve it, he stepped on a mine, injuring himself badly. Seemed to me that this was a better spot for a dog than for men on a night combat patrol. We again moved back to reserve. The war ended here. Two weeks later I rotated home with a total of 50 'points'. 36 combat points was supposed to be enough to go back home. Not always! I had a lot of company.

Right. A GI with the 61st Searchlight Company stands next to his 'moonbeam' light. Left. With each light producing 800,000,000 candlepower, night no longer hid Chinese activity, effectively curtailing surprise attack. Below Right. Trucks of the 61st Searchlight Company after the cease-fire. The earlier method of using the lights was to bounce them off the clouds, creating an imitation moonlight. It was found to be much more effective to place them within a mile or two of the MLR beaming them directly onto enemy positions. This irritated the Chinese and often drew their fire. Lower Left. This propaganda leaflet did not paint a rosy picture for Chinese troops. Photos and leaflets from Herbert Scheer.

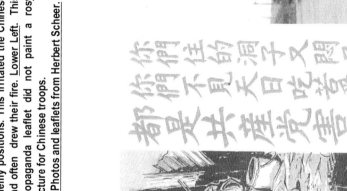

你住的洞子又閒又髒
你們不見天日吃盡苦罪
都是共產党害的

RED DRAGON
The SECOND ROUND
FACES OF WAR II

Herbert	L.	Scheer	US 56 117 689
First Name	MI	Last Name	Serial Number
Hugh	3166	28 Oct 1928	S/Sgt
Nickname	MOS	Birthday	Grade / Rank
61st Searchlight Company		Oct 1952- Sept 1953	CaveJunction, OR
Unit (s)		Duty Tour (s)	Home Town

Korean Campaign Service Medal w/2 stars National Defense Service Medal

Medals & Awards

United Nations Service Medal Republic of Korea Korean War Service Medal

800,000,000 CANDLE POWER

I was selected by my friendly local draft board for Army induction in the May 1952 draft lottery. I reported to the induction center where I was given a series of tests. I was then sent to the San Luis Obispo Signal Corps Training Center for 6 months training as a power generator operator, MOS 3166. In Korea I found MOS 3166 translated as front line operator of a carbon arc 800,000,000 candle power searchlight. Battlefield illumination is what it was all about. I was assigned to the Signal Corps 61st Searchlight Company then located east of the Imjin River on the western front. In my first week of duty in mid October '51, I was placed on 'Able' Light located on the MLR. After a week of OJT training, I was transferred to 'Dog Light', a mile or so west of ' Able'. These positions were on hilltops so searchlights could be focused directly on valleys and other hills. Earlier practice had been to bounce the light off cloud cover. This method had been discarded as ineffectual. Direct illumination of the target was now the method employed to light up Chinese positions at night, and to illuminate in front of the MLR when the Chinese employed their standard tactic of night attack. There was heavy fighting going on at this time, lots of green and red flares at night in areas 'Dog' Light could not focus on or reach.

February 1st '53 Bill Price and I were sent on DS (Detached Service) to Seoul's Kimpo Airfield, a base for F-86 Sabre Jets. The airfield had been attacked by enemy aircraft. Our job was to train Air Force personnel in operation of a searchlight. Light on the airplane target gave the flyboy ack-ack gunners a much increased probability of a target kill. We were there for 8 days, then back to the MLR. We were students as well as instructors, carrying away with us the lesson learned that airmen ate better food, in mess tents, slept dry on cots, not in foxholes, and in general led a comfortable existence with movies being shown twice a week after "duty hours."

On return from Seoul I was given the job of driving supplies. Originally there were 8 lights. I worked them all except 'Baker' light. 'Charlie' light had been captured by the Chinese. 'George' light was in the British sector. 'How' light was renamed 'Item' light as the Koreans could not pronounce 'How.' Driving up those Korean hills in low gear made me feel like one of those ducks in a carnival shooting gallery. Flat tires were a daily hazard. I never had less than one, often two, once three. There were a lot of shrapnel shards scattered around! Made a morning trip to "Dog" light which had recently moved near "Old Baldy." It was under light mortar fire. A new man was missing from the bunker. I was asked to locate him as the rest of the crew was busy working on the light preparatory for nightfall. I located him. He was frozen in fear, unable to move. Dragged him back to the bunker to regain his composure.

In March, a complete change of command took place. Although we were Signal Corps trained, we had been under control of the Corps of Engineers. Our new look put us into Field Artillery. An immediate bonus was our new company commander, Capt Albert Gilbert, a Field Artillery officer who was the best officer I encountered in my army service. He knew nothing about searchlights, but he knew how to command and how to gain cooperation from his men. As an example, my truck had a power winch often used to get the loaded truck out of soft spots in the steep mountain roads made almost impassible by spring thaws. On several supply runs Capt Gilbert came with me on familiarization visits to the various lights. When we encountered a monstrous chuck hole, Capt Gilbert would grab a shovel and help me fill it in. You have to love an officer who will pitch in to help out! He was unique in my experience.

One night during the heavy fighting on "Old Baldy" 'Dog' light truck blew a manifold gasket as the light moved to a new position. About 10PM after I had sacked out from a hard day, Capt Gilbert roused me to winch 'Dog' light into a new position. He accompanied me and using only black out lights only, pulled cable while I operated the winch from my truck. The light was soon in operation in its new position. The next night while it was quiet on the MLR, Jim Saint New, the 'Dog' light commander asked me to help him get the truck back to company for repairs. I checked with Lt Francis Gauss back at company who authorized the move. Coming down off the steep grade on a ridge next to 'Old Baldy', the tow chain came loose. I was not immediately aware what had happened, but noticed my truck was pulling real easy. I stopped and went hunting for Jim. When I found him, he threw his arms around me and made me promise to never leave him in the dark by himself again! We finally got the 'Dog' truck back for repair. That did it for me. I asked to be taken off supply runs. Russell Mc Swain, a replacement took over. I was assigned to 'Easy' light.

Above.   Tanks are firing WP on Chinese positions in front of the 223rd Regt. of the 40th Inf. Div.,1952.   Photo by Don Gardner This dug-in 'quad 50" is supporting the 160th Regt. of the 40th Inf Div, 1952.
                    Photo by Robert Riggs.
Bottom Left This bunker is home for a water cooled .30MG currently occupied by members of the 279th Regt. of the 45th Inf Div, 1952.
             Photo courtesy of Boyed Burnley.
Bottom. A soldier of the Belgian Bn checks a recent battle field, taking head count.
             Photo courtesy Francois Cuypers.

RED DRAGON
The SECOND ROUND
FACES OF WAR II

Ronald	J.	Demers	RA 11 242 455
First Name	MI	Last Name	Serial Number
Ron	Artillery Fwd Obsvr (FO)	9 Oct 1932	Cpl
Nickname	MOS	Birthday	Grade / Rank
1st FA Obsvn Bn		Nov 1952-Sept 1953	Peace Dale, RI
Unit (s)		Duty Tour (s)	Home Town

Good Conduct Medal   Korean Campaign Service Medal,2 stars United Nations Service Medal

Medals & Awards

National Defense Service Medal   Republic of Korea War Service Medal

ARTILLERY FORWARD OBSERVER

A few days after my high school graduation in June 1951, I enlisted in the US Army. Eight weeks basic training at Ft Dix, NJ was followed by 8 weeks advanced training at Ft Bliss, TX. After another ten months of training at Ft Sheridan, IL, I went to Camp Stoneman, CA, to await passage to Korea. Eleven days aboard a troopship took me to Japan. After three days in 'process' at Camp Drake, I again boarded ship, this time for passage to Pusan, South Korea. From there I went overnight by rail to Yongdong-po on the outskirts of Seoul. A group of us boarded a GI truck which transported us north to Yonchon, nearer the fighting front. Another GI 6x6 truck shuttled me to my new unit, 1st FA Obsn Bn just to the rear of the fighting front. Two days prior to Thanksgiving Day '52 I was on line as an Artillery Forward Observer. Civilian to combat soldier in 58 weeks. At that, I had more training than others!

My new home was a front line bunker, used also as an OP atop Hill 355, near the Imjin River, west of Chorwon. Facing us were the Chinese. The first day on line I left my rubber mattress outside my bunker to air out. A couple of hours later I looked for it. Vanished! I learned fast, but a bit late! The MLR at that time was quite stable. Both sides were dug in behind barbed wire with land mines strewn everywhere in front of their positions. Every day, and every night, both sides employed their artillery and mortars in intermittent harassing fire on the enemy. FO's in my unit routinely spent one week on the MLR, one week in the rear. In the winter months infantry action was light. Truce talks were going on at Panmunjom. Hopes were high the war would soon be over. It was a cold winter with much snow. March came in cold and blustery. The 23d Infantry of the 2d Div now held Hill 355. On 1 March the Chinese in Bn strength hit us all along the MLR on Hill 355. A few of the attackers managed to reach our trenches but were quickly killed. A M-19 halftrack with its synchronously fired single platform four .50 cal MGs, was dug in to the right of our FO position. The tremendous firepower of this murderous weapon, originally intended for anti-aircraft use, was of enormous help in our defense.

Things quieted down a bit for a couple of weeks. Some action, but no large scale attack or major effort was made to penetrate our positions. On the night of 17 March 1953 I was in a rear area, 'enjoying my week off.' The Chinese mounted an attack in full battalion strength. This time, regardless of losses, they pushed through the mine fields, barbed wire and our deadly defensive fire to reach our trenches atop the hill. Their casualties were extremely high as was to be expected in the "human sea" tactics employed by Chinese armies. Our casualties, in deep dug defensive positions were much less, but unacceptable by American army standards.

At dawn I was ordered back to Hill 355. I accompanied a rifle company of the 23d Infantry as they climbed to retake our MLR trench positions. The Chinese withdrew under heavy attack, leaving many dead, theirs and ours. Our casualties, surviving wounded and dead, were taken off the hill by litter and transported to the rear. Our few wounded men overlooked by the Chinese were loaded into an ambulance, the dead into GI trucks to be conveyed back to Quartermaster Graves Registration. The Chinese were buried in a mass grave. I had not had a chance to eat before accompanying men of the 23d in their dawn attack of Hill 355. I dug into the side cargo pocket of my GI fatigue pants for a belated C-Ration breakfast. Luckily, it was a can of 'Meat and Beans', the only edible item in my opinion, of any of the C-Ration menus. While eating, a dead Chinese on a stretcher was carried past. His severed foot fell off. It was promptly picked up by one of the litter bearers and thrown back onto the stretcher. I kept on eating. At that time, I felt nothing. It was just a part of war. Looking back, I marvel that I could continue eating. War deadens all the normal senses we usually feel as human beings. Death is so prevalent, so commonplace, it becomes part of the scenery like the clouds above or trees on a hillside.

That was the last major fight. Activity settled down into routine patrols and small probing attacks. None of these reached our trench positions. The probe attacks were easily beaten with artillery and mortar fire, and a stubborn infantry defense by men of the 23d Inf. Regt. A truce was signed on 27 July 1953. I left Korea in September of 1953. The troopship took 18 days to return to California in contrast to the 11 days it took going over! My two year enlistment was up. Discharged at Ft Devon, MA, I reenlisted in the US Army in 1955. Most of this 3 year service period was spent with the 25th Infantry Division in Hawaii. Quite a contrast to Korea. In 1958 I returned permanently to civil life. Today I am a retired police sergeant living in the town where I was born, Peace Dale, RI.

Above. The HU-1 helicopter was similar to the one Lt. Hunt flew in Korea. Photo by Robert Hunt. Above. These F9F pilots were always glad to see the HU-1s around. More than one fighter pilot owed his life to the fast response of these 'copter pilots. The bottom photos show a pilot being pulled out of the harbor at Wonsan for return to his carrier. More than any of the other new technologies, the helicopter proved its worth in Korea. Photos, National Archives.

RED DRAGON
The SECOND ROUND
FACES OF WAR II

Robert	D.	Hunt	553344 USN
First Name	M	Last Name	Serial Number
Bob	**1315-Pilot**	**1 July 1925**	**LT USNR**
Nickname	MOS	Birthday	Grade / Rank
HU-1		**Jan '53- Aug '53**	**Whittier, CA**
Unit (s)		Duty Tour (s)	Home Town
Air Medal with 4 stars	**Korean Campaign Service Medal with 1 star**		**United Nations Medal**
Medals & Awards			
National Defense Service Medal	**Navy Presidential Unit Citation**		**ROK KWSM**

WONSAN RESCUE PILOT

I was attached to HU-1, the first operational helicopter squadron in the US Navy. We were stationed at Ream Field, near San Diego. HU-1 had units aboard all Naval ships in the Pacific fleet that could accommodate a helicopter. We were a utility squadron, doing whatever needed to be done, mail delivery, personnel transfer, cargo or sea rescue. In January of 1953 I was assigned to an LST anchored offshore the North Korean harbor of Wonsan, just beyond range of the North Korean shore batteries. Among our many missions, we picked up downed pilots, and transferred personnel between the several islands in Wonsan harbor held by US Marines. Another of our duties was to dispose of floating mines ripped loose by weather to keep them from endangering our fleet at sea.

I particularly enjoyed one rescue. When I looked down the cable I saw the grinning face of a flight training classmate, Ted Korsegren. His plane had taken a hit. He made it to the Korean east coast where he bailed out. He was in a life raft when I located him, a boatload of North Korean soldiers hot after him. We reached him first and winched him to safety. We did not get much of a chance to visit. His ship sent a 'copter for him as he was slated to fly the next day. No rest for those guys. Shot down and then fly again. No parades, no hero celebrations in the media. I had a couple of tough attempted rescues inland. On one, I was despatched almost at sundown to a point just north of the "Bomb Line." I located the area where the pilot was pinpointed by parachute flares from circling friendly aircraft. By now it was full dark. Our 'copters were not equipped for night flying, no panel lights for one thing. As I dropped down to his location I received heavy automatic fire from the spot where I thought he was. He had apparently been captured and they were after another score. Lucky for me and my crewman none of 23 holes were disabling. My LST was not equipped for a night landing, so I set down on Yodo Island, spending a night with Marines in their cave. Next day, in fun, my crew circled the holes in yellow paint.

Another attempt, same location. The enemy were waiting for me with a 37mm AA gun "cocked and ready." They bracketed me. The sky lit with shell bursts around us. A dud hit the engine compartment, spinning us around. I lost some altitude but recovered and returned to "mother" on the LSD. My flight crew found the dud had entered on the left side of the cowling, tore through the starter motor, ripping it off the engine. It took with it one of the magnetos. The starter motor was left hanging by a battery cable. This was a tough fix for my crew. They welded the exhaust manifold, patched it, replaced the starter and magneto, and repaired the carburetor. It was a good thing the crew kept the engine compartment spotless, otherwise I would have gone down in flames. I kept the starter motor as a memento. It had a hole through the case and armature that a crack machinist would have been proud of.

My crew enjoyed the "Mine Patrol." We would fly up and down the coast looking for mines torn loose by wind, weather and tide. They would shoot at the mines with an M-1 rifle. The mine would sink. I lost track of how many were sunk, but more than 100. Those were 100 mines that would not menace our ships in the offshore patrolling Pacific Fleet. On one occasion we found a string of submerged mines in the harbor. We enlisted a UDC crew (Navy Seals) to set TNT charges with two minute fuses to the submerged TNT and tie a connecting rope from the TNT to a float. We hovered over the mines and enjoyed the thrill of blowing them up. We had one last interesting assignment. My crew and I were slated for stateside duty. July 3, 1953, my skipper hailed the Missouri, "Big Mo" patrolling southward. They hove to while we climbed up a rope ladder. It is hard to visualize the size of a ship that big. I didn't have to visualize. My arms told me it was a long way up! We hitchhiked south on several patrolling ships and finally caught a mail plane to Japan.

The 'Cease Fire' announced on 27 July 1953 that the war was over. Many men were listed as MIA and as POWs. The war was not yet over for them. Our missions and efforts would not have been successful were it not for the dedication and hard work of my flight crew. In the bitter cold of a Korean winter in the Sea of Japan, they never faltered, never complained, the helicopter was ready at all times. Never did I have to wait when ordered on a mission. The 'helo' was always ready, rotors ready to whirl. They did their job with great honor. Looking back, I have always been sorry it was called it a "Police Action." It was a war. It cost 34,000 American lives.

Above. In anticipation of the prisoner exchange, a Freedom Village is constructed to welcome our POWs back to civilization, July 1953. **Below Left.** BG Robert Bare, Asst. Div. C.O. of the 1st Marine Division inspects a ' pre-fab' bunker. This two man bunker weighing over two tons is being transported to a forward outpost,1953.
Both photos from the Internet.
Below Right. Bronze Star medal is awarded to M/Sgt. Rhinehart by Lt. Col. Beaty, "Somewhere in Korea," 1953.
Photo courtesy Richard Rhinehart.

RED DRAGON
The SECOND ROUND
FACES OF WAR II

Richard	A.	Rhinehart	RA 16 300 476
First Name	MI	Last Name	Serial Number
Rich	1502	29 Apr 1931	Major, then M/Sgt
Nickname	MOS	Birthday	Grade / Rank
185th Engineer© Bn		6 Jan '53-24 Mar '54	Hartford, MI
Unit (s)		Duty Tour (s)	Home Town

Bronze Star Commendation Medal GCM KCSM Presidential Unit Citation Navy PUC UNSM

Medals & Awards

Meritorious Unit Citation AFRM Occupn Medal,G Meritorious Svc Medal Jnt Svc Cmdn Medal

FO BUNKER INSPECTOR

Early January 1953 I was assigned to the 185th Engineer© Bn, 1169th Engineer Group in X Corps Sector. At that time the Bn was positioned in the Northeast corner of South Korea just above the 38th parallel. The 185th along with the 13th Engineer© Bn was assigned to build and repair roads and bridges. We were also charged with responsibility for laying and clearing mine fields. I was a young SFC recently assigned to the Bn. One of my tasks was to teach clearing and laying of mine fields. My previous 4½ years military experience had been with the Infantry and Artillery so my experience with mines and demolitions was limited. I boned up on Engineer Field Manual 5-34 and proceeded with the class. I felt the pride of accomplishment when I was commended for an excellent course of instruction. It gave me a sense of soldierly satisfaction to prepare the lesson plans and teach the course.

It was an impressive looking at the lines of soldiers translating a lesson plan into the reality of searching for mines. They exuded confidence in accomplishing a dangerous and difficult task. Then tragedy struck. I can still see our first casualty as training was translated to practicality in our initial mine clearing operation. It is a sight that has never left my mind's eye in all these years. What went wrong, we of course never knew, but we all witnessed the result. A headless soldier with both arms and one leg blown off. It hit me very hard, and of course affected the others in the mine clearing detail just as bad. What was noteworthy, after the medics body bagged our dead comrade, the detail returned to their task. They continued and completed the clearance of the mine field.

In early April of 1953 Major Cannon, our Bn S-2, asked me to accompany him on a tour of the Forward Observer bunkers in our area. Though inspection of bunkers was not one of our primary missions, it turned out to be an interesting assignment. I had no idea of what was expected of me. About an hour later I was aware of being back with the infantry, so to speak. I don't recall the height of that mountain, but I remember in spades how difficult it was to claw my way up that steep slope. With my steel helmet, back pack, armored vest, rifle and waist belt gear, I felt I carried twice my weight up hill. It didn't help my ego to see Korean laborers behind us pulling long 3" and 4" thick planks stamped "USA" up that mountain side. Where did they get the muscle on 'rice power' to do it?

I soon learned the purpose of the long planks. Previous inspection of the FO bunkers had determined that the small timbers holding up the sandbagged roof of the bunkers were too small to withstand the impact of even a close mortar or artillery round, let alone a direct hit. A close hit would have caved in roofs and buried the FOs under the weight of dirt and sand bags. The excuse given by the FOs was that they did not have time to find larger timbers if they were to maintain observation and do their job of spotting for their guns. Major Cannon observed that FOs were, in general, lax in properly constructing bunkers. This apparently was where the Engineers came in. I had visions of our Bn becoming bunker builders all along the front lines. I had not long to wait for the fireworks.

The North Koreans chose that particular moment to attack. It was a hairy two hours. I had a chance to see our infantry in operation. The initial attack was repelled. The skies began to clear. The Air Force was called on to strafe and bomb the attackers. It seemed like an eternity before they showed up. Actually, it was but a short time. Until that time I had little respect for the Air Force, but that viewpoint was quickly changed as the fighter jocks soon routed the North Korean attackers, sending the few survivors back to their entrenchments on the mountain opposite from us. After they showed up it was like having seats in a grandstand, at least until enemy shelling started hitting our lines. While I never felt secure in my personal safety as a combat engineer, I wouldn't want to change places with any of the Forward Observers. In their position on the front line they are sitting ducks for enemy snipers, as well as their opposite FO numbers in the enemy line. They do a hell of a job in their support of the infantryman on the MLR. They are a true elite.

During my fourteen months in Korea I was promoted to Master Sergeant and recommended for a Battlefield Commission. But the payoff was I made it safely home in contrast to many of my comrades who made the supreme sacrifice, giving their lives in the cause of freedom. South Korea is a free nation today as the result of those Americans who fought the good fight to maintain their status as a free nation among the free nations of the world. Their fight was not in vain. I wish all Americans could see that simple truth.

<u>Above</u>. Chinese positions at Ungok, near Carson, Reno, and Vegas are 'softened up' in preparation for an assault by A Co. 5th Marine Regt. <u>Bottom</u>. Marines can be seen on the ridge line making the final assault.

<u>Right</u>. Aftermath. This assault of positions a mile past the MLR would undoubtedly prove to the Chinese that we were as willing to throw away lives as they were. Final Marine casualties totaled 95 WIA, 15 KIA, and a minor miracle, no MIAs. <u>Photos courtesy of Bill Hawkins</u>.

RED DRAGON
The SECOND ROUND
FACES OF WAR II

William	G.	Hawkins	O 55897 USMC
First Name	MI	Last Name	Serial Number
Bill	0305	24 Jan 1930	Capt, then Lt
Nickname	MOS	Birthday	Grade / Rank
A2/1/5th Marine Regt 1st MarDiv		Oct '52- Oct '53	Stuart, FL
Unit (s)		Duty Tour (s)	Home Town
Silver Star Medal	Purple Heart Medal		Korean Campaign Service Medal, 3 stars
Medals & Awards			
National Defense Service Medal		United Nations Service Medal	ROK War Service Medal

JARHEAD TOURS THE LAND OF MORNING CALM

In Nov 1951, it became obvious I would be drafted. Volunteering, I opted for the US Marine Corps. I was sent to Quantico where in a 10 month period the transition from 'Joe College' to 'Jarhead' took place. Then it was staging at Camp Pendelton. A lot was crammed into 15 days we spent there, including a few 'Tom Collins' at Virginia Beach. We boarded the lovely USS Marine Serpent for a 17 day cruise to Kobe, Japan where we loaded fuel and provisions and, for 8 hours, off loaded the horniest men in the USMC. Two days later, dry, recovered from inebriation, and only 2 AWOLs we disembarked at Inchon for a look at the aftermath of war. We boarded a train through devastated Seoul to Munsan-ni. Trucks took us to our new home near Panmunjom. I was assigned to Able Co 5th Marines in 60 mm mortars, a weapon about which I knew little. My tenure at the CP was uneventful except for an explosion of a can of beans which had been left too heat to long in a Yukon stove. It took about two hours to extricate the Company Commander, a nervous type, from beneath his bunk. I learned quickly from intelligence briefings that combat was not fun and games.

The line had stabilized resulting in a WW I scene of trench lines, bunkers, mines, miles of commo wire, barbed and concertina wire. Incoming rounds harassed us on a 24 hour round- the- clock schedule. We spent 90 days on the line before going into 'reserve.' The line ballooned out around Panmunjom and a misnamed 'neutral zone' which in theory was a non combat zone. Actually it was a battle zone dotted with outposts, mine fields, booby traps and plotted artillery target sites. Well worn patrol routes left obvious paths atop rice paddy dikes. Our left flank tied into the Korean Marines who quickly won our respect by their gung-ho decorum. It was comforting to know they were on our side. We maintained listening posts(LPS) in front of our lines, usually at night, regardless of severe weather. Wire telephone lines were often cut by enemy mortars or artillery which could vary from an occasional round to a full blown barrage of 5000 rounds in an hour. We recorded and identified incoming rounds, giving us an insight what the Chinese were stockpiling and their possible attack plans. What they did not shoot at us was more informative than what they did fire at us.

It fell to my lot to take a group of "Chioga Bearers," drafted Korean Army laborers, to Outpost Kate about one mile in front of our lines to dig trenches, bunkers and lay wire. The procession consisted of me in front with my carbine, laborers in a group followed by my interpreter, Rhim, with his M-1. Kate was manned day and night by a squad of Marines. On one occasion, a Chinese patrol got in between me, my unarmed "chiggy bears" and our main line. They were challenged by the LP at the gate in the wire who mistook them for our "chiggies" returning. They were keeping warm in their sleeping bags, and were bayoneted in them. On the theory that a miserable Marine is an alert Marine, sleeping bags were then absolutely prohibited at an OP or LP. Ergo, the responsible platoon leader was banished to the rear to live happily ever after. I inherited his job. Shortly thereafter, our company commander, a man of questionable intellect, sent me and a squad to lay wire in full daylight on the forward slope of Kate. The Chinese considered this act of wanton aggression should be appropriately rewarded. One Marine KIA and one WIA was the result of the enemy mortar barrage.

When our Bn went into reserve, some one up the command chain decided Marines are an amphibious force. Such skills must be kept well honed. We loaded aboard the USS Lenawee to do cargo- net to landing- craft drill with frozen gear to boot. We did get 2 hot meals, a warm, dry bed and a shower out of it. The brass also felt we should retaliate for the fierce battles and casualties on Outposts Reno, Vegas, Carson, Bunker, The Hook and others. By golly, we'll assault one of their outposts! Able company was tasked for the assault. My platoon was 'honored' as point of the spear. Outfitted with flame throwers, bazookas, tanks and backed by close air support, we jumped off at 0700 and overran the hill mass at Ungok. The Chinese retreated into a honeycomb of caves. The fight then became a WW II island type combat, mopping up with flame throwers, satchel charges and grenades. We withdrew as planned after a day long fight, suffering 15 KIA and 95 WIA. While we were miles in front of our lines, we had no MIAs. Chinese casualties were put at 400. This must have included traffic accidents in Hong Kong! I was fortunate to receive only a mortar fragment and one burp gun slug in my hide. Seems a Chinese in his cozy cave resented my door knock and let loose with what sounded like an endless burst. After a few weeks in a Mash unit I was as good as new, and rejoined what was left of my company back on line. Life went on.

Left. An F-86 Sabre Jet on patrol in Mig Alley. Archive Photo.
Above. 51st Fighter Group Hqs,1953. Lower Left. Flight line of
16th Fighter Interceptor Squadron ready for a trip to Mig Alley.
Below. Sgt. Jeremiah Crise stands in front of one of the jets
on which he was crew chief.   Near Suwon, Korea, 1953.
Photos courtesy of Jeremiah Crise.

RED DRAGON
The SECOND ROUND
FACES OF WAR II

Jeremiah	G.	Crise	AF 22998109
First Name	MI	Last Name	Serial Number
"Jere"	43150	23 October 1930	S/Sgt
Nickname	MOS	Birthday	Grade / Rank
16th FIS/51st FIG/51st FIW		Jan 1953-December 1953	Terre Haute, IN
Unit (s)		Duty Tour (s)	Home Town
Good Conduct Medal, 2 clusters	US Presidential Unit Citation	KCSM 2stars	NDSM UNSM

Medals & Awards

AF Longevity Medal   Cross of Combat Volunteers(France)   ROK PUC & KWSM&Freedom Medal

CREW CHIEF

In 1947 I enlisted in the 38th Infantry Division of the Indiana National Guard, continuing a family military tradition dating back to 1776. 27 July 1950, I was discharged from the Guard and enlisted in the newly named US Air Force. Basic Air Force training was at Lackland AFB San Antonio, TX. Upon completion of basic I was assigned as drill instructor. After a bit more than a year in this slot, I volunteered to attend jet fighter aircraft and engine school at Amarillo AFB, Texas. I had been promoted to Staff Sergeant. The school accepted 150 NCO candidates. I was happy to be one of that select number. I remember the base commander saying in his speech he would never accept a group of young staff sergeants as they were too difficult to handle. After graduation from A&E school, I was transferred to Selma AFB in Alabama as crew chief. On arrival at Selma, I volunteered for duty in Korea. In the Air Force group at the POE staging area in Camp Stoneman, California, there were about 100 crew chiefs awaiting a flight for the trip to Korea.

On arrival in January 1953 at Yokohama, Japan I processed for Korea in a paperwork blizzard at FEAFCOM Base B. I was assigned to the 16th Fighter Interceptor Squadron (FIS), 51st Fighter Interceptor Group (FIG), 51st Fighter Interceptor Wing (FIW). The 51st FIG, based at Suwon, 30 road miles south of Seoul, had a proud and enviable WW II record. It had served with distinction in the China-Burma-India Theater where they eliminated the threat of Japanese Zero fighters in the Burma theater of operations. We flew from Tachikawa to Taegu, South Korea, landing on an unlit runway. It was an introduction to wartime conditions. The runway on both sides was lined with .50 caliber machine guns, gun crews on full alert against the threat of possible ground attack by North Korean guerillas. We took off in full darkness for Kimpo AFB at Seoul, K-16, landing in the middle of an air raid, courtesy of "Bedcheck Charlie." Again, no runway lights. Our pilot landed using his landing gear lights to set us down safely. We spent the rest of the night shivering in a cold Quonset hut. We left for Suwon at dawn, crammed into the rear of an old WW II '6x6' truck that had seen better days. It must have been one of the trucks retrieved from some South Pacific battlefield and rehabilitated in a Japanese work shop. It seemed to run well, but the metal truck bed was rusted out. We ate dust which boiled up from the unpaved road for the whole 30 road miles to Suwon. There were two pilots in the group with us. One remarked, "Being a dust eater was not his idea of breakfast."

The 51st Fighter Interceptor Group consisted of three fighter squadrons, 16th, 25th and 39th. We shared the base with the 8th Fighter Bomber Wing and a squadron of F-94s. The fighter group was made up of 75 F-86 jet fighter aircraft. Generally maintenance and availability of spare parts enabled us to keep an average 88% of our jet fighters operational on any given day, 66 of a 75 plane total. The goal was to have sufficient strength to fly two missions daily to "Mig Alley," located on the Yalu River boundary between North Korea and Chinese Manchuria. One of the oddities of the "rules of engagement" in the Korean War prohibited USAF pilots from pursuing MIGs into a Manchurian sanctuary, yet Russian backed Chinese and North Koreans encouraged daily raids southward.

The 16th FIS was grounded at the time I joined. Our squadron commander had been shot down in Manchuria. Although forbidden to cross into China, it was difficult in the heat of a fighter engagement to keep track of ground boundaries. May 26th was a sad day in my tour. The death of Capt Frank E. Miller, Jr. of the 16th FIS, killed in action on a mission in North Korea, affected me deeply. He was a fine officer, mourned by all. Another depressing day occurred when a transport crashed at Tachikawa, Japan. The plane was loaded with personnel returning from their last R&R before going home. Our base lost a number of air man due to accidents and wartime mishaps during my tour. The 51st shot down 312 MIGs, over 100 of them during my tour. The 16th shot down the first and last MIG of the war. The war's Ace of Aces, Capt Joseph McConnell was a member of the 51st. I was present when he was recognized for that honor. Buzz Aldrin flew with the 16th during my service in the unit. John Glenn flew with the 25th FIS. The 51st CO had commanded the Tuskegee Airmen in WW II. I was fortunately able to serve in company with some of America's most famous airmen.

I remember vividly the year of my life I spent in Korea. I have never for one minute regretted my service there. The defense of Korea was vital to the defense of world democracy. The spread of Russian Communism was halted. I often think of friends, especially those in the 51st FIG, some not as lucky as I to return to our American homeland. For those who did not, may they rest in everlasting peace.

Above. A tank-infantry patrol gets ready to start out on a patrol in the 279th Regt, 45th Division sector, Spring 1952.
Below. An 8 inch SP howitzer supports the 45th Division, 1952.   Photos courtesy of Glenn Ed White.

RED DRAGON
The SECOND ROUND
FACES OF WAR II

James	W.	Newland	ER 56 114 613
First Name	MI	Last Name	Serial Number
Jim	Tank Tow Operator	12 Mar 1929	Corporal
Nickname	MOS	Birthday	Grade / Rank
Don't remember.		10 Feb 1952-14 Jan 1954	Monroe, WA
Unit (s)		Duty Tour (s)	Home Town
Good Conduct Medal	Korean Campaign Medal w/4 stars		National Defense Service Medal

Medals & Awards

United Nations Service Medal   Republic of Korea War Service Medal   ROK Peace Medal

TRADE SCHOOL- APPRENTICE TO JOURNEYMAN

Twenty two years old, a recent college graduate, also newly married, and employed at his first teaching job, what in the hell was I doing here at Fort Ord? I was being taught to jump through the hoops, that's what! A course the army euphemistically called 'Basic Training' in reality was a basic trade apprentice course in mayhem and murder. Eight weeks of learning the lesser art of being a soldier! Those eight weeks were enough for many. However, my Enlisted Reserve status 'entitled' me to a 'Masters Degree' course in applied assassination. In sixteen short weeks I learned things I never thought possible. How to kill. How to use knives, wires, high and low explosives, and those failing, how to use my fingers in the killing trade. My new trade, merchant of death in the first person. To unlearn what twenty two years of Christianity, civility and the ethos of decency had instilled in me. How would these skills sound on my resume? History major, school teacher, has Masters degree in Artistry of Death and Destruction. Would the Mafia be hiring?

Sixteen weeks later I received orders to join in a struggle going on in a far away place called Korea. I learned that Korea was pronounced "Korearer" by those knowledgeable sergeants that had taught us so thoroughly. Off into the 'pipeline' that began in San Francisco then dumped us off at Camp Drake in Japan. That is where our lives as soldiers truly started. Daily, often hourly, formations were held, names called, men would disappear into a further, more mysterious branch of the 'pipeline.' After a few days about thirty of us were left. A final formation was held explaining that some had been selected as corpsmen, those remaining were to become Track Vehicle Mechanics. Corpsman sounded like lifting and carrying, bedpans and stretchers. I had never liked to be around hospitals anyhow. Too reminiscent of one's own mortality! Track Vehicles sounded like tanks. I knew soldiers didn't have to carry tanks. Oh Lord, I thought, have "them" choose me as one of those Track Vehicle trainees. That way I won't have to apply or put into practice my Masters degree in Artistry of Death and Destruction. Did God hear me, or was it fate? My number was called. Off I went to be taught how to be a Track Vehicle Mechanic. Two dozen of us were in the group sent to Tokyo Ordinance Depot(TOD).

"Men. You gunna learn a real trade heah. You guys gunna learn all 'bout fix'n tanks. This be a wrench." And so it began. In a few brief weeks we did indeed learn there are heavier things than bedpans or stretchers. They are called tank treads. Everything involving a tank ranges from heavy to impossible. I was launched into a whole new career opportunity called 'Tank Retrieval. A tank is disabled. It is then our task to return it to a place of safety for repair. A heavy duty tank has been modified by having the turret removed. An A frame is attached, cables connected. Presto! We now have a Tank Retriever which in essence is a heavy duty tow truck. There is a small problem barely mentioned in the instructional period. When a tank is 'disabled' in a war situation, it is generally because another tank or anti-tank artillery shell has made point blank contact. Chances are the same people that 'disabled' the tank still have it their gun sights hoping to bag the Tank Retrieval Vehicle. Get out, hook up, and vamoose! First, save those poor guys inside. That's the job. Not one for which you can buy adequate insurance coverage. If a tank is hit things go bad. Items in a tank burn, or explode. The first tank I pried open had what I thought was a bowling ball resting on what was left of the seat. It wasn't a bowling ball at all. It was all that was left of the head of some American mother's son. "What do I do with this, sergeant?" "Put it in the 'Parts Box'-- that foot locker over there. The Graves Registration guys from the Quartermaster Corps will pick it up."

The foot locker was filled and emptied with 'American' parts and other unidentifiable 'parts' which could be oriental, animal, vegetable or mineral. Hard to tell the difference. My crew mates dwindle in number. I am sent back to the Tokyo Ordinance Depot to aid in the resurrection of reclaimed battlefield parts. I am now a reclaimed parts expert, an on-the-job-trained specialist, no longer an apprentice, now a full fledged journeyman. All my training involving the finer points of how to dispense death while avoiding the same, to graduation as journeyman Track Vehicle Mechanic[read that as Tank Tow Operator] now ends in Tokyo as a clerk typist without either skills or a typewriter to practice on. The war drags on to its sad end. After one and a half years of service in Far East Command, I return to what I was before, a classroom teacher with a wife and a home. No banners, no waving flags. Home was enough.

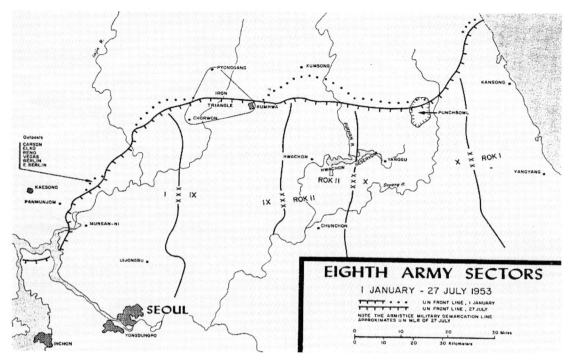

Above. Corps areas of responsibility during the final phase of the war. **Below.** An 8 inch howitzer from the 17th FA BN 'Persuaders' fire in support of Little Gibralter actions, 1953. **Map and photo from the Internet and Archives.**

William	J.	Dillon	US 21 917 740
First Name	MI	Last Name	Serial Number
Bill	1745	6 June 1932	Corporal
Nickname	MOS	Birthday	Grade / Rank
Mike Co,15th Inf,3d Div & 5th Cav,1stCav Div		Mch 1952-Sept 1953	Sayville, Long Island, NY
Unit (s)		Duty Tour (s)	Home Town

Combat Infantry Badge   Purple Heart   Korean Campaign Svc Medal, 4stars   ROK PUC UN Medal

Medals & Awards

National Defense Service Medal   NYS Conspicuous Service Cross   Korean War Service Medal

RATS AND BUNKERS

I had received my unit assignment. With several others, I was on my way to join Mike Company of the 15th Infantry. We stopped at a 'blocking' position. I watched a helicopter being loaded with dead and wounded for evacuation or medical treatment. I wondered whose place would I be taking, one of the dead or one of the wounded? I remembered as a kid I would quit things like school or jobs if I didn't relish what I was doing. At this point, I guess I recognized for the first time, my quitting days were over. I can't quit. I imagined going to my commanding officer, telling him, "I quit." He would have my ass thrown into the stockade or maybe here at the front, just have me shot for desertion, or wanting to desert. Definitely, my quitting days were over. A new era opened in my life.

I had been with Mike Company several months when we took this bunker over from another outfit. Rats made a move to any new position quite an adventure. In the bunker when we blew out the candles to sleep, the rats came out in the darkness. The squealing noises they made! It was like being in the middle of an Alfred Hitchcock horror movie. We were on their turf. It scared the hell out of me. I kept saying to myself "I am a combat soldier and must not be afraid of anything." Didn't work. Those damn ugly scaly tailed beasts. I was in the top bunk in the bunker. I hung my head, face down over the edge, so rats could not get at my face. I could feel those big rats walking on my back as they scurried to and fro. One guy woke up screaming, a rat had eaten a hole in his sleeping bag. It took six of us to hold him down and get him out of his sack. Amazingly he was not bitten. The rat was pounded to death with fists and pistol butts. Made a hell of a mess in his sleeping bag. One of the nightmares I still have is about a rat trying to get down my throat. I occasionally sleep breathing through my mouth when I have a cold. In Korea, everybody had colds. I awaken, choking and gagging, trying to get a rat out of my throat. This is the first time I ever told anyone that it actually happened to me.

When the heavy rains came, bunkers of logs and dirt dug into a hillside began to slump and fall in. We dismantled and rebuilt, keeping an ear open for incoming rounds. A huge 10 foot snake slithered out. It didn't bother us. Its body had two bulges showing it had eaten two big rats. It apparently was in the bunker with us all the time. One night a shell with a delayed impact fuse apparently hit near a nest of rats, causing them to scoot in panic everywhere. Although the shelling continued, men turned their weapons on the rats that kept them awake at night, more intent on killing rats than concern for their own safety. Rats made for a terrorized existence.

Were I asked, could I undergo the whole war again, I could honestly answer yes as for the combat part of war, but not for the filthy, foul living conditions. Sanitary facilities on the line were 'homemade.' Take a wooden ammunition box. Place a helmet on the box, draw an outline around the helmet. Cut out the resulting circle. Dig a pit. Place box over pit. After use, use GI belt shovel to cover the deposit. Dig new pit and move box as necessary. Seldom was toilet paper available. With a C-ration issue, a small roll was included in the can. This fundamental item was kept dry by tucking it inside the helmet liner. Using the GI toilet is another matter. First, the user is exposed to enemy observation and gunfire when sitting on the throne. Seeing a dead comrade topple from the throne, hit by a sniper's bullet, one tends to use his shovel to dig a 'cat hole' and cover it. Dig a new hole each time nature calls. With this new army of guys and dolls, this old combat infantryman wonders how the liberated sex handles this problem.

A shell with a delayed impact fuse hit near me, digging deep into the ground. When it went off, huge boulders went high into the air. Coiling myself into a fetus-like ball, I prayed none of the boulders would hit me. None did, but the concussion caused my ears to bleed. That quickly stopped, but the ringing was so loud hours passed before I could hear people speak. When we came off line, I asked the doctor to check it out. He said I had some hearing loss, but not enough to make changes, whatever that meant. The ringing finally went away, but even today if there is any background noise, I have great difficulty in hearing people, particularly children's higher voices. On discharge, I was given a Purple Heart and a pair of hearing aids. I'd gladly give them up if I could just have my hearing. It is as if I have been convicted of a crime in which we jointly serve a life sentence. She's innocent, but still pays.

Left. Sgt. Scheer and a ROK Major from the 12th ROK Regt. Above. It is not known if this war dog was named after our President, but his name was 'Ike'. Below. Psychological warfare was big business in Korea. Some of the surrender leaflets like this one were real 'works of art.' Photos and leaflets courtesy of Herbert Scheer.

空軍掩護!
隨要隨到!
只要聯軍士兵要,
飛機應聲就到!

6018°

RED DRAGON
The SECOND ROUND
FACES OF WAR II

Herbert	L.	Scheer	US 56 117 689
First Name	MI	Last Name	Serial Number
Hugh	3166	28 Oct 1928	S/Sgt
Nickname	MOS	Birthday	Grade / Rank
61st Searchlight Company		Oct 1952- Sept 1953	Junction City, OR
Unit (s)		Duty Tour (s)	Home Town
Korean Campaign Service Medal w/2 stars			National Defense Service Medal
Medals & Awards			
United Nations Service Medal			Republic of Korea Korean War Service Medal

WAR WARMS UP AS IT WINDS DOWN

Capt Albert Gilbert authorized my transfer from supply truck driver to NCO in charge of 'Item' light. This position, west of the Imjin River, was high on a ridge facing Chinese held Hill 317. The light faced northwest to shine on Chinese positions. We were a 5 man team assigned to operate 'Item' light, myself as NCOIC and Paul Orta, an old comrade. We had served together on 'Able' light before my TDY Air Force stint in Seoul. Three KATUSA completed our team, Kim Que-Hun was the lead ROK, the other two both were named Bok, hence Bok one and Bok two. None of the three ROKs had ever worked on a light before. We had an intensified OJT session for the first week. None of us got much sleep since we worked during hours of darkness operating the light and had OJT instruction during the day. Kim had some English so he passed on instruction to the two Boks. All three caught on fast. Our light was in direct support of the 11th and 12th ROK Regiments. 'Item' light was a stationary light, in contrast to the other company lights which were truck mobile. Korean Army Engineers built an enclosed bunker for the light. Another bunker was built as living quarters.

The ROKs operated the light at night in 2 hour shifts, 2 on and 4 off. We 2 GIs were 4 hours on, 4 hours off, but the other GI was on call as were the other 2 ROKs. It was a watch system that seemingly worked well. The 60 inch search light was a carbon arc device originally designed in WW II as an aircraft spotter light. The two interacting carbons, a negative inside the light, the positive outside the light, produced an arc light reflected off a spherical mirror. The result was a directed 800,000,000 candle power beam which was aimed like an artillery piece. It was one bright light! The light would shut down about once every hour, just long enough to change carbons used up in making the illumination. In the freezing cold of winter months, I would have to shed my parka to crawl inside a small hole in the bottom of the light to mount a new negative carbon. The positive was easier to replace as it was outside the light. The elevation and degree bands would have to be reset to get back on target. To illuminate a close in target such as Hill 317 we changed focus from a spot beam to a flood. The rifle companies on the MLR supplemented our efforts with parachute flares to light up pockets our beam did not penetrate. Our light was on dusk until dawn. On the last day of June, Capt Gilbert who was a "mustang" officer, came up to 'Item' light with orders promoting me to S/Sgt. He brought some faded S/Sgt stripes which he had himself worn before he became an officer. He pinned one on my right sleeve, then told me to get busy with a needle and thread!

Going into July, pay day was nigh. Paul Orta had not been paid for 3 months, illegible signature. I had him practice signing his signature. Pay day, 'The eagle screamed," his signature was legible to the pay officer. On some nights action was heavy, other nights not so bad. On one of the bad nights, in midst of heavy artillery and mortar fire I left the light bunker and to go to the living bunker for a crucial light operation item I had forgotten. I ran, all crouched over, with shrapnel buzzing in the air all about me. While "running for my life" I heard a voice, "Why are you running crouched over like that? No harm will come to you." I made the bunker without being hit. Turned me from a "Believer" to a "Knower" in my faith in God. Since then my faith has never faltered. A GI radar outfit moved in below our light position. Paul and I would bum a hot meal off them when time and duty permitted. They kept tally of the number of artillery hits our position took. They were always surprised the next time we came to mooch a meal to find us still alive.

The last 2 nights before "Cease Fire," 27 July 1953, action on the MLR was the heaviest I had ever witnessed. The night of the "Cease Fire," heavy artillery fire, both from our guns and Chinese artillery, continued until about 10:15 PM. After that, total silence. We had been told to keep generators running in case of an attack. Next morning at dawn, I heard oriental music. Donning my flak jacket, jamming my steel pot onto my head, I left the bunker to look over at the Chinese. There were several hundred Chinese soldiers, clad in black uniforms wandering about with no obvious purpose I could see. Perhaps they were just as glad to still be alive as I was. We were told by Capt Gilbert to pull back 2000 meters. A crew tore down the bunkers. All the big fir timbers from American west coast sawmills were salvaged, loaded aboard trucks and taken to the rear. We left the sandbags. The 61st Signal Co was reformed. We held formations next day! I left Korea on 10 Sept 1953, spending the intervening years until 1 May 1960 in the Enlisted Reserve.

The first helicopter assault was made by the Marines in 1953 on the Jamestown Line. Few of us then could imagine that this concept would become a major part of warfare in only a few short years. The skill of these pilots to maneuver their helicopters into tight spots was miraculous.   <u>Photos from the National Archives and the Internet.</u>

RED DRAGON
The SECOND ROUND
FACES OF WAR II

Jerome	None		Konsker		US 51201603
First Name	NMI		Last Name		Serial Number
Jerry		1745	22 Aug 1933		Corporal
Nickname		MOS	Birthday		Grade / Rank
Love Co/32/7, HQ7Div & 7th Signal Co.			May 1953-Sept 1954		Bronx, NY
Unit (s)			Duty Tour (s)		Home Town

Combat Infantry Badge   Korean Campaign Service Medal/1star   National Defense Service Medal
Medals & Awards
United Nations Service Medal   Presidential Unit Citation, Republic of Korea   Peace Medal, ROK

DEMONS OF WAR

At age 18 in accordance with the law I registered for the draft. Age 19 found me in Korea, a young soldier assigned to an infantry rifle company, 'Love' Company, 32d Infantry 7th Division. 'Love' was in fighting position on the Main Line of Resistance (MLR), or "the line," as it was often termed. I arrived in time to take part in the third round of fighting for possession of Pork Chop, that notorious Hill that changed hands three times in the last few months of the war. I was there for the third Chinese "human sea" attacks on 'Pork Chop'. In consequence, I made Corporal rather quickly. The fighting ended on 27 July 1953. Troops in Korea were expected to serve one year in overseas service at that time. One week after fighting ended, I was able to convince an officer in Love Company I could better serve as correspondent on the "The Bayonet," the 7th Division newspaper. I suspect he felt sorry for me. The officer was a 'Battlefield Commission' type and probably felt closer to an infantry grunt than most officers. I became a military photographer and correspondent the remainder of my time in Korea. The war changed my life as it did for many other young soldiers. War robs young men of their youth, they either become inured veterans or live a life of revulsion, recoiling from the horrors they have witnessed.

For too many of us, war does not end as guns go silent. Then and forever more we must go on, fighting forces of imagined demons that come in all colors and hues. We see the cold gray of the dead in the dawn of morning light and in the vivid burst of a nighttime flare. There are demons that shout and demons that stare. There are demons that hide deep in our psyche, not to be ousted from memory. Some demons are positive catalysts, propelling men and women to great things in public service, in science, in making this earth a better place to live. Other demons, in other people, eat into the fiber of a person's mind, leading to eventual destruction.

There was the demon called "rotation jitters." It is a demon haunting veterans of all wars, not only Korea. It is a demon that takes them from home and destroys too many of their brothers in arms. The psychology is simple. We left home and were subjected to events and sights that could never be anticipated, and even now, things we do not truly understand. We changed radically, both in mind and body. We were no longer the person who left home months, even years before. The world we now knew was no longer filled with vibrant color. It had grayed! However, the world we left behind, the world indelible in our memories, had not changed at all. It stood still like a snapshot, or the stop button on a VCR. Only we had changed. We were squared, triangled, hexagoned, no longer round, we fit in no hole at all. How do we return home? How do we fit in? This is where "rotation jitters" rears its ugly head.

I was fortunate to have transferred from the 32d Infantry to an assignment as official US Army correspondent immediately after the truce was signed. Later while attached to the Th Signal Photo Section I met "Bert." He was a Hungarian who had enlisted in Europe to gain citizenship for him and his mother. His father had been killed by the Russians in an uprising. He too was a refugee from the infantry and now an army photographer. He had seen enough combat time to earn his sergeant's stripes, a Combat Infantry Badge and a bunch of ribbons. Somehow, during his time in Korea, he developed a romance with a young lady in the United States. Exactly where he was to go, once out of the army, he could not visualize. What lay ahead of him was beyond his comprehension. It was frightening. He was nervous. How would he fit in, where could he fit in, earn a living in a new country where he had never lived? I went to relieve him one morning as CQ (Charge of Quarters) a job in company HQ, essentially a night watch duty. Bert had put a bullet through his head. Bert was not Jewish. I am. On the Jewish holiest day, Yom Kippur, I still say Kaddish (the memorial prayer for the dead) for my friend Bert. He died of "rotation jitters," truly a waste of a fine human being. Just another of war's casualties.

The war changed my life. I returned to the US, no longer a youth, but a man saddled with his personal demons. I threw myself into study, using every nickel of the GI Bill to become a writer with a master's degree in Theater and Play writing. Fifty years later, my demons have yet to be excised. In semi retirement I spend my spare time writing poetry which still reflects my combat experiences. Even though a half century has past, my time in Korea still haunts me. I am not a pacifist. I understand the need for a strong defense, even solid offensive capabilities. Even so, the thought of sending young men and women into the hell we saw in Korea is odious.

In February of 1954 the Marilyn Monroe USO show toured Korea. At this show performed in the Chorwon Valley she was at her best. Photos courtesy of Francois Cuypers of the Belgian Battalion.

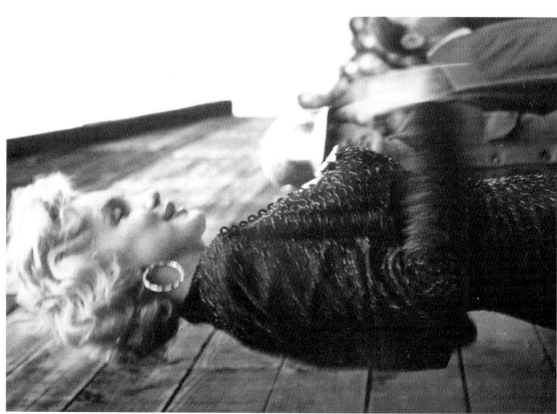

RED DRAGON
The SECOND ROUND
FACES OF WAR II

Leonard	O.	Loethen	US 55 337 9999
First Name	MI	Last Name	Serial Number
Len	1502	29 Nov 1932	Sgt
Nickname	MOS	Birthday	Grade / Rank
45th MASH (Mobile Army Surgical Hospital)		Jan 1953-Dec 1954	St Thomas, MO
Unit (s)		Duty Tour (s)	Home Town
Meritorious Unit Citation Korean Campaign Service Medal			National Defense Service Medal
Medals & Awards			
United Nations Service Medal			ROK Korean War ServiceMedal

POST WAR REFLECTIONS OF A MASH MEDIC

Drafted into the Army in 1953 and trained as a dental assistant at Ft Sam Houston, TX I ended up in Korea shortly before war's end assigned to 45th MASH Hospital. In my job as a clerk typist I worked in that section of personnel and administrative HQs which was responsible for incoming and outpatient record transfers as well as administrative functions of the hospital. Because the unit moved often, we worked out of tents. The equipment showed signs of dust, dirt and mud, which to me meant that the people servicing the hospital patients had fared worse than the equipment. A Sgt Major was in charge of administration. When he rotated stateside, I was asked to take over his job. As a Pfc, I didn't think much of the idea. Much work and responsibility, not commensurate with the pay of a Private First Class, at that time $54 per month. A special meeting was held which promoted me to Cpl. This caused a peer problem since almost all of the other PFCs had been in grade for quite some time, most much longer than I. That's the Army for you! About that time a movie was filmed called "Battle Circus," based on MASH units like ours. Our commanding officer acted as advisor.

We were located near the Chorwon Valley, direct invasion route to Seoul from the north. For some reason, we were ordered to climb the mountain near our base. At the top, I saw machine gun emplacements and infantry foxholes, going up, tangles of communication wire. It was a tough time climb with no equipment to carry. I can imagine the ordeal the infantry had, toting all their gear under fire. Chorwon, the scene of bitter fighting was devastated. I could see the shells only of two buildings in the area. Cardinal Spellman came at Christmas to give mass. The nurses in our hospital drew the attention of newsreel cameramen. This was prior to television. I was seen in newsreels on theater screens back home. I also witnessed Marilyn Monroe brave the rigors of a Korean December to give a USO show. Because our hospital cared for many wounded GIs, the USO shows came to us. Our officers club provided a place for line officers to visit their wounded men. In relaxation, they mingled with MASH medical personnel and performers from USO shows.

Many stories are associated with 45th MASH in the early days of the war. Incidents like MASH personnel and hundreds of wounded men were almost captured by the Chinese in December 1950. Others such as the triage decisions made necessary by a flood of wounded men overwhelming medical facilities and personnel. Patients sedated, placed outside hospital tents, wrapped in blankets against the cold, until time and personnel were available to care for them. There was the story of the GI captured by the Chinese, his boots taken from him, then turned loose to fare for himself. He survived for 3 weeks with only snow to eat. When he was brought into the hospital, he weighed 65 pounds! The unit was constantly on the move. As far north as Kunu-ri near the Manchurian border of North Korea in early December 1950. As far south as Taegu in South Korea in the dark month of January 1951 before the drive to again retake South Korea was launched, this time against both Chinese and North Korean armies. A sidelight was the wood carving of a nude Korean woman, a fixture of the officers mess. She is now on display at Ft Sam Houston in the Medical Museum.

After the truce was signed, the DMZ was still in turmoil. Shortly after the truce, our tent quarters were replaced by Quonset huts, palatial in comparison to drafty tents. Almost every night we were awakened by blare of sirens and noise of tank engines. Because we were a hospital unit we were privileged to have support units provide hospital guard duty. In return guards had visiting rights in our EM club. The hospital rations we drew gave us good food, the best that could be expected in Korea. One of the unfortunate things I witnessed several times was the sad affair of a wounded GI, a married man, receiving notice his wife was filing for divorce. This caused very decided attitude changes, complicating recovery of several wounded soldiers who were already suffering from the hardships of war. During the last months of the hospital's existence in Korea, our patients were soldiers wounded in training, Koreans, often children, wounded by exploding mines, and gunshot accidents due to careless handling of weapons. By the time our hospital closed shop I was actually drawing pay as a Sgt Major. It was my responsibility to work and to supervise the task of closing out and packing up all records, medical and personnel, and crating them for storage. It was amazing how many X-Rays were stored in the records. Statistically, more than 42,000 wounded soldiers were processed through 45th MASH. Looking back, It was a great honor and a great privilege to have served with the many distinguished doctors, nurses and other highly talented people in this unit.

<u>Above</u>. Picture was titled '4 eyes are better than 2'. A little sick humor from the Belgian Battalion. Also qualifies as one of the 'Faces of War.' <u>Photo by Cuypers</u>. <u>Left</u>. A wounded Lieutenant makes his way back to an aid station. He was with the 38th Regt. and wounded in the battle for Hill 1171, July 1951.

<u>Below.</u> The hospital ship Repose is seen in this photo taken in 1952. <u>Photos courtesy of the National Archives</u>.

RED DRAGON
The SECOND ROUND
FACES OF WAR II

David	P.	Whisnant	US 55 248 057
First Name	MI	Last Name	Serial Number
Dave	1745	7 March 1931	Sgt
Nickname	MOS	Birthday	Grade / Rank
1/1B/1/31/7		Sept '52-19 June '53	Detroit, MI
Unit (s)		Duty Tour (s)	Home Town

Purple Heart Medal   Combat Infantry Badge   Korean Campaign Service Medal, 2 bronze stars
Medals & Awards
Nat'l Defense Service Medal   United Nations Svc Medal   Korean War Svc Medal   ROK PUC

DRAFTEE TO VETERAN--TEN MONTHS.

Sept 1952, basic training finished, I shipped to Korea. My initiation into the hazards of military life were brought home as I went down the cargo net 'ladder' draped over the side of the troopship to board the LCVP at the port of Inchon. Loaded with 90 lbs of military gear, one slip, and I would have plummeted to the bottom of the sea, dead on arrival. On the way to B/31/7, the truck broke its steering gear as we crossed a rickety bridge over a deep chasm. Only a sagging cable kept us from going over the side into the depths below. It was hours before a wrecker towed us in. Arriving at "B" company rear, we were told, "Go to bed." Somebody said, "Where?" "Damn recruits! Here," pointing at the dirt floor, "Use your sleeping bags." A few hours later we were roused. Three guys did not get up. Looking closer, I saw three dead Chinese on stretchers. We joined the company which was located in the Iron Triangle near the tits on Jane Russell. Posted that night in a bunker, my squad leader, Sgt George, put me on guard. He told me, "Shoot anything that moves." I didn't blink an eye all night. He slept the night snuggled in his sleeping bag at my feet. Live and learn.

We occupied several positions on the MLR in the next 9 months. 7 March 1953, we were on 'Dales' outpost. Sgt George had rotated. I was now acting sqd ldr. The Chinese started shelling us with their big 120 mm mortars. It was intensive enough that it caused several bunker cave-ins, including mine. Thankfully, I was not in it. Our platoon sized outpost was hard hit. More than half our men were wounded or killed. We received a lot of raw replacements. A couple of nights later, my plat ldr told me we could expect to be hit that night. "Keep 90% of your men on all night alert." The mortar fire let up about 2 AM. I checked the men. I found the new men in the chow bunker with 'old-timer,' Jack Considine. "What the hell you guys doing in here?" Jack started swearing at me, "It's your idea, this 90% alert!" He had told the newbies to come into the chow bunker! I invited him outside into the trench, where I proceeded to kick his butt. I broke my thumb, either on his hard head, or the side of the trench. Next morning, my thumb was badly swollen. On sick call, the medics sent me to the Swedish Hospital in Pusan. There I was X-rayed, for 4 weeks I wore a cast on my thumb. My stay there was a pleasant one day interlude. Those Swedish nurses were nice people. Lots of TLC. As I left the hospital, Considine came in with a neck wound. I see Jack at our 31st reunions. We are good friends now, we do not mention the time 'we duked it out.'

In May I was promoted to Sgt and 4th sqd ldr. A 20 man combat patrol was sent out. I zeroed my .30 caliber LMG to cover the frontal area where the patrol was to set their ambush. The battle started about 1 AM. The flashes from Chinese Burp guns and our M-1s were continuous. I travered my LMG back and forth, left and right, between two pegs set as stops. The enemy switched some of their mortar fire onto my position. They fired until day light, never hitting me, a minor miracle. Lost my hearing for 2 weeks as a result of firing over 8000 rounds. I oiled my MG, switching barrels as each became red hot. My trigger finger had a blood blister all the way to the palm. None of the 20 men came back alive. When the squad showed at the chow bunker for rations issue in the morning, one ROK soldier was missing. I went to his bunker, yelled at him. He didn't move. He was sitting, M-1 across his lap, his back had a hole in it the size of a gravy bowl. Mortar shrapnel. Had to pry his fingers loose from his M-1, rigor mortis had set in, he was stiff in a sitting position. The next night a detail was sent out to bring back bodies of the patrol. Commo wire tied to an arm or leg was pulled dragging a body a short distance to make sure it was not booby trapped. All 20 bodies were retrieved for honorable military burial.

June '53 I was on Old Baldy's North View outpost, counting my 11 days short of rotation. Four of us were on the LP at the bottom of our hill. A spotlight behind us highlighted the hill crest. The Chinese were dug in behind the crest. About 1 AM the Chinese began playing old songs. Every 15 minutes a high-pitched sing-song voice would tell us they were going to take a break. Then their mortars would shell us. The singing would start again. I sure hated it when they took their breaks! The rain had started when I took a hit in the shoulder. I notified our CP via radio. I was told to lie low, too much incoming. I couldn't get any closer to the ground. I had already crawled into my helmet. Another mortar round hit me in the left knee, another guy got it in the foot. I radioed the CP that we were coming in, notify our LMGs not to shoot. We crawled back to the trench. They treated me at 44th MASH, then flew me to Japan. I spent 3 months in the 279th General Hosp, then was sent home and released from active duty on 21 November 1953. It was over.

Below. A Marine takes a smoke break before putting his 3.5 rocket launcher to work, the Nevada cities area, 1953. Photo from the National Archives.

Right Another propaganda leaflet. **Courtesy of Herb Scheer.**

Below Right. Lt.Markey, receives handshake and letter of appreciation from Commanding General of the USMC in Korea, 17 October 1953.

RED DRAGON
The SECOND ROUND
FACES OF WAR II

Christian	E.	Markey, Jr.	O-52113 USMC
First Name	MI	Last Name	Serial Number
Chris or Burr	2502	27 Oct 1929	Capt, then Lt
Nickname	MOS	Birthday	Grade / Rank
4th Bn11th Marines		June 1952-June 1953	Whittier, CA
Unit (s)		Duty Tour (s)	Home Town

Letter of Appreciation from Commanding General USMC in Korea.
Medals & Awards
Korean Campaign Service Medal w/ 3stars   Five other service ribbons

THE QUEEN, OUR CAPTAIN GENERAL!

At age 22, I was fresh out of college, officer's basic and communication schools and now, for this past two weeks, a newly engaged man. Flying out of Alameda NAS, my destination was Korea. I arrived late at night in the last week of June 1952, totally unfamiliar with where I was, where I was going, and to what type of outfit I would be assigned. Communication Officers (Commo) were in short supply, and badly needed. Having just finished Comm school I was accorded a warm welcome and assigned to 4th Bn 11th Marines. The 11th Marine Regt consisted of 4 Bns, three of these fired the 105 howitzer, while my 4th Bn fired the 155 howitzer, a much larger caliber weapon. The 1st MarDiv was dug in near Panmunjom and was positioned both north and south of the Imjin River. Our OPs looked directly down on the area where the interminable peace talks were taking place. The Communication platoon TO&E called for 1 officer and 90 men. Except for a minor relocations, 4th Bn remained in place even when 1stMarDiv went into Reserve in the spring of 1953. We stayed to support the British Commonwealth Division, the Turkish Brigade and the Korean Marine Corps(KMC).

During my year in Korea I had the pleasure and privilege of serving with many good marines. As any Marine will tell you, there are no other kind! 'Tho dimmed by the passage of almost 50 years, I have joyful memories of good friends and yes, of fallen comrades, of heat, dust, rain, mud and cold. Korea didn't seem have any weather in between those extremes. Manning the OPs, located well in front of the MLR was not that easy, nor all that healthy, for that matter. I am very proud, and lucky, to have served with those men.

With the Division in reserve except for the artillery, it was easy to get to know the British. Their chow was miserable. They found ours to be a great improvement--everything is relative. The British artillery officers were a hearty, cheerful, somewhat rowdy group of carefree professionals, quite used to overseas duty tours of 2½ to 3½ years. Marine Corps rotation was 6 months in the early part of the war but seemed to increase a month every month I was there. The British envied our short tours of duty and our food. They were frequent chow time guests. To the British, this was simply another tour of duty overseas. However, a historical event was taking place in England. If memory serves, in February King George VI died and Elizabeth ascended the British throne. The pomp and circumstance of the Royal Coronation also took place in the British mess on 2 June 1953 in Korea. The occasion provided me with a rather unique opportunity to celebrate the Queen's Coronation in the British manner. I've had almost 50 years to think about it, but have yet to figure out how the British managed to call off the war that one day in proper celebration of the Queen's Coronation. There was no war that day in the British sector, but there was one helluva celebration. I know because I was there! Having received an invitation to attend, I bummed a ride to their Division HQ as a 'special' guest. I guess they really did like the food in our mess!

Red, white and blue flares were visible high in the sky. The Durham Light Infantry quick stepped to the wails of what seemed to be a full company of bagpipers. It was a remarkable display of British military tradition. A banquet had been prepared in a large Quonset hut, one long table seating some 80 officers. The table was covered with beautiful linen tablecloths. Each place setting was arranged with fine china, sterling silver; 2 knives, 3 forks, 3 spoons and 4 crystal wine glasses. It was the most elaborate setting this marine had ever seen, let alone used. At our assigned seats and while still standing, we all raised our glasses and drank several toasts to "The Queen, Our Captain General." Once seated, the toasts continued into the afternoon, "To The Queen, Our Captain General."

The Commanding General sat at the head of the table enjoying himself immensely. He was a big man, perhaps 6' 3", 260 lbs. Two nurses from the hospital ship, one on either side, sat with the General. As the meal progressed he turned to play a piano, of all things, that had been placed there. He was quite good, playing lively tunes. Some good group singing took place. The General, with an arm around each nurse, continued to play the piano. A very talented man, that General! Of course, my eyesight may have become blurred by then. I believe I thanked my hosts for a memorable afternoon. I returned to my Bn, but don't remember how I got there. I do recall being told my orders back to the States were at Division. My relief was expected within a couple of weeks. The orders were there, my replacement arrived on schedule. I hitched rides to Inchon, Itami, Japan, Kwajalein, Pearl Harbor and on to Alameda NAS where I had shoved off a year ago. I was back home with unforgettable memories of Korean duty. The wedding took place 27 June 1953.

Above A Navy AD Skyraider [upper left] makes an air strike within 100 yards of 40th InfantryDivision positions, north of the Punchbowl, 1953.   Photo from the Internet.

Below.   Gen. James Van Fleet, CG 8th Army, welcomes Santa Claus to the 40th Division Hqs. He is accompanied on his left by by Maj. Gen. Cleland, 40th Div. C.O. and Lt. Gen. White, X Corps C.O. Last but not least is Santa Claus, aka Lt. William Nelson.   Photo courtesy of William J. Nelson.

RED DRAGON
The SECOND ROUND
FACES OF WAR II

William	J.	Nelson	0-996 017
First Name	MI	Last Name	Serial Number
Bill	1542,1560,2622	17 Jan 1930	Col AUS (Ret), then 1st Lt
Nickname	MOS	Birthday	Grade / Rank
E Co 223 Inf & HQ Co 224 Inf, 40th Div		May 1952-June 1953	Piedmont, MO
Unit (s)		Duty Tour (s)	Home Town

Medals & Awards: Combat Infantry Badge Army Commendation Medal Good Conduct Medal Natl Def Svc Medal
KCSM,3 stars Meritorious Service Medal Meritorious Unit Citation UN Medal ROK PUC

PRIVATE TO COLONEL

Big for my age, I enlisted in 1946 in the Regular Army at age 16. When my true age was exposed, I was bounced with a "Minority" Discharge. I waited until the following January and legally enlisted at age 17. I had made Cpl in C Co, 32d Med Tank Bn, 3d Armored Division when the Korean War began. There was a high turnover of personnel as many EM, as well as most WW II vets, were being sent to Korea to bolster those divisions shifted from occupied Japan. On 25 July '50 I was promoted to S/Sgt as Platoon Sgt, and in August to SFC, Field 1st Sgt. As a birthday present when I turned 21, my company commander, Cpt Hugh M. Mattoon, told me he had recommended me for a direct commission as 2d Lt. An approval authorized on 24 April '51 also assigned me to the 101st Airborne Division, Camp Breckinridge, KY. On arrival 3 June '51 I was assigned as plat ldr, G Co 516th Infantry Regt. After several months training I transferred to the 43d Inf Div, Co A, 169th Inf Regt, Camp Pickett, VA. This New England NG division was been activated for service in Europe due to the uncertainty of Russian intentions. In November, as the 43d prepared for NATO shipment, orders came from Department of the Army requiring all Combat Branch Lts be sent to their basic Branch Officers Course before being sent overseas. This order was the result of extremely high casualty rates among inadequately trained 2d Lts sent to Korea.

In April '52, a request made at Camp Pickett for Korean War duty was granted after I completed 4 months attendance at the Associate Infantry Company Officers Course at Ft Benning, GA. In May, after a 30 day leave spent with wife and new baby, I processed at Camp Stoneman, CA. I was flown from Fairfield-Suisan AFB, to Tachikawa AFB in Japan. We took ship to Inchon, Korea where we boarded a train for 40th Division Rear at Chunchon. At Regt HQs in the Kumwha Valley we could hear the thunder of artillery a mile or so away. I was assigned to E Co. Finally, I was in Korea in a combat zone! It was the fruition of young dreams which prompted my enlistment at age 16, wrapped in teen age idolatry of our soldiers in WW II. Under enemy fire qualified me for the Combat Infantry Badge, and promotion to 1st Lt. Both realized. I soon knew that there was no glory in combat, or in war. In summer it was either hot and dusty, or wet and miserable. In winter, the cold could quickly freeze to death any soldier too careless to adhere to cold weather discipline.

In 13 months in Korea, mostly spent in patrolling, small unit actions and manning MLR positions, the only things I gladly anticipated were letters from my wife and QM bath facilities. My service at Kumwha, Heartbreak Ridge and in the Sandbag Castle-Punchbowl areas were similar, no different from thousands of other men. When time came to return home, a number of 1st Lts were in a group being briefed for rotation. Our Regt'l CO, Col George C. Duncan, later Lt Gen, offered several of us promotion to Captain if we would extend our stay in Korea. Only one man, 1st Lt Edward Meyer, a 1951 USMA graduate, accepted. Later, as a 4 star general, he served as Army Chief of Staff. We were blessed with a top Division CG, MG Joseph P. Cleland, called the "Great White Father" due to his white hair. Capt David Hackworth, CO of F Co 223 Inf later gained fame when, as a LtCol commanding a battalion in Vietnam, his newly awarded decorations added to those of post WW II in Trieste and in Korea made him the most highly decorated US soldier.

My next four years were a chronicle of typical military service assignments. July 1953, 10th Infantry Division, Ft Riley, KS, Co Cmdr, division deactivated May 1954. May-Sept 1954, Ft Leonard Wood, MO, Co Cmdr, training Engineer replacements. Aug-Sept 1954, Co Cmdr, Command B, 6th Armored Division. Nov 1954-July 1957, US Army Europe, Mainz, Germany. Assigned 2d Armored Division, 42d Armored Infantry Bn, served as XO in Companies B and C and as A Co Cmdr. Spent my last year as Asst S-3, Operations. I returned to the US at a time when the Army was in one of its periodic personnel cutbacks as Congress tightened the purse strings. My efficiency reports were good, but lack of a college degree was a killer. In a process termed 'Riffing,' I was released from active duty and assigned to the Ready Reserve. It was a wake-up call. August 1957, I enrolled in the Forestry School at the Univ of Missouri, graduating in June 1960 with a BS in Forestry. Went immediately to work for the US Forest Service, spending the next 24 years in a variety of assignments, Missouri to West Virginia, retiring as District Ranger of Willow Springs District, Mark Twain Nat'l Forest. With a college degree under my belt, I became active in the US Army Reserve, retiring in 1981 with rank of Colonel. Today, retired from the US Forest Service and from the US Army Reserve, I'm thankful I could pursue two satisfying careers in my lifetime.

<u>Above</u>.   Location of POW camps in South Korea where thousands of POWs were allowed to escape rather than being forcefully exchanged.
<u>Right</u>.   A North Korean POW by the name of Kim [?] who designed and crafted a beautiful ring for his friend, PFC Noble.
<u>Below</u>.   Some G.I. humor from Stars and Stripes. In many cases it was more truth than fiction.   <u>Photos and map from Rollin Noble</u>.

← "TODAY'S THE FIRST DAY OF SPRING. ALL WINTER CLOTHING MUST BE TURNED IN. WE DON'T WANT OUR MEN TO BE BURDENED DOWN WITH A LOT OF HOT CLOTHES."

RED DRAGON
The SECOND ROUND
FACES OF WAR II

Rollin	B.	Noble	US 55 162 396
First Name	MI	Last Name	Serial Number
None	4641	26 Aug 1929	PFC
Nickname	MOS	Birthday	Grade / Rank
8th Army, 5th MP POW Command #5		Apr 1952-Aug '53	Mount Ayr, IA
Unit (s)		Duty Tour (s)	Home Town

Good Conduct Medal Korean Campaign Service Medal, 3stars National Defense Service Medal

Medals & Awards

Korean Service Medal Cold War Medal Korean Presidential Unit Citation United Nations Medal

FRIENDS AMONG ENEMIES

Fifty years ago, as a young man in my early twenties growing up in Mount Ayr, Iowa, war was the furthest thought in my mind. I was in my mid teens when WWII ended in complete victory for the United States. This time, most Americans believed it was truly the war that would end all wars, unlike WW I which contained the seeds of WW II. When the Korean War broke out, it was dubbed a "Police Action" in which the newly organized United Nations would soon bring the matter to an end. I of course had registered for the draft after the Selective Service System resumed its draft function in 1948. As 'the police action' in Korea dragged on, my number came up. I was drafted into the Army of the United States and sent through an 8 week Infantry Basic Training Course, then assigned to the Signal Corps for further training in military communications. Arriving in Korea I was sent to 8th Army, then reassigned to the 5th Military Police Command whose initial function was to erect, build, maintain, service and later internally guard a Prisoner of War camp. The camp was given the name POW camp No. 5. It was located in the area between Kwanju and Song Jong-ni in South Korea.

My job was to establish and maintain phone lines between Camp HQ and the outlying posts making up the 3 holding camps housing over 10,000 'North Korean POWs', who all claimed a South Korean origin. The camp was intended as a provisional camp. As the interminable peace talks continued for another 18 months, the camp took on the appearance of a permanent installation. Matters settled into a routine of communication checks and guard. POWs were often used as camp labor. As a result of this intermingling, we became acquainted with a few POWs. I befriended one, a younger POW who seemed out of character with some of the others. He held his name of Kim in common with several million other Koreans. Bars of soap, candy, tooth paste, tooth brushes and such were exchanged for extra detail work. Kim learned some English, probably more than I suspected. I learned a few words of Korean. In the course of this barbed wire friendship, Kim said he would make me a ring. However, before the ring was finished, the South Korean government, with help of South Korean soldiers guarding the camp perimeter, liberated the POWS. In making my check of commo lines after the breakout, I discovered Kim still in the compound. He had not made a break with the others.

He gestured to me. I went over to him and asked, "Why did you not leave with the rest of the POWs?" In almost perfect English, he replied, "Your ring is not finished. Tomorrow I will finish it and then go! Sayonara, Number One GI." I finished my line inspection thinking no more of the remarks Kim had made, knowing that a now redoubled guard would find him still behind the wire. Not so. True to his word, Kim and the remainder of the Korean prisoners that night fled the prison area, while South Korean perimeter guards kept American personnel pinned down by machine gun fire! In a full inspection of all three camps not one Korean prisoner was to be found. The search disclosed a package with my name in beautiful cursive script on it. In it was my ring. I have it yet and will pass it on to my grandchildren. I often wonder why Kim chose me for the gift of a ring. I cherish it to this day as a memento of my service in Korea. Was he able to rebuild his life? He is quite often in my thoughts as I grow older and more immersed in old war memories.

Editorial note: The US Army as part of the on-going "peace talks" at Panmunjom had questioned almost every POW, North Korean and Chinese as well as those South Korean young men who had been drafted into the North Korean army. North Korea drafted thousands of South Koreans during the three month period following the North Korean invasion of South Korea on 25 June 1950.

Almost all South Korean young men were determined not to be "repatriated" to North Korea as North Korean and Chinese negotiators insisted in the Panmunjom discussions. It took many months to sort out the prisoners. Each was asked where he wanted to go when repatriated. Die hard North Korean and Chinese Communists POWs were segregated in separate camps. North Korean and Chinese POWs who did not want to return to North Korea or China were placed in other camps Those professing to be South Koreans were placed in separate camps. These were closely watched since many Communist 'sleeper' spies were placed in their midst in an effort to control them. In crowded prison camp conditions, many South Koreans were murdered by Communists in their midst. American authorities were slow to act. South Korea took care of its own by "liberating" POWs as described in this vignette. AWW,Ed.

Above. A Korean laborer takes a break sitting next to his A-frame. Near the R R depot in Seoul, 1952. Photo courtesy of Glenn Ed White.

Left. A G.I. surveys destroyed R.R. rolling stock, handiwork of the US Air Force, near Chorwon, 1953

Below. A tank from the 64th Tk Bn. going south from Chorwon on Route 3, 1953. If 'might makes right' this big fellow has the right of way.

Photos courtesy of Art Elkington.

The SECOND ROUND
FACES OF WAR II

Arthur	George	Elkington	US 56 201 899
First Name	MI	Last Name	Serial Number
Art	1014	11 April 1932	Corporal
Nickname	MOS	Birthday	Grade / Rank
HQ Co 3d Bn 65 Inf 3d Div		22Jun 1953-19 Aug 1954	Salinas, CA
Unit (s)		Duty Tour (s)	Home Town
Combat Infantry Badge		Korean Campaign Service Medal with star	UN Medal	ROK PUC

Medals & Awards

Good Conduct Medal   National Defense Service Medal   PUC with star   Korean Service Medal

LAST DAYS OF WAR IN THE LAND OF MORNING CALM

In mid June 1953 the troop ship General A.W. Brewster took us to Inchon, harbor for the city of Seoul. We debarked onto a floating dock, then to an LST which took us to the beach where we boarded an elevated train that took us to the railhead. We looked down on scenes of utter destruction. Clusters of tents and a few Quonset huts had been erected in cleared areas. The train took us to Yongdongpo, then over a rickety, hastily repaired Han River bridge onto tracks posted for a 'super sonic' speed of 10 mph. Passing through the outskirts of Seoul we saw a devastated land, populated by poor people trying to locate shelter and eke out a subsistence. Along the track were many children, hands outstretched in supplication, pleading for scraps of food. We gave away all our rations. Their need was greater. From Uijongbu we traveled north to the railhead at Chinchon. Looking north up the damaged rail line into the narrow valley used by North Koreans in the 1950 invasion of Seoul, we could see the signs of war in a sky lit by tracers and flares. As it grew darker, "Moon Beams," huge searchlights bouncing light off overhead cloud cover, lit the battlefront ahead. Here we boarded trucks for unit assignment at the 'Repo-Depo.'Next morning we went north, dropping off men en route as "replacements."

We passed through Kumwha into the Iron Triangle area. I was the last one off the truck, destined for HQ Co 3d Bn 65th Inf. Bn HQ was in an area called the "The Boomerang," an area on the northeast side of "Pikes Peak,"Hill 454, about 100 yards below the hilltop. Looking northeast was Hill 1062, held by the Chinese and aptly named Papa San .It dominated the countryside. When our 155 artillery shelled the top of Papa San, it sounded like a jet plane overhead. It took a while for me to learn where I was. By scuttlebutt and maps at Bn Hqs, I eventually located myself geographically. The firefight I had seen the night before was going on at OP Harry, Star Hill, OP Dick, Hill 422 and the near vicinity of that area of the Iron Triangle. My company was just outside, about half way up the eastern leg of the triangle. A few nights later, I was riding shotgun on a supply truck destined for the staging point of the assault on OP Harry and Hill 422. We were in the middle of the action. Outgoing fire from our Quad 50's, twin 40's and rockets passed over our heads. Artillery and mortars were firing at almost point blank range. The entire scene was illuminated by flares and "Moon Beams" in the midst of the continuous din of a boiler factory. Luckily, no counter battery fire came our way. Going to the unloading point was easy, vision was good, "Moon Beams" were pointed at the enemy. Returning, we were almost blinded by the glaring light in our eyes.

About a month later the 65th Reg't went into reserve. Next day the Chinese began their last offensive of the war using 5 divisions in assault of the "Kumsong Bulge." Elements of the 3d Division were quickly placed in a blocking position at "Sniper Ridge." ROK positions and the 555 "Triple Nickle" FA were overun before the attack was stopped just north of the Kumwha valley. We stayed there until the truce. Enemy artillery fire hit us almost daily. Learning the day before that the truce was to be effective 27 July 1953, my buddy and I decided to take no chances. We grabbed shovels and began to dig foxholes into the north river bank. We got a lot of laughs directed our way, "Don't you know the war is over?" As we both suspected, next day the Chinese opened fire with everything they had, from1200 hours until the truce went into effect at 2200 hours. We did the same. The new silence was spooky!

The war over, we moved around in the Triangle area. One move took us a mile west of Chorwan. Overlooking our front to the southwest we could see Arrowhead Mt, Whitehorse Mt, T-Bone, Porkchop, and Old Baldy. To our right and north about 3 miles across the Chorwan valley was Ironhorse Mt, Jackson Heights, and OP's Tom, Dick and Harry. Further to the east was Papa San Mt. Kumwha was to the south. With the MLR silent, but not deserted, I was able to get some great photographs showing one third of the central MLR front. Looking back, Korea has some of the worst living conditions imaginable. Hot, choking dust in the summer, followed by fall rains and mud, a winter of unbelievable bone aching cold, then spring with an eruption of insects and snakes. I ran over one of those 5 ' long black snakes. The jeep bounced, the snake slithered off unharmed! My most vivid impression of Korea was the plight of the wretched Korean people in their desperate struggle to stave off starvation. My young years in the depression were luxury in comparison. I returned home in August 1954. I was not long in the war, but was decidedly glad it had ended! In retrospect I am proud to have served in the US Army. It was a priceless experience. It taught me to be grateful for all that America offers its citizens.

你們遭災受難
精神痛苦
都是共產黨害的

8725*

Above. An artillery battery is dug- in on the Central Front, 1952.
Below. Marines begin to utilize the helicopter for combat operations.
Photos courtesy of National Archives. Right. 'Psych war leaflet'
depicts a Chinese soldier sick of war. Leaflet from Herb Scheer.

RED DRAGON
The SECOND ROUND
FACES OF WAR II

Hubert	S.	Coose	US 55 306 147
First Name	MI	Last Name	Serial Number
Hub	1844	7 November 1931	Sgt
Nickname	MOS	Birthday	Grade / Rank
Btry A 75th FA Bn		Jan 1953-Jan 1954	Lockwood, MO
Unit (s)		Duty Tour (s)	Home Town
Korean Campaign Service Medal, 2 stars			National Defense Service Medal

Medals & Awards

United Nations Medal   Korean War Service Medal

'REDLEG' REMEMBERS WAR'S FINAL DAYS

Inducted in early Sept 1952, my basic training at Camp Chaffee, AR was spent in fathoming the mysteries of a 105 howitzer. I was then flown to Japan in with a planeload of officers. We spent 3 days in Tokyo, receiving winter clothing, M-1 rifles, and completed 'processing.' A ship took us to Korea, where we off loaded to a barge at 3 AM at some Korean port. Sound of bombs and shells exploding in the distance signaled our destination. We marched a short distance surrounded by hundreds of kids begging for something to eat. We gave what we had. Trucks took us to the front lines. Some guy grabbed me, took a gander at my orders, and led me to a bunker housing the gun crew of a 155mm howitzer. My welcome from one guy was, "Here's my replacement!" I had been there less than 5 minutes when the shout, "Fire Mission!" emptied the bunker. I had never seen a 155 howitzer before and did not know what to do. I was the new kid on the block and was given the job of loading the 96 lb shell into the breech of the howitzer. The first shell was not so bad, but as firing went into hours my arms felt as they were of lead and no longer belonged to me. What kept me going, I think, was the counter battery fire of the enemy trying to knock us out. The adrenaline of fear gives a man a lot of strength!

My fear continued in greater or lesser degree for the next 7 months. It certainly never went away. It was like ebb and flow of the tide, ever present. We maintained a constant harassing fire schedule every night. In event of an enemy night attack we fired all night long and tried to snatch a little sleep during the day. Every night a slow flying enemy plane would come over trying to locate lights for his artillery to fire at. This intermittent firing action went on for five months. I now knew our battery firing position was in the Kumwha valley. On several occasions we went on "night patrol." We would move our guns forward to get into range to hit an enemy position. Twice we were attacked by Chinese infantry. My M-1 rifle got so hot the gun oil kept in the rifle stock ran down the barrel, but my M-1 never let me down. Another occasion when we were hurriedly moving back, the 10,000 lb howitzer got away from us and cut off a man's foot. Another time, we moved less than 100 yards back when a round screamed in and cratered the position we had vacated. Some said 'soldier's luck', others, "God cares for us." Summer came, as hot in summer as it was cold in winter. In June the Chinese initiated their heaviest infantry and artillery attacks of the war in an effort to retake territory before a truce was signed.

75,000 Chinese were reported attacking down the Kumwha valley. We fired continuously for 9 days and nights, no rest or sleep. We fired like zombies, asleep on our feet. Incoming rounds exploded all around us, but miraculously our gun positions were not hit. The sandbags took a beating, sand spilled out so we had to rebuild the gun bunker under fire. We could hear the MG fire coming closer. The sky to the north was lit up as if by a terrible lightning storm that had no end. Trucks could not haul ammo to us as fast as we fired it. The man next to you says this may be the last day we have to live, and you wonder why you didn't say it to him first! The longer we fired, it seemed, the greater the number fighter planes and bombers circled overhead, adding an additional roar of war to din of battle. Once a plane was shot down in front of us. Two fighters circled the pilot who had bailed out, covering him with MG and rocket fire until a helicopter daringly rescued him. To the downed pilot that 'copter must have been like an angel from heaven.

In July it started again. This time the Chinese were reported attacking in 100,000 man strength. The action went on for 11 days and nights, again without sleep or rest for the gun crews. Our howitzers got so hot the rifling in the barrels wore out. Two guns in the Bn exploded, killing and wounding their crews. Replacement barrels were not always available. There were so many spent shell casings piled around the guns it was hard to get ammo to us. Korean laborers loaded them into trucks to be hauled away. That was usually our job, but this was an unusual time. We were all completely exhausted. I could not help but wonder, did it matter anymore, was this war we were fighting worth the pain and agony? The enemy kept coming for 11 days. They wiped out every thing to our front. Flank counterattacks, artillery and air power finally stopped them. I think the Chinese ran out of enough men available on the spot. They used their men like we used ammo. They kept coming until all were dead. When 'cease fire' was announced July 27th, every man in our gun crew fell to the ground, asleep within seconds. Where we were was bad, bad, but nothing like what our front line infantry faced. How any of them survived I have never been able to understand. God must have held them tightly in his hands

Above. GIs of the 7th Cav. Regt. are heavily engaged with enemy forces north of Uijongbu. They were in support of the Greek Battalion fighting a fierce battle with Chinese troops, May 1951. Below. The 2nd Ranger Company is seen on the move near Chunchon. The Ranger Companies were always in the thick of the fighting and were always on call if a situation became critical. They were great warriors but paid a terrible price as a 'fire brigade.' Photos from the Internet and Archives.

Above. Forward position of A Co. 13th Combat Engineers was located at the base of Pork Chop. They performed a bridge building miracle in impossible weather, under constant direct fire from the Chinese. One Engineer was awarded the Medal of Honor for his direct support of the 17th Regt. Right. Two engineers in the trenches at Pork Chop. Middle, Sgt Goudy at work reinforcing trenches and bunkers on Pork Chop. Bottom. A Company CO, Capt. Brettell, with Plt Ldr Lt Larkin. After fighting for the hill most of the month it was finally given to the Chinese as not worth further casualties. Members of D Co, 13th Engineers remained to destroy fortifications and set booby traps. 22 Bronze Stars were awarded in that final action. Photos courtesy of Jim Brettell and James Goudy.

RED DRAGON
The SECOND ROUND
FACES OF WAR II

James	A.	Brettell	O-69600
First Name	MI	Last Name	Serial Number
Jim	1331(Combat Cmdr)	27 Jan 1928	LtCol, then Capt
Nickname	MOS	Birthday	Grade / Rank
A /13th Engr(C)/7th Div		Mar '53- Jun-'54	Tyler, TX
Unit (s)		Duty Tour (s)	Home Town
Bronze Star with V and Oak Leaf cluster		Korean Campaign Service Medal with one star	
Medals & Awards			
National Defense Service Medal		United Nations Service Medal	Korean Freedom Medal

MURPHEY'S LAW THWARTED BY FIGHTING ENGINEERS(C).

By days end on the Fourth of July 1953 the summer Korean rains had poured steadily for 24 hours. Roads become quagmires. This presented an enormous maintenance problem for engineer troops. It doesn't just rain in Korea, it comes down hard, hours on end. It was not uncommon to schedule 24 hour round-the-clock road maintenance lest roads wash out overnight. They needed constant attention. The rains also created serious problems for infantry units in defense positions on the MLR. This was especially true at outposts such as Pork Chop Hill. The heavy rains masked noise that would alert our troops to enemy approach. Streams ordinarily inches deep became raging torrents, too deep and swift to allow passage of wheeled or track vehicles such as M-46 tanks or APCs.

On 6 July, under cover of darkness and torrential rain, the Chinese began their last major attack of the war on Pork Chop. The attack was ferocious and unrelenting. The Chinese were heedless of their own casualties. The 17th Infantry in defense of Pork Chop also suffered heavily. Counter attacks were immediately launched. A squad of engineers from A/13 were assigned to each rifle company in the 17th. They had regularly practiced counter attack procedure and were ready. Each engineer squad had a basic load of ammo, satchel charges, bangalore torpedoes, mines, radios and rations which they carried in event of counter attack. Their load was mule heavy. In these counterattacks, continuous rain complicated our routine road maintenance so badly we considered use of a Bailey bridge to span a small, usually fordable stream, flowing diagonally northwest, crossing the only supply route to Pork Chop. The 17th Inf, 7th Div was defending Pork Chop, A Co of the 13th Engineers attached. On the morning of 6 July, M/Sgt Jim Goudy and I made a reconn to determine if a Bailey bridge could be used to span the stream. We decided it could be done, and so reported to Engineer Bn HQ, setting wheels in motion. Our Bn HQ informed us an engineer bridge unit, normally assigned from I Corps, was not available.

This meant A Co/13 Eng was in the Bailey bridge business. Every engineer soldier is trained in bridge construction. We were rusty on procedure. No time for retraining. A Bailey section weighed 560 lb, and was 5 ft x 10 ft. M/Sgt Goudy dug into his bag of tricks and came up with the tech manual needed. The stream was rising rapidly. First order of business was to determine bridge length and exact location. We took a jeep to make a second reconn to locate a suitable site. Once we were in the general area of the proposed bridge site we would be in line-of-sight observation of the Chinese on Old Baldy. We parked the jeep out of sight, then moved on foot toward the area where the proposed bridge might be located, hoping the pouring rain would disguise our movement.

At the general site area of the bridge, M/Sgt Goudy stepped on something that emitted a very loud CLICK. We both knew it was a pressure release mine. M/Sgt Goudy had great presence of mind. He stood stock still, his weight on his left foot so as not to release pressure on the switch. Goudy caught his breath. He said, "Now what?" "I told him, "Stand still, let me think." We had very few options. We were still under observation, had been here quite some time, and were within small arms range of Old Baldy. As I looked around there, nothing was in sight except some boulders. They gave me the germ of an idea. I told M/Sgt Goudy to be patient, keep perfectly still and maintain his weight on his left leg. Soldier that he was, he mustered courage to do so while I placed boulders to build a parapet wall close to his leg. When I finished, I told him I could do nothing more. I said, "I'll get behind that big boulder."

Whenever you're ready, fall over that wall, and drop to the ground as quickly as you can." In a voice typical of his calm and confident nature, he said, "OK." Knowing he was standing on an explosive charge that could kill or take his leg off didn't seem to faze him. His voice never wavered. This man was cool! We both knew a mine of this type was designed to fly upward with a 1 to 3 second delay before exploding, spraying a fan shaped fragment pattern. Seeing that I was in place, he took a deep breath and jumped over the parapet of boulders. It seemed like an eternity before we both realized that the explosion blew the mine diagonally up and away from us. Neither of us had more than a scratch! We assumed the mine was an M-2 Bouncing Betty. The Chinese had nothing like it. It must have been placed there earlier by our own troops. In retrospect, it passes understand why the Chinese did not fire on us or attempt to capture us from their positions on Old Baldy. Was it because they knew the position was mined?

Or, were they just watching in amusement waiting for us to be blown sky high? Was it because they had bigger fish to fry, having only a few days earlier captured the Commander of the Columbian Battalion with enough documentation to cause the burning of a great deal of midnight oil at Chinese Division and Army HQs. Or was it just one of those vagaries of war for which there is no explanation? All of the problems and unexpected happenings of the past three days since the rains began, and which made necessary the erection of a Bailey bridge, were good examples of Murphy's Law in operation.

There is an old, old adage in the annals of warfare. It is in two parts. "If it can be misunderstood, it will be misunderstood!" The other, "If something can go wrong, it will go wrong!" These accidents-waiting-to-happen are usually referred to as Murphey's Law. The mishaps resulting from Murphey's principles have caused many military disasters in the long history of warfare. In this case, the gods of war took pity. We recovered quickly. What a way to start the construction of a Bailey bridge! 'Murphy' must have enjoyed a sardonic laugh at our plight! In spite of this difficult beginning we kept our eyes on the mission. We had come to select a bridge site and determine the length of the Bailey bridge to provide a life line for troops defending Pork Chop Hill. As it turned out, it was a good thing we performed that chore when we did. A few hours later continuing rains would have made it impossible.

Quickly we began to move components to a staging area near the site chosen for the bridge. 'Murphy' was waiting for us. The space in the staging area was very limited. The approach to the bridge site was on a side hill cut. We had to stay behind the nose of the hill to mask our activity from the Chinese on Old Baldy. It was most difficult and time consuming to maneuver those huge trucks in the limited space available to us for concealment. By dark we had begun the construction. Fortunately we had assistance in our task. In addition to the engineer soldiers in A Co 13th Eng, we had a number of Korean Army soldiers integrated into our company. These soldiers were called KATUSA, Korean Army Troops with United States Army. In addition we had assistance from the KSC, Korean Service Corps, to aid in our task. These older men, some volunteers, some conscripted by the South Korean government, performed miracles of supply lugging their A frame packs up the Korean hills to supply troops with the necessities of warfare. They were of great help in this bridge construction, working as they did, civilians under fire.

The darkness and the rain were serious handicaps for our project. The Chinese added to our problems by firing mortars directly into the bridge site. 'Murphy' had again put in an appearance! As if building a bridge in darkness and torrential downpour were not enough of a problem, it quickly became apparent that due to the language barrier, communication with the KATUSA soldiers and KSC laborers was extremely difficult. 'Murphy' was having a field day! Nevertheless, unloading and assembly of bridging units continued apace. No one faltered. Bridge construction was underway in spite of the language barrier problems posed by 'Murphy'!

After the first three sections of the bridge were assembled, we could not lo push the joined sections toward the far shore. Slick footing and incessant incoming mortar fire in combination with tired men made it impossible with the personnel available to get the bridge any further forward. 'Murphy' was shoved aside as we moved a Caterpillar D-7 to the site. With that piece of equipment in use, the bridge was rapidly pushed toward the suspended end of the bridge. A wounded KATUSA was brought back from the other side to safety. The men performed heroically time after time, exposing themselves to deadly mortar and small arms fire to continue assembly of the bridge so essential to the success of the infantry mission. In spite of the succession of casualties, work on the bridge continued as engineer soldiers, KATUSA and KCS labored together. Their mutual persistence resulted in a 60 foot span bridge across that rain swollen stream. The vital supply route was reopened by 0600 on the morning of 7 July. 'Murphy' lost the argument!

During that night there were many trips made moving wounded men to the Infantry Battalion aid station which was located just to the rear. On one such trip, M/Sgt Goudy, who was himself wounded, drove another wounded soldier to the aid station. After the medics treated Goudy, he was told that the other soldier would have to be moved to the division level hospital immediately if his life were to be saved. All the ambulances were in use. There was no way for the clearing station to evacuate him back further to the rear. M/Sgt Goudy 'jeeped' the man back to the Division hospital. By the time he returned to the bridge site, his platoon leader was pretty grumpy about his delayed return until he realized M/Sgt Goudy was wearing a new Purple Heart.

By the next morning, 8 July, the rising stream threatened the abutments of the bridge. So it was back to work while keeping a wary eye out for 'Murphy'. We decided we had better extend the bridge another 30 feet, making a 90 foot span. The bridge materials were on site. We were able to begin work at once. Although mortar fire was still a major problem and caused us more casualties, we were able to reassemble a launching nose on the far shore. With this in place we assembled additional sections on the near shore and completed the extension, delaying vital supply traffic for only two hours. When we finally finished the additional 30 feet, we heaved a huge sigh of collective relief and took stock of our assets. We had suffered 38 casualties in the previous 36 hours. There were 21 awards for valor in this single operation! The men had turned in a magnificent performance. It was my pride and privilege to have commanded this company of valiant engineer soldiers and Korean allies. 'Murphy' had won a few skirmishes, but he lost the war!

M/Sgt James Goudy and Lt Edward Larkin, platoon leader of A Co, worked in collaboration with me in writing this historical record.

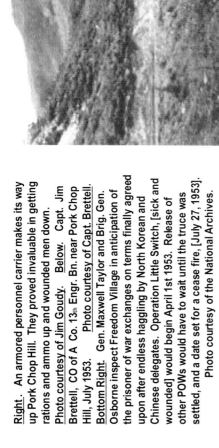

Right. An armored personnel carrier makes its way up Pork Chop Hill. They proved invaluable in getting rations and ammo up and wounded men down. Photo courtesy of Jim Goudy. Below. Capt. Jim Brettell, CO of A Co. 13th Engr. Bn. near Pork Chop Hill, July 1953. Photo courtesy of Capt. Brettell. Bottom Right. Gen. Maxwell Taylor and Brig. Gen. Osborne inspect Freedom Village in anticipation of the prisoner of war exchanges on terms finally agreed upon after endless haggling by North Korean and Chinese delegates. Operation Little Switch, [sick and wounded] would begin April 1st 1953. Release of other POWs would have to wait until the truce was settled, and a date set for a cease fire, [July 27, 1953]. Photo courtesy of the National Archives.

RED DRAGON
The SECOND ROUND
FACES OF WAR II

Robert	C.	Wickman	325-93-22 USN
First Name	MI	Last Name	Serial Number
Wick or Doc	8404	25 March 1931	HM3 to HM2
Nickname	MOS	Birthday	Grade / Rank
Item Co 3d Bn 7th Marines 1st Mar Div		June 1953-June 1954	Keizer, OR
Unit (s)		Duty Tour (s)	Home Town

Combat Action Ribbon   Presidential Unit Citation   Navy Unit Commendation Ribbon   NDSM

Medals & Awards

USN Good Conduct Medal   Korean Campaign Service Medal,1star   ROK PUC   UNSM   KWSM

LAST DAYS OF WAR

I enlisted 28 Sept 1950. I specifically joined the US Navy to "see the world," have a clean bunk, and eat hot chow. It looked as if it would all work out until I took the placement tests at NTC Boot Camp. Because my vision was not the best, (I memorized the eye chart to enlist) I wasn't qualified for Naval Air. My second choice was Hospital Corpsman since I had a desire to pursue a career in medicine. The interviewer, who knew a lot more about the services than I did said, "Are you sure?" I told him I was sure. I went to Hospital Corps School at Navy Hospital, San Diego. A little more than 2 years later, I received orders to the Field Medical Service School at Camp Del Mar in Camp Pendleton, CA. I shipped to Korea aboard the MSTS Meiggs in June of 1953, arriving in Korea about three weeks later. The Medical Corpsmen, a part of the 33d Replacement Draft, were assigned where needed. I went to Item Company 3Bn, 7th Marines. When I joined the 7th Marines as a Corpsman the 1st MarDiv was in Corps reserve. On the 4th of July after a huge Independence Day celebration, we moved to the 'Boulder City' area where the 25th Army Division was waiting to be relieved.

For some unknown reason, I was sent to make a sanitation inspection of an area the army was leaving. During the process, I spied a brand new, latest style flak jacket laying on a bunk in a vacant tent. There was no doubt the jacket needed a more careful owner. I left the worn and tattered flak jacket issued to me on the bunk. I tried the new jacket for fit. It could have been larger, but it covered me in the vital spots. A few steps away from the vacant tent, an Army Lt stopped me and inquired about my "new" flak jacket. I knew I had been had. At this most appropriate moment in an awkward situation, the Chaplain's driver drove up to tell me a Corpsman was needed to go to East Berlin. I had been assigned for that duty. The Army Lt wished me "good luck" as he held my old flak jacket in his left hand and waved goodby with his right. The driver took off for the Item Company CP as soon as I could climb in the jeep.

The first relief patrol took a wrong path ending in a heavily mined saddle between Berlin and East Berlin. A mine detonated. A Lt was killed. Corpsman Jack Stanfield, and several Marines were severely wounded. The wounded were treated and sent to the rear. We went on to East Berlin. An almost constant H&I fire battered us. Days were hot and bodies were bloating. The stench was terrible. In front of our rebuilt 'crab hole' was a mound. It didn't take long to find out what it covered. Shrapnel gouged the mound. The bloated body in the mound was in full decay. The blow flies came. My 'crabhole' was on the forward slope, toward "gooney land." Nature called. I asked Pfc Chas Taylor, a seasoned Marine, "Where do I go to relieve myself?" All he said was, "Stand up, Doc." The trench parapet was only 3 feet high, there wasn't much cover. I had just begun a good stream when I noted puffs of dirt "walking" toward me. I had been zeroed in on by a gook MG. Immediate problem solved. The gooks were experts with mortars. They would "walk" our trench line at their leisure. I lost my hearing for about 8 hours. An area where I was treating a wounded Marine was too close to their "incoming" fire. My ears have rung incessantly ever since. A four"holer" was in an area targeted by their mortars. One Marine had just positioned himself on the "throne." I have never seen anyone run so fast with his pants hanging below his knees. He dove into the trench just as a direct hit on the '4-holer' scattered its contents over a wide area.

Several days before the 'cease fire', fighting intensified. The 'goony' attacks penetrated our trench lines. Our casualties were heavy. At times my hands were so slick with blood I could barely start an IV. Corpsman HM3 George Takagi of George 3/7 carried ammo to the lines and returned wounded to the rear although he had taken a shrapnel hit in the leg. I have since learned from our Company XO that the final battle for 'Boulder City was one of the most severe of the entire war. Lee Brydon, a machine gunner of Weapons 3/7 attached to Item was one of the casualties I treated. We visit every few years. At reunions, I come in contact with several Marines who say I treated their wounds. These are very emotional moments. I returned to the states aboard the MSTS Collins. There were better ships sailing in our Civil War 100 years ago! I lost 17 lbs on the voyage. The ship's menu was heavy on liver stew and the like. The spaghetti, beans and breakfast cereals were all I could eat. In my book, liver is never good at any time, certainly not in stew.

I feel privileged to have survived the last battles of the Korean War, and to have been on the "hill" the night the Cease Fire flares were fired at 2200 hours on 27 July 1953. I am proud to have served my country as a Navy Corpsman with the United States Marine Corps.

Above. The ' tall and the short ' of it is Lt. Mueller and his ROK friend. Taken in June of 1953.   Photo by Lt. Mueller.
Above Right. A G.I. reads the latest Chinese propaganda delivered 'air mail', in the mortar shell he is holding. He may be looking for the crossword puzzle? Photo courtesy of Glenn Ed White.   Below. A wounded G.I. is being delivered to an Army MASH unit for treatment. The value of quick evacuation of wounded had been realized as early as August 1950, when General Stratemeyer requested 25 H-5 helicopters and trained medical personnel to handle front line medical evacuations. Army handled evacuations from the lines to the MASH units. The Air Force then flew them from the MASH units to base hospitals farther to the rear, or to Japan.   Photo courtesy of the National Archives.

RED DRAGON
The SECOND ROUND
FACES OF WAR II

David	S.	Mueller	O-1934840
First Name	MI	Last Name	Serial Number
None	1542	14 Oct 1929	2d Lt
Nickname	MOS	Birthday	Grade / Rank
G/224/40th Div		May '53- Nov '53	Montebello, CA
Unit (s)		Duty Tour (s)	Home Town

Medals & Awards
Combat Infantry Badge   Bronze Star   Korean Campaign Service Medal w/2 stars
Nat'l Defense Service Medal   United Nations Medal   KWSM   Korean 5O Peace Medal

THE CALM AFTER THE STORM

I was drafted in January 1951. After 13 weeks of basic infantry training at Camp Roberts, California, I was selected for OCS at Fort Benning, Georgia, graduating in Sept 1952. I was given several routine assignments with troops over the next few months before receiving alert orders to report to FECOM (Far East Command). In Yokohama the staging center for FECOM assignments, I received orders to report to HQ 40th Infantry Division. In early May 1953, I reported to Div HQ and was assigned to the 224th Infantry Regiment, thence to 'G' Company. The 40th Division was then manning a sector of the MLR on the eastern front. A well known terrain feature in this sector was 'The Punchbowl,' located in the high mountains north of Inje above the 38th parallel. It was a sharp lipped extinct volcanic crater with an almost level area in the bowl. Beginning in June '51, battles for the Punchbowl and the high ridges to the north, 'Bloody Ridge' seized on 5 Sept, and 'Heartbreak Ridge' taken on 13 Oct, became the scenes of the bloodiest, toughest and hardest fought battles of the Korean War. The highest casualty rates of the war occurred in these engagements, notably in the 2d Division, which suffered 3700 casualties on 'Heartbreak' alone in addition to those at Bloody Ridge a month earlier.

UN casualties in this period numbered almost 60,000 men, 22,000 of them American. The 2d Division with the French Bn attached was the major attacking force in these battles. The Turkish Brigade was involved in the June assault on the Punchbowl. Other UN troops in action were the 1st Marine Division with ROK 1st Marine Regt attached and the 5th and 7th ROK Divisions. Enemy opposition in this area was primarily North Korean. Chinese and North Korean casualties June to Nov 1951, in the 'Punchbowl' sector were estimated at 234,000 men. The 4 to 1 casualty ratio in this period, rather than 10 to 1 in the war's first year, showed the enemy's increasing tenacity in holding his positions. The Chinese had developed a rapid learning curve, making them a more formidable foe.

I checked in at G Company, replacing Richard Mayer as platoon leader, 2d platoon. Mayer would move up to XO, as soon as I was deemed qualified. Our fighting trenches were located on the forward slope of our hillside position, sandbagged squad bunkers and platoon CP on the reverse slope. It was my first night in command, as well as my first night on line. I was aware of the bloody history of our sectors so was most vigilant in execution of my duties. Incoming mortar fire impelled me to inspect all squad positions in the event an attack was in the offing. While standing next to a squad sentry, we heard a thud. In the dark we could not tell the source. Next morning a dud 120mm mortar round was spotted, lodged in the dirt about 4 feet from where we had stood. Luck!

A couple of days later I felt stomach cramps and started for the platoon latrine slit trench. We all suffered from diarrhea. Lt Mayer, who I was replacing, jumped to his feet saying, "Gotta go!" An incoming mortar round hit near the latrine, wounding him in both legs. Luck again! The remainder of our time at the Punchbowl was a routine of calm days and hazardous night patrols. Later we were replaced by a ROK unit. We move to a rest area for a few days. We were then sent to the Satae valley to replace a Phillipine unit. Our mission was to protect a bridge over a river which our company positions straddled. Lt Meyer rejoined us there. Nightly, we sent out patrols on both sides of the river. One night, one of our patrols sat all night in their bunker, reporting they had patrolled. The squad was placed under arrest and sent to the rear for courts-martial. Lt. Mayer was assigned escort duty, but arranged with the Company Commander for me to replace him, taking over a patrol I was to have led. Lt Mayer was seriously wounded on that patrol.

Luck, or fate, was again at my side! The rest of the war was fairly quiet. The usual night patrols occupied our time. I had the privilege of leading the last night patrol on the night the "Cease Fire" took effect. When we took up our position, we were told a "Turkey Shoot" would take place. Every gun and mortar we had fired over our heads. It was deafening. When it stopped, there was an eerie silence. It felt odd the next morning to walk in broad daylight back to our lines without the risking death. It was over.

I was lucky to be in Korea in a period of relative quiet. Troop morale was good, the men were confident and capable. We had about a dozen ROK GIs with us for training. They were exceptional soldiers. I owe my well being to luck and to a Lt who took hits perhaps meant for me. I never saw Lt Mayer again, either to commiserate, or thank him for a whole skin with no holes in it. Luck of the draw!

Above. The MLR in July of 1953. The center dark ridge is Whitehorse Mountain [Hill 395], the Chorwon Valley to the right. Upper Right. Our troops fight to take the near ridge line. Some WP can be seen in the middle, with troops in lower middle, the top of an ambulance in seen in the lower left edge of photo. Lower Left. Tankers of the 64th Tank Bn prepare to move into action. These three photos courtesy of Art Elkington. Lower Right. James Pitzer is seen at the entrance of his bunker on the MLR. This was on the Jamestown Line, July 1953. Photo courtesy of James L. Pitzer.

RED DRAGON
The SECOND ROUND
FACES OF WAR II

James	L.	Pitzer	4 305 850 USN
First Name	MI	Last Name	Serial Number
Jim	Field Medical Tech	24 July 1933	HM2
Nickname	MOS	Birthday	Grade / Rank
H-3-7 1st MarDiv		Apr 1953-Jul 1954	Portland, IN
Unit (s)		Duty Tour (s)	Home Town

Purple Heart Medal   Combat Ribbon   Naval Unit Citation   China Service Medal   UN Medal

Medals & Awards
Korean War Campaign Service Medal,1 star   National Defense Service Medal   ROK KWSM

THE BERLIN GATES

I was an 19 year old Field Medical Technician, US Navy trained as a corpsman for assignment as Field Medic to the USMC. My "Adventure in Korea" began in May when I arrived at a reserve area in the 1st Marine Division. I survived that first night in reserve. However, it rained so hard that when I awakened, I found my boots floating inches deep in the water on the squad tent floor. Life had been good! That would soon change. I spent the next few weeks doing my job as a field corpsman (medic) in How Company of the 1st Marine Division manning a MLR (Main Line of Resistance) sector of the Western front. We went into reserve several weeks later. In reserve we received new gear, refurbished old gear and trained replacements in preparation for going back on line.

On 8 July the Division moved to the Jamestown Line near Panmunjom. How Company was placed in a blocking position behind outposts Berlin and East Berlin. The old adage that "Misery Loves Company" surely applied here. We could see the MLR was bright with exploding ordnance. We stayed in that blocking position until the next morning. Before sunup the order was passed to move up to the MLR. As we unloaded from trucks, the gooks welcomed us with the usual random 'incoming' rounds. Before I had a chance to get my bearings, I heard the call, "Corpsman." A marine told me his platoon leader had been hit. "He's in a bunker in one of the trenches leading to the East Berlin gate." After searching for 30 minutes, "dodging" mortar rounds in the process, I located the Lt in a destroyed bunker. He had a leg wound which had clotted so that his leg looked like a big chunk of liver. After securing the wound I helped him stand. Of course he was a typical movie type marine, well over 6 feet tall and 220 lbs. I was 5'9" and weighed in at 180.

He used me like a crutch, in this way we got back to the CP. By then, my company had been placed on the MLR. I did not know where they were, so I started looking for a familiar face. Before I could locate the company, I heard the familiar, "Doc!" I had just entered the trench when a buck sergeant called again, "Hey Doc, come with me!" He was leading a fire team to man one of the "Berlin" gates. I never knew whether it was Berlin or East Berlin gate. Not that it really mattered, my job was medical, not tactical. The 'incoming' was rapid and really accurate. We ran, stooping low, along the trench until we reached the gate. While momentarily stopping to catch our breath, a round hit, wounding both of us. The force blew mud into multiple shrapnel lacerations on the left side of my face, gashed my legs and ruptured my left eardrum. I yelled like a bull, not from pain, but in release from adrenaline buildup and stress. The sergeant had been hit with shrapnel in his right knee. He was down, out of the fight. After treating him, we looked for a place to put him until a stretcher team came. We found somebody's sleeping hole into which he fit nicely. As a matter of fact there was room for two. I joined him and used water from my canteen to wash the mud from my face and, best I could, treat the shrapnel gashes in my face. As the day wore on, the call for "Doc" or "Corpsman" was heard several times. I don't remember how many wounded I treated that day. My saddest memory was finding a good friend, Ed Rigley, fellow corpsman, dead in the trench. Under him was another man from the platoon, a new man in the company. I had not learned his name. Both were killed instantly.

The 'incoming' increased as did calls for a stretcher. Over a 15 minute period my count on 'incoming' varied from 5 to 10 rounds per minute. Calls for "Corpsman" kept pace with the 'incoming.' Fortunately, I was able to move up and down the line without being hit again. The big Lt was doing OK, but the morphine was wearing off. He was going to be in intense pain before long. The big problem I feared was shock, the silent killer of the wounded. Sometime that afternoon, one of the few times I had been able to return to the sleeping hole and take cover, a Marine Officer stuck his head in the hole and asked if someone had called for a stretcher. I was surprised, it was our company commander, Jim Allison. My movie marine went off in good hands to treatment by competent Navy doctors in a rear area clearing hospital. It sticks in my mind as strange, but I never did know the names of any of the men in the fire team or of the sergeant whom I accompanied on that dash to the gate. I'm sure the same goes for them. While names are important, the comradeship of the Corps meant that we could depend on each other. That is all that counts. It is the true spirit of the Corps.

I was relieved by a fellow Corpsman 48 hours later. I will always remember the date. It was the last time I ever heard clearly in my left ear. Really, I was lucky. Sulfa powder in my kit, surgical cleansing by a doctor and suturing enabled quick healing.

Above. Reinforcing and repairing trenches and bunkers on Pork Chop Hill is hot work for these GIs from Able Company, 13th Combat Engineers. **Right.** Destroyed by Chinese artillery fire, these fortifications are being rebuilt. **Lower Right.** The deeper the better. All photos courtesy of Jim Goudy. **Below.** This badly wounded GI is being checked over by the first medic on the scene. Photo courtesy of the Internet.

RED DRAGON
The SECOND ROUND
FACES OF WAR II

Dan	D.	Schoonover	Unknown
First Name	MI	Last Name	Serial Number
Danny	Demolitions Engineer	8 Oct 1933	Cpl
Nickname	MOS	Birthday	Grade / Rank
Company A 13th Engineer Combat Bn		March '53- 10 July '53	Boise, ID
Unit (s)		Duty Tour (s)	Home Town

Congressional Medal of Honor — Korean Campaign Service Medal, 1 star

Medals & Awards

National Defense Service Medal — United Nations Service Medal

COMPANY COMMANDER RECOMMENDS AWARD OF MEDAL OF HONOR

He came to A Company, 13th Engineer Bn(C), not quite 20 years of age, transferred at his request from another company in our Bn to be near his brother Pat, a member of A Co.. He asked to be in the same platoon, but as his company commander, I considered it too dangerous o their family line to have them both exposed at the same time to the same risks. Dan Schoonover was a blonde haired, fresh faced young man, a poster picture of the good soldier. He was an intelligent, curious and willing student of the duties and responsibilities of the engineer squad leader in a counterattack. We practiced preparations for that role over and over on a regular basis. He was well liked by the men in his squad. When he appointed squad leader and promoted to Corporal his men were very pleased. He was the kind of soldier every company commander hopes for. When the officers, then the NCOs in the infantry rifle company to which his squad was attached were killed or wounded, he took over command of the remaining infantrymen, exercising the kind of leadership a few American soldiers always seem to have reserved somewhere in the psyche of their personality.

Fighting became heavy in early July as negotiators at Panmunjom wangled their way toward a truce after 2 years of acrimonious discussion. It was particularly heavy in our sector near Pork Chop Hill, so named by GIs because it resembled a pork chop. Its Korean was Sokkogae. From numerous statements we collected after the action in which he gave his life for his country, he moved without fear from position to position firing his weapon, tossing grenades and directing others until a mortar round landed close enough to kill him. The number and consistency of those statements prompted me to write the recommendation for the Medal of Honor and the accompanying citation that appears in General Order No 5 of 14 January 1955. At daily roll call after the battle ended, and in his honor, for 5 successive days we called Schoonover's name. His brother, Pat, was very distraught. We watched him closely, concerned he might launch a one man war to kill all the Chinese in Korea. His remains were recovered later for burial in the Military Cemetery in Hawaii. The citizens of Idaho have erected a memorial in his memory in Boise. A 500 man barracks at Ft Belvoir is named in his honor. Two of his fellow soldiers built a brick monument there to display a bronze plaque in his memory. It was my privilege to serve with this outstanding American soldier.   Capt James A. Brettell USA, Cmdg, Company A 13 Engineers© 1953.

DEPARTMENT OF THE ARMY GENERAL ORDER NUMBER 5 14 JANUARY 1955

CITATION: Corporal Dan D. Schoonover, United States Army, a member of Company A 13th Engineer combat Battalion, 7th Infantry Division, distinguished himself by conspicuous gallantry and outstanding courage above and beyond the call of duty in action against the enemy near Sokkagae, Korea from 8 to 10 July 1953. He was in charge of an engineer demolition squad attached to an infantry company which was committed to dislodge the enemy from a vital hill. Realizing that the heavy fighting and intense enemy fire made it impossible to carry out his mission, he voluntarily employed his unit as a rifle squad and, forging up the steep barren slope, participated in the assault on the hostile positions. When an artillery round exploded on the roof of an enemy bunker, he courageously ran forward and leaped into the position, killing one hostile infantryman and taking another prisoner. Later in the action, when friendly forces were pinned down by vicious fire from another enemy bunker, he dashed through the hail of fire hurled grenades into the nearest aperture, then ran to the doorway and emptied his pistol, killing the remainder of the enemy. His brave action neutralized the position and enabled friendly troops to continue their advance to the crest of the hill. When the enemy counterattacked he constantly exposed himself to heavy bombardment to direct the fire of his men and to call in an effective artillery barrage on hostile forces. Although the company was relieved early the following morning, he voluntarily remained in the area, manned a machine gun for several hours, and subsequently joined another assault on enemy emplacements. When last seen he was operating an automatic rifle with devastating effect until mortally wounded by artillery fire. Corporal Schoonover's heroic leadership during the two days of heavy fighting, his superb personal bravery, and willing self sacrifice inspired his comrades and saved many lives, reflecting lasting glory on himself and upholding the honored traditions of the military service.

Photos from upper left. Cleaning a 155 howitzer after a firing mission. - A 155 in full recoil. - G.I. relaxing on top of 'old smokey'. Bottom. A fire mission in the Kumhwa Valley. W. P. is the 'special of the day,' A Battery is dishing it out. At left, Jim has autographed a 155 round to 'Joe Chink.' A Btry of the 75th F.A. Bn. - All photos courtesy of Jim Vitali.

RED DRAGON
The SECOND ROUND
FACES OF WAR II

James	H.	Vitali	US 55 255 633
First Name	MI	Last Name	Serial Number
Jim	1844	27 Sept 1931	Corporal
Nickname	MOS	Birthday	Grade / Rank
75th FA Bn-(155mm howitzer)	Dec 1952-Jan 1954	Cuba, MO
Unit	Duty Tour (s)	Home Town

Good Conduct Medal   Korean Campaign Service Medal, 2 stars   United Nations Medal

Medals & Awards
National Defense Service Medal   Korean Presidential Unit Citation   Korean War Svc Medal

KUMSONG SALIENT

Like so many Americans of my age group, I was drafted as my lottery number came up. My local draft board had me reporting to the induction station shortly after my 19th birthday. I found myself in the good company of many other young Americans of similar circumstance. Following the Chinese intervention in the Korean War the casualty lists had out paced the volunteer rate for both the Army and the Marine Corps. I heard that the ratio of draftees to volunteers was now better than 20 to 1. I have no idea if these were true figures, but I do know that when I reached Korea and was assigned to my unit, most new men in my FA Bn had serial numbers beginning with US 5. Our NCOs were somewhat older men, many of them Regular Army, with experience in firing an artillery piece.

The troop ship USS General W. A. Mann took me to Japan. In mid December my replacement group boarded the USNS Ballou which carried us to Pusan, near the tip of Korea. Next we loaded onto flat bed trucks which shuttled us to a rail siding. We climbed aboard ancient wooden cars pulled by an equally ancient coal burning engine. With every chuff-chuff, soot spewed over the cars. Soot, dust and dirt came into the cars through the shot up windows. If glass had ever been in those windows, it was long gone. The seats were made of the hardest wood I ever sat on. To add to the misery, we loaded at 1:30 AM in a temperature of 19 degrees below zero. Huddling together for warmth on those hard seats and dirty floors didn't seem to make much difference. Our train crossed the 38th parallel into North Korea. After unloading we processed for assignment to our units. My outfit was to be the 75th FA Bn, firing 155mm howitzers. The Bn was located in the Kumwha valley sector of the Iron Triangle. Over the next 6 months I became quite proficient in my battery duties. This stood me and the battery in good stead when the Chinese launched their last, and greatest attack, of the war on the 'Kumsong Salient.' I was able to do my part in stemming the attack, preventing it from becoming a UN rout.

The Iron Triangle was a name given to an area of a figurative triangle having as its base Chorwon on the west, Kumwha on the east, and Pyonggang at the apex. Kumsong was located on a road and rail network 20 miles northeast of Kumwha and 30 miles east of Pyonggang. It was a dagger poised at the solar plexus of North Korea were the UN ever to decide to renew the offensive. Possession of Kumsong allowed an east-to-west flanking attack on Pyonggang, which, if launched with an attack north from Kumhwa, could drive west toward the North Korean capital of Pyongyang. It was one of the two only all weather roads bisecting North Korea across the peninsula. The Chinese agreed to an armistice but before signing the pact, they decided to first eliminate the Kumsong salient. The Chinese launched their attack on the salient 13 July. It was the costliest battle in terms of UN and US Army casualties of the entire war. A raging battle was fought over the next 13 days until the guns on both sides were silenced by the "armistice" on 27 July 1953.

The MLR in this eastern sector was manned by 3 divisions of the ROK Army backed by numerous American artillery units. When the Chinese struck, the 3 ROK divisions dissolved in panic, leaving supporting artillery units of all 3 Army Corps I, IX and X Corps unprotected. Salvation lay in continuing to fire their guns behind defensive perimeters manned by men from their own gun batteries. They were eventually relieved by hard fighting American infantry after the second day of the attack. Had it not been for the valor of these beleaguered American artillerymen, the 6 Chinese divisions in the attack would undoubtedly have made a greater advance than the 5 mile penetration they did achieve. However, they were successful in their primary objective. The Kumsong Salient was retaken. Unofficial casualty figures for 13-25 July are 14,000 UN killed, wounded and missing, and 35,000 Chinese dead. It was a bloody time.

During those 13 days from 13 July to 25 July we fired day and night, the first 2 days firing shells stockpiled at our guns. Once our rear was again in friendly hands, ammo was trucked to us through Chinese artillery fire. As a matter of record, American artillery fired more rounds in this battle than were fired during the 1944 Battle of the Bulge. At night with exploding bombs, shells and flares lighting the sky, it was a glimpse into the yawning gates of hell as they might appear to a sinner. Before the attack on Papasan hill, a preliminary Chinese barrage showered half a dozen rounds very close to our guns. One man was scared so stiff he couldn't stir. He said later he tried hard to move but his feet just would not obey! I know when I heard the scream of a shell sounding like it was coming right at me, I jumped the gun trails and slid in the dirt. We all hit the dirt, shoveling with our noses as those rounds came in!

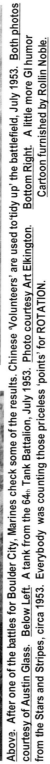

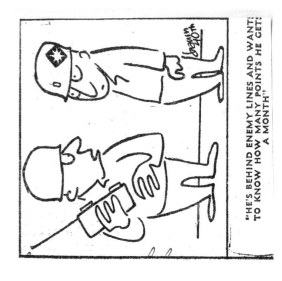

"HE'S BEHIND ENEMY LINES AND WANT! TO KNOW HOW MANY POINTS HE GET! A MONTH"

Above. After one of the battles for Boulder City, Marines check some of the results. Chinese 'Volunteers' are used to 'tidy up' the battlefield, July 1953. Both photos courtesy of Austin Glass. Below Left. A tank from the 64h Tank Battalion, July 1953. Photo courtesy Art Elkington. Bottom Right. A little more GI humor from the Stars and Stripes, circa 1953. Everybody was counting those priceless 'points' for ROTATION. Cartoon furnished by Rollin Noble.

Austin	H.	Glass	420-02-30 USN
First Name	MI	Last Name	Serial Number
Doc	8404	18 Sept 1930	HM 2
Nickname	MOS	Birthday	Grade / Rank
I/3/1/1st MarDiv		May 1952-August 1953	Hammond, LA
Unit (s)		Duty Tour (s)	Home Town

Bronze Star Medal with V   Navy Good Conduct Medal   Korean Campaign Service Medal, 3 stars

Medals & Awards

National Defense Service Medal   United Nations Service Medal   Korean War Service Medal

LAST BATTLE OF THE WAR

On 23 July 1953 I had been in Korea for over 13 months, when as a Navy Corpsman attached to the 1st Marine Division, I was ordered to that area of the Berlin Complex known as 'Boulder City' located above the 38th parallel in Chinese territory. In our approach to 'Boulder City' we were subjected to very intense mortar fire. Several casualties were treated and sent to the rear before we reached our objective. The approach route was, if I remember correctly, called 76 Alley, possibly named after the high velocity, 76mm flat trajectory "whiz- bang" gun, so deadly effective in line-of-sight fire. Akers, the other Corpsman in our relief group, was wounded at 76 Alley and sent back to the Battalion Aid Station. This left me as the only Corpsman to attend the wounded of Item Company. In that approach march to Boulder City and the next night of 24 July, it was estimated we took 27000 rounds of mortar and artillery fire. Chinese were everywhere, in our trenches, tunneling into holes in the sides of trenches, hiding, ready to pop out when their bugles sounded the attack. We had 46 killed and 316 wounded in that short 40 hour period There were about 60 of us left the next day.

During the night of the 24th, the Chinese and North Koreans came at us in swarms. The reason we survived was probably because we were better equipped and wore flak jackets which they did not have. Most of them did not have helmets. On the morning of the 25th plans were being made to fight our way out of an untenable situation. Our CO, Capt Louis Sartor, had been hit in the face by flying debris but had refused evacuation. Our only other officer was Lt Peeler or Pevey, I'm not sure of the name, but he certainly was one fighting son-of-a-gun. Armored Personnel Carriers accompanying a Bn of Marines arrived. Fighting was still very intense. The relieving Bn CO told us to go, they would take over. The Armored Personnel Carriers loaded us aboard. We were taken somewhere rearward, stripped of clothing which was burned, given showers, and issued new battle fatigues. We rested all night the 25th, received fresh stateside Marine replacements, and on the 26th went back to the lines, Hill 111 or Hill 119, I'm not sure which.

On the 26th until the Cease Fire took effect at 10PM on the 27th, we sustained more casualties. We knew the Demilitarized Zone would be established after the truce. We tried to use up all the ammo so it would not have to be hauled back. It was apparent the enemy had the same idea. My most vivid war memory is the morning of 28 July. We were still in our holes and trenches, not really believing the war was over. I heard someone call my name from the bottom of the hill. It was my best friend, Alfred C. Covino, who had been sent back to Bn Aid days before. We ran and hugged each other like long lost brothers. Covino who could always be counted on for food, produced two bottles of root beer. We used my entrenching tool to bury the root beer to cool it best we could. We cried, laughed, enjoyed our friendship and drank our root beer. He swears he doesn't remember where he got them. Possibly they were the only two bottles in Korea, and the very best I ever tasted. Al lives in Martha's Vinyard, MA. We visit each other almost yearly and drink a couple of bottles of root beer together. Somehow it never tastes as good as those two bottles we shared in Korea.

CITATION: UNITED STATES MARINE CORPS, HQ 1ST MARINE DIVISION. IN THE NAME OF THE PRESIDENT OF THE UNITED STATES THE COMMANDING GENERAL OF THE 1ST MARINE DIVISION (REINF) FMF TAKES PLEASURE IN AWARDING THE BRONZE STAR MEDAL TO HOSPITAL CORPSMAN AUSTIN H. GLASS, HOSPITAL CORPSMAN THIRD CLASS USN, FOR SERVICE AS SET FORTH

For heroic achievement in connection with operations against the enemy while serving with a Marine infantry company in Korea on 24 July 1953. Serving as a corpsman, Hospital Corpsman Third Class Glass displayed exceptional courage Initiative and professional skill in the performance of his duties. During the approach phase when the company was moving toward the main line of resistance to reinforce another company, they were suddenly subjected to an intense barrage which inflicted many casualties. Expressing complete disregard for his personal safety, he proceeded from man to man administering to their wounds and giving words of comfort. Upon arrival at the main line of resistance he discovered that the company already occupying the position had insufficient corpsmen to attend to the many wounded. He then covered the entire company front giving aid and helping to evacuate the wounded. During this period the supply of medical dressings became exhausted but he unhesitatingly improvised bandages and tourniquets from empty bandoleers. When surrounded by hostile forces, he fearlessly engaged in hand to hand combat in order to get wounded marines to the aid station. His exceptional skill and steadfast devotion to duty were directly responsible for saving many lives. Hospital Corpsman Third Class Glass' attention to duty and conduct throughout served as an inspiration to all who observed him and was in keeping with the highest traditions of the United States Naval Service. Hospital Corpsman Third Class Glass is authorized to wear the Combat Distinguishing Device R. McC. Pate, Major General, U.S. Marine Corps Commanding.

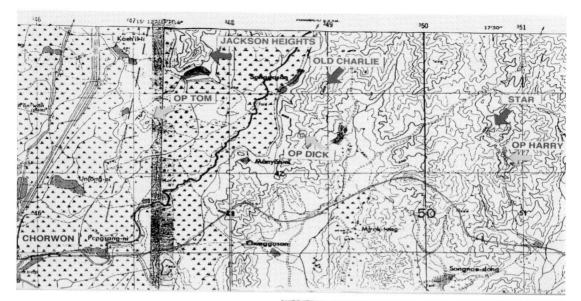

Above. Many fierce battles in the final days of the war of were fought in the Iron Triangle area. Shown in the upper left is Jackson Heights and Outpost Tom, while at the right is infamous Outpost Harry. Right. In the trenches of an outpost is Don Chase [left] and a buddy. Below.. Some troops of I Co, 15th Regt. of the 3rd Division are in one of the trenches. Sgt .Don Chase is on the right, July 1953. Map from the Internet.

Photos courtesy of Donald Chase.

RED DRAGON
The SECOND ROUND
FACES OF WAR II

Donald	A.	Chase	RA 31 467 752
First Name	MI	Last Name	Serial Number
Don	3745	11 January 1926	S/Sgt
Nickname	MOS	Birthday	Grade / Rank
I Company 15th Infantry 3d Div		November 1952-July 1953	Natick, MA
Unit (s)		Duty Tour (s)	Home Town
Combat Inf Badge w/star Bronze Star w/V, OLC Purple Heart, 2OLC GCM,2knots NDSM			
Medals & Awards			
EAME,2stars WW II VM ACSM KCMS,5stars UN Medal ROK PUC Korean War Service Medal			

PURPLE HEART THREE

We returned to the line in mid May, still in the Iron Triangle, but a different sector. 'Happy' Valley lay to our front, a broad expanse of paddy fields east and west of us. Pyongyang lay at the north apex of the triangle, the railroad ran north from there. Stalemated peace talks after two years of vicious fighting left both sides about where they were when the talks began. The main differences between the lines of two years ago were well fortified positions, bolstered with fortified bunkers and trenches, protected by barbed wire and dug in tanks with only their long 90mm barrels exposed. If a soldier was moving in a trench when a tank gun was fired, the blast would rattle his eyeballs. Two to three hundred yards in front of the trenches were outposts Dick and Harry. Dick, located on a ridge pointing at enemy positions, was the responsibility of my company. Two enemy hills, 'Star' and 'Old Charlie' dominated the valley. To protect us from enemy fire, we dug connecting trenches to the two outposts. The enemy was very aggressive in this area.

There were constant night patrols, both reconn and ambush, resulting in perpetual frayed nerves. A 100 percent alert status at the outpost was maintained every night. No one slept at night on outpost duty! Duty on 'Dick' was rotated among the platoons. To get to 'Dick' it was necessary to make a long difficult climb through a connecting trench. After a rain, the trench was a mud swamp. Each boot seemingly weighed 50 pounds. A soldier arrived at the top exhausted by the climb. One dry day while making the climb I chanced on a head and a hand severed at the wrist, the only remnants of some unlucky soldier. Which side? Only God knew.. Another time we stumbled on a body. At night the identity of a body could be determined only by its feet. Sneakers or combat boots?

Combat boots. One of ours, it must be brought in. I looped a piece of commo wire around one foot, backed off a short distance and yanked on the wire. No explosion, no booby trap. Daylight identified the body of a Greek soldier whose Bn at one time manned OP Dick. The body was a rippling mass as maggots wriggled beneath the skin of the corpse. No matter how many times I washed my hands later that day, I could not erase my feeling of the revulsion I experienced bringing the corpse back for burial by his comrades.

My promotion to Sgt 1st Class, the pay rating for platoon sergeant, came through several weeks before we were pulled off line. In reserve we trained in preparation for a for a raid. Lt Nester in one L5 light observation plane, I in another, flew over enemy positions. The pilots knew their business, returning us all safely in spite of a lot of small arms fire aimed at us. We returned to learn the raid had been aborted. A South Korean division had been badly mauled. The Third Division was ordered to replace them line. This new sector was in extremely rugged terrain which necessitated a long hard climb to take up positions. It was a backbreaking job for the Korean Chioggis to lug C-rations and water to us. Nevertheless, on July 4th they brought us 6 5 gallon cans of hot coffee, a real treat.

I took one 5 gallon can of coffee and crawled from foxhole to foxhole, filling each mans canteen cup. As was the custom, the other plat sgts had done the same thing. Our coffee distribution, finished we took shelter in a shallow depression to have a cup for ourselves. Suddenly, a red, yellow and an orange blast of light was instantaneously followed by an explosion which killed one sgt outright and severely wounded the other three of us. The side of my head had been ripped open. I also took two hunks of shrapnel in each leg, high up near the groin. As with previous wounds, I did not lose consciousness. Lt Nester was one of the men who helped carry me down the mountainside to a litter jeep for the short trip to the aid station where a helicopter flew me to a rear area surgical hospital. I was then put on a hospital train heading south. En route a medical officer checked each man, assigning him to a hospital.

I asked for the Swedish Hospital saying I had been there two years before and would like to see if anyone I knew was still there. My request was granted. I spent the next eight weeks there, renewing acquaintance with the shy Korean girl who had befriended my first time there. It was a pleasant reunion, but I had a hard time explaining why I had come back to Korea. I was released from the hospital in late September for return to my company. There I awaited orders for San Francisco where I processed for my Army discharge.

Troops of C Co. 19th Regt. 24th Div. re-enter Taejon on September 28, 1950. Lt. Funchess is on the right, carrying a flag.

Lt. Funchess on phone, in a defensive position on the Kum River Line. North of Taejon. July 15,1950

Above. Captured in his summer uniform, Lt. Funchess is shown above in his new Chinese uniform, <u>one year later.</u> He is second from right in this photo. **Photos courtesy of <u>Lt. Funchess.</u>**
Below Wounded or sick American POWs are air-lifted from Freedom Village directly to a hospital. **Photo courtesy**

Lt. Funchess is greeted by his wife, Sybil at the Columbia, S.C. airport on his return to the U.S.

RED DRAGON
The SECOND ROUND
FACES OF WAR II

William	H.	Funchess	O-956203
First Name	MI	Last Name	Serial Number
"Bill"	1542	8 Nov 1927	1st Lt.
Nickname	MOS	Birthday	Grade / Rank
C/19/24		5 Jul '50-7 Sep '53	Clemson, SC
Unit (s)		Duty Tour (s)	Home Town
POW Medal	Purple Heart	Good Conduct Medal	Combat Infantry Badge	Occupation-J

Medals & Awards

National Defense Service Medal   UN Service Medal   Campaign Service Medal w/2stars

AMERICAN WAR CRIMINAL

I graduated as a 2d Lt from Clemson College, SC 1n 1948. After a year at Fort Jackson, SC, I was assigned occupation duty with the 19th Inf Regt, 24th Div at Beppu, Japan. On outbreak of the Korean War, our two under strength 19th Inf Bns were sent to Pusan, South Korea, arriving 5 July 1950. We were lightly armed with ancient 2.34 bazookas, ineffective against Russian T-34 tanks and heavily armed North Koreans. Our few 76 mm gun light tanks were equally useless against thick T-34 armor. For the next 2 months we hopscotched over South Korea, trading our dead and wounded for space and time. American troops arriving over the next 2 months enabled the Pusan Perimeter to hold. The 15 Sept perimeter breakout and pursuit of retreating North Korean troops back into North Korea ended the war's first phase. The loss of young American soldiers, the cost in dead and wounded had been frightful.

In our northward pursuit of the fleeing North Koreans we passed through Anok, a city north of Pyongyang, North Korea. A North Korean civilian robed in white met us. "Russian Advisors left Anok a half hour ago. We non-Communist North Koreans have liberated the city." At a halt, Capt Louis Rockwerk, my company commander, sent for me. We met in the town square. A large grave had been opened, bodies were being removed. Other men, also white robed, hands tied behind their backs, were huddled in a group. Armed white robed men suddenly opened fire. All bound men were killed, their bodies rolled into the emptied grave. Other men, not white clad, began throwing dirt on the corpses. I had been summoned to witness a grave opening. Instead I was witness to murder! On 2 Nov at Anju, NK, we set up a road block to allow a South Korean division to pass. Before daylight on 4 Nov I sent Sgt Hartwell Champagne on patrol to our west. He returned in a rush to report massive movement of Chinese troops crossing the river a half mile away. The last remnants of the South Koreans had passed. We were alone. I radioed Bn to say that Chinese were in attack. "No, Lt, those are South Koreans!" In less than 5 minutes firing broke out near BN HQ. Chinese swarmed my 50 man platoon. We opened a heavy fire but were soon overwhelmed. Wounded by a bullet in my foot, and out of ammo, I took flight with several of my men, also wounded. We were soon bagged, hands tied behind our backs with telephone wire. A small fur hatted Chinese said in perfect English, "We are not mad at you, only at Wall Street!" I asked if he was Chinese. "No, I'm Korean!" Liar. His equipment was Chinese!

Wounded GI's were prodded with bayonets to make them rise. If they could not, they were shot in back of the head. For 3 weeks we hobbled, tottered, staggered and stumbled northward. For those unable to keep up the grueling pace set by the guards, a bullet in the head was the recipe of the day. Men tried to help me, but were restrained by guards. Finally, after two weeks, exhausted, starved and hobbling on one leg, using a tree limb crutch, I told the men to leave me. I expected a bullet in the head, but apparently, since I was still trying to keep up, although slipping and falling every 100 yards or so, a guard was assigned to me so I could tag along.

In camp 5 at Pyoktong in winter 1950/51, I estimate between 1000 and 1600 men died of wounds, cold, starvation and lack of medical care. On one winter visit to the EM compound I saw three rows of frozen dead bodies 30 feet long, stacked 4 feet high. No matter our sad clothing condition or sub-zero freezing weather, we were given a daily outdoor brainwash of political indoctrination. Gen Deng, Camp Commander, was lecturing. He showed a 3 foot high photo which I immediately recognized as the Anak grave site. Deng ranted and raved about 'American atrocities' at Anak. He kept on. I could stand it no longer. I jumped to my feet, "It's a damned lie!" "How do you know?" the startled interpreter demanded. "I was there! Those North Koreans were murdered by North Koreans!"

The instant the words left my mouth I knew I had made a big mistake. I was grabbed, led to an isolated hut, stripped to my shorts and ordered, "Stand at Attention." Shortly I heard vehicles and caught glimpses of high ranking Chinese and North Korean officers. I expected to be shot. Instead I was taken back to camp and ordered, "Keep Silence." My mail was stopped. I spent 30 days in isolation. In July of '53 the Chinese told us, "War is over." A 60 day POW exchange ended 5 Sept. On 6 Sept I asked why I was not released. "You are a war criminal, remember Ana!" The next day I was put on a narrow trail, kicked in the butt, "Stay on the trail and go south." An American Major who met me said, "You are one lucky man. Yesterday both sides agreed to release war criminals!"

409

Above. American POWs are seen in this photo from a Russian news agency. They seem to have already received the benefits of Chinese 'hospitality.' Right. These just freed American POWs have shown their defiance by throwing away their Chinese prison garb. Sgt. Jones is on the right. Below. Wounded POWs are being exchanged. Commies in the left photo and GIs in photo on the right.

Photos courtesy of Internet and Sgt. Jones.

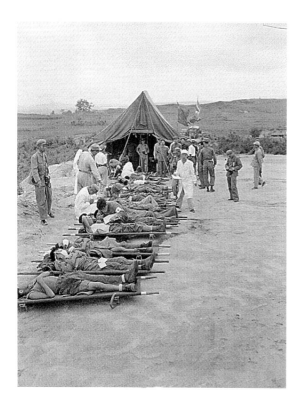

RED DRAGON
The SECOND ROUND
FACES OF WAR II

Nyle	T.	Jones	RA 19334833
First Name	MI	Last Name	Serial Number
None	745	25 March 1931	Sgt
Nickname	MOS	Birthday	Grade / Rank
Btry D 15th AAABn SP/31st Inf/7thDiv		Sept 1950-Aug 1953	Twin Falls, ID
Unit (s)		Duty Tour (s)	Home Town

Purple Heart Medal   Combat Infantry Badge   Prisoner of War Medal   Good Conduct Medal

Medals & Awards

Korean Campaign Service Medal 3stars   National Defense Service Medal   UN Medal   ROK PUC

PRISONER OF WAR

I was a child of the depression. Born in Idaho, my parents moved to California in an effort to better their life. I had escaped unharmed from a car I had been thrown into after being grabbed by a child molester and his Mexican accomplice. My mother said that was too close. We moved back to Idaho where such incidents were then almost unheard of. I had to quit school to help my Dad who had resumed farming as the depression drew to an end. After several years of this, I decided if I wanted to make something of my life, I had to leave the farm. My best bet was to join the Army, complete my education, grow into maturity and learn some skills which would better fit me for employment. I enlisted at age 17 and was sent to Japan where I served in the Army of Japanese Occupation.

After almost 2 years in the Occupation Army my unit, 15th AAA SP, part of the 7th Inf Div, landed at Inchon in mid September. Battery D was attached to the 31st Inf Regt. When the Chinese intervened we had just relieved the 5th Marines on the east side of the Chosin Reservoir in North Korea. The night of 27 Nov, the Chinese hit our 2Bn Task Force McLean with a two division sledge hammer. On Nov 30, I was wounded in thigh and left knee. Two buddies, Jim Mathis and Bill Dunford put me in a truck with other wounded men. I was captured 2 December by the Chinese along with another hundred or so "walking wounded." "Hobbling wounded" might be a better description of the column of wounded GIs force marched to a place we called "Death Valley." We stayed there 54 days. Deaths from wounds, dysentery and gangrene occurred daily. One of the wounded, Tully Cox had frozen feet which turned gangrenous. A North Korean guard loaned us a small saw. With that and a small knife, we did what we had to do. We took off our T-shirts and bound the stubs of his legs as best we could. I made a mental vow I would leave this place alive. One day, in mid January the Chinese told us that anybody who could walk would be sent to a POW camp. My own boots had been "liberated" by a Chinese guard when I was captured. One of our dead provided me with a much too large pair of boots, but better than walking in rag clad feet. We walked 10 days, no rest and little food or water to reach Kanggie, North Korea. It was called POW Camp No. 5.

At Kanggie, I refused an order to sign a letter denouncing our government. Another guy also refused. In early February the Chinese took the two of us in an oxcart to a North Korean Army camp 10 miles away and put with a lot of other GI "incorrigibles" already there. The North Koreans were a much worse than the Chinese. They systematically starved us. On the 1st of March, a Chinese officer came to the camp and told us we would be marched south to be released. Men fell out from wounds and hunger. We had to keep going, we were not allowed to help. We would hear a shot from the rear and know that another GI had been murdered. We moved mostly at night. The Chinese were afraid of American fighter aircraft that strafed and bombed them in daylight. First we marched south, then turned and went north again. By this time we had lost all hope. The Chinese had lied to us. Finally, about the 1st of May, we reached POW Camp No. 1 at Changsong, North Korea near the Yalu River. To my surprise, Tully Cox greeted us when we arrived!

There were 6 of us from Btry D at Camp No.1; Sgts Frank J. Celusniak and Banford, PFCs Calvin Hansen, Frederick Higgins, Tom Duncan and myself. Banford and Higgins both died while prisoners. When prisoners fell sick they were taken to the "Death House." Few returned. I fell ill. When the Chinese guards came to take me away, the guys in my room told the guards they would take care of me. The guards relented. I was deathly sick. That night in a dream my Grandfather, told me, "Don't worry son, everything will be alright." The next day I asked friends on work detail to pick dandelion leaves. That night, I boiled them in a tin can, drank the broth, ate the leaves. I got over my sickness. We all lived one day at a time. Each day we told each other think positive, there would be a tomorrow. I cannot describe the hunger, pain and torment we endured. Words are inadequate. With God's help I made it. After more than 32 months we were released, 14 August 1953. We rode in Chinese trucks to the American lines. As we neared we could see Americans waiting for us. We stripped off our Chinese issued uniforms and threw them over the side. We returned to freedom in our underwear. It was the last gesture of defiance we could display to our captors. My God, how glad we were to be free!

Memories of friends killed in battle, those who died of wounds and starvation have been with me every day since we were freed. I can never forget them. As for me, I am just a lucky survivor who made it home. No hero, just an average GI who had God's blessing.

411

Above. **American POWs arriving at Freedom Village for Operation
Big Switch.** Photo from National Archives. _Left._ Water points # 4 and 5,
established by the 428th Engr. Water Supply Co. of the 44th Engr. Group,
February of 1954. _Below._ Col. Paul Carroll is shown receiving a medal.
Photos courtesy of Col. Paul Carroll.

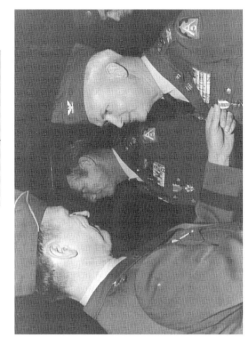

RED DRAGON
The SECOND ROUND
FACES OF WAR II

Paul	F.		Carroll	O 960 509
First Name	MI		Last Name	Serial Number
None	4110, Eng Staff O		July 1920	Col USA Ret, then 1st Lt
Nickname	MOS		Birthday	Grade / Rank
428 Eng Water Supply Co,378th Eng Util Det			Dec '52-Apr '54	Brockton, MA
Unit (s)			Duty Tour (s)	Home Town

Legion of Merit   Army Commendation Medal,3 OLC   Meritorious Service Medal   UN Medal

Medals & Awards

Korean Campaign Service Medal,1 star   NDSM, OLC   Vietnam Service Medal, 1 star   KWSM

THE HONEY BUCKET MAFIA

Shortly after the war ended 27 July 1953, our utility detachment received a call from a medical officer of First Logistical Command about a recent outbreak of hepatitis. The cause was traced to a popular Pusan night club, the 'Metropolitan.' The hepatitis carrier was the water used in drinks served to military personnel. My CO told me to contact the club manager and make arrangements to deliver potable water and ice. My Ops Sgt was acquainted with the club location. We set out, winding our way through numerous back alleys. The driver stayed to guard the vehicle, lest we return to find it stolen or stripped. We climbed the stairs and entered a dimly lit hall. We were immediately greeted by several attractive Korean girls in evening dress. They chorused, in unison, "You buy me drinkee?" "No, thanks, we'd like to speak to the manager." The manager was quite agitated. I'm sure he thought we were there to place his establishment off limits. After assuring him we were not there to blacklist his club, he eased in his manner, but kept a guarded attitude. We told him we wanted to make a daily 'presento' of treated water and ice. His demeanor changed. A tablecloth and several bottles of whiskey appeared. The number of nubile young women doubled. The manager said he would always use nothing but the water and ice we would provide. He added we would be his honored guests any time we cared to visit his club.

After reporting back to my CO I suggested we have a similar club on a smaller scale in our compound. As we already had an enlisted mans club, I was appointed president of a board of governors to hire a bartender and acquire a stock of beverages. To pay the salary of a bartender and other related club costs, I doubled prices. A fifth of Canadian Club was raised from $1 to $2, mixed drinks from 10 cents to 20 cents. Other liquor prices were raised accordingly and new prices posted: Seagram's VO, $2; IW Harper, $3.10; Napoleon Cognac, $2.75; Cresta Blanca Champagne, $2.25; Cresta Blanca Dry Vermouth, $1.00; Gordon's Gin, $1.50; Black&White Scotch, $2.75; Carioca Rum, $1.50; Benedictine D.O.M. $3.00; Santiago Portuguese Wine, $1.30, Balalaika Vodka, $1.75; Old Grandad, $3.00. To insure that water and ice deliveries proceeded smoothly at the Metropolitan Club, I volunteered to make monthly inspections. I was always greeted with open arms by the manager and employees. As the old saying has it, "It's hard to beat American know-how." The club carried on for years until all such recreational facilities were consolidated in the "Seoul Hilton."

Central sewage systems were unknown in Pusan. Sewage was handled by Korean contractors who serviced military compounds with "Honey Bucket" trucks, carts, or with two buckets, one hung at each end of a yo-yo stick balanced on a man's shoulder. It all depended on the size of the installation. Our contractor was called "Smiling Sam Construction Company." Shortly after "Smiling Sam" began operation, his company was 'acquired' by a competitor who called himself "Cheerful Charlie Construction Company." We never knew if the take over was legitimate or whether "Smiling Sam" had received an offer he couldn't refuse. Due to the daily urgency of sewage removal, we went along with the change as it became apparent "Cheerful Charley" was unlikely to have competition. "Charlie" appeared weekly to hand us his bill, escorted by his upper echelon. His entourage dressed like something out of "Guys and Dolls," pin stripe suits with broad lapels, grey snap brim Stetson hats and pointed toe shoes complete with spats.

Sewage collection proceeded smoothly until we received a call from the Replacement Depot that population had doubled with arrival of a Turkish contingent. The next day we were told sewage pickup had slowed. Latrines were filling up. The situation obviously was about to hit the fan. I contacted "Cheerful Charlie" who agreed to mobilize all available 'honey wagons' to take care of the emergency. I met "Charlie." He had mobilized his troops. Like Caesar, I led the vanguard to the Replacement Depot. After going a short distance, I realized my relief troops had halted. I turned back, "What's the problem?" "Cheerful Charlie" smiled and in his most friendly manner said in effect, "Due to unexpected expense caused by emergency mobilization, the price per bucket should be doubled." Faced by impending disaster this close to the gates of Rome, I quickly negotiated a raise in pay for Charlie's legions. I'm sure "Charlie" went on to bigger and better things. He probably became Director of the South Korean Environmental Protection Agency.

Later in civilian life while filling out a resume, I was tempted to list under previous experience, "engaged in environmental cleanup and supervised a collection agency. It would have jibed perfectly with the puffery I have reviewed in other resumes since that time.

Right. The 'Atomic' cannon was ready for duty. This 280 mm monster was considered for deployment to Korea several times. Can anyone imagine the ramifications IF it had been used ? Photo and news clippings courtesy of Jarvis Barrett. Below. Hard-core communist POWs make one final 'statement' on their way to repatriation. They burn their made in the U.S.A. clothing.
Photo from the National Archives.

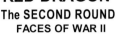

RED DRAGON
The SECOND ROUND
FACES OF WAR II

Jarvis	M.	Barrett	US 55 258 723
First Name	MI	Last Name	Serial Number
None	1151	29 July 1928	Corporal
Nickname	MOS	Birthday	Grade / Rank
868th FA(Atomic) Bn		Sept 1953-June 1954	Aurora, MO
Unit (s)		Duty Tour (s)	Home Town

Occpn Medal, Germany National Defense Service Medal Rated 'Best Mechanic', Bn Motor Pool.
Medals & Awards
Soldier of the Week, 15 consecutive awards. Honor Graduate Ordnance Dept Mechanics School

THE ATOMIC CANNON

Married, I entered military service at the ripe old age of 24, courtesy of my local draft board which was of the opinion travel would broaden my horizons. They were correct in ways I am sure were not suspected. I took my basic training on 105mm howitzers with the 34th Tng Bn, 87th Infantry. I was then shanghaied to Ft Bragg as one of 50 hand picked men selected for 8 weeks of infantry training and an additional 8 weeks of light (105mm) artillery instruction. Later, I was assigned to serve as an ammunition loader on the new atomic cannon slated for NATO service. My first look at that huge 11 inch (280mm) monster cannon was one of amazement. It weighed 85 tons. The barrel was 40 feet long. Overall the cannon was 85 feet in length. The range was 20 miles, later extended to 40 miles as experience was gained firing non- atomic shells. The hydraulically loaded shell weighed 600 lbs. The relatively small projectile was about 3 feet long and packed the explosive equivalent of the A-bomb dropped on Hiroshima, or 20,000 tons of TNT.

The trucks that carried the atomic cannon were called T-10's. One cab was in front of the cannon, the other in the rear. The two cabs easily accommodated 14 fully equipped battle ready soldiers. The tires were better than six feet in diameter. When the trucks were started up and began running they sounded like the roar of a jet plane on take off. The sound was deafening. Firing procedure for the gun crew required the lanyard man to dig a standing fox hole 75 yards behind the cannon, deep enough for him to be shielded, but in sight of the cannon breech. The recoil occurred in three stages to break up the concussion. Other foxholes of the same proportions accommodated the rest of the gun crew. One man got into the wrong foxhole, scrambled out to get to his own, the blast caught him, blew him 15 feet high. He landed unhurt but with the wind knocked out of him. It was a lesson for every man in the Bn!

When I arrived at Ft Bragg, a 13 week training course was being offered for crew assignment to the atomic cannon. We all sewed on the 868th Field Artillery Battalion shoulder patch depicting 7 steps to hell on a descending staircase to Gehenna. The symbolism of the patch was that it took 7 steps of readiness to fire, and firing meant hell for the enemy. After a few firing exercises, I decided if I wanted to retain my hearing, I needed to change jobs. I asked HQs for a change in assignment and was transferred to the motor pool. The pool maintained 129 trucks including trucks medics, a Sherman tank, a radar van and several other specialized vehicles as well as the T-10 cabs used in transport of the cannon. I never touched the T-10. These were handled by a specialized crew. I trained further with the Ordnance depot near Atlanta, GA. When I returned to the 868th one morning ,I was greeted with news we were going to Korea. Orders were changed four different times that day before movement to Korea was canceled. Why or what were the reasons I had then, or now, no idea, unless it was for propaganda purposes to discourage our enemies. We were never allowed to talk about it among ourselves, yet newspaper articles saved by my family show it was public knowledge here in the United States.

Six Atomic FA Bns, were slated for deployment to the Bonn Republic of West Germany. Each Bn was a unit of 900 soldiers who composed the six gun crews in each battalion of six guns. By my arithmetic that meant that there were 36 atomic cannon destined for deployment to West Germany. On the demarcation line separating West Germany from East Germany, 36 atomic cannon could quickly wipe out any Soviet offensive. What would happen if the Soviets also deployed atomic cannon in counter threat? Only the Good Lord has the answer to that question. My unit, the 868th FA Bn (Atomic) was first to go overseas. We sailed aboard the Navy Transport USS General McRae. We then deployed to Baumholder in Germany in June of 1953. Service was arduous, but uneventful.

I returned to my home in Aurora, MO having completed my two years of army service in June 1954, in accordance with the selective service law of my country. I then resumed a marriage placed on hold, and to continue preaching the gospel for my Lord Jesus Christ.

By any measure, the Korean War was, in part, a response by the United States to the aggressive threat of Soviet Russia and its satellites to supplant democracy and establish a world wide hierarchy of satellite communist countries answering to Moscow's plan for world dominion. While the hot war was fought in Korea, the US maintained forces and weapons world wide to counter the threat. The soldier who authored this vignette was one of several million young Americans who helped furnish the deterrence. ....Editor.

Above. The major effort of the Air Force was to stop supplies from reaching the Chinese front line troops. That made railroad bridges a prime target, and one of the Air Forces best 'bridge busters' was the trusty B-26 bomber. **Below.** It may just be superstition, but this 'good luck' hand shake before missions can't hurt. These six Air Force gunners seem to think it's a good idea. <u>All Photos courtesy of the National Archives</u>.

RED DRAGON
The SECOND ROUND
FACES OF WAR II

Richard	L.	Johnston	US 56 121 356
First Name	MI	Last Name	Serial Number
Dick	1648 (Fld Radio Rpr)	27 Oct 1930	PFC
Nickname	MOS	Birthday	Grade / Rank
Co.2 KCZLLSG		Aug 1953-Sept 1954	Portland, OR
Unit (s)		Duty Tour (s)	Home Town
Good Conduct Medal		Korean Service Medal	US Meritorious Unit Emblem

Medals & Awards

National Defense Service Medal   United Nations Service Medal   ROK Presidential Unit Citation

SIGNAL CORPS LONG LINE COMMUNICATIONS

I was inducted into the Army 20 October 1952 at Portland, Oregon. At Ft Lewis, WA I was given a series of tests which assigned me to the Signal Corps Replacement Camp at San Luis Obispo, CA for a 24 week course in Field Radio Repair. In July of 1953, it was off to Korea, arriving a few days after effective date of the truce, 27 July 1953. I was assigned to 518th Relay Company of the Korean Communication Zone Long Line Signal Group in Pusan, originally designated GHQ Long Lines Signal Group ALL8226. Shortly, I was transferred to Signal Service Company No. 2, in Pusan. The Korean Signal Group had its origin in 10 men and 10 truckloads of signal gear from the 71st Signal Battalion stationed near Tokyo, sent to Korea two days after the war broke out 25 June 1950.

Korean Communication Zone Long Line Signal Group was charged with operations and maintenance of cable from Tokyo to Mukden in Manchuria. This cable had been installed by the Japanese in 1937 prior to WW II. Communication lines had been extended from Seoul to the truce site talks at Panmunjon. The 10 terminal and repeater stations located 30 to 40 miles apart on the MSR from Pusan to Seoul were the responsibility of Signal Service Company No. 2. Some of the stations had been almost completely destroyed. Station personnel at these installations used a parked van containing new Japanese cable equipment. Stations were located on the MSR at Song Do near Pusan, Miryang, Taegu, Kumchon, Yong Dong, Yusong near Taejon, Chonan, Osan-ni, Yong Dong Po and Seoul.

Initially we set up in a derelict grade school. With a shaky peace in place, the South Korean government required use of the school as an educational facility. We gladly vacated the school and began building our own station structures and personnel quarters. Because of an engineering background, my buddy, Dale Sipple, a carpenter from Coos Bay, OR, and I were placed in charge of the building project. We erected Quonset Huts, tropicals, and a number of other smaller buildings needed for company operation and storage of equipment. We completed the project in about two months. The truce seemed to be holding. The prisoner exchange had been completed except for 27000 POWs released by order of President Syngman Rhee of South Korea. There were still about 8000 North Korean guerillas yet at large who must be dealt with before citizens of South Korea would be safe in their farms and villages.

At year's end I was transferred to the Osan Repeater Station which proved to be the final duty assignment of my tour in Korea. The Osan Repeater Station is about 35 miles south of Seoul. It changed hands twice during the Korean War requiring station facilities to be rebuilt each time after recapture. The station provided telephone service via open line wire to K-13 Airbase near Suwon and K-55 Airbase to the south. Most of the stations on the cable network had a station complement of 5 to 8 GIs. A typical crew consisted of a cable splicer, power man and two or three carrier and repeater men. The stations also were staffed with Korean personnel from the Korean Ministry of Communications and a work crew of cooks and laborers as well as an armed South Korean military guard.

It was a little after midnight in late January or early February 1954 when we heard an explosion near our Osan station. It sounded, we estimated the sound to be about a mile south of us on the rail line. Four of us were dispatched to investigate. What we found was a scene of horror, wreckage of a passenger train carrying two hundred people. The train had been running backward, pushing the tender of the engine ahead of it. The lead car had hit a truck at a road crossing. The truck had rolled over, derailing the train and blocking forward movement, successive cars compressed back over the engine. The passenger cars were of wood. There were shattered boards, splinters and jagged nails making rescue work slow and tedious. Fortunately the cars had not caught fire. We began rescue work immediately on our arrival. We worked all night, being joined at intervals by Air Force Medics assembled to help extricate the living passengers caught up in the shattered jumble of dead bodies and splintered wood. Sixty people were killed, 120 injured. All four of us were put in for the Soldiers Medal. Two were awarded that medal. Two of us, the Meritorious Service Emblem.

I landed in Seattle, rotating home in September 1954, imbued with the belief that intervention by the United States and the United Nations was a just cause. South Korea was saved from the pitiful life that North Koreans still endure. Had we not saved South Korea from the clutches of communism, my daughters could not have adopted my three Korean grandchildren as loved family members.

Above. The Navy is laying an air strike on the Punchbowl. Above Right. Our Infantry have taken this trench line. They are trying to get it secured, ready to repel the next Chinese counter attack. Below Right. The battle for Sandbag Castle is still in progress, but this GI manages to show the Stars and Stripes. Below Left. Infantry assaulting another hill. There was always another hill. All photos from the National Archives and the Internet.

RED DRAGON
The SECOND ROUND
FACES OF WAR II

Charles	W.	Bowar	US 55 305 849
First Name	MI	Last Name	Serial Number
None	1745	3 Sept 1932	Cpl, then Pvt
Nickname	MOS	Birthday	Grade / Rank
B Co. 24th Inf Regt 25th Div		April 1953-May 1954	Reliance SD
Unit (s)		Duty Tour (s)	Home Town

Combat Infantry Badge   Good Conduct Medal   Korean Campaign Service Medal, 1 bronze star

Medals & Awards

National Defense Svc Medal   United Nations Medal   ROK Korean War Service Medal   ROK PUC

CONCUSSION!

Drafted 24 November 1952, I was not eager to volunteer, but felt it was my duty and responsibility as an American citizen to serve when my country called on me to help bear the burdens of our country at war. While it was not then termed a war, but rather a "police action," I had read the weekly newspaper enough to recognize that the lengthy casualty lists meant something more deadly than the term being used by politicians. My sixteen weeks basic training completed, the Army gave a one week "Delay in Route" which I spent at home with my sisters and friends. I reported to the San Francisco Port of Embarkation [POE] where I boarded a troop transport for Japan. There I was placed on a troopship which took me to Inchon where I was assigned to the 25th "Tropic Lightning" Division. A few days afterward, in late April, I joined Baker Company, First Bn of the 24th Infantry, as a replacement rifleman. The regiment was in reserve in the IX Corps area of western Korea. In early May the regiment was moved west into I Corps where we relieved the 5th Marine Reg't. The Turkish Brigade occupied a series of low hills some 10 miles east of Panmunjom. The defense of the "Nevada Cities," Outposts Carson, Elko, Reno and Vegas and the 2 "German" Outposts, Berlin and East Berlin, were a Turkish responsibility.

The Turkish Brigade was greatly outnumbered. They were confronted by the 120th Chinese Division's 3 regiments, 38th, 359th and 360th. On 25 May the Chinese began a heavy shelling of Turkish positions. The shelling increased in intensity, every day for 3 days. It was the heaviest artillery preparation yet mounted by the Chinese in the Korean War. On 28 May the Chinese mounted a four battalion assault on the Turks. About 10 PM night of 28 May, we were given orders to sharpen our bayonets because we were going to move up on line with the Turks. My immediate reaction was, "You've got to be kidding." Nobody was kidding. We sharpened! We moved out at midnight, arriving at the MLR about 2 AM. We passed burning artillery emplacements which was almost as scary being shelled. The Chinese took "Carson" on 28 May after a hard fight with the Turks. Our 1st Bn 24th Inf including B Co, my outfit, was attached to the Turks as reserve. This allowed the Turks to call up their own reserves to join them in the raging fight. The morning of the 29th of May, Baker Co was ordered to reinforce 'Elko' and to retake 'Carson.' We moved through 'Baker Cut' which was open to fire from the Chinese now holding 'Elko'. We had to move across 600 yards of open terrain. Chinese fire was murderous.

Nevertheless, we took 'Elko' after a 25 minute firefight. Our attack was then directed at 'Carson.' We got about half way there but were stopped by fire from automatic weapons, artillery and mortars. We regrouped on 'Elko,' and prepared for a second attack on 'Carson.' We almost reached the foot of Outpost Carson that attempt. Enemy fire forced us to withdraw. Our third attack reached the base of 'Carson.' We fought there for 30 minutes but were again forced to withdraw to 'Elko.' During the next 10 hours B Co on 'Elko' endured six Chinese counterattacks plus terrific barrages of artillery and mortars. Several of those counterattacks were thrown back in hand-to-hand combat. Sharpened bayonets sure came in handy. That afternoon, a platoon from A Company tried to break through but were stopped by Chinese fire. Early that evening, Division ordered B Company to withdraw from 'Elko.' In my opinion, it was a shocking blow from our own brass hats. We had spent 14 hours holding 'Elko,' a lot of good American blood was wasted.

Baker Company incurred very heavy losses. Almost a third of our company strength were listed as casualties in defense of the "Nevada Cities," 'Vegas,' 'Carson' and 'Elko.' I have no idea of the Turkish casualties, but they must have been very heavy as they took the initial brunt of the battle. Chinese casualties were estimated at 3,000 men in those two days of fighting, almost a third of the men in the Chinese 120th Division. It was later estimated the Chinese fired 65,000 rounds of artillery and mortars at us and the Turks. The US Army and 11th Marines together, by record, fired 173,280 rounds at the Chinese. The Air Force flew 67 missions. Marine Corsairs flew 99 close support missions in the same two day period. It was an all out effort by the two air support arms.

I don't remember the withdrawal from Elko. Sometime late that afternoon, in the fifth or sixth attack by the Chinese, I must have been knocked out by a Chinese concussion grenade or a mortar shell. A day later when a buddy saw me after the withdrawal, he blurted, "I thought you were dead! You were covered with blood and lay there like a dead man!" It's true I was all bloody, but it was the blood of someone else. Other than that, all I remember is a terrific headache. That's about all I do recall, nothing of the next week or so.

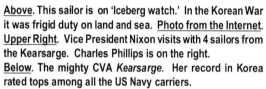

Above. This sailor is on 'Iceberg watch.' In the Korean War it was frigid duty on land and sea. Photo from the Internet.
Upper Right. Vice President Nixon visits with 4 sailors from the Kearsarge. Charles Phillips is on the right.
Below. The mighty CVA *Kearsarge.* Her record in Korea rated tops among all the US Navy carriers.

Photos courtesy Chuck Phillips.

RED DRAGON
The SECOND ROUND
FACES OF WAR II

Charles	N.	Phillips	426 93 82 USN
First Name	MI	Last Name	Serial Number
Chuck or Phil	Gunnery & Supply	28 Dec 1930	SK-3
Nickname	MOS	Birthday	Grade / Rank
USS Kearsarge CVA 33	1953-'55(Taiwan Combat Zone)		West Los Angeles, CA
Unit (s)	Duty Tour (s)		Home Town
Korean Service	National Defense	Good Conduct	United Nations	ROK PUC

Medals & Awards

China Service	Korean War Service	Combat Action Ribbon	Cold War Certificate

FLAT TOP SAILOR

My service in the US Navy began with basic training at the Naval Training Center in San Diego, CA, 4 June 1951. Upon completion, I was assigned to the Office of the Station Provost Marshall. My duties included maintenance of gate security, guard at the prison cell block, and at the barracks where the Waves were quartered. My toughest jobs, and saddest, were the funeral details. I never got over the lump-in-the throat feeling at these ceremonies, or my pity for weeping families as they received the folded American flag. In March 1953 I was assigned to the aircraft carrier USS Kearsarge CVA 33, referred to as "The Mighty Kay." by her crew. She was an Essex class carrier, as was her sister ship, USS Oriskany CVA 34, known to some as "Big Risk," to others as "The Fighting Lady."

Little known is the USS Kearsarge was the third warship of the US Navy christened with that name. The first Kearsarge, a USS sloop-of-war was named after a mountain which, in the Abnaki Indian language, means 'Heaven.' During our Civil War she cornered and sank the CSS Alabama, a commerce raider, off the French coast near Cherbourg. The second Kearsarge was a post Civil War battleship, the only battleship not named after a State of the Union. When I joined the crew of the "Mighty Kay," she was part of Task Force 77 operating out of Yokosuka, Japan. Until the Korean Truce was signed 27 July 1953, we, as part of Task Force 77, patrolled Korean waters so her aircraft could provide air reconnaissance, surveillance and attack capabilities. While still on line we took a group of soldiers, including ground combat veterans to Hong Kong for R&R. On the hangar deck I noticed one man standing alone. He had a bewildered look on his face. I introduced myself and welcomed him aboard with the hope he would enjoy his rest and relaxation furlough in Hong Kong. He had to think hard to recall his name. I cannot remember it, but have often wondered about him. I had never before understood the meaning of the expression, "The Thousand Yard Stare." I learned from the look in his eyes.

At the time of the armistice we were anchored in Manila Bay. While on liberty we were in a restaurant. A waitress, tears in her eyes, asked if the Japanese would now come back? Her expression and tears spoke volumes. I did my best to assure her WW II was over, and America was still acting as protector of her country. Another personal incident in Manila was my encounter with Vice President Richard Nixon. Four of us were allowed a brief visit after introductions and a handshake. He asked me how I liked the Navy, where I was from and what ship. I told him "Hollywood , the Kearsarge and that I was not too thrilled. "I wish my tour of duty were over as I belong at home with my wife and baby." He smiled and said, "I understand." I thought later, what a dumb thing to say to the Vice President . However, he had asked me an honest question, he got an honest answer! Returning to Japan, the chaplain arranged a Christmas party. We adopted 105 Japanese orphans for the day. What a time they had, movie cartoons and a big Christmas dinner. Santa had gifts of clothing and a toy for each child. It was a memorable day for all. The crew enjoyed it as much as the kids did!

After the Korean truce, Kearsarge and Oriskany were used in the filming of several movies. " Mighty Kay" was flagship for the "Caine Mutiny. Among the stars aboard was Fred McMurray. We had been casual acquaintances when I was a paramedic in LA prior to the war. The encounter allowed us to bring each other up-to-date. A great morale booster for this sailor! Other movies involving the "Mighty Kay" were the "The Eternal Sea," "Bridges at Toko-ri," and the "Fighting Lady." The ship's crew were the real stars!

In 1955, another liberty in Manila was cut short by Chinese Communist threats to Formosa and attacks on Quemoy and Matsu. On 22 January we headed for the Tachen Islands. "Condition Three" watches prevailed for two weeks. On 5 February our ships' captain announced evacuation of Nationalist troops had begun. Our planes provided air cover for the operation. For the next week, planes launched around the clock. On 13 February we received the welcome news, " Operation Complete." We stood down and sailed next morning for Hong Kong to complete our interrupted R&R. On 5 March I received orders for return stateside. I was discharged 27 April 1955 to return to civil life, military service completed. I realize how fortunate I was to return unscathed. I am truly grateful for the opportunity to have served my country. USS Kearsarge CVA 33, "Mighty Kay," was scrapped in May 1973. The San Diego Naval Training Center closed In March 1977. Those two events marked the end of an era in the lives of men who had served in the US Navy.

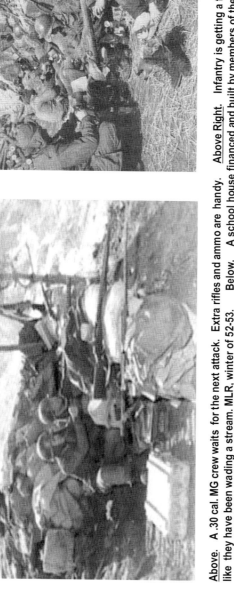

Above.   A .30 cal. MG crew waits for the next attack.   Extra rifles and ammo are handy.   Above Right.   Infantry is getting a foot inspection and dry socks.   Looks like they have been wading a stream. MLR, winter of 52-53.   Below.   A school house financed and built by members of the 40th Division is dedicated and turned over to the village elders. This project, located in Kapyong, South Korea, was completed in October of 1967.

RED DRAGON
The SECOND ROUND
FACES OF WAR II

Walter	Cox	Benton	RA 15 379 680
First Name	MI	Last Name	Serial Number
Walt	13250	18 Aug 1932	1st Sgt E-8
Nickname	MOS	Birthday	Grade / Rank
3d Div		1950-'51, 1957, !967-'68	Lakeland, FL
Unit (s)		Duty Tour (s)	Home Town

Bronze Star,OLC Purple Heart Good Conduct, 6 knots Meritorious Service PUC KCSM 3stars

Medals & Awards

OM,J&G NDSM AFRM UNSM ROKFM KWSM, 50th Aniv AFEM VSM 3 stars RVN 60 device

FLASHBACK

A lot of water has flowed under the bridge since that spring day in March 1951. It was one of those things which cannot be forgotten, no matter how hard you try. Those who have spent time in combat have seen things they would rather forget but cannot put out of their minds. This March day, spring thaw had just started in Korea. I was then about 100 miles north of Pusan. We had ended here after our three day 'cruise' from the evacuation off the beach at Hungnam on Christmas eve. On that particular day, one of the L-19 pilots had spotted some bodies lying by the side of a mountain creek. Below, at the bottom of the hill, a QM unit had set up a shower tent. Six of us were detailed to clear the bodies from the water and creek bank. It took us the better part of an hour to climb the steep hill to where the bodies lay. What I saw has been indelibly burned into my memory all these years. It was not a pleasant sight.

There were 30 Korean civilians, old men and women, young women, and several children. All had their hands bound with commo wire then lined up on the creek bank and shot. By North Koreans or Chinese, there was no way we could tell. Their bodies had fallen into the creek. Several bodies had been pulled from the creek when I noticed the NCO in charge of the detail was down in the hole we had dug for the bodies. He was using his bayonet to extract the gold from the teeth of the dead. It pissed me off. As a Pfc I could only ask him to stop. He gave me a sickly smile but continued placing pieces of gold in a tobacco sack. The next body I retrieved was of a young woman, perhaps 20 years old. She had fallen face up into the water. I lifted her body to the creek bank. In doing so, I turned her over. I saw where the bullet had made its exit. Strapped to her back was a baby. The bullet had torn the back out of that poor infant. Returning to the grave site I saw him still extracting gold from mouths of the dead. Seeing that, I lost it.

Unslinging the carbine strapped across my back, I clicked off the safety, placed the muzzle between the eyes of the NCO and told him, "You son-of-a-bitch, you touch one more person, and I'll blow your brains all over this hill." He took me at my word. We finished our grim job and returned to our unit. I cooled down and had started to worry what I had done to that NCO and what would happen to me. Thanks Be To God, no one, including the NCO, ever mentioned the incident. I think back, realizing only by the Grace of Our Lord I did not pull that trigger. Had I done so, I would probably still be serving time in Leavenworth.

I don't know why, but that memory always triggers another, happier memory. In 1967-'68 I was 1st Sgt of HQ & Svc Battery, 76th FA Bn. We were located a few miles south of the DMZ in the small village of Kun Kok-ni. There was a Korean orphanage on the hill above. My outfit built a two story vocational building using donated material and money given by soldiers in our unit. It was located on a hill behind our unit compound. Every Wednesday, my driver and I would make a run through 'Artillery Valley' picking up food and supplies donated by various sources, including Army mess Sgts. In my orderly room I kept a bell and a jar. If a soldier entered without knocking, removing his hat, or other uniform violation, I would ring the bell and fine him ten cents. Money was used to buy candy and gum at our little PX for orphanage kids. Looking back, I know some of the men used my rules as an excuse to contribute.

Each Wednesday we would drive our jeep on the winding dirt trail up the hill. All the way up we could hear children excitedly shouting, "Benton come, Benton come!" All the effort that everyone had put into making this place a refuge for those children, giving them a chance to grow up, was repaid many fold each week. Seeing the smiles and sparkling eyes of those kids, how they had filled out to become healthy children, was a matter of rejoicing for all our outfit. Men made excuses to go to the orphanage to see them. It was a lesson in psychology to watch these tough young American soldiers soften up when they were on a visit with these kids.

A few days before I rotated back to the states, Mr. Chin, the orphanage director, came to my orderly room and presented me with a brass plaque with the inscription, "In appreciation from Chin and 109 children of Ken KKK Orphanage for Meritorious Service 22 May 1968." Today it hangs on the wall of my den bringing back happy memories and also reminders of other Korean hills I wish I could forget. In review of my memories in a lifetime of military service, I find mine are a combination of many things, bad and good.

Above.   Memorial services are being held at at this cemetery which has many new graves. This 'Face of War' shows the high cost of freedom.   Photo from the Internet.
Left. The day after the war, Chinese and North Korean soldiers line the road that is the dividing line, to get a close look at their ex-enemy.
Below. A ROK soldier keeps a wary eye on curious Chinese soldiers, testing out this new thing called 'peace', July 28, 1953.
                Two photos courtesy of Art Elkington.

RED DRAGON
The SECOND ROUND
FACES OF WAR II

Eugene	P.	Moser	O-52 299 569
First Name	MI	Last Name	Serial Number
Gene	Artillery	Oct 1943	Lt Col, then 1st Lt
Nickname	MOS	Birthday	Grade / Rank
HHQ Co 1st Bn 38th Inf		May 1967- June 1968	None claimed- 'Army Brat'
Unit (s)		Duty Tour (s)	Home Town

Medals & Awards
MSM,OLC ARCOm,OLC AAM ARCAM, 4OLC NDSM w/ star AFEM DMZ Imjin Scout Badge
AFRM, hourglass ASR VaNG Bronze Star VaNG Com VaNG Svc Medal FA Order of St Barbara

BORDER WAR

I'm an Army Brat. Having no home town, I grew up living on military posts everywhere. I followed the footsteps of many prior 'Brats,' graduating from College of William and Mary, taking ROTC to gain a commission. Entering the army in June 1966, I then attended the Artillery School at Fort Sill. My first assignment was to Fort Gordon, GA and from there I went to Korea in May 1967. I was not particularly happy about the Korean assignment as I anticipated boring duty with nothing happening to liven the year I was slated to spend there. I had hoped to be sent to Vietnam where my training could have been put to good use. I consoled myself with the knowledge I was going to the 2d Infantry Division, not the 7th Infantry, then in reserve. My first unit was 'C' Battery, 5th Battalion, 38th Artillery in direct support of 3d Brigade, 2d Infantry Division. In July I was attached to 3d Bde HQs as the Artillery Liaison Officer. I held down the job for about month but was replaced by a more senior Lt in the liaison slot, resulting in my transfer to 1st Bn, 38th Inf Bde. In spite of the apparent demotion, I was happy with the assignment as I liked working with the Infantry.

I now knew Korea was a place where much was happening. People were being killed and wounded in a border war of raid and ambush. In the fall of 1966 North Korea began a systematic series of probes, ambushes and night time forays into encampments near the (DMZ). A Co, 1st Bn, 38th(A/1/38) Infantry was one night attacked by sappers who placed satchel charges under soldier's bunks, killing several and wounding several more. In the short time I had been attached to 3d Bde(Brigade) there had been a couple of incidents. I was given the duty of inventorying personal effects of the Brigade S-2 who was seriously wounded by North Korean machine gun fire while visiting a guard post. The DMZ at that time was guarded by platoon sized posts. These posts were girded by concertina wire and connected by a trench system linking Command Posts (CPs) to small observation / fighting posts. This stationary system was augmented by reconnaissance patrols or ambush patrols as occasion might demand in this strange no-war of skirmish and kill. We were instructed to call these North Korean attackers 'Unidentified Individuals', or "UIs," to use the GI term.

The United Nations Command began to build a 10 foot tall woven barbed wire fence across Korea, inside 'our' side of the Demilitarized Zone, ringed at top and bottom by concertina wire. Both sides of the fence had a raked dirt area to detect penetration attempts. Guard towers placed at intervals provided visual and electronic surveillance. A company of Construction Engineers© were bivouacked on the grounds of the Joint Security Area Support Base where Americans assigned to Panmunjom duties had billets and mess halls. In early afternoon, 28 August 1967, the engineers were attacked. When I got there it was all over. It had lasted but a short time because 2 men, noticing strange activity, went to investigate. This caused the North Koreans to begin an impromptu attack while many of the engineers were still in the chow line. It was a mess, especially to one who had never before seen combat casualties. Several engineers were dead, covered by ponchos. One sergeant had taken a round through the buttocks. It looked as if a butcher had used a knife to carve off the cheeks of his butt. There was little blood, just raw meat. A mama-san working at the mess hall had been gut shot. She screamed and cried in agony. All over the area, men were loading M-14 magazines into their weapons. The Quick Reaction Force, equipped with M-113 personnel carriers and an M-114 Scout Track, came roaring up in an attempt to quash the attack. The Battalion S-2, Lt Jim Rodden, and I jumped into one of the M-114s as it headed out in an attempt to block the flight of the 'UIs.'

Suddenly, an explosion. Lt Rodden, manning the M-60 in the second hatch of the track, tumbled to the floor. I pulled him out, his face bloodied. I was sure he was dead. He surprised me by sitting up! The M-113 behind us had hit a mine. The blast threw the 113 driver out of his track. No one was killed. I will never forget the splinter punctured vegetation or the acrid smell of explosives. Between November 1966 and October 1969 casualties of US forces were 75 Killed in Action, and 111 Wounded in Action. There were more than 300 firefights. South Korean losses were about three times those of the American units. In those two days of action, August 28th and 29th, 1967, we had 7 Killed in Action and 28 Wounded in Action plus at least one civilian dead. Some truce! Korea was not at peace. We were in a skirmishing type war, replete with dead and wounded, a truth unknown to Americans back home.

Above. An MP offers two Commie POWs a drink of water. Right. This North Korean POW being exchanged at Freedom Village insults an American Major, calling him a 'war criminal.'
Below, 1954. Barb-wire barricades and mine fields are quickly installed. Fifty three years later, they still divide North Korea from South Korea.
Photos from the Archives and Internet.

426

Left. Highly reinforced bunkers and OPs were sited along the DMZ in the early '60's. Yet, these were not able to prevent infiltrators or North Korea's constant sneak attacks.
Photo courtesy of Gene Moser.
Above. GIs plant the Stars & Stripes on a newly won hilltop,1952. Below. Returning American POWs show off their pet magpie at a news conference.
Photos from National Archives and Internet.

Kee-Tae		Choi	122955 ROK
First Name	MI	Last Name	Serial Number
None	Corps of Engineers	Capt, then Pfc to Lt	
Nickname	MOS	Birthday	Grade / Rank
12th Div ROK		Oct 1950-December 1969	Seoul, Korea
Unit (s)		Duty Tour (s)	Home Town
Gold Star Hwarang Award	Commander's Award, 1st Corps		
Medals & Awards			

Commander's Award, Army Corps of Engineers   7 other Medals & Awards

A WAR PILGRIMAGE

On graduation from high school in 1945 I went to work as a clerk in the office of the Japanese Government General. We were under Japanese occupation. After the surrender of Japan, I carried on in the same job under auspices of the Marshall Plan as administered by the US Army. When the new government of the Republic of Korea was established in 1948 I held the same position. We South Koreans were going through a rough time in our struggle to reestablish our country as a free nation after the two generation occupation by Japan beginning in 1905. Most of us held the high hope that we would establish a new democratic country. Those Koreans of Communist persuasion were determined that Korea would be governed by Communist ideology. The Communist slogan was "Achieve Total Independence through Revolution by the People." To those of us who believed in freedom of the individual and the philosophies of democracy, Communism was a doctrine of slavery. It was a schism that led to Civil War in less than two years.

North Korea invaded the South Sunday morning, 25 June 1950 with six Russian trained armored divisions of well equipped soldiers. Most of the northern part of our country was overrun within the first week by troops of the Democratic Peoples Republic of Chosun. [DPRC]. Most South Koreans opposed a communist take over but without organization, did not know what to do. Some fled south, but an untimely destruction of the only bridge across the Han River kept most of Seoul in the city. As a government employee I was also concerned for my own safety. During the next few weeks our 8 family members went hungry as we tried to ration what little food we had. Three weeks later, we were desperate. I returned to the government administrative office where I had been employed. The Communists put me back to work and authorized a rice ration. At the same time they were rounding up young men for service in their so-called "Volunteer Army." Those who resisted were tagged "Anti-element," and were the first targets of their "press gangs."

At the end of July, two North soldiers came to the office. It ended my civil life. My classification was now " Anti-element." I was taken to the Hee Mun High School, a three story rectangular building with a large open playground in front, surrounded by a 12 feet high wall. It had been converted for use as a North Army basic military training site. Hundreds of us were held there. I was not ready to yield to North Korean brutality. I used every opportunity to look for a chance to escape, carefully observed every part of the structure and the posts of the soldiers on guard. The third night, about 2 AM, I made a sneak exit from the school. Several of us working together managed to get over the wall after the guard passed on his way to his turn-around point. I tiptoed through the dark streets of Seoul to my home, barely getting there before sunrise. I hid in the homes of friends and relatives, moving only at night until the Inchon landing by troops of General MacArthur's command liberated Seoul on 28 September. We hoped the war was over!

Following the liberation of Seoul, I volunteered as an enlisted man in the ROK Army 3d Division, commanded by a distant family 'uncle,' Gen Seok-won Kim. The division was in the Yangyang area when we started our northward drive to Hamkyung Buk Do. I participated as an infantryman. Our retreat from the North was ordered in mid December. Navy ships evacuated us from Seomjin Harbor, Hamkyung Buk Do[Hamhung]. We returned to South Korea, where we debarked just south of Gang-Neung City. There we regrouped and established a new front line. We were now well within South Korea, below the 38th parallel which had marked our boundary with the North. In May 1951 I was captured by the Chinese when my company was surrounded during a battle in the Hyun Ree area of Gangwon Do Province. My life as a prisoner of Communism started all over again. The Chinese used us as labor to carry wounded soldiers to the rear, to bury dead bodies and to carry ammunition and food for their troops. It was a miserable existence.

North Koreans acted as interpreters between POWs and the Chinese, eliminating communication problems, and insuring all Chinese orders were obeyed. We were kept near the front line, never more than 3 or 4 miles behind it, always on call for any labor task needed on the fighting front. They called us "Liberation Fighters" and tried to brain wash us into accepting communism. We were also taught numerous North Army songs, including the popular song praising KIM II Sung, the North Premier, who actually was a Dictator. I again began observations in preparation for an escape. Since I was near the front line, I also had to assess the risk of being shot by troops of my own side should I escape the Chinese. I began hiding rice and scorched Bab as a preliminary step to escape.

I adopted the role of a soldier accepting what I was told in the brain washing classes. I participated in "self help" teaching schedules and began leading discussions as if I were accepting Communist dogma. In my assessment of risk was the certainty that it would be easier to escape, here, near the front line, than if I were taken further north. One dark night in early August I squeezed between adjoining straw mats hung on poles. The mats were strung together as fencing around the POW enclosure. I wasn't as quiet or as careful as I should have been. A noise must have alerted the Chinese guard. He shot at me. I thought he had missed. He shot several more times, merely adding faster wings to my heels as I ran for my life through the concealing brush. I crossed over two ridges on the mountainside, running for several hours before I stopped to listen for the sound of any pursuit. I heard none, but noticed that the pant leg covering my left thigh was stiff with dried blood. I tore a piece off the lower pant leg and bound the wound. Luckily it was not deep or serious. I hid that day and reached the front line that night. The area was hilly and thickly wooded. I could see no soldiers around. Artillery shells were dropping in the area, coming from the south. Ours. Somehow I had passed through the Chinese lines and was headed directly into lines manned by American troops. Luckily, I was found by a FO team of American soldiers. However, they could not identify me as a South soldier. My clothes were ragged. I was wearing North Army sneakers.

They put me in a temporary POW camp near Wang which was set up next to a supply depot. I had been in the camp for about two weeks when the camp authorities in mid August began shipping POWs to other prison camps. I was very uneasy about the situation. The risk of misidentification as a North soldier was very probable, considering the circumstances of my capture. Were that tag to be hung on me, I would be a North POW for the duration of the war. The obvious solution was to escape the POW camp, go to Seoul where I was known and could be properly identified. I would then again be a soldier of the Republic of Korea. One rainy evening I eluded the guard who huddled inside his poncho to keep dry in the downpour. I could not help but feel the irony of the situation. I was attempting escape from the US Army who were aiding us, fighting in our behalf against communism in my own country.

I hid near the main road leading south, keeping my eyes open for a chance to swing aboard a passing truck. A lone truck for some reason slowed as it passed. I grabbed the tail gate and tried to swing aboard. Somebody inside grabbed my arms and helped me aboard. The truck was filled with KATUSA, but a special category of KATUSA. They were Korean student volunteers from the Korean community in Japan. They did not understand the Korean language very well.. I explained my long story to them in Japanese. They let me stay with them without sounding an alarm. I thanked them with much gratitude when I left them after we arrived in Seoul.

As soon as I got back home in Seoul, I contacted my family "uncle," to ask his advice and assistance so I might resolve my difficult situation before it worsened. He very generously contacted Army HQ, and recommended, without any request on my part, that I be considered as a candidate officer in the Army Corps of Engineers. My educational background, two years service in the government prior to the war, my service as an enlisted man, and my escape from the North Army were all factors which were considered. After several days of debriefing by the Military Police concerning my knowledge of the Chinese Army picked up in my captivity, I was released to enter Officer's Training School. I received my commission on 31 March 1952 and was immediately assigned to the 12th ROK Division then fighting in the Inje area north of the 38th parallel. We were fighting the North Army here, not the Chinese.

It was truly a civil war as we fought the Communists in this mountainous area near our eastern coast. Both sides fought from deep dug trenches. An attack by either side on the trench system of the other made for a bitter struggle with high casualties. Night patrols between the lines took its toll in dead and wounded also. My platoon was usually involved in laying mines on likely areas of enemy approach to our trench system. We were also charged with the responsibility of clearing mines laid by North soldiers which would hinder our attacks on enemy positions. It was tedious, dangerous work, which must be carefully done lest a mine be set off. This work was at times done under enemy fire which added to the innate dangers involved in mine clearing. At other times we would be involved in constructing bridges or roads to allow the passage of supplies. The next eighteen months of my participation ended as the truce was signed on 27 July 1953. As it turned out, the war was over although border flare ups occurred for years. The border is still heavily guarded and buttressed by s 40,000 American soldiers to this day. While the fighting war was over, the reconstruction of our war ravaged country loomed as a gigantic task. It is a task which will never end as we participate in the world economy.

I continued my military career until 1969 when I resigned my commission as Captain. Recollecting all these wartime incidents confirmed my thinking I made the right decision to be a freedom fighter for my country. I also realize how lucky I was. I could have met the same fate as 2d Lt Cho Chang-Ho who lived 43 years as a North POW. Lt Cho was a fellow high school alumni, a few years junior to me in Kyunggi Commerce High School in Seoul. He made his escape from the North into Manchuria, and with help from the Manchurian-Korean community, returned to his home in our Korean Republic in October 1994. His story saddened and frightened me. I wondered how many other men from the South, both soldiers and civilians, had met same fate, but died unknown in captivity.

I firmly believe that wars like our Korean Civil War should never be fought again. No one should ever have to experience such ugliness and horror again. On the other hand, I am proud of the role I played in fighting a Communist government which used people as tools, rather than to protect and benefit them. The soldier spirit in our country has made us a free nation in this world we live in.

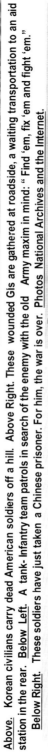

Above. Korean civilians carry dead American soldiers off a hill. Above Right. These wounded GIs are gathered at roadside, awaiting transportation to an aid station in the rear. Below Left. A tank-Infantry team patrols in search of the enemy with the old Army maxim in mind: " Find 'em, fix 'em and fight 'em." Below Right. These soldiers have just taken a Chinese prisoner. For him, the war is over. Photos National Archives and the Internet.

Jean	NMI	Kirnak nee Bowen	N792-948
First Name	MI	Last Name	Serial Number
None	"Nurse"	6 Sept 1925	1st Lt ANC
Nickname	MOS	Birthday	Grade / Rank
8076 MASH		Nov '50-Aug '51	Mosby, MT
Unit (s)		Duty Tour (s)	Home Town

Korean Campaign Service Medal, 3 stars   United Nations Service Medal

Medals & Awards

National Defense Service Medal   Republic of Korea Peace Medal

AFTER FIFTY YEARS

October 2000. In San Francisco I boarded a Korean Air Boeing 777 on a 13 hour non stop flight to Seoul. An invited guest of the Republic of South Korea, I was honored by an invitation to attend the Korean War 50th Anniversary Commemoration. My memory flashed back to October 1950. On that war time trip, our small prop plane landed twice to refuel. Our flight time was 36 hours to Yokohama. A small plane took me to Pyongyang, North Korea on to Sunchon where I reported to MASH 8076, then by ambulance to Kunu-ri, 20 miles shy of the Chinese border. It was to be a short stay. On 28 Nov, the Chinese entered the war, creating havoc in a surprise attack resulting in thousands of dead and wounded GIs, POWs, and some unfortunate soldiers listed as 'Missing in Action.' It was a brutal indoctrination to the horrors of war. I can never forget the 600 wounded soldiers brought into Mash that fateful day. 8076 Mash, and all our wounded soldiers barely escaped capture as we fled for our lives.

The airport at Seoul was my first returning glimpse of Korea. It was a modern skytropolis. A different world from the wartime runways I last saw when in Seoul in 1950. Korea was the first war fought under the banner of the United Nations. Twenty three polyglot nations from both hemispheres fought in common cause to save South Korea from the jaws of the Red Dragon. As I looked around I could hardly believe this was the same nation I left in shambles 50 years ago. The hard working Korean people had transformed a ravaged countryside into a modern nation. Looking out the windows of the bus, everywhere we saw modern industry, the bustle of city of commerce, swarms of people pursuing business activities. It was life in the fast lane, no different than any large American City. I asked, "How was it possible?" The answer was simple. An industrious people, working cooperatively in a six day week had transformed an agrarian economy into one ranked eleventh on the world scale. Average yearly income is $8700, yet every one seemed well fed and happy. As a nurse and mother one thing stood out. The children, even at the age of two, were incredibly well behaved. We saw groups everywhere, toddlers through mid grades, under supervision of nursemaids or teachers being taught the civics and mores of their society and the cooperative culture of their country. It had an awesome effect on child behavior.

Our guides showed us the monuments and memorials to the fallen of the Korean War. What impressed me was memorials always included American soldiers and Marines as well as South Korean soldiers. Korea wants its people and its future generations to remember the Korean War and to keep alive the national gratitude to the 17 nations that sent their men and women to fight for their freedom. In our tours we crossed the Han River a number of times. It seemed as if we crossed on a different bridge each time. At the time of the Korean War there was but one bridge across the Han. In 1951 it was blown with a terrible loss of life. Through some coordination error, the bridge was crowded with fleeing refugees at the time of the blast. Today there are 24 modern bridges. The river banks have been revetted with huge concrete slabs. Both sides of the river for miles have been landscaped, providing benches and picnic areas in a park like setting. Trolley tracks parallel the river banks, allowing easy access for Seoul's 11 million people.

We visited the DMZ at Panmunjom, site of the interminable peace squabbles which preceded the truce in July 1953. We were fortunate to have as lecturer a well informed tall, muscular black Army Colonel. In a powerful command voice he gave us a brief history of Korea culminating in an aftermath WW II decision between the US and Russia which divided Korea into separate zones of influence. The political division of Korea into two countries at the 38th proved to be a tragedy. It led to civil war 5 years later when the Russian backed Communist North invaded the South that fateful day of 25 June 1950. The aftermath of that "Cease Fire" truce of 27 July 1953 ending the fighting exists with North Korea today poised on the border with over 900,000 troops, the third largest standing army in the world. The United States maintains a force of 37,000 men as a backup for the South Korean Army. The Colonel talked of the hopeful reunification of the two Korea as as a result of peace talks then going on. To date little has resulted except for a token visit by 100 South Koreans allowed to visit relatives in North Korea. In exchange, the South has given thousands of tons of fertilizers and foodstuffs. The tragedy endures for over one million Koreans separated from relatives for 50 years. Were the reunification of Korea to take place, one of the world's tinder boxes would cease to exist. The inexorable passage of time continues.

Above. Wounded 2nd Infantry Division troops are being carried by litter jeep to the nearest aid station. Right. Two wounded G.I. buddies make it back as far as the aid station together. They are happy with their 'good fortune'?   Photos courtesy of the Internet. Below. Jean Kirnak Bowen, in Korea for the 50th anniversary celebration of the Korean War in July 2000, poses with these Ethiopian soldiers.
          Photo courtesy of Jean Kirnak Bowen.

Left. A wounded G.I. is rushed to an airplane for evacuation at the burning Yonpo Airfield, North Korea, December 1950.

Below Left. Marines hold a memorial service for their fallen comrades.

Below. An Infantry patrol searches the frozen mountains in search of the enemy. The Chinese, masters of camouflage, had infiltrated almost a half million troops into North Korea. without detection.

All Photos from the Internet.

RED DRAGON
The SECOND ROUND
FACES OF WAR II

Maurice	NMI	Siskel, Jr.		ER 15 246 312
First Name	MI	Last Name		Serial Number
Maury	7776 & 4740	30 May 1928		Cpl
Nickname	MOS	Birthday		Grade / Rank
HM/31/7		Dec 1950-July 1951		Bedford, IN
Unit (s)		Duty Tour (s)		Home Town
Parachutists Badge	World War II Victory Medal	Combat Infantry Badge		Good Conduct Medal
Medals & Awards				
Korean Campaign Service Medal, 3 stars		National Defense Medal	UN Medal	KWON

ON WAR: A OLD SOLDIER TO HIS DAUGHTER.

In my reply to you, many things I may say will reinforce the opinions you already hold as to the barbarity of those who fight in wars. By definition, war usually involves horrible behavior at all levels of the primate kingdom. Current thinking in many areas of our society denigrate the soldier-warrior as 'baby killer' and 'legalized murderer.' This is specifically true of those anti-war individuals whose views are often described as "Dove" or "Peacenik." Before I really get into an explanation based on personal experience, I will make one simple statement. "Scratch the skin of any combat soldier, and beneath you will find feathers of a "Dove." There is no one more anti-war than the veteran who has survived the horrors of front line combat. What is overlooked or forgotten, is the reality that it takes but one side to start a war. Acting in self defense results in the "other side." In my thinking, that is a defensible position. I will add there is one other justification for fighting a war: In defense of personal and national freedom. A wise Athenian statesman some 2500 years ago made a statement that has since become an axiom for free men everywhere. "Better a free man in his grave than a slave on his knees." I postulate that statement is as true today as it was then. The lust for power produces men like Hitler who perpetrates a "Holocaust," a Saddam Hussein, who gasses his own Kurdish citizens, men, women and children. I do not defend war, I merely comment on it as a survivor of war. And, I believe, as one more qualified to do so than the current crop of media commentators who "studied" war in Poly Sci 101 under some liberal academic who also had never faced the fire of an enemy.

I ask you to pull back and try to understand better just what war is when it is faced squarely. Arguably, behavior in warfare is partly a function of the desperation of the participants. In any case, war is a fight for keeps. One opponent lives, the other dies. The dying, on either side, is neither clean nor quick, nor merciful, in terms understood by non combatants. Some of this was shown vividly and well in the first part of the movie, "Private Ryan." To those involved, war is a fundamental and forever significant experience whether ever discussed or not. It is difficult to know, no matter how hard one tries, that one has conveyed the feeling and emotions of a war time soldier to someone who has not shared the experience. War is so ugly and so final. It entails horrendous pain, whether experienced or inflicted. It is overwhelming in its effect on the soldier and the civilian caught in the middle. At the time, it is all consuming. There is no time to think of anything except doing what must be done in terms of survival. It is a canopy which shuts out all else while the soldier is supremely and intensely busy doing his job. At such crucial moments, there is no silliness about God or atheists in a foxhole, or a high minded philosophy being expressed as, "I'm transmitting this fire message to our mortars as my part in saving the world for democracy." Those kinds of important philosophical considerations do arise, but not when a soldier is in the process of killing someone. There simply is neither time nor willingness to consider anything but survival.

Emotions in war are very personal. They command a person's total being in ways never experienced in any other realm of human activity. In some instances, war can have a surprisingly dispassionate event. In others, it boils with a superheated hatred difficult to imagine. In most of the Western World, we are so frightened by real honest-to-God hatred that we try to make it "'impossible' by 'outlawing' it," by enacting "hate-crime" laws which stem from our fears. Can enacting such laws really make a difference? Fear, not desire for justice or even of revenge drives the hate-crime absurdity. Similarly driven and motivated are many aspects of war.

In some parts of the world, wars are inspired by the experience of seeing loved ones killed quickly, and sometimes, slowly by enemies. Hate is acquired; it is not innate behavior. In Palestine, kindergarten kids are taught the glory of suicide by blowing themselves in places crowded with Jews. In Afghanistan, rival tribes have inflicted such pain on each other for centuries that peace has become almost an impossibility. These first hand experiences and teachings persist in many societies for generations. When you see your great grandfather killed in the courtyard, your grandmother slaughtered as she tries to comfort the great grandfather, your father and brother tied and slowly put to death while your mother is being raped, you learn hate with all your being. You teach your kids to hate those who exhibited such behavior. These kinds of feelings are so intense that they frighten us deeply. Few of us ever experience such hate emotions. But these feelings are common throughout the Middle East, and the Balkans as well.

It is taken in with their mother's milk. We are "civilized"; we do not hate like that, thus it scares us senseless. We believe ourselves incapable of such acts until an American Civil War, a Jewish Holocaust or a My Lai in Vietnam occurs to demonstrate again that we have not really changed- even in our civilized West. We do not cope well with hate because, to us, it is a great unknown. Hate has persisted so long in some regions that there can be no prospect of peaceful coexistence until the sequence of learned hatred is broken. In my view, this is why we will not know peace in the Middle East in your lifetime. The curricula in kindergarten must change. Today's 5 year olds must die of old age before the chain can effectively be broken. We have yet to reach complete accommodation with our own Indians, right? And, I suspect, some of our black citizens could add a few old scores as well.

I'm asking you to understand, not forgive or condone, the insensate cruelty that dominates the news about Afghanistan. I suspect what horrifies you is killing, the ruthless taking of human life. War by its very nature is cruelty. In the process, modern war develops taking of human life into a macabre science. We try to alleviate those cruelties by educating our 'allies' in more humane ways of waging war the west has developed in the last few hundred years. We don't kill prisoners, nor torture them. Read the rules of war laid out in the Geneva Convention. They are the most humane procedures yet governing armed conflict. We still have committed only our treasure, not our blood in Afghanistan. We have insufficient men there either to control the warlords or the country side on any large scale. A different ethos guides life in tribal societies such as Afghanistan. The media in our country, raised in our way of life, is as horrified as you. It is is reflected in personal bias as they 'report' the news. We look upon rats somewhat as the various tribes over there view each other. They bait traps for enemies, kill their prey, and think little of it.

Earlier in an E-mail, I described some of the inherent complexities involved in apprehension of Osamma bin Laden. It is extremely complex as so many aspects of area, race and religion are involved. We commit war materiel but are reluctant to commit our people. The faith an ally has in us is not inspired as we appear ready to fight to his last man. We are too ready to impeach our leaders every time a man is lost a "friendly fire incident." These are terrible mistakes, but wars are fought by fallible humans who make mistakes. We are so damned dainty we cannot accept that lethal errors are an inherent aspect of war. We are so sheltered, our government and media go to extremes trying to make death acceptable. It is not acceptable- it just is! Death is a part of life, war merely accelerates the process for great numbers of people. We have become so mother protected in our thinking that we fail to realize we live in a real world, not in some Hollywood fantasy portrayed in a Shangri-La movie. Soldiers, having lived in a real world of kill or be killed, are more direct and pragmatic. Most of us lack the capability of explaining to our loved ones why we feel as we do.

Currently, it is a 'baby powder war.' It is no more a war than was the war on drugs, the war on poverty, or any of the other 'wars' I listed recently. Yet on the grounds of this non-war, we are turning our society upside down as we endeavor mightily to continue our normal lives. What a schizophrenic joke. So, bide your time; know history in order to preserve constitutional principles as much as possible, and notwithstanding, support your government and fellow Americans as best you can in spite of all the seeming incongruities. It will work out. Right will always triumph if might and right are on the same side. In the circumstances we now find ourselves, we now are in the very beginning of a war in which as Americans, we are not only right but have the requisite might. I know you think that these acts of terrorism will soon be over. They will not be over in my lifetime nor, I suspect, in yours either. This, I believe is an era of history that will consume several generations before the world again finds the path to a lasting peace. It has the connotations of a religious war involving three of the world's principal religious beliefs. That, I know, is difficult to accept. As I type this to you, it is easy to discern the beginning of a much larger arena of war as I read of the inflamed passions throughout the Arab world, fanned by fanatic mullahs who incessantly call for "jihad" against the Infidel American Satans. In the next year I think we may well see anti--American riots in every country in the Arab World as well as calls for a 100% complete oil embargo to cause our American economy to topple. I suspect that this statement will be considered an alarmist, paranoid thought.

We have torn up Afghanistan better than the Russians, at lesser cost and with weaponry which the Russians neither had nor could afford. Our goals are more limited in scope than those of Russia. Finally, it should be noted that this is a fight in progress. It promises to be a much more complex and time consuming conflict than it now appears. So be prepared for a long and bumpy ride!

Over the past forty years I have thought many times, as you and your brother grew into maturity, I should attempt to convey to you the safe and secure world you live in probably would not last. But I am neither prescient nor a prophet. Perhaps I was wrong in my gut instincts. If so, how would it help to pass my nagging doubts onto your shoulders as they might never come to pass? In the light of September 11, my thinking has changed. I should have done so many years ago.

Love, your dad,   Maury Siskel, Jr   E-mail 9 March 2002

Above.. These wounded soldiers, huddled around a stove, all show their own 'face of war.' They had all been held by the enemy until rescued. Below.   This medic has done all he can for the wounded G.I. The chaplain is standing by if needed, to perform the last rites.

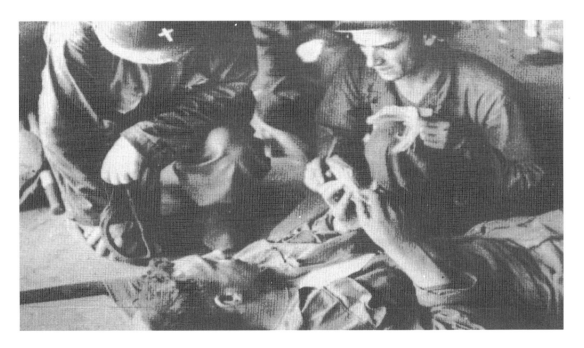

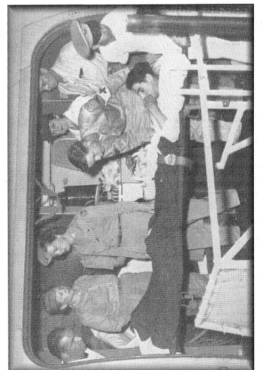

Right. A column of Infantry moves forward in their constant search for the enemy. Then their job becomes very serious.

Lower Right. A determined jeep driver hauls his POW passengers to a rear area, while a buddy keeps a sharp eye on them. It looks like one of them has had some first aid for a hole in the chest. His expression shows he is still feeling some pain.

Below. This wounded G. I. has made it back far enough to get loaded on an airplane. He is now in the good hands of medics and nurses and will soon be in a hospital in Japan. His chances look pretty good. Photos from Archives Internet.

RED DRAGON
The SECOND ROUND
FACES OF WAR II

Thomas	F.	Marker		RA 13 281 295
First Name	MI	Last Name		Serial Number
Tom	1561	10 January 1927		Corporal
Nickname	MOS	Birthday	Grade / Rank	
Hvy Mortar Co 31st Inf Regt		18Sept1950-12 Dec 1950		Deptford Twnship, NJ
Unit (s)		Duty Tour(s) in Korea		Home Town

Distinguished Service Cross Purple Heart Medal Good Conduct Medal   KCSM,2 stars
Medals & Awards
Combat Infantry Badge   Occupation Medal-Japan   NDS Medal   UN Medal   KWS Medal

FLASHBACK

Editorial note: Corporal Thomas F. Marker was a badly wounded survivor of Task Force Faith who managed to cross the ice of the Chosin to reach Marine Corps positions at Hagaru-ri. The previous day a Chinese 120mm mortar round had killed his platoon leader, 1st Lt James R. Grist, Gunnery Officer HM/31/7, who stood less than three feet in front of Marker. Lt Grist took the full effect of the blast, partially shielding Marker. Marker was hit on the right side of the face, losing his right eye. He suffered severe facial lacerations as well as several non-disabling shrapnel wounds but was still ambulatory. On his trip across the reservoir, he had fallen through a weak spot in the ice, just above his knees. He was able to pull himself out and continue toward Marine Corps positions. He attributes his ability to continue to the cold wind which dried his pant legs sufficiently that he could knock the ice off. The exercise of walking warmed him with enough body heat, though suffering severe frost bite, to yet move about. Arriving in Hagaru-ri, he was drafted into a Marine Corps ammo detail carrying ammo to East Hill. Each man toted two 500 round metal boxes of machine gun ammo, one in each hand. He was air evacuated from Hagaru-ri the day after his encounter with General Almond and Lt Haig.

General Alexander Haig,

November 16, 2002

My name is Thomas F. Marker, Sr. I live in Deptford Township, NJ. I was watching the Fox News channel anchored by Rita Cosby. You were her guest and had been asked to comment on the upcoming war with Iraq. I have not seen you personally for fifty two years, and was very pleased to see you looking so well. For a man of your years you did not drool or mumble. (Ha Ha!) At the end of the show you mentioned you had fought at the Chosin Reservoir in North Korea in 1950. A long forgotten memory kicked in. I was standing at attention in front of General Edward M. Almond and 1st Lt Alexander Haig. I was the only soldier in a long file of Marines, each of us carrying two boxes of .30 cal machine gun ammo to East Hill.

I heard the General tell the driver to stop. He got out of the jeep,motioning with his hand for me to come to him. He had two stars on his fur cap. I stood in front of him, putting down the ammo cans so I could salute. He asked, "Where is your parka? I told him I was one of the few survivors of Task Force Faith from the east shore of the Chosin Reservoir, adding the Army never issued winter clothing to us even though the temperature dropped to forty two degrees below zero at night." All the Marines in the ammo detail remained at a halt, waiting to see what was going to happen to me. All the Marines had big parkas and other winter clothing for upper and lower body. My right eye was covered with a bloody rag. I had shrapnel wounds on my face. I wore a steel helmet instead of a fur hat. A mortar shell the day before had exploded in front of me, then later I had gone through the reservoir ice up to my knees.

I was covered with some ice still on my legs up to my knees and my uniform clothing was all torn up from the blast. General Almond said to you, "Get a DSC medal out of your map case." He took off the big warm parka he was wearing, and told me, Put it on. He then pinned the medal on me and said, "When you get back from East Hill, go to the airstrip to be flown out to a hospital in Japan." Later that day when I came to the airstrip, my platoon officer, Lt Jerome McCabe who was from Baltimore, Maryland, and who was himself wounded in the shoulder, helped me to get up and into the plane. Lt McCabe is still alive and has retired as a Colonel of the US Army. To shorten a long story, I just wondered if you remembered the good deed that General Almond did that day? Also, I want to wish you and your family Happy Holidays.

Your friend,

s/ Cpl Tom Marker
PS: You look almost as handsome as me, but thats the way the mop flops! (HaHa!

Thomas	F.	Marker	RA 13 281 295
First Name	MI	Last Name	Serial Number
Tom	1561	10 January 1927	Corporal
Nickname	MOS	Birthday	Grade / Rank
Hvy Mortar Co 31st Infantry Regt		18 Sept 1950- 12 Dec 1950	Deptford Township, NJ
Unit (s)		Duty Tour(s) in Korea	Home Town

Distinguished Service Cross Purple Heart Medal Good Conduct Medal Combat Infantry Badge

Medals & Awards

Occupation Medal-Japan National Defense Service Medal Korean Campaign Svc Medal, 2 stars

A MEMORY RECALLED

Office of
Alexander M. Haig, Jr.
March 24, 2003

Mr. Thomas F. Marker
P. O. Box 5061
Deptford, NJ 08096-5061

Dear Tom,

Thank you for your letter of November 16 which recalled our meeting at the Chosin Reservoir in 1950. I was and remain very familiar with Task Force Faith and its heroic fighting along with the U.S. Marine Corps.

As you may know General Ned Almond held LTC Faith in the highest regard and was badly shaken at his loss. Actually, General Almond made herculean efforts to relieve the Task Force with nearby Marine Corps reinforcements but was unable to do so because of the enemy attacks against the 1st Marine Division.

I do recall the incident you described in your letter and was heartened by the fact that you recalled the incident so vividly. The air evacuation General Almond set up apparently saved your life. He also made the decision to withdraw almost 100,000 North Korean citizens to freedom in the South. General Almond's bravery was never in question, although it was seldom recounted in post mortems of the conflict.

I was also delighted to learn that you survived it all and apparently still retain the feisty edge you demonstrated at the Frozen Chosin. My very best wishes to you and yours. You are a true American hero.

Sincerely,
S\ Al Haig
T\Alexander M. Haig, Jr.

Editorial comment: Cpl Tom Marker spent 6 months in a military hospital in Sendai, Japan before being sent home to the USA to complete his recuperation. Loss of his right eye prevented continuation of the military career he had planned. While at Sendai, he was located by Mrs James Grist, who, as a military wife, had remained in military quarters in Japan while her husband was fighting in Korea. In her visit, she told him she had learned from others that I was in very close proximity to her husband at the time of his death. It was only after several urgent pleas from Mrs Grist that he divulged the facts of his officer's death. Both wept in common grief at their loss. Cpl Marker told me it remains as probably the saddest moment of his life.

Above. Wounded GIs lie on litters and wait for treatment and evacuation to the rear.   Right. An LST transports these wounded GIs to a hospital ship off shore.   Below The Navy performs the final rites for one of their own.   Below Right. The Infantry still in pursuit of their elusive foe, somewhere in those forbidding mountains. Photos from National Archives

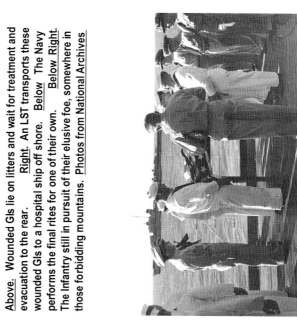

440

POETRY PENNED BY SOLDIERS IS AS DIFFERENT AS THE FACES OF MEN IN THE RANKS. AN AMERICAN ARMY IS COMPOSED OF ALL THE DIVERSE ETHNIC GROUPS OF AMERICAN SOCIETY. IN THE MAKING OF MILITARY DISCIPLINE, AS THE LEGENDARY PHOENIX ROSE FROM ITS OWN ASHES, A SPIRITUAL BOND OF COMRADESHIP IS BORN WHICH REFLECTS A SOLDIERLY PRIDE.

'MILITARY' POETRY EXPRESSES THE FEELINGS AND EMOTIONS, THE FEARS, SENSIBILITIES AND YEARNINGS FOR HEARTH AND HOME IN THE MINDS OF YOUNG MEN EXISTING IN THE CAULDRON OF WAR. WAR FROM TIME IMMEMORIAL HAS ALWAYS BEEN FOUGHT BY YOUNG MEN IN THE FLOWER OF YOUTH. THEY ARE THE ONLY ONES WITH THE STAMINA TO ENDURE THE EXIGENCIES OF COMBAT. AMERICA IS FORTUNATE THAT OUR NATIONAL BACKGROUND OF INDIVIDUAL FREEDOM HAS ENDOWED OUR YOUNG CITIZENRY WITH THE CAPABILITIES TO MAINTAIN OUR NATIONAL FREEDOM OVER THE GENERATIONS.

A SOLDIER'S PRAYER

Look, God
I have never spoken to you
But now I want to say,
"How do You do!"

You see God,
I was told You did not exist,
And like a fool,
I believed all of this.

Last night from a shell hole
I saw your sky,
I figured right then
I had been told a lie.

I wonder, God
If you will shake my hand,
Somehow I feel
That you will understand.

Strange, I had to come
To this hellish place,
Before I had time
To see your face.

Well, I guess there isn't
Much more to say,
But I am sure glad, God
That I met you today.

I guess the zero hour
Will soon be here,
But I am not afraid
Since I know You are near.

I hear the signal, well God,
I will have to go,
I KNOW I love You lots
This I want you to know.

Looks like this will be
A horrible fight,
Who knows, to your house
I may come tonight.

Though I wasn't friendly
With You before,
I wonder, God
Would you wait at the door?

Look, I am crying!
Me, a soldier! shedding tears!
I wish I had known you
These past many years.

Well, I have to go now, God
Goodbye.
Strange, since I have met you
I am no longer afraid to die.

.......author unknown. The poem was found on the body of a nineteen year old American soldier.

SOLDIER

I WAS WHAT OTHERS DID NOT WANT TO BE
I WENT WHERE OTHERS FEARED TO GO
AND DID WHAT OTHERS FAILED TO DO

I ASKED NOTHING FROM THOSE WHO GAVE
NOTHING, ACCEPTING THE THOUGHT OF
ETERNAL LONELINESS SHOULD I FAIL.

I HAVE FELT THE FACE OF TERROR
FELT THE STINGING COLD OF FEAR
ENJOYED THE SWEET
TASTE OF A MOMENT'S LOVE

I HAVE CRIED IN PAIN AND HOPE
BUT MOST OF ALL, I HAVE LIVED
TIMES OTHERS SAY ARE BEST FORGOTTEN.

BUT TODAY, IN THE VAULT OF MY MEMORY,
I AM PROUD OF WHAT I WAS,
A SOLDIER.

IT IS THE SOLDIER, NOT THE POET
WHO HAS GIVEN US
FREEDOM OF SPEECH.

.................Charles M. Province

MARINES AND SOLDIERS OF WORLD WAR II AND KOREA HELD A COMMON BOND IN THEIR ANTIPATHY FOR C-RATIONS, AND A MUTUAL LOVE FOR THE M-1 GARAND RIFLE. "TAKE CARE OF IT AND IT WILL TAKE CARE OF YOU," WAS INDELIBLY IMPRESSED ON EVERY RECRUIT. INSTRUCTORS WERE GENERALLY SILENT ON THE SUBJECT OF C-RATIONS. THAT CAN OF WORMS WAS BEST LEFT UNOPENED UNTIL OVERSEAS. THERE, HUNGER AND THE 'CHURCH KEY'– A UTILITY CAN OPENER, USUALLY ATTACHED ALONG WITH HIS DOG TAGS TO A NECK CHAIN– INITIATED a SOLDIER TO THE ERSATZ FOODS OF THE QM DEPARTMENT'S ' LOWEST BID' CONTRACTORS.

C-RATIONS
.....................Robert A. Gannon

JOHNNY REB SANG THE PRAISE
0F EATING GOOBER PEAS,
BUT AS HIS MODERN COUNTERPART
I'LL SING THE PRAISE OF C'S.

LUSCIOUS MORSELS ENCLOSED
IN CANS OF BLACK AND GREEN,
THEY GRACED THE DINNER TABLE
OF MANY A MARINE.

OF COURSE, I DIDN'T LIKE THEM
WHEN I WAS IN THE CORPS,
THEY HAVEN'T SEEN MY MESSKIT
IN THIRTY YEARS OR MORE.

FOR AT A BUSINESS LUNCHEON
WE VERY OFTEN DINE ON LOBSTER,
STEAK AND MUSHROOMS
WITH A CRYSTAL GLASS OF WINE.

AND IT'S TRUE THAT SUCH A REPAST
IS FIT TO SERVE THE TABLE OF A KING
BUT AS FOR TRIM AND A SNAPPY
IT DOESN'T DO A THING.

I LOOK AROUND THE FESTIVE BOARD
AND SOMEHOW SLIP AWAY,
TO A TIME WHEN LIFE WAS BETTER
THAN IT SEEMS TODAY.

MY MEMORY CAN CONJURE UP MOST
ANY SCENE I PLEASE,
BUT THE ONE I SEE MOST OFTEN
IS AN OPEN CAN OF C'S.

THE FACES GATHERED AROUND IT
ARE YOUNG, AND HARD, AND LEAN.
FOR ONE PRECIOUS MOMENT
I CALL MYSELF "MARINE."

WE'D SWAP, TRADE AND CRITICIZE
EACH GRUDGING LITTLE BITE,
AND BORROWING FRUIT COCKTAIL
\WOULD SURELY START A FIGHT.

WE ATE THEM IN THE BROILING SUN
IN COLD AND RAINY WEATHER,
IF THERE WASN'T ENOUGH FOR ALL
WE SHARED THEM ALL TOGETHER.

WE NEVER HAD TOO MUCH OF WHAT
THE WORLD CALLS WEALTH,
BUT WE COULD TWIST A TIGER'S TAIL
AS WE BRIMMED AGLOW IN HEALTH.

I WOULD TRADE MY GOURMET FARE
AND ALL THE LINEN NAPERIES,
FOR THE LOYAL FRIENDS AND PRIDE
I HAD WHEN I WAS EATING C'S.

.................Robert A. Gannon

M-1 RIFLE

DO YOU WONDER WHY THAT RIFLE
IS HANGING IN MY DEN?
YOU KNOW I RARELY TAKE IT DOWN
BUT I TOUCH IT NOW AND THEN.

IT'S RATHER SLOW AND HEAVY
BY STANDARDS OF TODAY,
BUT NOT TOO MANY YEARS AGO
IT SWEPT THE ENEMY AWAY.

IT HAS HELD ITS OWN IN BATTLES
THROUGH SNOW, IN RAIN AND SUN
I HAD ONE JUST LIKE IT
THIS TREASURED OLD M-1

IT WENT ASHORE AT BOUGAINVILLE
IN NINETEEN FORTY THREE,
IT STORMED THE BEACH
THROUGH BULLET RIDDLED SEAS.

SAIPAN KNEW ITS STRIDENT BARK
KWAJALEIN FELT ITS STING,
THE ROCKY CAVES OF PELELIU
RESOUNDED WITH ITS RING.

IT CLIMBED THE HILL ON IWO
WITH MEN WHO WOULD NOT STOP
AND LEFT ITS BANNER
FLYING AT ITS TOP.

WELL, TIME MOVES ON
AND THINGS IMPROVE,
WITH RIFLES AND WITH MEN.
AND THAT IS WHY THE TWO OF US
ARE SITTING IN MY DEN.

BUT SOMETIMES ON A WINTRY NIGHT
WHILE THINKING OF MY CORPS
I CANNOT HELP BUT REFLECT THAT IF
THE BUGLES WERE ONCE MORE TO BLOW
WE WOULD A TEAM BE ONCE MORE.
[M-1rifle- Gas operated,firing an 8 round clip]
A BEAUTY OF THE GUNSMITH'S ART.....Ed]

TAPS

DAY IS DONE. GONE THE SUN FROM
THE LAKES THE HILLS, THE SKY
ALL IS WELL, SAFELY REST
GOD IS NIGH.
FADING LIGHT DIMS THE SIGHT
AND A STAR GEMS THE NIGHT
GLEAMING BRIGHT FROM AFAR
DRAWING NIGH, FALLS THE NIGHT.
THANKS AND PRAISE FOR OUR DAYS
NEATH THE SUN, NEATH THE STARS
AS WE GO, THIS WE KNOW
GOD IS NIGH.
.....ORIGINAL VERSION

TAPS

THERE WILL BE A GREAT ENCAMPMENT
IN A LAND ABOVE THE CLOUDS TODAY
THERE IS A MINGLING AND A MERGING
OF OUR BOYS WHO HAVE GONE AWAY
THO' ON EARTH THEY ARE DISBANDING
THEY ARE VERY CLOSE AND NEAR
THOSE BRAVE AND HONORED HEROES
SHOW NO SORROW, SHED NO TEAR
THEY HAVE LIVED A LIFE OF GLORY
HISTORY PINS THEIR MEDALS HIGH
LISTEN TO THE THUNDER ROLLING
THEY ARE MARCHING IN THE SKY.
.......ARTHUR NOTTINGHAM CHAPPUS

ODE TO A VETERAN

I CANNOT WRITE WITH A POET'S FLAIR
AND WHEN I PASS ON, NO ONE WILL CARE
BUT AS LONG AS I BREATHE AND LIVE
I SING THE PRAISES OF THOSE WHO GIVE
THOSE WHO SERVED OUR COUNTRY TRUE
ARE ENTITLED TO THEIR RIGHTFUL DUE
FOR THOSE WHO SACRIFICE FOR THE CAUSE
LET US HONOR, PRAISE AND GIVE SALUTE
TO THE MEN WHO WEAR THEIR NATION'S SUIT
WHETHER OLIVE DRAB OR NAVY BLUE
MARINES AND AIRMEN, I SPEAK ALSO OF YOU
TO ALL MEN WHOSE HEARTS WERE TRUE
PATRIOTS, WE THANK YOU, ONE AND ALL
FOR ANSWERING YOUR COUNTRY'S CALL.
.................................HARRY JOE EVANS

AS AN OUTFIT CLIPS OFF THE MILES IN A LONG MARCH TO A NEW OBJECTIVE, AN INFANTRYMAN NEEDS TO THINK OF SOMETHING OTHER THAN SORE FEET AND PROBABLE RECEPTION AT HIS DESTINATION. THIS IS THE WAY ONE MARINE KEPT FOCUS ON THE PRESENT---BY NOT ANTICIPATING THE FUTURE.

PACKS

SLOGGING THRU' THE BOONDOCKS
BEHIND YOUR BUDDY'S BACK

YOU GET TO RUMINATING
ON THE CONTENTS OF HIS PACK

YOU KNOW HE'S LUGGING ITEMS
VERY MUCH THE SAME AS YOU
BUT IN A LITLE CORNER
THERE'S A PRIVATE THING OR TWO.

A D ECK OF CARDS, A PICTURE,
A SPECIAL TREAT FROM HOME,
A NOTE THAT SAYS I LOVE YOU,
A TOOTHBRUSH OR A COMB.

AN INEXPENSIVE SOUVENIR
A LOCK OF GOLDEN HAIR,
A PAPERBACK OF POETRY,
A BOOK OF COMMON PRAYER.

I THINK MARINES RESEMBLE
THOSE CANVAS PACKS THEY WEAR.
EXTERNALLY, THEY ALL LOOK ALIKE
BUT A DIFFERENCE IS THERE.

THEY MAY HAVE DIFFERENT VALUES
AND COME FROM VARIED PLACES.
THEY DIFFER IN RELIGION
AND BELONG TO DIFFERENT RACES.

SOME DO THEIR JOB WITH RIFLES
WHILE OTHERS USE A TANK.
SOME LEAD OR FOLLOW READILY
DEPENDING ON THEIR RANK.

BUT ALL ARE TRAINED AS WINNERS
IN ANYTHING THEY DO
FROM FIRE TEAM TO TYPIST
OR IN A CHOPPER CREW.

ON BEACHES HOT WITH BATTLE
OR PLAYING JUST A GAME
THEIR DOUGHTY FIGHTING SPIRIT
IS REALLY QUITE THE SAME.

THEY NEVER THINK ABOUT ODDS
OR HOW THE BETTING LEANS.
THEY JUST GO IN AND WIN IT
BECAUSE THEY ARE MARINES.

IF A WOMAN GOES TO WAR

THERE ARE NO THOUGHTS OF GLORY
        WHEN A WOMAN GOES TO WAR
THERE ARE NO SOARING ANTHEMS
        TELLING WHAT SHE'S SERVING FOR
HER THOUGHTS ARE NOT OF VALOR
        OR OF BATTLES WON OR LOST
BUT OF THE HUMAN SUFFERING
        THAT IS A BATTLE'S COST
SHE DOES NOT SEE A CONFLICT
        AS A MILITARY GAIN
BUT LOOKS ON ITS AFTERMATH
        OF HORROR, DEATH, AND PAIN
SHE HAS NO GRAND ILLUSIONS
        OF WHAT HER ROLE IS FOR
BUT WORKS AND PRAYS WITH ALL HER HEART
        TO BRING AN END TO WAR
SO IT HAS BEEN THROUGH HISTORY
        AND WILL BE, WITHOUT CEASE
A MAN MAY FIGHT FOR GLORY
        BUT A WOMAN FIGHTS FOR PEACE.

THE OLD MAN

HE KNELT AND BOWED HIS HEAD
BESIDE THE TORN AND SILENT DEAD
BATTLE SMOKE STILL LINGERED WHERE
HE TOUCHED THE BLOODY, MATTED HAIR.
A SHATTERED HELMET LAY BESIDE
THE FALLEN FIGHTER WHERE HE DIED
AND ON THAT LITTERED BATTLE FIELD
HIS SENSES CHURNED AND REELED
SO MANY TIMES HE'D SEEN BEFORE
THIS SENSELESS LEGACY OF WAR
WHERE PAIN, BLOOD AND LONELY DEATH
WERE COMMON AS A SUDDEN BREATH
HE PRAYED THAT HE MIGHT LIVE TO SEE
HIS NATIVE LAND WHERE MEN WERE FREE
SO HE COULD TELL THE BRUTAL STORY
OF MEN WHO DIED IN PRIDE AND GLORY
HE DID NOT PRAY FOR ENDLESS YEARS
TO CALM HIS HEART OR DRY HIS TEARS
JUST LONG ENOUGH FOR HIM TO NOTE
WHEN HE'D BE OLD ENOUGH TO VOTE.

VERSE USED BY PERMISSION OF THE AUTHOR, ROBERT A. GANNON   FROM *THE LAUGHTER AND THE TEARS*© 1997

"THEY ALSO SERVE WHO ONLY STAND AND WAIT.".........JOHN MILTON, 1608-1674   SONNET XV , "ON HIS BLINDNESS."

THERE ARE AT LEAST A DOZEN DIFFERENT KOREAN WAR VERSIONS OF MAJOR HENRY J. LIVINGSTON'S [1748-1828] CLASSIC *'TWAS THE NIGHT BEFORE CHRISTMAS.* IF MEMORY SERVES, THE INFANTRY VERSION WAS PRINTED SOMETIME IN 1951, IN "THE BAYONET," WEEKLY NEWS SHEET OF THE 7TH INFANTRY DIVISION. THE POEM, FAMILIAR TO ALL, WAS A NATURAL VEHICLE FOR SOLDIER POETS TO USE IN IRONIC PARODY OF THE KOREAN YULETIDE SEEN THROUGH EYES OF GIs SERVING IN KOREA.

KOREAN CHRISTMAS CAROL

DOGFACE VERSION

'Twas the night before Christmas, and all through the tent,
W as the odor of fuel oil, the stove pipe being bent.
Worn and wet boots were hung by the oil stove with care,
In hope that QM Santa would issue each man a new pair.
The weary GIs were sacked out in their homemade beds,
With visions of sugar babes dancing in their heads.
But up on the ridge line began a noisy and loud clatter,
A Chinese machine gun started an ominous chatter.

I rushed to my rifle and threw back the bolt,
The rest of my tent mates awoke with a jolt.
Outside we could hear Platoon Sergeant Kelly,
He was an old Army man with a little pot belly.
Come Yancey and Clancy, come Connors and Nixon,
Up Miller, Up Shiller, Up Dunder and Blixen.
We tumbled outside in hurried mass confusion,
So damn cold each man required a transfusion.

Get up on that hilltop there and silence that pesky Red
And don't come back until you're sure he is stone dead.
Then putting his thumb in front of his red nose,
He took leave of all his cold and shivering GI Joes.
But we all heard him say, in a voice so merry and light
Merry Christmas to one and all.
May you live through the night!
...............................Contributed by Lulan E. Gregg 8076 MASH

KOREAN CHRISTMAS CAROL

REDLEG VERSION

'Twas the night before Christmas, all through the bunker
Hung the sickening odor of fuel oil, hanging heavy in the air.
GI Shoe-Pacs had been hung by the oil stove with great care,
In hopes Santa had boots and would leave a new pair.
Weary 'redlegs' were sacked out in their hard bunker beds.
They had visions of luscious Hollywood starlet sugar babes,

Dancing, dancing around hopefully, in their fevered heads.
Then about midnight on my watch, the bunker phone rang
A distant gun in gooney land echoed with a colossal bang.

I clamped on my steel pot, jumped into cold boots,
Yelled to my buddies, it is time for us to go shoot.
Outside we could hear FDC Chief, CWO Officer Maxxon,
Getting quick shooting orders from Captain Hanson.
Come Jansky and Chamski, come Donners and Bonnors,
Up with Killer and Diller, Up with Dixon and Nixon.
Get on your guns, set your fuses, make it charge five,
Blast those damn Reds, don't leave one of them alive.

Then, CWO Maxxon did spryly leap into his idling jeep,
Orders home held in his hand, he'd been here 52 weeks.
Making like Santa, he roared in voice jolly and gay,
His finger to his nose, in a parade ground sort of way,
Merry Christmas, one and all, may you live through your stay!
......*With apologies to Arny Anderson B Battery 96th FA Bn*

QUIET HEROES

Although you walk among us
We hardly know you are there.
Because you've lived a part of life
That we can never share.

Yet there are times and feelings
When our lives are in touch.
Those quiet, private moments
That seem to matter much.

We sense the pride within you
When the flag is on parade.
We see your sad and haunted eyes
When Taps is played.

We know you've faced the horrors
That we can't understand.
And gave your youth for freedom
to protect our sacred land.

From Valley Forge to Trenton
From Shiloh to Bull Run.
From Manila Bay to Cuba
From Haiti to Verdun.

From South Pacific islands
To European snow.
The story of your glory
Was quick to spread and glow.

From frozen mountain ridges
To beaches rich with palm.
From the skies above Korea
To the jungles of Vietnam.

From the island of Grenada
The list goes on and on.
To the city streets of Panama
And bloody Lebanon.

You charged across a desert
Ruled by violence and hate.
Bringing blessed independence
To the people of Kuwait.

So, although we may not say it
We hope you know it is true.
That each time we see Old Glory
We're looking straight at you.

Another excerpt from
The Laughter and The Tears

Robert A. Gannon VMA 132 USMC
Korea 1952-1953

In the halcyon days of Selective Service, every draftee was given an intelligence and skills aptitude test on arrival at the induction center. These tests were used to assign men to various service branches. Those with prior skills, knowledge or "innate" potential ended up in such technically oriented branches as the Signal Corps, Chemical Warfare Service or Ordnance Department. In such a system, Infantry manpower quotas were often filled with men who did not 'fit' the IQ slots determined by the Binet and Inkblot psychologists of that era. Thankfully, the fallibility of those procedures contributed to the long term vigor of the infantry. Many men of high IQ escaped the dragnet set by the 'shrinks' to become leaders in the infantry, that branch of military service often termed the "Queen of Battles." Poetry, one of the fine arts of the English language, is well represented in these pages by Donald A. Chase, a thrice wounded infantry soldier of the Korean War. His poetry reflects the many facets of an infantryman's war.

Infantryman

The attack would commence at the break of day
All of us involved knew it was time to pray.
No more false bravado, voices became subdued or still
Thoughts full of consequences in taking an enemy held hill.

Four grenades per man, two extra M 1 bandoliers
This was the outer load we carried, along with inner fears.
Daylight was still dawning as we approached the jump off line
Heartbeats increasing in tempo, nerves on edge were easy to find.

Supporting tanks fire on the hilltop, enemy shells begin to fall
The waiting time for orders is over, time to heed our leaders call.
We advance in skirmish line formation, pressing forward in attack
Casualties rise in number, but no thought is given to turning back.

Then in one final surge, enemy positions are at last overrun
For the lifeless bodies still in place, nothing can be done.
Another battle is over, we all knew there would be more
Pause, regroup, move out, the infantryman's only lot in war.

Darkness Brought Death

Each time the daylight faded, and darkness filled the sky
The waiting would begin, for the night to hurry by.
Darkness was the time the enemy chose to strike
Knowing eyes grow weary as they strain to pierce the night.

There was little sound or movement, weather took its toll
Bodies ached and stiffened from winter's bitter cold.
Hours slowly passed, all senses were fatigued
Endurance has its limits, sleep was the crying need.

Suddenly, with no warning, flames and thunder rock the scene
Shells and bullets hit their targets, the night is rent with screams.
Man made moonbeams lit the sky, flares added their glow
Shadows twisted and danced as in some weird picture show.

Chattering machine guns sang their deadly serenade
Shrapnel whined and howled from exploding hand grenades.
From frozen snow filled holes, men would fight to stay alive
Sadly, though some did see the sun rise, many others died.

Fallen Comrades

No matter what I am doing, or where my steps may roam
I think about comrades who never came home.
Many years have passed, but memory hasn't dimmed
A picture in my mind still clings and lies within.

I see their unlined faces which never grow old
The shy, timid, ones and also those so bold.
Still I hear their youthful banter, brightening a dreary day
Keeping all his fears inside, each one in a different way.

Yet all did their duty, as good soldiers do so well
Existing under conditions that oft' times were sheer hell.
I remember sharing rations and the packages of wives
This generosity of spirit in them was always alive.

All of this stays within me, ever turning in my mind
Faces drifting pass my eyes, of another time and place
Many times have I wondered, why them instead of me?
Perhaps in some future world, I'll be allowed to see.

Veterans

Whenever our country has gone to war
There comes forth a special breed
Of men and women from all walks of life
To serve their country in the hour of need.

Like the minutemen of old, they rallied
To defend our flag 'round the world.
And even today, though aged and gray
Stand tall when our nation's banners unfurl.

There are tears for departed comrades
Whose bodies lie far and wide
Yet always remembered down the years
So in a sense they still walk side by side.

Those men and women are veterans
Whose bodies carry scars of many a fight
Some outside, but mostly on the inside
In defense of our nation's birthright.

..............DONALD A. CHASE

IT IS AN EXERCISE IN IRRELEVANCY TO SAY THAT WAR AFFECTS EVERY INDIVIDUAL INVOLVED. HOWEVER, THE EFFECT OF WAR ON THOSE WHO FIGHT SIDE BY SIDE, CAN BE STRIKINGLY DIFFERENT. HERE, SOME DIFFERENT PERSPECTIVES.

AN AWAKENING

I thought it was grand,
This shiny weapon in my hand,
Its range was long , its aim was true,
It had the power to pass through
Any fleshy barrier in its way
................Jerome A. Konsker

I was still but nineteen that day,
When it did then become abhorrent
To flood my brain with a torrent of
Images, or to make sense of any kind,
Of the turmoil racing through my mind.
L/32/7 KOREA 1953

No, it crawled in on hands and knees
Each time I held and slowly squeezed
A round into the night, at a target
Whose unseen face won't let me forget
The horror of what I have done.
I wish never to use another gun.

AT THE KOREAN WAR MEMORIAL

Once I went to visit a war. To serve a cause I knew not why.
I arrived to find men who, unknowingly, came here to die.
They lay on cold, damp ground, Motionless, not a sound.

And I still did not understand what I was to do in this land.
Some will say "You were just a lad." That makes it more sad,
Those faces staring up at me, not destined evermore to see,
If their sacrifice and pain had been a mission made in vain.

History sometimes provides reasons,
although blurred by the passage of seasons.
I stand here, with my eyes full of tears,
My mind chaotic with mem'ries not blunted by the years.
Hoping, the silent bronze patrol might hear a man, holding
The hand of his son, thanking them for what they had done.
....Jerome A. Konsker L/32/7 Korea 1953

WAR'S LEGACY

FROM BOYHOOD TO ADULTHOOD CHANGES TAKE PLACE
BUT THE SCARS OF WAR ARE NEVER ERASED
WHEN YOU ANSWER THE CALL TO BECOME PART OF THE FIGHT
THEN YOU LEARN OF WAR'S HORROR AND ALL ITS FRIGHT.

HOW SHELLS CRASH DOWN WITH SPINE CHILLING SOUND
YOU CROUCH IN FEAR IN A HOLE YOU DUG IN THE GROUND
HOW BULLET AND SHELL ZING AND WHISTLE PAST
HOW A FRIEND SLUMPS DOWN AND BREATHES HIS LAST.

THE ENEMY SOLDIER, JUST ANOTHER MAN
DOING HIS DUTY AS BEST HE CAN
NO GLORY EXISTS, AND GRUESOME SIGHTS SEEN
HAUNT ME FOREVER TO BECOME PART OF MY DREAMS.

WHEN AT LAST IT IS OVER AND YOU SAIL FOR HOME
YOU CARRY SCARS THAT ARE YOURS ALONE
SCARS ON THE OUTSIDE, EASY TO FIND
SCARS INSIDE, ETCHED DEEP IN THE MIND.

THE YEARS PASS BY AND SOME MEMORIES DO FADE
BUT THOUGHTS STILL TURN TO THE FRIENDS YOU MADE
TO THOSE WHO SURVIVED IT AND TO THOSE CUT DOWN
WHO TODAY REST QUIETLY IN THEIR SPOT IN THE GROUND.

REMINISCENCE

WE CLIMBED THE HILL IN SILENCE
LISTENING TO THE SOUNDS OF WAR
EACH IN HIS OWN WAY AND MANNER
TRYING TO GET READY FOR WHAT IS IN STORE..

ALL HEARTBEATS START TO QUICKEN
THINKING OF WHAT COULD GO WRONG
WHEN SHELLS AND BULLETS START TO SING
THEIR ALWAYS DEADLY, OFTEN FATAL SONG.

WE'VE HEARD THIS SONG OF DEATH BEFORE
FOR MAN A NIGHT AND MANY A DAY
FORTUNATE INDEED THOSE AMONG US
WHO WERE ABLE TO WALK AWAY.

THE SIGHTS AND SCENES ENCOUNTERED
AS LONG DAYS AND NIGHTS WENT BY
LIVE FOREVER DEEP IN YOUR MIND
AND AT ODD TIMES, MAKE YOU CRY.

TIME WILL ERASE ALL WOUNDS, 'TIS SAID
BUT SOMETIMES THAT IS NOT TRUE
FOR WHEN THE WOUNDS ARE DEEP INSIDE
THE BECOME PART OF YOU.

REMEMBER
........................FATHER DENNIS O'BRIEN USMC

It is the veteran, not the reporter,
Who has given us freedom of the press
It was the veteran, not the poet,
Who has given us freedom of speech.

It is the veteran, not the lawyer
who has given us the right to a fair trial.
The veteran, not a campus organizer,
Who gives us the right to demonstrate.

It is the veteran who salutes the flag,
Who served under the flag,
Whose coffin is draped by the flag,
Who allows the protester to burn the flag

TO A FALLEN KOREAN WAR FRIEND.................Richard I. Kirk Lt Col USA Ret

DO NOT WEEP FOR ME, I AM NOT DEAD
AND WEATHER SLAYS THE HEATHER
THEN YOU AND I, AGAIN, AT LAST
SHALL ONCE MORE BE TOGETHER.

BUT WHEN THE MEMORY IS PAST
THERE IS NO LAST DYING EMBER
I SHALL LIVE WITH YOU MY FRIEND
SO LONG AS YOU REMEMBER.

MOTHERS OF THE CORPS

WE'D BUILT A FIRE TO HEAT A POT OF JOE
THE GROUND AROUND WAS FROST BOUND
THE AIR WAS KISSED WITH SNOW
FAINTLY IN THE DISTANCE
WE COULD HEAR THE RUMBLING GUNS.
BUT NOW WE ARE SAFE BEHIND THE LINES.

FOR NOW, WE, THE LUCKY ONES.
AROUND OUR LITTLE CIRCLE
WERE FACES YOUNG AND OLD
SIPPING CANTEEN CUPS OF COFFEE
AS A GUARD AGAINST THE COLD.

NO ONE SPOKE. WE GLUMLY SAT
THINKING IN ACHING HEARTS
OF COMRADES WHO WERE MISSING.

AND THEN A SERGEANT BY MY SIDE
SAID, GOD, I JUST REMEMBERED
TODAY'S THE BIRTHDAY OF THE CORPS
THE TENTH DAY OF NOVEMBER.

HOW SWIFT OUR THOUGHTS WENT SWIRLING
IN THAT DIM FIRE'S FLICKERING GLOW
ON MENTAL JOURNEYS TO CAMP LEJUENE
AND ON TO PENDLETON AND QUANTICO.

WE DREAMED OF TABLES LADEN
WITH THE VERY BEST OF FOOD
OF LAUGHING GIRLS WITH GOLDEN CURLS
IN HAPPY, FESTIVE, JOYFUL, MOOD.

WE COULD ALMOST HEAR THE MUSIC
FLOATING SOFTLY ON THE NIGHT
AS WE MOVED ACROSS THE DANCE FLOOR
WITH AN ARMFUL OF DELIGHT.

BUT SUCH THINGS ARE FOR DREAMERS
AND WE ARE FIGHTING MEN
OUR THOUGHTS MUST BE ON WHAT IS NOW
NOT WHAT MIGHT HAVE BEEN.

AND SO WE ASKED THE GUNNY
TO SPIN A YARN OR TWO
ABOUT STORIES OF THE CORPS
AND HEROES HE KNEW.

GUNNY GRINNED, STRETCHED HIS LEGS
AND PUT HIS COFFEE DOWN
HIS EYES SEEMED SOMEWHAT DREAMY
AND HIS GRIN BECAME A FROWN.

NO TALE I'LL TELL, GUNNY GROWLED
OF HEROES I'VE KNOWN
LIKE DIAMOND, PULLER, JOEY FOSS
OR JOHNNY BASILONE.

INSTEAD I'LL TELL A STORY
ABOUT TRUE COURAGE I HAVE SEEN
OF THE MOTHERS OF YOUNG MARINES.

"A DOZEN TIMES I'VE SAILED AWAY
AND LEFT THEM ON THE SHORE
WATCHING PROUDLY, FEARFULLY
AS THEIR SONS WENT OFF TO WAR.

"YOU THINK YOU'RE TOUGH," HE SAID,
"SO YOUR WAYS ARE WILD AND HARD
WELL, MAYBE SO, BUT BACK AT HOME
TO HER, YOU'RE JUST A CHILD.

"JUST STOP AND THINK A MINUTE
OF WHAT HER LIFE MUST BE
WHILE SHE IS WAITING SAFE AT HOME
AND YOU ARE ACROSS THE SEA.

"EVERY TIME THE PHONE RINGS
SHE HOPES IT MIGHT BE YOU
THO' IN HER HEART SHE SADLY KNOWS
THAT DREAM JUST CAN'T COME TRUE.

"AND EVERY TIME A LETTER COMES
SHE READS BETWEEN THE LINES
WONDERING HOW YOU REALLY ARE
THO' YOU SAY YOU'RE DOING FINE.

"BUT STILL SHE HAS A JOB TO DO
SHE HAS A HOME TO RUN
ALTHOUGH HER WORLD IS TORN APART
AND SHE'S FRIGHTENED FOR HER SON.

"SO SHE KEEPS ON SMILING BRAVELY
WHILE COVERING HER FRIGHT
AND ONLY LETS HER LONELY TEARS
SLIP SOFTLY OUT AT NIGHT."

THE GUNNY PAUSED. NOBODY SPOKE
AND IN THE FIRE'S GLOW
WE WATCHED THE PALE ICE CRYSTALS
OF THE SOFTLY FALLING SNOW.

"MEN," HE SAID, "THE TIME HAS COME
FOR US TO DRINK A TOAST
WITH OTHERS OF OUR BROTHERHOOD
WHO SERVE FROM COAST TO COAST.

AND I PROPOSE, THIS SOLEMN NIGHT
THAT WE LIFT OUR CUP OF CHEER
TO THOSE LONELY, GALLANT LADIES
WHO SUFFER WHILE WE ARE HERE.

WITHOUT THEIR PRAYERS AND COURAGE
WE COULD NEVER WIN A WAR.
I RAISE MY CUP IN HOMAGE AND TRIBUTE
TO THE MOTHERS OF THE CORPS."

SEMPER FI !
TO OUR MOTHERS!
SEMPER FI !

ROBERT A. GANNON IN THESE POEMS
AGAIN EXHIBITS HIS STRIKING
VERSATILITY AND POETIC ARTISTRY IN
THE INTERPRETATION OF TWO WIDELY
DIFFERENT MOODS AS HE TRANSLATES
HIS THEMES INTO POETRY.

.................Robert A. Gannon © 1997

HELMET ON A RIFLE

THEY BUILT A MARBLE MONUMENT
IN TOWN THE OTHER DAY
THEY PUT IT ON THE VILLAGE GREEN
ON PROMINENT DISPLAY.

IT HOLDS A LIST OF NATIVE SONS
WHO LEFT TO FIGHT A WAR
IN TRIBUTE TO THE MEN WHO DIED
WHO WALK THESE STREETS NO MORE

IT IS A GRAND AND NOBLE SYMBOL
RAISED BY A GRATEFUL LAND
BUT I REMEMBER A SIMPLER ONE
OF STEEL, WOOD AND SAND.

A DAY WHEN I WAS YOUNG
WHEN THE WORLD WAS FIRE LASHED
AND LIFE IN THE BALANCE, HUNG.

I REMEMBER THE PUFFS OF DUST
THAT SWIRLED AROUND OUR FEET
AND THE WAY THE RIFLE BARRELS
SHIMMERED, GLOWED IN THE HEAT.

OUR ADVANCE STARTED AT DAWN
WITH THE SUN LOW AT OUR BACK
ALL OUR THOUGHTS THAT MORNING
WERE ATTACK! ATTACK! ATTACK!

MY EYES WERE ON THE POINT MAN
HE WAS THE FIRST TO GO DOWN
I SAW HOW THE BULLETS HIT HIM
AND SLAMMED HIM TO THE GROUND.

IT WAS A SIGNAL TO TURN US LOOSE
AND DROVE US FORWARD AT A RUN
COULDN'T STOP FOR THE POINT MAN
TOO MUCH WORK TO BE DONE.

THAT DAY LASTED ALMOST FOREVER
BUT FINALLY CAME TO AN END
I WALKED BACK TO THE POINT MAN
WHERE I HAD SEEN HIM FALL
WHERE NOW THE LAND WAS QUIET
WITH THE PEACE OF GOD ON ALL.

COVERED HIM WITH MY PONCHO
AND TO MAKE SURE HE'D BE FOUND
I TOOK HIS RIFLE AND BAYONET
AND JABBED IT INTO THE GROUND.

MUCH MORE I COULD NOT DO
MY TRIBUTE SEEMED SUCH A TRIFLE
SO I TOOK A BATTERED HELMET
AND PLACED IT ON THE RIFLE.

YEARS HAVE FLOWN SINCE THAT DAY
AND NOW I READ HIS NAME
CARVED ON A MARBLE MONUMENT
ENSHRINED ON A ROLL OF FAME.

YET, THAT HELMET ON A RIFLE
WAS A FAR MORE FITTING SHRINE
FOR THE RIFLE WAS MY BROTHER'S
AND THE HELMET WAS MINE.

DONALD CHASE EARNED HIS FIRST COMBAT INFANTRY BADGE IN WORLD WAR II, AS A GLIDER TROOPER IN TWO ETO INFANTRY CAMPAIGNS. HIS SECOND CIB RESULTED FROM TWO COMBAT TOURS IN KOREA, THE FIRST, IN 1951 WITH BAKER COMPANY 19th INFANTRY REGT, THE SECOND IN 1952-'53 WITH ITEM Co 15th INFANTRY REGIMENT. HE WAS BADLY WOUNDED TWICE IN HIS FIRST TOUR. HE NEARLY LUCKED OUT IN HIS SECOND TOUR, ONLY TO BE ALMOST MORTALLY WOUNDED 26 JULY 1953, THE DAY BEFORE THE END OF HOSTILITIES. HIS POETRY VOUCHES FOR THE TRUTH OF A TWO WAR EXPERIENCE.

SCENES AND SOUNDS

MY MIND IS FILLED WITH MANY SCENES AND SOUNDS
FROM TWO WARS LONG AGO, IN MY LIFETIME PAST
A BULLET'S CRACK AS BY YOUR EAR IT WHIZZES
AND BARKING HOWITZERS WITH AN ECHOING BLAST.

THERE IS THE WHISPERY CHUFF OF DEADLY MORTARS
COUGHING UP THEIR SILENT SHELLS OF DEATH.
THE LOW, CLOSE WHOOSH OF FLAMING NAPALM
WHICH LEAVES ONE GASPING FOR BREATH.

I CAN STILL SEE THE SHATTERED TANKS
WITH THEIR CREWMEN LYING HERE AND THERE.
YET NEITHER FRIEND OR FOE WILL AGAIN FIGHT
FOR DEATH IS WHAT THEY NOW ALL SHARE.

THE SKY IS FILLED WITH VAPOR TRAILS
LEFT BY THE BOMBERS PASSING OVERHEAD.
CITIES AND TOWN JUST PILES OF RUBBLE
WELL MARKED BY THE SMELL OF THEIR DEAD.

ALSO REMEMBERED IS THAT FRANTIC CRY, MEDIC!
SOUNDING LOUD OVER THE COMMOTION AND DIN.
AND THAT INVOLVES THE GRIMNESS OF SEEING
A COMRADE'S BLOOD LEAKING FROM WITHIN.

THESE THINGS HAVE CONTINUED TO HAUNT ME
NEVER CEASING WITH THE PASSAGE OF YEARS.
EVEN DURING MOMENTS OF QUIET REFLECTION
THEY CAN SOMETIMES RESURRECT OLD FEARS.
...........................Donald A.Chase

KOREAN HILLS

LISTEN FOLKS TO MY TALE OF WOE
FROM A LAND FAR ACROSS THE SEA
A RUGGED PLACE FOR THE HUMAN RACE
THEY'VE GOT THE BEST OF ME, KOREAN HILLS!

YOU CLIMB ALL DAY, YOU CLIMB ALL NIGHT
YOU GO UPHILL ON ONE SIDE TO FIGHT
DOWN THE OTHER, AFTER AN ENEMY IN FLIGHT
THEY'LL MAKE YOU LOOK A SIGHT, KOREAN HILLS!

I KNOW A GUY WHO STARTED OUT
TO CLIMB A KOREAN HILL ONE DAY
TWO WEEKS HAVE PASSED WITH NO WORD
I THINK HE LOST HIS WAY, KOREAN HILLS!

I'D GIVE THE WORLD IF I COULD SEE
JUST ONE FLAT STRETCH OF GROUND
A WOMAN'S FACE IN A CIVILIZED PLACE
AND A BRIGHTLY LIT UP TOWN, KOREAN HILLS!
.....................Fred E. Proft 1st FA Obsvn Unit

KOREAN HILLS

THE MOUNTAINOUS BATTLEFIELDS IN KOREA
HAD NUMBERS, SOME HAD WELL KNOWN NAMES.
WHERE DEADLY FIGHTING TOOK PLACE
SOMETIMES FOR A FIGHT ALL IN VAIN.

JACKSON HEIGHTS WAS SUCH A PLACE
WHERE A LOT OF BLOOD WAS SPILLED.
THE END RESULT WAS MANY DEATHS
AND THE ENEMY STILL CONTROLLED THE HILL.

OUTPOST TOM AND OUTPOST DICK
WERE PLACES OF MUCH LESSER FAME.
YET, THERE TOO, MEN SUFFERED AND DIED
AS ENEMY SHELLS POURED DOWN LIKE RAIN.

OUTPOST HARRY WAS A CRITICAL HILL
ONE TO BE HELD AT ALL COSTS.
THERE, MANY MEN WENT TO THEIR MAKER
TO MAKE CERTAIN IT WOULD NOT BE LOST.

HISTORY BOOKS ON THE KOREAN WAR
WILL HAVE A SHORT PARAGRAPH THAT WILL TELL
ABOUT THE MEN WHO DEFENDED OUTPOST HARRY
AND HOW WELL IT WAS DEFENDED, IT NEVER FELL.
...........................Donald A.Chase

SILENT MOUNTAINS

IF THE BARREN MOUNTAINS OF KOREA COULD TALK
WHAT MEMORABLE TALES THEY WOULD TELL.
OF MEN WHO FOUGHT IN A FORGOTTEN WAR
WHICH GAVE THEM A PREVIEW OF HELL.

THEY WOULD SPEAK OF THINGS THAT TRIED MEN'S SOULS
LEAVING THE SURVIVORS TO REMEMBER SO WELL.
THE COLD WITH ITS SNOW, AND MUD FROM THE RAIN
AND UNDERGROUND HOLES WHERE THEY DWELT.

THERE WOULD BE STORIES OF HUMAN ENDURANCE
BROUGHT OUT BY THE WILL TO SURVIVE.
BRAVERY, COURAGE AND UNTHINKING SACRIFICE
FOR WARFARE DEMANDS THAT SOME MUST DIE.

THE BARDS WILL ALSO TELL OF THE BURIAL PLACE
OF SOLDIERS NOW LOCKED IN ETERNAL SLEEP.
WHOSE GREY-WHITE BONES LIE SILENT AND STILL
THOUGH LOVED ONES AND COMRADES STILL WEEP.

VOICELESS MOUNTAINS WITH THEIR UNTOLD TALES
HAVE A FAR GREATER MEANING TO MOST.
OF THE MEN WHO FOUGHT AND EXISTED THEREON
THEY ARE A SEPARATE WORLD FULL OF GHOSTS.
...........................Donald A. Chase

THESE POEMS REPRESENT THE TWO SIDES OF THE COIN EVERY COMBAT SOLDIER SEES IN HIS MIND'S EYE.
THE HARD ROAD OF WAR HE TREADS IN HIS FIGHT FOR SURVIVAL, OR THE ETERNAL FLAME OF ARLINGTON.

THE INFANTRYMAN

IT'S BEEN A LONG AND FREEZING WINTER
WITH THE ELEMENTS HARD TO BEAR,
WITHOUT SHELTER WE WITHSTOOD IT
WITH WHAT CLOTHES WE HAD TO WEAR.

WE'D SLEEP IN HOLES WHILE A BUDDY GUARDED
AGAINST AN ENEMY THAT MIGHT ATTACK,
And IF HE CAUGHT BOTH OF US NAPPING
WE'D LIKELY GO HOME IN A SACK.

AT LAST MORN CAME, BEANS FOR BREAKFAST
CHIPPED FROM A CAN FROZEN HARD AS ICE,
AND IF A FIRE YOU WERE PERMITTED
TO BREW INSTANT COFFEE, HOW NICE!

TO REMAIN HERE WE'D BE LUCKY
BUT SOON AFTER IT BROKE DAYLIGHT,
OFF WE MARCHED, TO JOIN WITH OTHERS
OFF TO JOIN IN ANOTHER FIGHT.

NOW MY MIND BEGINS TO WANDER
WITH MORBID THOUGHTS I HOLD MY BREATH,
FOR I REALIZE EACH STEP I'M TAKING
MAY BRING ME CLOSER TO MY DEATH .

I'D NEVER FELT THIS SCARED BEFORE
THIS GUT WRENCHING FEAR I GET,
THE FIRST TIME I FACED THE ENEMY
AND THAT FEAR STAYS WITH ME YET.

FROM AN E-MAIL SENT TO THE EDITOR by "CHARLIE."
CHARLIE WHO? I WISH I KNEW. I'D GIVE CREDIT DUE! *Ed*

EVERY HUMAN TREASURES LIFE
AND I'VE OFTEN WONDERED WHY
WE'D RUSH HEADLONG TOWARD THE ENEMY
WITH EVERY CHANCE THAT WE MIGHT DIE.

I'VE SEEN LOOKS ON MANY FACES
OF MY COMRADES AND I KNOW,
WHEN THE ORDER "MOVE OUT" WAS GIVEN
'TWAS ONLY PRIDE THAT MADE THEM GO.

YOU CAN TALK ABOUT OLD GLORY
AND MOM'S SWEET APPLE PIE,
BUT I THINK IT'S PRIDE THAT DROVE US,
WHEN CHANCES WERE THAT WE COULD DIE.

I DON'T SAY WE'RE NOT PATRIOTS
FOR THAT'S THE BASIS OF OUR PRIDE,
PRIDE OF SELF AND HOME AND COUNTRY
AND WITH THIS PRIDE, MANY OF US DIED.

SO WITH MINDS TURNED NUMB IN ANXIOUS FEAR
WE FOLLOW THE ORDERS WE ARE HANDED,
BETTER DIE AN HONORED SOLDIER'S DEATH
THAN GO HOME A COWARD BRANDED.

FOR ANY THAT MAY WONDER FREEDOM'S COST
LET THEM IN COMBAT SPEND ONE DAY WITH ME,
AMID EXPLODING SHELLS AND WHISTLING BULLETS ,
AND THEY WILL LEARN FREEDOM IS NOT FOR FREE.

THIS POEM WILL REVERBERATE IN THE HEART AND MIND
OF EVERY DOGFACE INFANTRY SOLDIER........IN ANY WAR.

DREAMS

LIFE IS PLEASANT IN SUNSHINE'S BRIGHT LIGHT
BUT APPREHENSION SETS IN WITH COMING OF NIGHT
I FALL ASLEEP BUT DREAMS FILL MY MIND
OF DAYS OF TERROR ONCE THOUGHT LEFT BEHIND.

ON DAYS ON OUTPOST IN NO MAN'S LAND
SEEING THE PIECES OF WHAT WAS ONCE A MAN
WHO HE WAS, WHICH SIDE, NO ONE KNEW
ONLY PART OF HIS HEAD AND ONE HAND SHOW.

THE UNSEEN MORTAR COUGHS UP ITS SHELL
FOLLOWED BY THE BLAST THAT CASTS ITS SPELL
NOWHERE TO GO, NOWHERE TO HIDE
SCREAMING SHRAPNEL SPREADS FAR AND WIDE.

AT LAST ALL IS QUIET, BUT I STILL HUG THE GROUND
SHOCKED AT FIRST BY THE ABSENCE OF SOUND
THE HEARTBEAT SLOWS AND I AWAKE TO FIND
JUST ANOTHER DREAM, PLAYING TRICKS WITH MY MIND.

THOSE SCENES OF BATTLE FROM DAYS LONG AGO
ARE KEPT BURIED INSIDE SO NO ONE KNOWS
THOUGH I TRY WITH ALL MY MIGHT
I CAN'T STOP DREAMS THAT COME WITH THE NIGHT.

UNWANTED MEMORIES

OFTEN WHEN I SIT ALONE AND TWILIGHT FILLS THE SKY
I FIND MYSELF RECALLING SCENES FROM YEARS GONE BY
MEMORIES OF A WAR IN KOREA STILL CLUTTER UP MY HEAD
DREARY DAYS AND HELLISH NIGHTS, FRIENDS LONG DEAD.

THE MANY HILLS WE FOUGHT ON, SEEMINGLY WITHOUT END
AND THE FEAR INSIDE ME, OF DEATH JUST AROUND THE BEND
THE CLASHES WITH AN ENEMY WHO SOMETIMES FLED AWAY
BUT FOR EVERY HILL WON WITH MANY LIVES WE HAD TO PAY.

PERHAPS ONE WAS LUCKY, WHEN A BULLET FOUND AN ARM
THEN FOR A LITTLE WHILE, ONE WAS SAFE FROM HARM
MY MIND RECALLS ICY WEATHER AS DISEASE TOOK ITS TOLL
FROZEN FEET WERE COMMON BY WINTER'S NUMBING COLD.

THE TRENCH LINES, BUNKERS AND GRIMY FACES THERE
IF YOU WERE OBSERVANT, YOU SAW THE BURNT OUT STARE
THE PATH FROM TRENCHES THAT LED TO NO--MAN'S LAND
A TORN PIECE OF GROUND, DESTROYED BY HUMAN HAND.

ALWAYS THERE ARE THOSE WHO FELL, NEVER AGAIN TO RISE
TO THIS DAY, I STILL SEE THE SHOCK IN STARTLED EYES
VIVID PICTURES LOCKED INSIDE, THO' THEY DO NOT SHOW
NEVER LEAVE MY THOUGHTS, NO MATTER WHERE I GO.

THE CHOSIN RESERVOIR©, A TONE POEM by ROBERT F. HAMMOND, WAS INSPIRED BY HIS ATTENDANCE AT DEDICATION OF THE KOREAN WAR MEMORIAL IN WASHINGTON, DC. IN HIS WORDS, "AS SOLE SURVIVOR OF MY GUN SECTION, "A"BATTERY 57TH FA BN, I FELT I SHOULD DO SOMETHING IN HONOR OF THE GUYS WHO DID NOT COME BACK. I PLACED A NOTE IN REMEMBRANCE AT THE WALL, 'YOU ARE FINALLY REMEMBERED, *BUT I NEVER FORGOT.* IT WAS NOT ENOUGH, MY THOUGHTS HAUNTED ME. WHAT FINALLY EMERGED WAS A TRIBUTE TO MY LONG DEAD COMRADES, *GONE, BUT NOT FORGOTTEN.*"

Editorial Note: The Chosin Reservoir was also a feature of the poetry section in Korean Vignettes, Faces of War© which preceded Red Dragon. It is reprinted as probably the most descriptive verse to come out of the Korean War. It is a haunting reminder of the cost in American lives and blood spilled in a war fought to stop the onslaught of Communism and save South Korea as a free nation.

THE CHOSIN RESERVOIR ....Robert F. Hammond

IN THE HILLS OF NORTH KOREA
BY A LAKE OF AZURE BLUE,
RIDES A FARMER IN HIS OXCART
ON THE ROAD TO HAGARU.

HE IS SINGING SONGS OF HISTORY
THAT HIS FATHER TAUGHT TO HIM,
AS HIS EYES SURVEY THE SCENERY
THAT'S NO LONGER GRAY AND GRIM.

IN HIS MIND HE HEARS THE CANNONS,
THE RECOILLESS RIFLE'S ROAR
AND THE CHATTER OF THE BURP GUNS
ALL AROUND THE RESERVOIR.

MORTARS CRASHING, CARBINES
FLASHING,
SCREAMING MEN AND BOYS,
BUGLES, FLARES AND HOWITZERS
A SYMPHONY OF NOISE.

HE IS THINKING OF HIS CHILDHOOD
WHEN HE SAW THE SOLDIERS COME,
TO THIS PEACEFUL MOUNTAIN VALLEY
THAT HAD NEVER HEARD A GUN.

AND HE'S NEVER UNDERSTOOD IT
HE WILL ALWAYS WONDER WHY,
SO MANY MEN HAD COME THERE
FROM SO FAR AWAY, TO DIE.

HOW THEY FOUGHT WITH SAVAGE FURY
AGONIZING THROUGH THE SNOW,
FINGERS TURNINGBLACK WITH FROSTBITE
DEATH WAS SWEEPING TO AND FRO.

COL FAITH, COMMANDER McLEAN, MEN
AND OFFICERS, AND THOUSANDS MORE,
FOUGHT, FROZE AND BLED TO DEATH
AT CHOSIN RESERVOIR.

IN THE HILLS OF NORTH KOREA
BY A LAKE OF ICY BLUE,
THERE'S NO MONUMENT TO WITNESS
AND NO CROSSES ARE IN VIEW.

JUST SOME LAND OF LITTLE VALUE
COVERED WELL BY FALLEN SNOW,
BUT THEY SAY TO LISTEN CAREFULLY
WHEN THE WIND BEGINS TO BLOW.

YOU WILL HEAR THE GHOSTLY BUGLES
FROM THE MOUNTAIN PASS, NEARBY.
YOU MAY HEAR THE BATTLE SPREADING
FROM THE MOUNTAINS TO THE SKY.

LIVES WERE ENDING, FUTURES
PERVADING,
FATE WAS CASTING DICE.
SOME WOULD LIVE, SOME WOULD DIE,
KARMA CARVED IN ICE.

THE BATTLE LONG IS OVER NOW,
BUT FOUGHT EACH NIGHT ANEW,
BY MEN WHO CAN'T FORGET,
THEY'RE CALLED THE 'CHOSIN FEW.'

SO LET VETERANS TELL THEIR STORIES
LET THE LEGEND LIVE AND GROW,
LET THE CHOSIN BE REMEMBERED
WITH THE MEN OF THE ALAMO.

WITH BASTOGNE AND WAKE ISLAND
AND THE BUNKER HILL COMMAND,
WHEREVER THERE'S COURAGEOUS
MEN TO TAKE A VALIANT STAND.

ONCE THEY FOUGHT TO SAVE A NATION
THEY COULD NOT HAVE OFFERED MORE
THAN THE SACRIFICES MADE THERE
AT THE CHOSIN RESERVOIR.

IN THE HILLS OF NORTH KOREA
BY A LAKE OF AZURE BLUE,
MARINES FOUGHT BLOODY BATTLES
DEPARTING THE CHOSIN RESERVOIR.

IN THE HILLS OF NORTH KOREA
BY A LAKE OF AZURE BLUE,
SOLDIERS FOUGHT TO STAY ALIVE
AT THE CHOSIN RESERVOIR.

THAT SCRAP OF RIBBON

I FOUND A SCRAP OF RIBBON
IN THE CORNER OF A DRAWER,
A MEMORY OF A TIME GONE BY
A SYMBOL OF A WAR.

A LITTLE SCRAP OF RIBBON
COLORED BLUE, EDGED WITH WHITE,
A LITTLE SCRAP OF RIBBON
TO COMMEMORATE A FIGHT,

SO MANY DIFFERENT RIBBONS
SO MANY DIFFERENT WARS,
SO MANY MEMORIES HIDDEN
IN THE CORNER OF A DRAWER

THOUGHTS OF LOVE, THOUGHTS OF HATE
THOUGHTS OF LABORED BREATH,
MEMORIES OF MUD AND BLOOD
PAIN AND WOUNDS AND DEATH.

UNKNOWN ACTS OF VALOR
IN THE LIVES OF FIGHTING MEN,
POINTLESS THINGS THAT MATTER
THE LAUGHTER OF A FRIEND.

BURNING IN THE SUMMER HEAT
THE WATER BOTTLE DRY,
CURSING WITH FRUSTRATION
AS YOU WATCH SOMEBODY DIE.

CROUCHING IN A FOXHOLE
AS THE WORLD IS TORN APART
AND YOU KNOW EACH SEPARATE,
SCREAMING SHELL IS SEARCHING
FOR YOUR HEART.

JUST A LITTLE SCRAP OF RIBBON
JUST A SIMPLE PIECE OF CLOTH
BUT GOD, OH MY GOD,
THE AWFUL PRICE WITH WHICH
THAT RIBBON'S BOUGHT.

..........Robert A. Gannon

THE DRAGON STRIKES

AS NIGHT FADES INTO THE PRE-DAWN MURK
A CUNNING AND AGE OLD ORIENTAL GAME
BY SONS OF CATHAY COMES INTO PLAY
TALONS CLUTCHING, A RED DRAGON LURKS.

WHISTLES AND BUGLES SHRILL IN NOISY FANFARE
WHITE PHOSPHORUS FUMES WAFT ACRIDLY IN AIR
A STEALTHY ROADBLOCK LAID WITHOUT FAULT
BRINGS A BATTALION COLUMN TO A HALT.

IN FULL DAYLIGHT A SNIPER TAKES DEADLY TOLL
A GI HELMET IN HIS GUN SIGHT, HIS GOAL
GI SOLDIERS LIE PRONE ON A PADDY SLOPE
THE ROAD TO THE SOUTH THEIR ONLY HOPE.

TRUTH AND ETERNITY VIE FOR FORTUNE'S HAND
DOES EAST OR WEST PRODUCE THE BETTER MAN?
SLANT EYED CHARLIE AND HIS RUSSIAN BURP GUN
OR AN AMERICAN SOLDIER AND HIS TRUSTY GARAND

INTO AN M-1 GUN SIGHT AT A DEAD RUN COMES CHARLIE ONE
AN M-1 GARAND BARKS SHARPLY, ONE DEADLY ROUND
IN FINAL SALUTE TO CHARLIE ONE, NOW HOMEWARD BOUND
HIS LIFE DESTINY ENDED BY A GI'S SMOKING GUN.

TIGHT INTO HIS SHOULDER THE RIFLE STOCK
AIMING, FIRING ROUNDS TWO, THREE AND FOUR
NO COWARD, CHARLIE KEEPS COMING FOR MORE
NOW FOUR SONS OF HAN LIE IN THEIR GORE.

AN EYE AIMED IN THE SIGHT OF AN M-1 GARAND
RETURNING TO CHINA SOME SONS OF HAN
SENT TO THIS RUGGED MOUNTAIN LAND
WILLING TO FIGHT TO THEIR LAST MAN.

CHINESE 'BOO BINGS' IN DEATH DO LIE
THEIR SOULS ASCENDING, PONDERING
MUST THEY COME SO FAR, WONDERING
WAS IT ONLY TO DIE? ....'A SOLDIER OF THE 31ST REGIMENT'

FROM CHOSIN TO THE SEA

THE HIKE FROM CHOSIN, SEVENTY MILES ON ICE AND SNOW
WITH TEMPERATURES READING MORE THAN FORTY BELOW
WITH FROSTBITTEN HANDS AND CLUMSY FROZEN FEET
NOTHING TO EAT AND NOR TIME FOR SLEEP
WILL WE REACH HAMHUNG, ONLY GOD KNOWS
IN FIERCE BATTLE OUR DEAD LAY ALL AROUND
SNIPERS FIRING AT US FROM THE HIGH GROUND
AMMO GONE, NO WAY TO GET MORE
OUR TRUCKS, RIDDLED BY ENEMY FIRE WILL NOT GO
ON WE TREAD THROUGH THE FROZEN SNOW
THROUGH THE DAY AND THROUGH THE NIGHT
O, MY GOD, WE'RE FACING ANOTHER FIRE FIGHT
FOUGHT THAT ONE 'TIL WE BROKE THROUGH
THEY SAY THE BIG WATER IS JUST AROUND THE BEND
ANOTHER NIGHT IN THIS HELL MARCH WE MUST SPEND
I SEE THE WATER, I SEE THE SHIPS
MY PRAYER IS SAID WITH FROZEN LIPS
I THANK OUR LORD FOR HELPING ME FINISH THIS TRIP.
..............MERVALE JONES 185TH COMBAT ENGINEER BN 1950

CHRISTMAS IN KOREA

HE CROUCHES IN HIS FOXHOLE, COLD
AND PEERS AT MOUNTAINS BLEAK AND OLD
AROUND THE SNOW LIES THICK AND WHITE
IT IS A SOLDIER'S CHRISTMAS NIGHT.
SOME STRANGERS FOUGHT AND SOME DIED
FOR ANGEL'S SONGS, A WHISTLING SHELL
NOT "PEACE ON EARTH, BUT THE HELLISH YELL
OF KILLERS, DRUGGED WITH ASSIGNED HATE
DEAR GOD, DID CHRISTMAS COME TOO LATE?
SOME STRANGERS FOUGHT AND SOME DIED
"OH, LITTLE TOWN," THE THOUGHT IS BLURRED
AS CHILDISH MEMORIES ARE STIRRED
WELL TAUGHT HANDS THE DEATH MARCH PLAY
AGAINST THE FOE THIS CHRISTMAS DAY
SOME STRANGERS FOUGHT AND SOME DIED
THE DEAD ASK "WHY" AT CHRISTMAS TIDE
FOR PEACE ON EARTH AND GOOD WILL TO MEN
THE HOMESICK SOLDIER CRIES, "WHERE, O WHEN."
................REVEREND L.T. NEWLAND KOREA DECEMBER 1950

THE OLD PARADE GROUND ....Robert A. Gannon

I WALKED THE OLD PARADE GROUND
OF MANY YEARS AGO
WHILE MEMORIES FLOODED BACK
OF MEN I USED TO KNOW.

I WALKED THE OLD PARADE GROUND
EMPTY BUT FOR ME
EXCEPT FOR HIDDEN LEGIONS
THAT I ALONE COULD SEE.

I HEARD THE CRUNCHING FEET
I FELT THE BURNING SUN
I SAW THE RIFLED GREEN CLAD LINES
PASS BY ME, ONE BY ONE.

AGAIN I LIVE IN YESTERDAY
WHEN I WAS WEARING GREEN
ONCE MORE I COUNTED THE COST
OF BEING CALLED MARINE.

I THOUGHT OF DAYS IN DISTANT LANDS
WHERE CHERRY BLOSSOMS BLOOMED
I THOUGHT OF GRIM AND LONELY NIGHTS
WHEN CANNONS ROARED AND BOOMED.

I FELT THE SALT ON MY FACE
I SAW THE OCEAN ROLL
I HEARD THE MELANCHOLY TALE
THE SINGING SEABIRD TOLD.

THEN FROM THE ROLLS OF YESTERDAY
CAME NAMES I USED TO KNOW
LIKE GUY AND BOB AND ACE AND BULL
ROLAND, NORT AND BO.

I WALKED THE OLD PARADE GROUND
QUITE LOST IN REVERIE
WHILE ALL AROUND PHANTOMS MARCHED
THAT I ALONE COULD SEE.

I WALKED THE OLD PARADE GROUND
BUT I WAS NOT ALONE
I WALKED THE OLD PARADE GROUND
AND KNEW THAT I WAS AT HOME

FOUR POEMS OF DONALD CHASE'S WORLD WAR II EXPERIENCE ARE INCLUDED IN AMPLIFICATION OF HIS KOREAN SERVICE.

A MEMORABLE DAY

THE SOLDIERS TROOPED ABOARD THE SHIP
SEEMINGLY, IN ONE LONG ENDLESS FILE.
THEIR YOUTHFUL BANTER FILLED THE AIR
LAUGHTER IN THE AIR, FACES CRINKLED IN SMILES.

BUT BEHIND THE SMILES AND FRIENDLY BANTER
WAS A KNOWLEDGE THEY WERE ON THEIR WAY TO WAR.
WHEN THIS SHIP COMPLETED HER SEA JOURNEY
AND LANDED THEM ON A DISTANT FOREIGN SHORE.

EVER PRESENT WAS THE NAGGING THOUGHT
THAT MANY IN THIS SHIP MIGHT NEVER RETURN.
AND JUST HOW FATE WOULD DECIDE THIS GAMBLE
MADE FEELINGS INSIDE EACH MAN TOSS AND CHURN.

IN TIME THE SHIP IS LOADED AND AWAY
FROM THE DOCK STARTS TO SAIL.
WHILE OBSERVERS STANDING ON THE PIER
SEE THOUSANDS LINING THE SHIP'S RAIL.

MANY LOOKED THROUGH GLISTENING EYES
AS THESE YOUNG MEN SAILED AWAY
BUT WHETHER ABOARD SHIP OR ON THE PIER
ALL WOULD LONG REMEMBER THIS DAY.
..................Donald A. Chase

GLIDER TROOPER

LITTLE HAS BEEN WRITTEN ABOUT GLIDERMEN
FOR THEY WERE THE UNHERALDED GI'S.
OVERSHADOWED BY THEIR PARACHUTE BROTHERS
EVEN THOUGH EQUAL NUMBERS WOULD DIE.

THEY WERE AN UNUSUAL MIX OF SOLDIERS
SOME WERE DRAFTEES; OTHERS, VOLUNTEERS.
BUT ONE THING THEY ALL SHARED
WAS GUT COURAGE, COMMON TO THE LOT.

BEING AIRBORNE IN SMALL FLYING GLIDERS
WAS NOT FOR THE FAINT OF HEART.
KEEPING COMPOSURE WAS ITSELF AN ORDEAL
WHILE WAITING FOR THE TOW ROPE TO PART

WHEN AT LAST CUT LOOSE FROM THE TOW 'PLANE
THERE WAS A HURRIED RUSH TO GET DOWN
MANY OF THE LANDINGS WERE TRAGIC
BONE BREAKING CRASHES WERE COMMON ALL AROUND.

LUCKY SURVIVORS WOULD GATHER ROUND LEADERS
THEN MOVE OUT TO FIGHT TILL THE END.
GETTING LITTLE OF THE CREDIT RICHLY DESERVED
SUCH WAS THE LOT AND THE FATE OF GLIDERMEN.
..........................Donald A. Chase

NIGHT JUMP

THE NIGHT WAS DARK WITHOUT A MOON
YET FILLED WITH A RUMBLING ROAR.
THE SOUND OF TRANSPORT 'PLANE ENGINES
CARRYING NERVOUS YOUNG MEN OFF TO WAR.

INSIDE SOME OF THE PLANES THERE WAS SILENCE
WHILE IN OTHERS, BRAVADO HELD SWAY.
SERVING AS COVER FOR INNER FEARS
PROTECTING EACH MAN IN HIS OWN PERSONAL WAY.

HEARTS BEAT FASTER WHEN CAME TIME TO HOOK UP
WAITING FOR THE JUMP LIGHT TO TURN GREEN.
A COMMAND, "GO", THEN OUT THE 'PLANE DOOR
JUMPING, HOPING TO CLEAR THE PROP'S SLIPSTREAM

THE ENEMY SEARCHLIGHTS DANCED TO AND FRO
WHILE HIS ACK-ACK BARKED ITS DEADLY SONG.
HERE, THERE, FLAMING OBJECTS HURTLED TO EARTH
LIT UP EVIDENCE OF SOMETHING GONE WRONG.

A FORTUNATE FEW SURVIVED THAT NIGHT
BUT NEVER HAVE THEY FORGOTTEN THE PAST.
THOUGHTS OFTEN TURN TO FALLEN COMRADES
FOR WHOM THAT JUMP WAS THEIR LAST.
..........................Donald A. Chase

MILITARY REUNIONS

OLD COMRADES MEET WITH WARM HELLOS
REMEMBERING WARM FRIENDSHIPS FROM THE PAST
OF CAMARADERIE, WAR FORGED IN TRYING TIMES.
THAT THROUGH A LIFETIME OF YEARS DOTH LAST.

AGE AND TIME JUST ROLL AWAY
ONCE AGAIN WE ARE ALL YOUNG MEN.
RELIVING THE DAYS OF YOUTH IN WAR
AND WHAT TOOK PLACE BACK THEN.

ALL KNOW THEY WERE THE LUCKY ONE
WHO LIVED TO COME BACK HOME.
FOR MANY FELL AND ARE NO MORE
LEAVING ONLY THEIR SPRITS TO ROAM.

THE STORIES FLOW BRINGING SMILES
THOUGH MEMORIES MAY HAVE DIMMED.
MISSING FRIENDS ARE NOT FORGOTTEN
SINCE THEY TOO IN HEART ARE KEPT WITHIN.

BUT SADNESS MUST ALSO PLAY ITS PART
FOR COMRADES WILL CONTINUE TO FALL.
LEAVING THINNER RANKS WITH EMPTY SPACES
UNTIL FINALLY, THE LAST SILENT ROLL CALL.
..........................Donald A. Chase

BURY ME WITH SOLDIERS

I'VE PLAYED A LOT OF ROLES IN LIFE
I'VE MET A LOT OF MEN.
i'VE DONE THINGS I'D LIKE TO THINK
I WOULDN'T DO AGAIN.

AND THO I'M YOUNG, I'M OLD ENOUGH
TO KNOW SOMEDAY I WILL DIE.
TO THINK ABOUT WHAT LIES BEYOND
AND BESIDE WHOM I WILL LIE.

PERHAPS IT DOESN'T MATTER MUCH
STILL, IF I HAVE MY CHOICE
I'D WANT MY GRAVE 'MONGST SOLDIERS
WHEN DEATH AT QUELLS MY VOICE.

I'M SICK OF POLITICAL HYPOCRISY
AND OF LECTURES BY THE WISE
I'LL TAKE THE MAN WITH ALL HIS FLAWS
WHO GOES, THOUGH SCARED, AND DIES.

THE TROOPS I KNEW are COMMON MEN
THEY DIDN'T WANT THE WAR
THEY FOUGHT BECAUSE THEIR FATHERS
AND THEIR FATHERS HAD BEFORE.

THEY CURSED AND KILLED AND WEPT
GOD KNOWS, THEY'RE EASY TO DERIDE
BUT BURY ME WITH MEN LIKE THESE
WHO FACED ENEMY GUNS AND DIED.

IT'S FUNNY WHEN YOU THINK OF IT
THE WAY WE GOT ALONG
WE'D COME FROM DIFFERENT WORLDS
TO LIVE IN WHERE NO ONE BELONGS.

I DIDN'T EVEN LIKE THEM ALL
I'M SURE THEY'D ALL AGREE
YET I WOULD GIVE MY LIFE FOR THEM
I KNOW SOME DID FOR ME.

SO BURY ME WITH SOLDIERS, PLEASE
THOUGH MUCH MALIGNED THEY BE
YES, BURY ME WITH SOLDIERS, FOR
I MISS THEIR COMPANY, YOU SEE.

WE'LL NOT SEE THEIR LIKES AGAIN
WE'VE HAD OUR FILL OF WAR
BUT BURY ME WITH MEN LIKE THEM
'TILL SOMEONE ELSE DOES MORE.
.... UNKNOWN
Contributed by Charles A. Lonsford B/31/7

THE BATTLEFIELD

BATTLEFIELD SOUNDS, SMOKE AND FIRE
DAYS IN TRENCHES IN FRONT OF BARB WIRE.
DIRT AND COLD, SNOW, SLEET, ICE AND RAIN
A BATTLEFIELD TO A SOLDIER BRINGS PAIN.

COMBAT SOLDIERS KNOW THIS LIVING HELL
TERRIBLE SOUNDS OF INCOMING ROUNDS.
EXPLODE ON IMPACT AS THEY HIT GROUND
MORE SOLDIERS DIE, A FATE KNOWN WELL.

MANY SOLDIERS HAVE GONE INTO COMBAT
IN THEIR YOUTH, WHEN THEY WERE YOUNG.
YOUNG MEN TO OLD MEN, AGEING FAST
A SHORT LIFE PROSPECT, UNDER THE GUNS.

LOSS OF A BUDDY, DEATH OF A FRIEND
I CAN'T FORGET THE PAIN AND TERROR
OF HIS LIFE IN THE ARENA OF COMBAT
I HAD HELD HOPES FOR A BETTER END.

HIS MEMORY WILL BE WITH ME TILL I DIE
HE SURVIVED BATTLE AND TIME ON LINE.
HIS HOPE FOR ANOTHER DAY OF SWEET LIFE
DASHED FOREVER BY A PLUNGING SHELL.

REMEMBRANCE OF HIS DAYS IN COMBAT
THE HARD TIMES HE WENT THROUGH.
HE HAS EARNED HIS PLACE IN HISTORY
FIGHTING FOR THE RED, WHITE AND BLUE.
..........Boyed H. Burnley 45th Division

TOMORROW IS TODAY

SO THEY MARCHED, THOSE LAUGHING BOYS
MARCHED OFF TO WAR'S TATTERED GLORY.
TO THE SOUND OF MILITARY FIFE AND DRUM
MARCHED OFF TO LIVE A SHINING STORY.

INSTEAD THEY FOUND A FIELD OF RED
PILED WITH DEAD BODIES, TORN AND GORY
GONE NOW THOSE BOYS, LAUGHING BOYS.

GONE WITH LIVES OF PAIN AND SORROW
GONE TOO, THOSE PRECIOUS YOUNG LIVES
THE LIVES OUR COUNTRY HAD TO BORROW.

SO TELL ME, FRIEND, AS WARS NEVER END
OR THE WORLD WE LIVE IN APT TO MEND
WHO WILL DEFEND US TOMORROW?

..................Richard L. Kirk 58th Armored FA Bn

SOLDIER'S LAMENT

WHEN I AWOKE THIS MORNING
THE GROUND WAS MIGHTY COLD
JOINTS WERE STIFF, HEAD DID ACHE
I KNEW I WAS GETTING OLD!

NOW IF YOU SEE MY CAPTAIN
TELL HIM I WANT TO GO HOME
AIN'T HAD NO FUN OR LOVIN'
AND I'M COLD DOWN TO MY BONES!

I'VE TRIED EVERYTHING I KNOW
TO SURVIVE IN THIS LAND
BUT I CAN TELL YOU RIGHT NOW
IT WASN'T MADE FOR MAN!

I NEED TO LEAVE THIS PLACE
AND GO BACK TO THE US OF A
BACK WITH PEOPLE I LOVE
THAT'S WHERE I WANT TO STAY!

AND IF YOU THINK I'M KIDDING
I'LL TELL YOU WHAT YOU CAN DO
SIGN MY ROTATION PAPERS
AND ITS GOOD BY, I'M LEAVING YOU!
......Fred E. Proft 1st FA Obsvn Bn

NEW DAY DAWNING

THERE IS A NEW DAY DAWNING
ON THIS HILL SO FAR AWAY.
WHERE GI'S SPENT A WEARY NIGHT
AND NOW LOOK EAGERLY TO DAY.

THE WATCH WAS LONG, INTENSE
SLEEP HAD PASSED US BY.
TIRED, WEARY EYES LOOKED UP
TO AWAIT THE DAWNING SKY.

WE, FAR AWAY, ACROSS THE SEA.
FOLKS BACK HOME NEVER KNOW
WHAT IT IS TO MISS THE BLESSING
A NIGHT SPENT IN RESTFUL SLEEP.

NO GUNS ROAR, OR SHELLS FALL
NO SOUNDS TO BREAK THE NIGHT.
TO WAKE, RESTED IN EARLY MORN
AND START THE DAY OK, ALRIGHT.
IN THANKS TO THAT I SAY AMEN!

........Fred E. Proft 1st FA Obsvn Bn

WE ARE THE COMBAT ENGINEERS

WE ARE CALLED UPON TO CLEAR THE WAY FOR THE INFANTRY
WE ARE CALLED WHEN TANKERS BREAK THROUGH A BRIDGE
WE ARE CALLED UPON TO PLANT AND CLEAR MINE FIELDS
WE BUILD ROADS, WE BUILD BRIDGES, WE BLOW BRIDGES
AND SOMETIMES WE ALMOST WALK ON WATER.
WE ARE LEADERS, WE ARE PATRIOTS ,WE ARE RIFLEMEN

WE ARE CALLED UPON IF PERIMETER DEFENSE IS NEEDED
WE FIGHT AS INFANTRY WHEN WE ARE CALLED UPON
WHEN THE GOING GETS ROUGH THEY CALL ON US
WE ARE THE COMBAT ENGINEERS.
WE SERVE THE FLAG, WE SALUTE THE FLAG.
IF WE DIE IN BATTLE, OUR BODIES ARE DRAPED IN THE FLAG.

FROM PUSAN TO THE YALU

THE WAR STARTED UP NORTH
IN THIS FAR ASIAN LAND,
DEMOCRACY AGAINST COMMUNISM
THE SOUTH MUST MAKE A STAND.

SO THE NORTH KOREANS STRUCK
ON THAT ALMOST FATAL DAY,
PUSHING BACK THE AMERICANS
WHO STOOD STEADY IN THEIR WAY.

IN TO THE FAR SOUTH THEY DID PUSH
A PINCHED PUSAN PERIMETER,
COMPRESSED BY THE FOE SO SMALL
AMERICANS FOUGHT, GIVING ALL.

OUR TROOPS HELD THAT PUSAN LINE
FIGHTING, DYING, DAY AFTER DAY
WHILE HELP WAS RUSHED TO THEM
FROM BASES HALF A WORLD AWAY

WE LANDED AT TIDE RIPPED INCHON
THE MIDDLE OF THIS MOUNTAIN LAND
PERIMETER TROOPS PUSHED NORTH
AS MACARTHUR HAD PLANNED.

PUSHED TO THE BORDER RIVER YALU
THE RED ENEMY WAS ON THE RUN.
OUR GOAL, HOME BY CHRISTMAS
TO JOIN OUR FAMILIES IN NOEL FUN.

CHINESE CROSSED THE YALU RIVER
IN STEALTH THAT INVASION DAY
DOWN TO THE CHOSIN RESERVOIR
SECRETLY, THEY MADE THEIR WAY.

SURROUNDING AMERICAN TROOPS
IN THAT GHASTLY, FROZEN WASTE,
PRESIDENT TRUMAN SAID IN HASTE
THEY'LL NEVER LEAVE THAT PLACE.

THOSE HEROIC, HARD FIGHTING MEN
WILL HAVE TO BE WRITTEN OFF BY A
STROKE OF THE PRESIDENTIAL PEN
WHAT A WASTE OF AMERICAN MEN.

BUT THOSE HARD FIGHTING MEN
WERE NOT ERASED BY A TRUMAN PEN.
THEY FOUGHT HARD BY DAY AND NIGHT
AND EVEN HARDER IN THE MOONLIGHT.

MANY, MANY CHINESE WERE KILLED
AS THEY FOUGHT THEIR WAY OUT
THEIR STEADY COURAGE AND GLORY
WILL LONG BE TALKED ABOUT.

CHOSIN RESERVOIR SURVIVORS
NOW CALLED THE 'CHOSIN FEW'
WILL ALWAYS BE REMEMBERED
AS AMERICA'S FIGHTING CREW.

OUR TROOPS WERE PUSHED SOUTH
BY THAT MIGHTY ENEMY DRIVE
BUT OUR FIGHT AGAINST COMMUNISM
WAS STILL VERY MUCH ALIVE.

OUR MEN STOOD STEADFAST
NEAR THAT 38TH PARALLEL BASE
ONLY LOANING SEOUL TO THE REDS
AS A TEMPORARY LEND-LEASE CASE.

AMERICANS STOOD ON THEIR GROUND
AWAITING OTHER AMERICAN TROOPS
TO JOIN IN A MIGHTY PUSH TO RETAKE
KOREA IN A GREAT MILITARY REBOUND.

THAT SPRING CLANGOROUS CANNONS,
IN ARTILLERY DUELS OF BARKING GUNS.
SOLDIER'S AND MARINE'S EARS DID RING
AS SEARCH WAS MADE FOR KIM- IL SUNG.

FOUND THEM IN CAVES AND HOLES
BURROWED IN THEM LIKE MOLES
TWO WEEKS OF GUERILLA WARFARE
MADE THEM A PART OF HISTORY PAST.

THEN THE CHINESE HAD THEIR TURN
BURP GUN AGAINST M-1 GARAND,
M-1 RIFLES WON, BRINGING SURCEASE
AND FINAL PEACE TO SONS OF CATHAY.

THE MARINES JOINED ARMY TROOPS
WHO NOW WERE FIGHTING UP NORTH
TO RETAKE ALL LOST KOREAN GROUND
SOON OUR ARTILLERY WOULD SIGNAL

THE START OF A GREAT PUSH TO SMITE
THE SONS OF HAN A MIGHTY BLOW
THE ENEMY STOOD THEIR GROUND,
IN VAIN, THEY MADE A VALIANT FIGHT.

AGAIN IN ONE VIGOROUS, LAST DRIVE
VICTORY REJUVENATED MORALE
OUR ARMIES AGAIN AT STRENGTH
MEN REVELED IN SPIRIT AND FELT ALIVE.

THE ENEMY MOUNTED A SECOND ATTACK
IN THE SPRING OF NINETEEN FIFTY ONE
THEY PAID FOR EVERY MILE WE LOST
THE GAIN THEY MADE WAS HIGH IN COST.

THE HOT SUMMER WAS SPENT TAKING
FROM ENEMY HANDS, HILL AFTER HILL
THE ENEMY FOUGHT LONG AND HARD
THE CHINESE REALLY TESTED OUR SKILL.

ALL FALL THE STORY WAS THE SAME
HARD FIGHTING EVERY SINGLE DAY,
MORE HILLS TO TAKE, A PRICE TO PAY,
A REPETITION OF THE SAME OLD GAME

THE YEARS FIFTY TWO AND THREE
SAW TOUGH FIGHTING IN THE TRENCHES
AS WE FOUGHT OFF THE CHINESE ENEMY
FROM BEHIND OUR BARBED WIRE FENCES

WHEN THE ARMISTICE FINALLY CAME
AND THE LONG FIGHTING WAS OVER.
THE SPREAD OF COMMUNISM WAS DONE
THEIR EVIL CREED WAS PUT ON THE RUN.

THAT WAR WILL NEVER BE FORGOTTEN
AS LONG AS MEN LIKE ME SHALL LIVE,
FOR THOSE WHO DIED IN THAT PLACE
THEIR BUDDIES REMEMBER EVERY FACE.

.............Sgt Arthur T. Laporte, aka 'The Iron Frenchman' 1950-51 Item Company 3d Bn 7th Marines, 1st MarDiv USMC

ANOTHER TAKE-OFF VERSION OF "TWAS THE NIGHT BEFORE CHRISTMAS." PROBABLY BECAUSE THE ORIGINAL POEM WAS SO OFTEN COMMITTED TO MEMORY IN SCHOOL BY THE GENERATIONS WHO FOUGHT IN WWII AND KOREA, IT WAS AN APT POEM FOR A SOLDIER POET TO ADAPT FOR USE IN POETIC VERSE ABOUT CHRISTMAS.

'TWAS THE NIGHT BEFORE CHRISTMAS ....Unknown

'TWAS THE NIGHT BEFORE CHRISTMAS
HE LIVED ALL ALONE
IN A ONE BEDROOM HOUSE
OF PLASTER AND STONE.

DOWN THE CHIMNEY I HAD COME
WITH PRESENTS TO GIVE
CURIOUS TO SEE WHO
IN THIS HOME DID LIVE.

AS I LOOKED ALL ABOUT
A STRANGE SIGHT I DID SEE
NO TINSEL, NO PRESENTS
NOT EVEN A TREE.

NO STOCKING BY THE MANTLE
JUST BOOTS FILLED WITH SAND
ON THE WALL HUNG PICTURES
OF FAR DISTANT LANDS.

FADED MEDALS AND BADGES
AWARDS OF ALL KINDS
A SOBER THOUGHT
CAME THROUGH MY MIND.

FOR THIS HOUSE WAS DIFFERENT
IT WAS DARK AND DREARY
I FOUND THE HOME OF A SOLDIER
ONCE I COULD SEE CLEARLY.

THE SOLDIER LAY SLEEPING
SILENT, ALL ALONE
CURLED UP ON THE FLOOR
IN THIS ONE BEDROOM HOME.

HIS LINED FACE WAS GENTLE
THE ROOM IN SUCH DISORDER
NOT HOW I PICTURED
A UNITED STATES SOLDIER.

WAS THIS THE ARMY HERO
OF WHOM I'D JUST READ
CURLED UP ON AN OLD PONCHO
WITH THE COLD FLOOR FOR A BED.

I REALIZED ALL THE FAMILIES
THAT I SAW THIS NIGHT
OWED THEIR LIVES TO SOLDIERS
WHO WERE WILLING TO FIGHT.

SOON 'ROUND THE WORLD
THE CHILDREN WOULD PLAY
AND GROWNUPS CELEBRATE
A BRIGHT CHRISTMAS DAY.

THEY ALL ENJOYED FREEDOM
EVERY MONTH, EVERY YEAR
BECAUSE OF SOLDIERS
LIKE THE ONE LYING HERE.

I COULDN'T HELP BUT WONDER
HOW MANY LAY ALONE
ON THIS COLD CHRISTMAS EVE
IN LANDS FAR FROM HOME.

THE VERY THOUGHT
BROUGHT A TEAR TO MY EYE
I DROPPED TO MY KNEES
AND STARTED TO CRY.

THE SOLDIER AWAKENED
I HEARD HIS ROUGH VOICE
"SANTA, PLEASE DON'T CRY
THIS LIFE IS MY CHOICE.

I FOUGHT FOR FREEDOM
I DON'T ASK FOR MORE
MY LIFE IS COMPLETE
COMRADES, COUNTRY AND GOD.

THE SOLDIER THEN ROLLED OVER
AND QUIETLY DRIFTED TO SLEEP
I COULDN'T CONTROL IT
I CONTINUED TO WEEP.

I KEPT WATCH FOR HOURS
BOTH SILENT AND STILL
AND WE BOTH SHIVERED
IN THE COLD NIGHT'S CHILL.

I DID NOT WANT TO LEAVE
ON THAT COLD DARK NIGHT
THIS GUARDIAN OF HONOR
SO WILLING TO FIGHT.

THEN THE SOLDIER ROLLED OVER
AND IN A VOICE SOFT AND PURE
WHISPERED, "CARRY ON ,SANTA
IT'S CHRISTMAS DAY, ALL IS SECURE."

I LOOKED AT MY POCKET WATCH
AND KNEW HE WAS RIGHT
MERRY CHRISTMAS, OLD SOLDIER
TO ALL OLD SOLDIERS, GOOD NIGHT.

A NIGHT IN COMBAT ....Boyed H. Burnley

THOSE ICY KOREAN BATTLEFIELDS WE ALL REMEMBER WELL,
WE RECALL THE SOUND OF AN EXPLODING ARTILLERY SHELL.
IN MIDST OF NIGHT WHEN A ROUND HAS HIT COMES A YELL,
MEDIC, MEDIC, COME QUICK, I'M HIT, AS A SOLDIER FELL.

THE MEDIC COMES TO HIS FEET, AT A RUN GOES TO HIS SIDE,
FOR THIS IS COMBAT IN KOREA, NOT A CAMP TRAINING GUIDE,
MANY SHELLS ARE STILL FALLING ON THIS BLOODY GROUND,
SOLDIERS DIE BY SHELLFIRE ERE THEY CAN MAKE A SOUND

THE INCOMING MORTAR SHELLS RAIN DOWN THICK AND FAST,
TO SOFTEN US UP IN AN ATTACK THAT WILL NOT BE THE LAST
IN THE NEAR DISTANCE IS HEARD CHATTER OF A BURP GUN,
CHINESE CLOSE IN ON OUR WIRE, AN OUTPOST IS OVERRUN.

HERE ON THIS BATTLEFIELD IN THE MIDDLE OF A DARK NIGHT,
ONLY A QUARTER MOON TO SEE BY, NOT ENOUGH LIGHT
SUPPORTING ARTILLERY FIRE PLACED ON OUR BARBED WIRE
WE ARE AT "FIX BAYONETS!" YET OUR HOPE IS ON SHELL FIRE

SHELLS ARE ON TARGET, THE CHINESE BREAK, BEGIN TO RUN,
WE STAND TO IN OUR TRENCHES, STAYING IN OUR POSITIONS.
IN TRUE CHINESE STYLE A SECOND ATTACK IS SURE TO COME,
CHINA HAS UNLIMITED MANPOWER FOR WASTE BY OUR GUNS.

WE STAY IN OUR TRENCHES, THEY CANNOT BREAK THROUGH,
HALTED BY RIFLE AND MACHINE GUNS, A GRENADE OR TWO.
AT DAYBREAK COMES THE CALL, "STAND DOWN, ALL CLEAR!"
WE MADE IT THRU THE NIGHT. OH, GOD! WILL IT EVER END?

THIS SIMPLE LITTLE MEDAL ....Robert A. Gannon

IT'S A SIMPLE LITTLE MEDAL
DISTINGUISHED IN ITS WAY
REFLECTING STANDARDS
OF A NEAR FORGOTTEN DAY.

NO CROSSES, SYMBOLS OR
STARS OF MILITARY MIGHT
OR WREATHS OF VICTORY
ARE ANYWHERE IN SIGHT.

ITS COLOR SPEAKS SACRIFICE
WITH UNRELENTING PAIN
SELFLESS ACTS OF COURAGE
NO LOGIC CAN EXPLAIN.

THIS SIMPLE LITTLE MEDAL
IS VALOR'S COUNTERPART
ONLY BLOOD AND SUFFERING
CAN WIN THE PURPLE HEART.

SOLDIER POETRY OFTEN EXPRESSES EMOTIONS AND SENSIBILITIES WHICH ARE SELDOM, IF EVER, MENTIONED WHEN IN ACTIVE SERVICE. THE MILITARY POET USUALLY TAKES FORM LATER IN LIFE AS THE PASSAGE OF YEARS GIVES THOUGHT AND VOICE TO FEELINGS KEPT DEEPLY BURIED IN THE LONELY RECESSES OF THE MIND.

BOYS BECOME SOLDIERS

Called into the army while young and naive,
Visions of adventure not hard to conceive,
Filled minds with awe at this new chapter of life,
All determined to make good, whatever the strife.

The settings were strange, many things were new,
Men of all walks of life, in common bond, soldiers too,
Those who were bashful, timid and somewhat shy,
Each in his own manner, learning how to get by.

This getting "used to" took some a while,
But for every solemn frown there was a happy smile.
Good friendships developed as men slowly found
That there were many others of like mind all around.

The days passed quickly, sometimes it was fun,
Learning about soldiering under a warm sun.
Training sessions ended, men scattered everywhere,
Experiencing new adventures which all will share.

Battlefields claim most where they see first hand,
The brutality of war as it scorches the land,
Scenes and experiences leave them all, much older,
and complete the transition from boy to soldier.
........................Donald A. Chase

BRUTAL GAME OF WAR

First comes the scream for a medic,
Too late, to his maker he must yield.
Sent there by whistling bullets,
That crisscross the battlefield.

Other men shake and grit teeth,
As the deadly shells crash down.
A certain sense of soldier's honor,
Makes men hold their ground.

Sometimes fighting is so savage,
Dead men lie in a jumbled heap
In minds of many is the question
Was the price paid too steep?

Yet when the battle is won,
There is a feeling of great pride.
Though you cannot see it,
It is private and held inside.

In a soldier's life oft it happens,
In the mind scarring game of war.
All who served and endured it,
Lives are changed forever more.
........................Donald A. Chase

COMBAT VETERANS

At night, their sleep is restless,
For they have never known real peace,
Brutal warfare has left its ugly memories
And a roiling turmoil, yet to cease.

Scenes of battles fought long ago,
Remain as vivid as they were at the time.
When rifle bullets were exchanged,
And every man's life was laid on the line.

There lie the lifeless broken bodies,
Of men whose fate it was to die.
Carried by comrades to collection points
In neat rows, in lonely solitude they lie.

These unwanted pictures creep into my mind,
From another time and a faraway place.
And the ever scrolling passage of years,
These painful images have never erased.

Countless and ever pressing battlefield images,
Are forever flickering across my mind's screen.
They are a haunting, sad reminder of a past
Which to others is unknown and unseen.
....................Donald A. Chase

PRISONERS OF WAR

Off to one side, somber and silent,
They squat, mute, with downcast eyes,
Not knowing what their fate will be
Will they live, or will they die?

One has blood running down his face,
Where a bullet has creased his head.
Another has an arm that has been mangled,
With a bandage stained in blood's bright red.

A third man with feet black and discolored,
Seen through canvas sneakers full of holes.
His feet and toes swollen and useless,
Frozen stiff in winter's bitter cold.

They were all enemy soldiers,
Yet human, like you and I.
And one cannot but help notice
The anguished pain in their eyes.

That scene of pain, distress and misery,
For me, has defied the passage of time.
It is another unwanted souvenir,
Of a war that has left scars on my mind.
........................Donald A. Chase

AN OLD SOLDIER DIED TODAY

HE WAS GETTING OLD AND PAUNCHY
AND HIS HAIR WAS FALLING FAST,
AS HE SAT AROUND AT THE REUNION
TELLING STORIES OF HIS PAST.

OF A WAR HE ONCE FOUGHT IN
AND THE DEEDS HE HAD DONE,
IN EXPLOITS WITH HIS BUDDIES
THEY WERE HEROES EVERY ONE.

SOMETIMES TO HIS NEIGHBORS
HIS TALES BECAME A JOKE,
HIS BUDDIES LISTENED QUIETLY,
THEY KNEW WHEREOF HE SPOKE.

BUT WE'LL HEAR HIS TALES NO LONGER
FOR OL' BOB HAS PASSED AWAY,
THE WORLD'S A LITTLE POORER
FOR A SOLDIER DIED TODAY.

HE WON'T BE MOURNED BY MANY
JUST HIS CHILDREN AND HIS WIFE;
FOR HE LIVED AN ORDINARY
AND VERY QUIET SORT OF LIFE.

HE HELD A JOB AND RAISED A FAMILY
GOING QUIETLY ON HIS WAY,
THE WORLD WON'T NOTE HIS PASSING
'THO A SOLDIER DIED TODAY.

WHEN POLITICIANS LEAVE THIS EARTH
THEIR BODIES LIE IN STATE,
THOUSANDS NOTE THEIR PASSING
AND PROCLAIM THEY WERE GREAT.

NEWSPAPERS TELL THEIR LIFE STORIES
FROM THE TIME THEY WERE YOUNG,
BUT THE PASSING OF A SOLDIER GOES
UNNOTICED AND UNSUNG.

WHO IS THE GREATEST CONTRIBUTION
TO THE WELFARE OF OUR LAND.
A POLITICIAN WHO BREAKS A PROMISE
AND CONS HIS FELLOW MAN?

OR THE ORDINARY FELLOW
WHO IN TIMES OF WAR AND STRIFE,
GOES OFF TO SERVE HIS COUNTRY
AND OFFERS UP HIS LIFE?

THE POLITICIANS STIPEND
AND THE STYLE IN WHICH HE LIVES,
ARE OFTEN DISPROPORTIONATE
TO THE SERVICE HE GIVES.

WHILE THE ORDINARY SOLDIER
WHO OFFERED UP HIS ALL,
IS PAID OFF WITH A MEDAL
AND PERHAPS A PENSION, SMALL.

IT'S SO EASY TO FORGET THEM
ALL THE ALS AN D JIMS AND BOBS
WHO FOR US WENT INTO BATTLE
TO DO THEIR COUNTRY'S JOBS

IT'S NOT THE WILY POLITICIANS
WITH THEIR PROMISES AND PLOYS
WHO WON FOR US THE FREEDOM
THAT OUR COUNTRY NOW ENJOYS.

SHOULD YOU FIND YOURSELF IN DANGER
WITH YOUR ENEMIES NEAR AT HAND
WOULD YOU CHOOSE SOME COP-OUT
WITH HIS EVER WAFFLING STAND?

OR WOULD YOU WANT A SOLDIER
HIS HOME, HIS COUNTRY, HIS KIN,
JUST A COMMON ORDINARY SOLDIER
WHO WOULD FIGHT TO THE BITTER END?

JUST A COMMON ORDINARY SOLDIER
AND HIS RANKS ARE GROWING THIN,
BUT HIS PASSING SHOULD REMIND US
WE MAY WELL NEED HIS LIKE AGAIN.

FOR WHEN COUNTRIES ARE IN CONFLICT
WE FIND THAT IT IS THE SOLDIER'S PART
TO CLEAN UP ALL THE TROUBLES
THAT THE PINSTRIPE POLITICIANS START.

IF WE CANNOT HONOR HIM IN LIFE
WHILE HE'S HERE TO HEAR PRAISE,
COULD WE NOT PAY HIM HOMAGE
AT THE ENDING OF HIS DAYS?

A SIMPLE HEADLINE ON A SECOND PAGE
OF THE DAILY NEWSPAPER MIGHT SAY,
WE'LL SHED A TEAR TODAY IN MOURNING
AN ORDINARY OLD SOLDIER DIED TODAY.
One of many versions E-mailed on the inter-
net. This version is attributed to an irritated
veteran waiting his turn at the Chicago VA
Clinic. Contributed by Roy Oxenrider A/32/7

FORGOTTEN SON

HE WAS JUST ONE OF MANY OF OUR FORGOTTEN SONS,
WHO ANSWERED HIS COUNTRY'S CALL TO CARRY A GUN.
A BOY WHO BELIEVED IN THE GRACE OF OUR LORD,
AT SEVENTEEN, HE BECAME A MAN, A BOY NO MORE,
FIGHTING FOR KOREA'S FREEDOM ON THAT FOREIGN
SHORE.

HE CAME ASHORE AT INCHON IN HIS TANK, THEN SOUTH
TO SUWON, HIS BRAVE EFFORT HELPED SAVE A NATION.
AT KOTO-RI IN NORTH KOREA, APART OF THE CHOSIN FEW
WHERE COMRADES SLEEP IN ICY GRAVES FOR ME AND
YOU.

AS A BOY HE RISKED HIS LIFE THAT I MIGHT HAVE MINE
NOR HAVE HIS SCARS HEALED WITH PASSAGE OF TIME.
THIS, MY HUMBLE ATTEMPT TO HONOR HIS SACRIFICE,
TO LET HIM KNOW THE DIFFERENCE HE MADE IN MY LIFE.

LIKE SO MANY OTHERS, HE WAS A FORGOTTEN SON,
NOW HE BRINGS SUNSHINE TO THE HEART OF HIS
GRANDSON.

Another unknown poet, obviously not a Korean War soldier,
who has composed a message of love, admiration and respect
for his Grandfather who served during the Korean
War.........UNKNOWN

POTPOURRI

POETS COME IN ALL RACES, COLORS AND RELIGIONS.
THE AMERICAN MILITARY SERVICES, CHEFS WIELDING THE
SPOON THAT STIRS THE GREAT AMERICAN MELTING POT.

WHO YOU CALLING COLORED?

WHEN I BORN, I BLACK
WHEN I GROW UP, I BLACK
WHEN I GO IN SUN, I BLACK
WHEN I COLD, I BLACK
WHEN I SCARED, I BLACK
WHEN I SICK, I BLACK
WHEN I DIE, I STILL BLACK

YOU WHITE FOLKS..................
WHEN YOU BORN, YOU PINK
YOU GROW UP, YOU WHITE
YOU GO IN SUN, YOU RED
WHEN YOU COLD, YOU BLUE
YOU SCARED, YOU YELLOW
WHEN YOU SICK, YOU GREEN
WHEN YOU DIE, YOU GRAY.

SO WHO YOU RED NECKS CALLING COLORED?
......From the scrapbook of Jack E. Wright, George Company
......George Company 3rd Battalion 5th Marine Regiment
......First Marine Division, United States Marine Corps.

THE MORTARMAN'S SONG

BLESS 'EM ALL, THE LONG, THE SHORT AND THE TALL,
SHELLS HEAVY AND LIGHT, BIG AND SMALL,
BLESS THE HIGH EXPLOSIVES WITHIN, PULL THE PIN,
CHECK ALL THE CHARGES AND DROP THE SHELL IN,
SILENT DEATH IS GIVING TOJO A FRIENDLY CALL,
THE BIG AND LITTLE, THE SHORT AND TALL, BLESS 'EM ALL!

WE FIRE THE WEAPON THAT NOBODY SAYS THEY LOVE,
WE LUG ALL THAT HEAVY AMMO UP THESE DAMN HILLS,
TO HELP YOU GUYS GIVE HASHIMOTO A HEARTY SHOVE,
WHEN WE'RE THROUGH, TOJO WILL BE ON THE RUN,
WE'RE GONNA FIX HIM GOOD WITH 'DOC' SHANKER'S PILLS,
THE BIG AND LITTLE, THE SHORT AND TALL, BLESS 'EM ALL!

SO CHUFF, IT'S OUT OF THE GUN WITH A WHAM,
WHERE IT LANDS WE DON'T GIVE A DAMN,
IT MAY BE OVER OR IT MAYBE UNDER,
IF IT HITS ON TARGET, IT'S A WONDER,
MAKES A GUNNER CUSS AN OBSERVER'S COMPASS!
PITY THE LIFE OF A POOR MORTAR MAN!

WE COME UP TWO HUNDRED AND TWO HUNDRED MORE,
AND WHEN IT LANDS IN THE SAME DAMN PLACE,
THEY YELL OUR GUN IS A DOGFACE DISGRACE,
STILL OUR DEVOTION IS FOR THIS PIG IRON BASTARD,
THE BEST DAMN GUN THIS 'CROSS EYED' ARMY EVER HAD!
PITY THE LIFE OF A POOR MORTARMAN!

THIS DOGGEREL WAS UNDOUBTEDLY 'INSPIRED' BY THE BRITISH WW II SONG, "BLESS 'EM ALL MY LADS, BLESS 'EM ALL." I HAVE NO IDEA WHO WROTE IT OR GAVE IT TO ME BACK IN 1944. IT WAS RETRIEVED FROM AN OLD FOOTLOCKER WHILE RUMMAGING FOR SOME BURMESE-JAPANESE OCCUPATION CURRENCY. FORTUNATELY, T WAS WRITTEN IN PENCIL ON BACK OF AN OLD 81 MM MORTAR RANGE CARD, STILL LEGIBLE IN SPITE OF MOLD. THOUGHT IT MIGHT BE OF INTEREST, WORTH SHARING WITH READERS OF THIS BOOK.....ED

OLD SOLDIERS

THEIR FACES ARE WELL WEATHERED
AND NOW THEIR STEPS ARE SLOW.
YET EACH MAN CAN PROUDLY SPEAK
OF HONORABLE SERVICE LONG AGO.

BEHIND EACH FURROWED FACE
THERE IS A STORY TO BE TOLD.
FOR A WARRIOR ONCE RESIDED WITHIN
PERFORMING DEEDS BRAVE AND BOLD.

AT A TIME WHEN THEY WERE YOUTHFUL
AND ANSWERED THEIR COUNTRY'S CALL.
MUSTERING FAITHFULLY TO HER COLORS
FULLY COMMITTED TO GIVING THEIR ALL.

THE MANY HARDSHIPS SUFFERED
THEY, AND THEY ALONE, WILL KNOW
BUT HERE AND THERE A MISSING LIMB
IS THE SILENT EVIDENCE THAT SHOWS.

THESE OLD SOLDIER RANKS ARE THINNING
NO LONGER DO THEY PASS IN REVIEW.
YET THEIR VALIANT DEEDS LIVE FOREVER
THO' KNOWN OR REMEMBERED BY FEW.
.... Donald A. Chase

THE HELMET

IT'S NOT A THING OF BEAUTY
MOST GI's WOULD HAVE TO SAY.
A HELMET ON A BATTLEFIELD
HAS SAVED MANY A LIFE EACH DAY.

THIS HELMET OF STEEL IS USED
FOR MANY THINGS BY FRONT LINE GI's
GIVES THE HEAD GOOD PROTECTION
AND HAS SAVED MANY LIVES.

IT IS ALSO USED FOR BATHING
AND THE WASHING OF YOUR FEET.
SOMETIMES FOR HEATING WATER
OR FOR COOKING SOMETHING TO EAT.

WHEN THE SHELLS COME CLOSE
ONE THING THAT IS FOR REAL
YOU FEEL ALMOST BUCK NAKED
WITHOUT YOUR HELMET OF STEEL.

IT'S NOT LIKE AN EASTER BONNET
MOST GI's WOULD HAVE TO SAY
THANK GOD FOR A ' POT' OF STEEL
IT SAVES LIVES EVERY BATTLE DAY.
...........Boyed H. Burnley

ODE TO TINY BOUCHARD

OLD SOLDIERS NEVER DIE, THEY SAY
THEIR HEARTS ARE VOID OF FEAR.
BUT NEVER LIVED A SOLDIER YET
WHO HASN'T SHED A MANLY TEAR.

I KNOW A MAN, A MAN OF WORTH,
A SOLDIER THROUGH AND THROUGH
WHOSE SHOW OF MANLINESS
DISSOLVED LIKE THE MORNING DEW.

NO, SOLDIERS NEVER DIE, THAT'S TRUE
BUT THEY CAN BE HEIR TO GRIEF
DEATH AT HOME CAN GRIEVE SO DEEP
THAT A BRAVE SOLDIER MUST WEEP.

WHEN MY FRIEND LEARNED
OF DEATH OF ONE LOVED SO DEAR
LIKE A SOLDIER HE BORE HIS GRIEF
YET HE SHED A SOLDIERLY TEAR.

OLD SOLDIERS NEVER DIE THEY SAY
THEIR HEARTS ARE VOID OF FEAR.
BUT NEVER LIVED A SOLDIER YET
WHO HASN'T SHED A TEAR.
S/Sgt Steve Palatnick Co A 7th Cav Regt

THE CAISSONS GO ROLLING ALONG

OVER HILL, OVER DALE
AS WE HIT THE DUSTY TRAIL
AND THE CAISSONS GO ROLLING ALONG
IN AND OUT, HEAR THEM SHOUT
COUNTERMARCH AND RIGHT ABOUT
AND THE CAISSONS GO ROLLING ALONG
THEN ITS HI! HI! HEE!
IN THE FIELD ARTILLERY
SHOUT OUT YOUR NUMBERS LOUD AND STRONG
FOR WHERE E'ER YOU GO
YOU WILL ALWAYS KNOW
THAT THE CAISSONS GO ROLLING ALONG
THAT THE CAISSONS GO ROLLING ALONG!

OVER HILL, OVER DALE
AS WE HIT THE DUSTY TRAIL
AND THE CAISSONS GO ROLLING ALONG
IN AND OUT, HEAR THEM SHOUT
COUNTER MARCH AND RIGHT ABOUT
AND THE CAISSONS GO ROLLING ALONG
THEN IT'S HI! HI! HEE
IN THE FIELD ARTILLERY
SHOUT OUT YOUR NUMBERS LOUD AND STRONG
FOR WHERE E'ER YOU GO
YOU WILL ALWAYS KNOW
THAT THE CAISSONS GO ROLLING ALONG!
THAT THE CAISSONS GO ROLLING ALONG!

The LAUGHTER AND The LOVE ....RICHARD I.. KIRK LT COL US ARMY, RET.

I SEE THE MARKERS STRETCHING OVER THE HILL,
NAME PLATES IN THIS FASHIONABLE DWELLING,
THEIR RANKS BROKEN BY AN OCCASIONAL GAP,
AS THOUGH A TIRED SOLDIER HAD LAID DOWN,

IN COOL, SOFT GRASS MIDST SCATTERED FLOWERS,
FOR A SHORT REST, NAPPING. THEN I HEARD THE WIND,
AS IF MY KINSHIP WITH THE DRAGON'S TEETH,
WERE SUDDENLY, SOFTLY, A VOICE ON THE WIND.

HEAR THE WIND'S SOFT TONGUE,
FEEL THE COOLNESS NEAR,
FEEL AND LISTEN, THEY SAID TO ME,
FOR WE, WHO NEITHER SEE OR HEAR.

'TIS NOW TO SAY THAT ONCE WE LAUGHED,
WHO QUIETLY LIE HERE WHILE SOFT THE EARTH ABOVE
AND, GENTLY RESTING, SOFTLY DREAM
TENDERLY REMEMBERING THE LOVE AND THE LAUGHTER.

I WAS DARK HAIRED THEN AND LIGHT OF HEART,
MY LOVE'S OWN TRUE LOVE'S NOT FOR MOURNIN,'
I TOLD HER SO THE NIGHT I LEFT, OUR LOVE HAS DIED ABORNIN'.
I WAS GENTLE, SOFT AS SUMMER, MY HEART WAS THISTLE DOWN

I LEAVE LOVE UNHURT, WEEP NOT FOR ME, I SEEK MY CROWN.
I LOVED AND WAS LOVED, IT WAS HARD TO LEAVE,
TO TURN FROM ALL, TO FEEL DARKNESS NEAR, BUT THIS I KNOW
MY HEART'S OWN HEART RESTS, DREAMING, SLEEPING HERE.

WITH ALL THIS THE WIND'S SOFT VOICE,
FROM OUT OF THE CLOUD HIGH POPLAR TREE,
LAVED MY CHEEK, CARESSED THE GRASS,
AND WHISPERED TENDERLY TO ME.

I LEFT THAT PLACE OF SILENT SLEEP AND GENTLE DREAMS,
MY STEPS BRUSHED THE SCATTERED FLOWERS,
BUT, AS I LEFT, ONCE MORE ON THE WIND
A TENDER VOICE SAYING. YOU WILL YET BE OURS.

DMZ GUARD BOYD H. BURNLEY LOVE CO MEDIC, 279 INF 45TH DIV SURVIVOR

ON THE MOUNTAINS AND HILLS IN THIS FARAWAY LAND,
OUR MEN ARE ON GUARD WHERE WE MADE A STAND,
WITH A DIVIDED LINE AND NO MAN'S LAND,
THEY STAND WATCH WITH GUN IN HAND.

TIME AGAIN MAY COME, THEY MAY BE CALLED UPON
TO DEFEND THIS LAND WE SO HARDLY WON
OUR MEN STAND GUARD NIGHT AND DAY
FOR THE KOREAN PEOPLE AND FREEDOM'S WAY

THEY WALK THE LINES, THEY PATROL THE HILLS,
TO SEE THAT ALL IS QUIET, ALL IS STILL,
IN THIS WAR TORN LAND OF MANY YEARS AGO,
THERE IS NOW A PEACE THAT WE ALL KNOW.

LOOK AT SOUTH KOREA AS THEY LIVE TODAY,
THE FREEDOM THEY HAVE, AND WHAT THEY SAY.
THEY THANK US FOR THE RIGHT TO LIVE THEIR WAY
AND REMEMBER OUR FALLEN VETS EACH AND EVERY DAY.

THIS LAND OF SOUTH KOREA WHERE WE FOUGHT AND DIED
WE STILL STAND GUARD AND WATCH WITH GREAT PRIDE
CITIES THE SOUTH KOREANS REBUILT NEW AND BRIGHT
IN THIS LAND OF SOUTH KOREA WHERE EVERYONE IS FREE.

FROM MY FIRST DAY IN KOREA UNTIL THE DAY I LEFT THE LINE,
I NEVER THOUGHT I'D MAKE IT THROUGH THE WINTER TIME.
STANDING IN A TRENCH O'ER LOOKING SNOW COVERED GROUND
MADE ME LONG TO BE HOME WITH MY FAMILY SAFE AND SOUND

THERE ARE TIMES IN COMBAT THAT YOU CANNOT FORGET,
LIE UNDER SHELL FIRE, KNOWING YOU MAY BE CLOSE TO DEATH
LYING IN A FOXHOLE IN THE GROUND, SHELLS FALL ALL AROUND
YOU LIE THERE AND WONDER, "WILL I EVER LIVE TO GO HOME?"

FEET WARMED BY A STOVE MADE OF AN AMMO CAN WE FOUND,
A STOVE PIPE OF C-RATION CANS PICKED UP OFF THE GROUND.
FOOD NOT THE BEST, CAME FROM THE SAME C-RATION CANS,
BUT SOMETIMES A CUP OF COLD COFFEE TO WASH IT DOWN.

LONG DAYS AND ICY WINTER COLD HERE I CANNOT FORGET,
FOR ON THESE KOREAN HILLS I THOUGHT I'D FREEZE TO DEATH.
THERE WAS A TIME WE SPENT FORTY FIVE DAYS ON THE LINE,
NO CHANGE OF CLOTHES, NO SHOWER OR BATH IN THAT TIME.

WELCOME WAS SLEEP THOSE DAYS IN THE REAR,
KOREAN HILLS WHERE I SURVIVED COLD AND WAR,
MEMORIES OF KOREAN HILLS ARE WITH ME YET
THE GOOD LORD IN HIS ARMS BORE ME SAFELY HOME.

SARGE ....Robert A. Gannon

I'VE HAD MUCH SUCCESS IN LIFE
I'VE GOT A HOME AND A WIFE
GOOD JOB THAT PAYS ME WELL
AND I'M IN CHARGE.

BUT THROUGH ALL THE THICK AND THIN
THE PRIZE I WORKED MOST TO WIN
WAS TO HAVE A SQUAD OF GYRENES
CALL ME SARGE.

SINCE THE DAY I LEFT THE CORPS
I'VE WON TROPHIES BY THE SCORE
HAD MY NAME ENGRAVED IN BRONZE
AND RANKED WITH STARS.

BUT ALL MY WINNINGS PALE BESIDE
A SUDDEN SURGE OF HONEST PRIDE
WHEN A SQUAD OF GYRENE RIFLES
CALLED ME SARGE.

MY BOYS WEREN'T MEN OF LETTERS
I HAVE NEVER MET THEIR BETTERS
ON A CAMPUS, IN AN OFFICE
OR AT LARGE.

AND I THINK IF WE SHOULD MEET
ON THE CORNER OF THE STREET
THEY'D SMILE AND SLAP MY BACK
AND CALL ME SARGE.

SURE, WE HAD OUR DAYS OF FUN
BUT WHEN WE HAD TO FACE THE GUN
MY SQUAD WAS ALWAYS FIRST
TO LEAD THE CHARGE.

AND WHEN IT CAME TO A TIME FOR DYING
THERE WAS NEVER ANY CRYING
FROM THAT SQUAD OF LEATHERNECKS
WHO CALLED ME SARGE.

SO WHEN GOD TOTES UP MY SCORE
I HOPE HE'LL THINK ABOUT THE CORPS
SINCE I'M BETTING TEN TO ONE
I'VE HELPED KEEP HIS OLD WORLD FREER

BY FIGHTING IN KOREA WITH A SQUAD OF LEATHERNECKS WHO CALLED ME SARGE.

SHORTLY AFTER THE END OF WORLD WAR II, THE ARMY ADOPTED "THE BALLAD OF RODGER YOUNG" AS THE OFFICIAL SONG OF THE UNITED STATES INFANTRY. ITS LYRICS NEVER CAUGHT FIRE IN THE HEART OF THE INFANTRY DOGFACE. THE SONG LINGERED ON BUT WAS SELDOM HEARD. THE ARMY HAS SINCE ADOPTED THE ROLLICKING OLD ARTILLERY SONG, "AS THE CAISSONS GO ROLLING ALONG" AS ITS OFFICIAL 'ANTHEM'. "CAISSONS" WAS COMPOSED BY EDMUND GRUBER, THEN SERVING AS A GUN BATTERY LIEUTENANT IN THE 5TH FIELD ARTILLERY, AT THAT TIME STATIONED IN THE PHILLIPINES.

THE BALLAD OF RODGER YOUNG...©1944 Frank Loesser

THEY'VE GOT NO TIME FOR GLORY IN THE INFANTRY
THEY'VE GOT NO USE FOR PRAISES LOUDLY SUNG
BUT IN EVERY SOLDIER'S HEART IN ALL THE INFANTRY
SHINES THE NAME, SHINES THE NAME OF RODGER YOUNG.

SHINES THE NAME, SHINES THE NAME RODGER YOUNG
FOUGHT AND DIED FOR THE MEN HE MARCHED AMONG
TO THE EVERLASTING GLORY OF THE INFANTRY
LIVES THE STORY OF PRIVATE RODGER YOUNG.

CAUGHT IN AMBUSH LAY A COMPANY OF RIFLEMEN
JUST GRENADES AGAINST MACHINE GUNS IN THE GLOOM
CAUGHT IN AMBUSH TILL THIS ONE OF TWENTY RIFLEMEN
VOLUNTEERED, VOLUNTEERED TO MEET HIS DOOM.

VOLUNTEERED, VOLUNTEERED, RODGER YOUNG
FOUGHT AND DIED FOR THE MEN HE MARCHED AMONGIN THE
EVERLASTING ANNALS OF THE INFANTRY
GLOWS THE LAST DEED OF PRIVATE RODGER YOUNG.

IT WAS HE WHO DREW THE FIRE OF THE ENEMY
THAT A COMPANY OF MEN MIGHT LIVE TO FIGHT
AND BEFORE THE DEADLY FIRE OF THE ENEMY
STOOD THE MAN, STOOD THE MAN WE HAIL TONIGHT.

SHINES THE NAME, SHINES THE NAME RODGER YOUNG
FOUGHT AND DIED FOR THE MEN HE MARCHED AMONG
TO THE EVERLASTING GLORY OF THE INFANTRY
LIVES THE STORY OF PRIVATE RODGER YOUNG.

ON THE ISLAND OF NEW GEORGIA IN THE SOLOMONS
STANDS A SIMPLE WOODEN CROSS ALONE TO TELL
THAT BENEATH THE SILENT CORAL OF THE SOLOMONS
SLEEPS A MAN, SLEEPS A MAN REMEMBERED WELL.

SLEEPS A MAN, SLEEPS A MAN, RODGER YOUNG
FOUGHT AND DIED FOR THE MEN HE MARCHED AMONG
IN THE EVERLASTING SPIRIT OF THE INFANTRY
BREATHES THE SPIRIT OF PRIVATE RODGER YOUNG.

FREEDOM OF SPEECH   ....Unknown

A PROTEST RAGED ON THE COURTHOUSE LAWN
ROUND A MAKESHIFT STAGE THEY RALLIED ON.
FIFTEEN HUNDRED OR MORE THEY SAY,
HAD GATHERED TO BURN A FLAG THAT DAY.

A YOUTH HELD UP A FOLDED FLAG
CURSED IT, AND CALLED IT A DIRTY RAG.
ON SHOULDER, A RUSTY SHOTGUN HELD PROUD.

HIS UNIFORM JACKET WAS OLD AND TIGHT
EACH BUTTON POLISHED SHINY AND BRIGHT,
HE CROSSED THAT STAGE WITH SOLDIER'S GRACE
UNTIL HE AND THE YOUTH STOOD FACE TO FACE.

"FREEDOM OF SPEECH THE OLD MAN SAID,
IS WORTH DYING FOR, GOOD MEN ARE DEAD,
ALLOWING YOU TO STAND ON THIS LAWN
AND TALK US DOWN FROM DUSK TO DAWN.

"BUT BEFORE ANY FLAG IS BURNED THIS DAY
THIS OLD MAN IS GOING TO HAVE HIS SAY.
MY FATHER DIED ON A FOREIGN SHORE,
IN A WAR THEY SAID WOULD END ALL WAR.

TOMMY AND I WEREN'T EVEN FULL GROWN
BEFORE WE FOUGHT IN A WAR OF OUR OWN
TOMMY DIED ON THE SAND OF IWO JIMA'S BEACH
IN SHADOW OF A HILL HE COULDN'T QUITE REACH
WHERE FIVE GOOD MEN RAISED THIS FLAG SO HIGH
THE WHOLE DAMN WORLD COULD SEE IT FLY.

AND AGAIN, IN KOREA, IN MY SECOND WAR
I GOT THIS BUM LEG I STILL DRAG AROUND
FIGHTING FOR THIS SAME OLD FLAG.
NOW THERE IS BUT ONE SHELL IN THIS OLD GUN
SO NOW IT'S TIME FOR YOU TO DECIDE WHICH ONE?

WHICH ONE OF YOU WILL FOLLOW OUR LEAD
TO STAND AND DIE FOR WHAT YOU BELIEVE?
FOR AS SURE AS TOMORROW'S RISING SUN
YOU'LL BURN IN HELL 'FORE THIS FLAG DOES, MY SON.

NOW THIS RIOT NEVER CAME TO PASS
THE CROWD GOT QUIET AND THAT CAN OF GAS
WAS SET ASIDE AS THEY WALKED AWAY
THINKING ABOUT WHAT THEY'D HEARD THIS DAY.

AND THE YOUTH WHO HAD CALLED IT A DIRTY RAG HANDED THE OLD SOLDIER THE FOLDED FLAG.
SO THE BATTLE OF THE FLAG WAS THIS DAY WON BY A TIRED OLD SOLDIER WITH A RUSTY GUN.
WHO ONE LAST TIME HAD TO SHOW THAT THE FLAG MAY FADE, BUT THE COLORS NEVER RUN.

I REMEMBER........................Boyed H. Burnley

I HAVE STOOD ON THE BATTLEFIELD
IN THE MIDST OF DEADLY SHELLFIRE
AND HIGH UP IN THE KOREAN HILLS
I'VE SEEN FEAR IN A SOLDIER'S EYES
AND WITNESSED LOSS OF MANY LIVES.

I HAVE STOOD IN A TRENCH AT NIGHT
IN THE MOON'S DIM LIGHT, WAITING
FOR THE ENEMY TO STRIKE
IN DARK OF NIGHT THERE ARE SOUNDS
TO MAKE A BEATING HEART TREMBLE.

LIVE IN AN ICY FOXHOLE IN THE GROUND
AT 30 BELOW, NO PLACE ELSE TO GO
FALLING SNOW, AN ANIMAL IN HIS HOLE
THE LORD'S HELP I'M STILL AROUND
YET, I REMEMBER OTHERS WHO DIED.

A Marine has the toughest job of all, telling his wife and child goodbye. The question of why there is a war and why does he must go can never be answered to their satisfaction. A 'face of war' seen only by Veterans.

These two sailors are paying their respect to the war dead at this U. N. Cemetery in Pusan, Korea. This photo was taken in 1951. There would be more and much larger cemeteries in the final two years of this brutal war. Archive Photos.

461

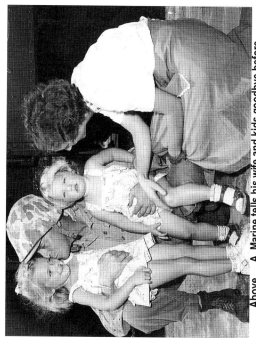

Above. A Marine tells his wife and kids goodbye before boarding a ship for Korea. Below. This wife and kids in Japan get to tell their daddy goodbye as he leaves for work. If he is lucky he will be having dinner with them tonight.

At a Memorial service at one of the many cemeteries in Korea, this little Korean girl places flowers on a grave, while soldiers present arms in a final salute. Archive photos.

The total destruction of Seoul, Korea, the hopelessness and despair of its citizens, is shown in these pictures. Having changed hands four times, the suffering of those civilians that survived, was monumental. Like the mythical Phoenix rising from its own ashes, Seoul has matured into a great modern city. A tremendous tribute to the Korean people. All photos from the National Archives or the Internet.

LOOKING BACK

Fifty years later, the question is often asked, "Was it worth it?" A peace treaty has never been signed with Communist North Korea. Thirty five thousand American soldiers are still in Korea to help enforce a very fragile truce. More than 250 Americans have been killed in border clashes since 1953. The price we paid in American lives for the three war years exceeded 34,000 combat deaths. An additional 20,000 deaths are attributed to war related "other causes." Total combat deaths on both sides, numbered almost 750,000. Civilian casualties are estimated in excess of 2,000,000 Korean men, women and children.

American losses in the three Korean Wars years of 1950-1951 were nearly equal to our losses during the 12 year long war in Viet Nam. South Koreans have rebuilt their shattered country into a modern nation with a high standard of living. North Koreans are starving under their cruel Communist regime, surviving by eating grass and bark in the worst of times, and somewhat better at other times on food doles from the US, South Korea and other humanitarian nations.

On the 50th anniversary of the Korean War a nation wide effort is being made to remember all veterans who served. Why was it called the "Forgotten War" for 50 years? Survivors of that war, serving their country, fought and came home to get on with their lives. They found jobs, married, raised families. Few of them bothered friends or neighbors with war stories of misery and agony endured during those war years. Who are they, these men you are asked to pay tribute to?

Most likely they are your friends, neighbors or acquaintances, who at a young age,50 long years ago, went off to do a job they were asked to do. The survivors returned home to try and pick up on a normal life. They well deserve a simple "Thank You." All six million of them. Norman L. Strickbine

PAGE	FACES OF WAR	UNIT
153	Peter T. Aguilar	Heavy Mortar Co 31st Infantry Regiment 7th Infantry Division
281	Sung-sup An	Tank Co 31st Infantry Regiment 7th Infantry Division
103	James H. Appleton	I tem Co 3d Battalion 5th Marine Regiment 1st Marine Division
125	James H. Appleton	I tem Co 3d Battalion 5th Marine Regiment 1st Marine Division
135	James H. Appleton	I tem Co 3d Battalion 5th Marine Regiment 1st Marine Division
125	James H. Appleton	I tem Co 3d Battalion 5th Marine Regiment 1st Marine Division
137	James H. Appleton	I tem Co 3d Battalion 5th Marine Regiment 1st Marine Division
143	James H. Appleton	I tem Co 3d Battalion 5th Marine Regiment 1st Marine Division
155	James H. Appleton	I tem Co 3d Battalion 5th Marine Regiment 1st Marine Division
159	James H. Appleton	I tem Co 3d Battalion 5th Marine Regiment 1st Marine Division
179	James H. Appleton	I tem Co 3d Battalion 5th Marine Regiment 1st Marine Division
181	James H. Appleton	I tem Co 3d Battalion 5th Marine Regiment 1st Marine Division
193	James H. Appleton	I tem Co 3d Battalion 5th Marine Regiment 1st Marine Division
237	James H. Appleton	I tem Co 3d Battalion 5th Marine Regiment 1st Marine Division
253	James H. Appleton	I tem Co 3d Battalion 5th Marine Regiment 1st Marine Division
263	James H. Appleton	I tem Co 3d Battalion 5th Marine Regiment 1st Marine Division
203	Roger G. Baker	3d Platoon A Co 1st Tank Battalion 1st Marine Division
205	Roger G. Baker	3d Platoon A Co 1st Tank Battalion 1st Marine Division
167	Ashok Banerjee	60th Indian Field Ambulance Company Republic of India
415	Jarvis M. Barrett	868th Field Artillery (Atomic) Battalion (Germany)
107	Kenneth F. Barwise	12 Plat Dog Co Princess Patricia's Canadian Light Infantry Regiment
265	Denzil Batson	2d Platoon Fox Co 15th Infantry Regiment 2d Bn 3d Infantry Division
323	Clarence D. Beaver	HQ Co 31st Infantry Regiment 7th Infantry Division
169	Joaquin B. Benitez	I/tem Co 3d Battalion 7th Marine Regiment 1st Marine Division
99	Joseph J. Bennett	D Btry 15th AAA Automatic Weapons Battalion Self Propelled
423	Walter Cox Benton	3d Military Police Company 3d Infantry Division
285	David B. Bleak	Medical Co, 223d Infantry Regiment 40th Infantry Division
341	Harley Bogart	539th Quartermaster Laundry Company 8th Army
131	Melvin James Boland	Baker Co 1st Bn 1st Marine Regiment 1st Marine Division
27	Louis W. Bontempo	G Co 32d Infantry Regiment 7th Infantry Division
83	Paul E. Bouchard	Co A 7th Cavalry Regt 1st Cavalry Division & 6147 TAC Air Sqdrn
419	Charles W. Bowar	B Co 24th Infantry Regiment 25th Infantry Division
287	George F. Bray	Baker Co 1st Bn 180th Infantry Regiment 45th Infantry Division
392	James A. Brettell	Able Co 13th Engineer Bn(C) 7th Infantry Division
197	Melvin W. Bromby	Motor Torpedo Boat Squadron 1 & MTB Sqdn 2 United States Navy
189	Henry D. Buelow	16th Reconn, 1st Cav Div & 45th Reconn, 45th Infantry Div. & USN
247	Thomas Riley Bunner	Item Co 223d Infantry Regiment 40th Infantry Division
293	Boyed H. Burnley	Attached Love Co 279th Infantry Regiment 45th Infantry Division
311	Ernest L. Buschjost	2d Chemical Mortar Battalion Attached C Co 461st Infantry Battalion
97	James F. Byrne	George Co 3d Battalion 1st Marine Regiment 1st Marine Division
325	Robert B. Campbell	Weapons Company 1st Bn 1st Marine Regiment 1st Marine Division
81	John T. Carrig	1st Platoon Able Co 1st Bn 17th Infantry Regiment 7th Inf. Div.
413	Paul F. Carroll	428th Engineer Water Supply Co 378th Engineer Utility Detachment
38	Larry M. Casilac	Fox Co 2d Battalion 9th Infantry Regiment 2d Infantry Division
213	Esper K. Chandler	Able Co 2d Plt 27th Infantry Regiment 25th Infantry Division
91	Donald A. Chase	B Co 19th Infantry Regiment 24th Infantry Division
121	Donald A. Chase	B Co 19th Infantry Regiment 24th Infantry Division
133	Donald A. Chase	B Co 19th Infantry Regiment 24th Infantry Division
339	Donald A. Chase	I Company 15th Infantry Regiment 3d Infantry Division

AUTHOR CONTRIBUTOR INDEX

PAGE	FACES OF WAR	UNIT
407	Donald A. Chase	I Company 15th Infantry Regiment 3d Infantry Division
428	Kee-tai Choi	12th Infantry Division Army of the Republic of Korea
351	Gilbert H. Clausen	Headquarters Company 187th Airborne Regiment 8th Army
93	Richard E. Coate	E Company 15th Infantry Regiment 3d Infantry Division
109	Richard E. Coate	E Company 15th Infantry Regiment 3d Infantry Division
161	Donald M. Cohen	Charlie Co 1st Battalion 38th Infantry Regiment 2d Infantry Division
389	Hubert S. Coose	Battery A 75th Field Artillery Battalion 8th Army
61	Richard Eyre Coote	16th New Zealand Field Artillery Regiment
25	John Covach	Co A 31st Infantry Regiment 7th Infantry Division
35	John Covach	Co A 31st Infantry Regiment 7th Infantry Division
111	John Covach	Co A 31st Infantry Regiment 7th Infantry Division
145	John Covach	Co A 31st Infantry Regiment 7th Infantry Division
243	John Covach	A Co 31st Infantry Regiment 7th Infantry Division
367	Jeremiah G. Crise	16th FIS 51st FIG 51st Fighter Interceptor Wing USAF
47	Kenneth G. Crump	36th FBS 8th Fighter Bomber WING 5th AF United States Air Force
331	James W. Davis	Easy Co 2d Bn 5th Marine Regiment 1st Marine Division
359	Ronald J. Demers	1st Field Artillery Observation Battalion Eighth Army
309	William J. Dillon	Mike Co 15th Inf Regt 3d Div & 5th Cav Regt 1st Cavalry Division
371	William J. Dillon	Mike Co 15th Inf Regt 3d Div & 5th Cav Regt 1st Cavalry Division
112	Arthur F. Dorie	M Company 3d Battalion 23d Infantry Regiment 3d Infantry Division
301	Arthur F. Dorie	Mike Co 3d Battalion 23d Infantry Regiment 3d Infantry Division
207	Lynn W. Dorsey	343d Squadron 98th Bombardment Wing United States Air Force
19	Donald D. Down	3d Platoon Co F 2d Bn 7th Cavalry Regiment 1st Cavalry Division
147	Jacques K. Doyle	179th Infantry Regiment 45th Infantry Division US National Guard
227	Jacques K. Doyle	179th Infantry Regiment 45th Infantry Division
291	Jacques K. Doyle	179th Infantry Regiment 45th Infantry Division
55	Charles W. Edmond	Co "B" 15th Infantry Regiment 3d Infantry Division
387	Arthur George Elkington	Headquarters Co 3d Bn 65th Infantry Regiment 3d Infantry Division
43	Glenn V. Ellison	Fox Co 27th Infantry Regiment 25th Infantry Division
150	Ronald C. Feldkamp	Heavy Mortar Co 31st Infantry Regiment 7th Infantry Division
201	Richard E. Fordyce	C Co 31st Infantry Regiment 7th Infantry Division
321	Richard E. Fordyce	C Co 31st Infantry Regiment 7th Infantry Division
64	Paul A. Freeburger	Intell & Reconn Platoon 14th Infantry Regiment 25th Infantry Division
329	Paul A. Freeburger	Intell & Reconn Platoon 14th Infantry Regiment 25th Infantry Division
409	William H. Funchess	C Co 19th Infantry Regiment 24th Infantry Division
295	Robert A. Gannon	VMA 132 United States Navy
283	Donald F. Gardner	George Co 2d Bn 223d Infantry Regiment 40th Infantry Division
15	Gerald D. Gingery	H Co 5th Cavalry Regiment 1st Cavalry Division
405	Austin H. Glass	Item Co 3d Bn 1st Marine Regiment 1st Marine Division
127	Lulan E. Gregg	8076 MASH (Mobile Army Surgical Hospital)
73	James R. Grove	Baker Co 13th Engineers(C), 7th Infantry Division
129	Charles L. Grove	USS Ajax (AR6) United States Navy
123	Levi O. Haire	HQ & Service Co 13th Engineer (C)Battalion 7th Infantry Division
233	Chae-soo Han	Korean War Correspondent Seoul Newspaper
365	William G. Hawkins	2d Plat Able Co 5th Marine Regiment 1st Marine Division
269	Carl L. Hempen	2d Chemical Mortar Battalion 8th Army
275	Carl L. Hempen	2d Chemical Mortar Battalion 8th Army
299	Jay E. Hibberts	1st Sqd 3d Plat Fox Co 279th Regimental Combat Team 45th Div
225	John W. Hill	Fox Co 279th Infantry Regiment 45th Infantry Division
240	James J. Hill	Co H 2d Bn 196th Regimental Combat Team Alaska Frontier Guard

AUTHOR CONTRIBUTOR INDEX

PAGE	FACES OF WAR	UNIT
221	Paul Z. Hinson	3dPlatoon Fox Co 279th Infantry Regiment 45th Infantry Division
219	Lawrence Hochfeld	504th Transportation Truck Co 8th Army US Army
68	Hung-bae Park	Lt Col Ret Med Corps Air Force Republic of Korea
361	Robert D. Hunt	HU-1 (Helicopter Unit One) United States Navy
260	Ha-lyong Hwang	Guerilla Intel: KLO G-2, KMC G-2, HID, SOU 105, AISS 6006-SAU 53
417	Richard L. Johnston	Co 2 KCZLLSG US Signal Corps US Army
85	Kerstin Jonasson	Swedish Red Cross Field Hospital Based in Pusan, South Korea
141	James A. Jones	Item Co 3d Bn 7th Marine Regiment 1st Marine Division
411	Nyle T. Jones	Btry D 15th AAA Bn SP Atchd 31st Infantry Regt 7th Inf Division
176	Billie G. Kanell	Company I 35th Infantry Regiment 25th Infantry Division
95	LaFayette F. Keaton	Love Co 1st Battalion 187th Airborne Regimenal Combat Team
185	Dale W. Kember	1092 Engineers(C) Battalion Eighth Army
215	James D. Kennicutt	Mike Co 279th Infantry Regiment 45th Infantry Division
58	Tay S. Kim M.D.	Love Co 8th Cav Regt 1st Cavalry Division & 24th Infantry Division
43	Jean Kirnak nee Bowen	8076 MASH (Mobile Army Surgical Hospital)
375	Jerome Konsker	Love Co 32d Inf Regt HQ 7th Div & 7th Signal Co 7th Inf Division
289	Walter Kosowan	54th Transport Coy 2d Royal Canadian Regiment CANADA
305	George W. Langdale	2d Platoon Able Co 27th Infantry Regiment 25th Infantry Division
71	Leonard LaRue (Brother Marinus OSB)	MSTS "Meredith Victory"
217	Gerald E. Lawrence	Item Co 3d Battalion 31st Infantry Regiment 7th Infantry Division
33	Bae -suk Lee	3d Military Police Company 3d Infantry Division
75	Bae-suk Lee	2d Battalion 15th Infantry Regiment 3d Infantry Division
11	Bae-sun Lee	10th Fighter Wing Air Force Republic of Korea
343	Bae-sun Lee	10th Fighter Wing Air Force Republic of Korea
6	Jae-won Lee	Fox Co 32d Inf Regt 7th Inf Div & 5th Regimental Combat Team
347	Robert E. Levulis	B & HQ Cos 1st Bn 279th Infantry Regiment 45th Infantry Division
139	David F. Link	HQ Co 2d Bn 17th Infantry Regiment 7th Infantry Division
377	Leonard O. Loethen	45th MASH (Mobile Army Surgical Hospital)
21	Benjamin S. Luci	C & D Batteries 3dAAA AW Bn (Self Propelled)
223	Roger J. Lueckenhoff	A Co 160th Infantry Regiment 40th Infantry Division
273	John A. Lynn	King Co 3d Bn 31st Infantry Regiment 7th Infantry Division
277	John A. Lynn	King Co 3d Bn 31st Infantry Regiment 7th Infantry Division
280	Chun-sun Ma	Heavy Mortar Co 31st Infantry Regiment 7th Infantry Division
438	Thomas F. Marker, Sr.	Heavy Mortar Co 31st Infantry Regiment 7th Infantry Division
439	Thomas F.Marker Sr, &	Heavy Mortar Co 31st Infantry Regiment 7th Infantry Division
439	General Alexander M. Haig Jr.	Then 1st Lt, Aide to Major Gen Ned Almond, Cmdg X Corps US Army
381	Christian E. Markey, Jr.	4th Battalion 11th Marine Regiment 1st Marine Division
255	Edwin E. Marshall	How Co 160th Infantry Regtl Combat Team 40th Infantry Division
313	Benito Martinez	Co A 27th Infantry Regiment 25th Infantry Division
87	John D. Matthews	Co's E and G 2d Bn 7th Cavalry Regiment 1st Cavalry Division
29	John P. McBride	Easy Co 7th Cavalry Regiment 1st Cavalry Division
41	Jean F. McCrady	B Co 31st Infantry Regiment 7th Infantry Division
425	Eugene P. Moser	HHQ Co 1st Battalion 38th Infantry Bde (Brigade)
303	Lloyd R. Moses	CO HQ 31st Infantry Regiment 7th Infantry Division
397	David S. Mueller	George Co 2d Bn 224 Infantry Regiment 40th Infantry Division
271	Arnoldo A. Muniz	Service & Tank Cos 224th Infantry Regiment 40th Infantry Division
319	Paul G. Myatt	Able Co 27 "Wolfhounds" Infantry Regiment 25th Infantry Division
383	William J. Nelson	Easy Co 223 Inf & HQ Co 224 Inf Regiment 40th Infantry Division
333	James W. Newland	Don't remember
369	James W. Newland	Don't remember

AUTHOR CONTRIBUTOR INDEX

PAGE	FACES OF WAR	UNIT
337	Thomas M. Nielsen	4th Fighter Interceptor Wing United States Air Force
0385	Rollin B. Noble	8th Army 5th Military Police POW Command #5
187	Daniel Northup	A Company 31st Infantry Regiment 7th Infantry Division
173	William V. Palizzolo	Baker Co 1st Battalion 7th Marines 1st Marine Division
235	Theodore S. Perry	George Co 223d Infantry Regiment 40th Infantry Division
421	Charles N. Phillips	Kearsarge CVA 33 1953-'55 (Taiwan Combat Zone) US Navy
89	Marvin L. Pearson	17th Heavy Tank Co 17th Infantry Regiment 7th Infantry Division
399	James L. Pitzer	H (Weapons) Company 3d Bn 7th Marine Regiment 1st Marine Division
164	Fred E. Proft	1st Field Artillery Observation Battalion X Corps 8th Army
31	Charles C. Rakestraw	A Company 32d Infantry Regiment 7th Infantry Division
45	James P. Ramsey	A Company 32d Infantry Regiment 7th Infantry Division
251	John O. Rem	Battery B 780th Field Artillery Bn 8th Army
245	Max R. Reynolds	Head Quarters Company 2d Engineer Battalion(C) 2d Infantry Division
363	Richard A. Rhinehart	185th Engineer(C) Bn Eighth Army
249	Robert L. Riggs	M Company 160th Infantry Regiment 40th Infantry Division
349	Keith E. Roberts	2d Field Artillery Bn 4.2 inch Rockets US Army
23	Richard P. Roderick	HQ 5th Air Force United States
105	Angelo Rosa	Service Battery 955th Field Artillery battalion Bn Eighth Army
195	Joseph W. Russo	A 15 AAA & 2d Ranger Co & 32d Inf Regt 7th Infantry Division
257	Christopher E. Sarno	1st Tank Bn 1st Marine Division Fleet Marine Force
357	Herbert L. Scheer	61st Searchlight Company 8th Army
373	Herbert L. Scheer	61st Searchlight Company 8th Army
401	Dan D. Schoonover	Company A 13th Engineer Combat Bn 7th Infantry Division
79	Maurice Siskel Jr.	Heavy Mortar Co 31st Infantry Regiment 7th Infantry Division
434	Maurice Siskel, Jr.	Heavy Mortar Co 31st Infantry Regiment 7th Infantry Division
101	Boris R. Spiroff	G Company 7th Cavalry Regiment 1st Cavalry Division
317	John J. Stevenson	Item Co 223 Infantry Regiment 40th Infantry Division
307	Stanley Stoyanof	3dTM Railway Service Transportation Corps Eighth Army
199	Dennis D. Strickbine	C Company 1st Motor Transport Battalion 1st Marine Division
353	Leroy I. Strope	Baker Company 15th Infantry Regiment 3d Infantry Division
315	LeVern E. Sundet	Able Co 27 "Wolfhounds" Infantry Regiment 25th Infantry Division
355	LeVern E. Sundet	Able Co 27 "Wolfhounds" Infantry Regiment 25th Infantry Division
183	Anthony Tavilla	Fox Company 2d Bn 23d Infantry Regiment 2d Infantry Division
267	Edward H. Utley	Weapons Company 1st Battalion 1st Marines 1st Marine Division
209	Emery A. Vallier	E Company 7th Cavalry Regiment 1st Cavalry Division
191	Joseph C. Violette	Tank Company 31st Infantry Regiment 7th Infantry Division
403	James H. Vitali	75th Field Artillery Battalion (155mm howitzer) Eighth Army
171	Blaine B. Wallin	Love Company 1st Bn 32d Infantry Regiment 7th Infantry Division
119	Pat N. Westfall	Heavy Mortar & Fox Cos 31st Infantry Regiment 7th Infantry Division
297	Marion C. Wheeler, Jr.	Company C 728th Military Police Battalion
379	David P. Whisnant	1st Squad 1st Platoon Baker Co 1st Bn 31st Infantry Regt 7th Inf Div
50	Clarence A. White	B Co 32d Infantry Regiment 7th Infantry Division
230	Glenn E. White`	Love Co 279th Infantry Regiment 45th Infantry Division
395	Robert C. Wickman	Item Co 3d Battalion 7th Marine Regiment 1st Marine Division
17	Harry Wiedmaier	USS Mansfield DD278 United States Navy
335	Peter J. Worthington	12 Platoon Dog Co 3d Bn Princess Patricia's Light Infantry CANADA
157	Chesley Q. Yahtin	Ambulance Co 7 th Medical Battalion 7th Infantry Division
13	Keun-sup Yoon	Maintenance Officer Air Force Republic of Korea
327	Roy E. Zittle	C Company 1st Battalion 224th Infantry Regiment 40th Infantry Div

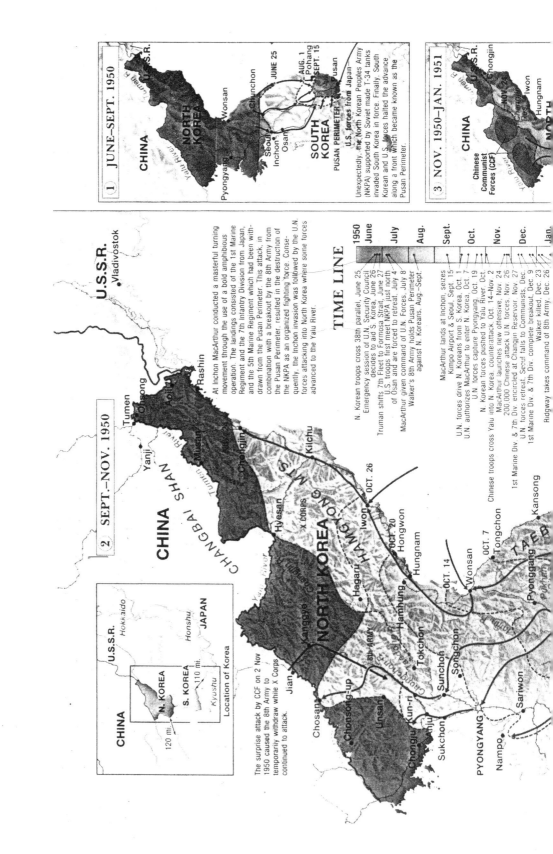

① JUNE–SEPT. 1950

Unexpectedly, the North Korean Peoples Army (NKPA) supported by Soviet made T-34 tanks invaded South Korea in force. Finally, South Korean and U.S. forces halted the advance along a front which became known as the Pusan Perimeter.

CHINA
NORTH KOREA
Pyongyang
Wonsan
Chunchon
JUNE 25
Seoul
Inchon
Osan
AUG. 1
Pohang
SEPT. 15
Pusan
SOUTH KOREA
PUSAN PERIMETER
U.S. forces from Japan
Yalu River

③ NOV. 1950–JAN. 1951

CHINA
Chinese Communist Forces (CCF)
Chongjin
NOV. 24
Iwon
Hungnam
NORTH
Yalu River
U.S.S.R.

② SEPT.–NOV. 1950

U.S.S.R.
Vladivostok

At Inchon MacArthur conducted a masterful turning movement through the use of a bold amphibious operation. The landings consisted of the 1st Marine Regiment and the 7th Infantry Division from Japan, and the 5th Marine Regiment which had been withdrawn from the Pusan Perimeter. This attack, in combination with a breakout by the 8th Army from the Pusan Perimeter, resulted in the destruction of the NKPA as an organized fighting force. Consequently, the Inchon invasion was followed by the U.N. forces attacking into North Korea where some forces advanced to the Yalu River.

Tumen
Yanji
Oesong
Aoji
Rashin
Musan
Chongjin
CHANGBAI SHAN
TUMEN RIVER
CHINA
Hyesan
Kilchu
OCT. 26
X CORPS
Iwon
OCT. 20
Hongwon
Hungnam
Hagaru
Chosan
Changjin
Jian
NORTH KOREA
HAMGYONG
Hamhung
OCT. 14
Wonsan
OCT. 7
Tongchon
TAEB
Kansong
Chongsong-up
Unsan
Kujang-dong
Kun-ri
Anju
Tokchon
Sunchon
Songchon
Pyonggang
Sukchon
Chongju
Sariwon
PYONGYANG
Nampo

CHINA
U.S.S.R.   Hokkaido
Honshu
JAPAN
N. KOREA
S. KOREA   110 mi.
Kyushu
120 mi.
Location of Korea

The surprise attack by CCF on 2 Nov 1950 caused the 8th Army to temporarily withdraw while X Corps continued to attack.

TIME LINE

1950

June
N. Korean troops cross 38th parallel, June 25.
Emergency session of U.N. Security Council decides to aid S. Korea, June 26.
Truman shifts 7th Fleet to Formosa Strait, June 27.

July
U.S. troops first meet NKPA just north of Osan and are forced to retreat, July 4.
MacArthur given command of U.N. Forces, July 8.
Walker's 8th Army holds Pusan Perimeter against N. Koreans. Aug.–Sept.

Aug.

Sept.
MacArthur lands at Inchon, seizes Kimpo Airport & Seoul, Sept. 15.
U.N. forces drive N. Koreans from S. Korea, Oct. 1.
U.N. authorizes MacArthur to enter N. Korea, Oct. 7.

Oct.
U.N. forces capture Pyongyang, Oct. 19.
N. Korean forces pushed to Yalu River, Oct.
Chinese troops cross Yalu into N. Korea counterattack Oct. 14–Nov. 2.

Nov.
MacArthur launches new offensive, Nov. 24.
200,000 Chinese attack U.N. forces, Nov. 26.

Dec.
U.N. forces retreat, Seoul falls to Communists, Dec.
1st Marine Div. & 7th Div. encircled at Changjin Reservoir, Nov. 27.
1st Marine Div. & 7th Div. complete breakout, Dec. 9.
Walker killed, Dec. 23.
Ridgway takes command of 8th Army, Dec. 26.

Jan.